# Pro SharePoint 2010 Search

**Josh Noble**
**Robert Piddocke**
**Dan Bakmand-Mikalski**

Apress®

**Pro SharePoint 2010 Search**

ISBN-13 (pbk): 978-1-4302-3407-4

ISBN-13 (electronic): 978-1-4302-3408-1

President and Publisher: Paul Manning
Lead Editor: Mark Beckner
Technical Reviewer: Lars Fastrup
Editorial Board: Steve Anglin, Mark Beckner, Ewan Buckingham, Gary Cornell, Jonathan Gennick, Jonathan Hassell, Michelle Lowman, Matthew Moodie, Jeff Olson, Jeffrey Pepper, Frank Pohlmann, Douglas Pundick, Ben Renow-Clarke, Dominic Shakeshaft, Matt Wade, Tom Welsh
Coordinating Editor: Anita Castro
Copy Editor: Mary Ann Fugate
Production Suppoer: Patrick Cunningham
Indexer: John Collin
Artist: April Milne
Cover Designer: Anna Ishchenko

Distributed to the book trade worldwide by Springer Science+Business Media, LLC., 233 Spring Street, 6th Floor, New York, NY 10013. Phone 1-800-SPRINGER, fax (201) 348-4505, e-mail orders-ny@springer-sbm.com, or visit www.springeronline.com.

For information on translations, please e-mail rights@apress.com, or visit www.apress.com.

Apress and friends of ED books may be purchased in bulk for academic, corporate, or promotional use. eBook versions and licenses are also available for most titles. For more information, reference our Special Bulk Sales–eBook Licensing web page at www.apress.com/info/bulksales.

# Contents at a Glance

# Contents

# About the Authors

**Josh Noble** has made a career on the front lines, diagnosing business pains and alleviating them with technology. As the sales manager for SurfRay Inc., Josh has worked with global clients, such as the American Bar Association, Best Buy, Intel, the US Coast Guard, and Conoco Phillips, to build solutions to business problems through expertly designed search on Microsoft CMS and SharePoint. His unique background allows him to assist teams to bridge the gap between the business unit's project goals and the technical unit's project design. Josh is from Fort Worth, TX, where he received his Bachelor of Science degree from Texas Christian University. He is currently studying for his MBA at his alma mater. Josh can be contacted on e-mail at josh@prosharepointsearch.com.

**Robert Piddocke** has worked with search technology for over a decade and has implemented hundreds of site and enterprise search solutions, including solutions for the Holy See, the London Stock Exchange, Lloyds of London, Microsoft Xbox, MetLife, and many more. Robert has worked for several search vendors and implemented a range of enterprise and site class search products. Currently, Robert is technical lead in North America for SurfRay Inc., the leading search add-on vendor for SharePoint. Robert has lived and worked in Japan and Denmark and speaks English, Danish, and Japanese. He is originally from Vancouver, BC, where he now lives with his wife and two children. He has his degree from the University of Victoria, in Victoria, BC. Robert can be reached at Robert@prosharepointsearch.com.

**Dan Bakmand-Mikalski** works with research and development at the global Danish company SurfRay Inc., a market leader in search technology on the SharePoint platform. First-hand experience with customers and SharePoint professionals has given him a unique insight into the core challenges you are likely to face when doing advanced customizations and extensions to native SharePoint search. Specializing in understanding the SharePoint search engine characteristics and the search interfaces, his experience offers relevant insights for newcomers as well as experienced SharePoint administrators and developers on how to leverage unused potential in SharePoint. Dan has an academic background as a civil engineer in the fields of computer science and mathematical modeling from the Technical University of Denmark. Dan was born in Copenhagen, Denmark in 1978, where he also currently lives and works. Although Dan has written several articles on SharePoint and search technology, this book is Dan's debut as a published author and professional writer. Dan can be contacted on e-mail at bakmand@gmail.com.

# About the Technical Reviewer

**Lars Fastrup** is an independent contractor offering software development and advisory services for SharePoint products and technologies, the .NET Framework, and Microsoft SQL Server. Until the end of 2007, he worked for the search technology company Mondosoft, where he headed the conception and development of the popular Ontolica search add-ons for SharePoint Portal Server 2003 and SharePoint Server 2007. Lars also co-authored the book *Inside the Index and Search Engines: Microsoft Office SharePoint Server 2007*. Besides his consulting business, Lars also develops and sells add-on products for SharePoint from his web site, www.sharepointproducts.com.

# Acknowledgments

When Apress editor Mark Beckner reached out nine months ago, asking me to bring a team together to write this book, I thought he must have lost his mind. Matt, I would like to thank you for placing your faith in us. Without your drive to convince me that we were capable of taking on such an ambitious project, none of this would have been possible.

I would like to thank my co-authors, Dan and Robert. The time and dedication you invested into not only writing this book but also putting up with me should be considered saintly. Dan, I don't know how you survived so many late nights still working in Denmark past the hours I fell asleep in the United States. Robert, I would like to thank you for never ignoring me when I wanted to chat about the latest new idea or vent about problems with our test server. It has been an amazing journey uncovering all the hidden valleys of search in SharePoint with you, and I could not have asked for a better team.

They say that behind every great man there is a great woman. While I am not yet a great man, I am fortunate to be halfway there with a great woman. To my amazing fiancée, I want to thank you for placing me on loan to this project for the past several months. For all the late nights and exhausting weekends researching and writing, your support grounded my sanity. Thank you for always pretending to care when I rambled about the latest feature we found or challenge we encountered.

To my family, friends, and colleagues, thank you for supporting me over these many months. I would like to thank my father for instilling my work ethic, exposing me to technology from a young age, and always pushing me to seek the next challenge. To my mother, I would like to thank you for providing me with a good upbringing while striving to make me compassionate, dedicated, ethical, and humble. For my many supportive friends and MBA team, I thank you for your constant encouragement. To my partners, clients, and peers, thank you for always asking the hard questions and challenging me to learn.

To our technical editor, Lars, I want to thank you not only for correcting us when we were wrong and pointing out everything we missed, but also for writing the amazing resource that this book built upon. Without your book, *Inside the Index and Search Engines*, we would still be planning our table of contents. To our colleagues at SurfRay and CEO Soren Pallesen, I would like to thank you for allowing us to share our knowledge of SharePoint search with the world, even when doing so was uncomfortable. Finally I would like to thank our coordinating editor, Anita Castro, development editor, Jim Markham, and marketing manager, Leo Cuellar, for your dedication to this book. If it weren't for the support of everyone around me, this book would have never been possible.

Josh Noble

Writing this book was a lot of fun. It was also a lot of work, work that was done during time I should have been paying attention to my wife and kids. So I want to thank Maya, Pavel, and Joanna, first and foremost, for supporting me for the six months of evenings I spent writing, testing, and editing, and not with them. Additionally, special thanks go to my good friend and our technical editor, Lars Fastrup, for his guidance, support, and great and helpful edits. Thanks also to the team at Apress, including Anita, Jim, Leo, and Mark for picking us up, dusting us off, and keeping us on track. Finally, thanks to my great co-authors, each with their own style: Josh, who kept us on track and hassled us when deadlines approached, and Dan, for his technical insight and fun attitude. Thanks guys! A better team I could not have hoped for. I hope this book is as much fun to read as it was to write and useful for those interested in getting the most out of SharePoint Search.

Robert Piddocke

Special thanks go to Robert and especially Josh for their work in managing the editorial and publishing process and their gentle reminders and encouragement during the busy days and nights of writing. Special appreciation goes toward my family and friends, whom I have seen much less of during the writing process than I would like. Thank you for showing great interest and understanding during a busy period. It has been a great motivation.

Dan Bakmand-Mikalski

# Introduction

## Why Is This Book Useful?

This book has been written to address what no other single resource has been dedicated to tackle, search in SharePoint 2010 (SPS 2010). While there are other books that spend a brief chapter to touch on search in SharePoint 2010, scattered information in Microsoft documentation and on blogs, and SharePoint search books that actually focus more on FAST Search Server 2010 for SharePoint than SharePoint's own search capabilities, at the time of this book's publication, there are no other books devoted explicitly to the search offering included in SharePoint 2010. General SharePoint resources may spend 50 pages summarizing the Microsoft documentation on search, but they cannot do more than scratch the surface in such an abbreviated space. Other search-focused books explain the theoretical concepts of enterprise search, or jump heavily into Microsoft's new product, FAST Search Server 2010 for SharePoint. This book, by contrast, is beneficial to all deployments of SharePoint 2010. The information presented throughout is applicable to standard and enterprise editions of the platform. Due to the great amount of overlap, it is also widely useful for deployments of Search Server 2010 and Search Server 2010 Express.

While there are many technical resources about SharePoint 2010 available that were produced with Microsoft oversight, this is not one of them. As a result, this book is able to dive into the hard-to-find details about search in SharePoint 2010 that are not widely exposed. We hope this book will help teach you how to do what consultants charge a fortune to do, and help you understand the best way to do it. We share our years of experience maximizing SharePoint and other enterprise search engines. We not only take a look inside the machine and show you the gears, but also explain how they work, teach you how to fix the problem cogs, and help you add efficiency upgrades.

This book is an end-to-end guide covering the breadth of topics from planning to custom development on SPS 2010. It is useful for readers of all skillsets that want to learn more about the search engine included in SharePoint 2010. After reading this book, you will be able to design, deploy, and customize a SharePoint 2010 Search deployment and maximize the platform's potential for your organization.

## Who Is This Book Written for?

Quite a bit of energy was put into insuring this book is useful for everyone with an interest in SharePoint 2010 Search. It was purposefully written by a SharePoint developer, a SharePoint administrator, and a business consultant so that each could contribute in his respective areas of expertise. The chapters have been designed to evenly cater to three primary readers: users, administrators, and developers.

We recognize that most readers will not utilize this book cover to cover. To make it more useful for the varying areas of interest for reader groups, instead of meshing topics for various groups into each chapter, we have designed the chapters to primarily touch on topics for one reader group. For example, Chapter 5 was written to teach users about using the search user interface, Chapter 10 sticks to the administrator topic of utilizing farm analytics to improve search relevancy, and Chapter 9 teaches developers how to build custom connectors for the BCS. No matter your level of expertise, there are topics in this book for anyone with an interest in getting the most out of search in SharePoint 2010.

The following are some of the key topics throughout the book that will be useful for readers with various needs.

# Topics for Users

- *Components of the search interface*: Chapter 5 provides a thorough walkthrough of the various components of the search interface, including the locations of features and how they work.

- *Setting alerts*: Chapter 5 explains alerts and provides a guide on how to use and set them.

- *Query syntax*: Chapter 5 provides a full guide to the search syntax, which can be used in query boxes throughout SharePoint to expand or refine searches.

- *Using the Advanced Search page*: Chapter 5 outlines the Advanced Search page and how it can be used to expand and scope queries.

- *Using people search*: Chapter 5 teaches the components of the people search center and how to use the people search center.

- *Using the Preferences page*: Chapter 5 explains when the Preferences page should be used and how to use it.

# Topics for Administrators

- *Managing the index engine*: Chapter 3 goes into detail on setting up the crawler for various content sources, troubleshooting crawl errors, and using iFilters.

- *Deploying search centers*: Chapter 4 explains the techniques and considerations for deploying search centers.

- *Configuring the search user interface*: Chapter 6 builds on Chapter 5 by providing a detailed walkthrough on configuring search Web Parts, search centers, and search-related features.

- *Setting up analytics and making use of analytical data*: Chapter 10 focuses on the setup of SharePoint reporting and using the data to improve business processes and relevancy.

- *Tuning search result relevancy:* Chapter 10 provides detailed instruction regarding how to improve search result relevancy by using features such as authoritive pages, synonyms, stop words, the thesaurus, custom dictionaries, ratings, keywords, and best bets.

- *Managing metadata*: Chapter 10 dives into the uses of metadata in SPS 2010 Search, how to set up metadata, and how to use it to improve relevancy of search results.

- *Creating custom ranking models*: Chapter 10 ends by covering the advanced topic of utilizing PowerShell to create and deploy custom relevancy ranking models.

- *Enhancing search with third-party tools*: Chapter 11 discusses commercial third-party tools that enhance search beyond functionality available with light custom development.

## Topics for Developers

- *Adding custom categories to the refinement panel Web Part*: Chapter 6 discusses the most essential search Web Part customizations, including how to add new refinement categories to the refinement panel Web Part.

- *Designing custom search layouts*: Chapter 7 covers subjects necessary to design a search interface with a custom look and feel. Topics necessary for this include manipulation of master pages, CSS, and XSLTs.

- *Modifying the search result presentation*: Chapter 7 provides instruction for changing result click actions and editing the information returned for each search result with XSL modifications.

- *Improving navigation in search centers*: Chapter 7 gives detailed instruction for adding site navigation to the search interface, which is disabled by default.

- *Advanced customization of the refinement panel Web Part*: Chapter 7 provides instruction for advanced customization of the refinement panel Web Part.

- *Creating custom search-enabled applications*: Chapter 8 covers topics such as the search API and building custom Web Parts with Visual Studio 2010.

- *Creating Business Connectivity Services components*: Chapter 9 exclusively covers end-to-end topics on connecting to external content sources through the Business Connectivity Services (BCS).

# What Topics Are Discussed?

This book covers the end-to-end subject of search in SharePoint 2010. We start with a brief background on the available Microsoft search products and follow with key terms and a basic overview of SPS 2010 Search. The book then guides readers through the full range of topics surrounding SharePoint search. We start with architecture planning and move through back-end setup and deployment of the search center. We then jump into an overview of the key user-side features of search, followed by how to configure them. More advanced topics are then introduced, such as custom development on the user interface, leveraging the BCS to connect to additional content sources, and how to use search analytics to improve relevancy. The book is capped off with a chapter on how improve search beyond the limitations of the base platform.

While this provides a general overview of the path of the book, each chapter contains several key topics that we have found to be important to fully understand SharePoint 2010 Search from the index to the user experience. These are the key concepts learned in each chapter.

# Chapter 1: Overview of SharePoint 2010 Search

This chapter introduces readers to search in SharePoint 2010. It provides an overview of the various Microsoft search products currently offered and their relation to each other as well as this book. A brief history of SharePoint is given to explain developments over the last decade. The chapter lays the groundwork of key terms that are vital to understanding search in both SharePoint and other search engines. It explains the high-level architecture and key components of search in SPS 2010. It also provides a guide for topics throughout the book that will be useful for various readers.

# Chapter 2: Planning Your Search Deployment

This chapter provides further details of the core components of SharePoint 2010 Search, and issues that should be taken into account when planning a deployment. Each component of search and its unique role are explained at further length. The function of search components as independent units and a collective suite is addressed. Hardware and software requirements are outlined, and key suggestions from the authors' experience are given. Scaling best practices are provided to help estimate storage requirements, identify factors that will affect query and crawl times, and improve overall search performance. Redundancy best practices are also discussed to assist in planning for availability and avoiding downtime.

# Chapter 3: Setting Up the Crawler

This chapter dives into setup of the index engine and content sources. It provides step-by-step instructions on adding or removing content sources to be crawled as well as settings specific for those sources. It covers how to import user profiles from Active Directory and LDAP servers and index those profiles into the search database. Crawling and crawl rules are addressed, and guidance on common problems, including troubleshooting suggestions, is given. The chapter also explains how crawl rules can be applied to modify the connection credentials with content sources. Finally, the chapter explains the setup of iFilters to index file types not supported out of the box by SharePoint 2010.

# Chapter 4: Deploying the Search Center

This brief chapter provides step-by-step instructions on deploying SharePoint search centers. It explains search site templates and the difference between the two options available in basic SPS2010. A guide on redirecting the search box to a search center is given, as well as notes on how to integrate search Web Parts into sites other than the search center templates.

# Chapter 5: The Search User Interface

This chapter is an end-to-end walkthrough of the search user interface in SPS2010. A wide range of topics is discussed to provide a comprehensive user guide to search. It explains how to use the query box and search center to find items in SharePoint. It explains the different features of SharePoint search that are accessible to users by default, such as the refinement panel, alerts, and scopes. A full guide on search syntax is given for advanced users, and a guide of the people search center is provided for deployments utilizing the functionality.

## Chapter 6: Configuring Search Settings and the User Interface

This chapter expands on Chapter 5 by diving into configuration of the search user interface. It provides advice on how to accomplish typical tasks for configuring the search user experience in SPS 2010. The first part of the chapter explains the common search Web Parts and their most noteworthy settings. The following parts of the chapter focus on understanding concepts such as stemmers, word breakers, and phonetic search. The chapter provides details on configuring general search-related settings such as scopes, keywords, search suggestions, refiners, and federated locations. Information on administrative topics related to user settings, such as search alerts and user preferences, is also described in detail.

## Chapter 7: Working with Search Page Layouts

This chapter is the first of two that focus on advanced developer topics related to search. It explains best practices for design and application of custom branded layouts to the search experience. Topics such as manipulation of the CSS, XSLTs, and master pages are all specifically addressed. A detailed discussion of improving navigation within the search center is also provided. The chapter continues with guidance on manipulating the presentation of properties and click action of search results. It ends with instruction for advanced customization of the refinement panel Web Part.

## Chapter 8: Searching through the API

This is the second of two chapters that focus on advanced developer topics related to search. It delivers the fundamentals of the search application programming interfaces (APIs) in SharePoint 2010. A thorough re-introduction to the query expression is presented from a development perspective, and guidance is provided on how to organize the query expression to get the desired results. The chapter also contains an example of how to create a custom search-enabled application page using Visual Studio 2010.

## Chapter 9: Business Connectivity Services

This chapter is an end-to-end guide for developers on the SharePoint 2010 Business Connectivity Services (BCS) with a special focus on the search-related topics. It explains the architecture of this service and how it integrates both within and outside SharePoint 2010. A guide is given on how to create BCS solutions and protocol handlers, including a full step-by-step example. Specific examples are also provided of how to use SharePoint Designer 2010 to create declarative solutions and Visual Studio 2010 to create custom content types using C#.

## Chapter 10: Relevancy and Reporting

This chapter is a guide for the user of SharePoint analytics and applications to improve search relevancy. It teaches readers how to view and understand SharePoint search reporting and apply what it exposes to enhance the search experience. A guide to the basics of search ranking and relevancy is provided. The key settings that can be applied to manipulate items to rise or fall in search results are explained. Reporting and its ability to expose the successes and failures of the search engine are explained, along with techniques that can be applied to modify the way the search engine behaves. A guide to utilizing the SharePoint thesaurus to create synonyms for search terms is also provided. The chapter ends with advanced instructions for utilizing PowerShell to create and deploy custom ranking models.

## Chapter 11: Search Extensions

This chapter explains the limitations of SharePoint 2010 and various options for adding functionality to the platform beyond custom development. It is the only chapter that explores topics beyond the capabilities of the base platform. It explores the business needs that may require add-on software, and reviews vendors with commercial software solutions. It takes a look into free add-on solutions through open source project communities, and provides general outlines of when replacements to the SharePoint 2010 Search engine, such as FAST Search Server for SharePoint 2010 (FAST) or Google Search Appliance, should be considered.

# This Is Not MOSS 2007

While skills picked up during time spent with MOSS 2007 are beneficial in SPS 2010, relying on that expertise alone will cause you to miss a lot. There have been significant changes between MOSS 2007 and SharePoint 2010. Search not only received improvement, but also underwent complete paradigm shifts. The old Shared Services Provider architecture has been replaced with the SharePoint 2010 service application architecture, creating unique design considerations. The MOSS 2007 Business Data Catalog (BDC) has been replaced with the Business Connectivity Services (BCS), unlocking new ways to read and write between SharePoint and external content sources. Index speed, capacity, and redundancy options have all been improved to cater to expanding enterprise search demands. Even the query language has been completely revamped to allow for Boolean operators and partial word search.

Throughout this book, we have taken special care to note improvements and deviations from MOSS 2007 to assist with learning the new platform. Captions pointing out changes will help you to efficiently pick up the nuances of SharePoint 2010. Direct feature comparisons are also provided to assist with recognizing new potential opportunities for improving search.

# The Importance of Quality Findability

If you are reading this book, then most likely your organization has decided to take the leap into SharePoint 2010. Unfortunately, more often than not the platform is selected before anyone determines how it will be used. This leaves a large gap between what the platform is capable of achieving and what is actually delivered to users. The goal of this book is to bridge the gap between what SharePoint can do to connect users with information, and what it does do for your users to connect them with their information.

By default, most of the world's computer owners have a browser home page set to a search engine. Search is the first tool we rely on to find the needle we need in a continuously expanding haystack of information. People expect search to quickly return what they are looking for with high relevancy and minimal effort. Improvements catering to effective Internet search have raised user expectations, which should be seen as a call to action for improved web site and portal design, not an opportunity to manage expectations. If this call to action is not met, however, business will be lost to completion for web sites, and intranet users will find shortcuts to the desired content management practices.

Consider your own experiences on your favorite global search engine. If the web site you are looking for does not appear within the first (or maximum, second) page of search results, then you most likely change your query, utilize a different search engine, or simply give up. Users on SharePoint portals exhibit the same behavior. After a few attempts to find an item, users will abandon search in favor of manual navigation to document libraries or the shared drives that SharePoint was designed to replace. Users eventually begin to assume that once items find their way into the chasm of the intranet, the only chance of retrieving them again is to know exactly where they were placed. It is for these reasons that implementing an effective search experience in SharePoint 2010 is one of the most important design considerations in SharePoint. If users cannot easily find information within your SharePoint deployment, then they cannot fully leverage the other benefits of the platform.

# The Value of Efficient Search

It is obvious that in today's economy it is more important than ever to make every dollar count. Organizations cannot sit back and ignore one of the largest wastes of man-hours in many companies. According to a 2007 IDC study, an average employee spends 9.5 work-hours a week just searching for pre-existing information. What's worse is that six hours a week are spent recreating documents that exist but cannot be found. With this information, combined with the statistic that users are typically successful with their searches only about 40% of the time, the cost of a poor search solution can quickly compound to quite a large burden on a company of any size.

Let's say that an employee is paid $75,000 a year for a 40-hour work week and 50 weeks a year (2,000 hours). Based on this, the employee earns $37.50/hour before benefits. Applying the statistics just cited, you can see that the cost per week to find information is $337.50/week ($16,875 annual), and the cost to recreate information is $225.00/week ($11,250 annual). This being said, the cost per employee at this rate would be $28,125/year for a poor findability and search solution. In a different deployment scenario, assume 500 employees earning $20 per hour, with just one hour loss per user/month. In just three months, the waste due to poor search is $30,000 in wasted wages. That is an extra employee in many companies.

From these statistics, it is clear that well-designed search is a key driver of efficiency within companies. This book helps you to achieve this efficiency with search. It provides a full range of topics to help you design a SharePoint search portal that quickly connects users with their information. We pull from our experience working with SharePoint search every day to provide expert advice on the topics that matter when building a SharePoint search center that really works. Although designing and implementing a quality search experience does take time, this book places the ability within the grasp of every SharePoint 2010 deployment.

# Note from the Authors

Our goal is not only to teach you the facts about search in SharePoint 2010, but also to give you the basic tools to continue your learning. Creative applications for SharePoint search are always evolving. Use the knowledge gained in this resource to explore the continuing evolution of knowledge throughout your company, peers, and the Web. As you build your SharePoint search environments, make sure to always keep the users' experiences in mind. Solicit feedback, and continue to ask yourself if the search tool you are creating will help users change *search* into *find*.

This book is the product of countless hours of planning, research, and testing. It is the combined efforts of many people, including Apress editors, Microsoft, SharePoint consultants, bloggers, clients, and our colleagues at SurfRay. With these people's support, we have designed this book's content and structure to teach you all the essentials of search in SharePoint 2010. As you continue on to Chapter 1, we hope that you enjoy reading this book to the same extent we have enjoyed writing it for you.

# CHAPTER 1

■ ■ ■

# Overview of SharePoint 2010 Search

After completing this chapter, you will be able to

- Distinguish between the various Microsoft Search products

- Understand the search architecture in SharePoint 2010

- Translate integral terms used throughout the rest of the book

- Know how to effectively use this book

Before taking the journey into this book, it is vital to gain a firm understanding of the ground-level concepts that will be built upon throughout. This chapter is designed to bring together several of the core concepts necessary to understand the inner workings of SharePoint 2010. Many of these are universal to all search engines, but some may be foreign to those readers new to SharePoint.

It is important to keep in mind that a few of the terms used throughout this resource may be different than those used on public blogs and forums. The terminology presented in this chapter will assist the reader in understanding the rest of this book. However, it is more important to understand the core concepts in this chapter as they will prove more helpful in your outside research. As discussed in the introduction, this book will not address every possible topic on search in SharePoint 2010. The most important subjects are presented based on the experiences of the authors. The dynamics of SharePoint, however, create a potentially unending network of beneficial topics, customizations, and developments. While this book does not cover everything, it will provide all of the basic knowledge needed to effectively utilize additional outside knowledge.

Microsoft has a wide range of enterprise search product offerings. With new products being released, and existing products changing every few years, it can become quite cumbersome to keep track of new developments. To lay the foundations of the book, the chapter starts with a brief review of this product catalog. Each solution is explained from a high level with specific notes on the key benefits of the product, technological restrictions, and how it fits into this book. While it is assumed that every reader is using SharePoint 2010, a large amount of the topics discussed will be relevant to other products in the Microsoft catalog.

The second half of the chapter first focuses on a few of the most important soft components of search. These include components such as the search center, the document properties that affect search, and the interactive components for users. The second half of the chapter then outlines the basic architecture of SharePoint 2010 Search. While this topic is discussed at length in the following chapter, the depth of detail provided here is sufficient for readers not involved with the infrastructure setup. Finally, the chapter is capped with a guide to a few of the most important topics in this book for various reader groups.

# Microsoft Enterprise Search Products: Choosing the Right Version

As mentioned in the introduction, Microsoft has been in the search space for over a decade. In that time, they have developed a number of search products and technologies. These range from global search on Bing.com, desktop search on Windows 7, search within Office 14, and a wide range of "enterprise" search solutions. Each of these products is designed to handle specific types of queries, search against various content sources, and return results using various ranking algorithms. No two search technologies are the same, and a user being fluent in one does not translate to effective use or deployment of another. For the purpose of this book, we will be focusing on Microsoft SharePoint 2010, and as the weight of this book indicates, this subject is more than enough information for one resource.

Due to the overlap between many of Microsoft's enterprise search technologies, we will make side notes throughout this book indicating where the information is applicable to solutions other than SharePoint 2010. Throughout the book there will also be notes on technology limitations, where the use of an additional Microsoft technology or third-party program may be necessary to meet project goals. These side notes should not be considered the definitive authority on functionality outside the scope of this book, but they are useful in recognizing key similarities and differences between products.

## Microsoft SharePoint Server 2010

SharePoint Server 2010 is Microsoft's premier enterprise content management and collaboration platform. It is a bundled collection of workflows, Web Parts, templates, services, and solutions built on top of Microsoft's basic platform, SharePoint Foundation, which is discussed further in the following section. SharePoint 2010 can be used to host a wide variety of business solutions such as web sites, portals, extranets, intranets, web content management systems, search engines, social networks, blogs, and business intelligence databases.

SharePoint 2010 deployments can be found in organizations with a massive difference in scale and requirements. User counts in implementations as small as single digits are seen in small intranets and expand into the millions with large extranets and public-facing sites. The beauty of the solution comes in its ability to be deployed relatively quickly and easily, and its ability to be customized to cater to a wide range of needs with various workflows, Web Parts, templates, and services. The out-of-the-box functionality can cater to generic needs of organizations, but the power of the tool comes in the building blocks that are able to be inserted, combined, and customized to meet a variety of usage scenarios. While the most obvious use of SharePoint 2010 is intranet portals, the platform is now seeing a greater push to the public domain with wider-range Web 2.0–focused tools.

SharePoint 2010 is available both on-premise, off-site, and in the cloud through Microsoft as well as several third-party hosting firms. On-premise refers to deployments of software that run locally on in-house hardware, as opposed to those that are hosted in a remote facility, such as a server farm or on the internet. Historically, most software has been managed through a centralized on-premise approach, but in recent years, advances in cloud computing, the rise of netbooks, and the availability of inexpensive broadband have grown the popularity of decentralized off-premise deployments. While both approaches can produce the same experience for users, each presents its own set of IT challenges. On-premise deployments require the procurement, maintenance, upgrade costs, and potential downtime associated with server hardware. Off-premise deployments at hosting centers allow companies to avoid these challenges for a fee, but present their own challenges in the way of bandwidth, security, and more limited functionality depending on the hosting center. Off-premise options for SharePoint 2010 are available through various hosting centers. Many of these hosts simply maintain reliable off-site deployment of the same software available internally and provide remote access to full configurability options. Other hosted versions, such as SharePoint Online offered by Microsoft, may provide only a subset of the features available through on-premise deployments. Due to the variable features available in the off-premise offerings, this book will target the on-premise version of SPS 2010.

Unlike SharePoint Foundation 2010, which will be discussed in the next section, SharePoint Server 2010 requires additional software licensing. Licensing costs may deviate depending on a particular client's licensing agreement and procurement channel. Microsoft may also deem it necessary to change licensing structures or costs from time to time. As a result, this book will not discuss licensing costs, although this should be taken into consideration during the planning stages discussed in Chapter 2.

Before learning about the current version of SharePoint, it may be helpful to know the background of products it has been derived from. SharePoint 2010 stems from a decade and a half of development history. During this time, Microsoft has taken note of the platform's pitfalls and successes to continuously produce improved platforms every few years. Fueled by the need to be able to centrally share content and manage web sites and applications, the earliest version of SharePoint, called Site Server, was originally designed for internal replacement of shared folders. Site Server was made available for purchase with a limited splash in 1996 with capabilities around search, order processing, and personalization.

Microsoft eventually productized SharePoint in 2001 with the release of two solutions, SharePoint Team Services (STS) and SharePoint Portal Services (SPS 2001). SharePoint Team Services allowed teams to build sites and organize documents. SharePoint Portal Services was focused primarily on the administrator and allowed for structured aggregation of corporate information. SPS also allowed for search and navigation through structured data. Unfortunately, the gaps between these two solutions created a disconnect between the end users using SharePoint Team Services to create sites and administrators using SharePoint Portal Services to manage back-end content.

In 2003, Microsoft released the first comprehensive suite that combined the capabilities of SharePoint Team Services and SharePoint Portal Services. Much like today, the 2003 version of SharePoint came in two different flavors, Windows SharePoint Services 2.0 (WSS 2.0), which was licensed with Windows Server, and SharePoint Portal Server 2003 (SPS 2003). Due to the inclusion of WSS 2.0 in Windows Server, and the large improvements over the 2001 solutions, adoption of SharePoint as a platform began to skyrocket. SharePoint 2003 included dashboards for each user interface, removed much of the tedious coding required in previous versions, and streamlined the process for uploading, retrieving, and editing documents.

In 2006, Microsoft released Microsoft Office Server 2007 (MOSS 2007) and Windows SharePoint Services 3.0 (WSS 3.0), following the same functionality and licensing concepts of their 2003 counterparts. By leveraging improvements in the underlying framework, SharePoint 2007 ushered in the maturity of the platform by introducing rich functionality such as master pages, workflows, and collaborative applications. MOSS 2007's wide range of improvements from administrative tools to user interfaces positioned SharePoint as the fastest growing business segment in Microsoft.

In May 2010, Microsoft released SharePoint Server 2010 (SPS 2010) and SharePoint Foundation 2010, the successors to MOSS 2007 and WSS 3.0. SharePoint 2010 builds on MOSS 2007 by improving functions such as workflows, taxonomy, social networking, records management, and business intelligence. It is also noteworthy to point out Microsoft's noticeable improvements to features catering to public-facing sites and cloud computing.

In regards to search, improvements in SharePoint 2010 can be found across the board in areas such as improved metadata management, the ribbon, inclusion of the Business Connectivity Services (BCS) in non-enterprise versions, a significantly more scalable index, expanded search syntax, and search refiners (facets). With the exception of metadata management, these are the types of subjects that will be addressed throughout this book. Although throughout this book there will be side notes touching on comparisons between MOSS 2007 and SharePoint 2010 Search components, it will be generally assumed that readers are new to SharePoint in 2010. For a comparison of the important changes between MOSS 2007 and SharePoint 2010, please see Table 1-1.

# SharePoint Foundation 2010

SharePoint Foundation 2010 (SPF 2010) is the successor to Windows SharePoint Services 3.0 (WSS 3.0). It is the web-based collaboration platform from which SharePoint Server 2010 expands. SharePoint Foundation provides many of the core services of the full SP 2010, such as document management, team workspaces, blogs, and wikis. It is a good starting point for smaller organizations looking for a cost-effective alternative to inefficient file shares, and best of all, access to SharePoint Foundation 2010 is included free of charge with Windows Server 2008 or later.

In addition to being a collaboration platform for easily replacing an outdated file share, SharePoint Foundation can also be used as a powerful application development platform. The prerequisite infrastructure, price, and extensibility create an ideal backbone for a wide range of applications. Developers can leverage SharePoint's rich application programming interfaces (APIs), which act as building blocks to expedite development. These APIs provide access to thousands of classes, which can communicate between applications built on top of the platform. The attractiveness of SharePoint Foundation 2010 as a development platform is compounded by its wide accessibility, which lowers barriers to access by non-professional developers. This increased accessibility consequently expands information sharing about the platform and has facilitated a rapidly growing development community.

SharePoint Foundation does have support for very basic indexing and searching. Although not as powerful as the search capabilities made available in SharePoint Server 2010 or Search Server 2010, it will allow for full-text queries within sites. Without any additions, SPF 2010 allows access to line-of-business (LOB) data systems through a subset of the BCS features available in full SPS 2010. It can also collect farm-wide analytics for environment usage and health reporting. For more extensive search functionality, the upgrade to SharePoint 2010, FAST for SharePoint 2010, Search Server 2010, or the addition of the free Search Server Express 2010 may be necessary. Without the recommended addition of the free Search Server Express product or SharePoint 2010, functionality such as scopes, custom property management, query federation, and result refiners is not available. A full chart of the major differences in search functionality between these products can be found in Table 1-1.

While SPF 2010 will not be the focus of this book, some of the information presented in later chapters overlaps. Major differences between SharePoint Foundation and SharePoint 2010 include the available Web Parts, scalability, availability, flexibility, and administrative options. In addition, the people search center is not available in SharePoint Foundation. Tables 1-1 and 1-2 provide a more detailed comparison of major features and scalability considerations for SPF 2010. For a full list of the available search Web Parts in SharePoint 2010, please see Table 1-3.

An important note if upgrading WSS 3.0, which allowed for both 32- and 64-bit compatibility, is that SharePoint Foundation 2010 requires a 64-bit version of both Windows Server 2008 and SQL Server. While SPF 2010 is outside of the scope of this book, a few important notes on infrastructure and prerequisites can be found in Chapter 2. Since SharePoint Foundation is an underlying core of SharePoint Server 2010, it stands to reason that if you have the hardware and software prerequisites required for SPS 2010, you will also meet the needs of SharePoint Foundation.

# Microsoft Search Server 2010 Express

Microsoft Search Server 2010 Express (MSSX 2010) is the successor to Search Server 2008 Express. It is an entry-level enterprise search solution that provides crawling and indexing capabilities nearly identical to SharePoint Server 2010. This free search server is available for anyone using Windows Server 2008 or later, and it should be the first addition considered when search functionality beyond that available in SharePoint Foundation is necessary.

Although frequently deployed on top of SharePoint Foundation, Search Server 2010 Express is able to isolate the infrastructure from other Microsoft SharePoint technologies. This allows for an enterprise search solution without the need for SharePoint Foundation or SharePoint Server 2010.

Search functionality of Search Server 2010 Express that is not included in SharePoint Foundation ranges from the types of content that can be crawled to how the user interacts with search results and refines queries. A full chart of the major differences in search functionality between these solutions can be found in Table 1-1. Because MSSX 2010 is built from a subset of SPS 2010 search functionality, there are some limitations, most notably around searching on people due to the lack of the underlying "people" element in Foundation. Other limitations resolved by moving to the purchasable Search Server 2010 are addressed in the next section.

# Search Server 2010

Microsoft Search Server 2010 (MSS 2010) is the more robust and scalable version of Search Server 2010 Express. MSS 2010's feature set is nearly identical to that of its free counterpart. It can function independently of SharePoint, index federated content through the BCS, and provide a robust end-user search interface.

The major differences and the price justification to move from the free version to the full Search Server 2010 are the scalability for enterprises. Microsoft has placed limitations on the Search Server 2010 Express index capacity. The maximum capacity of full-text index in MSSX 2010 is approximately 300,000 items with Microsoft SQL Server 2008 Express, or 10 million items with SQL Server. To index content above this limitation, Search Server 2010 is necessary, which can manage about 100 million items.

In addition to the significant difference in index capacity, scalability is drastically different. The topology component of any particular Search service application (SSA) must be on one server with Search Server 2010 Express. As seen in MOSS 2007 and Search Server 2008, this restriction can become a significant limitation for larger or more frequently accessed search environments. Alternatively, the full Search Server 2010 is capable of spreading its topology components across multiple servers, which allows for distribution of workload. Distribution of workload can lead to decreased indexing and crawling times, increased search speed, increased storage capacity, and greater accessibility. These topics will be addressed in more detail in Chapter 2.

Service applications are a new concept brought about by the service application model in SharePoint 2010. Similar to the way the BCS in SharePoint 2010 replaced the Business Data Catalog (BDC) from MOSS 2007, service applications replaced the Shared Services Providers (SSPs). SSPs in MOSS 2007 were a collection of components that provide common services to several Internet Information Services (IIS) web applications in a single SharePoint server farm. Unfortunately, while SSPs were acceptable for farms with simple topologies in MOSS 2007, they presented a large barrier to growth for larger deployments. Shared Services Providers grouped all services, such as Excel Services, MySites, and Search, together into one SSP unit, although service functions were all radically different. This presented significant challenges to scaling and flexibility.

---

■ **Note** In SharePoint 2010, service applications allow services to be separated out into different units. Unlike SSPs, which restricted a web application to be tied to a single provider, web applications can now use the services available on any of the service applications. Service applications can also be spread across multiple farms to further distribute services, and multiple instances of the same service application can be deployed.

In addition to redesigning the existing service model in SharePoint 2010, Microsoft added a number of new services. Out-of-the-box services include the BCS, Performance Point, Excel, Visio, Word, Access, Office Web Apps, Project Server, Search, People, and Web Analytics. The most important service for the purpose of this book, of course, is the Search Service Application, formally known as the Search Service Provider (SSP). While several of the other service applications are necessary to unlock the full range of capabilities around search in SharePoint 2010, at least one SSA is required for search to function. Further details on the Search service application will be found in the next chapter.

---

Search Server 2010 and the Express version will not be the focus of this book, but most of the information necessary to plan, deploy, configure, and customize these solutions is identical to SharePoint Server 2010. Throughout this book, there will be notes when there is a significant difference between the functionality of Search Server 2010 and SharePoint 2010.

# FAST Search Server 2010 for SharePoint

FAST Search Server 2010 for SharePoint is Microsoft's enterprise search add-on that replaces the search functionality of SharePoint. For the end user, it provides a wide range of additional features, such as improved search results navigation, expanded language support, and previews of Office documents. On the back end, it can index content sources and line-of-business applications not accessible by basic SharePoint 2010 and scales up to billions of items. It also gives developers the power to manually manipulate relevancy at the index level to force desired items to the top of result sets.

FAST should be considered when more than 100 million items need to be indexed, the search user interface cannot be customized or configured to meet the needs of end users, or there is a need to index line-of-business applications not accessible to SharePoint 2010. The item limit of 100 million is noteworthy as this is the upper limit for SPS 2010. Once this limit is approached or breached by the index, a more powerful search solution is necessary, which leads to the practicality of FAST as an option. It is important to note that FAST requires its own servers and cannot be installed on the same server as SharePoint 2010. In addition, at the time of writing this book, the FAST Search Server 2010 for SharePoint addition is available only for Microsoft SharePoint Enterprise clients (ECAL).

As stated previously, the scope of this book is to guide SharePoint administrators through the successful planning, deployment, and customization of SharePoint 2010 Search. While the previously mentioned Microsoft search technologies have a wide amount of overlap with the subject of this book, FAST Search Server 2010 for SharePoint replaces the SharePoint 2010 Search pipeline, and as a result this book will not be highly relevant to that platform. While there are notes throughout this book stating when an upgrade to FAST Search Server 2010 for SharePoint may be necessary, the most consolidated information on the subject can be found in Chapter 11.

*Table 1-1.* *SharePoint Search Product Feature Matrix*

| Feature | SharePoint Foundation 2010 | Search Server 2010 Express | Search Server 2010 | SharePoint Server 2010 | FAST Search Server 2010 for SharePoint |
|---|---|---|---|---|---|
| Basic search | X | X | X | X | X |
| Scopes | | X | X | X | X |
| Search enhancements based on user context | | | | | X |
| Custom properties | | X | X | X | X |
| Property extraction | | Limited | Limited | Limited | X |
| Query suggestions | | X | X | X | X |
| Similar results | | | | | X |
| Visual Best Bets | | | | | X |
| Relevancy tuning by document or site promotions | | Limited | Limited | Limited | X |
| Sort results on managed properties or rank profiles | | | | | X |
| Shallow results refinement | | X | X | X | X |

*Continued*

| Feature | SharePoint Foundation 2010 | Search Server 2010 Express | Search Server 2010 | SharePoint Server 2010 | FAST Search Server 2010 for SharePoint |
|---|---|---|---|---|---|
| Deep results refinement | | | | | X |
| Document preview | | | | | X |
| Query federation | | X | X | X | X |
| Windows 7 federation | | X | X | X | X |
| People search | | | | X | X |
| Social search | | | | X | X |
| Taxonomy integration | | | | X | X |
| Multi-tenant hosting | | | | X | |
| Rich web indexing support | | | | | X |
| Support for MySites, Profiles pages, social tagging, and other social computing features | | | | X | X |
| Access to line-of-business (LOB) data systems | X | X | X | X | X |

***Table 1-2.*** *SharePoint Search Product License and Scalability*

| | SharePoint Foundation 2010 | Search Server 2010 Express | Search Server 2010 | SharePoint Server 2010 | FAST Search Server 2010 for SharePoint |
|---|---|---|---|---|---|
| Allowable servers per Search service application | One | One | Multiple | Multiple | Multiple |
| Approximate Maximum Index Capacity (items) | 10M | 300K w/SQL Server 2008 Express; 10M w/ SQL server | 100M | 100M | 500M |
| Product Key Required | Included in Windows Server 2008 or later | Free download from Microsoft | Yes | Yes | Yes, requires enterprise edition of SPS 2010 |

# Getting to Know Search in SharePoint 2010

So far, this chapter has explained what this book will and will not cover. It has explained the range of search-related technologies and products in the Microsoft portfolio, and it has provided scenarios where each may be necessary. The rest of this chapter will serve as an introduction to the terms and concepts used throughout the book. This will help build understanding of the integral background necessary for understanding SharePoint 2010 architecture, services, and sites.

## The Search Center

For end users, the search center is the most important component of search. This is where users execute queries, view results, interact with search result sets, and make decisions on document selection. While the back-end components of search are equally important from an IT perspective, this is the user's front-end connection to all of the complex processes making search work, and without it, users could not search.

The search center can be accessed through two processes. The most direct is by navigating to the search tab in a SharePoint portal. In a standard out-of-the-box (OOTB) SharePoint environment, manually navigating to the search center through the search tab takes users to the query interface shown in Figure 1-1.

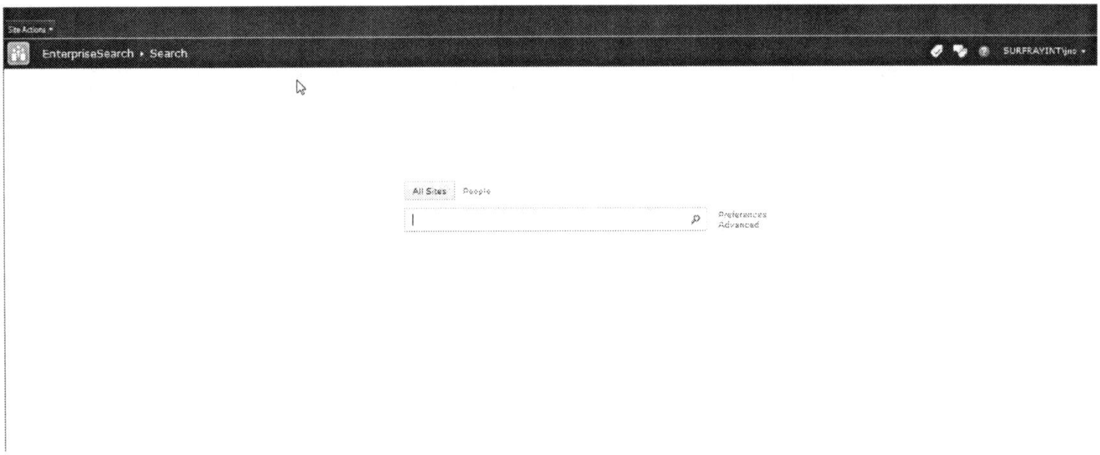

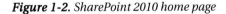

**Figure 1-1.** *SharePoint 2010 search center*

The other option for navigating to the search center is by executing a query through the search box. In an OOTB SharePoint environment, the search box can be found in the upper right-hand quadrant of sites and lists, as shown in Figure 1-2.

**Figure 1-2.** *SharePoint 2010 home page*

When a query is executed through either of these interfaces, it is passed to the search results page and executed. Unless specifically designed to work differently, both search interfaces will take users to the same search results page. If the executed search query matches to results, the results page will display results and allow interaction with them, as shown in Figure 1-3. If no results are found to match the query, then the user will still be directed to the results page, but a notification to this effect will be displayed along with a set of suggestions for altering the query.

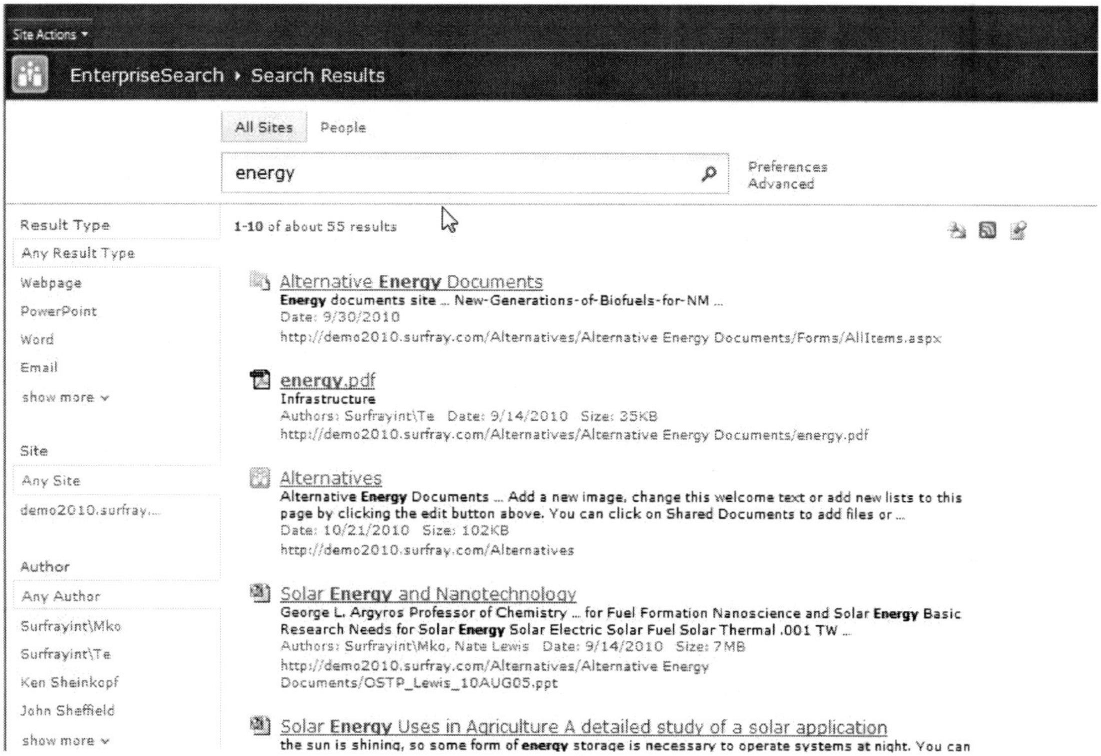

*Figure 1-3. SharePoint 2010 search results page with results*

Deployment, use, and configuration of the search center are discussed in detail in Chapters 4, 5, and 6, respectively.

# Metadata

Put most simply, metadata is data about data. It is the set of defining properties for a library, list, web site, or any other data file. If the writing within a Microsoft Word document is the unstructured content, metadata is the structured content attached to the document that defines it. For a Microsoft Word document, this information typically includes the modified date, author, title, and size, but may also include comments and tags. In SharePoint, metadata may also include properties such as the location of the document, team responsible for it, or the date an item was last checked out. This is the information that defines the document, and it is vital for search within SharePoint.

All search engines utilize metadata to catalog items much like a library. The SharePoint search index stores a wide variety of metadata associated with each item and utilizes this information when returning search results. Typically, since it is generally more reliable and structured, metadata is the first component analyzed by the search engine to determine an item's relevancy. For example, say a user is searching for a Microsoft Word document authored by a particular colleague and enters the keyword "energy" into the search field. The search engine will first consider only documents that have metadata designating them to be Word files and authored by the designated colleague. It will then look throughout the metadata and unstructured content of the documents to return only those that contain the term "energy." In SharePoint, documents that contain the term "energy" in the title are most likely more relevant than those that include it within the body of the writing. Consequently, those documents with "energy" in the title will appear by default higher in the result set than those that contain it in the body. The title of a document is a piece of metadata associated with the file.

As users mature past the most basic concepts of search, metadata becomes increasingly vital. It is what allows users to refine searches based on property restrictions. Metadata tags are what enable tag clouds and hit mapping for global search engines. The language of items and web pages is designated by metadata, and so is the file type. Without metadata, search engines would not be able to differentiate between the title of a document and the body. They would be unable to tell if a result is a Microsoft Word document or an AutoCAD rendering.

When users upload items to SharePoint, they are by default given the option to add a variety of standard metadata to documents such as the author and title. Depending on the design of a SPS 2010 deployment, different metadata may be set up to be requested or required from users before finishing an upload. This metadata is then stored in a database for use by the search index. As will be seen in Chapters 3 and 10, the management of metadata greatly affects relevancy, ranking, and the general ability to find items using search.

# Web Parts

Web Parts are ASP.NET server controls and act as the building blocks of SharePoint. They allow users to modify the appearance, content, and behavior of SharePoint directly from the browser. Web Parts allow for interaction with pages and control the design of a page. For users unfamiliar with SharePoint, Web Parts are also known as portlets and web widgets. These building blocks provide all the individual bits of functionality users may experience within a SharePoint environment.

Examples of Web Parts include those such as the refinement panel Web Part, which allows users to drill into search results, and the Best Bets Web Part, which suggests one or more items from within a search result set based on the entered keyword. In SharePoint 2010, there are over 75 Web Parts that come with the platform, 17 of which are dedicated to search. The options for available Web Parts are increasing daily as additional custom Web Parts can be created in-house, purchased from third-party vendors, or shared freely on sites such as CodePlex. Each can be enabled or disabled to change the available functionality, moved around the page to change layout, and reconfigured to change behavior.

The design and placement of Web Parts can be controlled by administrators. Most Web Parts have a number of settings that control their appearance and available user interactions. Administrators can also use Web Parts to control the layout of a page. For example, if the administrator wants the search refiners to appear on the right of the search results page instead of the left, he or she can move the refinement panel Web Part to the right zone. If the administrator wants to do something more extreme, like adding the advanced search page options to the search results page, he or she can add the advanced search box Web Part to the search results page.

The design and placement of Web Parts around a page is controlled by zones. Pages are broken into eight zones. Administrators can move Web Parts around the page by dragging them into different zones or placing them above or below each other within zones. Figure 1-4 shows the zones within a page that can be utilized for custom page layouts.

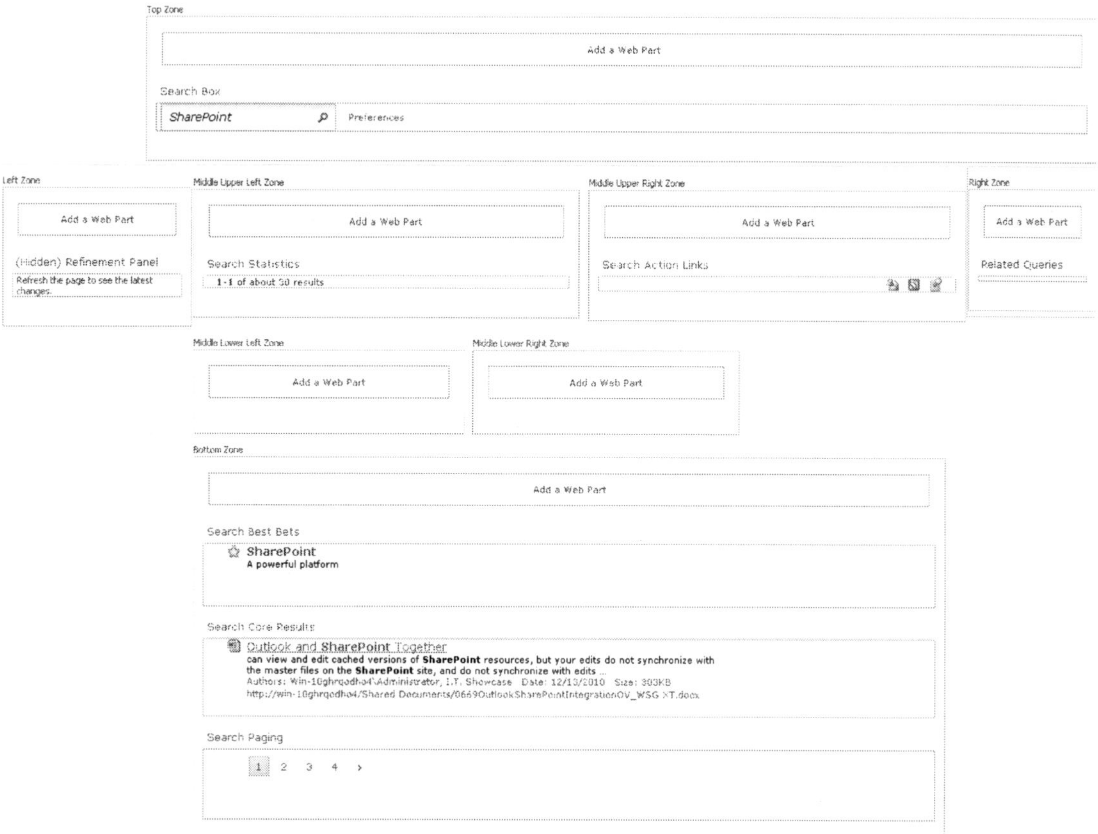

**Figure 1-4.** *SharePoint 2010 Web Part zones*

The available Web Parts are one of the major underlying differences between SharePoint 2010 and SharePoint Foundations 2010. Since Web Parts strictly control the available features within SharePoint, limiting the free SharePoint Foundations to only the basic Web Parts provides the functionality gap. Table 1-3 shows a list of all the out-of-the-box Web Parts available in both SharePoint 2010 and SharePoint Foundations 2010.

***Table 1-3.*** *SharePoint Web Parts List*

| Business Data | Media and Content |
|---|---|
| BusinessDataActionsWebPart.dwp | Media.webpart |
| BusinessDataAssociationWebPart.webpart | MSContentEditor.dwp |
| BusinessDataDetailsWebPart.webpart | MSImage.dwp |
| BusinessDataFilter.dwp | MSPageViewer.dwp |
| BusinessDataItemBuilder.dwp | MSPictureLibrarySlideshow.webpart |
| BusinessDataListWebPart.webpart | Silverlight.webpart |
| IndicatorWebPart.dwp | |
| KpiListWebPart.dwp | **Outlook Web App** |
| Microsoft.Office.Excel.WebUI.dwp | owa.dwp |
| MossChartWebPart.webpart | owacalendar.dwp |
| VisioWebAccess.dwp | owacontacts.dwp |
| | owainbox.dwp |
| | owatasks.dwp |
| **Content Rollup** | |
| CategoryResultsWebPart.webpart | |
| CategoryWebPart.webpart | **Search** |
| ContentQuery.webpart | AdvancedSearchBox.dwp |
| MSUserDocs.dwp | DualChineseSearch.dwp |
| MSXml.dwp | PeopleRefinement.webpart |
| RssViewer.webpart | PeopleSearchBox.dwp |
| siteFramer.dwp | PeopleSearchCoreResults.webpart |
| SummaryLink.webpart | QuerySuggestions.webpart |
| TableOfContents.webpart | Refinement.webpart |
| WhatsPopularWebPart.dwp | SearchActionLinks.webpart |
| WSRPConsumerWebPart.dwp | SearchBestBets.webpart |
| | SearchBox.dwp |

**Filters**

AuthoredListFilter.webpart

DateFilter.dwp

FilterActions.dwp

OlapFilter.dwp

PageContextFilter.webpart

QueryStringFilter.webpart

SpListFilter.dwp

TextFilter.dwp

UserContextFilter.webpart

**Social Collaboration**

contactwp.dwp

MSMembers.dwp

MSUserTasks.dwp

ProfileBrowser.dwp

SocialComment.dwp

TagCloud.dwp

SearchCoreResults.webpart

searchpaging.dwp

searchstats.dwp

searchsummary.dwp

SummaryResults.webpart

TopAnswer.webpart

VisualBestBet.dwp

**SQL Server Reporting**

ReportViewer.dwp

**Forms**

Microsoft.Office.InfoPath.Server.BrowserForm.webpart

MSSimpleForm.dwp

# SharePoint 2010 Search Architecture

The architecture of search in SharePoint can be somewhat complex to understand, specifically because the segmentation of functions between hardware and the way the functions are manipulated from a software perspective are quite different. In every search engine, there are four main components to search, although they may be named differently in each solution. These components include the crawler, indexer, query processor, and databases. Each of these plays a vital role in gathering, storing, structuring, and returning the items within a search environment. In every search engine, these major components hold the same role, but the differences in search engines are found in the way these components interact with each other and execute their own function. Understanding the differences between these functional units will be helpful when having conversations on this subject, tying together research from other sources, and graduating to topics beyond the scope of this book.

The search architecture in SharePoint 2010 has been redesigned from MOSS 2007 to allow for significantly greater scaling. The components of search can most simply be grouped into three functional components. These include query components, crawl components, and database components. Each can be scaled separately to meet the demands of a particular deployment. Before understanding how to plan, set up, configure, and customize search in SPS 2010, it is important to understand what these components do. Figure 1-5 provides a high-level overview of the components of search within SPS 2010 and how they interact with each other. Further details on these services will be found throughout this book, but the following figure provides an initial conceptual drawing to assist with understanding how each function connects.

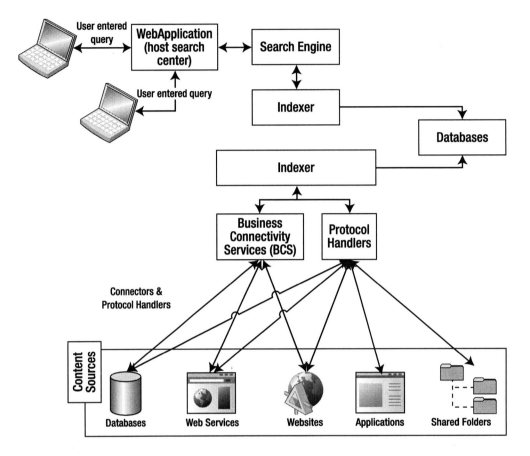

*Figure 1-5. SharePoint 2010 search service architecture*

## The Crawler

Crawling is the process of gathering data from content sources and storing it in databases for use by the query server. This process is the underlying plumbing of the search architecture and is located on the crawl server in SPS 2010. The crawler is responsible for gathering structured and unstructured content to be indexed. It is necessary for collecting all information into a searchable index, including content in SharePoint, content on shared drives, from web services, Exchange public folders, databases, and non-SharePoint hosted applications. Without a crawler, SharePoint would not be able to gather data from content sources, the Web, federated farms, other content management systems, or databases.

SharePoint's crawler can gather content from a variety of content sources. It has built-in capabilities to index its own documents as well as web content and content from directories. It can also index almost any other type of content. It does this through connectors and protocol handlers that essentially unlock a content source to indexing by translating the data into something that the SharePoint crawler can understand and store. Connectors in SharePoint 2010 are managed through the Business Connectivity Services (BCS). For those familiar with the Business Data Catalog (BDC) in MOSS 2007, the BCS is its replacement. The BCS provides read/write access to line-of-business (LOB) systems, so it not only manages the gathering of content but can also be used to manipulate or change content. By default, SharePoint 2010's pre-installed connectors can manage a wide range of content sources, such as Lotus Notes, Exchange, and Documentum. Connectors supporting access to databases, web services, and Windows Communication Foundation (WCF) can be created through the BCS without the need for code. In addition to the pre-installed and easily built connectors, external content sources can be accessed by writing a custom connector through the BCS. The BCS is such an important part of searching on external content sources that an entire chapter has been dedicated to it. Please see Chapter 9 for full details on using the BCS to crawl and index content sources. If crawling and indexing requirements are beyond the capabilities of connector creation through the BCS, protocol handlers can be coded with C# or purchased through third-party vendors. Purchasable protocol handlers will be discussed in Chapter 11, but C# coding is beyond the scope of this book and will not be discussed.

SharePoint 2010 can crawl, index, and search more than just document content sources; it can also do this for people. This can all be done on user profiles with connections to Active Directory (AD) and MySites while being security trimmed through Lightweight Directory Access Protocol (LDAP). These integrations allow searching for people with special skills, departments, teams, or any other data that may be associated with an employee. The LDAP security also insures that only users with the appropriate permissions can return sensitive information such as addresses, phone numbers, and social security numbers. More information about crawling and indexing this type of information can be found in Chapter 3.

## The Indexer

Indexing is the process of turning data gathered by the crawler into logical structured data that is usable by a search engine. This process is the second key component to any search engine. The indexer is responsible for making sense of crawled data. The indexer also collects custom metadata, manages access control to containers, and trims the results for the user when interfacing with the search engine. Unlike many other enterprise search tools, SharePoint 2010 allows only limited access to the indexing capabilities.* More detail on the capabilities of the SharePoint 2010 index will be found in the next chapter.

---

▓ **Note** *This is one of the major differences between FAST Search Server for SharePoint 2010 and SharePoint 2010.

---

Depending on the content being indexed, iFilters may be necessary. An iFilter is a plug-in for the Windows operating system that extracts the text from certain document types and makes a searchable copy of the files in a temporary folder, which allows the SharePoint crawler (and Windows desktop search) to index the content. Without iFilters, content could be gathered into SharePoint, but it could not be translated into data the search engine understands. Chapter 3 addresses pre-installed and third-party iFilters in more detail.

In most search solutions, especially enterprise search tools, the crawler and indexer are separate controllable processes. In SharePoint, Microsoft has consolidated these two processes into one logical component called the *index engine*. This does become complicated, however, when learning the physical server architecture of where these features reside. The crawler and indexer are mashed together to create an easier-to-manage and streamlined process in SPS 2010. As mentioned in the last section, the crawler is housed on the crawl server. The indexer function also occurs on this same server and is essentially tied to the crawler. These two components together are commonly referred to as the *index engine*. The index partitions created by the index engine are propagated out to all query servers in the farms. These query servers are home to the index partitions and the query processor discussed in the next section. Understanding where these different functions reside is not overly important once search is set up, but it is extremely important when planning for an initial implementation and making changes to a farm to improve performance. To review, the crawler and indexer functions reside on the crawl servers. The crawler gathers data from content sources; the indexer then processes and translates the data for use by SharePoint. The indexer function on the crawl server then pushes logical sections of the index out to index partitions on query servers. These query servers can then process queries against their partition of the index, as discussed in the next section.

The topic of planning server architecture and a more detailed walkthrough of search architecture will be found in the next chapter. Although the difference between the server location of a component and the way the components interact with each other may be difficult to understand this early into the book, these concepts will become clearer as you learn more in later chapters.

## The Query Processor

The query processor is the third major component of the search architecture. The query processor is the portion of the search architecture that users directly interface with. It is what accepts queries entered into the search box, translates them into programmatic logic, delivers requests to the index engine, and returns results.

Users interface with the query processor each time they enter a query to the search box or search center. The user provides the query processor with an instruction each time a search query is entered. The query processor accepts that query and applies programmatic logic to translate it into logic the index will understand. The search engine then liaises with the search index to pull a list of search results that correspond to the user's entered query. Using a relevancy algorithm, the search engine prioritizes search results and presents them back to the user.

Every query processor works in this manner, but each uses a different algorithm for liaising with the search index and prioritizing results. This is why SharePoint 2010, Google Search Appliance (GSA), and FAST for SharePoint 2010 can search against the same content sources but return different results or results in a different order. In SharePoint 2010, there are ways to manipulate the priority of search results, or relevancy, through document popularity, improved metadata, and no index classes. This topic is discussed in detail throughout the latter portion of Chapter 3.

As just mentioned, the query processor applies a layer of programmatic logic to queries to create a syntax that other portions of the search architecture will understand. In SharePoint, these techniques include word breaking, Boolean operators, wildcards, and stemmers. Word breaking is the process of breaking compound words into separate components. Boolean operators are user-entered syntax, such as AND as well as OR, which manipulate the way multiple terms in a query are handled. The wildcard operator, denoted by the character *, allows for the tail of a search term to be unfixed. An example of the use of a wildcard is that entering Shar* would return results for SharePoint, Sharon, or Shark. Stemmers are similar to wildcards but are used to recognize variations on a word. An example of this variation is returning planning for the entered word plan. Full details on query syntax, including a chart of available syntax, can be found in Chapter 5.

In the SharePoint 2010 architecture, the query processor is located on the query server. Since user-entered queries are handed directly to the index, this is the logical location for both the indexer and search engine to reside. By locating both within the same architectural unit, SharePoint 2010 decreases the time it takes for a query to pass to the index and for the index to hand results back to the search engine. Interactions with the query processor occur through user interfaces called Web Parts, located on the web server. The specifics of this architecture are discussed in detail in the next chapter.

---

▨ **Note** Although the query processor is a key component of search, and must exist for search to function, there is very little if any official Microsoft literature about the component. This is because, unlike some search tools, the SPS 2010 search engine is fixed and unable to be directly manipulated by developers without advanced knowledge of the interior workings of SharePoint. As a result, a formal title for this component is not well established. In other literature, blogs, and public forums, this component may be referred to by different names such as *query engine* or *search engine*. Throughout this book, we will remain consistent by using the term query processor.

---

## The Databases

The fourth and final components of the search infrastructure are databases. Almost all data in SharePoint is stored in SQL database instances. In regards to search, databases are used to store a wide range of information, such as crawled and indexed content, properties, user permissions, analysis reports, favorite documents, and administrative settings. When the crawler accesses a content source and brings data into SharePoint, it places that content into one or more databases. In addition, all of the data that administrators and users add to SharePoint through active actions, such as adding metadata, or passive actions, such as logs created from portal usage, is also stored in SQL databases. There are three primary SQL databases necessary to run the search service in SPS 2010.

> *Crawl databases* manage crawl operations and store the crawl history. Each crawl database can have one or more crawlers feeding it, in which case each crawler can attend to different content. The database both drives the crawl and stores the returned content. For those familiar with the database architecture of MOSS 2007, this database replaces the Search database.

> *Property databases* store the properties (metadata) for crawled data. This structured information is used by the index to organize files, indicate necessary permissions, and control relevancy.

> The *Search Admin database* stores the search configuration data and access control list (ACL) for crawled content. Unlike other databases, only one Search Admin database is allowed or necessary per Search service application. For those familiar with MOSS 2007, this is the replacement for the Shared Services Provider (SSP) database.

For any SharePoint environment, there will be a number of various databases, depending on factors such as how content is structured, the number of crawlers pulling from content sources, the types of analytics stored for business intelligence, and security trimming. Other databases that may be encountered include Staging and Reporting databases for analytics or Logging databases for diagnostics. Chapter 2 will discuss planning for databases in significantly more detail.

## Multilingual Support

SharePoint 2010 supports over 40 languages to cater to the global usage of Microsoft SharePoint product lines. The full extents of supported languages are not, however, automatically installed when SharePoint 2010 is deployed. For additional language support, language packs are made available through Microsoft and are available for free download. SharePoint Server 2010, Search Server 2010, Search Server Express 2010, and FAST Search Server for SPS 2010 all use the same language packs to provide consistency between solutions. Multiple language packs can also be installed on the same server without changing the underlying language of the Microsoft Server product. This allows multinational deployments to use one farm to host a large geography.

Language packs contain language-specific site templates. These templates allow administrators to create sites based on a specific language. Without these language packs, sites in languages other than those allowed in the installed product would be improperly displayed. It is also important to note that language packs do not translate an existing site or site collection; they simply allow administrators to build new sites or site collections in a different language.

For search, these language packs are vital for word breaking and stemming to operate correctly. By applying a language pack, one search interface can be used to search against multilingual content, while simultaneously recognizing the language being entered in the search box. Without language packs, word breaks would not be inserted in logical positions, a correlation would not be able to be made between a searched term and its various stems, and the SharePoint search engine would be unable to properly translate a query into a structured presentation for the index.

Microsoft is continuing to support additional languages to increase the ability for global companies to adopt SharePoint. The list of supported languages at the time this book is published and their Language IDs can be found in Table 1-4. Language packs are available through Microsoft for download.

*Table 1-4. SharePoint 2010 Supported Languages*

| Language | Language ID | Language | Language ID |
|---|---|---|---|
| Arabic | 1025 | Italian | 1040 |
| Basque | 1069 | Japanese | 1041 |
| Bulgarian | 1026 | Kazakh | 1087 |
| Catalan | 1027 | Korean | 1042 |
| Chinese (Simplified) | 2052 | Latvian | 1062 |
| Chinese (Traditional) | 1028 | Lithuanian | 1063 |

| Language | Language ID | Language | Language ID |
|---|---|---|---|
| Croatian | 1050 | Norwegian (Bokmål) | 1044 |
| Czech | 1029 | Polish | 1045 |
| Danish | 1030 | Portuguese (Brazil) | 1046 |
| Dutch | 1043 | Portuguese (Portugal) | 2070 |
| English | 1033 | Romanian | 1048 |
| Estonian | 1061 | Russian | 1049 |
| Finnish | 1035 | Serbian (Latin) | 2074 |
| French | 1036 | Slovak | 1051 |
| Galician | 1110 | Slovenian | 1060 |
| German | 1031 | Spanish | 3082 |
| Greek | 1032 | Swedish | 1053 |
| Hebrew | 1037 | Thai | 1054 |
| Hindi | 1081 | Turkish | 1055 |
| Hungarian | 1038 | Ukrainian | 1058 |

# Scaling

The query server, crawl server, and database server functions in SharePoint 2010 are extremely scalable. These functions can all be grouped onto a single physical server in small deployments, or spread across several different physical servers as necessary to cater to performance, availability, bandwidth, and security needs. There are two key concepts of scaling that need to be understood before considering the implications of physical server configurations. These concepts are scaling up and scaling out, each of which has distinct effects on a search deployment.

Scaling out is the concept of adding more hardware and software resources to increase performance, availability, and redundancy. Scaling out is done to handle more services, sites, applications, and queries. It is also done to achieve redundancy, which results in increased availability. *Availability* refers to the ability or inability of a system to respond predictably to requests. The result of failures in availability is *downtime,* which, depending on the severity, means the inability for users to properly leverage a SharePoint deployment. By scaling out, there are greater insurances against downtime, but increased license costs and hardware costs will be incurred.

Scaling up is the concept of improving each server by adding more processors, memory, storage, and faster disks to handle a larger workload. Scaling up allows for each server to perform a given task faster. Adding a faster query server, for example, allows for each query entered by a user to be accepted and results returned faster. Adding a faster crawl server improves crawl speed, and adding more storage space to a database server allows for retention of more content and metadata from crawled content sources.

Search in SharePoint 2010 is significantly more scalable than in previous versions of SharePoint. Unlike MOSS 2007, which allowed only one crawl server per farm, you can now deploy multiple crawl servers to increase indexing speed. In addition to redundant crawl servers, multiple query servers and database servers can also be deployed in one farm. Greater flexibility in both scaling up and scaling out is what drives SharePoint 2010's ability to crawl more content, store more data, and execute queries faster than MOSS 2007.

Before deploying SharePoint 2010, the physical server architecture should be carefully considered. The results of this decision will greatly affect the performance of a search deployment, but it will also drastically sway hardware costs, licensing costs, deployment time, and maintenance costs. Plans for future growth of a SharePoint deployment as well as limitations of the software should also be taken into account when planning the appropriate architecture. A full review of the considerations that should go into planning search architecture can be found in Chapter 2.

## Extensibility

SharePoint 2010 is not limited to the features and functions available out of the box. With the right skillset, there is a great deal of flexibility that ranges from basic customization, such as different site templates, to advanced concepts, such as custom workflows, search navigation, and crawler connectivity. The fact that functionality is not immediately apparent doesn't mean it cannot be added to a SharePoint farm.

The bulk of this book focuses on what can be done with SharePoint out of the box without additional development or third-party resources. It is, however, important to understand that SharePoint is just the backbone platform and building blocks. SPS 2010 is just the Christmas tree without lights or decorations. To get the leverage of the full potential of SharePoint, it may be necessary to dive into more advanced functionality by doing custom development, implementing freeware Web Parts, or purchasing a vended solution.

The latter portions of this book will discuss more advanced topics of extensibility. Chapter 7 provides the basics for customizing the look and feel of the search interface through master pages, CSS, XSLTs, and Web Part XML customization. Chapter 9 focuses on how to use the Business Connectivity Services (BCS), which is included with all SharePoint 2010 products, to index custom content and build custom connectors. Finally, Chapter 11 provides an overview of vended products, such as custom Web Parts and iFilters, which extend the search capabilities of SharePoint 2010.

## Summary

The first half of this chapter outlined the focus of this book, explored the background history of Microsoft SharePoint Server 2010, and provided a brief overview of the other products in the SharePoint search catalog. The second half of this chapter provided an introduction to the key concepts and architectural components that will be focused on throughout this book. These sections are vital for building the basics for the more advanced subjects discussed throughout the readings. The rest of this book will take an in-depth dive into the key topics necessary to plan, set up, configure, customize, and extend search within Microsoft SharePoint 2010.

# CHAPTER 2

■ ■ ■

# Planning Your Search Deployment

After completing this chapter, you will be able to

- Estimate content size and identify factors that will influence crawl times

- Determine how much storage space you will need to allocate to search

- Plan for an initial deployment of SharePoint 2010 Search

- Anticipate performance issues

- Scale for search performance

- Understand availability and plan to avoid downtime

- Provision search with Windows PowerShell

Microsoft SharePoint Server 2010 is significantly more advanced than previous versions of the SharePoint platform. Few areas were given more attention than the structure of the search components. This re-structuring has made the search piece of SharePoint vastly more scalable and robust for large- and small-scale deployments alike. With these changes, however, come added complexity and the need for more thoughtful consideration when planning a SharePoint Search deployment.

When determining planning strategies for deploying SharePoint Search, it is wise to consider the architectural and business environment as well as the available budget and availability of hardware and required software. What should be indexed and what should be delivered to the users are essential areas to consider before starting a deployment.

The simplest model, and the most common for development and testing purposes, is to install all the search components, including the database components, on a single server. But most companies will want to consider separating search (at least in part) from their base SharePoint deployment. Most implementations will naturally start with a single server with combined crawl and query roles, in addition to the web servers and database servers already in the farm, and then consider scaling out as search performance is identified as problematic.

The administrator should always be wary of the fact that performance issues, although not obvious, can cause frustration and stalled adoption of the platform. Therefore it is wise to think ahead and plan for high availability when at all possible. Some organizations can tolerate slower response times as search may not be considered a critical business tool. However, it is a best practice that the time it takes from entering a search term to the moment the result page is finished rendering should be no more than one second. Of course, there are many factors that may determine the result page rendering time, including custom Web Parts and design elements that are not directly related to search. However, if at all possible, care should be taken to limit the amount of time for any SharePoint page to be returned.

Administrators should optimally target all latency to sub-second levels. Poorly performing search in SharePoint often gives rise to questions such as, "Why does it take five seconds to search in our own systems when I can get results from the Internet in less than a second?"

Outlined in this chapter are the core components of SharePoint 2010 Search and considerations that should be taken into account when planning a deployment. Each component and its unique role are described, and how they can work independently or together is addressed. Hardware and software requirements are briefly outlined and references to more information given. Finally, scaling and redundancy best practices are discussed.

# SharePoint 2010 Components

SharePoint 2010 has a number of performance and redundancy features. The search capabilities have been redesigned to allow for a broader ability to scale and more points for redundancy.

The new architecture for SharePoint 2010 provides a more compartmentalized approach to search by dividing the tasks that the search mechanism performs into different roles that can also be spread out across physical or virtual servers, as well as further divisions within these roles. The four server roles for search are as follows:

- *Web server role*

- *Query server role*

- *Crawl server role*

- *Database server role*

The query server and crawl server roles are unique to the search component, whereas the web server and database server roles can be utilized by and are necessary for other components of SharePoint 2010.

## Web Server Role

Servers hosting the web server role host the web components of SharePoint 2010 that provide the user interface for searching. These components, such as search center sites, Web Parts, and web pages that host query boxes and result pages, are delivered from servers with the web server role to the end users. These components send requests to servers hosting the query server role and receive and display the result set. More details on customizing the search components that reside on the pages hosted by the web server role are discussed in Chapters 6 and 7.

The web server role may not be necessary in SharePoint farms that are dedicated for search, as other farms that are utilizing the search farm will handle this role and communicate with the search farm directly from their web servers. The web server role is often combined in smaller deployments with web servers serving content or with other search server roles.

## Query Server Role

The query server role serves results to web servers. Query servers receive requests from servers with the web server role and forward these requests to all servers in a farm with the query server role. They then process the query against all index partitions and return their results to the requesting server, which then forwards the results to the requesting web server.

On each query server, there is a query processor, which trims the result set for security, detects duplicates, and assigns the appropriate associated properties to each result from the property store. Any SharePoint farm providing search must have at least one server hosting the query server role. However, a farm may call search from another farm and therefore not need the query server role.

The query server role, like other application roles in SharePoint, can be hosted on a server with other application server roles. This makes SharePoint 2010 very versatile but may cause confusion when planning resource usage. Having all servers provide all roles is not optimal resource usage, as some demanding roles may cause other roles to perform poorly. Caution and consideration regarding the role and demand of each server and each task are therefore advised.

The query server holds the index on its file structure or a file structure relative to it. A query server can host either the entire index or index partitions—sections of the index that can be assigned to different query servers by the administrator for load, performance, and redundancy. Index partitions may be duplicated on a number of servers with the query server role to provide redundancy. Adding query servers with the index partitioned across those query servers will also increase search query performance and reduce result latency.

## Index Partitions

An index partition is a portion of the entire search index. Microsoft has designed the index to be broken into logical sections that can be distributed and mirrored across query servers. Generally, index partitions are spread across servers and represent an equal amount of crawled data. Indexes may also be partitioned on a single server. They can also be mirrored on another server or set of servers to provide redundancy.

Imagine, for example, that a SharePoint farm has 300GB of crawled data and three query servers. Each query server can hold a single index partition representing 100GB of crawled data. Query speed is increased because the load of searching the index is distributed over servers and divided by three. The query servers take time to look into the index for any given query, and therefore searching in smaller partitions across multiple servers is substantially more performant. An additional mirror of each partition can also be added to each query server to insure redundancy. Should any one query server fail, the remaining query servers still have all portions of the index and can continue to serve results. See Figure 2-1.

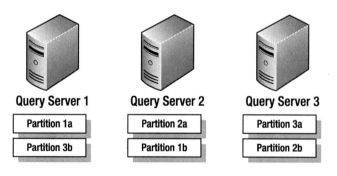

| Query Server 1 | Query Server 2 | Query Server 3 |
|---|---|---|
| Partition 1a | Partition 2a | Partition 3a |
| Partition 3b | Partition 1b | Partition 2b |

***Figure 2-1.*** *Three query servers with mirrored partitions*

# Crawl Server Role

The crawl server role is responsible for crawling content. This crawling mechanism is similar to other web crawling technologies, except that it is specifically designed to crawl and index SharePoint content, including user profiles from a directory, associated document metadata, custom properties, file shares, Exchange public folders, web content, and database and custom content through the BSC (as well as content via iFilters and protocol handlers).

The crawl servers host the crawler components, and, like the query server role, at least one server in a SharePoint 2010 farm providing search must host the crawl server role. Crawlers on the crawl servers are associated with crawl databases. Each crawler is associated with one crawl database.

It is recommended that the Search Administration component also be hosted on the server with the crawl server role. However, it can be hosted on any server in the farm. SharePoint 2010 hosts only a single Search Administration component per Search service application.

---

▓ **Note** Until sometime in the middle of 2010, the crawl server in SharePoint 2010 was known as the index server. In November 2010, Microsoft updated SharePoint 2010 documentation, changing the name to crawl server. However, many blog posts and references to SharePoint 2010 use the term index server to refer to what we call the crawl server in this book. We, as search engine professionals, believe the term crawl server is much more appropriate for what the server's role actually is, and obviously Microsoft came to think so as well. Administrators should just be aware that the crawl server and index server are the same in SharePoint 2010, and the actual index lives on the query server.

---

## Search Service Application (SSA)

SharePoint 2010 has its core services broken into service applications. These applications, which deliver much of the functionality of SharePoint 2010, are separated to provide granularity and scalability when managing many of the different features available in SharePoint 2010. These services include but are not limited to the User Profile service, the Business Data Connectivity service, the Managed Metadata service, and the Search service, among others. Additionally, third-party vendors or solution providers could provide custom service applications that plug into SharePoint 2010, although at the time of writing, there were not any good examples of a third-party service application.

The Search service application is the service application that is responsible for the search engine. It manages the crawler and the indexes as well as any modifications to topology or search functionality at the index level.

# Database Server Role

In a SharePoint 2010 Search deployment, the search databases are hosted on a server with the database server role. It is also possible to host other SharePoint 2010 databases on the same server or separate search and content database roles. Servers with the database server role can be mirrored or clustered to provide redundancy.

There are three types of databases utilized by a SharePoint 2010 farm providing search: property databases, crawl databases, and Search Administration databases.

Aside from disk size and performance limitations, there are no other considerations that limit hosting other databases, such as SharePoint content databases, on a SharePoint 2010 server with the database server role.

- *Property databases*: Property databases hold property metadata for crawled items. These properties can be crawled document metadata or associated custom properties from SharePoint 2010.

- *Crawl databases*: Crawl databases store a history of the crawl. They also manage the crawl operations by indicating start and stop points. A single crawl database can have one or more crawlers associated with it. However, a single crawler can be associated with only one crawl database.

- *Search Administration databases*: Search Administration databases store search configuration data such as scopes and refiners and security information for the crawled content. Only one Search Administration database is permitted per Search service application.

# Environment Planning and Metrics

When preparing to deploy SharePoint 2010 Search, there are several areas of consideration that need to be addressed. How many servers will be used, which roles those servers take, and how services are spread across them are dependent on how much content there is to index and what the performance expectations are. Another consideration, which often becomes the most critical, is how much of a budget the organization has to meet those requirements.

This section intends to give an idea of the factors to consider when planning a SharePoint Search deployment. Many administrators will not have many choices when it comes to infrastructure, so they must plan the best and most performant solution with the hardware they have.

*The key considerations for planning a deployment are as follows:*

- *Performance*: There are two main factors for performance when it comes to search—crawl performance and query performance. Crawl performance refers to how fast the search crawling components can collect text and metadata from documents and store them in the databases. Query performance refers to the speed at which results can be returned to end users performing searches and how that performance may be affected by query complexity and volume. SharePoint has several areas where performance can be improved by adjusting or adding search or crawl components.

- *Scalability*: Organizations grow and shrink as do their knowledge management requirements. Most often, we envision growth and prosperity, and this would correspond with increasing content in SharePoint and an increasing load on the services it provides. Search is a service that is generally seen as increasing in popularity and adoption, and therefore usually scaling up or out to handle demand is necessary. However, the opposite may sometimes also be a consideration. Scaling can be required to improve performance by adding additional hardware and/or software components as well as improving availability by providing redundant services across hardware. Any environment should be planned so that one can scale to improve these factors.

- *Security:* One of the most key concerns of organizations is the protection of data. Security is of paramount concern. Security is a broad topic and worthy of careful consideration. Security can be controlling access to servers from outside intruders, but it can also be controlling which authenticated users are allowed to see precisely what content.

- *Availability:* Critical business systems need to be available for use. Downtime of a key SharePoint site or its related services can result in hundreds or thousands of employees being unable to perform their jobs. This kind of downtime can quickly cost millions of dollars in lost productivity and undelivered goods or services. Making servers redundant and having failover strategies can help mitigate hardware and software problems that could cause downtime.

- *Budget:* Budget is always a key consideration. Organizations need to make careful calculations about what risks they are willing to take to reduce costs. Some risks are reasonable while others are not. For example, saving $10,000 by not making crawl servers redundant could be a feasible savings if company business is not adversely affected by not having an up-to-date index for several days should the crawl servers fail. However, having 10,000 employees not able to access information for even a day can easily outweigh the savings.

These considerations will be discussed in more detail in the following sections. First, it will be useful to get an idea of the minimum hardware and software requirements that Microsoft sets forth as well as calculate required disk size for the databases and understand the initial deployment options.

# Hardware and Software Requirements

SharePoint 2010's search components take their requirements from the base SharePoint 2010 server requirements, with the exception that query servers should have enough RAM to hold one third of the active index partition in memory at any given time. Therefore, care should be taken when planning query servers and the spread of index partitions to ensure there is sufficient RAM for the index.

## Hardware Requirements

The core recommendations for hardware hosting SharePoint search are as follows:

- All development and testing servers:

    - 4 core CPU

    - 4GB RAM

    - 80GB system drive

- All application servers:

    - 4 core CPU

    - 8GB RAM

    - 80GB system drive

- Database servers:
    - Small production deployments (less than 10 million documents)
        - 4 core CPU
        - 8GB RAM
        - 80GB system drive
        - Sufficient storage space for search databases
    - Medium to large deployments (more than 10 million documents)
        - 8 core CPU
        - 16GB RAM
        - 80GB system drive
        - Sufficient storage space for search databases

---

■ **Note** Microsoft Office SharePoint Server 2007 could be run on 32-bit servers. SharePoint 2010 requires 64-bit servers. Be careful that all the servers are 64-bit if upgrading from a previous version of SharePoint and all associated software (e.g., third-party add-ins) is also 64-bit compatible.

---

## Software Requirements

Microsoft has made major advancements in the install process of SharePoint. SharePoint 2010 has a surprisingly friendly installer that can check the system for prerequisites and install any missing required components. This makes installation of SharePoint 2010 for Search installations extremely easy.

There are some important things to note, however. SharePoint 2010 is available only for 64-bit systems. This will mean that all hardware supporting the operating system must be 64-bit.

SharePoint 2010 search application servers require one of the following Windows operating systems:

- 64-bit Windows Server 2008 R2 (Standard, Enterprise, Datacenter, or Web Server version)
- 64-bit edition of Windows Server 2008 with Service Pack 2 (Standard, Enterprise, Datacenter, or Web Server version)

*If Service Pack 2 is not installed, SharePoint 2010's installer will install it (cool!).*

SharePoint 2010 search database servers (non-stand-alone) require one of the following versions of SQL Server:

- 64-bit edition of SQL Server 2008 R2
- 64-bit edition of SQL Server 2008 with Service Pack 1 and Cumulative Update 2
- 64-bit edition of SQL Server 2005 with Service Pack 3

Whenever possible, it is recommended to use the R2 releases.

There are a number of other required software packages that the SharePoint 2010 installer's preparation tool will install as well.

- Web server (IIS) role

- Application server role

- Microsoft .NET Framework version 3.5 SP1

- SQL Server 2008 Express with SP1

- Microsoft Sync Framework Runtime v1.0 (x64)

- Microsoft Filter Pack 2.0

- Microsoft Chart Controls for the Microsoft .NET Framework 3.5

- Windows PowerShell 2.0

- SQL Server 2008 Native Client

- Microsoft SQL Server 2008 Analysis Services ADOMD.NET

- ADO.NET Data Services Update for .NET Framework 3.5 SP1

- A hotfix for the .NET Framework 3.5 SP1 that provides a method to support token authentication without transport security or message encryption in WCF

- Windows Identity Foundation (WIF)

---

■ **Note** For more up-to-date information and more details, visit Microsoft TechNet's hardware and software requirements page: http://technet.microsoft.com/en-us/library/cc262485.aspx.

---

## Database Considerations: Determining Database Size

When determining how much database to allot for search, it is important to consider each database and its purpose separately. Most search engine vendors' databases take between 15% and 20% of the total repository size for all search databases. Although a safe guideline is to always allow 20% of content size space for search databases, SharePoint's architecture is more complex and requires a little closer consideration. Microsoft gives some formulae to calculate the search database size. Although tests will probably not match these calculations, they are a good place to start.

Also, remember that index partitions do not reside in SQL on the database server. They reside on the file structure on or relative to the query servers. Their location can be set in the Central Administration under Manage Service Applications ➤ Search Service Application ➤ Search Administration ➤ Search Application Topology ➤ Modify. These databases could reasonably be on a high-performance disk array or storage area network. See Figure 2-2.

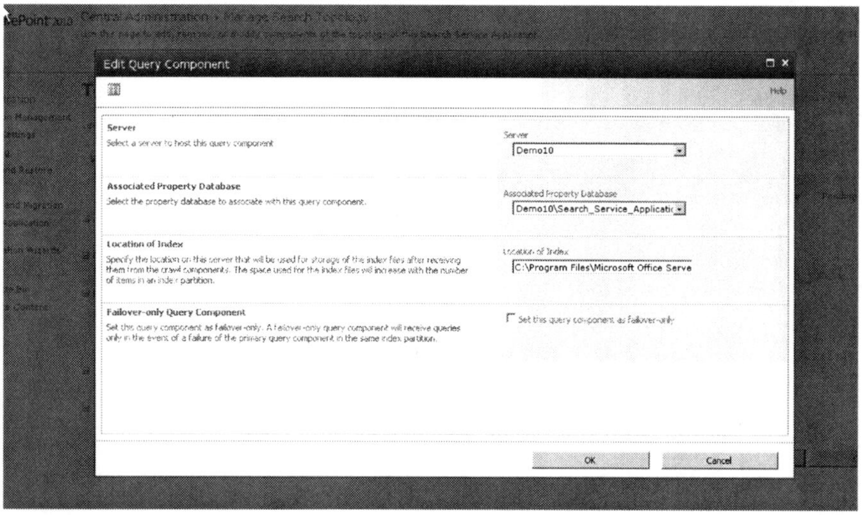

**Figure 2-2.** *The Edit Query Component page with index partition path*

There are three database types on the database server held in SQL: an Administration database, crawl databases, and property databases. The server may contain many crawl and property databases depending on the size and complexity of the deployment. It is essential to account for each one. Microsoft gives the following calculations to determine their sizes.

The Search Administration database stores only security information and search setting information and does not need more than 10GB of storage space. It will likely not take more than 1GB in any scenario, but it is allocated extra for good measure.

Crawl database size is relative to the size of the content database it is crawling. Content database size, if one is not already available to check, can be determined with the following calculation from Microsoft:

*Database size = ((Number of documents × Number of non-current versions) × Average size of documents) + (10KB × (List items + (Number of non-current versions × Number of documents)))*

---

▓ **Tip** For more details, see `http://technet.microsoft.com/en-us/library/cc298801.aspx`.

---

The crawl databases sizes are then determined by multiplying the size of the content database by 4.6%.

The property databases sizes are determined by multiplying the size of the content database by 1.5%.

Total database server size requirements for search are therefore as follows:

- Admin database = 10GB

- Crawl databases = Content database size × .046

- Property databases = Content database size × .015

A simple example of a SharePoint farm with a 100GB content database would require the following:

- Admin database = 10GB

- Crawl databases = 100 × .046 = 4.6GB

- Property databases = 1TB × .015 = 1.5GB

- Total space required = 16.1GB

Additionally, the input/output per second (IOPS) requirements on SQL for search are of importance. Search is extremely dependent on good seek performance.

- For the crawl database, search requires from 3,500 to 7,000 IOPS.

- For the property database, search requires 2,000 IOPS.

## Query Server Space Calculations

Index partitions are held on the query servers and not in the database server (unless the server with the database server role also has the query server role). The crawl database, Search Administration database, and property databases are held in SQL. Index partitions are held on the file structure. Microsoft suggests calculating space for the index partitions at 3.5% of the content databases. This space needs to be on the drive on which the query server is storing the index partitions. Space should be also allocated for the active search index and the data coming during a crawl as well as the total space required during master merge. Therefore, the query servers should provide at least three times the necessary space for the index.

---

■ **Note** When considering redundancy or if there is more than one index partition, additional space for each additional partition will be needed.

---

So, for example, if there is 100GB of content in the SharePoint content database, it can be expected that a single index partition will require 3.5GB of space. If there are two query servers, each holding a single active index partition and one index partition mirror, one should expect 7GB (3.5% × 2) of space or 3.5GB per server required to hold the index partitions.

- Content database size = 100GB

- Index partition = 100 × .035 = 3.5GB

- Index partition mirror = 100 × .035 = 3.5GB

- Space for master merge = All index partitions × 3
- Total = 21GB

# Initial Deployment Guidelines

It can be a difficult process to decide how large of a deployment and how many resources to dedicate to an initial search deployment. Generally speaking, if SharePoint 2010 is being installed as the first document management and collaboration tool, the search components can start out in their simplest form and scale out as documents are added and the adoption of SharePoint 2010 grows. However, this scenario is becoming rare, and most organizations will find themselves either upgrading to SharePoint 2010 from a previous version or migrating content from another system or from an ad hoc system, such as a file share. In these cases, initial deployment architectures and best practices can be useful.

Luckily, Microsoft gives some guidelines for what kinds of architectures can support different scenarios. These guidelines are based on the number of items that are indexed and searchable regardless of whether they come from inside or outside SharePoint 2010. The entirety of these documents is known as the *corpus*.

- *1 million documents or less*: All roles on a single server or one application server and one database server

- *1 to 10 million documents*: Web server and query server roles combined on one to two servers, one dedicated crawl server, and a dedicated database server

- *10–20 million documents*: Same architecture as 1 to 10 million documents model but with an additional crawl server and redundancy on the query servers—that is, use two query servers, each with two index partitions broken into half of the index partition on each and a mirror of the other server's half on each.

- *20–40 million documents*: For more than 20 million documents, a dedicated search farm is recommended. On a dedicated search farm, servers with the web server role are not necessary as long as the farm where searches are initiated has servers with this role and those servers are configured to direct queries to the dedicated farm. The farm should have a minimum of four query servers, each with a quarter of the index in an index partition. Each query server should also host a mirror of another server's partition for redundancy. In addition, two crawl servers, each with two crawlers, and two crawl databases, each with two crawlers associated with it, are recommended. In addition, it is recommended that two additional database servers be utilized to hold property databases and the Search Admin database.

- *40–100 million documents*: Any organization with more than 40 million documents will require a completely dedicated search farm with a high level of redundancy. The web server role should probably be handled by the content farm except if a dedicated web server is allocated for indexing (recommended). The farm should have six to ten query servers, each holding an equal portion of the index in an index partition, as well as a mirror of one of the other index partitions from another server. There should also be four crawl servers and four database clusters where the four crawl servers write to two crawl databases.

Use the following flowchart (Figure 2-3) to easily see how many servers will be required for a deployment.

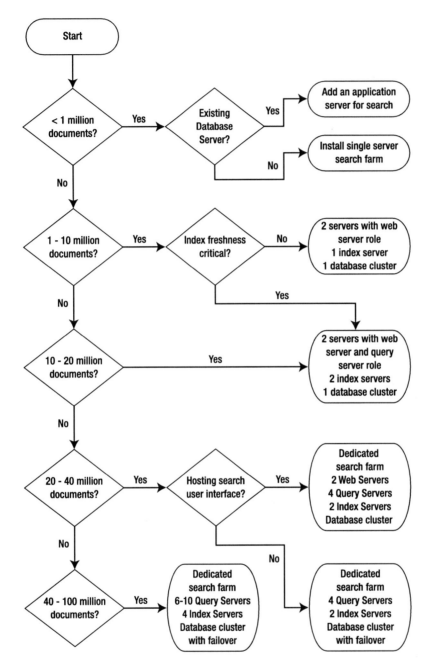

**Figure 2-3.** *Deployment sizing decision flowchart*

# Typical Server Configurations

Microsoft often refers to the way that it organizes servers working together as a topology, and the administrator can modify the search application topology from within SharePoint's Central Administration. Topology refers to the overall layout of the servers and the software components on those servers. We use the terms server configurations and topology interchangeably in this book.

The different ways in which servers can be configured to provide scalability, performance, and redundancy for SharePoint 2010 are vast and largely dependent on the particular environment of each business. We will not attempt to give an exhaustive example of each possible configuration but will attempt to outline the basic models and the points where these may be safely and most effectively modified to suit particular business needs.

As mentioned earlier, the most common and first type of deployment any SharePoint administrator will encounter will be the single server deployment, simply because this is the model where all testing and development will start. However, few organizations with serious document management and collaboration needs will utilize a single server in a production environment. Even small, departmental deployments will usually have at least a separate database server.

Which topology fits a particular organization is dependent on several factors, which we discuss later in this chapter. However, many considerations outside search, which are not covered in this book, are key in deciding the overall topology of a SharePoint deployment, so we encourage administrators to investigate this topic separately.

## Single Server

A single server implementation for very small corpora can be either part of an existing SharePoint farm or a stand-alone search server with crawl and query components on it. It may or may not have database components on the server. Most organizations will have an existing database cluster that they will utilize for performance and redundancy. Figure 2-4 shows a simple but typical single search server implementation with or without a database.

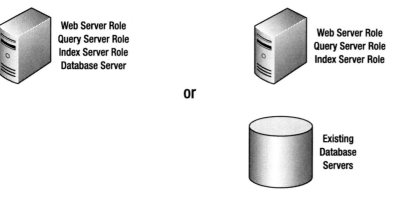

**Figure 2-4.** *A single server deployment*

## Small Farm

Many organizations will demand more performance and utilize a small search farm. This farm participates in overall SharePoint tasks as well as dedicated search tasks. One of the web servers may be outside of Network Load Balancing (NLB) to provide performance for indexing or may participate in content delivery. Both web servers also perform the query server role. The content serving portion of the farm will certainly have additional web servers. There is a single crawl server. See Figure 2-5.

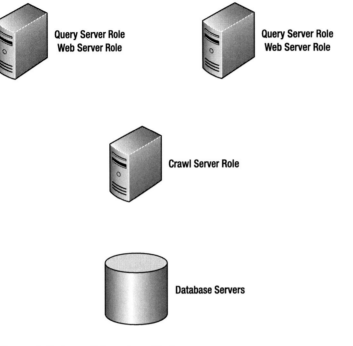

**Figure 2-5.** *A small farm installation*

## Medium Farm

In a medium-sized farm, there should be at least two servers with a shared query server role that can host the web server role. One of these may or may not be excluded from NLB for indexing performance. There are two crawl servers to provide redundancy for crawling. There is a single dedicated database cluster for storing the crawl database, property database, and Administration database. See Figure 2-6.

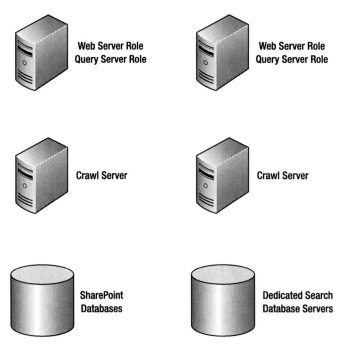

**Web Server Role**
**Query Server Role**

**Web Server Role**
**Query Server Role**

**Crawl Server**

**Crawl Server**

**SharePoint**
**Databases**

**Dedicated Search**
**Database Servers**

*Figure 2-6.* *A medium search farm*

## Medium Dedicated Search Farm

At a certain point, the search components will need to be separated from performing any content delivery tasks and dedicated to search. In a dedicated search farm, there can be web servers for delivering search requests and providing content to the crawl server; however, they should be excluded from participating in content delivery. Other components should be isolated to their own servers and dedicated to their own roles. Combining roles is still possible, but as the farm grows, dedicating the servers to individual roles will be the wisest use of resources. See Figure 2-7.

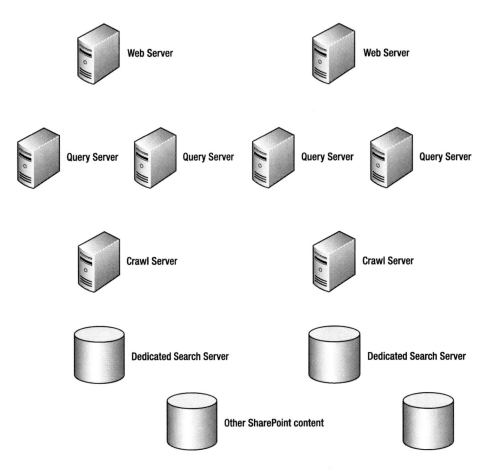

*Figure 2-7.* A medium dedicated search farm

## Large Dedicated Search Farm

For the largest deployments, all roles should be hosted on multiple dedicated servers. Dedicated web servers for indexing are still possible, but the focus should be on providing high-performance query components to handle queries from a large SharePoint farm. A large farm may have ten or more query servers, four or more crawl servers, and at least two database clusters dedicated to holding the search databases. As we saw in the SharePoint 2010 components section, index partitions can be separated across query servers and mirrored evenly. See Figure 2-8.

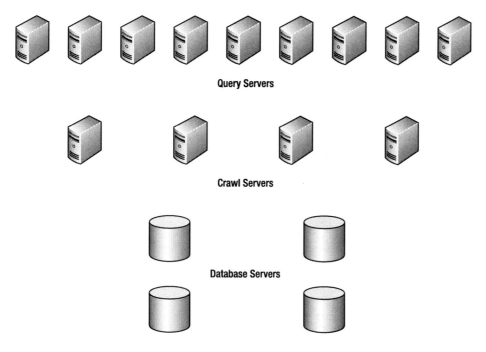

**Figure 2-8.** *A large dedicated search farm*

# Performance

Although performance is usually not a major consideration during initial software implementations, it is a critical aspect to consider. Most often, performance is in the back of the administrator's mind, and assumptions about how fast the responses will be are made without consideration of environmental variables and infrastructure limitations. Administrators are often surprised when pages load slowly, documents take seemingly forever to download, or searches are returned only after several seconds.

Search performance is additionally dependent on different factors than content display, and its requirements to perform can often be overlooked. There are unique areas that need to be considered to make search perform, and giving them proper consideration prior to deploying SharePoint Search implementation may help avoid user dissatisfaction at a later stage.

In most cases, the target for good search performance is that search result pages, under peak search load, are finished rendering in less than one second. Search should take no longer to complete and be actioned than any regular page. Also, as users will become accustomed to using the result page to some extent as an information source or an information target from where they can check out, edit, or share documents in and of itself, search should be seen as a core content display component.

There are two main areas of performance for a search engine:

*Query latency*: Query latency is the time it takes the query servers to receive a search request from the web server, check the index partitions for the given query terms, gather the result data from the search databases into a result set, and return it to the web server. Additionally, the web server must render this result set in the result page and display it with any special formatting, custom design, or custom Web Parts. Although the rendering and display mechanism is not strictly part of the query servers' performance, users will not differentiate when their result set is returned slower than expected.

There are a number of factors that can attribute to high query latency. These include slow hardware, or more often hardware with insufficient resources, a slow network connection, large indexes, and a high volume of queries. Monitoring these factors and pinpointing the bottlenecks can help determine and remedy the source of poor query times.

*Indexing speed*: How fast the crawl server can gather documents determines how fresh the content returned in search queries is. It also will determine if security values are updated in the result list. Users may make the assumption that search is a representation of the documents at any point and expect that the latest version of documents is searchable. Luckily, SharePoint 2010 has an excellent incremental crawl mechanism that will keep refreshing the documents on schedule without search downtime. However, poor performance on search indexing could mean that initial crawls take days to weeks to complete. Poor SharePoint performance in general could mean that incremental indexing during business hours could be undesirable. It is always desirable to scale the deployment to allow for better performance and availability as opposed to disabling or limiting indexing frequency. Of course, infrastructure and budget limitations must be balanced with business needs.

# Performance Reports

Measuring performance in SharePoint 2010 has been made much easier with the addition of SharePoint health reports. The reports are in the Administrative Report Library, which can be found in the Central Administration under Manage Service Applications ➤ Search Service Application ➤ Search Administration ➤ Administrative Reports. There are several reports to help diagnose performance issues. The starting point for investigating performance issues and the key performance reports available are as follows:

*Query Latency:* Query latency is the total time it takes for queries to be processed and returned to the web servers. The Query Latency report shows how long queries take to be returned. All queries are not equal, and queries for more common terms with larger result sets will generally take longer to process, assemble result sets, and return. The Query Latency report shows the different areas and how long it takes for the query to be processed in each area: the server rendering, at the object model, and on the back end (databases). More information can be found in the reporting section. See Figure 2-9.

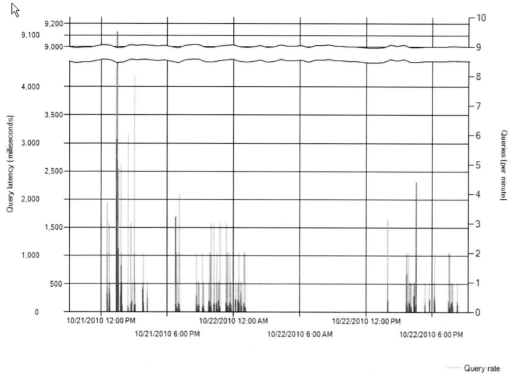

**Figure 2-9.** *Query Latency report*

*Query Latency Trend:* Latency is not a static consideration, so seeing the progression of performance and any increase or decline in performance over time can be useful. Also, it is wise to associate the given performance decline with other factors that may be affecting it, such as index size or crawling behavior, as well as other demands on key components, such as shared database servers. The Query Latency Trend report will show query latency over a given time period and display the latency for scaling proportions of the queries. So, the administrator can see the latency of all queries in the 95th percentile of all queries and in the 90th, 80th, 70th, 50th, and 5th percentiles. This gives the administrator the ability to see how quickly the queries are returned and how this scales. The crawl rate can also be seen in comparison for simultaneous periods. This will allow the administrator to determine if sub-second results are being achieved for the majority of queries. A best practice is to keep the 90th percentile of searches below 1,000 milliseconds (1 second), and the crawler should return between 200 and 400 items per second.

*Crawl Rate per Content Source:* The crawl rates can be seen in this report and will give an indication of how fast the crawler is collecting content. Although it will probably collect information fast enough for most organizations, the crawler can have issues with particular documents or at particular times, and this data can be seen here. See Figure 2-10.

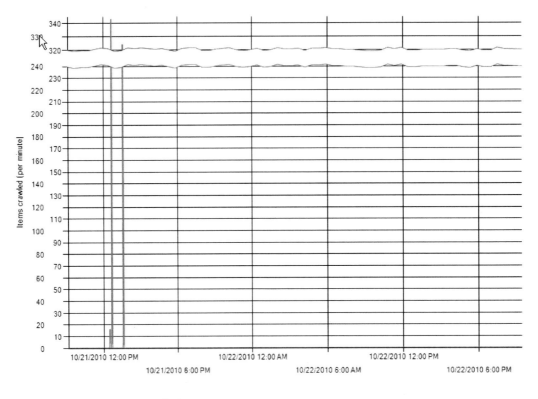

Local SharePoint sites    Anchor Crawl

*Figure 2-10. Crawl Rate per Content Source report*

*Crawl Rate per Type:* Some areas take more resources to crawl and the Crawl Rate per Type report can show this information. This information may be unique to an organization with a lot of document modification or a heavy check-in/check-out rate. See Figure 2-11.

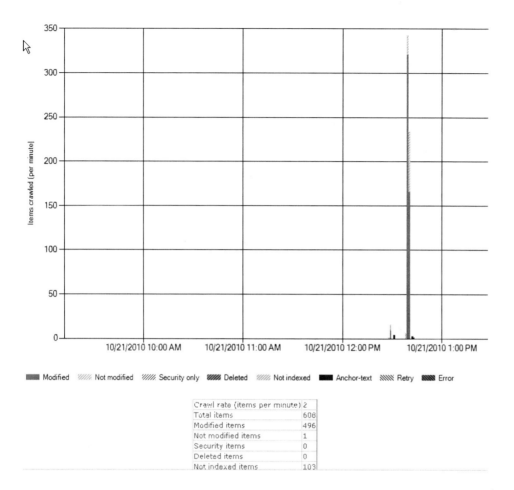

| Crawl rate (items per minute) | 2 |
|---|---|
| Total items | 608 |
| Modified items | 496 |
| Not modified items | 1 |
| Security items | 0 |
| Deleted items | 0 |
| Not indexed items | 103 |

**Figure 2-11.** *Crawl Rate per Type report*

## Acting on Performance Issues

Acting on performance issues is as important as identifying them. There are a few key areas where performance can be improved based on data from the health reports.

*High query latency*

1. Separate query server role, web server role, and crawl server role depending on where the bottleneck is or if another service is taking up too many resources.

2. Scale up by adding index partitions and if necessary RAM to handle the 33% of the index partitions being stored in memory.

3. Add query servers, and place additional index partitions on the new query servers to balance the query load.

*Query latency growing over time*

1. Add index partitions to spread load and check the performance trend.

2. Separate roles onto separate servers.

3. Add servers to handle query load as demand grows.

# Scaling

Scaling is the process of adding resources to IT systems to improve performance or handle additional load. Scaling is an important topic for mitigating poor performance and eventual end-user dissatisfaction. Scaling can prevent downtime and allow for reactive management of resources as well as control budget overruns by allowing for progressive addition of infrastructure as demand and corpus size grow.

As we saw in Chapter 1, there are two basic methods for scaling search:

- *Scaling up*: Adding more resources to a physical machine that is under heavy load

- *Scaling out*: Adding additional machines or segmenting tasks to better utilize existing resources

SharePoint 2010 is especially good at managing existing resources and scaling out to handle demand and alleviate bottlenecks.

## Why and When to Scale

The most critical point to consider scaling is when users begin to complain about missing content and slow response times from search. Missing content can indicate a problem with crawling that may be the result of a lack of resources (either in the crawler or in the target system). Slow response times usually indicate too heavy of a load on the query servers.

Basic scaling can be as simple as adding servers to effectively move from one level of deployment as content grows (as was outlined in the previous section) or a more reactive approach of addressing specific performance or capacity issues as they arise. In order to implement the latter technique, one should be aware of the triggers for identifying an issue and the steps to address it.

The following are some typical scaling trigger scenarios and their resolutions:

- *Scenario 1—Missing or stale content*: Content is missing from the repository, and the crawler rate is less than 15 documents per second from the Crawl Rate per Content Source health report. This health report can be found in Central Administration ➤ Administrative Report Library ➤ Search Administration Reports ➤ Crawl Rate per Content Source.

- *Scenario 2—Slow search responses*: Users complain of slow response times on search. Either SharePoint 2010 is performing well on basic page loads and search is not returning fast enough, or the entire search and result pages load slowly. First check that there aren't any poorly performing custom design elements or Web Parts that may be experiencing problems on the search result page. Check the Search health reports to identify slow query response times and latency, and consider scaling out the query servers by either partitioning the index and/or adding query servers to hold index partitions.

- *Scenario 3—No disk space on database server.* The good SharePoint admin always keeps his or her eye on the Central Administration and never ignores warning messages from SharePoint 2010. SharePoint 2010 is especially good at notifying the administrator of any issues. This includes database size issues. Should the database server run out of space, SharePoint 2010 will alert the administrator. This scenario most often happens during crawling when the database server has been set to automatically grow. The natural fix for database disk space issues is to add disks to the array or increase the size of disks on a server if the solution is not using RAID or some other redundant storage solution.

## Disk Recommendations

Search is an input/output–intense process. Basically, a search engine indexes all the content from a particular source (e.g., SharePoint site, web site, database, file share, etc.) and builds databases with the words indexed, the links to the documents, metadata found on the documents, metadata associated with the documents, time, size, type, etc. The crawling process writes all this information to databases. SharePoint stores some of these databases in SQL and some on the file structure in index partitions. The query components then access these databases, look for the terms that were searched for (these may be free text or property-based), and match the terms with the documents and their properties. To do this requires a lot of writing and reading to hard drives. Therefore having hardware that performs well is an important aspect of improving search performance.

Generally speaking, to support search well, databases will need to be in some kind of disk array. For write-intensive databases, such as a crawl database, RAID 10 is recommended. For added performance, the temp database should be separated to a RAID 10 array. (See more in the following sections, and consult external resources for more information on RAID.) In addition, there should be a redundant array to avoid downtime. More redundant arrays will slow performance but improve redundancy, so finding the right balance for the requirements is key.

RAID stands for redundant array of independent disks and is the technology of combining several disks into an array, where if one fails, the other will take the load and provide a mirror of all data. More complicated RAID configurations have more redundancy. They also improve performance.

Search queries require a lot of throughput, so having well-performing databases can help. On the database servers, it is recommended that the input/output per second (IOPS) capabilities be 3,500 to 7,000 IOPS and at least 2,000 on the property database. Therefore, at minimum, disk speeds of 7,200 RPM or better are required in a RAID configuration. Highly performant search implementations also make use of storage area networks and sometimes solid state drives (which may support up to 1,000,000 IOPS in a storage array vs. 90 IOPS for a single 7,200 RPM SATA drive).

---

■ **Tip** See more information from Microsoft on search database requirements and information about RAID architecture for SQL at http://technet.microsoft.com/en-us/library/cc298801.aspx.

---

## Availability

Availability in IT systems is the measure of how often servers and their services are available for users to access. Of course, all organizations would like to have 100% availability. This level of availability is either not possible, not practical, or too expensive for most organizations. Therefore, most organizations endeavor to achieve the highest availability possible for a reasonable cost. Generally, availability is measured by a number of nines. This is a reference to the closeness to 100% availability achievable by increments of additional nines from 90% to 99.999…%. A common expression is "5 nines of uptime" or 99.999%. This represents 5 minutes and 35 seconds of allowable downtime per year.

The main method to achieve high availability in IT systems is by making them redundant—that is, adding copies (or mirrors) of the systems that will take over the tasks should hardware or software fail (which it inevitably does). Redundancy in SharePoint deployments can insure uninterrupted service for end users. Redundancy in a SharePoint deployment can be deployed as a solution for failover scenarios (a server dies) but can also be deployed to ease maintenance tasks and allow for performance and server management without adversely affecting the uptime of the solution.

SharePoint 2010 handles redundancy in a number of ways by allowing for mirrored services over multiple machines. The farm architecture of SharePoint also allows for one server to compensate for another if one of the servers in the farm fails or is taken down for maintenance.

Each component in SharePoint 2010 Search represents a possible failure point. Therefore, the components are made capable of being mirrored. The most common areas to mirror are as follows:

- *Web servers*: Although not strictly part of the search engine, web servers deliver the content that SharePoint 2010 Search is indexing. If these servers fail and there is no redundancy, then the index will not refresh. However, if the web servers fail, there will be no site, so users will probably not be primarily concerned with the lack of search.

- *Query servers*: Multiple query servers can improve performance but also provide for redundancy by providing an alternative source for the queries to be processed. Mirroring index partitions across query servers insures that all portions of the index are available if one server should fail.

- *Crawl servers*: If constant index freshness is a critical business need, mirroring crawl servers can help the database and indexes stay up to date should one fail.

- *Database servers*: One of the most critical areas to provide redundancy in is the database servers. Database servers provide the data for the query components and the repository for the indexing components to write to. Database failure will cause search to fail completely, so it is essential to have databases constantly available.

## Why and When to Consider Making Services Redundant

Any service that is considered critical should have a failover component. Being able to search and receive results is a critical feature of SharePoint. Therefore, the services that allow users to query the index and receive results should have redundancy. This includes query servers and any index partitions on those query servers.

All servers with the query role should have some level of redundancy. Ideally, all index partitions should have a redundant instance. So, if there is one server with the query role and two index partitions on that server, a redundant query server with a second instance of both index partitions will be necessary.

This is considered minimum redundancy for SharePoint Search as it insures that given a hardware failure for a query server, search will not fail with an error for users.

Additionally, database servers should have a redundancy element as they hold the crawl and property databases essential to searching as well as the Administration database, without which search cannot be performed. Most organizations already have redundant database implementations, such as database clusters. Either the search databases should be installed in these existing database clusters, or a similar model should be employed to insure redundancy.

If freshness of content is considered critical, making crawl servers redundant is required. If freshness of content is not a critical factor, having a less strict redundancy model for indexing can be acceptable. However, should a failure happen, the crawl components must be re-provisioned on new or existing servers.

## Server Downtime Impact Chart

Although no one likes downtime, avoiding any downtime with full redundancy may be either too costly, too cumbersome, or too maintenance-intensive for some organizations. Therefore, it is valuable to understand the impact of downtime for the individual components of SharePoint 2010 Search and determine which may be acceptable to the organization. See Table 2-1.

■ **Note** A dedicated search farm need not have the web server role if this role is provided by a content farm, which connects to the search farm.

*Table 2-1.* Server Downtime Impact Chart

| Server Role | Severity | Impact of Downtime |
| --- | --- | --- |
| Web server role | Critical | Users cannot see the search page (and possibly not SharePoint content if the web server role is shared). |
| Query server role | High | Users will not be able to search for content. The search page may still work but return an error. |
| Crawl server role | Medium | The search will still work and results will be returned, but the content will not be up to date and indexes not refreshed. |
| Database server role | Critical | Users will not be able to search for content. The search page may still work but will return an error (SharePoint content may also not be returned if the database server role is shared). |

## Limitations and Hard-Coded Boundaries

All software has limitations and hard-coded checks and measures to avoid unforeseeable or untested behavior. SharePoint is no exception to this and has several hard-coded limitations as well as suggested boundaries for search in SharePoint 2010. These limitations are generally set to avoid poor or unsupportable behavior. Luckily, Microsoft has been so kind as to test SharePoint extensively and reveal some of the boundaries that exist for the product. Microsoft gives three types of limits:

- *Boundaries*: Hard-coded limits that are not possible to exceed—this should be interpreted as the software will cease to continue if this limit is reached. It does not mean it will cease to function but may stop continuing to grow or perform if this limit is reached.

- *Thresholds*: This is a configurable item that could possibly be exceeded if necessary, but it is not generally recommended to do so.

- *Supported limits*: To go where no one has gone before! Generally, this means that if one exceeds this limit and SharePoint breaks, one should not expect Microsoft to fix it (without a fee). Microsoft has tested the software to this limit and can support it to work at this level. These are defaults set.

Tables 2-2 through 2-6 show the known limitations and boundaries.

*Table 2-2. Database Limitations*

| Topic | Limit | Support | Notes |
|---|---|---|---|
| **Crawl databases** | 10 per SSA | Threshold | Each SSA can have ten separate crawl databases to record crawl data. It is unlikely that more would be necessary, but it is possible. |
| **Crawl database items** | 25 million items/database | Threshold | Crawl databases hold information about the crawl, not the crawled content, so having too many items will make seek and record time slow for this information. |
| **Property databases** | 10 per SSA | Threshold | Property databases are bound to index partitions and therefore have the same limitations. |
| **Property databases** | 128 maximum per farm | Threshold | The maximum number of property databases matches the maximum for index partitions. |
| **Index partitions** | 10 per SSA | Threshold | Chopping up the index partition into smaller chunks may seem like an infinitely good idea, but too many chunks will make the SSA work too hard looking through the individual partitions and not into each one. Keep this limit at a maximum of ten per SSA. |
| **Index partitions** | 128 maximum per farm | Boundary | Each search farm can hold only 128 index partitions. This is the maximum the SSAs can query. |

*Table 2-3.* *Topology Limitations*

| Topic | Limit | Support | Notes |
|---|---|---|---|
| **Search service applications (SSA)** | 20 | Supported limit | It is recommended to have a maximum of 20 SSAs per farm. More is possible but will possibly hamper performance. |
| **Crawl components** | 16 per SSA | Threshold | Two crawl components per crawl database and two per server are recommended. So a single SSA would require eight servers with this limitation. |
| **Query components** | 128 per SSA | Threshold | Crawl components must copy files to the index partitions on the query servers. These maximums match the other maximums of the index partitions. |
| **Query components** | 64 per server | Threshold | This threshold is based on the server's capacity to receive data from the crawler. |

*Table 2-4.* *Crawler Limitations*

| Topic | Limit | Support | Notes |
|---|---|---|---|
| **Indexed items** | 10 million per index partition | Supported limit | Microsoft recommends limiting the number of items in a single partition to 10 million. In most cases, this should probably be much less for performance reasons. |
| **Indexed items** | 100 million per SSA | Supported limit | Although SharePoint can probably index more than 100 million documents and successfully search them, Microsoft has set the supported limit at 100 million. For more, they recommend you buy FAST for SharePoint. |
| **Concurrent crawls** | 20 per SSA | Threshold | Several crawlers can run simultaneously, but each takes resources, and having too many will reduce the overall performance of each. Fewer crawlers will often index faster than too many. We always want to avoid maxing out our server capacity as Windows will compensate by using less performant memory (page file), to the detriment of the whole system. |

*Table 2-5. Administration Limitations*

| Topic | Limit | Support | Notes |
|---|---|---|---|
| **Crawl log entries** | 100 million per SSA | Supported limit | Each indexed item will have a log entry, so this limit is in accordance with the indexed items limit. |
| **Scope rules** | 100 per scope | Threshold | Each scope rule must be mapped in the database and data allocated to it. Having many rules will inhibit the index's ability to maintain freshness. |
| **Scope rules** | 600 per SSA | Threshold | This limit is also to maintain freshness in the crawled data. |
| **Scopes** | 200 per site | Threshold | Scopes take time and effort to assemble in the result list. Too many scope rules will inhibit performance. |
| **Display groups** | 25 per site | Threshold | This is a limit for a reasonable list limit in the Search Administration user interface. |
| **URL removals** | 100 removals per operation | Supported limit | URLs supported for each removal operation |
| **Authoritative pages** | One top level; few second and third level per SSA | Threshold | Authoritative pages adjust ranking values. Adding too many can make the ranking very complicated and probably won't meet expectations. The boundary for authoritative pages is 200 per SSA. An iterative approach is recommended. Try adding some and checking the outcome on each adjustment. |
| **Keywords** | 200 per site collection | Supported limit | Keywords manage synonyms and best bets. If you use 5 best bets per keyword, the boundary is 5,000, which is imposed by ASP.NET. This boundary can be increased by editing the `web.config` and `client.config` files. |
| **Alerts** | 1,000,000 per SSA | Supported limit | This is the outer limit of alerts that Microsoft has tested. More is certainly feasible. |
| **Content sources** | 50 per SSA | Threshold | More starting points can cause more troubles for the crawler and a more difficult diagnostic experience. Although 500 is the actual boundary, keeping the starting points for the crawler low will aid in crawling and avoid problems. |
| Start addresses | 100 per content source | Threshold | Again, having more starting points will bog down the crawler. Microsoft recommends using an HTML link list (web page of links) and setting it as a starting point instead of adding many starting points. The boundary is again 500. |

| Topic | Limit | Support | Notes |
|---|---|---|---|
| Crawl impact rules | 100 | Threshold | Crawl impact rules increase or decrease the number of threads that the crawler uses to crawl a specific site. You can increase the number of rules over 100, but you should be careful to consider the actual impact of the rules. The threshold is based on how many rules can be displayed on the page without it becoming unresponsive. The tested limit is 2,000. |
| Crawl rules | 100 per SSA | Threshold | SharePoint 2010 can accept many more crawl rules but will have trouble displaying all the rules if too many more are added. If you can't see the rules, working with them or modifying them could be difficult. |

**Table 2-6.** *Property Limitations*

| Topic | Limit | Support | Notes |
|---|---|---|---|
| **Managed properties** | 100,000 per SSA | Threshold | Metadata crawled from documents, lists, web pages, or any other source can be mapped to managed properties. They must be mapped to a managed property to make them searchable. The suggested limit for these mappings is 100,000. |
| **Metadata properties** | 10,000 per item | Boundary | Absolute maximum number of crawlable properties per document |
| **Managed property mappings** | 100 per managed property | Threshold | Many crawled properties can be mapped to a single managed property. This helps combine similar metadata into a single searchable property. Too many mappings can cause a slower crawl and slower queries as the mappings must be made at the crawl and each search must call the diverse values from the properties. |
| **Crawled properties** | 500,000 per SSA | Supported limit | SharePoint's crawler can pick up many different pieces of metadata, and being able to crawl properties from metadata is an especially powerful feature. These properties can be later used for search and filtering. Microsoft sets a supported limit of 500,000 for these properties, but in many cases, many more could be expected. |

---

■ **Note** For more information on these limits and a complete list of software limits for SharePoint 2010, see `http://technet.microsoft.com/en-us/library/cc262787.aspx`.

---

# PowerShell

Those already familiar with SharePoint 2010 will certainly be familiar with Windows PowerShell. PowerShell is a command line shell built on the .NET Framework that allows commands (called cmdlets) to be made directly to the object model of SharePoint 2010. Although using the graphical user interface (GUI) of SharePoint is arguably easier and more user-friendly, repeated tasks and automation can be achieved using PowerShell scripts.

PowerShell has a large number of available cmdlets included with SharePoint 2010 that can provision the search service, adjust topology, create index partitions, manage crawl rules (see Chapter 3), and even change relevancy models (see Chapter 9). Administrators who need PowerShell will need to understand it on a larger scale for unattended installations and provisioning of SharePoint.

We will not go into or list all the available commands or describe how they are called. Instead we will outline a few useful cmdlets and provide references to more information on the vast world of PowerShell.

The cmdlets most useful for deploying search in SharePoint and covered in this chapter are as follows:

- `Get-SPEnterpriseSearchServiceInstance`

- `Start-SPEnterpriseSearchServiceInstance`

- `New-SPServiceApplicationPool`

- `New-SPEnterpriseSearchServiceApplication`

- `Get-SPEnterpriseSearchServiceApplication`

- `New-SPEnterpriseSearchServiceApplicationProxy`

- `Set-SPenterpriseSearchAdministrationComponent`

- `New-SPEnterpriseSearchCrawlTopology`

- `New-SPEnterpriseSearchCrawlDatabase`

- `New-SPEnterpriseSearchCrawlComponent`

- `Set-SPEnterpriseSearchCrawlTopology`

- `New-SPEnterpriseSearchQueryTopology`

- `Get-SPEnterpriseSearchIndexPartition`

- New-SPEnterpriseSearchQueryComponent
- New-SPEnterpriseSearchPropertyDatabase
- Set-SPEnterpriseSearchIndexPartition
- Set-SPEnterpriseSearchQueryTopology

# Provisioning Search with PowerShell

Provisioning any service application can be a complicated task. There are several prerequisites that need to be met before any service application can be provisioned in a SharePoint farm and also a number of additional parameters that need to be identified in order to allow the cmdlets to successfully and appropriately run. If the variables are not set properly, the cmdlets could fail. Luckily, PowerShell will prompt with any missing required parameters and stepping through them at the command prompt in PowerShell can help the administrator build a script with the variables to deploy the search. Be aware that PowerShell requires a managed account to run the SharePoint cmdlets. This can be set with Set-SPManagedAccount. For the purpose of these examples, we will use the Administrator account.

The following is a step-by-step guide showing how to provision search using PowerShell and an example script based on these steps. Use the following steps to provision the Search service application:

1. Start the Search service (SharePoint Server Search 14). The Search service will already be installed on the machine, so it is just a matter of starting the service. It will need to be running to perform the provisioning, so it's the first place to start. In order to start it, however, it is necessary to know what it is called.

2. Get the local instance name:

   ```
   Get-SPEnterpriseSearchServiceInstance -local
   ```

3. The identity, in this case, will be the Globally Unique Identifier (GUID) in the ID field, so this can be copied, and Start-SPEnterpriseSearchServiceInstance -Identity (GUID here) can be called or placed in a variable for later use:

   ```
   $SearchServiceInstance = get-spenterprisesearchserviceinstance –local
   ```

4. Next, start the service:

   ```
   Start-SPEnterpriseSearchServiceInstance -Identity $SearchServiceInstance
   ```

▦ **Note** For this example, parameters are filled, where possible, with their actual values for clarity's sake. However, it is best to set variables for these values in the script and call them later. This will allow the values to be re-used and also provide the content of some of the parameters to be called where necessary.

5. Create an application pool. To create an application pool, give it a name and an account. In this case, we will use administrator, but an organization will likely want to use a different account depending on how search is deployed. The user will need the `SharePoint_Shell_Access` role on the configuration database and will need to be a member of the Administrators and WSS_ADMIN_WPG local groups on the server where SharePoint is installed.

```
New-SPServiceApplicationPool -name Search_Service_App_Pool -account Administrator
```

6. Create the Search service application. To do this, create a new `SPEnterpriseSearchServiceApplication`, give it a name, call our previously created application pool, and assign a database name for the admin database.

```
New-SPEnterpriseSearchServiceApplication -Name "Pro Search Service Application"↵
 -applicationpool Search_Service_App_Pool -databasename ↵
Search_Service_Admin_Database
```

7. Create a service application proxy. A proxy is required to interact with the service and expose search to the front-end search Web Parts. To create a proxy, use the `New-SPEnterpriseSearchServiceApplicationProxy` cmdlet. It will require a name and the absolute URI of the Search service application that was created. To get the absolute URI, make a variable, place the Search service application, and then call the URI as follows:

```
$SearchServiceApplication = Get-SPEnterpriseSearchServiceApplication
New-SPEnterpriseSearchServiceApplicationProxy –nam Search_Service_App_Proxy↵
 -Uri $SearchServiceApplication.Uri.AbsoluteURI
```

8. Set the Administration component so Central Administration can interact with the Search service. This will require knowing the GUIDs as these will be taken as parameters. The IDs can be seen by using the `Get-SPEnterpriseSearchServiceInstance` and `GetSPEnterpriseSearchServiceApplication` cmdlets (see Figure 2-12).

```
Administrator: SharePoint 2010 Management Shell                          _ □ X
PS C:\Users\Administrator> Get-SPEnterpriseSearchServiceInstance -local

TypeName         : SharePoint Server Search
Description      : Index content and serve search queries
Id               : aaa2e28b-287d-44c4-a01b-8c831ea0c1a4
Server           : SPServer Name=WIN-10GHRQODHO4
Service          : SearchService Name=OSearch14
Role             : None
QueryComponents  : {}
CrawlComponents  : {}
AdminComponents  : {dbfa12ad-7718-4dbf-8513-28065a031108}
Status           : Online


PS C:\Users\Administrator> Get-SPEnterpriseSearchServiceApplication

Name                 : Pro Search Service Application
Id                   : d8240341-a272-45af-9d3c-451dd0d9d0cd
ServiceName          : SearchQueryAndSiteSettingsService
QueryTopologies      : {fc1430bc-fc28-4738-b7e3-0c805013f3e0}
PropertyStores       : {Search_Service_Admin_Database_PropertyStore}
CrawlTopologies      : {c137f9d3-cc2f-4b3d-94d4-2951fc9c09b4}
CrawlStores          : {Search_Service_Admin_Database_CrawlStore}
SearchAdminDatabase  : SearchAdminDatabase Name=Search_Service_Admin_Database
Status               : Online
SearchApplicationType : Regular
DefaultSearchProvider : SharepointSearch
Properties           : {Microsoft.Office.Server.Utilities.SPPartitionOptions}


PS C:\Users\Administrator> Set-SPEnterpriseSearchAdministrationComponent -Search
Application d8240341-a272-45af-9d3c-451dd0d9d0cd -SearchServiceInstance aaa2e28b
-287d-44c4-a01b-8c831ea0c1a4_
```

***Figure 2-12.*** *Setting the Search Administration component using the IDs of the Search service instance and Search service application*

9.  Obviously, it will be more practical to use the variables we have already set and set new variables to easily pass the required values.

    ```
    Set-SPenterpriseSearchAdministrationComponent -SearchApplication ↵
    $SearchServiceApplication -searchserviceinstance $SearchServiceInstance
    ```

10. In order to crawl, a crawl component is required. But before a crawl component can be provisioned, there needs to be a crawl topology in which to place it. So the next step is to create a crawl topology.

    ```
    $CrawlTopology = $searchserviceApplication | New-SPEnterpriseSearchCrawlTopology
    ```

11. Now, a crawl component can be created. But first, a new crawl database should be created.

    ```
    $CrawlDatabase = $searchserviceApplication | New-SPEnterpriseSearchCrawlDatabase↵
     -DatabaseName CrawlDatabase
    New-SPEnterpriseSearchCrawlComponent -CrawlTopology $CrawlTopology↵
     -CrawlDatabase $CrawlDatabase -SearchServiceInstance $SearchServiceInstance
    ```

12. Next, set the new crawl topology as active. Several crawl topologies can exist on a single server, but only one can be active. Before one can remove a crawl topology, an alternative must be created and set as active. Then content sources will be crawlable.

```
$CrawlTopology | Set-SPEnterpriseSearchCrawlTopology –Active
```

▓ **Note** Use `Remove-SPEnterpriseSearchCrawlTopology` to remove any old crawl topologies.

13. Create a new query topology, index partitions, and query component to query the Search service application. The number of partitions on the server can be set using the `–partitions` parameter.

```
$QueryTopology = $searchServiceApplication | New-SPEnterpriseSearchQueryTopology ↵
-Partitions 1
```

14. It gets a bit complicated now, so the partition ID will need to be placed into a variable and then passed with the other information to create the new query component.

```
$Partition = Get-SPEnterpriseSearchIndexPartition -querytopology $QueryTopology
New-SPEnterpriseSearchQueryComponent -indexpartition $Partition –QueryTopology↵
 $QueryTopology -SearchServiceInstance $SearchServiceInstance
```

▓ **Note** It is recommended to create failover partitions of all index partitions. If multiple partitions are created, each partition will require its own query components. To set a partition as failover, add the parameter `–failoverOnly`.

15. Finally, the query component will need a property database. For order's sake, create a new database and assign the new partitions to it. And then activate the query topology.

```
$PropertyDatabase = New-SPEnterpriseSearchPropertyDatabase –searchapplication↵
$SearchApplication -databasename Search_Property_Database
$Partition | Set-SPEnterpriseSearchIndexPartition -PropertyDatabase ↵
$PropertyDatabase
$QueryTopology | Set-SPEnterpriseSearchQueryTopology –Active
```

▓ **Note** Search topologies can also be imported and exported for re-use with the `$searchserviceapplication | Export-SPEnterpriseSearchTopology -Filename c:\Search\Topology.xml`.

Listing 2-1 provides the complete sample script.

***Listing 2-1.** Sample Script* ProvisionSSA.ps1

```
#Set Database and Service Names here - set them as desired
$SearchServiceAppPool = "Search_Service_Application_Pool"
$SearchApplicationName = "Pro SharePoint Search Service Application"
$SearchAdminDatabase = "Search_Service_Admin_Database"
$CrawlDatabase = "Crawl_Database"
$SearchPropertyDatabase = "Search_Property_Database"

#Set the search service instance name in a variable and start the service.
$SearchServiceInstance = Get-SPEnterpriseSearchServiceInstance -local
Start-SPEnterpriseSearchServiceInstance -Identity $SearchServiceInstance

#Set a user for the service and create a new application pool for search
$Search_Service_Account = "Administrator"
$ApplicationPool = new-SPServiceApplicationPool -name $SearchServiceAppPool↩
 -account $Search_Service_Account

#Create the search service application
New-SPEnterpriseSearchServiceApplication -Name $SearchApplicationName↩
 -applicationpool $ApplicationPool -databasename $SearchAdminDatabase

#Create the Search Service Application Proxy
$SearchServiceApplication = Get-SPEnterpriseSearchServiceApplication
New-SPEnterpriseSearchServiceApplicationProxy -name Search_Service_App_Proxy↩
 -Uri $SearchServiceApplication.Uri.AbsoluteURI

#Set the Search Service Administration Component
Set-SPenterpriseSearchAdministrationComponent -SearchApplication↩
 $SearchServiceApplication -searchserviceinstance $SearchServiceInstance

#Create a Crawl topology
$CrawlTopology = $searchserviceApplication | New-SPEnterpriseSearchCrawlTopology

#Create a new crawl database and crawl component and then Set the new Crawl Topology Active
$CrawlDatabase = $searchserviceApplication | New-SPEnterpriseSearchCrawlDatabase↩
 -DatabaseName $CrawlDatabase
New-SPEnterpriseSearchCrawlComponent -CrawlTopology $CrawlTopology -CrawlDatabase↩
 $CrawlDatabase -SearchServiceInstance $SearchServiceInstance
$CrawlTopology | Set-SPEnterpriseSearchCrawlTopology -Active
```

```
#Create a new query topology
$QueryTopology = $searchServiceApplication | New-SPEnterpriseSearchQueryTopology -Partitions
1
$Partition = Get-SPEnterpriseSearchIndexPartition -querytopology $QueryTopology
New-SPEnterpriseSearchQueryComponent -indexpartition $Partition –QueryTopology↵
 $QueryTopology -searchserviceinstance $SearchServiceInstance

#Create a database for properties and assign it to the query partition
$PropertyDatabase = New-SPEnterpriseSearchPropertyDatabase -searchapplication
$SearchServiceApplication -databasename $SearchPropertyDatabase
$Partition | Set-SPEnterpriseSearchIndexPartition -PropertyDatabase $PropertyDatabase

#Activate the Query Topology
$QueryTopology | Set-SPEnterpriseSearchQueryTopology -Active
```

## PowerShell for Scaling

PowerShell can also be effectively used to scale out the search components of SharePoint 2010. Topology changes are not allowed on a stand-alone installation, so make sure the installation is appropriate. PowerShell scaling capabilities for SharePoint Search include the following:

- *Adding query components*: Query components can be added only to an inactive query topology. Therefore, a new query topology must be created with the desired structure before adding query components. All query components should be added before the query topology is activated.

    ```
    New-SPEnterpriseSearchQueryComponent
    ```

- *Adding index partitions*: The number of index partitions must be defined when creating the query topology. After creating the query topology with the desired number of index partitions, query components should be set to the appropriate partition.

    ```
    New-SPEnterpriseSearchQueryTopology -Partitions 2
    ```

- *Adding property databases*: Property databases can be added to the specific Search service application to support large amounts of metadata. It only requires the Search service application as a parameter.

    ```
    New-SPEnterpriseSearchPropertyDatabase
    ```

- *Adding crawler components*: A crawl topology can contain multiple crawl components that will aid in crawl performance.

    ```
    New-SPEnterpriseSearchCrawlComponent
    ```

# Summary

In this chapter, we looked at factors to consider when deploying search infrastructure. We also looked at the key components for the search model in SharePoint 2010 and how they work together to scale and load balance. Planning an initial deployment was covered, and suggestions and diagrams for that planning were given. There are no clear rules to match every possible configuration, but the guidelines given should help administrators find architecture to get them started.

The chapter also addressed performance and availability topics and gave suggestions and best practices for what to do if these areas become an issue. Some limitations were addressed and outlined to help avoid unrealistic expectations for SharePoint 2010 Search. And finally, Windows PowerShell for search was introduced and a brief overview of the available commands was given. A step-by-step guide to a simple provisioning SharePoint search and a sample script were given.

# Further Reading

Here are some suggestions for further reading or more details on the topics covered in this chapter.

## SharePoint Components

Microsoft's Russ Maxwell has some good blog posts on architecture and scale here: `http://blogs.msdn.com/b/russmax/archive/2010/04/16/search-2010-architecture-and-scale-part-1-crawl.aspx` and `http://blogs.msdn.com/b/russmax/archive/2010/04/23/search-2010-architecture-and-scale-part-2-query.aspx`.

## Environment Planning and Metrics

Microsoft's guide on hardware and software requirements can be found here: `http://technet.microsoft.com/en-us/library/cc262485.aspx`.

Microsoft's guide on performance and capacity planning can be found here: `http://download.microsoft.com/download/7/F/0/7F069D0B-B6BD-4692-868B-E8555BB72445/SearchforSPServer2010CapacityPlanningDoc.docx`.

A guide on search usage reports can be found here: `http://technet.microsoft.com/en-us/library/ee808861.aspx`.

## Performance

Information on storage capacity planning and RAID can be found here: `http://technet.microsoft.com/en-us/library/cc298801.aspx#Section33`.

## PowerShell

A general description of Windows PowerShell for SharePoint can be found here: `http://technet.microsoft.com/en-us/library/ff628968.aspx`.

A short and useful list of Windows PowerShell cmdlets for search can be found here: http://social.technet.microsoft.com/wiki/contents/articles/sharepoint-server-2010-search-windows-powershell-cmdlets.aspx.

A complete list of available cmdlets is listed on TechNet here: http://technet.microsoft.com/en-us/library/ee906563.aspx.

Search topology cmdlets are described here: http://technet.microsoft.com/en-us/library/ff696763.aspx.

# CHAPTER 3

■ ■ ■

# Setting Up the Crawler

After completing this chapter, you will be able to

- Set up the crawler to index SharePoint content

- Add and remove content sources

- Import and index user profiles

- Crawl file shares and Exchange public folders

- Troubleshoot crawler errors

- Install iFilters to crawl additional document types

- Set up federated sources

After the SharePoint 2010 environment has been successfully planned and installed, the next steps are to set up the crawler, define the content sources, and apply any special rules or filters to ensure all appropriate content is indexed.

This chapter will dive into the indexing process and how to define and set up each content source. It will give step-by-step instruction on adding or removing content sources to be crawled as well as settings specific to those sources. It will cover how to import user profiles from Active Directory and LDAP servers and index those profiles into the search database.

Crawling and crawl rules will be addressed, and some guidance on common problems and how to troubleshoot them will be addressed. We will also see how crawl rules can be applied to modify the credentials used to connect to content sources.

The chapter will also cover the use of iFilters to index file types not supported out of the box by SharePoint 2010. Third-party iFilters, in detail, will be covered later in the book, so we will cover only the installation and setup in this chapter and give a couple of quick examples of the most common file types, PDF and RTF.

Finally, adding federated sources will be covered. Displaying results from these sources will be covered later in the book, but this chapter introduces the concept of adding either a new federated source or importing a federated location from Microsoft's Federated Search Connector Gallery.

# The Search Service Application

SharePoint 2010 is designed to achieve many business tasks, and a logical structure is important to control and organize all those functions. For this reason, SharePoint is broken into separate services. Many of the essential services delivered by SharePoint are broken into what Microsoft has called service applications, which can control, independently, the different tasks that SharePoint performs. They can also be individually configured for performance and scaling. As we saw in the previous chapter, this compartmentalization makes SharePoint extremely scalable and performant.

The Search components of SharePoint 2010, for many reasons, including scaling, configurability, and performance, are therefore isolated into the Search service application, which is an application layer for configuring the back-end functionality of SharePoint search. Almost all the configuration directly related to the search components is done in the Search service application. However, as we will see, a great deal of supporting configuration may be required in the User Profile service application, the Managed Metadata service, or the Business Data Connectivity service. These services help extend SharePoint 2010 Search to address a variety of business needs.

This chapter will refer often to the Search service application and the menu items in the left navigation of the Search Service Application page. There are often many ways to get to the same pages in SharePoint. The most direct route is outlined here.

1.  Open Central Administration. On the main page of SharePoint Central Administration, there are eight sections. Under Application Management (as shown in Figure 3-1), choose "Manage service applications".

***Figure 3-1.*** *Choose "Manage service applications" from the Application Management menu.*

2.  The Service Applications page shows all the service applications running in the SharePoint farm and their status. Scroll down and choose the Search Service Application option (Figure 3-2).

| | | |
|---|---|---|
| Search Service Application | Search Service Application | Started |
| Search Service Application | Search Service Application Proxy | Started |

**Figure 3-2.** *The Search Service Application option*

3.  The Search Service Application page shows a System Status and a Crawl History section as well as a navigation to the left with four sections: Administration, Crawling, Queries and Results, and Reports. Examine the information in the System Status section. This is the starting point for most Search-related administration tasks.

## Default Content Access Account

SharePoint's crawler requires a user to access content and makes requests to SharePoint and other content sources. It makes standard requests to these content sources much the same way that a user requests content through a browser and waits for a reply. The reply it gets often depends on what user it makes those requests with. Some content sources may restrict access to specific content based on user credentials, and having the wrong user applied to SharePoint's default content access account (Figure 3-3) can adversely affect the outcome of crawls.

Make sure a user with appropriate permissions to crawl SharePoint is set on the default content access account on the Search Service Application page. This user should have read access to all content that should be crawled. This user should not be an administrator, as documents in an unpublished state would be crawled.

| | |
|---|---|
| Propagation status | Idle |
| Default content access account | DEVELOPMENT\SP_SSPServiceAccount |
| Contact e-mail address | someone@example.com |
| Proxy server | None |

**Figure 3-3.** *The default content access account*

If there are content sources that do not recognize the default content access account, special crawl rules can be created to use a different user for those sources. See more in the "Using Crawl Rules" section.

# Indexing

Indexing is the process of collecting data and storing it in a data structure that can be accessed by an application that can query the index and point to data in a database. This data structure is usually called a search index. Some indexes contain all the searchable information. Others, such as SharePoint's, store the words found in the documents and pointers to more information about those documents in another database. In SharePoint the index is held on the query servers, and the document data and data related to the crawler and its administration are held on the database servers. However, for the purpose of this section, we will discuss only indexing as the process to create both the indexes and the related search databases.

SharePoint 2010 can crawl and index a number of different file types and content types from different sources. In this section, we will discuss the different content sources and how to set up the crawler to index each one.

Out of the box, SharePoint can index the following content sources:

- Web content (HTTP and HTTPS)

- SharePoint user profile databases

- Lotus Notes

- Exchange public folders

- File shares

- Business Connectivity Services–connected content

- Other sources where a connector is provided (e.g., Documentum)

These different sources can be divided into two different types: structured and unstructured content.

## Structured Content

Structured content is content that has a defined structure that can generally be queried to retrieve specific items. Relational databases, such as Microsoft SQL Server, are structures that allow their content to be retrieved if you know the row and column ID of the cell where that data sits. Databases allow their content to be retrieved if the user or the user interface knows how to acquire the location of the data. Most relational databases have their own indices to help locate these IDs. These are generally not very performant and do not support free text search well. A search engine database structure will perform much better at finding all of the occurrences of a particular term in a timely manner.

When we marry unstructured and structured content or even two disparate structured content sources, we lose the ability to simply look up cell IDs to find the specific data. Additionally, different databases' indices seldom, if ever, work together. This is where a search engine becomes crucial. SharePoint's search components can index both unstructured and structured content, store them together, return them in a homogenized result set, filter based on determined metadata, and lead the end user to the specific source system.

SharePoint 2010 has a powerful feature for indexing structured content. This feature, called Business Connectivity Services, allows administrators to define connectors to structured data sources and index the content from them in a logical and organized manner, making that data searchable and useful from SharePoint.

BCS is capable of collecting content out of the box from

- MS SQL Databases
- .Net assemblies

Additionally, custom connectors can be created to allow it to index almost any other content source, including

- Other databases
- Line-of-business applications such as Seibel and SAP
- Other enterprise resource planning (ERP) systems
- Many other applications and databases

## Unstructured Content

Unstructured content refers to content that is not set in a strict structure such as a relational database. Unstructured content can be e-mails, documents, or web pages. Unstructured content is the biggest challenge for searching as it requires the search engine to look for specific terms across a huge corpus of free text. Unstructured search is often referred to as "free text" search.

Out of the box, SharePoint 2010 can index the following unstructured content sources:

- SharePoint sites
- Lotus Notes sites
- File shares
- Exchange public folders
- External and internal web sites
- Other sources where a connector is available

## Crawling SharePoint Sites

Setting up target sites to crawl in SharePoint is easy. The Content Sources section in the Search service application allows the administrator to add any type of supported content source. By default, when installed, the content source of the local web applications associated with the SharePoint site will be defined. If a SharePoint installation is dedicated solely to search the target, SharePoint site collection should be explicitly defined as a content source.

In order to do this, navigate to the Search Service Application page in the Central Administration under Manage Service Applications. On the left-hand menu, there are several search-specific items, one of them being Content Sources. On this page, there is a full listing of all the content sources being indexed by SharePoint (see Figure 3-4).

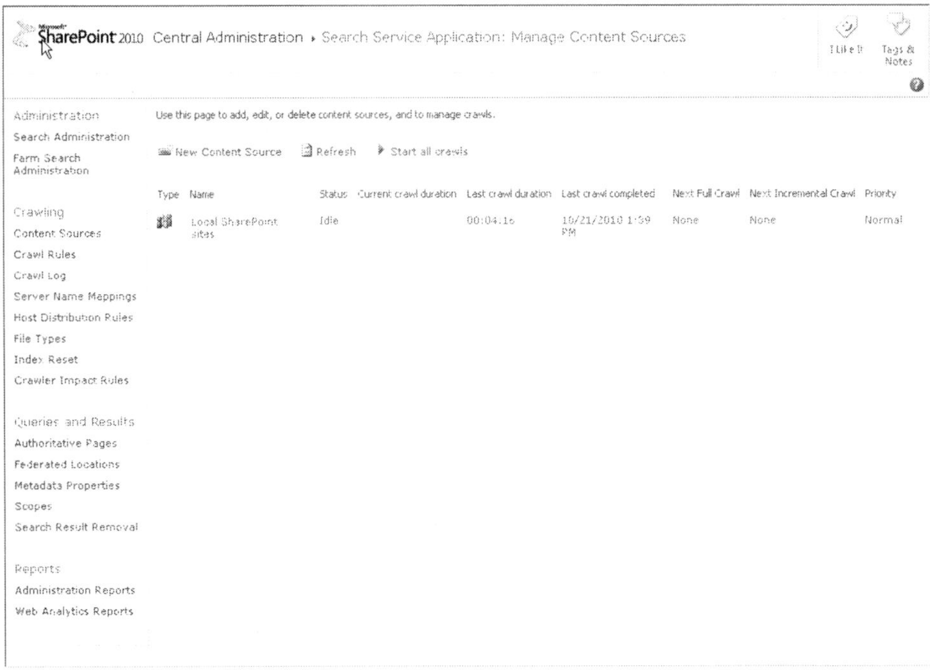

**Figure 3-4.** *Content Sources page*

---

■ **Note** The type of content source should be chosen so SharePoint's crawler knows how to connect and handle the documents it is crawling. If a SharePoint site is being indexed, the crawler can connect and retrieve all the documents, lists, list items, libraries, and any associated metadata.

---

■ **Note** Notice the SPS3 protocol in the Start Address definitions on the Content Sources page (Figure 3-5). This is the protocol by which SharePoint connects to the User Profile repository and indexes user data. If user data is to be indexed, this protocol and target should be defined. If there are issues searching for people, check in this section first.

---

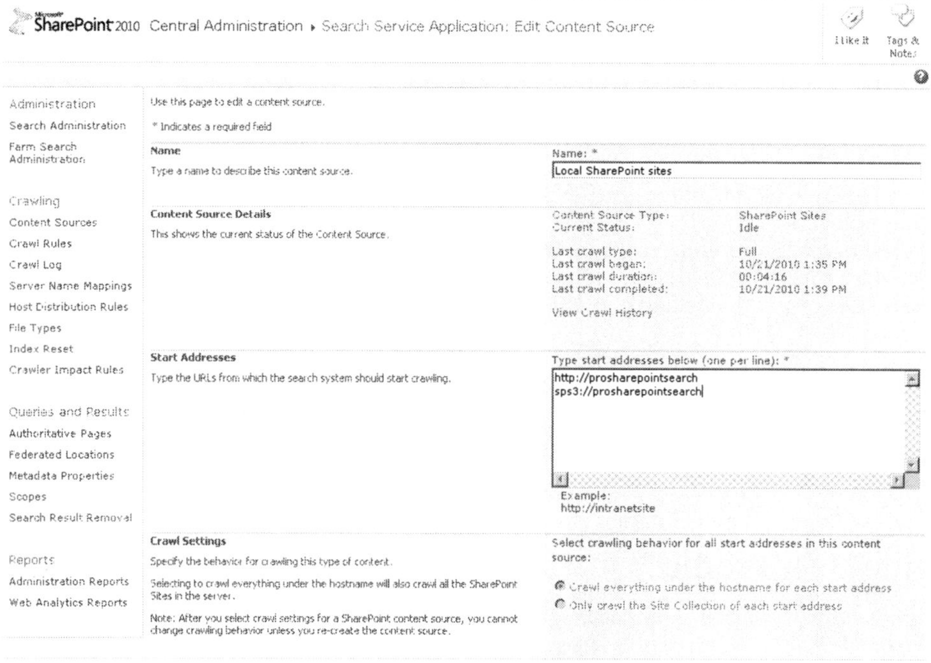

**Figure 3-5.** *Defining start addresses in a content source*

# Crawling Users Profiles

Enough cannot be said about the power of connecting people for business. For most organizations, their people and those people's expertise are their biggest assets. Finding people and expertise in a company can be a challenging task at the best of times, and experience and skills can go largely unexploited because people with the right knowledge cannot be found—or worse, their colleagues don't even know they exist.

SharePoint's People Search is a powerful feature to expose people in an organization and their expertise, making them findable and accessible. The people search mechanism, although a simple enough concept, requires the identification of people in the organization, their expertise, and their contact information. In order to expose this information and find the relevant people, SharePoint must first be able to crawl the information about these people.

People data in SharePoint comes from indexing user profiles. User profiles are held in SharePoint and hold the information about all the users of SharePoint as well as other potential SharePoint users that may have profile data imported from Active Directory or some other directory server service. User profile data can be entered manually, either by the administrator or by the users themselves in their personal site (MySite). Additionally, other data sources can be used to populate user profile data.

Usually the starting point for an organization is to synchronize the existing information they have in their organization's directory with SharePoint and then allow connected users to enrich that information on their MySite pages. This will allow for rich metadata and social search functionality in People Search. However, this is not strictly necessary, and data from a directory server is not required to have a rich people search experience as long as users are aware of the MySite feature and have the time and interest to keep it up to date.

User profile data is managed by the User Profile service application in the Service Applications section of Central Administration. For the purpose of this book, we will only go into crawling user profiles and synchronizing them with Directory Servers, but it is important to note that a great deal of rich user information can be managed from this service application. Additionally, the User Profile service application makes it possible to share user data across multiple sites and farms. This can allow for a rich and effective people search and expose expertise in areas of the organization not previously accessible to many employees.

The protocol used to crawl data collected from the User Profile service is called SPS3. It can be seen set in the default content source for SharePoint sites as `sps3://servername`. If user profiles are not crawled, check if this site is set in the default content source.

---

■ **Tip** If your Mysite definition uses Secure Sockets Layer or Transport Layer Security (https), it may be necessary to set the SPS3 protocol to use secure sockets (sps3s) as well.

---

## Synchronizing User Profiles

To synchronize user profiles, navigate to the "Manage service applications" page in Central Administration (Figure 3-6).

Application Management
Manage web applications
Create site collections
Manage service applications
Manage content databases

*Figure 3-6. The Application Management menu*

Then choose the User Profile Service Application link (see Figure 3-7). Check if the service application is started in the right-hand column.

User Profile Service Application

    User Profile Service Application

*Figure 3-7. Choosing the User Profile Service Application link*

The sources for user profile information are managed in the Synchronization section, where different user data sources can be defined and synchronization schedules defined (Figure 3-8).

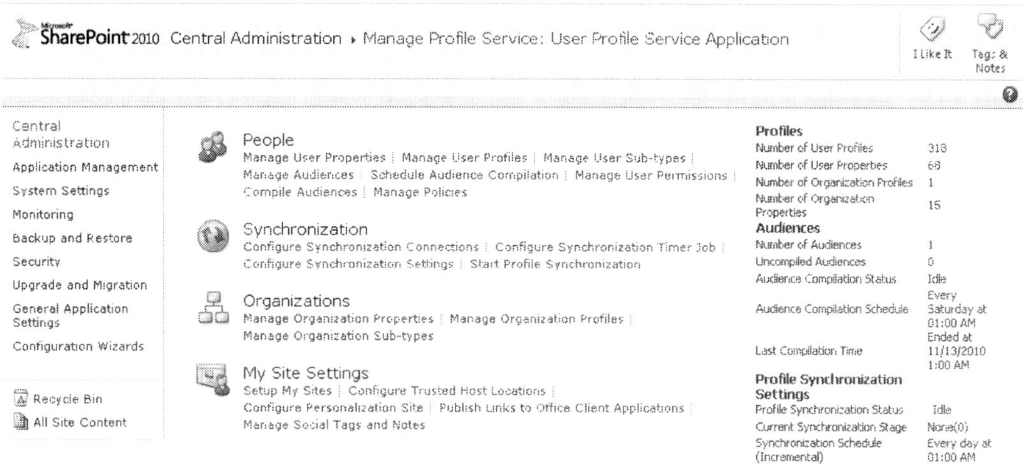

**Figure 3-8.** *The User Profile Service Application page*

Selecting the Configure Synchronization Connection menu item will display the page where additional user profile data sources can be added. To add a new source to synchronization, select Create New Connection. The following source types can be selected:

- Active Directory

- Active Directory Logon Data

- Active Directory Resource

- Business Data Connectivity

- IBM Tivoli Directory Server

- Novell eDirectory

- Sun Java System Directory Server

■ **Note** The Synchronization Connection page returns relatively good errors if the connection fails, but the Populate Containers button will still function even if all the required fields are not filled out. Make sure you have the correct domain, server, and user information to connect and retrieve the directory data.

# User Accounts

The synchronization connection settings should use an account that has access to the data source. The account should be able to read all the user profile data on the directory server being synchronized. How this account is set up may vary depending on the source system. The source systems are defined on the Add Synchronization page and can be set by choosing the correct system (listed here) in the Type drop-down menu, shown in Figure 3-9. When using Business Data Connectivity Services, an account is not required as the accounts set in the Business Data Connectivity entity will be used.

- *Active Directory.* The user must have Replicate Directory Changes permission on the target domain. For Windows 2003 Active Directory installations, the user should be a member of the Pre-Windows 2000 Compatible Access group. For domains with a different NetBIOS name, the `cn=configuration` container in Active Directory should be checked to make sure the user has Replicate Directory Changes permission. As exporting property values is also likely, the user should also have Create Child Objects and Write All Properties permissions.

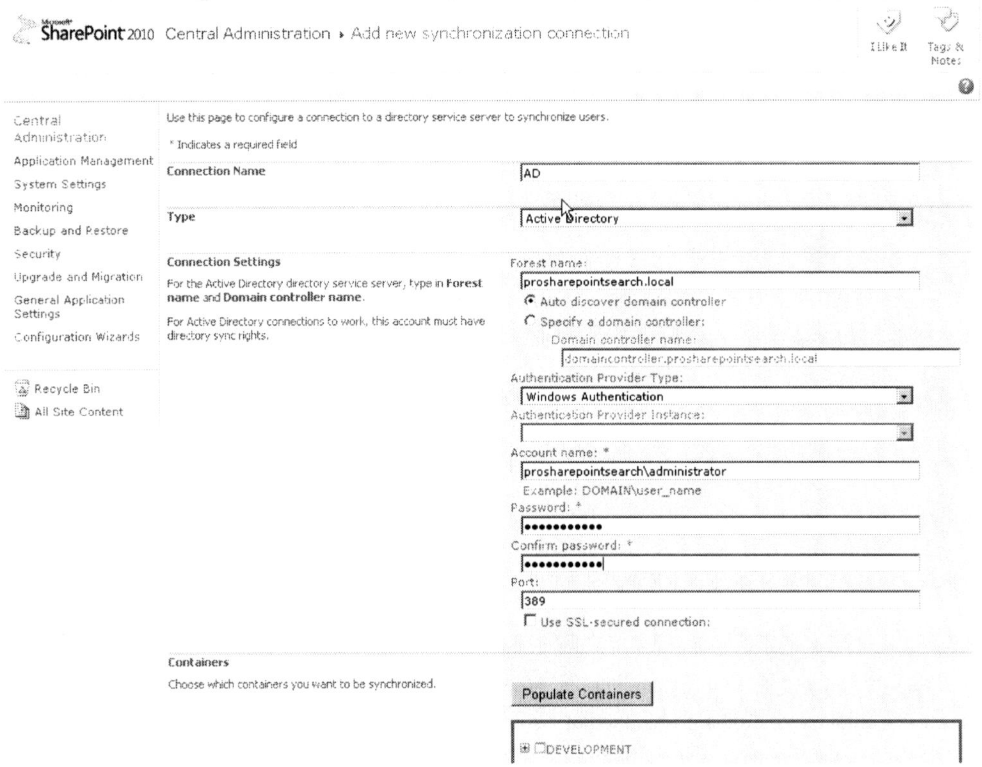

*Figure 3-9. Adding a new Directory Server source for synchronization*

- *Novel eDirectory*. Novel eDirectory should be configured to allow the specified user to browse in the Entry Rights property for the directory tree where the users to import are listed. Additionally, it should give the user Read, Write, and Compare rights in All Attributes for the same directory tree.

- *Sun Java System Directory Server*. In the Sun Java System Directory Server, Anonymous Access to RootDSE should be enabled with Read, Write, Compare, and Search rights. If the intention is to incrementally synchronize (recommended for large directories), the account should also have Read, Compare, and Search permissions on the `cn=changelog` object.

- *IBM Tivoli*: The account specified to synchronize with IBM Tivoli should be a member of the administrative group.

---

■ **Note** To configure synchronization with a Lightweight Directory Interchange Format (LDIF) file, see the how-to guide provided by Microsoft on TechNet: `http://technet.microsoft.com/en-us/library/ff959234.aspx`.

---

## Excluding Directory Tree Nodes

SharePoint allows the administrator to choose which levels of the directory and which nodes to synchronize. All other nodes will be excluded. The administrator can select the entire directory by choosing Select All or choose each organizational unit separately. Since, generally, current user data is interesting only to an organization, it is recommended that care is taken to select only organizational units that have current users in them. Exclude former employees, service users, computers, etc. See Figure 3-10.

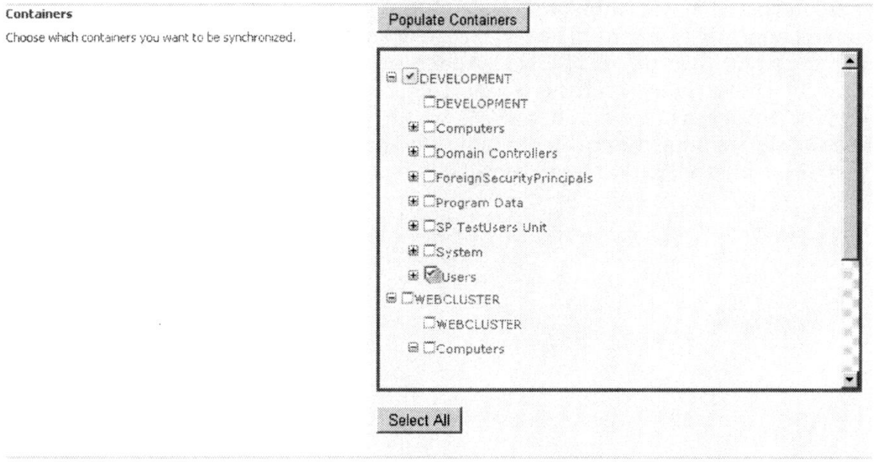

*Figure 3-10. Selecting the directory containers and users to be synchronized for user data*

■ **Note** The User Profile service must be set to synch before any user profiles can be crawled. Be sure to initiate an initial synch before crawling and expecting users to be searchable.

## Searching from MySites

Each MySite has its own search box that is similar to all the pages in a SharePoint site. However, this MySite search box can have a different target search center. Designating the target search center for MySites is done in the User Profile services application under MySite Settings (Figure 3-11).

*Figure 3-11. Setting the appropriate target search center for MySites*

# Crawling File Shares

SharePoint 2010 Search is truly designed as an enterprise search tool. Many do not appreciate the extensive search capabilities of SharePoint because of all its other enterprise functionality. SharePoint 2010 has extensive indexing capabilities, and one of the most useful is the indexing of file shares. We have yet to encounter an organization without hoards of data stored away on file shares. Some or all of this data may not be interesting, and care should be taken as to what is included in an index. We will cover this in detail in Chapter 10. However, the ability to index and expose the potential treasure troves of information locked away in these data graveyards is vast. This section will outline how to quickly and easily set up the SharePoint crawler to index file shares.

Like adding SharePoint sites, setting the crawler to index file shares is done in the Add Content Sources page in the Search service application (see Figure 3-12).

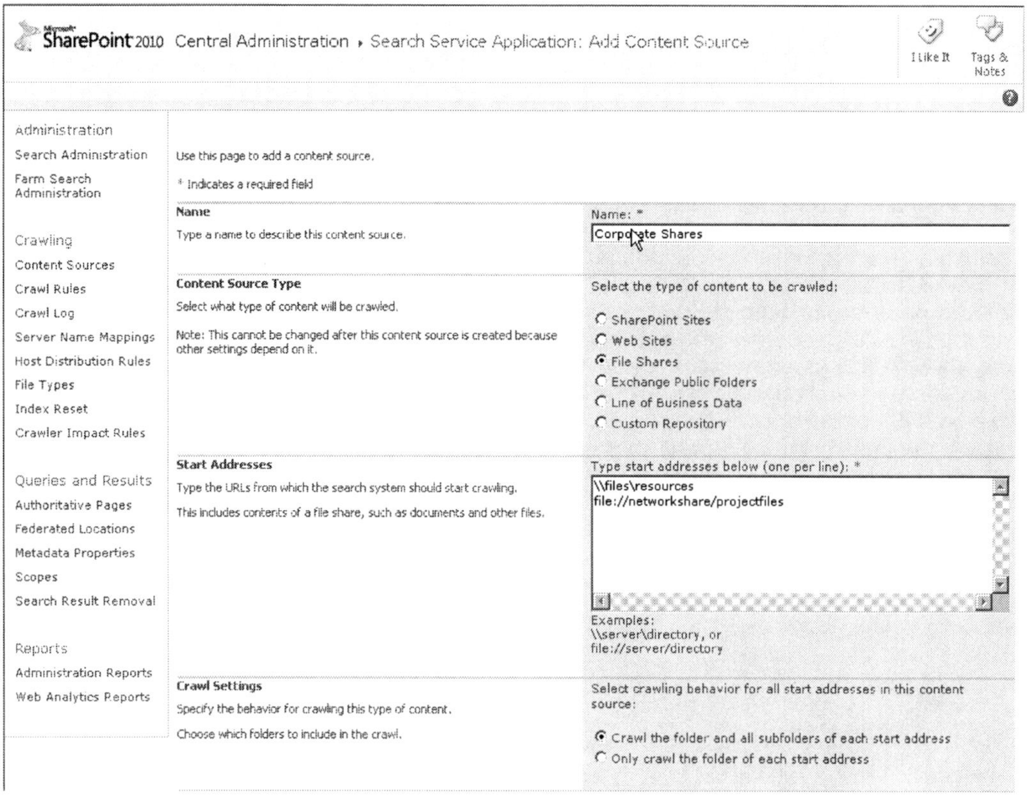

**Figure 3-12.** *The Add Content Source page defining file shares to crawl*

Defined paths in the Start Addresses section must be either UNC paths or paths using the file protocol (`file://fileshare`). Testing the paths by mapping the drives on the server is advisable before adding them as content sources. Make sure the crawl user has read access to the file shares.

Crawled files may also contain metadata that can be used by the search refiners in SharePoint 2010 or in scopes. This metadata is usually not made available by default in SharePoint, unlike many of the document properties in documents managed by SharePoint in document libraries. Making sure this metadata is crawled and mapped to managed properties in SharePoint can allow for this metadata to be used in refiners and scopes. See the section later in this chapter on crawling and mapping metadata for more details on how to map this crawled metadata.

---

■ **Note** File shares are often filled with document types that are not indexed by default by SharePoint's crawler. Luckily, SharePoint has the ability, via the Windows operating system, to convert and crawl text from other file types using iFilters. iFilters can be programmed for custom file types or purchased from third-party vendors. We will address iFilters later in this section and later in the book.

---

# Crawling Web Sites

SharePoint 2010 can also crawl web sites and has a unique crawling mechanism for indexing web content. Although SharePoint itself is essentially a very powerful web site for portal usage, the crawling mechanism differs insomuch as the web crawling mechanism of SharePoint 2010 has special capabilities for parsing HyperText Markup Language (HTML) and extracting content from HTML tags. When crawling SharePoint sites, the crawler uses a different application programming interface (API) to collect documents and a rich amount of associated information such as custom properties.

It is generally recommended that SharePoint sites, even those that are used as external web sites, should be indexed as SharePoint sites. If indexing a web site built on some other content management system or indexing all or part of an external web site, the web site definition should be used. Crawling sites as web sites will limit the crawler to indexing content retrievable on the presentation tier of the web site—that is, the web sites as anonymous visitors will see them.

There are times when it may be necessary or desirable to index SharePoint sites as web sites, and this is also possible—for example, if the SharePoint site is for a public site not owned or operated by the organization, if the site is behind a firewall, or if the SharePoint site is based on a different version of SharePoint and it is not possible to index it as a SharePoint site.

Web sites should be added by adding the entire HyperText Transfer Protocol (HTTP) or HTTP with Secure Socket Layers (SSL) path (HTTPS). See Figure 3-13.

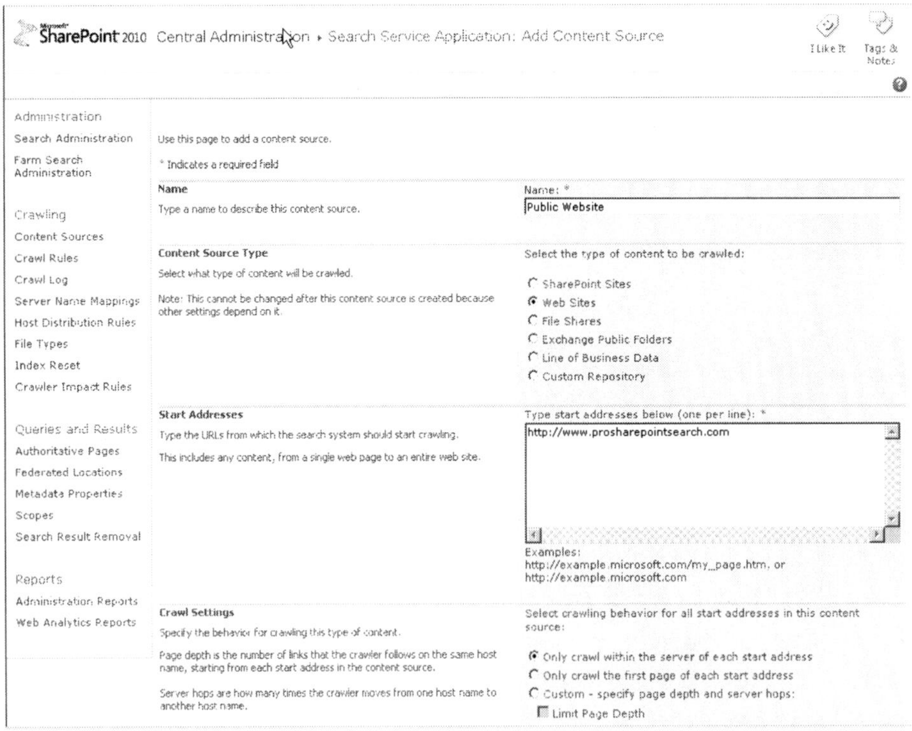

**Figure 3-13.** *Adding a web site content source*

Web sites are anything but a standard group of items. There are nearly as many variations of how web sites are built as web sites themselves. Even though standards exist for HTML and web content, it is very difficult to find a site that follows these standards. Respect should be given to browser developers for giving end users such a rich experience, given the state of most web sites. With that said, the argument exists that if browsers were not as forgiving, web developers would be more careful. Most crawlers are usually not as forgiving. This is usually due to the fact that a crawler needs to make sense of the content it is getting in the HTML, not just display it.

Many factors make crawling web pages tricky, including

- *JavaScript*: Crawlers generally cannot understand JavaScript and will ignore it.

- *Flash*: Crawlers will not index the content of Flash objects in most cases.

- *Images*: Web crawlers do not make sense of images outside of their metatags or alt tags. Scanned text is a special problem—although users see text, crawlers see only an image.

- *Broken HTML*: Although browsers will display poorly formatted HTML, crawlers can often stumble on it.

- *Poor or missing metadata*: Web pages can hold metadata, and this can improve the richness of the content. However, most content management systems do a poor job of managing and publishing metadata. Custom sites are even worse.

- *Page or site-based crawl rules*: Robots metatags or `robots.txt` files

These issues make crawling web sites difficult and the content collected from them often not as good as that from a SharePoint site. If the administrator has control of the web site, correcting these issues can make the web content more accessible to SharePoint Search as well as to global search if the site is exposed to the World Wide Web.

# Crawling Exchange Public Folders

SharePoint 2010 can also crawl Exchange public folders. Like file shares, public folders have enjoyed a certain level of popularity for storing shared documents. Exchange has the handy capability of sharing e-mail messages and documents by placing them in shared public folders. Since many information workers are actively using Outlook, having shared documents and e-mail in Exchange can be very useful. Of course, SharePoint is the next-generation solution, and there are many advantages to moving this content directly into SharePoint. However, if moving them is not desirable, indexing that content and making it available in SharePoint's search is possible.

Setting up the crawler to crawl public folders is similar to the previous content sources, except you will need to be aware of what user rights the crawler account has. If it does not have read access to the public folders that need indexing, a crawl rule will need to be added that defines this user.

Follow these steps to add Exchange public folders as a content source (see Figure 3-14):

1. In the Search Service Application page in the Central Administration, select Content Sources and New Content Source.

2. Fill out the fields with the appropriate information, and select Exchange public folders as the content source.

3. Set the Exchange server and the path to the public folders to be indexed in the Start Addresses field. Internal sites can use the NetBIOS name in place of the fully qualified domain name (FQDN). If Exchange Web Access is running under Secure Socket Layers, be sure to use the HTTPS protocol in the path. If the server is Exchange 2007 SP2 or later versions, the path to the public folder can be identified by accessing the public folders via Exchange Web Access and copying the path in the address bar from the browser.

4. Fill out the other fields with appropriate choices (index subfolders, schedule crawl, etc.).

5. Ensure the crawl user has read access to the public folders *or* create a new crawl rule that has the credentials of a user that does have access. See the following section on crawl rules for more guidance.

Once again, the crawler will communicate with the Exchange server in a different way than other content sources. For this reason, it is important to make sure that the content source is correctly defined.

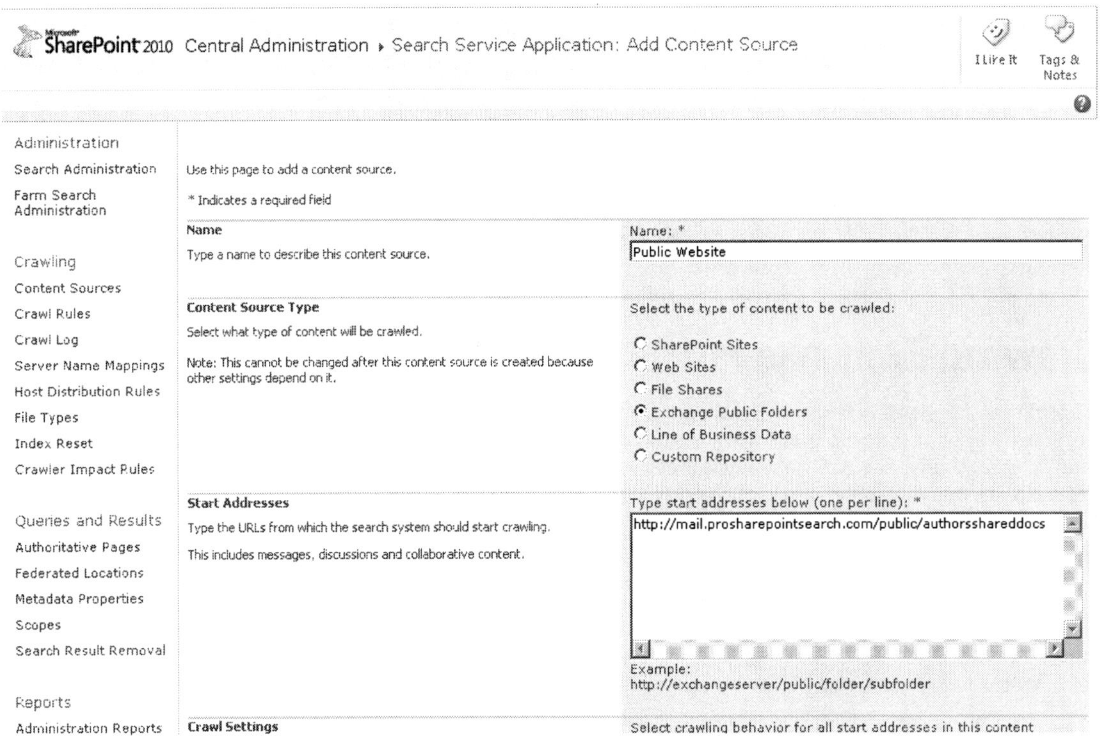

*Figure 3-14. Adding Exchange public folders as a content source*

# Crawling Line-of-Business Data

Line-of-business (LOB) systems are those systems in an organization that perform tasks critical to the operation for the business. Although this definition is relatively broad, generally, systems such as enterprise resource planning (ERP), accounting, and customer relations management (CRM) systems are included in this definition. For many organizations, SharePoint is quickly becoming an integral part of these systems. Since SharePoint is a relatively new and lightweight tool for many organizations, bringing data from larger, older, or more core business systems can be important.

The ability to crawl line-of-business data from other IT systems is one of the features that makes SharePoint a true enterprise search tool. This ability is made possible by the powerful Business Connectivity Services, which has an entire chapter in this book dedicated to it (Chapter 9). If it is the intention to include line-of-business data in SharePoint and utilize a Business Data Connectivity service, there should be a content source defined for that data. Here are the steps to add a Business Connectivity Services content source.

1. Navigate to the Search service application and select Content Sources on the left-hand menu.

2. Give the content source a name and choose Line-of-Business Data as a Content Source Type.

3. Select the appropriate Business Data Connectivity service if there is more than one. Selected external sources or all external sources can also be chosen. This may be necessary if there are several external sources defined in the service but all are not interesting to crawl.

4. Set a crawl schedule and a priority.

The crawler is now ready to crawl and index the Business Data Connectivity service (Figure 3-15).

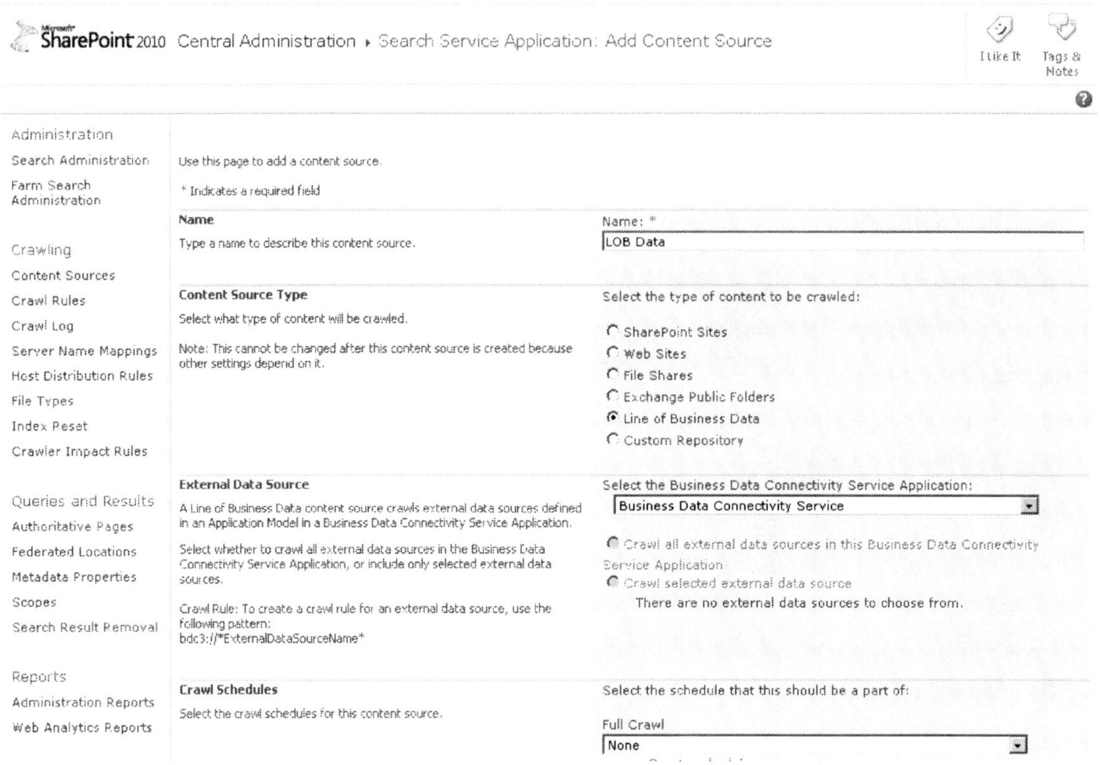

**Figure 3-15.** *Setting up a Business Connectivity Services content source*

# Using Crawl Rules

SharePoint 2010's crawler communicates with the content sources that are defined in a very standardized manner. It indexes the content as the user that it is specified as and collects information from all the links that are specified. If subfolders are set to be indexed, it will navigate to those folders, collect the links, and gather the content. It is not always desirable or possible, however, to have SharePoint crawl the content sources in the same way with the same accounts. Therefore, SharePoint 2010 has a powerful feature to specify rules for given paths that may be encountered during crawling. These rules can include or exclude specific content as well as pass special user credentials to those specific items in order to gather them correctly.

Crawl rules are applied in the Search service application on the Crawl Rules page, which is under the Crawler section of the left-hand navigation. Adding a new crawl rule is as easy as navigating to the Crawl Rules page and selecting new crawl rule. Because regular expressions and wildcard rules can be applied, a testing feature is made available on the Crawl Rules page. This feature will allow a particular address to be entered and tested to see if there is a rule already designated that affects the crawling of this address. Since many rules can be applied and the effect of rules is not always obvious, this testing feature is very useful (Figure 3-16). If a page is not being crawled, administrators are encouraged to check for conflicting rules.

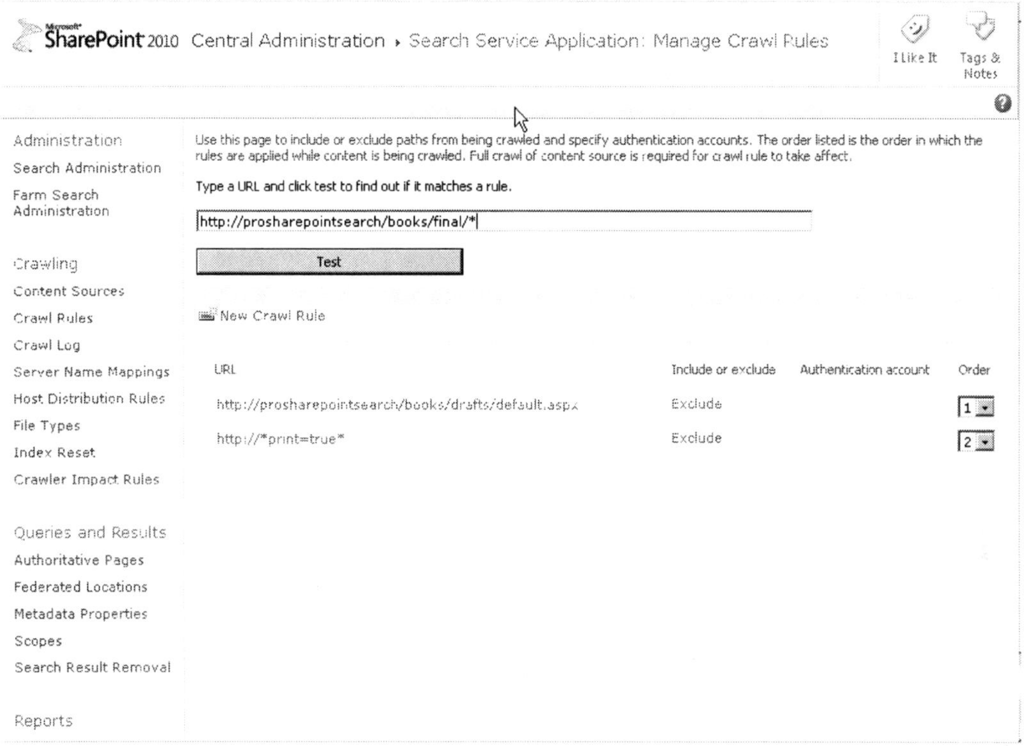

*Figure 3-16. Testing a crawl rule*

To add a crawl rule, navigate to the Search service application and choose Crawl Rules in the left-hand navigation under Crawler. On the Crawl Rules page, select New Crawl Rule. On the Add Crawl Rule page, paths can be added to either explicitly exclude or include. Wildcards or regular expressions can be used to create complicated inclusion or exclusion rules. This gives a powerful way to find undesirable or desirable content and make sure it is or isn't crawled.

Adjusting the crawler with crawl rules can go a long way toward improving the relevance and quality of the search result set. All too often, search result lists are polluted with unnecessary or irrelevant content. Setting this content in crawl rules to be excluded from the crawl can help to remove unnecessary documents from the crawl database and consequently the result lists. Some typical examples of this are documents of a certain type or in a certain location. Although many serious scenarios can be imagined where documents with a certain file name or in a certain path need to be excluded, one of the most common situations is when crawling a public web site with print versions for each page. Setting a crawl rule to set the print version (e.g., print=true pattern in URL) can easily allow these to be removed from the crawled content and remove this noise. Some simple inspections of the search results and the patterns in URLs on the content source sites will help to determine what kinds of rules are appropriate.

# Using Regular Expression in Crawl Rules

SharePoint 2010 has the added feature of supporting regular expressions in crawl rules. The administrator must be sure to select the "Match regular expressions" check box and formulate the expressions properly, but this feature opens vast new possibilities for controlling what is crawled and what isn't.

SharePoint 2010 supports the following regular expression operators listed in Tables 3-1 through 3-3.

*Table 3-1. Acceptable Grouping Operators in SharePoint 2010*

| Operator | Symbol | Description | Example | Valid match | Invalid match |
|----------|--------|-------------|---------|-------------|---------------|
| Group | () | Parentheses will group sets of characters. Operators for the group will be applied to the entire group. | | | |
| Disjunction | \| | This pipe operator is applied between two expressions and returns true when only one is valid. It is a logical OR. | \\prosharepointshare \((share1)\|(share2))\.* | \\prosharepointshare \share1\<files> OR \\prosharepointshare \share2\<files> | \\myshare\ share1share2\ <files> |

*Table 3-2. Acceptable Matching Operators in SharePoint 2010*

| Operator | Symbol | Description | Example | Valid match | Invalid match |
|----------|--------|-------------|---------|-------------|---------------|
| Match any character | . | The period or dot operator matches any character. It will not match with a null character, which means the number of dots should correspond to the number of characters matched. | http://prosharepoint search/default.as. | http://prosharepoint search/default.aspx | http://prosharepoint search/default.asp |

| Operator | Symbol | Description | Example | Valid match | Invalid match |
|---|---|---|---|---|---|
| Condi-tional match | ? | The expression can be tested to either exist or not. It will not expand the expression. | http://prosharepoint search/default(1)?.ht ml | http://prosharepoint search/default.aspx AND http://prosharepoint search/default1.aspx | http://prosharepoint search/default11.aspx |
| Wildcard match | * | A single character can either exist or repeatedly exist based on the operator's expansion. | http://prosharepoint search/default(1)*.asp x | http://prosharepoint search/default.aspx AND http://prosharepoint search/default111.asp x | http://prosharepoint search/def.aspx |
| Match one or more times | + | It requires the expression on which it is applied to exist in the target address at least once. | http://prosharepoint search/default(1)+.as px | http://prosharepoint search/default1.aspx AND http://prosharepoint search/default111 .aspx | http://prosharepoint search/default.aspx |
| List match | [<list of chars>] | This operator is a list of characters inside square brackets "[]". It matches any characters in the list. A range of characters can be specified using the hyphen "-" operator between the characters. | http://prosharepoint search /page[1-9].htm | http://prosharepoint search/page1.htm OR http://prosharepoint search/page2.htm OR http://prosharepoint search/page3.htm OR ... | |

*Table 3-3.* *Acceptable Count Operators in SharePoint 2010*

| Operator | Symbol | Description | Example | Valid match | Invalid match |
|---|---|---|---|---|---|
| Exact count | {num} | This operator is a number inside curly brackets"{}", e.g., {1}. It limits the number of times a specific match may occur. | http://proshare pointsearch/(1){5} -(0){3}.aspx | http://proshare pointsearch/11111-000.aspx | http://proshare pointsearch/111-00.aspx |
| Min count | {num,} | This operator is a number inside curly brackets "{}" followed by a comma ",", e.g., {1,}. It limits the number of repetitions a specific match can have and places a minimum amount on that match. | http://proshare pointsearch/(1){5, }-(0){2}.aspx | http://proshare pointsearch/11111-00.aspx AND http://proshare pointsearch/11111-00.aspx | http://proshare pointsearch/1111-00.aspx |
| Range count | {num1, num2} | This operator holds two numbers inside curly brackets"{}" separated by a comma ",", e.g., {4,5}. The first number defines a lower limit, and the second number defines an upper limit. It limits the number of repetitions in a URL between the two values, num1 and num2. The first number should always be lower than the second to be valid. | http://proshare pointsearch/(1){4} -(0){2,3}.aspx | http://proshare pointsearch/1111-00.aspx AND http://proshare pointsearch/1111-000.aspx | http://proshare pointsearch/9999-0000.aspx |
| Disjunc- tion | \| | This pipe operator is applied between two expressions and returns true when only one is valid. It is a logical OR. | \\proshare pointshare \((share1)\| (share2))\.* | \\proshare pointshare \share1\<files> OR \\proshare pointshare \share2\<files> | \\myshare\ share1share2\ <files> |

| Operator | Symbol | Description | Example | Valid match | Invalid match |
|---|---|---|---|---|---|
| List | [<list of chars>] | This operator is a list of characters inside square brackets "[]". It matches any characters in the list. A range of characters can be specified using the hyphen "-" operator between the characters. | http://proshare pointsearch /page[1-9].htm | http://proshare pointsearch/page1.h tm OR http://proshare pointsearch/page2.h tm OR http://prosharepoin tsearch/page3.htm OR ... | |

When adding regular expressions to match crawl paths, it is important to know that the protocol part (e.g., `http://`) of the path *cannot* contain regular expressions. Only parts of the path after the defined protocol may contain regular expressions. If the protocol is excluded, SharePoint will add `http://` to the hostname and any attempts at regular expressions.

By default regular expression matches are not case-sensitive. Additionally, SharePoint 2010's crawler normalizes all discovered links by converting them to lowercase. If it is necessary to match case or use regular expressions to exclude documents based on character case in the path, the "Match case" check box should be checked. Otherwise, leave it empty. It may be necessary to match case if crawling Apache-driven web sites where pages are case-sensitive, Linux-based file shares, or content from Business Connectivity Services that preserves case. Creating crawl rules for case-sensitive file types allows them to be crawled and recognized as unique.

## Using Crawl Rules to Grant Access

Crawl rules can also be used to grant access to specific content or parts of content by defining the user that will crawl that content. Generally, the crawler should be given full read access to content and allow SharePoint's permissions filtering to determine what users can see.

■ **Note** Be careful when applying blanket permissions across large document repositories. Although giving the SharePoint crawler read access to everything is usually a good idea in well-managed SharePoint sites, doing it on other systems can often expose security risks such as documents without correct permissions that are never found solely due to obscurity. A search engine is a great tool for finding things, even those best left hidden.

It is also possible and sometimes necessary to define a special user for indexing external sites or independent systems such as file shares or Exchange. In these cases, a special user with read access to the content can be defined in the crawl rules. For example, if indexing Exchange public folders, a separate user can be defined to allow read-only access to those folders. This user can be set in crawl rules to be the user to index that content, thereby protecting other Exchange content from unauthorized crawling (Figure 3-17).

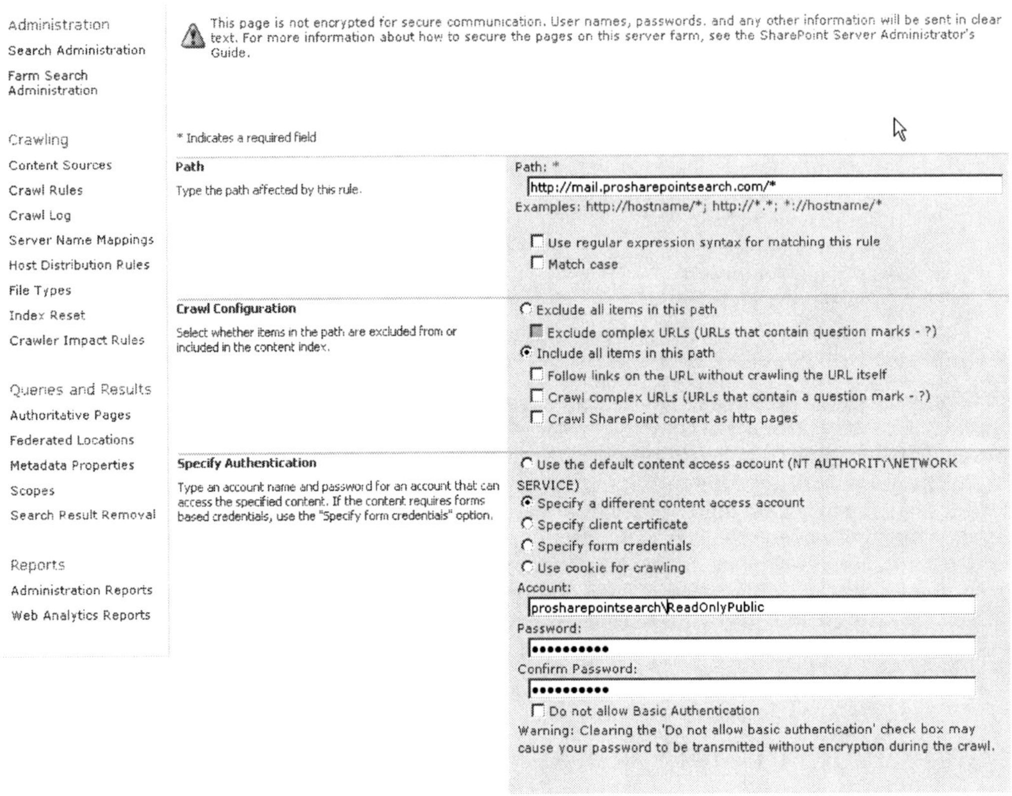

**Figure 3-17.** *Specifying a crawl rule that applies a specific user to the crawler*

---

■ **Note** Many content management systems allow for web-based authoring. Authors can click a link to add, edit, and delete content. With some crawler technologies, it is possible for the crawler to delete all the content on a site as the crawler clicks every link. The authors of this book saw this often with Microsoft's previous CMS product. However, SharePoint's crawler will submit only GET form requests, and modifications and deletions via web-based authoring systems are usually triggered by POST forms. So the likelihood of SharePoint's crawler modifying or deleting content is slim. However, it is still wise to use crawl rules to specify a read-only user to index such sites.

---

# Troubleshooting Crawl Errors

All too often, users complain about missing content in search engines. Either impatient users expect their content to appear immediately or some crawling issue causes the content to be skipped during indexing. Undefined file types, documents without any text, documents left checked out, or just corrupted files can cause SharePoint's crawler to fail.

Luckily there is a way to investigate and identify crawl problems in SharePoint (although it still leaves a certain amount of guesswork necessary). The SharePoint crawler logs can show a lot of information about what was crawled, what wasn't, errors that were encountered, and even warnings.

Administrators can investigate the crawl logs in SharePoint Central Administration in the Search service application, under the Crawler menu on the left navigation. By default the crawl log shows a list of content sources and their top-level warnings. By clicking each content source, the administrator can dig into the particular content source's error overview. For more details on specific documents or pages, the administrator will need to choose one of the links at the top of the page to view crawl logs by hostname, URL, crawl history, or error message.

The Host Name crawler log page shows all the hostnames defined across the different content sources. Clicking individual hostnames takes the administrator to the URL page, where individual URLs are displayed with their crawl result. This can be a success, an error, or a warning. It will also show documents deleted from the crawl database.

The crawler log will report the following status messages (see Figure 3-18):

- *Success*: The item was successfully crawled. The item has been added to the index and databases and already made searchable or the content was already in the index and has not changed.

- *Warning*: A warning message indicates some issue with the crawl. This could mean that the content was crawled, not crawled, or partially crawled. A good example of this is when a file type is defined but an appropriate iFilter for that file type is not present or is not functioning properly. A warning indicates that the document and its associated metadata from SharePoint (properties) have been crawled but not the content from within the document.

- *All Errors*: This message indicates there was a problem with the item and it, therefore, wasn't crawled. If it is a new item, it will not be searchable. Old items presently in the index will not be removed until the error has been resolved and the item can be identified as deleted. The item will also not be updated.

- *Deleted*: Deleted refers to all items that, for any reason, were removed from the index. These items will no longer be searchable. Items are generally deleted from an index in response to a deletion on the site or a crawl rule or a Search Result Removal (more on Search Result Removal in Chapter 10).

- *Top-Level Errors*: Top-level errors are a subset of the errors group and therefore are not counted in the hostname view. They are errors at the top page or entry point of the crawler that restricted it from crawling further. These errors are important as they can indicate why an entire site or content source is not indexed.

- *Folder/Site Errors*: These errors are like top-level errors but represent errors only at the start page of folders or sites. Again, these errors can be useful when diagnosing errors at a lower level or on a particular site and no error for the specific item exists.

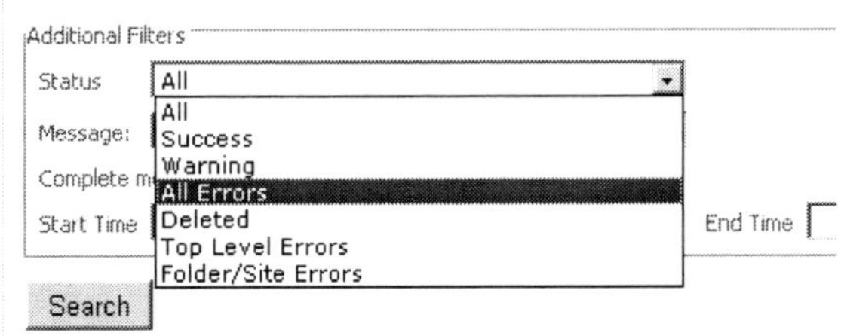

**Figure 3-18.** *Filtering on status messages in the crawl logs*

Crawl errors can be very difficult to decipher. SharePoint admittedly still does not have the best error logging. However, there is much that can be gleaned from the crawl logs and corrections made based on the information presented. Here are some common scenarios:

- *Warning message*: "The filtering process could not load the item. This is possibly caused by an unrecognized item format or item corruption."

  This message is most likely caused by one of two problems:

  1. The iFilter for this file type is not installed or is not functioning properly. In this case, install the iFilter. Citeknet has an iFilter Explorer that can help diagnose these problems.

  2. Although the iFilter is installed and functioning properly, this document is created in a manner not supported by this iFilter or there is formatting in this document that the iFilter does not like. In this case, investigate a third-party vendor's iFilter as an alternative.

- *Warning message*: "This item and all items under it will not be crawled because the owner has set the NoCrawl flag to prevent it from being searchable."

  1. This message indicates that during crawl, the crawler was instructed by the server that this content should not be crawled. For SharePoint this can mean that the site was set to not allow crawling. This is set in the site under Site Settings, Search and Offline Availability.

  2. A particular list or library can also be set to not be visible in search results. This is set in Advanced Settings on the List or Library settings page of the list or library in question.

  3. For non-SharePoint content, this can be caused by a Robots metatag or a `robots.txt` file. If the tag `<META NAME="ROBOTS" CONTENT="NOINDEX, NOFOLLOW">` appears on the page, SharePoint will respect it and not crawl the page. If the page is listed in a `robots.txt` file at the root of the site, SharePoint will likewise respect this rule and not index the page.

- *Error message*: "Object could not be found."

  This message indicates that when crawling a file share, the name of the file share is correct but the file to be crawled is not correct. The file will be deleted from the index. Check the file share, and make sure the content is correct and accessible by the correct user.

- *Top-level error message*: "Network path for item could not be resolved."

  This message points to a problem with the file share or the resolution of a domain name. Check that the share is available or the content source is resolvable from the crawl server. Content previously crawled under this content source that is not subsequently found will not be deleted from the index.

- *Error message*: "Access denied."

  "Access denied" is one of the most common error messages and indicates that the content is not accessible to the crawler. Check the permissions on the document against which user has be set as the default content access account in the Search service application.

# Server Name Mappings

Sometimes, it is desirable to crawl one source and have the link refer to another source. For example, I have a dedicated crawl server called SPCrawlWFE, which is a mirror of my web servers that are providing content to my users. I want to crawl the SPCrawlWFE site but have the users click through to the other server (SPProdWFE). By using server name mappings, one site can be crawled and the server names on the result page links change to another server.

To add a server name mapping, navigate to the Server Name Mappings page under the Crawler section of the Search service application. Click New Mapping. On the Add New Mapping page, add the name of the site that was crawled and the name of the site users should click through to. See Figure 3-19.

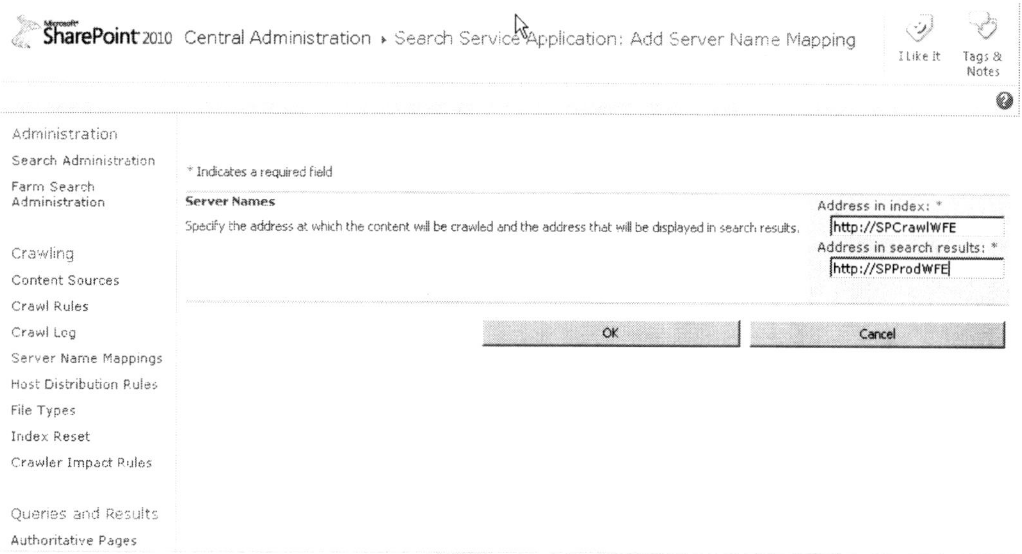

*Figure 3-19. Configuring server name mappings*

# Crawler Impact Rules

Crawler impact rules can allow the administrator to dictate whether the crawler requests content from a site more or less aggressively than default. This is useful if a site does not have a mirror for dedicated crawling or if the site is outside of the SharePoint farm and may not handle the load. In cases where it is desirable to crawl an external web site, it may be wise to limit the load put on that external site, as the administrator of that site may block the crawler due to the load and fear of a possible denial of service attack on the site. On the other hand, it may be desirable in environments that are especially performant to increase the load the crawler puts on the content servers during crawl to speed up the crawler and reduce crawl time.

Adding crawler impact rules is easy but requires consideration. The authors of this book recommend thorough testing in development systems before dedicating crawler impact rules to production. To add a rule, click Crawler Impact Rules under the Crawling section of the left navigation on the Search service application. Choose Add Rule. Enter the name of the site or content source that the rule should apply to. If it is desirable to restrict the impact on the site, lower the number of requests (default is 8). If it is possible to increase the load on the target source, increase the number. If the site is particularly sensitive to load, choose "Request one document at a time and wait the specified time between requests." Add a time in seconds that it will take the site to recover from delivering the request. Remember that limiting the number of connections and adding a pause between requests will substantially slow the crawl time. See Figure 3-20.

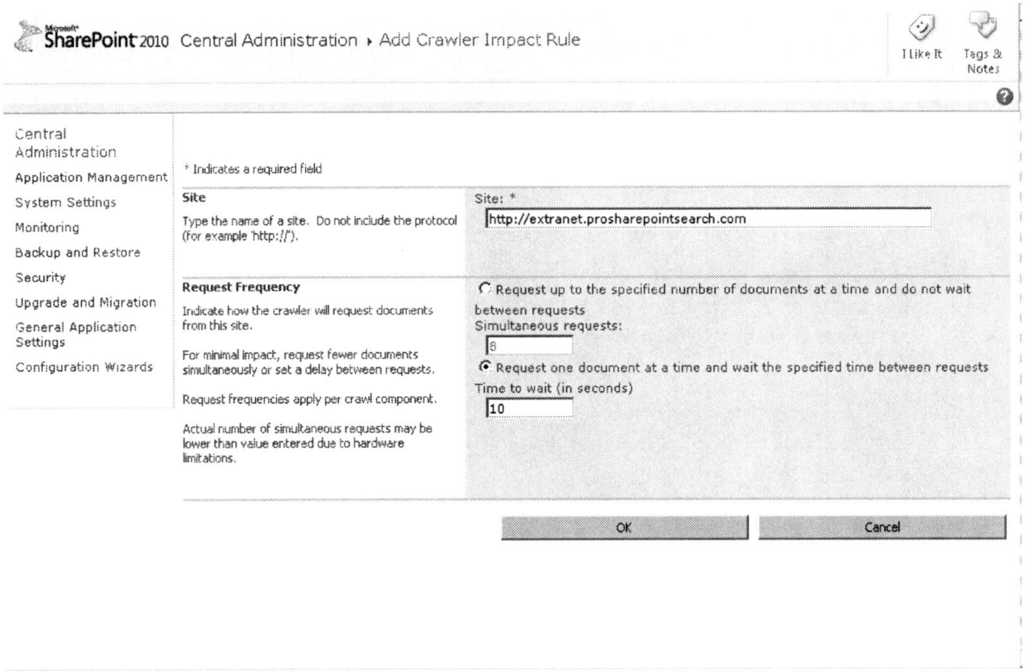

***Figure 3-20.*** *Adding a crawler impact rule*

# Crawler Scheduling

SharePoint's crawlers can be scheduled to perform full and incremental crawls at different intervals and for different periods. This is done separately for each content source, allowing for static content to be isolated from recurring crawls and dynamic or frequently updated content to be constantly refreshed. The scheduling configuration is done on the Edit Content Source page of each content source at the end of the page.

It is recommended that SharePoint content have a relatively aggressive incremental crawl schedule while taking into consideration actual update frequency and possible hardware limitations. Other content sources should have their respective usage considered before scheduling incremental crawls.

It is wise to schedule a full crawl on a regular basis to ensure database consistency. However, this regular schedule will depend largely on the time it takes to perform a full crawl. Some organizations with large repositories may choose to avoid full crawls after their initial index is populated. At the time of writing this book, the reliability of the SharePoint index is unknown, but it should be noted that search databases, like other databases, are subject to corruption and a full crawl may be periodically required.

Figures 3-21 and 3-22 show the part of the Edit/Add Content Sources page where a full crawl or incremental crawl can be scheduled and the Manage Schedules page (accessed through the "Create schedule" and "Edit schedule" links) with the options for scheduling those crawls.

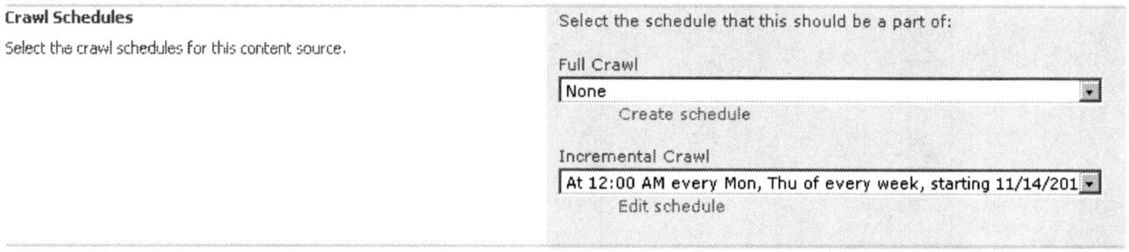

**Crawl Schedules**

Select the crawl schedules for this content source.

Select the schedule that this should be a part of:

Full Crawl

None

    Create schedule

Incremental Crawl

At 12:00 AM every Mon, Thu of every week, starting 11/14/201

    Edit schedule

*Figure 3-21. The scheduling section of the Edit/Add Content Source page*

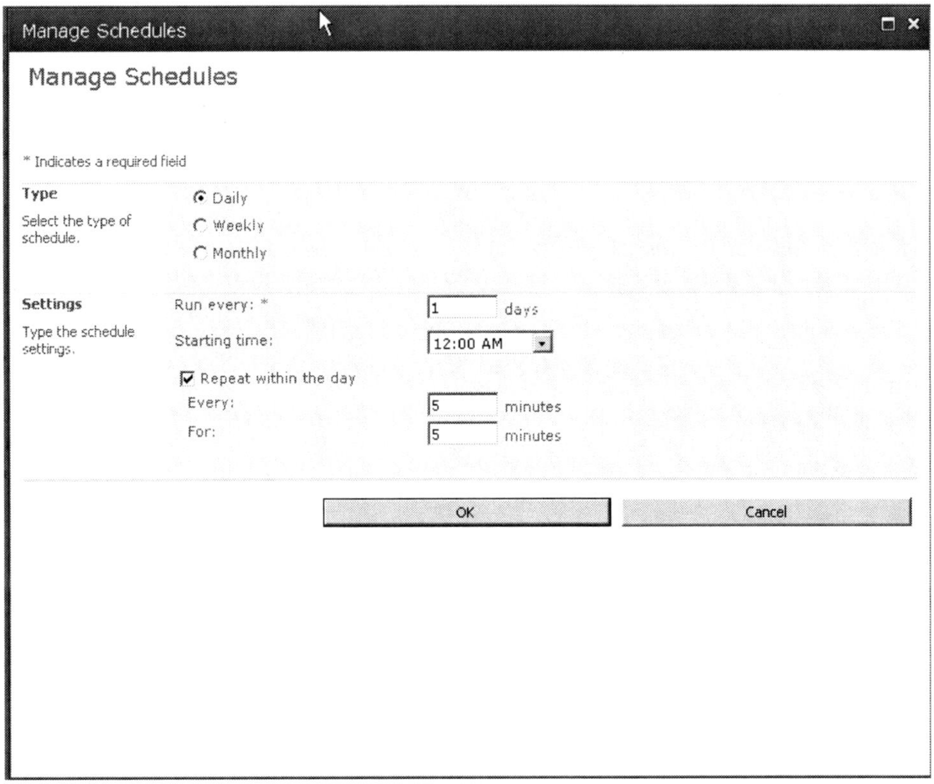

**Figure 3-22.** *The Manage Schedules page*

# Full vs. Incremental Crawls

SharePoint 2010 has two types of crawl mechanisms, full and incremental. Incremental crawls perform more efficiently and can keep the index up to date in near real time (Figure 3-23). However, at least one full crawl of a content source is always required and there may be other occasions when a full crawl is required.

During a full crawl, the crawler queries the content source and requests all the content for the first time. It then saves that data in the index and crawl database with date stamps and item IDs. Every time a full crawl is launched, this process is begun from scratch and old data is abandoned.

A full crawl is required when

- A new content source is added—any new content source requires a full crawl initially.

- A new file type is added—new file types cannot be picked up on an incremental crawl.

- A new managed property is mapped from a crawled property.

- Managed property mappings are changed or a new crawled property is added to an existing managed property.

- New crawl rules are added, changed, or removed—crawl rule modification requires a full crawl to take effect.

- The index becomes corrupted or performs irregularly—this should almost never happen but should not be ruled out.

During an incremental crawl, the crawler looks at the crawl database to determine what has been crawled or not crawled, and then requests updated information from the source depending on the content source type. In this way, the crawler can collect only documents that have been added or updated since the last crawl or remove documents from the index that have been removed from the content source.

If a situation exists where an incremental crawl is inappropriate or not possible, SharePoint will start a full crawl instead. In this way, the search index will not allow for the crawler to stop crawling on schedule and will not launch a crawl that will corrupt the index.

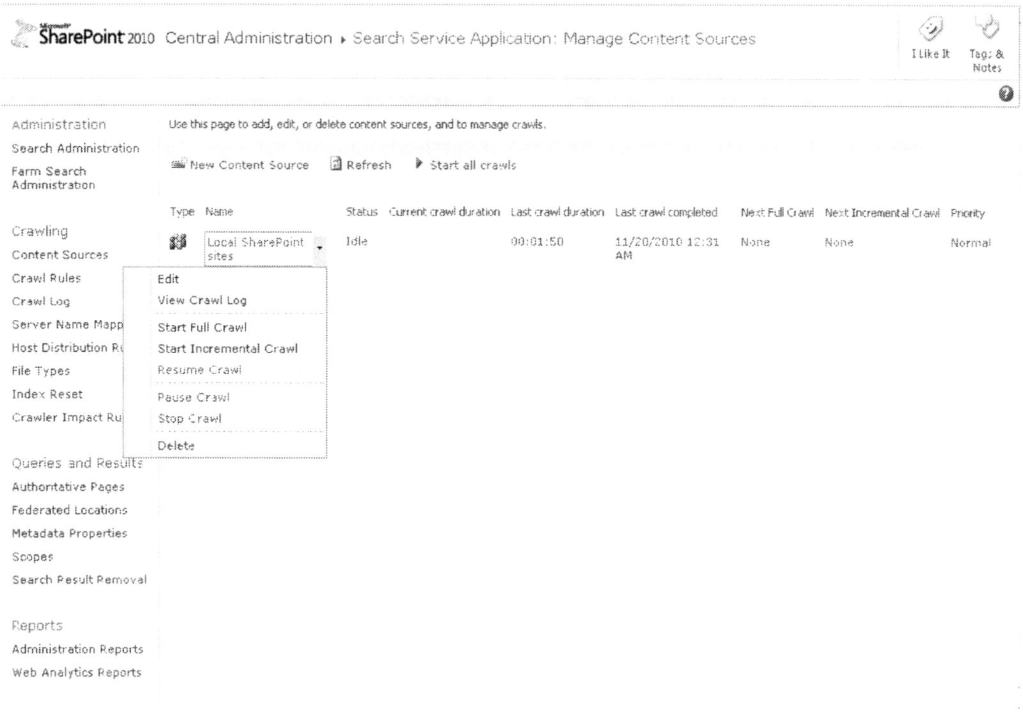

*Figure 3-23. Crawl control in SharePoint 2010*

# Crawling Metadata

Metadata is information that is associated with a document or file that is not necessarily an explicit part of the visible document. Often, metadata is held in hidden tags on a document or with files or records associated with that document. SharePoint 2010 has a powerful mechanism to assign a large number of properties to lists and documents, which is configurable by the administrator and updatable by authors and collaborators. The management of metadata will be discussed later in this book where it is considered relevant for improving or expanding search. SharePoint 2010 has a rich, new Managed Metadata service application that adds a great deal of configurability and relevancy to search, which will be covered.

In this section, we will cover how to crawl metadata such as metatags, document properties, and SharePoint custom properties, as well as see how to map that metadata to managed properties to make them available in search.

The first step to working with metadata in SharePoint search is to get familiarized with the existing property mappings and the crawled properties. In the Search service application under the Queries and Results section of the left navigation, there is a link to the Metadata Properties page. On this page, all of the managed properties and their mappings to crawled properties are listed. There are several default mappings. Many of the crawled property mappings are obvious—for example, People:AccountName (text). But others are not obvious—for example, Office:5 and Basic:6. Those beginning with OWS are from SharePoint list columns.

By selecting Crawled Properties at the top of the Metadata Properties page, a list of all crawled properties and their respective mappings is shown. It is possible to glean, in some cases, what the specific crawled properties mean. But in many cases, they are a mystery. However, this is generally of little consequence. It is important to name columns that contain custom properties with unique and telling names so that they may be easily identified and mapped to managed properties.

By default, columns are indexed by the crawler, but they are not all mapped to a managed property and so are not searchable. The exception to this is that crawled text properties are searchable as free text when included in the index but are not explicitly searchable as properties. To map a crawled property from a column to a managed property, navigate to the Metadata Properties page in the Search service application. Select New Managed Property at the top of the page (see Figure 3-24).

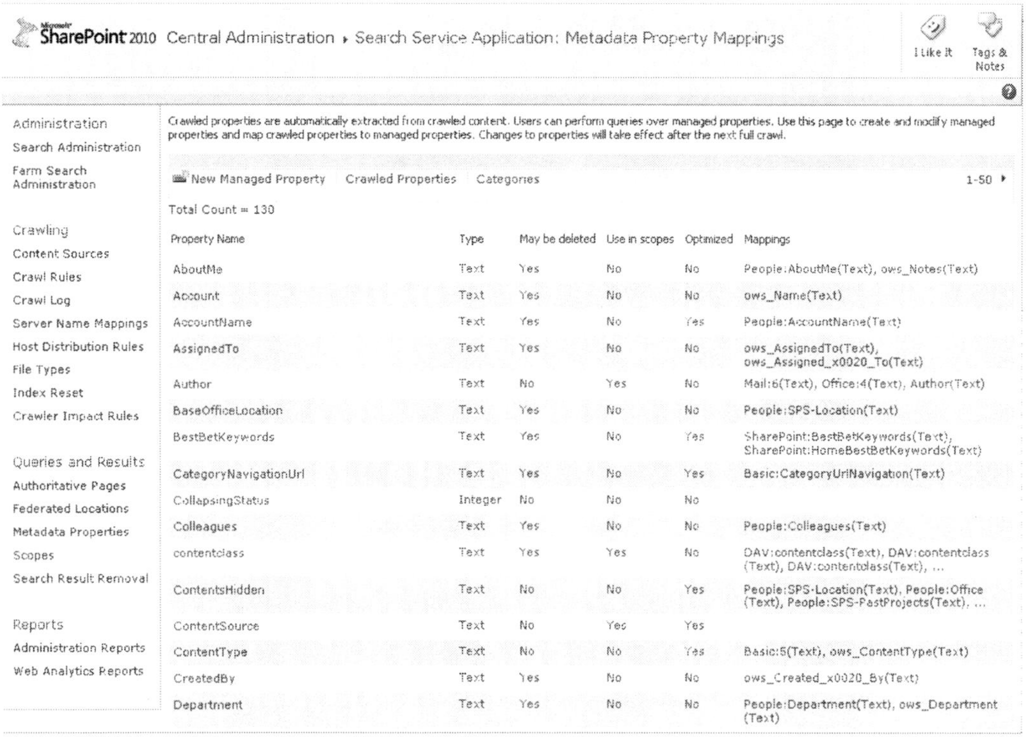

**Figure 3-24.** *The Metadata Properties page*

On the New Managed Property page, the property can be defined. The name should be indicative of the column and perhaps have the same name. The name cannot contain spaces. Users should be able to enter this term in the search box with appropriate search syntax to return documents with these properties. Using unusual codes or mysterious naming conventions should be avoided. Declare a type of property and whether individual properties in the columns will hold multiple values. The multiple values check box is not necessary if different records have a single value in the column but differ—only if a single property entry associated with a single record may have multiple values.

Multiple crawled properties can be mapped to a single managed property. This is useful when indexing several lists, or libraries with similar columns but different headings and hence different crawled property names. Also, different crawled properties from different document types or from other sites can be merged into a single, searchable managed property.

Select Add Mapping to find the crawled property to map to the managed property. The Crawled Property Selection dialog allows a category (such as SharePoint) to be chosen and a title filter applied to narrow a potentially long list of crawled properties. The title filter is controlled by the Find search box and uses a "contains" operator so that any property with the entered term in it will be returned (see Figure 3-25).

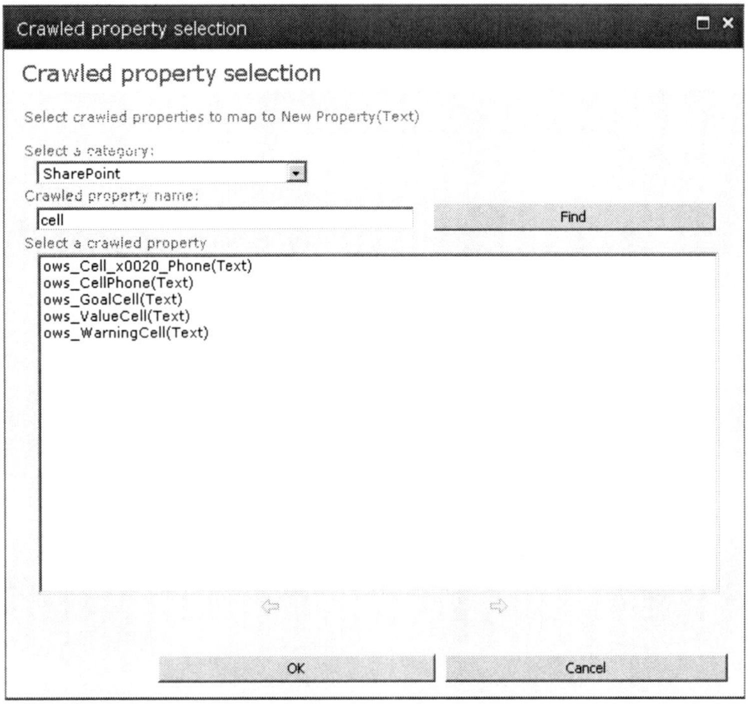

**Figure 3-25.** *The "Crawled property selection" dialog*

All managed properties can be allowed to be used in scopes to make logical division of the search index. This allows for searching in a particular set group of documents with specific properties. For example, People Search in SharePoint uses a scope that refines queries to only the People items in the index. See more on scopes in the next section.

Finally, managed properties that are text can be stored as hash in the database. To do this, set the "Reduce storage requirements for text properties by using a hash for comparison" check box when creating a new managed property. This will reduce the amount of space necessary to store the properties but will limit the search operators that can be used to find the properties to equality or inequality.

# Defining Scopes

Search scopes are a slightly confusing concept in SharePoint, as Microsoft has adopted the term "scope" to refer to a structure categorization of documents based on filtering of documents on their shared properties. It is best to think of search scopes as groups of documents that have shared properties.

When setting up the crawler, it is possible to create scopes based on managed properties. This will allow pre-determined filter sets to be applied on new search tabs and in search box drop-downs (must be enabled in the Site Collection Search settings). Care should be taken to create scopes that match business needs and possible future sectioning of the content. Any managed property can be made available for scopes, but properties must be explicitly defined as available for scopes in the Edit Managed Property page.

To create a new scope, navigate to the Scopes menu item under Queries and Results on the Search Service Application page. On the Scopes page, the existing scopes can be seen. In SharePoint 2010, there should be two default scopes, People and All Sites, as shown in Figure 3-26.

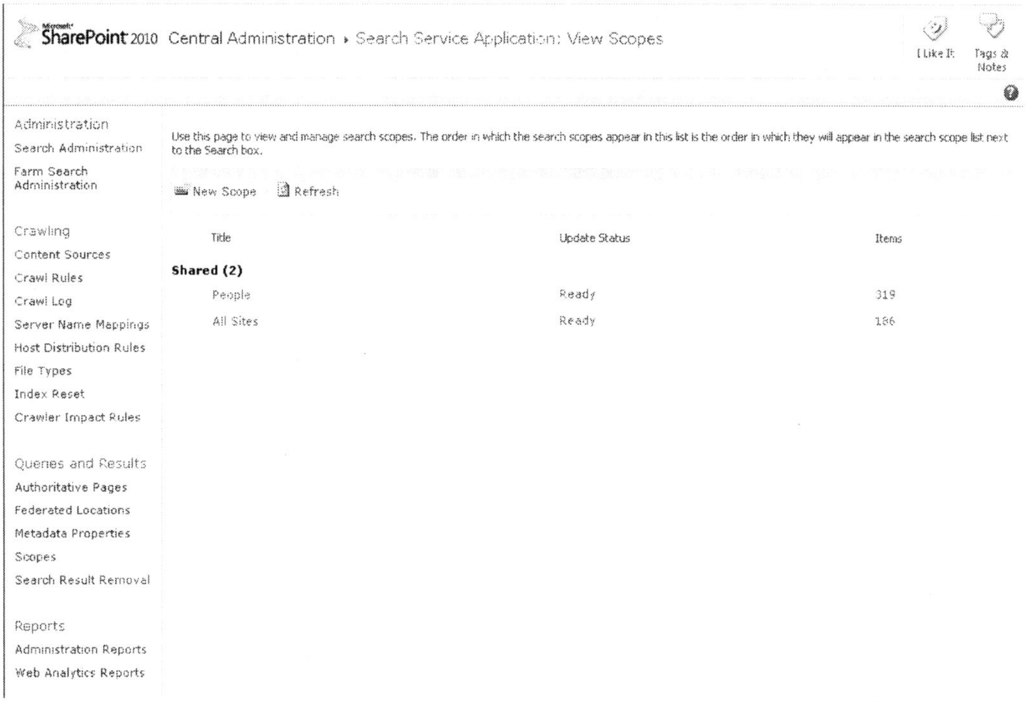

***Figure 3-26.*** *The View Scopes page*

# Adding or Editing Scopes

A scope can be edited by clicking it. Alternatively a new scope can be created by clicking New Scope. This will open the Create Scope page, where the scope can be given a name and description and a target result page set if the default search center is not being used for that particular scope. No rules for the scope will be applied on this page. This is done in the next step. After the new scope is created, the site will return to the View Scopes page. Here the new entry will appear with a link to add rules. If the Add Rules link is clicked, a new page where rules for that scope can be applied will appear.

There are four kinds of scope rule types:

- *Web Address*: Content can be delimited based on the URL of the site the content was found under. This rule type is based on the protocol and URL of the site (e.g., `http://server/path`). This rule can be applied on a folder, a hostname, a domain, or subdomain. Each setting has a unique field to apply the rule.

- *Property Query*: A scope rule can be created that filters documents based on common properties across documents. For example, a particular content type or author property can be used to isolate documents in a scope. The Property Query option gives a drop-down of all managed properties that have been set as available for use in scopes. The operator is always equal so the value placed in the field must be an exact match to the value in the property.

- *Content Source*: A scope can limit the result set to a particular content source. Choosing Content Source will give a drop-down menu of all the defined content sources in the Search service application.

- *All Content*: A scope can also be based on all content in the index. Choosing All Content will simply return all content in that scope.

In addition to these rules, specific behaviors may be applied for each rule except All Content. The available behaviors are Include, Require, and Exclude.

- *Include*: Items in this rule will be included in the results of this scope unless they are excluded by another rule applied to the same scope.

- *Require*: If Require is chosen, the scope will not include items that do not conform to this rule. That is, all items must match this rule regardless of other rules.

- *Exclude*: Items matching an exclude rule will not be added to the scope or included in the search result set of the scope.

Multiple rules may be applied for any given scope.

## Scope Update Schedule

Scope updates, as a rule, happen every 15 minutes if set to automatically refresh. If necessary, these updates can be changed to be made manually. This is done from the main page of the Search Service Application page under Scope Update Schedule.

## Setting Scopes with PowerShell

Scopes can also be managed with PowerShell cmdlets. It is possible to add, remove, and edit scopes with PowerShell as well as manage the rules associated with the scopes.

The following PowerShell commands are available for managing scopes:

- `Get-SPEnterpriseSearchQueryScope`

- `New-SPEnterpriseSearchQueryScope`

- `Remove-SPEnterpriseSearchQueryScope`

- `Set-SPEnterpriseSearchQueryScope`

Additionally, scope rules can be added, removed, and set using the following PowerShell cmdlets:

- `Get-SPEnterpriseSearchQueryScopeRule`

- `New-SPEnterpriseSearchQueryScopeRule`

- Remove-SPEnterpriseSearchQueryScopeRule

- Set-SPEnterpriseSearchQueryScopeRule

In order to set a rule, the scope's name must be passed as a parameter for the cmdlet for adjusting the scope rule. This is because rules are unique to individual scopes. For example, to create a scope called PDF and set that scope to include only items of the PDF file type, open the SharePoint 2010 Management Shell console and use the following PowerShell cmdlets:

```
Get-SPEnterpriseSearchServiceApplication | New-SPEnterpriseSearchQueryScope -name PDFs
 -description  "PDF documents only"  -displayinadminui  $true
```

This will create a new scope called PDFs. The `DisplayInAdminUI` parameter should be set to `$true` (or 1) if the scope should appear in the Search service application's Scopes page in Central Administration. Otherwise, set it to `$false` (or 0) to hide it.

After creating the new scope, it should have some rules applied to it. To do this, the ID of the scope is required. Otherwise, if creating a scope and adding rules to it at the same time, a variable can be assigned to the `New-SPEnterpriseSearchQueryScope` command like this:

```
$NewScope = Get-SPEnterpriseSearchServiceApplication | New-SPEnterpriseSearchQueryScope
 -name PDFs -description  "PDF documents only"  -displayinadminui  $true
```

Just like on the Scopes page in the Search service application in Central Administration, there are four rule types you can set with `New-SPEnterpriseSearchQueryScopeRule`. Here are the rule types and example cmdlets.

- *Web Address*: To create a web address rule in PowerShell, the cmdlet takes the URL value in the rule type parameter. The parameter `URLScopeType` must also be set. The values that this parameter takes are Folder, HostName, or Domain, just like in the Scopes page in Central Administration. Finally a value for the parameter `MatchingString` must be set. This is the string of the web address you want to set. The cmdlet would look something like this:

  ```
  New-SPEnterpriseSearchQueryScopeRule -ruletype Url -matchingstring
   http://prosharepointsearch/demos -urlscoperuletype Folder -filterbehavior
   Include -url http://prosharepointsearch -scope $NewScope
  ```

- *Property Query*: Creating a property query rule is probably the most common. This rule type requires a name for the managed property that will be used and the value that the managed property will check. It also needs a filter behavior as in the Scopes page, a URL, and the specific scope to apply it to and the search application.

  ```
  New-SPEnterpriseSearchQueryScopeRule -ruletype PropertyQuery
   -managedproperty filetype -propertyvalue pdf -filterbehavior Include -url
   http://prosharepointsearch -scope $NewScope
  ```

- *Content Source*: There is no specific rule type value for content sources. This is because content source is a managed property in SharePoint. To set the scope by content source, use the `PropertyQuery` value in the rule type parameter and set the name of the content source as the value.

  ```
  New-SPEnterpriseSearchQueryScopeRule -ruletype PropertyQuery -managedproperty
  ```

```
ContentSource -propertyvalue "Local SharePoint Sites" -filterbehavior Include⏎
-url http://prosharepointsearch -scope $NewScope
```

- *All Content*: The All Content scope rule is quite straightforward as it simply includes all content. Use the following cmdlet:

```
New-SPEnterpriseSearchQueryScopeRule -ruletype AllContent -url⏎
http://prosharepointsearch. -scope $NewScope
```

# Crawling Other Document Types with iFilters

Not all file types are crawled by SharePoint out of the box. Therefore, it is important to identify the file types that are important to the organization and make sure they are both crawled and searchable. It is probably not possible or desirable to crawl all file types found in an organization (especially those lingering on file shares); however, some thought should be given to which file types hold content relevant to the business's needs.

## Adding a File Type to the Content Index

The first measure to take after identifying a potentially unsupported file type is to add it to the content index. This is done in the Central Administration under the Search service application. On the left menu is displayed the File Types menu item under the Crawling section (see Figure 3-27).

Crawling

Content Sources

Crawl Rules

Crawl Log

Server Name Mappings

Host Distribution Rules

File Types

Index Reset

Crawler Impact Rules

***Figure 3-27.*** *The Crawling menu on the Search Service Application page*

The File Types page holds a list of all recognized file types for the SharePoint crawler (Figure 3-28). The most common files found in a SharePoint environment and all Microsoft Office file types are represented here. However, many file types common to most organizations, such as Portable Document Format (PDF) and Rich Text Format (RTF), are not added out of the box. Many other file types may also be found in organizations. Many are unique and complicated file formats. Others are just different names for plain text files. It would be a major undertaking for Microsoft to support even a fraction of them. Instead Microsoft has created a mechanism for adding new file types and converting them into something SharePoint's crawler can recognize.

To add a new file type, click the New File Type link at the top of the page. A new file type may already be a supported format, but the file extension might not be recognized by SharePoint. For example, there can be many variations of file name extensions for flat text files (e.g., .log). See Figure 3-29. Additionally, some file types will not appear by default but can be recognized and decoded by the default iFilters. If it is necessary to crawl these files, adding them is a simple but required task.

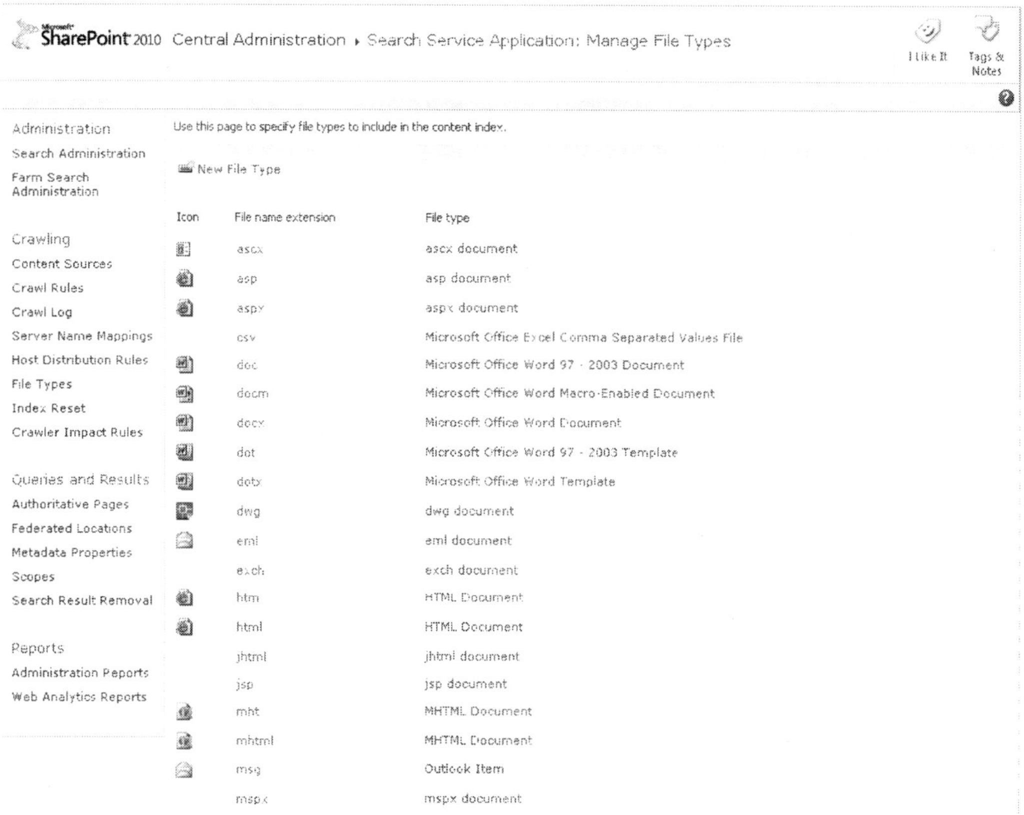

**Figure 3-28.** The File Types page

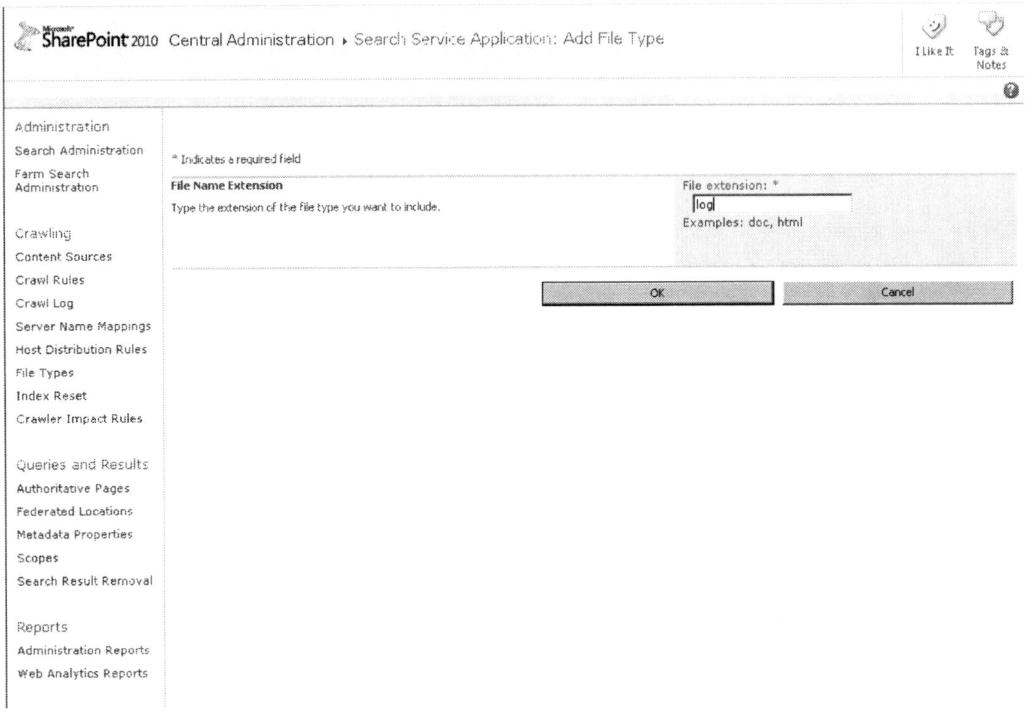

**Figure 3-29.** *Adding the Log File Format (*.log*) file type for SharePoint to crawl*

Some files will require the addition of an iFilter. An iFilter is a component that can decode a specific file type and allow the crawler to understand and store the text and metadata from it in its databases and index. Although many iFilters are provided for free from Microsoft and other sources, not all are installed by default by SharePoint 2010. Finding and installing these iFilters can be necessary to index certain file types. One of the most common file types found that is not supported by default in SharePoint is the Rich Text Format (RTF); another is the Portable Document Format (PDF).

To add the PDF format, it is recommended that you acquire an installable iFilter from Adobe or another third-party vendor. Other third-party vendors offer iFilters that have a larger range of compatibility with different PDF generation types and perform significantly better than Adobe's but come with a relatively modest price tag. Depending on what type of PDF file generator an organization uses and how many PDF documents it has, it may opt to use a third-party paid-for iFilter. Considering the relatively low costs of the iFilters, the authors of this book would highly recommend choosing iFilters from one of the vendors in Chapter 11.

## Installing Adobe's iFilter

Acrobat iFilter can be acquired from Adobe's web site. It will be necessary to download and install the 64-bit version available from `www.adobe.com/support/downloads/detail.jsp?ftpID=4025`. At the time of this book's publication, the latest version was 9.0. The installation requires some additional installation steps. These steps are outlined in the PDF guide available on the download link on Adobe's site (`www.adobe.com/special/acrobat/configuring_pdf_ifilter_for_ms_sharepoint_2007.pdf`). The guide is targeted for Microsoft Office SharePoint Server 2007, but the same instructions apply except for the location of the registry key. The basics of installing the 64-bit iFilter are as follows:

1. Download the iFilter.

2. Run the installer.

3. Open the registry (`Regedit.exe`) and add the `.pdf` file extension value to the filter extension container (Figure 3-30) at `\\HKEY_LOCAL_MACHINE\SOFTWARE\Microsoft\Office Server\14.0\Search\Setup\ContentIndexCommon\Filters\Extension`. The default value that should be applied is `{E8978DA6-047F-4E3D-9C78-CDBE46041603}`.

4. Add an icon to the iFilter install (see "Adding Icons to File Types").

5. Restart the Search service application by running `Services.msc` at the run dialog, finding the SharePoint Server Search 14 service, and restarting it.

6. Perform a full crawl.

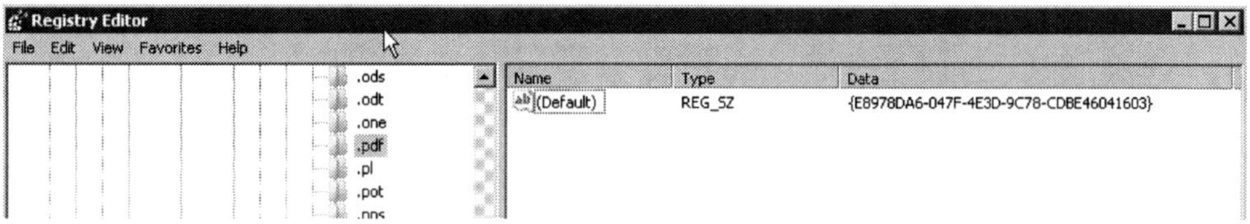

***Figure 3-30.*** *The new* `.pdf` *registry key in the registry*

Other iFilter vendors' installation programs perform these tasks automatically. However, it is always necessary to perform a full crawl to retrieve new file types. Please follow the iFilter vendor's instructions when adding a new iFilter.

Before PDF documents or any new file type can be crawled, the Search service application will need to be restarted. The easiest way to do this is to go to the Services snap-in by typing "services.msc" in the search box in the Start menu on the server, find the SharePoint Server Search 14 service, and restart it (see Figure 3-31). After the service is restarted, it will be necessary to launch a full crawl to pick up any PDF files. For this reason, it is wise to install the PDF iFilter before starting the crawler on a large document set for the first time.

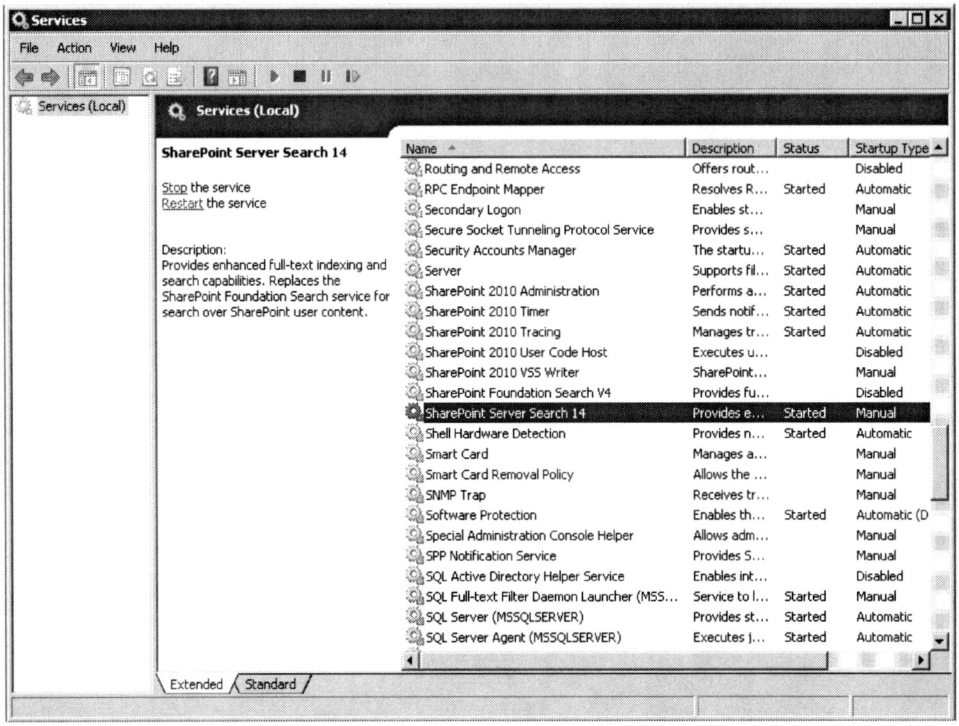

**Figure 3-31.** *Restarting the Search service in the Services snap-in*

■ **Note** The Search service application can also be restarted using the NET START and NET STOP commands from a command prompt. The name of the Search service application is OSearch14.

## Indexing Rich Text Format Files

Adding the Rich Text Format (RTF) file type requires finding the RTF iFilter on the server or on Microsoft's web site and installing and registering it on the SharePoint index server. Additionally, adding the RTF file type is necessary.

1.  Check if the RTF iFilter is on the server. It is called **rtffilt.dll** and is in the **%windir%\system32** folder (probably C:\Windows\System32). If it isn't there, the self-extracting RTF iFilter file **rtf.exe** can be downloaded from Microsoft's web site (http://support.microsoft.com/kb/291676/en-us).

2.  Register the iFilter with the **regsvr32** command at a command prompt by placing this line in the run dialog: regsvr32 rtffilt.dll.

3. Add the RTF file type to the File Types page in Central Administration, as shown in Figure 3-32.

4. Run `Services.msc` at the run dialog, find the SharePoint Server Search 14 service, and restart it.

5. Start a full crawl.

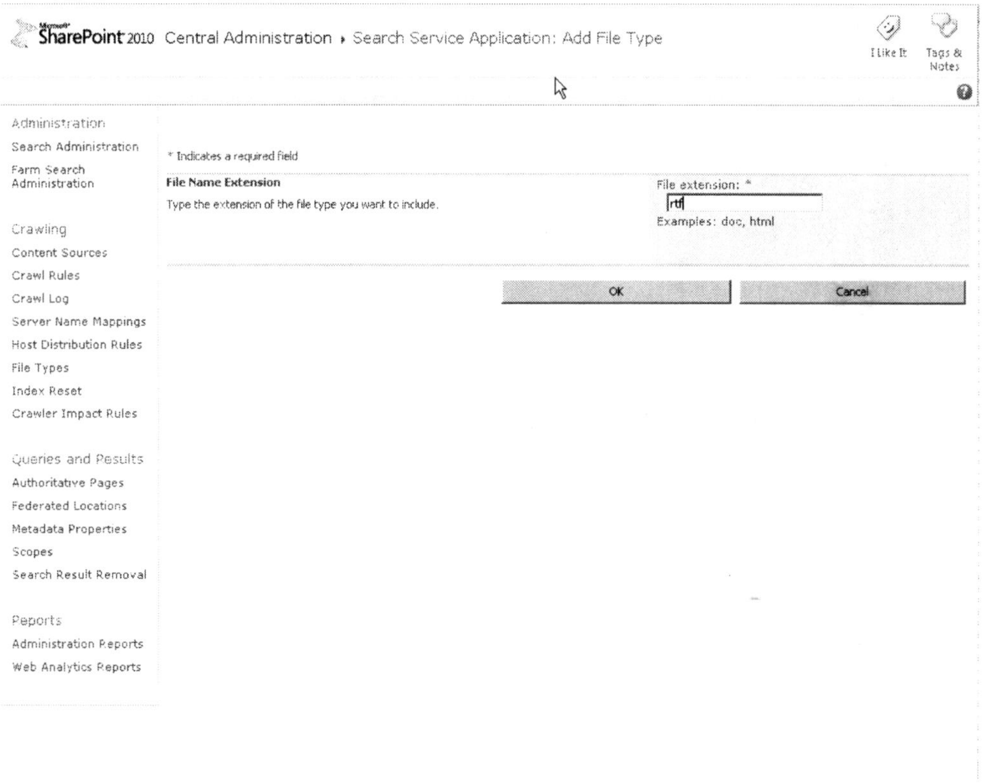

**Figure 3-32.** *Adding the Rich Text Format (*`.rtf`*) file type*

## Adding or Changing the File Type Icon

New file types will usually not have an icon associated with them. SharePoint Search will display a default blank icon in such cases after the file type has been added. Even if there is a definition already there, many organizations will want to adjust the icons to match their own style requirements.

To add a new file type icon or change the existing one, first the new icon must be copied to the `C:\Program Files\Common Files\Microsoft Shared\Web Server Extensions\14\TEMPLATE\IMAGES\` directory. Images can be downloaded or created. They should be icon size, roughly 16 pixels by 16 pixels. For PDF files, Adobe offers a free 17-pixel-by-17-pixel icon, with some legal restrictions, at `www.adobe.com/misc/linking.html#pdficon`. This will also work, but larger icons may cause formatting problems.

After the icon is added to the `IMAGES` directory, the `DOCICON.xml` file in the `C:\Program Files\Common Files\Microsoft Shared\Web Server Extensions\14\TEMPLATE\XML` directory needs to have a key added to tell SharePoint the name of the new file type's icon. For the PDF icon, the line should read `<Mapping Key="pdf" Value="pdficon.gif"/>`, where `pdficon.gif` is the name of the icon you saved to the directory.

---

■ **Note** Since a full crawl will be needed to include new file types, it is advisable to add any iFilters and file types before a full crawl in a large production environment.

---

# Federated Sources

Another great feature supported in SharePoint 2010 is the ability to add federated sources. Federated sources are those sources that are not directly crawled by SharePoint's crawlers but can still be searched by querying and accessing the indexes of external systems. This is done by querying the search mechanism of that external source, retrieving the result set, and then formatting and displaying it within the SharePoint search interface.

Federated sources can be either SharePoint sites or sites that conform to the OpenSearch 1.0 or 1.1 standards. These standards define how search queries should be passed and how the data is structured and returned.

New federated sources can be defined or an existing template can be downloaded and imported. To create a new federated source, click New Location and fill out the fields with the appropriate settings. Every source requires a name that will also be used in the search center.

## Creating a New Federated Source

When creating a new federated location, a name and a display name should be defined. The display name will be shown on the federated search Web Part. A description of the source is also required (see Figure 3-33).

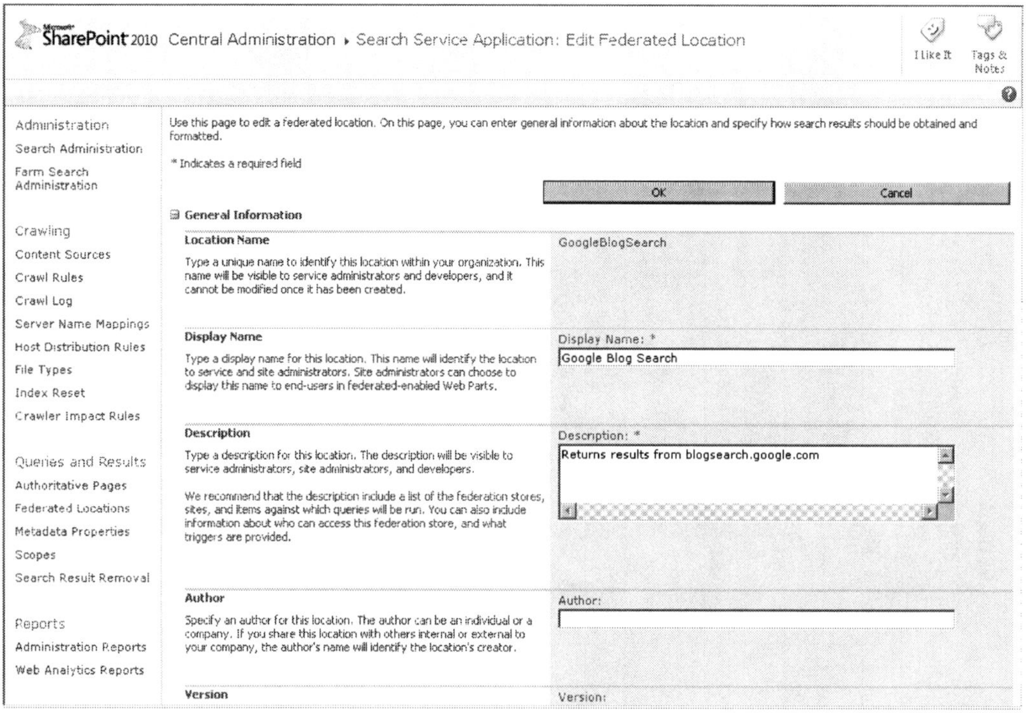

**Figure 3-33.** *Defining a new federated location*

Triggers can be set on all federated locations to dictate what queries are sent to the federated locations and how they are sent.

There are three basic triggers:

- *Always*: Send all queries.

- *Prefix*: Use a trigger prefix to send queries.

- *Pattern*: Use a pattern trigger to send both the trigger and the query in a new pattern that may be adjusted with regular expressions.

If Always is chosen, any search query or phrase will also be passed to the federated source; if Prefix is set, it will look for a particular term and then pass the following terms as the query. In this way, the first term (the trigger term) can be used to indicate which federated source should be queried to supply this information (Figure 3-34). So if the Prefix trigger is "pics", it might be advisable to federate in Flickr or some other image search engine. If the Prefix trigger is "weather", it might be advisable to send the query to weather.com. This will require a certain level of training for end users so they understand which triggers will action which information to appear. Federated search results appear in a separate Web Part on the results page. This is discussed in more detail in Chapters 6 and 7.

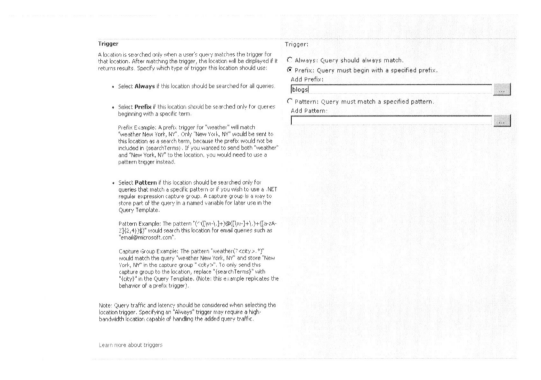

**Figure 3-34.** *Setting triggers in a new federated location*

Location information must be provided. If an OpenSearch-compliant site is being used, OpenSearch should be set here. Additionally, a query template should be specified. This query should be the URL to the OpenSearch-compliant RSS feed where the query term is replaced by the `{searchTerms}` value. This is called a query template in the standard. This offers a certain amount of flexibility, and the `{searchTerms}` value can be mixed with other accepted parameters to provide more exact results. For example, on Google's blog search feed, we can filter into the result set by clicking some of the options on the page. It is possible to sort the result set by date, and the parameter `scoring=d` is added to the query URI. This list of parameters can be captured from the address bar of the browser and modified with the `{searchTerms}` value to create a query template that returns results sorted by date. Not all parameters are supported by RSS feeds as they are generally separate applications that are not a main concern for the search providers. However, often RSS feeds and the OpenSearch definitions will support some added functionality.

For the OpenSearch-compliant RSS feed for blog posts, search from Google, `http://blogsearch.google.com/blogsearch_feeds?hl=en-us&q=sharepoint&lr=&ie=utf-8&num=10`; if we replace the query term "sharepoint" with the `{searchTerms}` value and add the parameter `scoring=d`, we will get the query template `http://blogsearch.google.com/blogsearch_feeds?hl=en-us&q=sharepoint&lr=&ie=utf-8&num=10&scoring=d`, which can be used to create a federated source that retrieves blog posts sorted by date.

The properties displayed can also be modified by modifying XSLT in the Display Information section. Depending on which provider is federated, it may be necessary to provide a custom XSLT. Providers do provide an OpenSearch declaration that can be used as a starting point, and the example XSLT definitions from the locations available for import will help.

---

▨ **Note** To federate search from SAP NetWeaver, SAP has a detailed how-to document here:

www.sdn.sap.com/irj/scn/go/portal/prtroot/docs/library/uuid/70bce92e-d355-2d10-9993-890bb7b19381?QuickLink=index&overridelayout=true.

---

## Importing a Federated Location from Microsoft's Federated Search Connector Gallery

To import a location, a preconfigured federated location must be downloaded and imported. The available federated location downloads are available for download from Microsoft's Federated Search Connector Gallery for Enterprise Search: http://technet.microsoft.com/en-us/enterprisesearch/ff727944.aspx. Two file types are given, an FLD file and an OSDX file. SharePoint 2010 requires the OSDX file. Earlier SharePoint search products require the FLD files. They are basically just XML files with the settings for the federated locations. They can be edited manually, but entering a new location will be easier.

After downloading the federated location definition file, it can be imported with the import command and eventually edited to match the required settings.

---

▨ **Note** You may have to restart the Search service application for changes to take effect.

---

It is also possible to define a federated location as a search index on this server. This will provide search results in the Federated Results Web Parts from a locally stored index. This is not the setting for federating results from a remote SharePoint site. To get federated content from another SharePoint server, use the OpenSearch specification and the RSS feed of the search results from the remote SharePoint site.

---

▨ **Tip** The Federated Sources page is a quick way to see an overview of the source groups for search, the number of queries each has received in the last 30 days, and their click-through.

---

# Summary

The goal of this chapter was to provide detailed guidance on setting up the crawler and adding content sources. In addition, it addressed crawling issues and additional settings in the Search service application necessary to crawling typical kinds of enterprise content. It also looked at how to configure the crawler for special document types and how to add iFilters for document types that are not supported out of the box by SharePoint.

It is wise, if not critical, to consider these settings before building too much of an enterprise search implementation with SharePoint, as crawling large document sets can take days, if not weeks, and many settings in this section require a full crawl after adjustment.

# Further Reading

Here are some suggestions for further reading or more details on the topics covered in this chapter.

## Indexing

To download the indexing connector for Documentum, go here: `www.microsoft.com/downloads/en/details.aspx?FamilyID=32D0980A-4B9A-4B0D-868E-9BE9C0D75435&amp;displaylang=en`.

To read about crawling case-sensitive URLs, see this blog post: `http://blogs.msdn.com/b/enterprisesearch/archive/2010/07/09/crawling-case-sensitive-repositories-using-sharepoint-server-2010.aspx`.

## Crawl Rules

To read more about regular expressions in crawl rules, see: `http://blogs.msdn.com/b/enterprisesearch/archive/2010/01/21/regular-expressions-support-in-crawl-rules.aspx`.

## Scopes

For a list of the parameters and more information on creating scope rules with PowerShell, see: `http://msdn.microsoft.com/en-us/library/ff608132.aspx`.

## Federated Sources

For more information on the OpenSearch project, visit `www.opensearch.org`.

A list of sites that list search engines and sites that support the formats is also available at `www.opensearch.org/Community/OpenSearch_search_engine_directories`.

■ ■ ■

# CHAPTER 4

# Deploying the Search Center

After completing this chapter, you will be able to

- Understand the out-of-the-box search user interfaces

- Deploy the Basic and Enterprise Search Centers

- Redirect the universal search box to a search center

- Add search Web Parts to a Web Part page

Before we can move forward with introducing the pieces of the search user interface, we need to outline the steps of setting up and deploying the search center. The search center is a site in SharePoint 2010 that provides search results and can be modified to meet an organization's particular search needs.

This chapter will introduce the templates available for deploying search to a SharePoint site collection. It will then highlight the differences between the different search centers and present step-by-step instructions on how to deploy each type. It will close things out by deploying Web Parts to standard pages.

## Understanding the Search Center

Strictly speaking, the search center is not a required element for search to function in SharePoint 2010. Individual search Web Parts can be added to any page on a site and perform a variety of search tasks. Also, SharePoint comes with a default results page that will display results from the queries to the standard search box on all pages. However, a good starting point for setting up and testing search is to use the search site templates provided and create a search center to which queries will be redirected.

Before that can be done, though, one must follow a short set of steps. Once SharePoint has been installed, some content added, and the first initial crawl run, the administrator can go to the default site collection and search. The search can be performed by the search box that appears on the top right of every page in the default SharePoint site collection and will appear on new site collections as they are created (Figure 4-1). It can be modified or removed by modifying the design elements of the site collection, but that will not be covered in this book.

**Figure 4-1.** *The search box*

If a search is performed from this search box, the search query will be passed to a search results page and search results will be displayed. However, this search results page, called OSSSearchResults.aspx, is the default search page and will display the results for the given site collection. However, most site administrators will want to create a custom search and results page that users can access both via the search box and via a search page. Although the individual Web Parts can be added to pages to create a totally custom search and results page anywhere within a site collection, this custom search and results page is usually deployed as a site under the site collection using either the Basic or Enterprise Search site templates.

There are several advantages to this. By creating a search center with a search site template, the SharePoint administrator can do the following:

- Give users a site to navigate to for search instead of using the search box to get to the results page

- Customize the search experience with advanced search capabilities

- Access search preferences

- Utilize tabs to create a custom search scoping experience

- Share a search center across sites or collections

- Separate search by collection

# Basic vs. Enterprise Search Centers

There are two site templates for search delivered with SharePoint 2010: the Basic Search Center and the Enterprise Search Center. The Basic and Enterprise Search Centers vary in several ways and both are included in the standard license for SharePoint. If the SharePoint Server Publishing Infrastructure feature on the site collection has not been activated, then the Basic Search Center is the only functional option. The Enterprise Search Center template will appear but will cause an error if chosen (see more in the section on deploying the Enterprise Search Center).

---

■ **Note** The Enterprise Search Center is the SharePoint 2010 replacement of the "MOSS 2007 Search Center with Tabs" publishing site template. The Basic Search Center is the SharePoint 2010 equivalent of the "MOSS 2007 Search Center Lite."

---

# The Enterprise Search Center

The Enterprise Search Center provides a tab-based interface in which users can jump between several search pages. An example of this can be seen in Figure 4-2. The two tabs, All Sites and People, are provided by default, but additional tabs can be added. These tabs can be fully customized to cater to the needs of a particular organization. By selecting the different tabs above the query field, users can direct their searches to different scopes.

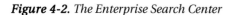

Site Actions ▾

search ▸ Search                                                                WIN-10GHRQODHO4\Administrator ▾

All Sites    People

|                                                     🔍   Preferences
                                                          Advanced

***Figure 4-2.*** *The Enterprise Search Center*

The most immediately apparent benefit of the Enterprise Search Center is the availability of the People Search tab. The Basic Search Center does not include a People Search tab, so if this is required, enabling the SharePoint Server Publishing Infrastructure feature and deploying the Enterprise Search Center are recommended. As will be shown throughout the book, the tabs provided in the Enterprise Search Center allow users to quickly execute searches against different scopes. Administrators can add one or more additional customized search centers when using the Enterprise template through these tabs. Customized search centers may add simple contrasts, such as directing searches to documents or people, but may be more advanced, such as searching against different physical locations or departments. This provides a range of flexibility for organizations with a central enterprise portal that needs to provide a search experience to a range of independent departments or user groups with distinctly different needs. For example, while the sales department needs to search against customer profiles and marketing documents, the accounting department needs to find information pertaining to contract dates, expense reports, and purchase history. The experience each department hopes to get from search is different. Creating separate search centers that display results based on different properties, provide different refinement panel categories, or even present results in a different format may provide a better experience for each of these groups.

Administrators can control access for each Enterprise Search Center tab. In the foregoing case, they may choose to allow only the sales and accounting departments access to the respective search tabs, while allowing the human resources department access to both. Properly established, security trimming in SharePoint ensures that employees can access only the sites that they are allowed to view.

## Deploying the Enterprise Search Center

If People search is required or desired, it is wise to deploy the Enterprise Search Center, which has a template with all the elements of People search already set. Although the Enterprise Search Center template is visible on standard SharePoint deployments, it requires the SharePoint Server Publishing Infrastructure feature.

To deploy the Enterprise Search Center, follow these steps and refer to Figure 4-3.

1.  Navigate to the top level of your site collection where you want the search center.

2.  Log in as a site collection administrator.

3.  Choose Site Actions, Create Site.

4.  Name the search center in the Title field.

5.  Give a path for the search center under Web Site Address.

6.  Choose the Enterprise tab under the Template section.

7.  Choose the Enterprise Search Center template.

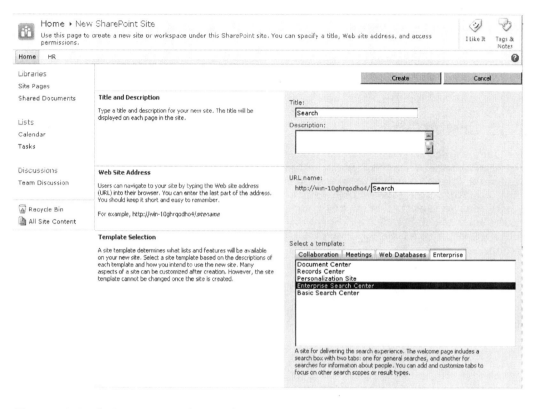

**Figure 4-3.** *Deploying an Enterprise Search Center*

---

■ **Note** If you get an error creating the site, it is likely the Publishing feature activation failed (Figure 4-4). If you copy the correlation ID from the error page and look in the most recent ULS log at `C:\Program Files\Common Files\Microsoft Shared\Web Server Extensions\14\LOGS`, you will find an error similar to this:

```
Exception: System.InvalidOperationException: The SharePoint Server Publishing Infrastructure
feature must be activated at the site collection level before the Publishing feature can be
activated.
```

This indicates the Publishing feature needs to be activated at the site collection level before the Enterprise Search Center can be used. Activate it, and try to deploy the search center again.

---

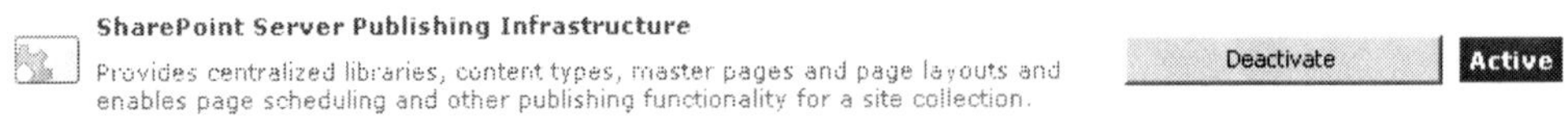

**SharePoint Server Publishing Infrastructure**
Provides centralized libraries, content types, master pages and page layouts and
enables page scheduling and other publishing functionality for a site collection.

Deactivate | **Active**

*Figure 4-4. The SharePoint Server Publishing Infrastructure feature*

## The Basic Search Center

Unlike the Enterprise Search Center, the Basic Search Center provides users only with the ability to
execute basic and advanced searches against one universal access search experience. The lack of built-in
tabs that allow for different search experiences can be seen in Figure 4-5. While the Basic Search Center
can be customized to provide a specialized experience for users, every user on the search center will
return results from the same content sources in an identical layout. In addition, as noted earlier, the
Basic Search Center does not provide a pre-deployed tab for People search. The main benefit of this
search center is simplicity, as it allows for quick deployment of search functionality on any SharePoint
site collection.

Site Actions ▾  Browse  Page

Search ▸ Search                                                WIN-10GHRQODHO4\Administrator ▾

Preferences
Advanced

*Figure 4-5. The Basic Search Center*

# Deploying the Basic Search Center

The Basic Search Center gives search and result functionality with advanced search and preferences but without a built-in, pre-defined People Search tab. See Figure 4-2.

To deploy the Basic Search Center, follow these steps and refer to Figure 4-6.

1. Navigate to the top level of your site collection where you want the search center.

2. Log in as a site collection administrator.

3. Choose Site Actions, Create Site.

4. Name the search center in the Title field.

5. Give a path for the search center under Web Site Address.

6. Choose the Enterprise tab under the Template section.

7. Choose the Basic Search Center template.

---

■ **Note** It is best to name your search center "Search". Although many administrators come up with clever names for search for their organization or portal, it is really best to keep it simple. The path can also be /search/ unless there is a good reason to name it otherwise.

---

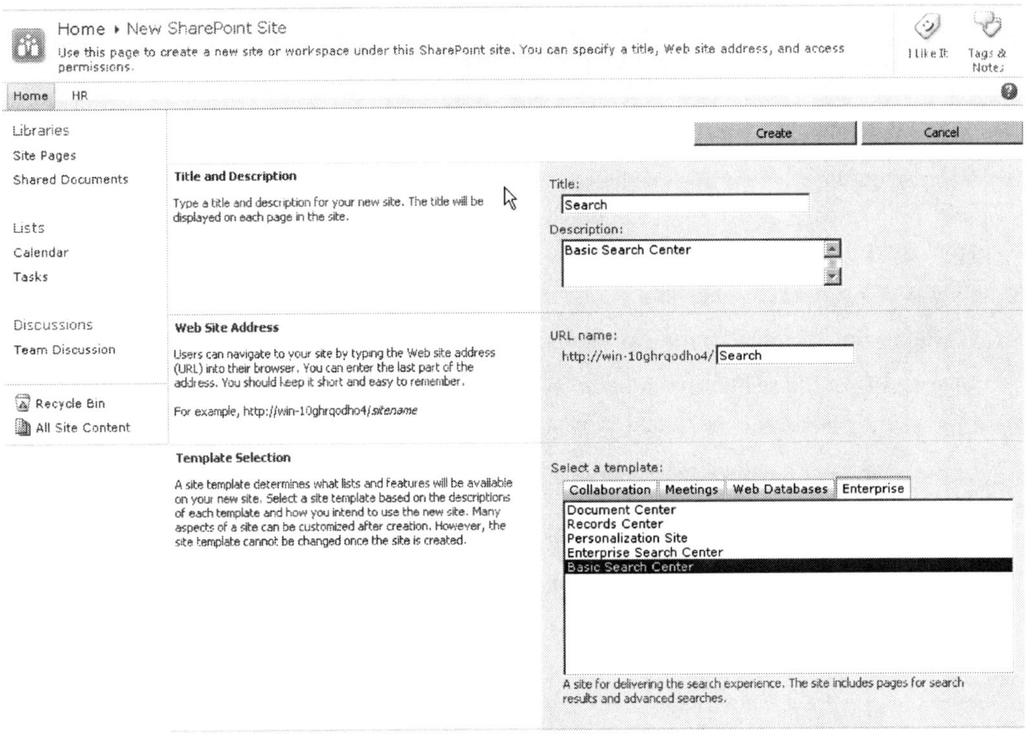

**Figure 4-6.** *Creating a new Basic Search Center*

# Redirecting the Search Box to the Search Center

After the search center has been deployed, it will be possible to make searches from the center's search page, modify preferences, and perform advanced searches from the Advanced Search page. However, the main search box that appears on all pages will still point to `OSSSearchResults.aspx`. So you'll need to direct these queries to the search center you have created. For multiple site collections that share a single search center, redirecting this search box to the shared search center can be extremely useful.

To modify the target of the search box, follow these steps and refer to Figure 4-7.

1. Navigate to the top level of the site collections.

2. Choose Site Actions, Site Settings.

3. Under Site Collection Administration, choose Search Settings.

4. In the Site Collection Search Result page field, define your new search results page. If you named your Basic Search Center "Search", this path will be `/Search/results.aspx`. If you created an Enterprise Search Center and named it "Search", the path will be `/Search/Pages/results.aspx`.

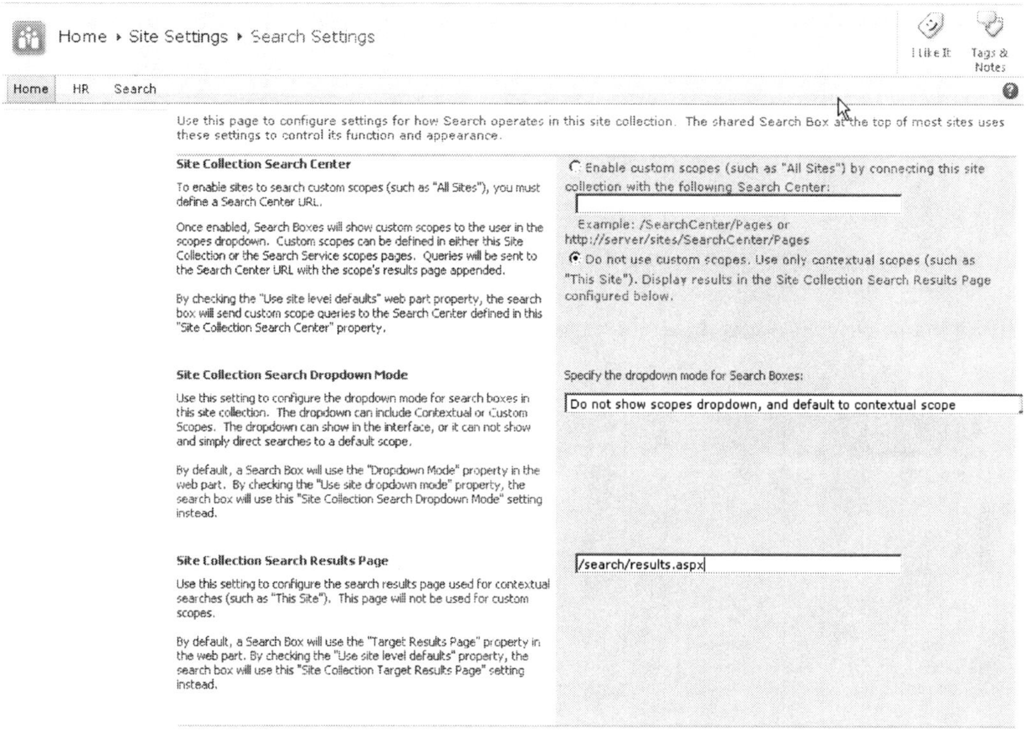

**Figure 4-7.** *Changing the search box target*

These are the basic steps necessary for deploying a search center to SharePoint 2010. Using one of the built-in search centers is the quickest way to get a feature-rich, customizable search user interface. However, as previously mentioned, search does work out of the box and many organizations can get by using the default `OSSSearchResults.aspx` results page. For others, even the search centers are not enough or perhaps not flexible enough. This will require them to create their own Web Part pages and deploy the search Web Parts individually to them—or perhaps deploy them to other site pages or even create their own Web Parts (as discussed in Chapter 8).

# Web Part Deployment

It is possible to deploy search on your SharePoint 2010 installation without actually deploying a search center. Both search and result Web Parts can be added to normal pages without using the built-in templates. The method of deploying the search Web Parts is the same as deploying any other Web Part on SharePoint 2010. In fact, all the functionality of the Basic and Enterprise Search Centers can be recreated by building a site with the search Web Parts. However, this is a lengthy task, and most if not all of the search functionality necessary for most organizations is available on the search centers. Therefore, unless extremely custom search usage is required, it is recommended to use the built-in templates and deploy a search center.

# Adding Web Parts

To add Web Parts to an existing page, do the following:

1. Choose Edit Page under Site Actions while logged in as a site administrator.

2. Select Editing Tools and Insert.

3. Click Web Part.

4. Choose the Search category and the search Web Part you want to add (Figure 4-8).

5. Save and close the editor under the page menu in the ribbon.

***Figure 4-8.*** *Adding search Web Parts*

After the Web Parts are added to the page, the target of the search box can be added by editing the Web Part or customizations to the parts made. In Figure 4-9, a search box and core results Web Part have been added to the home page of the default SharePoint site.

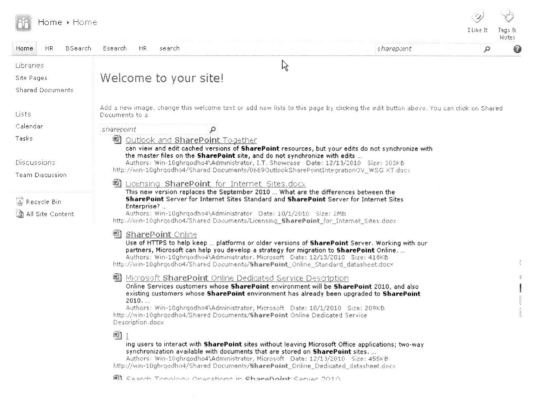

**Figure 4-9.** *A crude example of adding search Web Parts to a page*

A better example of when to add the search Web Parts to a non-search page would be for displaying a diverse set of documents or pages in a single list regardless of their location in SharePoint. This could be a list of the latest ten documents that have a given term in them or documents by a specific author. Using the result Web Part alone on a Web Part page and setting a fixed query for that Web Part can allow this information to be displayed anywhere on the site that the administrator deems useful. See Chapters 6 and 7 for more information about deploying and customizing the search Web Parts.

# Summary

In this chapter, we looked at the search user interfaces available for deployment to SharePoint site collections. We looked at the different functionality available in the Basic and Enterprise Search Centers and outlined the steps to deploy each one. Additionally, we briefly looked at deploying the search Web Parts to Web Part pages in SharePoint.

# CHAPTER 5

■ ■ ■

# The Search User Interface

After completing this chapter, you will be able to

- Navigate the search user interface in SharePoint 2010

- Create alerts and RSS feeds for search result sets

- Use federated results

- Filter search results with refiners and scopes

- Use advanced search syntax to adjust search queries

- Leverage the Advanced Search page to build custom search queries

- Look for people by using the People Search page

- Set search preferences for languages and suggestions

So far, this book has provided a thorough walkthrough of planning the search architecture in SharePoint 2010 with considerations of scalability and redundancy. It has walked through the installation and deployment of the search services with a deep dive into setting up the crawler for various content sources. By this stage in the reading, it is expected that the reader understands the basic terms of SharePoint 2010 Search discussed in Chapter 1, and has deployed infrastructure, installed the software, and configured the basic services for search. At this point, all of the basic building blocks should be established, and the ability to execute queries should be available.

This chapter discusses the search user interface, which refers to any end-user experiences tied to search. Unlike the rest of this book, the content of this chapter is designed to be a guide for end users as much as for administrators. A wide range of topics is discussed, such as the query box, search center, query syntax, search results, and manipulation of results. This chapter provides a front-end user walkthrough of the search experience to aid in the understanding of how to use SP2010 Search; it does not discuss the configuration and manipulation of the back end of this experience. The next chapter will provide detailed explanations on how to manipulate and configure the search centers and features discussed in this chapter.

This chapter starts with a more in-depth review of the query box, which was first introduced in Chapter 1. We then provide a thorough introduction to the search center along with the different tabs and pages it contains. The chapter then takes a deep dive into each page of the search center in detail, starting with the All Sites results page. The purpose and use of all the major search Web Parts are explained before moving into advanced query syntax. The chapter completes with walkthroughs of the Advanced Search page, People search page, and finally the Preferences page. The Advanced Search page,

People search page, and Preferences page leverage many of the same Web Parts and query syntax first introduced in regards to All Sites search. In addition, the Web Parts and query syntax introduced in this chapter form the core competencies that are built on for the rest of this book. As a result, it is very important to understand these topics in regards to All Sites search before moving into the later pages in the chapter.

For any users of previous versions of SharePoint, the search user interface is largely unchanged. For those fluent in MOSS 2007, picking up the end-user search experience will be easier, and much of the information in this chapter will be review. There are, however, several new features that should attract extra attention. These features include the addition of full Boolean search syntax, the addition of search refiners (facets), the addition of the Preferences page, and vast improvements to the People search page. As each subject is discussed, general differences between the search user experience in MOSS and SP2010 will be noted.

## The Query Box

The query box, also referred to as the small search box, is generally the first place a user can go to interact with search. In a standard deployment, the query box can be found in the upper right quadrant on any site outside of a search center. Examples of where the query box can be found include the home page, site collections, sites, subsites, team sites, and lists. Depending on the customizations done, the search center may be found in other locations on a page or can be found worked into various Web Parts. Unless the design of a site has been customized, the query box can be found in the location shown in Figure 5-1.

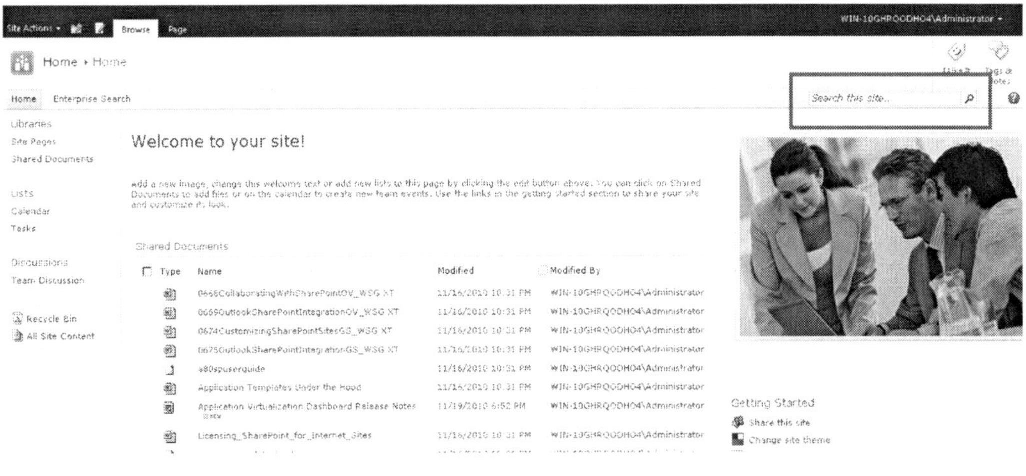

**Figure 5-1.** *The SP2010 query box*

The query box provides a free text field for entering search queries. In SharePoint 2010, the query box can be used to enter search queries for documents, people, sites, lists, and any other items found in crawled content sources. By default it is set to search the site the user is currently on, but depending on the configuration of the query box, and whether the administrator has made the scope picker available, the query box can be set up to search against any available site or site collection.

Due to the level of customizations that can be made to the search user interface, certain configurations have been made to the user interface we show throughout this chapter. These settings have been made to provide a thorough overview of the standard search features made available in SP2010. Although not automatically enabled with the deployment of a search center, these customizations are simple and standard to many deployments. They do not require any special custom development and can be easily enabled through the site settings. Several of the simple customizations that have been made to show the full range of search user interface features include the following:

- The Search Actions Web Part has been set to display the "relevance" and "modified date" sorting options in Figures 5-4, 5-9, 5-47, and 5-49.

- The Top Federated Results Web Part has been enabled for Bing.com in Figure 5-32.

- The Federated Results Web Part has been enabled and set to display results from Bing.com in Figures 5-9 and 5-29.

- The scopes drop-down on the Search Box Web Part to display the scope picker in Figures 5-2, 5-3, 5-4, and 5-45

- Additional tabs were added in Figure 5-8 and 5-31 to display federated search options.

- Query suggestions were enabled on the search box Web Part to show the feature in Figure 5-13.

- A best bet is established between the query "SharePoint" and the document *Collaborating with SharePoint* in Figure 5-28.

Details on how to enable these features as well as several others will be found in the next chapter.

The query box can accept the standard search syntax used throughout all search fields in SP2010. Unlike MOSS 2007, SP2010 supports advanced query syntax. Although not necessarily the most efficient place to build complex search queries, the query box can, in fact, execute all of the same search parameters as the Advanced Search page found on a search center. The details of the available search syntax are discussed in detail later in the chapter.

When users enter search queries in the query box and execute the search, they are redirected to a search results page with items relevant to the executed search returned. The returned search results are provided based on the entered query, scope, and user permissions. The search center the query box routes to is established by the chosen scope. The user can then interact with the search results as if the search had been executed through a search center. As stated earlier, if the default scope is used, the search results will return results only from the site the user was on when he or she executed the query. To search against a broader range of sites, the user needs to select a different scope, navigate higher in the site hierarchy, or execute the query through the search center. Searches entered through a query box without a different site selected will return results similar to those shown in Figure 5-2.

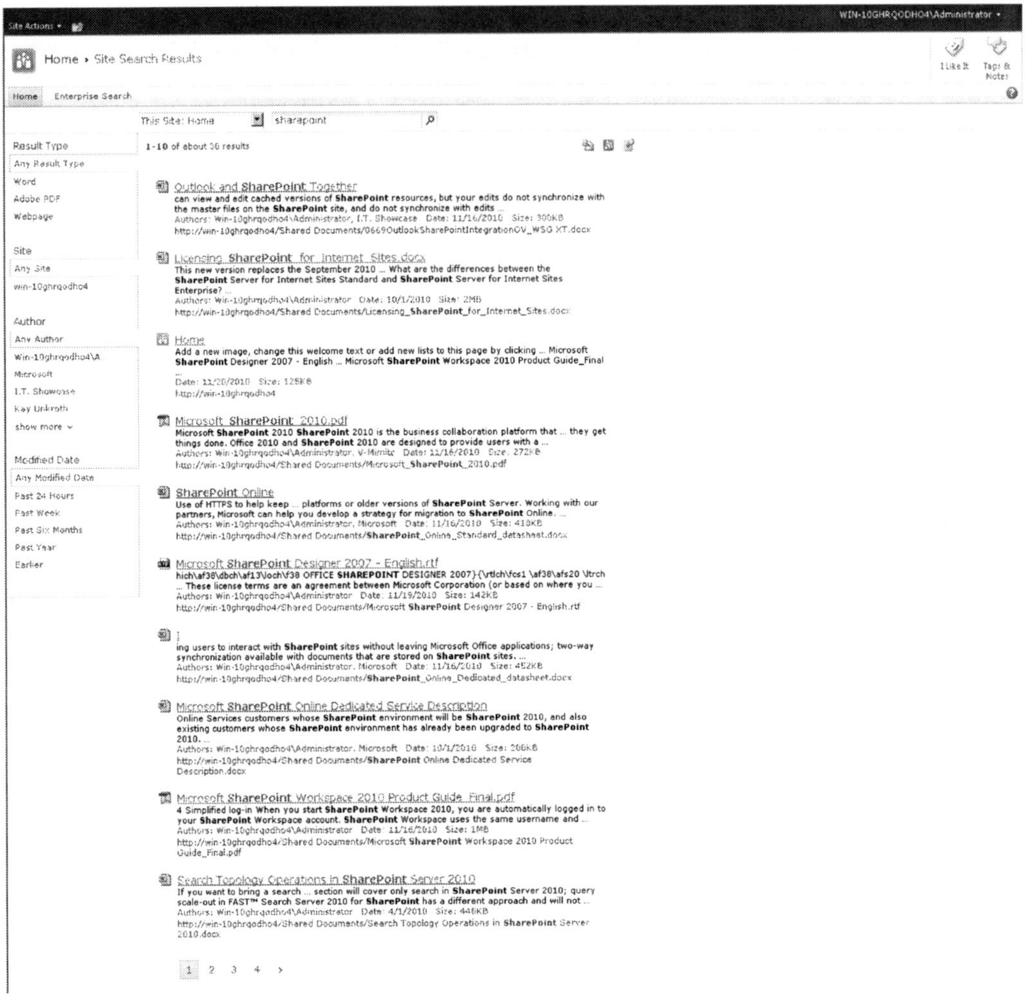

***Figure 5-2.*** *Site search results*

# Taking Advantage of the Scope Picker

To broaden or sharpen a search through the query box, the scope picker can be used. Scopes are set up by administrators and provide options for the application of pre-determined rules to a search. The most common application of scopes is to specify a target site or site collection, but scopes can also be used to select different search pages such as People search, as well as a combination of other parameters, such as those found on the Advanced Search page. Scopes are not generally created on the fly, but instead are created by the site administrator for the most commonly needed search parameters.

When available, scopes are accessed through a drop-down to the left of the query box as shown in Figure 5-3. By default, the site currently being accessed is chosen. To change the scope, click the drop-down and select the desired scope. When a scope for a different site or site collection is chosen, the executed query will return results outside of those available only through the current site.

***Figure 5-3.*** *Search scopes and the query box*

When the search is executed, the target site or site collection will be listed next to the search query above the results (Figure 5-4).

***Figure 5-4.*** *Search scopes and the results page*

After a result set is returned, the capability to change the selected scope or query is made available. By selecting a different scope and executing a different query, a new set of results will be returned. This provides the ability to change search parameters as needed without navigating back to the originating site or site collection.

# The Search Center

The search center is the second location users can leverage to execute searches and return results. Search centers are SharePoint sites dedicated to the function of search that hold all the search pieces, tabs, Web Parts, search pages, results pages, etc. They provide the end-to-end ability to enter advanced queries, select preferences, and retrieve, filter, and action search results.

SharePoint 2010 is not restricted to one search scope per search center. Depending on the needs of an organization, many scopes may be made available. The most common are "All Sites" and "People" search pages. In addition to these, specialized search pages may be created for different user groups, departments, sites, and federated environments, to name a few. Each search tab is designed around a fixed scope, so when the "People" search tab is accessed, it automatically applies the "People" scope.

Access to various search pages can be provided through a few paths. When a site-specific search is executed through the query box, the user is navigated to a search page for the target site. When a search is performed through the query box to a collection of sites or all sites, the user is directed to the corresponding search results page. When a user navigates to the All Sites center tab, the option can be made available to choose several search pages other than All Sites.

---

**Note** When queries are executed through the query box, the user is directed to a search center. In an out-of-the-box configuration, the difference between manually navigating to a search center and entering a site search through a query box is the availability of the Advanced Search page and the Preferences page. It is important to understand, however, that the query box can be directed to a site search results page or the same search center a user can manually navigate to.

---

The search center can be accessed just like any other site. Once the search center is selected, the landing page shown in Figure 5-5 will appear.

**Figure 5-5.** *Enterprise Search Center home page*

From this page, there are a few more options made available. Users can change the scope of their query through tabs above the query field, navigate to the Advanced Search page, navigate to the Preferences page, or enter a search query. The various tabs available here are generally set to different search scopes. They may be configured to execute queries against different content sets, and the search results page each tab returns can be configured for a customized look and feel. In the default SharePoint 2010 Enterprise Search Center shown in Figure 5-5, users can execute queries against content in the entire site collection, or select the People tab to execute a query against the people scope. The format of the search results page that returns for queries executed through each of these tabs is different. More customized deployments may offer search tabs that are specialized to the needs of a particular department or may direct queries to specific content sources.

Queries entered through the search center will function in the same manner as those entered in the search query box. By default, the standard search center home page is set to "All Sites" (Figure 5-6). "All Sites" is the broadest search scope available and includes all available content sources, items, and sites, with the exception of people. When a query is entered through the "All Sites" tab, the user will be navigated to the corresponding search results page.

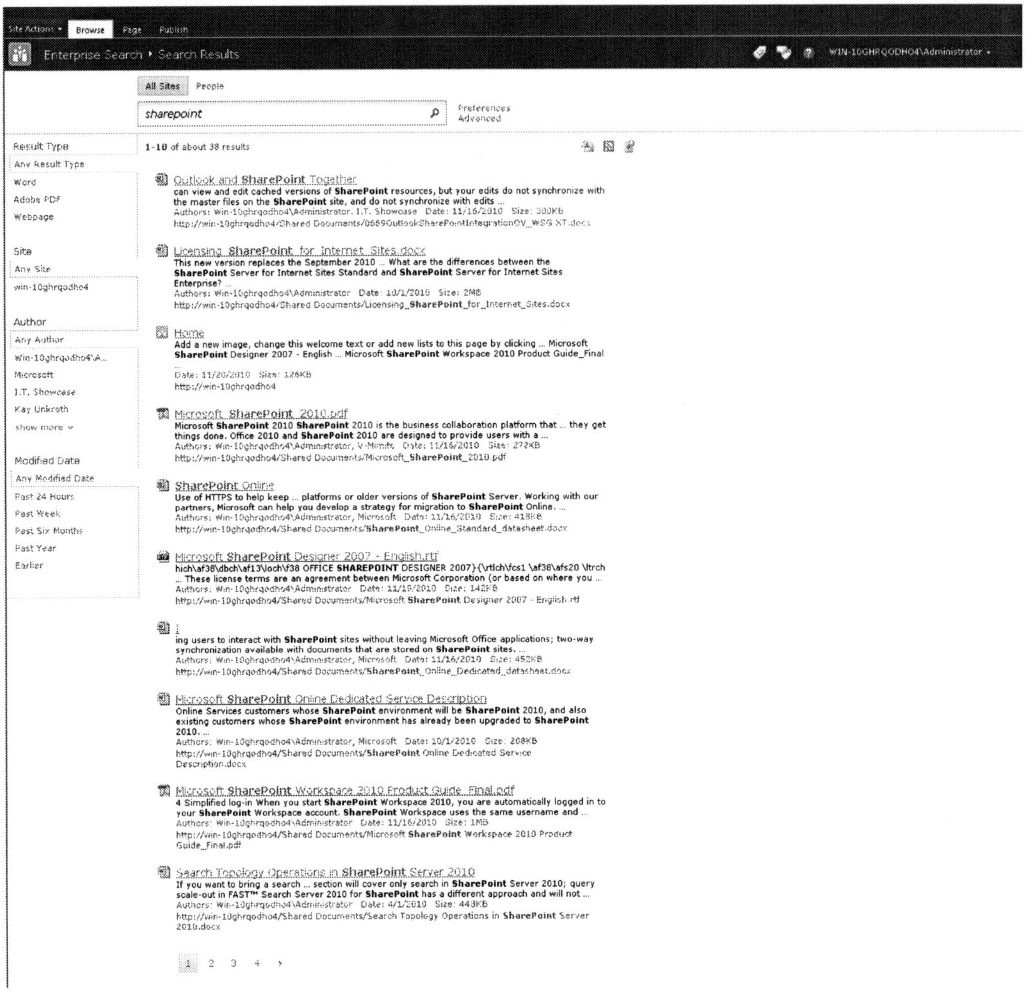

**Figure 5-6.** *Standard All Sites results page*

In addition to the All Sites search tab, the People search page can be accessed by selecting the People tab above the search field. By doing so, the scope of the search is redirected to the People search results page. Figure 5-7 shows a standard SPS2010 People search results page. Most of the functionality on the People search results page is similar to that of the All Sites results page. The notable differences are addressed toward the end of this chapter.

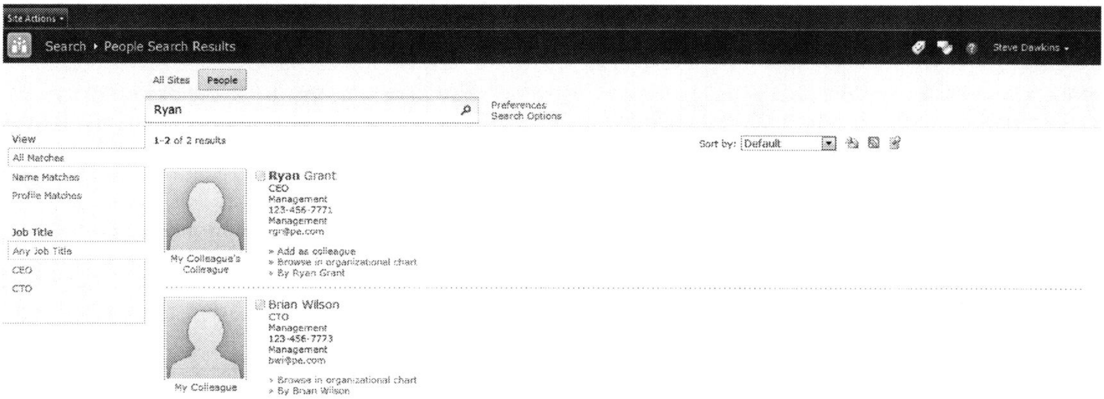

**Figure 5-7.** *Standard People search results page*

On both the All Sites and People search results pages, there is the option to tab between the available search scopes. In a fully developed SharePoint 2010 deployment, other search tabs may be made available.

In global companies with more than one SharePoint farm, it is common to provide access to search against federated environments through search center tabs. Chapter 3 discussed the topic of crawling federated environments in detail, but to review, federation is the ability to search on content that was not crawled by the farm being accessed. Federated searches may include content pulled from global search engines or other SharePoint deployments within a global company. With federated search, a query can be entered through one farm and passed to a different content source, where it is then processed by that respository's search engine.

Access to federated search is commonly provided through tabs on the search center. This allows users to search their own farms by default, but select to search against other content repositories as needed. An example of search tabs set up for federation is shown in Figure 5-8.

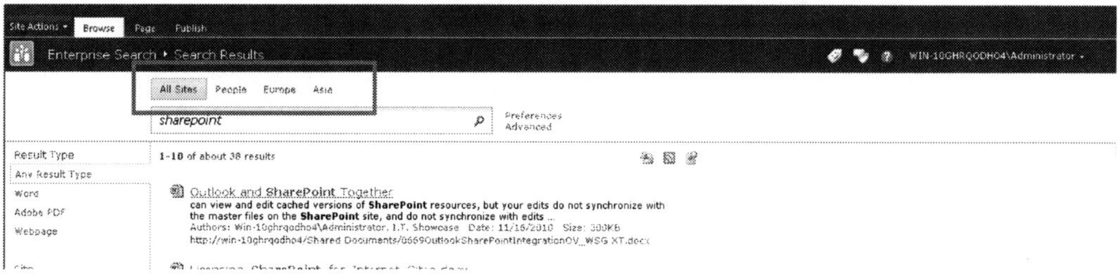

**Figure 5-8.** *Federated search tabs*

# The Search Results Page

Once a query is executed, either through the query box or a search center, the user is navigated to the corresponding search results page. The search results page is comprised of a number of Web Parts that, when combined, allow users to view and interact with the search results. The search results page presents a set number of results per page, and then allows users to move to additional pages by way of a navigator located at the bottom of the results page.

As shown in the screenshots in the previous sections, the results page for searches entered through the query box and search center vary slightly in the out-of-the-box configuration. The default search results page for queries entered through the query box does not provide access to the Advanced Search page or Preferences pages. It does, however, provide the scope picker drop-down. The features discussed in this section are available for searches made through the All Sites search page. These features can also be made available for searches entered through the query box.

The search results page is composed of many different components brought together by a collection of Web Parts. A Web Part is an ASP.NET server control that allows a designer to modify the content, appearance, and behavior of a web page directly from a browser. Web Parts are the building blocks that provide the wide range of customization allowed in SharePoint 2010. They present data, allow for interaction with pages, and control the design of a page. In SharePoint 2010, there are over 75 Web Parts that come with the platform, and additional custom Web Parts can be created. There are 17 Web Parts dedicated to search. Each can be enabled or disabled to change the available functionality, moved around the page to change layout, and reconfigured to change behavior. This chapter discusses the major search Web Parts that most users will interact with. The key Web Part components of the search results page are labeled in Figure 5-9.

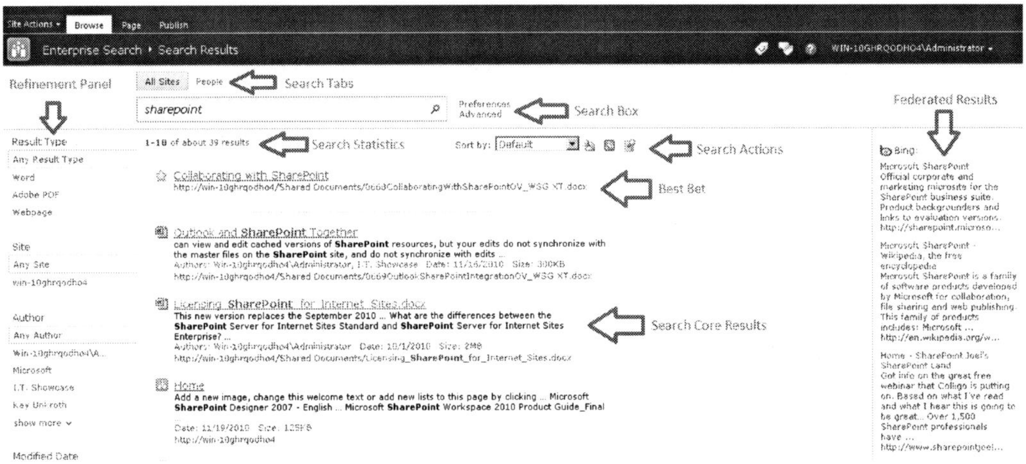

***Figure 5-9.*** *Labeled search results page*

Figure 5-9 displays features and Web Parts that may not be enabled in every environment. The following settings have been made to provide the broadest overview of available features.

- The Search Actions Web Part has been set to display the "relevance" and "modified date" view options.

- The Top Federated Results Web Part has been enabled.

- The Federated Results Web Part has been enabled and set to display results from the location Bing.com.

Search results pages may include Web Parts additional to those shown. Individual Web Parts may also be located in different zones on the page, or be configured to act differently than shown. This figure shows most of the standard available search Web Parts in the All Sites scope, with their default settings.

Starting from the top zone, the Search Box Web Part provides the ability to execute a new search query. It also provides access to the Preferences page and the Advanced Search page discussed later in this chapter. When triggered, the Search Summary Web Part displays alternative query suggestions for the current search query below the search box. As shown in Figure 5-10, this Web Part provides query suggestions based on SharePoint's dictionary to provide users with alternative query options.

*Figure 5-10. Search Box and Search Summary Web Parts*

Directly below the search box, the Search Statistics Web Part displays the numerical portion of the result set being displayed on the current page. It also provides the estimated number of results in the entire result set. Adjacent to the right of the Search Statistics Web Part, the Search Actions Links Web Part provides the ability to set alerts and create RSS feeds on the result set. If enabled, users can change the order of the search results by selecting a different sorting option from the "Sort By:" drop-down. Users can also use this Web Part to connect Windows Desktop Search to the result set. This provides the ability to search the result set at a later time without manually opening SharePoint again.

---

■ **Note** Due to security trimming, the search engine generally is unable to determine the exact number of results in large results sets. This is the reason the phrase "about" is used when displaying the total number of results. When a total result count is exact, the term "about" is omitted.

---

To the right of the Search Actions Links Web Part is the Related Queries Web Part. If available, this provides a list of suggested alternative search queries based on the aggregated experiences of users in the environment. Below the Related Queries Web Part is the People Matches Web Part. This Web Part, shown in Figure 5-11, displays the first three people that would be returned had the query been executed through the People tab. This is a useful tool that allows people to not be included in the All Sites results set, while still being able to see some of the top people-related results.

People Matches

Ryan Grant
CEO
Management

Ronald Brown
Project Engineer
Engineering

Randy West
Marketing
Coordinator
Marketing

View more people »

***Figure 5-11.*** *People Matches Web Part*

Users may also find the Federated Search Results Web Part in the right zone, which presents results from a federated content source such as Bing.com or blogs. To the left of the Search Statistics Web Part, the Refinement Panel Web Part allows users to drill into search results by selecting known metadata such as result type, the site the item is located on, or the author of the item.

Below the Search Statistics Web Part, the Best Bets Web Part can be found, which, if enabled, provides suggestions for the most likely items users may be looking for in a result set. Below the Best Bets Web Part, the Top Federated Results Web Part displays the most relevant search results from one or more federated environments. The Top Federated Results Web Part is not enabled by default, and if enabled, will be shown only if a farm is pulling content from federated content sources.

The focus of the search results page is, of course, the results themselves. The results can be found in the Search Core Results Web Part located in the center of the page. Each result contains several components, as shown in Figure 5-12.

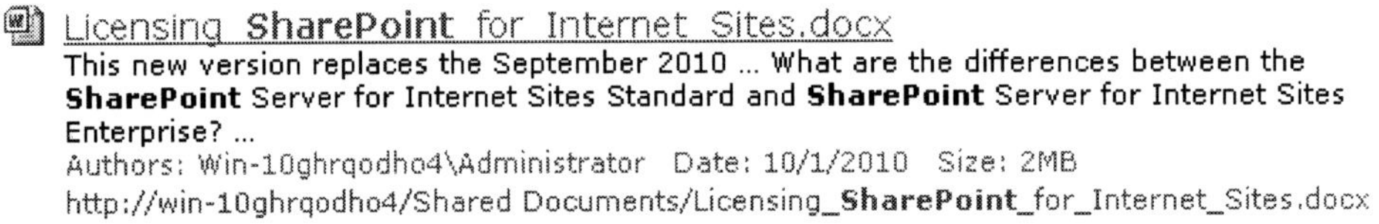

Licensing SharePoint for Internet Sites.docx
This new version replaces the September 2010 ... What are the differences between the **SharePoint** Server for Internet Sites Standard and **SharePoint** Server for Internet Sites Enterprise? ...
Authors: Win-10ghrqodho4\Administrator  Date: 10/1/2010  Size: 2MB
http://win-10ghrqodho4/Shared Documents/Licensing_**SharePoint**_for_Internet_Sites.docx

***Figure 5-12.*** *Individual search result*

Each result contains a clickable title, which, if clicked, will provide the ability to interact with the search result. Depending on the type of search result, the action taken when the title is chosen will change. If the item is a Microsoft Office document, a second window will appear, which provides the ability to save the document or open it with the corresponding Microsoft Office program. If the result is a document other than Microsoft Office, only the option to save the document is provided. If the result is not a document, choosing the result title will navigate the user to the location of the result. Examples of non-document results include SharePoint sites, lists, or web pages. The icon to the left of the search result title indicates the item type for the result.

Below the result title, a description is displayed. The description contains what the search engine believes are the most relevant blocks of text from within the content of the item. The blocks of content are not necessarily the first block of text in the result or adjacent to each other. The keywords from the search query are found in bold within the result description. Under the description, there is a list of key properties associated with the item. By default, the displayed properties are authors, date of last published edit, and size of the file. Finally, below the properties, an actionable link to the result's location is shown.

The final Web Part in a standard search results page is the Search Paging Web Part, found at the bottom of the page. This Web Part provides links for navigating to additional search results pages. By default, the number of results returned per page is set to ten, but this number can be adjusted by the administrator, as shown in the next chapter.

Depending on how an environment is being used, it may be advised to increase the number of results per page. Providing more results per page allows for faster browsing of large search results, but it does affect performance. Since SharePoint's search engine is returning information only about the results displayed on the current page, increasing the results per page will consequently increase the amount of information that needs to be processed and returned. Both the user experience and server performance should be taken into consideration before adjusting the results per page.

The final major factor that contributes to the search results page is the order of the results. The order of returned results is determined based on document relevancy and SharePoint's ranking formula. SharePoint ranks documents based on the frequency of query terms within the file as well as the overall comparative document value. Various ranking considerations are applied based on several values such as keyword matches, query proximity, static document properties such as file types, and user-driven weighting such as popularity. The result is that a single document becomes a collection of differently weighted ranking considerations. These weighted values are then used to produce the order of search results.

The topic of relevancy is one of great importance as it greatly affects the search user experience. The phrase "garbage in, garbage out" is quite applicable to the topic of search relevancy in that if users do not provide SharePoint with accurate properties, then SharePoint will produce bad search results. Insuring that users correctly tag, store, and rate documents will greatly contribute to successful relevancy. If users do not consistently attach properties to documents or store files in illogical locations, then the number of values SharePoint can consider for relevancy decreases along with accuracy. Companies should implement simple and consistent practices for tagging and storage so that users can contribute to their own success.

It is also important to understand that while the front-end diligence of document management is the shared responsibility of every user, the ranking formula is outside of end-user control. There are, however, many steps that SharePoint administrators and designers can take to improve result ranking. This is a topic of significant importance and is discussed at length in Chapter 10.

The combination of the various Web Parts discussed in this section create the net end-user search experience. To successfully leverage SharePoint's search experience, users must be comfortable with the use of most of these features. Each feature contributes to search success through a different function. The following sections drill into each of these features and their purpose within the search center in more detail. As mentioned at the start of the chapter, the goal of this chapter is to provide a thorough review of the end-user experiences for each component of the search interface. The following sections are in line with this goal and explain how to use each component, not how to customize each component. The focus of the following chapter is customization of each feature in the following sections.

# Search Suggestions

If enabled, SharePoint 2010 can provide search suggestions on any query box or search center dialog field (Figure 5-13). Search suggestions (called query suggestions on the Search Box Web Part) work similarly to Bing or Google search fields. As a user enters a search query, SharePoint presents suggested terms below the search box based on the partial entry of a query. By selecting a presented search suggestion, that query will be automatically initiated and the corresponding search results page will be returned.

**Figure 5-13.** *Search box with search suggestions*

Search suggestions are provided based on past user experience. Over time, SharePoint tracks search queries that result in a user clicking a result. Once a minimum number of clicks occur for a particular search query, it becomes an available suggestion. Only search terms that yield results that actually get clicked will go into the search suggestion pool. A minimum of six clicks per year is required for the term to show up as a search suggestion. As a result, search suggestions become more abundant and relevant over time.

Although it is possible to add and remove search suggestions manually, this cannot be managed by the end user. The next chapter discusses how an administrator can manually manipulate search suggestions. The topic of manually adding query suggestions and scoping them to create a custom experience based on the search page is covered.

## Alert Me

The Alert Me option found in the right zone below the search box provides the ability to set notifications when the result provides for a specific search query change (Figure 5-14). This is useful for users who need to know if new content relevant to a search query has been indexed, existing results are altered, or results are removed from the set. Alerts can be created to make one or more users aware of these changes. They can also be set to be delivered via e-mail or SMS text message.

To set an alert for a result set, first click the Alert Me button on the search results page. This will navigate the user to the new alert page.

**Figure 5-14.** *Alert Me button location*

The new alert page provides the ability to set the parameters of the alert (Figure 5-15). On this page, the following options can be configured.

- *Title*: The subject field of the e-mail or introductory text of SMS text messages

- *Recipients*: Which users should be alerted

- *Delivery method*: If an e-mail and or SMS text message should be sent to recipients

- *When to alert*: If the alert should trigger only when the search would yield new results, when content of an existing result is changed, or both

- *Alert frequency*: If checks for changes that will trigger the alert should be performed on a daily or weekly basis

Other users can also be added to this alert, which would then make a duplicate alert for them. Once another user has been added to the alert, the creator will no longer be able to edit it for that user.

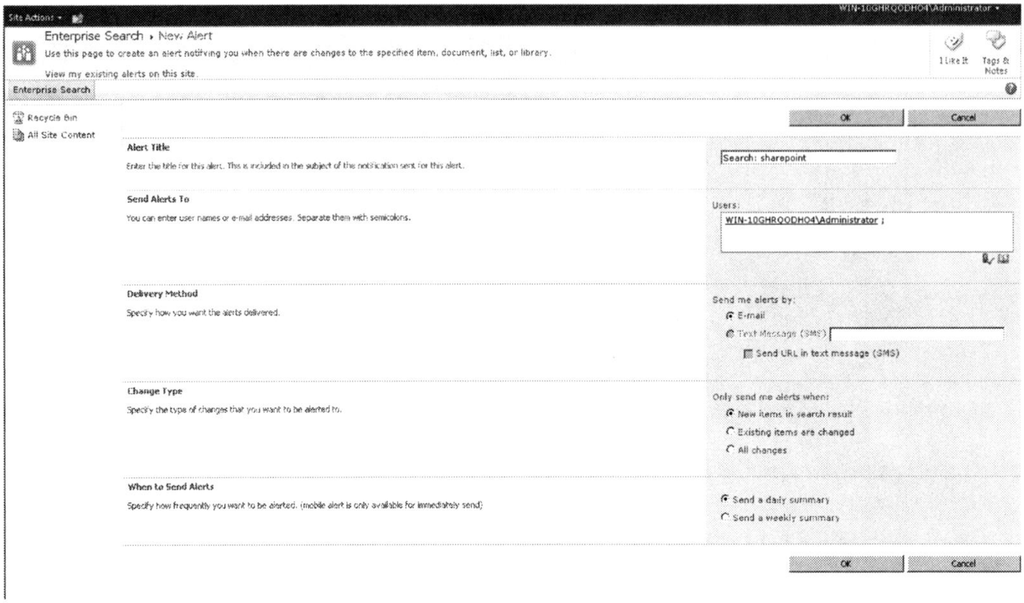

**Figure 5-15.** *New Alert page*

---

■ **Note** Changes that trigger search alerts are based on the crawled content. An alert can therefore never fire more often than the crawl intervals of the content sources that yield the search results for the specific search alert.

---

Once the desired settings are entered, clicking OK will create the alert. Alerts will continue to be delivered by SharePoint at the established delivery method and frequency until the alert is removed. To add, edit, or remove previously set alerts, select Manage My Alerts under the Page tab on the ribbon (Figure 5-16). This will provide access to manage only the logged-in user's existing search alerts.

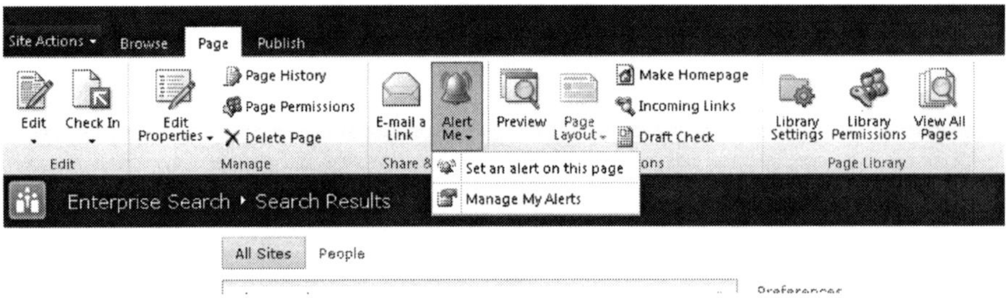

**Figure 5-16.** *Manage My Alerts option*

The alerts management page displays a list of all existing alerts and delivery methods for the logged-in user. To edit any alert, simply click the alert name. To delete one or more alerts, select the check boxes next to the alerts that need to be deleted, and then choose Delete Selected Alerts. To create a new alert, select Add Alert. Alerts created through the My Alerts page are not restricted to a set of search results. Alerts for any list, document library, or document can be created through this option (Figure 5-17).

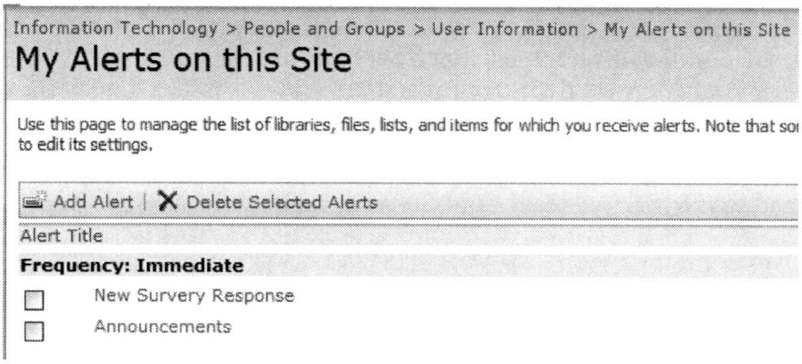

*Figure 5-17. My Alerts page*

By selecting an alert, the user is taken to a page that is almost identical to the New Alerts page. The only differing option is that only alerts for the current user can be edited (Figure 5-18). As a result, this page does not allow a user to add recipients. The other fields of the chosen alert can be edited and updated.

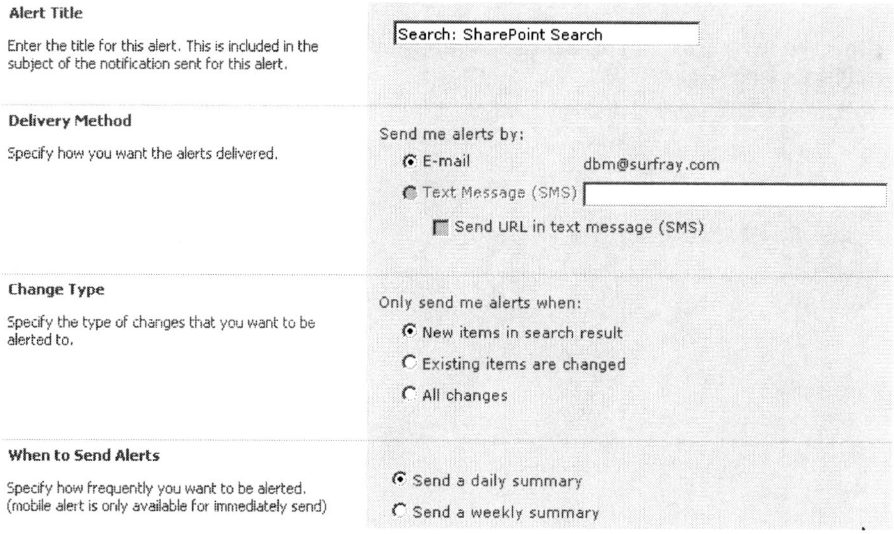

*Figure 5-18. Editing Alerts page*

# RSS

The Really Simple Syndication (RSS) option provides the ability to subscribe to a feed based on the current search query. This is similar to setting an alert, but instead of receiving an SMS or e-mail notice each time an item in the document changes, an RSS feed is established. Unlike alerts, which use a push-based model for notifying the user about changes to a search result set, RSS employs a pull-based model. Where alerts cause an e-mail to be pushed to a user's phone or e-mail when content changes, RSS allows users to decide when they want to pull and review changes to a result set from an RSS feed reader.

In regards to search, RSS feeds can push notifications to a user if content within a search result set changes. As information within the set feed is updated, it will download to the user's local computer for access through RSS-compatible programs. Examples of RSS-compatible programs include Microsoft Outlook 2010, the Feed Headlines gadget in Windows 7, and Internet Explorer. These RSS-compatible programs allow for the aggregation of several feeds and can provide a consolidated view of tracked information. As needed, a user can access an RSS feed reader and view any changes to the content of a search result set.

Setting an RSS feed is similar to establishing an alert. To set an RSS feed for the current query, select the RSS button after executing a query (Figure 5-19).

*Figure 5-19. RSS button location*

This will navigate the user to a page that displays the currently set RSS feeds and the ability to subscribe to the newly desired feed (Figure 5-20).

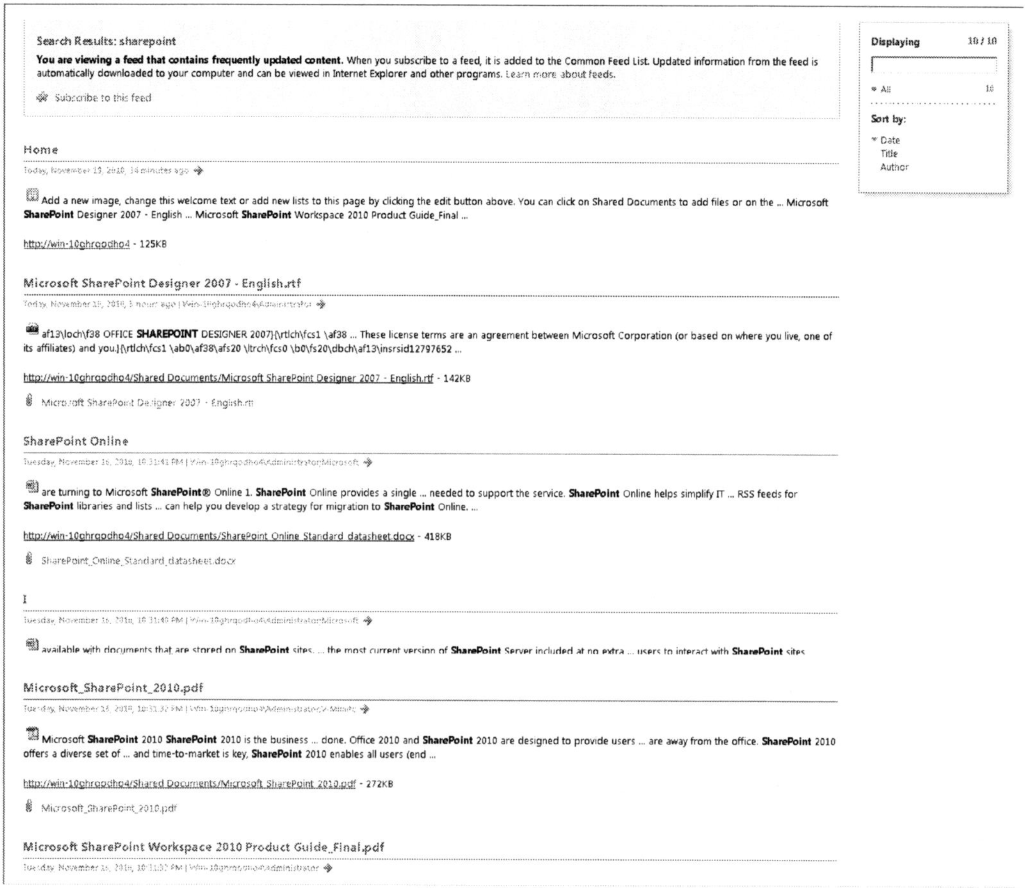

**Figure 5-20.** *RSS feed list*

Clicking the title of the RSS feed navigates back to the search result set for that query. Selecting "subscribe to this feed" allows the user to enter a name for the new feed and select the location where the feed will be created (Figure 5-21). After a feed is created, it is added to the common feed list.

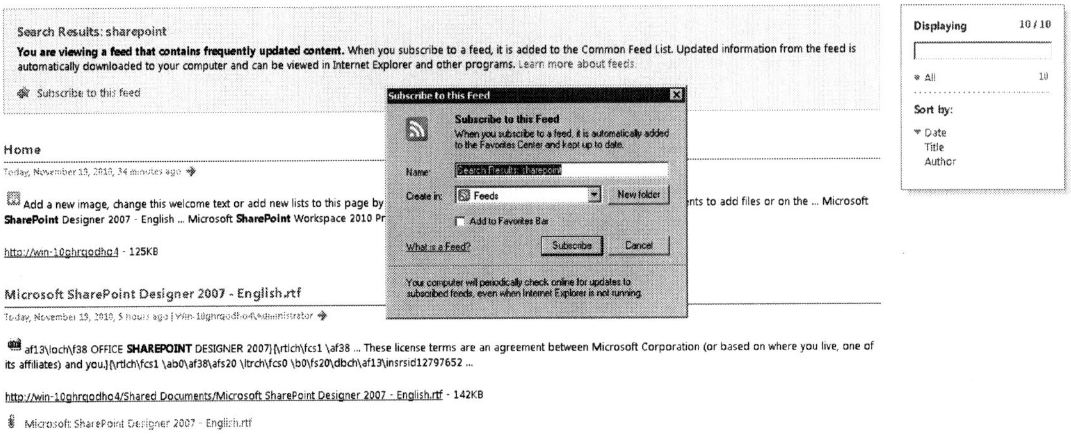

Search Results: sharepoint

**You are viewing a feed that contains frequently updated content.** When you subscribe to a feed, it is added to the Common Feed List. Updated information from the feed is automatically downloaded to your computer and can be viewed in Internet Explorer and other programs. Learn more about feeds.

Subscribe to this feed

Home

Today, November 19, 2010, 34 minutes ago ➜

Add a new image, change this welcome text or add new lists to this page by ... nts to add files or on the ... Microsoft
**SharePoint** Designer 2007 - English ... Microsoft **SharePoint** Workspace 2010 Pr...

http://win-10ghrqodho4 - 125KB

Microsoft SharePoint Designer 2007 - English.rtf

Today, November 19, 2010, 5 hours ago | Win-10ghrqodho4\administrator ➜

af13\loch\f38 OFFICE SHAREPOINT DESIGNER 2007]{\rtlch\fcs1 \af38 ... These license terms are an agreement between Microsoft Corporation (or based on where you live, one of
its affiliates) and you.]{\rtlch\fcs1 \ab0\af38\afs20 \ltrch\fcs0 \b0\fs20\dbch\af13\insrsid12797652 ...

http://win-10ghrqodho4/Shared Documents/Microsoft SharePoint Designer 2007 - English.rtf - 142KB

Microsoft SharePoint Designer 2007 - English.rtf

Displaying          10 / 10

All                  10

Sort by:
Date
Title
Author

**Subscribe to this Feed**

When you subscribe to a feed, it is automatically added
to the Favorites Center and kept up to date.

Name: Search Results: sharepoint

Create in: Feeds        New folder

Add to Favorites Bar

What is a Feed?        Subscribe        Cancel

Your computer will periodically check online for updates to
subscribed feeds, even when Internet Explorer is not running.

*Figure 5-21. Subscribing to a new RSS feed*

To view a subscribed feed in Internet Explorer, select the Feeds tab in the Favorites Center (Figure 5-22). This tab can be accessed by clicking Favorites and then Feeds. All feeds the current user is subscribed to can be found under this tab. Selecting a feed will navigate the user's browser to the chosen feed in SharePoint.

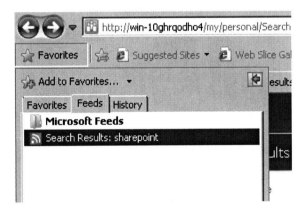

*Figure 5-22. Viewing subscribed feeds in Internet Explorer*

To change the properties of a feed after it has been created, select "View feed properties" on the right-hand side of the feed list. Doing so will open the window in Figure 5-23. The feed name, frequency of the user's computer checks for updates, and maximum number of updates to be stored can all be configured. Depending on the frequency of content updates within the search result set, system performance, and available storage space, the update schedules and archive options may need to be considered. If content frequently changes within a feed, frequent checks for updates will cause additional load on the user's local machine, connection bandwidth, and host servers. Setting a large number of items to be archived will require a larger amount of storage space.

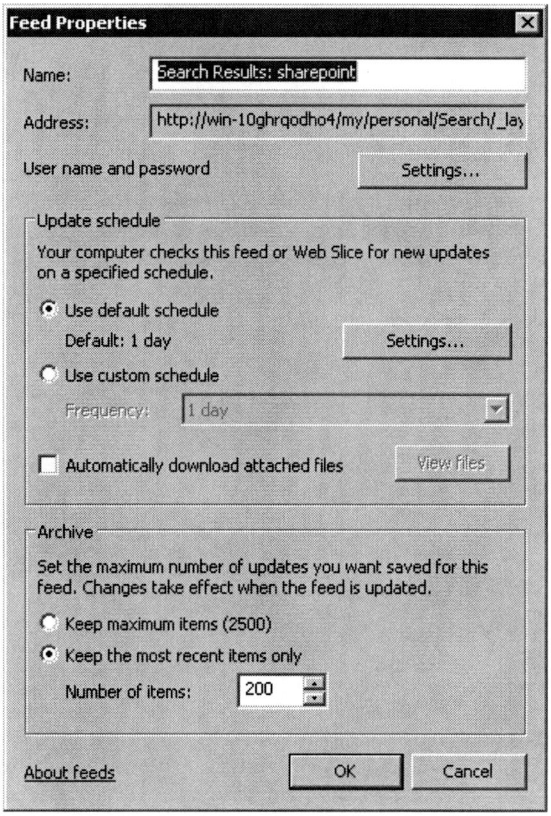

*Figure 5-23.* RSS Feed Properties dialog

# Search Later from Windows Explorer

The Search Action Links Web Part option provides the ability to search a location later from Windows Explorer in Windows 7. This allows for a user to establish federated search connections between the SharePoint 2010 Search Centers and the user's local machine. Once this connection is made, a user does not need to open SharePoint to search within the scope of the connection.

To establish a federated connector for the scope of the current search query, first execute the search query within the desired scope. On the search results page, select the search action on the far right as shown in Figure 5-24.

Preferences
Advanced

atingWithSharePointOV_WSG XT.docx

**Figure 5-24.** *Windows Explorer connection button location*

This action will download the connector and provide a prompt, asking if the user wants to establish the connection. The Add Search Connector prompt is shown in Figure 5-25. Choosing to add the connection will complete the handshake and open Windows Explorer on the local machine.

**Figure 5-25.** *Adding the connector*

By entering a search query into the Windows Explorer search box, queries can now be run against the established scope. When a query is executed, Windows passes the federated search to SharePoint 2010 and returns results in much the same way they would return in a SharePoint search center. Results return with actionable titles, keywords highlighted within the content snippets, and associated metadata. Figure 5-26 shows a set of federated search results with previews enabled in Windows Explorer.

**Figure 5-26.** *Federated search results in Windows Explorer*

Double-clicking a result will perform actions similar to clicking a result title in a search center. Microsoft Office documents will be opened in their corresponding programs. PDFs will open in Adobe Reader or other PDF viewer, and SharePoint sites will open in a new web browser window.

By default, the search result set in Windows Explorer will display only the first 20 results. To view the entire search results set, the search must be executed within SharePoint. A shortcut to executing the current query in SharePoint can be found at the top of the Windows Explorer Window. Selecting "Search on website" as shown in Figure 5-27 will open SharePoint in the browser and provide the full search result set in the corresponding search center.

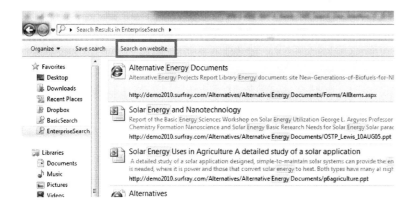

**Figure 5-27.** *"Search on website" button*

If multiple federated search connections have been established on the local machine, they can be accessed by selecting the desired scope on the left side of Windows Explorer under Favorites.

## Best Bets

Best bets are result suggestions pushed to users based on their search queries. Unlike the search suggestion functionality, which suggests a query, the Best Bets feature suggests a result. Best Bets suggestions occur based on specific keywords entered into the query and are presented as the first result(s) in a search result set. This result is slightly offset and marked with a star to stand out from the rest of the result set. For users, actioning a Best Bets result suggestion functions as any other search result of the same content type. The usefulness of the Best Bets feature for users is that if well managed, it drives the most relevant result to the start of a result set. Figure 5-28 provides an example of a best bet.

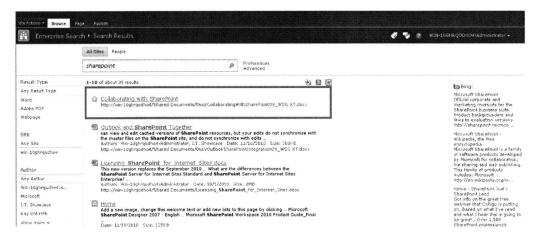

**Figure 5-28.** *Search results page with a best bet*

The Best Bets feature allows administrators to determine which results are most relevant for keywords. The goal of these is to feed content to the user based on the results that the administrators want the user to find first. Administrators can manually associate keywords with a Best Bets result. These are usually determined by analyzing the analytics for a given environment. SharePoint 2010 can also provide administrators with suggestions for Best Bets in a periodic report that factors in likely desired suggestions based on the aggregated metrics of an environment. Chapter 10 dives into administrative topics involving the Best Bets feature.

---

■ **Note** SharePoint 2010 Best Bets do not include HTML. For graphical best bets that use HTML, a third-party solution such as Ontolica Search or FAST for SharePoint 2010 is necessary. Public-facing SharePoint sites or those heavy on branding and marketing may want to consider this option.

---

# Federated Results

Search federation in SharePoint allows search results to be pulled from other search engines into a SharePoint search center. If set up, users can use one search center to pull information back from content outside of SharePoint. For example, if a user is logged into the North American SharePoint farm, but wants to also return results from the European farm, if federated search is set up, the user can achieve this. In the same search interface, the user could also return search results from an Internet search engine, such as Bing.com.

This concept was first highlighted in Chapter 1 and is essential for SharePoint environments that need to pull content from sources such as external silos, other SharePoint farms, blogs, and Internet search engines. Chapter 1 discussed how SharePoint can accept a query, pass it to another external search engine for processing, and return results from that external search engine into one aggregated interface. Chapter 3 discussed in detail how to set up the SharePoint crawler for search federation. Chapter 6 discusses how to customize the user interface for federated search results, and Chapter 9 discusses how to establish custom connectors through the BCS to crawl federated sources not supported by SharePoint out of the box.

## Federated Search Web Part Locations

Depending on the needs of a SharePoint environment, and the design choices made by the SharePoint administrator, federated search results may be displayed to users several different ways. Federated search results appear on the search results page through the Federated Results Web Part. Since this Web Part can be located in different zones on a search results page, and the content being federated is different for every SharePoint deployment, the user interaction with federated results is different for every environment.

Federated results are most commonly found in one of two sections of the results page. They may be found in the right zone of the page, as shown in Figure 5-29. This allows for a clear differentiation between federated results and the results being returned from locally indexed content sources. Blogs, wikis, and Internet search results are generally configured to appear in this zone.

**b** Bing:

Microsoft SharePoint
Official corporate and
marketing microsite for the
SharePoint business suite.
Product backgrounders and
links to evaluation versions.
http://sharepoint.microso...

Microsoft SharePoint -
Wikipedia, the free
encyclopedia
Microsoft SharePoint is a family
of software products developed
by Microsoft for collaboration,
file sharing and web publishing.
This family of products
includes: Microsoft ...
http://en.wikipedia.org/w...

Home - SharePoint Joel's
SharePoint Land
Got info on the great free
webinar that Colligo is putting
on. Based on what I've read
and what I hear this is going to
be great... Over 1,500
SharePoint professionals
have ...
http://www.sharepointjoel...

View more results »

***Figure 5-29.*** *Federated results in right zone*

Federated results may also appear above or below the locally indexed search results. Generally, content such as items from external databases and other SharePoint farms is displayed in this location (Figure 5-30). Content from these sources is more closely related to the content in the local search results, so including it as a more fluid portion of the search result set may be preferable.

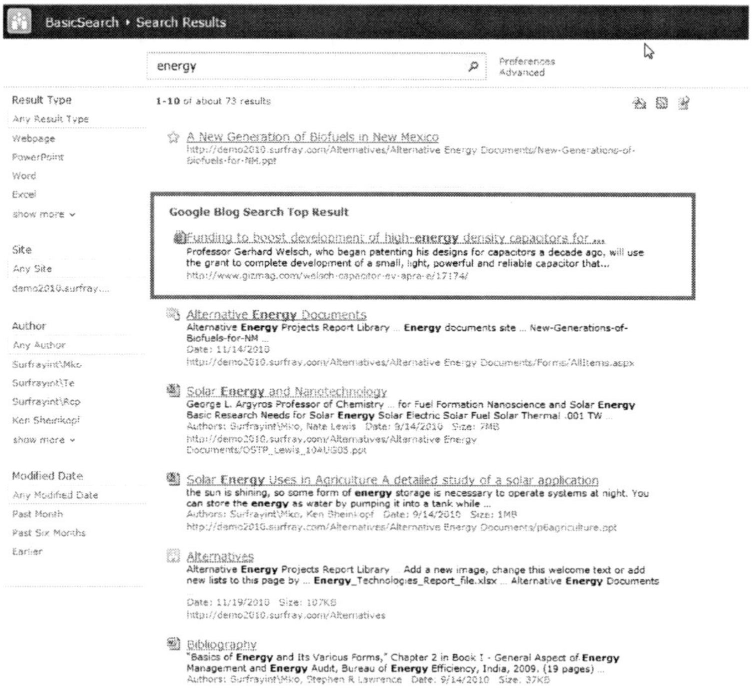

**Figure 5-30.** *Federated results in bottom zone*

Lastly, federated results may be so significant that they justify their own tab on the search center. This allows the administrator to create a search results page specifically for federated results, and not include locally indexed content. Additional tabs may be added to the search center adjacent to the All Sites and People tabs, as shown in Figure 5-31. Examples of this are common in environments such as international deployments with several SharePoint farms. A user can search locally indexed content by searching in the All Sites tab, but then select the Europe or Asia tabs to direct a search only to content federated from the European or Asian SharePoint farms. Federated search tabs with a dedicated search results page can provide a search experience that is the same as that for locally indexed content.

**Figure 5-31.** *Federated search tabs*

When adding federated results above or below the locally indexed results, and when creating a separate tab dedicated to the federated search results, it is advisable to use the Search Core Results Web Part and not the Federated Results Web Part. The Federated Results Web Part is formatted to present results in the right zone. Consequently, using the Federated Results Web Part in the bottom zone will present results in a tall, thin format, which doesn't present well. Instead, setting the "location" from which the Search Core Results Web Part returns results to the desired federated location will present results in a format more aligned with normal result sets. This topic is discussed further in the next chapter.

## Federated Result Presentation

If indexed by the federated search engine, SharePoint can display information about the content and properties of an item in the federated results. By default, when returning results from an Internet search engine such as Bing.com, the first three results that would return if the user executed his or her query through Bing.com are presented. The title of the results, a few lines of content, and the result's URL are all displayed. Clicking the actionable title of the result will navigate the user directly to the result's web site. Choosing to view more results will navigate the user to Bing.com and present the full result set for the query entered in the SharePoint search center. From here, users can use the Internet search engine in the same way possible if they had navigated to it directly.

In addition to displaying a list of multiple results from a federated environment, SharePoint 2010 can also display the top federated results as shown in Figure 5-32. If the Top Federated Results Web Part is enabled, the top one or more results from a federated location are displayed in a format similar to a best bet. Depending on the setting, the first result or the first several results from a federated location can be suggested. The suggestions are formatted to blend well above or below a core result set, and the title provides a link directly to the result. This suggestion option can be deployed by itself or in combination with the Best Bets feature.

*Figure 5-32. Top federated result from Bing.com*

As mentioned previously, due to the large amount of configurability surrounding search federation in SharePoint 2010, every environment will present federated search differently. The type of content presented in federated results and the way the results are presented on the page require significant consideration from the administrator based on the needs of users. Details regarding how to configure federated search for different needs are discussed in the following chapter.

# Search Refiners

The search refiners found on the left zone of the search results page provide the ability to drill into search results. These refiners, which are shown in Figure 5-33, are the major search navigation enhancement made available in SharePoint 2010. Although common to many search engines, this feature was not available in previous versions of SharePoint. Refiners, also called facets, allow users to select structured properties about the result they are searching for, and cut out results that do not contain that property. This feature allows for irrelevant search results to be quickly cut for a result set. If properly developed, users can filter from a massive result set littered with irrelevant results, down to a smaller and more manageable set of relevant results.

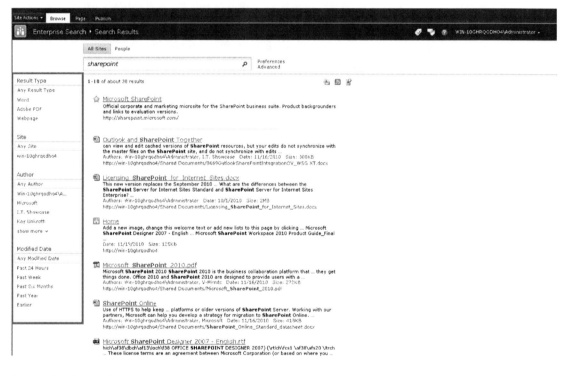

*Figure 5-33. Search refiners*

The importance of search refiners can be found throughout countless public-facing sites. Take an electronic retailer's web site, for example. When users navigate to an electronics retail site and search for a television, any site offering a reasonable number of TVs will most likely provide an initially overwhelming number of options for general search queries on TVs. Without the ability to filter through the large number of TVs, and narrow down to those relevant to a site visitor, potential buyers may become frustrated and leave the site in favor of competitors. Most users or site visitors will never navigate more than a few pages into a search result set. Fortunately, most successful electronics retailers provide refinement options. Sites allow users to select a TV brand, size, price range, or feature set. This allows buyers to quickly filter out TVs that are not applicable to their needs, and more importantly, return a smaller list of results for TVs that do meet their needs. This same need to filter results applies whether a site is catering to potential buyers or internal employees.

SharePoint 2010's refiners analyze the result set for particular sets of metadata. On a standard search results page, these metadata sets include Result Type, Site, Author, and Modified Date. SharePoint will look ahead at the first 50 items in the result set by default, not just the current page, and provide all the options within these categories. For example, if a result set contains Word and PowerPoint files, but not Excel spreadsheets, then an option for refining on the Excel file type would not be made available.

By default, only the four most frequent options for each category are displayed. If more than four options are available in a refinement category, the "show more" button at the bottom of each group can be selected. An example of this option is shown for the Author category in Figure 5-34. Clicking "show more" will expand the available refiners in each category and provide the full list for the result set. This option is provided so that the results page can be kept to a length in which minimal scrolling is needed. By clicking "show more", a potentially large number of options may become available, depending on the result set. If all options are presented by default, the results page would become very cluttered and lengthy in environments with large amounts of differing metadata in each refinement category.

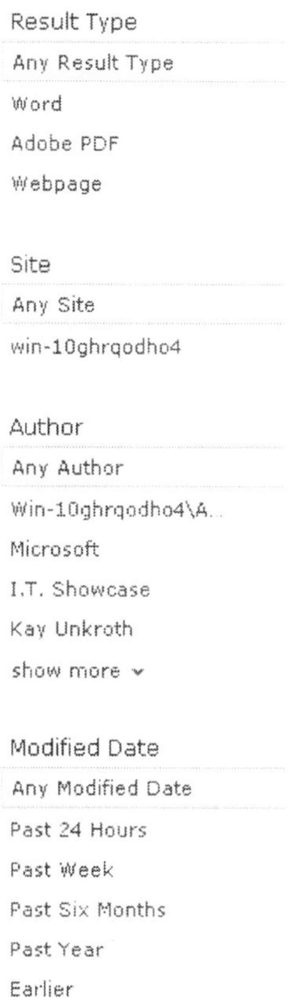

Result Type

Any Result Type

Word

Adobe PDF

Webpage


Site

Any Site

win-10ghrqodho4


Author

Any Author

Win-10ghrqodho4\A...

Microsoft

I.T. Showcase

Kay Unkroth

show more ˅


Modified Date

Any Modified Date

Past 24 Hours

Past Week

Past Six Months

Past Year

Earlier

*Figure 5-34. The search refinement panel with all results displayed*

## Selecting Refinement Values

When a user selects a refiner value, the search result set is updated to show only items that contain the selected value. For example, if a user selects PowerPoint from the set of available result types, all items that are not PowerPoint documents will be removed from the search result set. The currently selected refinement value is indicated by a three-sided box around the value. If additional result set refinement is needed, further refinement values can be selected in additional categories to continue elimination of unwanted results until one value has been selected for each category. It is also important to note that multiple values cannot be selected for each category. For example, if a user wants to return both PDF and Word documents in the search result set, but eliminate all other file types, this is not possible using the refinement panel. Figure 5-35 shows the search refinement panel with several values selected.

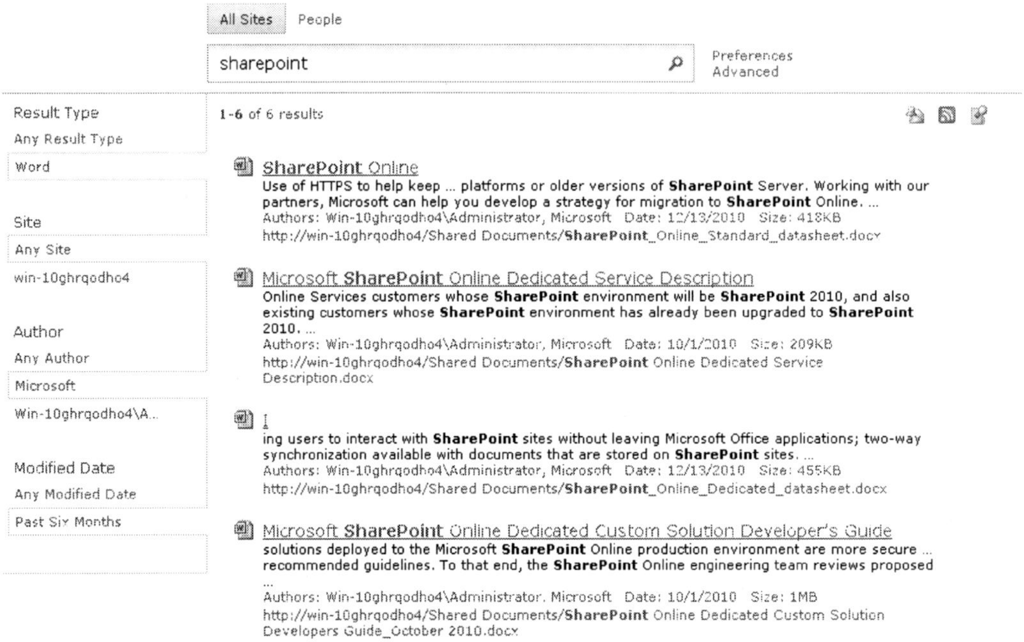

**Figure 5-35.** *Search refinement panel with selected values*

Users can also change the selected refinements as needed to adjust the search result set. For example, if a user has set the refinements shown in the previous figure, he or she has instructed the search results page to display only Word documents, authored by Microsoft, which were modified in the last six months. If the user recognizes that the document may in fact be a PDF document, he or she can simply select Any Result Type, which removes the selected value, and then select PDF as the new value. This same process can be done for any of the refinement categories to clear the selected restrictions.

## Refining by Site

The Site refinement option, which is shown in Figure 5-36, functions in a slightly different fashion than the other refinement categories. This category allows users to drill into the SharePoint site hierarchy and restrict the location of an item. For example, if a user is searching All Sites, by default the user will first be given the option to select a site collection. Once a site collection is selected, a list of the top sites where result items are located is provided. The users can select the appropriate site where the desired item is located, which then may present an option for a collection of subsites, depending on the farm's taxonomy. This process can continue through subsites and into lists and document libraries until the user has drilled into the bottom level of the SharePoint hierarchy. Like all refinement panel values, the available options will depend on the setup and content of your SharePoint deployment.

It is important to note that while users can drill into the SharePoint hierarchy, they cannot back out by just one level. To broaden the site refinement category, users must select *any site* and reset the entire collection of selected values. The web browser's back button does allow for a selection to be reversed, but utilizing this option is not generally recommended in practice, as the back button has negative consequences in other aspects of web browsing.

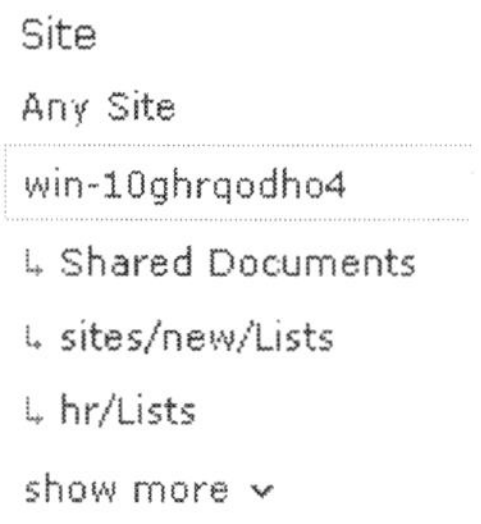

```
Site
Any Site
win-10ghrqodho4
  ∟ Shared Documents
  ∟ sites/new/Lists
  ∟ hr/Lists
show more ∨
```

***Figure 5-36.*** *Site refinement category*

Depending on the metadata within an environment, the available refinement options can be expanded. Additional categories can be displayed, the number of characters displayed per filter value can be adjusted, and the available actions can be restricted. The next chapter discusses this in more detail.

## Refiner Limitations

There are limitations to the base SharePoint 2010 search refiners. The primarily noticeable restriction is that refinements are presented based on the first 50 items in a result set by default. They are not based on an analysis of the entire result set unless the result set is smaller than the Web Part's *accuracy index*. The number of top search results that are analyzed by the Web Part can be increased, but the hard limit is 500 items. As a result, SharePoint 2010 refiners are considered "shallow." In addition, SharePoint 2010 OOTB can present refiners based only on managed properties. Managed properties must be mapped, crawled, and exposed in list and library metadata. For some environments, especially those with federated content sources, this may be restrictive. For cases requiring further entity extraction or refinements that analyze a larger set of results, a search extension such as Ontolica Search or FAST for SharePoint 2010 may be necessary.

# Search Query Syntax

SharePoint 2010 is capable of executing Boolean operators, suffix wildcards, and property queries in addition to the standard free text queries. For many end users, simply being able to execute suffix wildcard searches allows for a much easier transition to SharePoint from legacy platforms with this functionality. These capabilities are standard in most global and web site search engines, but have been lacking in SharePoint until the 2010 suite of search solutions. The inclusion of more advanced query syntax has significant impact on a user's ability to expand and narrow a search result set before using refiners or the Advanced Search page.

Users familiar with standard search query syntax should be able to easily adopt the advanced syntax available in SP2010. For those users who do not need to construct complex queries regularly, and consequently do not wish to learn the advanced query syntax, most of these options can be found on the Advanced Search page. It is important to mention that not all query syntax can be used for free text expressions, keyword queries, and property restrictions. As each operator is presented, the expressions that can be used will be noted.

## Search Query Operators

The wildcard operator can be used at the end of a keyword query or property query to enable prefix matching. This allows a user to broaden a search by entering the initial portion of a search query and indicating that SharePoint's search engine should fill in the remainder of the query. In SharePoint 2010, the wildcard operator is indicated by the asterisk character ("*"). A user can enter the initial portion of a search term followed by the wildcard operator as follows.

`shar*`

The resulting search results may include the terms SharePoint, sharing, Sharon, sharp, shark, and so on. The wildcard operator can be used only at the end of each term in a query. As a result, the query "*point" will search for "point" but not return "SharePoint". The search query "Share* AND Exp*" would allow the wildcard operator to work as expected, since it is inserted at the end of each term.

SharePoint 2010 supports the AND, OR, NOT, and NEAR operators, which allow for broadening or narrowing of a search query. To function as operators, these terms must be entered in all caps, as shown. The first three Boolean operators can be used with free text expressions, keyword queries, and property restrictions. The NEAR operator can be used only with free text expressions. The AND operator specifies that all of the search terms adjacent to the term "AND" must be included in the search result. Unless another operator is specified, the AND operator is entered between all search terms by default when a query is entered. In this example, both the terms "SharePoint" and "Expert" must be included in the search result, although the two terms do not need to be adjacent to each other.

`SharePoint AND Expert`

The OR operator specifies that a search result must include one of the terms adjacent to the term "OR", but both do not need to be included. In this example, either of the terms "SharePoint" and "Expert" needs to be included in the search result, but both do not need to be included.

`SharePoint OR Expert`

The NOT operator specifies terms that cannot be included in a search result. Items that contain the keyword that follows the NOT operator will be excluded from the result. In this example, results will include the term "SharePoint", but must not include the term "Expert".

`SharePoint NOT Expert`

The NEAR operator, also referred to as the proximity operator, specifies that search terms must be in a specific order and within a close distance to each other. Unlike the AND, OR, and NOT operators, the NEAR operator can be used only with text expressions and cannot be used in property restrictions. When placed between two search terms, only results containing the terms in the entered order and in close proximity to each other will be returned. If a user finds that search results being returned with the default AND operator are irrelevant because term 1 appears on page 1 of a document, and term 2 appears on page 15 of a document, the NEAR operator may provide the desired result set. In this example, only results that include the term "SharePoint" followed by up to eight other terms and then the term "Expert" will be returned.

```
SharePoint NEAR Expert
```

In addition to these Boolean operators, there are several other operators that are important to know. The first is the synonym operator that is initiated by the phrase WORDS. The WORDS operator allows a user to indicate that certain terms in a keyword query are synonyms of each other. This is similar in function to the OR operator, in that results need to contain one or more of the keywords, but these two operators differ in the rankings of the returned results. Also important to note is that unlike the OR operator, the WORDS operator is limited to free text expressions and cannot be used on property restrictions. In the following examples, the keyword query matches results that contain either the term "Children" or the term "Kids".

```
WORDS (Children, Kids)
```

```
Children OR Kids
```

The results that are returned by using these two queries may come back in a different order. This is because standard SharePoint 2010 ranking is being used. When using the WORDS operator, SharePoint considers the two terms to be the same for ranking purposes. When using the OR operator, SharePoint considers the two terms to be different for ranking. For example, if a document contains the term "Children" five times, and the term "Kids" five times, the WORDS operator causes that to be considered as ten occurrences of the same term. If the OR operator is used, SharePoint considers the document to have five occurrences of the term "Children" and five occurrences of the term "Kids". As a result, SharePoint would place the document with the assumed ten occurrences of one term earlier in the result set than five occurrences of each term.

Identical to the AND/NOT operators, SharePoint can accept the inclusion and exclusion operators. These are established by insertion of a + or – in the query, and can be used on free text search or property restrictions. Since it is identical to the AND operator, the inclusion (+) operator is the default behavior of search unless another operator is specified. In the following example, content containing the terms SharePoint and Expert is included in the search results, but content that contains the term MOSS is not.

```
SharePoint + Expert - MOSS
```

Quotation marks ("") can be entered around a phrase to specify that search results must contain the exact set of words in the provided order. This allows for phrases to be grouped together and considered as one search term. This is necessary when the terms need to be in a specific order without additional terms between them. If quotation marks are not used, the AND operator will be inserted between terms by default. This may cause results to be returned where keywords have many other terms separating them. Unlike the NEAR operator, which will return all the results produced by using quotation marks, the exact phrase operator returns only results where the terms are touching. The NEAR operator will return results where the terms are either touching or in close proximity to each other. In the following example, only results containing the phrase "SharePoint 2010 Expert" will be returned.

```
"SharePoint 2010 Expert"
```

Parentheses "( )" can be entered to combine parts of keyword queries. Just like a math equation, entering keywords between parentheses will allow terms or phrases to be grouped together. In the following example, all results will include the term SharePoint, but they must also include either the term "Expert" or "Genius".

```
(Expert OR Genius) AND SharePoint
```

## Property Restrictions

In addition to Boolean operators, wildcards, and other syntax operators, SharePoint 2010 users can execute queries based on property restrictions to narrow the scope of a search. Property restrictions allow users to limit results to those that contain properties, or metadata, that they specify in the query. In many cases, these properties may also be able to be restricted by building the parameters in the Advanced Search page. If the option to enter a property restriction has not been made available on the Advanced Search page, however, manually building a restriction into the query may be a user's only option for returning a specially refined result set. Property restrictions can be executed for any managed property value. Chapter 3 discussed how to map a crawled property to a managed property.

A basic property restriction is composed of the following components.

```
<Property Name> <Property Operator> <Property Value>
```

The property name is the particular property being addressed, such as author, file type, or upload date. The property operator is the symbol for the function a user wishes to execute. Property operators are generally mathematical operators and include functionality such as stating a property must be greater than, less than, or equal to a value. A full list of these is provided later in this section. Finally the property value is the numerical or written language character that must be associated with the property. For example, if the restriction is a date, the property value may be September 30, or it could be .docx in a file type restriction. These are a few examples of compiled keyword property restrictions.

```
author:"Josh Noble"
```

This returns only items authored by Josh Noble.

```
filetype:docx
```

This returns only Microsoft Word documents.

```
write>11/20/2010
```

This returns only items updated after 11/20/2010.

When building queries with property restrictions, it is important not to leave any white space between characters. As discussed in the section on Boolean operators, white space is assumed by the search engine to be the AND or inclusion character. As a result, the following queries would be treated as free text queries instead of the intended property restriction.

```
author:  "Josh Noble"
```

```
author  :"Josh Noble"
```

```
author  :  "Josh Noble"
```

All three of these examples would yield results for the free text query.

```
author "Josh Noble"
```

As mentioned earlier, property restrictions can be executed against any managed property. A secondary stipulation for searching on a managed property is that the administrator must have set the property to be either retrievable or full-text queryable. This is not a property setting that can be made by the end user, but it does affect the actions a user can perform on a managed property. Managed properties that are set to be retrievable are soloed in the property store database. Managed properties that are set to be full-text queryable are stored in the full-text index along with all of the rest of the content in a farm, such as sites, documents, and lists. As a result, managed properties that are full-text queryable can accept the same query syntax as a normal content query.

Only text properties, also called string properties, can be set to be full-text queryable. All other managed properties, such as numerical values (integers), dates, times, Boolean, and binary data types, are strictly retrievable. Full-text queryable properties can accept the full-range or keyword query operators.

```
author:Josh
```

```
author:Noble
```

For full-text queryable properties, both of these property restrictions will return items authored by Josh Noble. These properties can also accept suffix wildcard and exact phrase operators.

```
author:Jos*
```

This example would return items authored by Josh Noble as well as Joshua Hammond, Josef Smith, or Josline Heff if the result set contains those authors. Just like keyword queries, the wildcard operator can be used only at the end of a term. When the exact phrase operator is used on a full-text queryable property, the property must contain the specific phrase.

```
title:"SharePoint Expert"
```

```
title="SharePoint Expert"
```

In these examples, the document title must contain the phrase "SharePoint Expert". Returned results may include "SharePoint Expert gives search advice", "Become a SharePoint Expert", or "What the SharePoint Expert knows". The suffix wildcard operator can also be used in combination with the exact phrase operator.

```
title:"SharePoint Ex*"
```

This query would return items titled "The Best SharePoint Experience", "Who needs SharePoint Expertise?", and "SharePoint Express Search".

Property values stored in the property database can be queried only for the entire value of a property. Unlike free text queryable properties, those that are just set to be retrievable must match the property restriction query exactly. Again, this is not an option made available to the end user, and if the settings of a property are unknown, testing if something is set to retrievable, full-text queryable, or both may require some trial and error. For those that are only retrievable, and not also full-text queryable, the following query would be accepted.

`company:"APress Books"`

This query would return only items in which the company field is "APress Books". Unlike full-text queryable properties, if the company is "APress Books London", the result would not be returned. The term must match the field exactly. This same rule applies for numerical property values such as integers, decimals, dates, times, yes or no, and binary data types.

`size:50MB`

In this example, the returned results must have exactly 50MB in the size property. The other property operators can also be used against retrievable properties.

`size<50MB`

This property restriction returns only results in which the item size is less than 50MB.

`size>=50MB`

This property restriction returns only results in which the item size is greater than or equal to 50MB. A full list of the available operators can be found in Table 5-1. Depending on the managed property being used, different operators can be used. The table provides a full outline of the operators that can be used for each data type. All of the listed operators can be used for Integer, Decimal, and Datetime values. Text, or string, values can accept the : or = operators. Binary and Boolean (YesNo) values can be restricted only with the : operator.

**Table 5-1.** *Property Restriction Operators*

| Operator | Action |
| --- | --- |
| : | Results must contain the specified value. |
| = | Results must be equal to the value. |
| > | Results must be greater than the value. |
| > = | Results must be greater than or equal to the value. |
| < | Results must be less than the value. |
| < = | Results must be less than or equal to the value. |
| < > | Results do not equal the value. |
| " | Results must be within the range of the values. |

Although every environment will most likely contain custom managed properties, a list of common managed properties can be found in Table 5-2.

*Table 5-2. Common Managed Properties*

| Property Name | Description |
| --- | --- |
| FileExtension | File extension |
| Filetype | File type (same function as preceding) |
| Author | Author |
| DocComments | Comments |
| DocKeywords | Keywords |
| FileName | Item's file name e.g., docx or ppt |
| Size | File size in KB |
| Path | URL |
| Write | Last modified date |
| CreatedBy | Document creator |
| ModifiedBy | Last modifier |
| DocSubject | Document subject |
| Title | Document title |

It is also important to note that multiple property restrictions can be combined to create a string of restriction parameters in a keyword query. The length of a property restriction is limited to 2,048 characters, but within that limit, combinations of retrievable and free text queryable property restrictions can be created. Users can string together restrictions for several different properties and enter more than one restriction for each property.

When multiple values for the same property are entered, the search engine treats them as if they were separated by the OR Boolean operator.

```
author:"Josh Noble" author: "Robert Piddocke" author:"Dan Bakmand Mikalski"
```

This property restriction would return items authored by "Josh Noble", "Robert Piddocke", or "Dan Bakmand Mikalski". It is important to remember that standard keyword queries automatically use the AND operator, but the search engine assumes the OR operator between identical property restrictions.

```
author:"Josh Noble" filetype=docx size>50MB
```

```
author:"Josh Noble AND filetype=docx AND size>50MB
```

Both of these queries will return Microsoft Word documents that are larger than 50MB and authored by Josh Noble. Just like a keyword query, the search engine automatically enters the AND operator between restrictions for different properties.

Finally, combinations of free text keyword queries and property restrictions can be entered as one query string.

```
Share* AND author:"Josh Noble" NOT "Piddocke"
```

This query would return items that contain the keyword "Share", are authored by Josh Noble, and do not contain the phrase "Piddocke" within the content.

```
filetype=docx filetype=pdf AND "SharePoint Expert"
```

This query would return items that are either Microsoft Word or PDF documents and contain the phrase "SharePoint Expert". Using the rules outlined in this section, a wide range of advanced queries can be strung together to return a desired set of search results. As users become more advanced, and the need to produce more concise sets of search results increases, understanding the full capabilities of this search syntax becomes increasingly necessary. A full review of the available query syntax can be found in Table 5-3.

*Table 5-3. Search Query Syntax Overview*

| Operator | Example |
| --- | --- |
| Prefix matching for search keywords and document properties using the wildcard * operator | When searching for "nor*", results may include "Norcross", "north", "normal", etc. |
| The "AND" operator specifies a result must include both terms separated by "AND". | When searching for "Noble AND SharePoint", all results returned must contain *both* the term "Noble" and the term "SharePoint". |
| The "OR" operator specifies a result must include at least one of the terms separated by "OR", but does not need to contain both. | When searching for "Energy OR Nuclear", results will include items containing "Energy", "Nuclear", or both "Energy" and "Nuclear". |
| The "WORDS" operator specifies that terms in a keyword query are synonyms. This is similar to the "OR" operator. | When searching for WORDS (Kids, Children), results will include items containing "Kids" as well as "Children" and consider them to be the same term for ranking. |
| The "NOT" operator specifies a result must not include the term following the "NOT" operator. | When searching for "Energy NOT Nuclear", all results returned must contain the term "Energy", but never should contain "Nuclear". |
| The "-" (exclusion) operator works the same as the "NOT" operator. | When searching for "Energy - Nuclear", all results returned must contain the term "Energy", but exclude results containing "Nuclear". |

| Operator | Example |
|---|---|
| The "NEAR" operator specifies the adjacent search terms must be within close proximity to each other. | When searching for "Energy NEAR Nuclear", all results returned will contain "Nuclear" within a limited number of words after "Energy". |
| The use of quotation marks ("") for designating exact search phrases is supported. | The string "2009 financial report" will return all items that contain the exact phrase "2009 financial report". |
| Parentheses ( ) can be used to combine different parts of keyword queries and group search terms. | The string "(Nuclear OR Oil) AND Energy" will return all results containing "Energy" so long as they also contain "Nuclear" or "Oil" terms as well. |
| Property restrictions can be entered so that results match specific properties. | The query "author:Josh Noble" will return only documents authored by "Josh Noble". "filetype:pdf" will return only PDF-type files. |
| Any combination of the foregoing search tools is supported. | The query "plant AND filetype:pdf" will return only PDF documents containing the term "plant". Also "instru* AND (author:Josh OR author:Dan)" will return all items containing the term "instructions" authored by Josh or Dan. |

# The Advanced Search Page

So far, this chapter has provided a detailed walkthrough of entering search queries through the query box and search center. The actions that can be taken on the search results page have been discussed in detail, and the available query syntax has been explained. Stepping back to the query box and search center, there is a third optional location for building queries. The Advanced Search page allows users to build more complex search queries without manually entering an advanced search syntax string. For users who have not yet learned the available search query syntax and would like to refine the keywords, languages, and property restrictions included in a search result set, the Advanced Search page provides a set of options for building more advanced queries.

The Advanced Search page can be accessed by a link on the All Sites search center prior to entering an initial query or from the All Sites search results page after entering a query. Depending on the settings made by the administrator, it may also be possible to access the Advanced Search page by a link next to the query box or site search results page (Figure 5-37).

*Figure 5-37. Advanced search link*

If the user navigated to the Advanced Search page from a result set, the query that was already entered will be copied into the first field of the Advanced Search page in SharePoint 2010. If additional non-query restrictions were entered into the result set, such as a refinement, it will not be carried into the Advanced Search page. As shown in Figure 5-38, without customizations, this page allows for users to work in two primary areas. These areas include "Find documents that have…" and "Add property restrictions…"

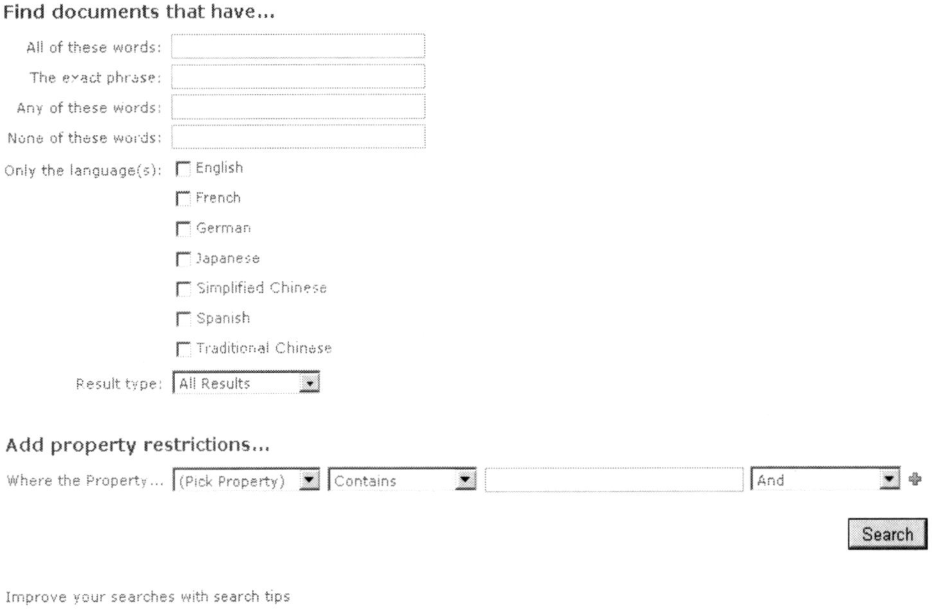

**Figure 5-38.** *Advanced Search page*

# Keywords on the Advanced Search Page

The two categories of query manipulation are aligned with search syntax discussed in the last section. The first, "Find documents that have…", is where the keywords for the query are entered. These fields allow the user to execute operators other than the AND operator by entering the search term in the corresponding free text field. By entering a search term into a free text field, the operator indicated by the field's description will be executed behind the scenes. The fields correspond to the operators in Table 5-4.

***Table 5-4.*** *Search Query Syntax Overview*

| Field Title | Operator |
| --- | --- |
| All of these words | AND |
| The exact phrase | " " |
| Any of these words | OR |
| None of these words | NOT |

All of the terms that should be in the search result are entered in the first text field, titled "All of these words". The AND operator will automatically be inserted between the words entered into this field. Any phrases that contain multiple words that need to occur in a specific order next to each other can be entered into the second field, titled "The exact phrase". The phrase will be treated as if it had quotation marks surrounding it. For example, SharePoint Expert will return results with this exact phrase in the order the terms are entered, unlike the "All of these words" field, which would return results that include "SharePoint" and the separated term "Expert". No quotation marks are necessary when entering a phrase into this field. The third field, titled "Any of these words", will treat all entered terms as if they were separated by the OR operator. Words that can but don't have to be in the search result are entered into this field. The inclusion of one, but not all, of the terms in this field is sufficient to indicate a desired search result. The final field, titled "None of these words", allows for the exclusion of the terms entered into the text field. Search results will not include any of the terms entered into this field.

The "Find documents that have…" section also now includes language restrictions and result type refinements. Selecting the check box next to one of the listed languages narrows the results to include only items that were authored in the chosen language. By default, the language field of an item is not factored into its availability as a result. All languages supported by the installed language packs are searched on. When a language restriction is chosen, SharePoint will exclude results not authored in the chosen language(s).

The last option in this section is to restrict the search results by a result type. This functionality is identical to the result type refinement on the search results page for the available refinements. By selecting a result type from the drop-down list, only items matching the chosen result type will appear in the search result set. When choosing a result type, SharePoint 2010 will include all versions of the format. For example, when Word Document is selected as the result type, files with the extensions `.doc`, `.docx`, `.dot`, `.docm`, and `.odt` will all be returned. The result types available for selection without customization of the Advanced Search page can be seen in Figure 5-39.

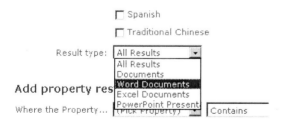

***Figure 5-39.*** *Advanced search result type refinement*

# Picking Property Restrictions

The section "Add property restrictions…" allows for the ability to create strings of property restrictions from a series of two drop-down boxes and a free text field. Using this option, users can string together queries with several property restrictions without learning how to enter them into the search box. Just like a property restriction entered as query syntax, each property restriction has three sections, which include the property name, the property operator, and the value. When multiple property restrictions are built into the advanced search, a fourth field, which allows for restrictions to be combined using the AND operator or the OR operator, appears. To add or remove additional property restrictions, simply select the + or – icon to the far right of the property restriction.

The first drop-down after the phrase "Where the property…" is labeled "(Pick Property)" and allows the user to choose the property that will be restricted (Figure 5-40). By default, the properties shown in the following figure are available when searching all result types. Additional properties are made available depending on the selected result type.

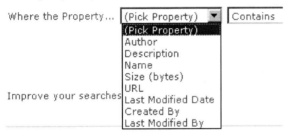

***Figure 5-40.*** *Pick Property options*

The second drop-down allows the user to select the operator to be used in the property restriction. Depending on the selected property type, the available operators will change. If the property is a text, or string, then the "Contains", "Does not contain", "Equals", and "Does not equal" operators will be available. If the property is an integer, then "Equals", "Does not equal", "Greater than", and "Less than" operators are available. If the property is a time or date, then the "Equals", "Earlier than", and "Later than" operators become available. Table 5-5 lists the available operators and their corresponding symbol for use in search query syntax.

***Table 5-5.*** *Advanced Search Property Restriction Operators*

| Field Title | Operator |
| --- | --- |
| Contains | : |
| Does not contain | < > |
| Equals | = |
| Does not equal | NOT |
| Greater than | > |
| Less than | < |
| Earlier than | <= |
| Later than | >= |

The last field is a free text field where the user enters the desired value of the property restriction. Depending on the property type, the values that will return results greatly differ. Author, Description, Name, URL, Created by, and Last Modified By property types will all accept text strings. The Size property type will accept a numerical value in bytes by default. The Last Modified Date property will accept a numerical date in the form DAY/MONTH/YEAR or MONTH/DAY/YEAR depending on how the SharePoint 2010 DateTime field is configured. This allows for flexibility in global deployments.

## Query Examples on the Advanced Search Page

Some of the examples of property restrictions found in the previous section on search query syntax can be found in the following screens. Figure 5-41 provides an example of utilizing the author property with the equals and OR operators. This search will return results with the authors Josh Noble, Robert Piddocke, and Dan Bakmand Mikalski. This is equivalent to the search query `author:"Josh Noble" author:"Robert Piddocke" author:"Dan Bakmand Mikalski"`.

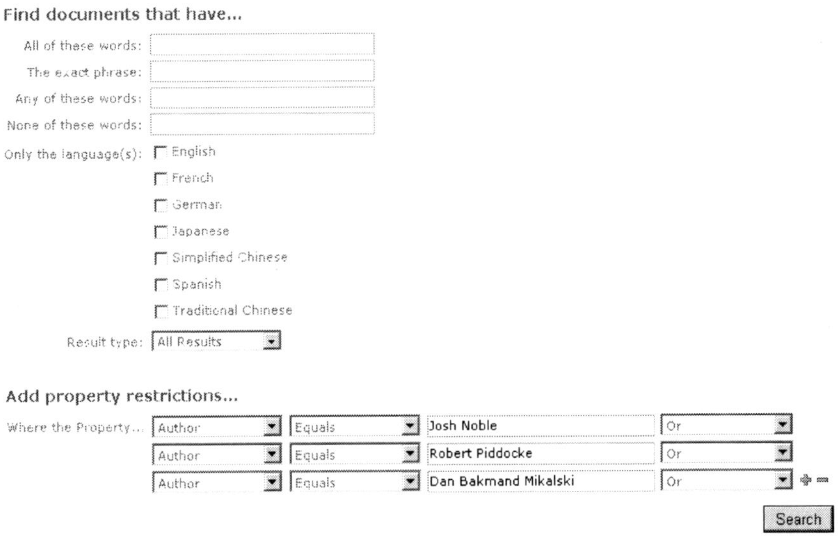

Find documents that have...

All of these words: _____
The exact phrase: _____
Any of these words: _____
None of these words: _____

Only the language(s):  ☐ English
                       ☐ French
                       ☐ German
                       ☐ Japanese
                       ☐ Simplified Chinese
                       ☐ Spanish
                       ☐ Traditional Chinese

Result type: [All Results ▼]

Add property restrictions...

Where the Property... [Author ▼] [Equals ▼] [Josh Noble            ] [Or  ▼]
                      [Author ▼] [Equals ▼] [Robert Piddocke       ] [Or  ▼]
                      [Author ▼] [Equals ▼] [Dan Bakmand Mikalski  ] [Or  ▼] ✛ ▬

                                                                      [Search]

*Figure 5-41. Configuring a query to return only items authored by Josh Noble, Robert Piddock, or Dan Bakmand Mikalski*

The parameters in Figure 5-42 will return results for Word documents over 50MB (52,428,800 bytes) authored by Josh Noble. This search is equivalent to the query `author:"Josh Noble" AND filetype=docx AND size>50MB`.

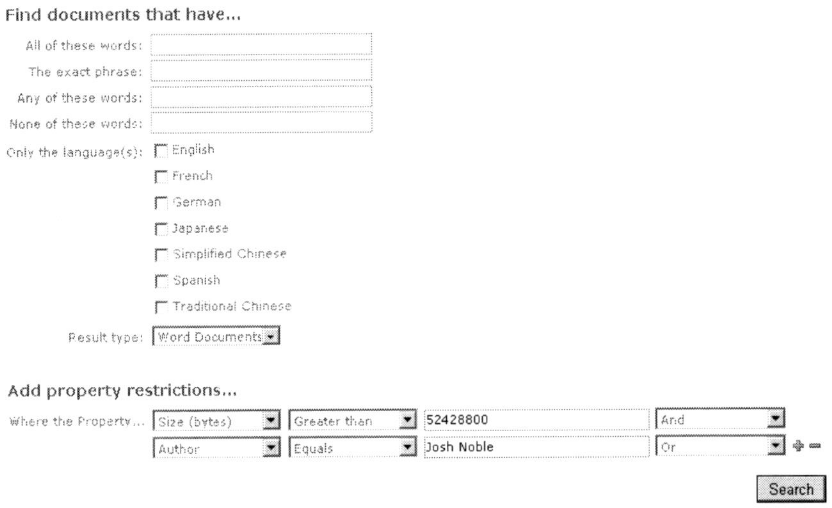

Find documents that have...

All of these words: _____
The exact phrase: _____
Any of these words: _____
None of these words: _____

Only the language(s):  ☐ English
                       ☐ French
                       ☐ German
                       ☐ Japanese
                       ☐ Simplified Chinese
                       ☐ Spanish
                       ☐ Traditional Chinese

Result type: [Word Documents ▼]

Add property restrictions...

Where the Property... [Size (bytes) ▼] [Greater than ▼] [52428800     ] [And ▼]
                      [Author       ▼] [Equals       ▼] [Josh Noble   ] [Or  ▼] ✛ ▬

                                                                      [Search]

*Figure 5-42. Configuring a query to return only Word documents over 50MB authored by Josh Noble*

The search in Figure 5-43 will return results for any English PowerPoint presentations, no matter the extension, that contain the phrase "SharePoint Search Expert". This search is the equivalent of entering the query (DetectedLanguage="en") (FileExtension="ppt" OR FileExtension="pptx" OR FileExtension="pptm" OR FileExtension="odp") AND SharePoint Expert.

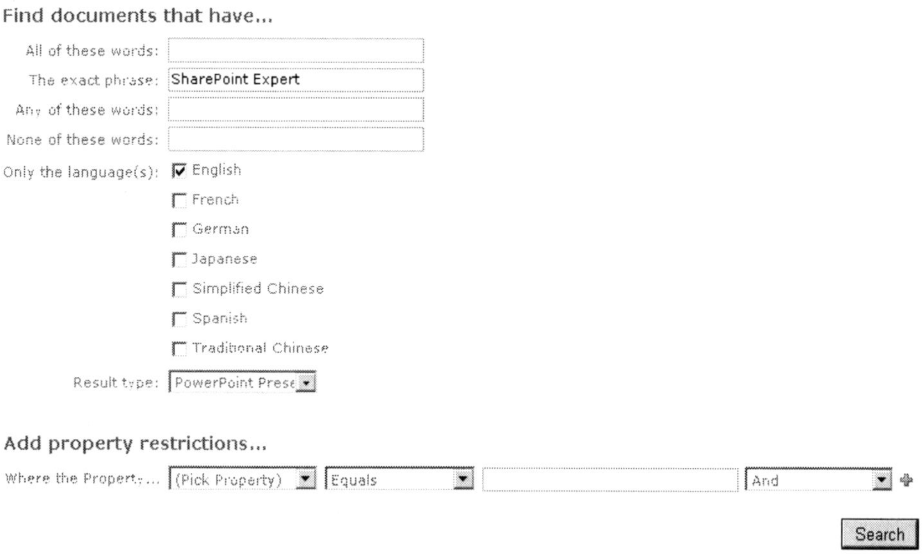

**Find documents that have...**

| | |
|---|---|
| All of these words: | |
| The exact phrase: | SharePoint Expert |
| Any of these words: | |
| None of these words: | |

Only the language(s): ☑ English
☐ French
☐ German
☐ Japanese
☐ Simplified Chinese
☐ Spanish
☐ Traditional Chinese

Result type: PowerPoint Prese ▼

**Add property restrictions...**

Where the Property... (Pick Property) ▼  Equals ▼  [                ]  And ▼  ✚

Search

**Figure 5-43.** *Configuring a query to return only English PowerPoint presentations containing the phrase "SharePoint Expert"*

For users that would like to learn the available search query syntax and become less reliant on the Advanced Search page, try this.

Build a search query in the Advanced Search page. Make sure to include the property restrictions and keyword syntax you would like to learn how to enter manually. Execute the search and take note of the content produced in the search field at the top of the search results page. Figure 5-44 shows an example of part of an advanced query syntax that would be produced by specifying a scope, last modified date, and file extension on the Advanced Search page.

All Sites    People

ALL(SharePoint)(Write=11/20/2010)(FileExtension=  🔎    Preferences
Advanced

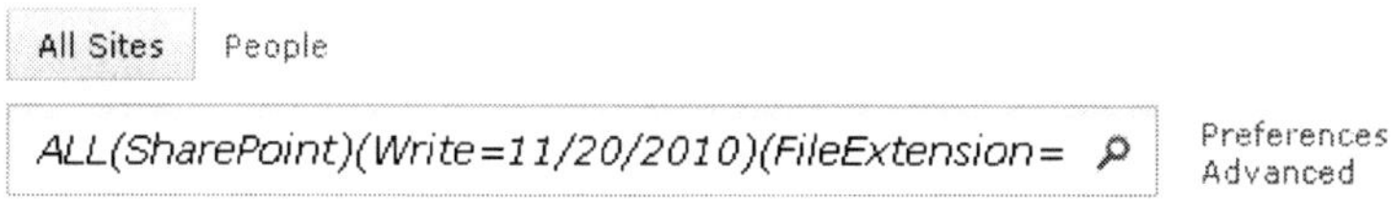

**Figure 5-44.** *Advanced search syntax after a query from the Advanced Search page*

This search syntax also contains all of the keywords, property, and scope restrictions built into an advanced search query. This syntax can also be entered into any SharePoint search field to reproduce the same results. The syntax is also useful to learn the structure of search strings, operators, and property restrictions. Taking note of this syntax will guide your knowledge of the search syntax through repetition. Eventually, you will not need to navigate to the Advanced Search page for your commonly entered expressions.

# The People Search Page

Working with documents, lists, and web pages is only one of the many reasons SharePoint 2010 is attractive as a portal and collaboration platform. Another part of the equation is SharePoint's ability to connect people with other people through its form of social networking. People have different skills, competencies, resources, and networks that are most likely not implicitly known to everyone in an organization. The aggregation of knowledge about people is what has made social networking Internet sites such as Facebook, MySpace, and LinkedIn such core experiences inside and outside of the office. The value of participating in these sites is not to find information stored within documents, but to find information stored within and about people.

Within a company, people are arguably the most valuable resource. Knowing who can provide the right expertise, who knows whom, and who works for whom can provide answers that a company directory cannot. Knowledge about people's competencies within an organization can produce greater efficiencies by directing answer seekers to knowledgeable experts, instead of reproducing research and answers. SharePoint 2010 can provide the platform for connecting people with this information. If a user needs a list of employees that know how to manufacture a widget, or create a specialized spreadsheet, or review a legal agreement, SharePoint 2010 can provide those answers through the People search page.

---

■ **Note** This section is not about how to direct SharePoint to crawl data about people, but instead it is about how to retrieve that data once it is crawled. For full details on how to crawl and index MySites, blogs, and collaboration sites, please refer to Chapter 3.

---

If set up, the People search page can provide access to data such as that found in MySites, user profiles, Active Directory, web sites, collaboration sites, as well as personal and professional blogs. This information can also be restricted by privacy protection rules such as LDAP and Active Directory security trimming on a per user basis, as discussed in Chapter 3.

The People search page can be accessed through the same pathways as an All Sites search page. To review, these pathways include navigating to the search center and selecting the People tab, or entering a search in the query box and selecting the People search scope. Figure 5-45 shows the selection of the People scope if this option is enabled on the query box.

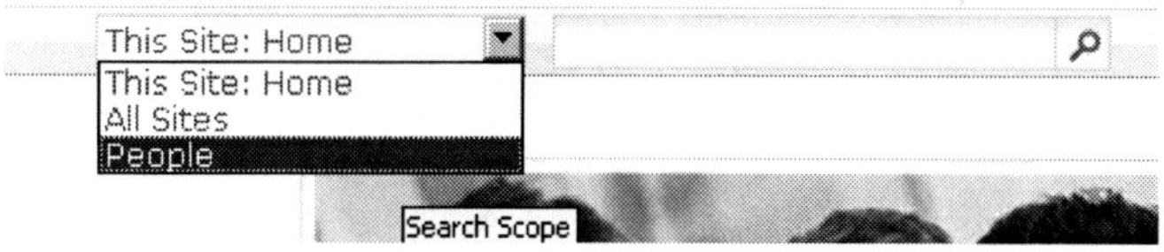

**Figure 5-45.** *People scope on the query box*

# People Search Options

Similar to the All Sites search page, navigating the the People search tab provides a few options not available by default from the query box. These include a link to the Preferences page and a link to open the search options. The Preferences page is by default identical to the Preferences page for All Sites search. Selecting Search Options opens up the People search equivalent of advanced search options. Unlike the Advanced Search page found on the All Sites search, however, selecting Search Options simply opens a set of free text fields to enter additional parameters to the query. The default fields for Search Options are shown in Figure 5-46.

**Figure 5-46.** *People search options*

The search fields that direct toward a People search results page work just like any other search field. A query is entered, in this case for a person, skill, job title, keyword, etc., the query is run, and the results are returned on the People search results page. As seen in Figure 5-47, the layout of this search results page is fairly similar to the All Sites search, with a few exceptions.

*Figure 5-47. People search results page*

The search field and the Preferences page still appear at the same location. The Search Options link replaces the Advanced Search page link, but simply opens up an additional set of options below the query field. These options are the same as a free text property restriction. The Last Name and First Name fields allow a user to search for a person's first or last name respectively. Search queries are not case-sensitive, so there is no need to capitalize the first letter of a first or last name in the query. The Last Name and First Name fields will search for exact matches to the entered query, so if a user enters the query "Sand" into the Last Name field, it will not return results for a user with the last name "Sanderson". To indicate that a query entered into the Last Name or First Name fields is intended to be part of a name, and not an exact match, the user must enter the wildcard character, "*". It is important to note that just like searching in All Sites, partial word searches are restricted to prefix matching in People search.

The Job Title and Keyword search fields will also match only an exact term unless the wildcard operator is inserted. Unlike first and last names, however, these fields in a result may include more than one term. Consequently, the entered keyword or job title must match exactly one term in the result, but the result doesn't need to match only the entered query. As a result, entering part of a job title, such as a query for "sales", would return people with the job title "Sales", "Regional Sales Manager", or "Sales Director", since each contains an exact match for the term "sales".

As mentioned earlier, the Search Options section functions just like the Advanced Search page and more specifically, property restrictions. Just like property restrictions for documents, not all users will be concerned with learning to use property restriction in People search, especially considering that search options occur as a drop-down instead of a completely different page. It may be useful, however, for some users and administrators to know the property names for the fields in this section. The reason for this is that the fields in the search options do not allow for multiple property restrictions on the same property as in the Advanced Search page. If a user enters the terms "Josh Robert", "Josh OR Robert", "Josh; Robert", or any other combination that may seem logical in a different search engine to denote two separate terms, the desired results will not be returned. This means that if a user wishes to return results for users with either the first name "Josh" or "Robert", the user is unable to do so without manually entering the property restriction syntax shown here.

```
FirstName:"Josh" OR FirstName:"Robert"
```

When multiple, different fields or property restrictions on the Search Options are completed, each field will be separated with the AND operator. This means that the query will return only results that match the terms entered in all fields, but will not return results that meet a portion of the query. To assist in the building of broader People search queries, the default property names can be found in Table 5-6.

***Table 5-6.*** *People Search Property Names*

| Property Name |
| --- |
| LastName |
| FirstName |
| JobTitle |
| Responsibility |
| Skills |
| Interests |

## Standard Web Parts in People Search Results

The People search results page does allow for the Alert Me, RSS, and Search from Windows actions provided in the All Sites search. These features operate the same in People search as they do in All Sites search. This search page also allows for faceted search refinements that function just like All Sites search, but the page also allows for filtering on properties relevant to the people scope. The default refiners in People search include View and Job Title, but these options can be expanded by the administrator depending on the managed properties with an environment. View allows for users to specify if the result was returned due to a query match in the person's profile or name. Depending on the type and amount of information provided within a person's profile, this provides a useful tool to specify whether a user is looking for a specific person, or someone that works with or knows a person. Refining by Job Title is useful for larger result sets in which the user generally knows the title of the person he or she is looking for, but may not be able to be specific enough to enter a search for Job Title in the Search Options. Information about mapping additional managed properties to People is discussed in Chapter 3, and information about adding additional refinements is provided in the following chapter.

## Using People Search Results

As with the All Sites search tab, People search provides a cluster of information about a person and highlights the queried keyword within the result. An individual item from the People search results is shown in Figure 5-48.

**Dan** Bakmand Mikalski
Software Developer
R&D
(+45) 31 63 14 14
dbm@surfray.com

» Add as colleague
» Browse in organizational chart
» By Dan Bakmand Mikalski

My Colleague's
Colleague

*Figure 5-48. Individual search result in the People search results page*

By default, each item in the results provides a person's name, title, department, and other information about the displayed person, such as contact information. The name of the person is actionable and, when clicked, will bring the user to the personal "MySite" of that person. Unlike the standard All Sites search result, however, there are many more actions that can be taken on People results. If configured, a person's MySite acts as a hub of information about that user and includes expanded information such as contact information, his or her organizational chart, shared content, tags and notes on sites, colleagues, and participating memberships, such as e-mail distribution lists. Much of this information is accessible directly from the remainder of the search result.

If a person has uploaded a profile picture, it will be displayed on the result. Between the person's name and picture, a small square box, acting as a link, provides access to the user's profile contact card. In SharePoint 2010 a user's profile is also called a presence. If a user is online, this box will turn green. Clicking the box will provide an additional set of options such as contact information, the ability to initiate an e-mail, instant message, or phone call, or schedule a meeting directly from the results page. The default actions that are available when clicking the contact card are shown in Figure 5-49.

*Figure 5-49. People search contact card*

# Taking Action on Results

On a default People search page, below the name and contact information of a person, there are three links. These links allow the user to take action on the result. The first available action is the Add to My Colleagues link. Each user's MySite has a page that supports this action. The end result of taking this action is that the selected person will be added to a user's Colleagues list on his or her profile. The Colleagues list is a shared list of colleagues similar to connections on LinkedIn or friends on Facebook. When choosing to add a colleague, the user is navigated to a page that allows the user to select the setting of the relationship. The settings that can be made include selecting the colleague, adding him or her to a team or group, and setting the groups that can see the relationship. The Add Colleagues page is shown in Figure 5-50.

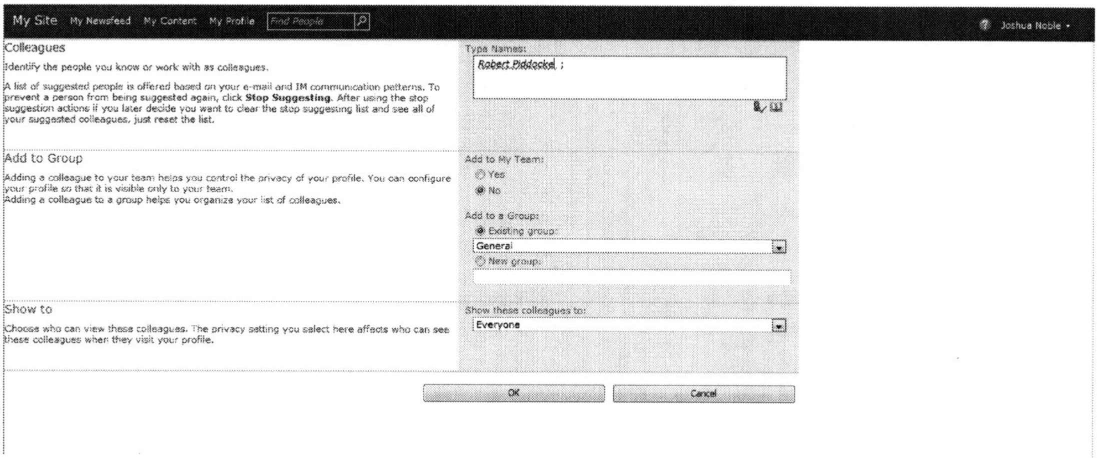

***Figure 5-50.*** *Adding a new colleague*

Selecting the option to Browse in Organizational Chart will navigate the user to the selected person's Organization tab on his or her MySite (Figure 5-51). If the organizational chart is established for the selected person, the user can view other people in the person's vertical and lateral hierarchy. Managers they report to, the people that report to them, and people at the same level of the hierarchy are displayed. People higher in the organizational hierarchy are shown above the current person's contact card, people they work with at the same level are shown to the left and right of the contact card, and people who report to the person are shown below the contact card. Using the selected person's contact card as a starting point, users can navigate through the contacts related to the person and view his or her contact cards. Users can continue to follow this structure of organizational hierarchy away from the initially selected person until they find the related contacts they may be searching for.

173

***Figure 5-51.*** *Organization chart*

The last option on each result allows the user to see a brief list of items "about" the person as well as items authored by the person. When clicking "By *person*", a window opens on the page that displays a list of five items from the All Sites search and provides the ability to show more results "about" the person from All Sites search. The list shown under *"person"* is the top five results that would be returned if the following query was entered into "All Sites" search.

```
person author:"person"
```

For example, if the person being actioned in the result was named Josh Noble, the top five results for the search query (Josh Noble author: "Josh Noble") would be returned. This query returns result items where the person's name is treated as a keyword and he or she is one of the authors. If the option to show more results is selected, a second window appears and a search results page is shown for the full list of results on the corresponding query. The results page can be treated just like any All Sites search results page. If a user tabs to more by "person," then the same actions occur but instead for the following query.

```
author:"person"
```

This query skips looking for items that include the person as a keyword and returns only items where the person is an author. Both of these options allow for a convenient social networking feature to find items related to people, teammates, and colleagues within an SP2010 environment.

## Expertise Search

SharePoint has one final and extremely interesting feature in SharePoint 2010 People Search. Users now have the ability to execute an expertise search for themselves with a special set of content. Expertise search, which is more commonly refered to as "vanity search," is similar to "googling yourself." In a strong effort to build out the social networking features in SharePoint 2010, when a user searches for his or her own profile, a few unique features are returned in addition to the standard People result content. These features can be seen in Figure 5-52.

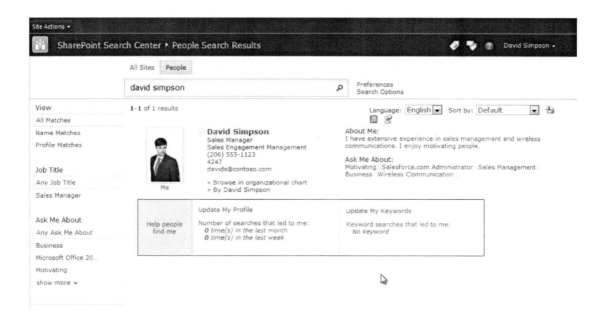

**Figure 5-52.** *Vanity search result*

When viewing your own People search result, you can find your About Me and Ask Me About "blurbs" to the right of the result. The "About Me" section is where you can provide a personal description of yourself. The "Ask Me About" section tells people about your interests, skills, responsibilities, and business specialties. Both of these sections are essentially an elevator pitch of yourself to all other SharePoint users. Keeping this information up to date is essential for organizations that rely on SharePoint to connect people with each other. If your profile is out of date, then other users may contact you about projects you are no longer involed with or may not be able to find you for the project you are currently working on. The content for both these sections can be edited on your MySite profile.

When returning your own People search profile as a result, you will also be presented with a uniqe box below the result. This box, conveniently titled "Help people find me", contains a few helpful tools and information to aid other SharePoint users in connecting to your profile. On the left side of this box is a link titled "Update My Profile", which lands on your My Profile edit page. Below this link are the statistics on the number of times other SharePoint users executed searches that returned your profile as a result. Statistics are presented for searches over the last month and the last week by default.

The right column of the "Help people find me" box is headed by another link to your My Profile edit page titled "Update My Keywords". Just like document searching, keywords are structured properties that SharePoint uses to connect search queries to relevant results. Consequently, creating accurate keywords for your user profile will help other users return your profile in their search results when appropriate. Keeping your keywords up-to-date is an easy way to improve your profile's relevancy. To aid in this keyword creation, an overview of the keywords that other users have entered that led to your profile are presented below the "Update My Keywords" link.

## The Preferences Page

The final link that can be selected next to the query field on both the All Sites and People search pages is the Preferences page. This page allows users to set user profile-specific settings for searching such as whether search suggestions appear and the languages that are used. The user-selected settings made on this site are applied to a user's entire SharePoint search experience, disregarding which computer the user uses to access SharePoint. Settings are tied to a user profile and not an IP address and are the same across all web applications. The Preferences page is accessed by clicking the Preferences link to the right of the search field (Figure 5-53).

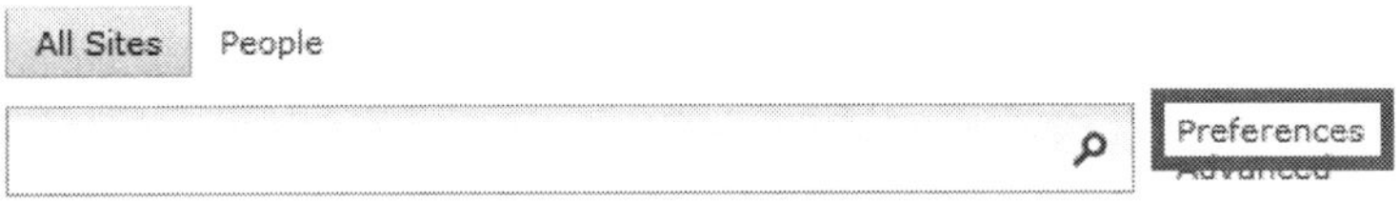

| All Sites | People |

Preferences
Advanced

***Figure 5-53.*** *Preferences page link location*

After clicking the Preferences link, the user is navigated to the Preferences page, shown in Figure 5-54. The Search Suggestions setting enables or disables search suggestions from the search box for the current user. This is especially useful if the user accesses the search box via the Internet on a connection with high latency. This would in some cases cause significant delay when showing search suggestions or otherwise disturb the user experience of the page—the reason being the round-trip between client and server is taking too long when entering text into the search box.

The Language setting in the Preferences page is used to define the stemmers and word breakers used for searching. Since different languages include different stemmers and word breakers, specifying the set that SharePoint utilizes, if more than one is available, can help to provide increased relevance to users searching on international installations.

---

▦ **Note** Manually selecting languages helps overcome the problem in MOSS 2007, where the current browser language setting would dictate which stemmer and word breaker were used. Modifying the preferences overrides the browser language setting, thus providing a solution to this problem.

---

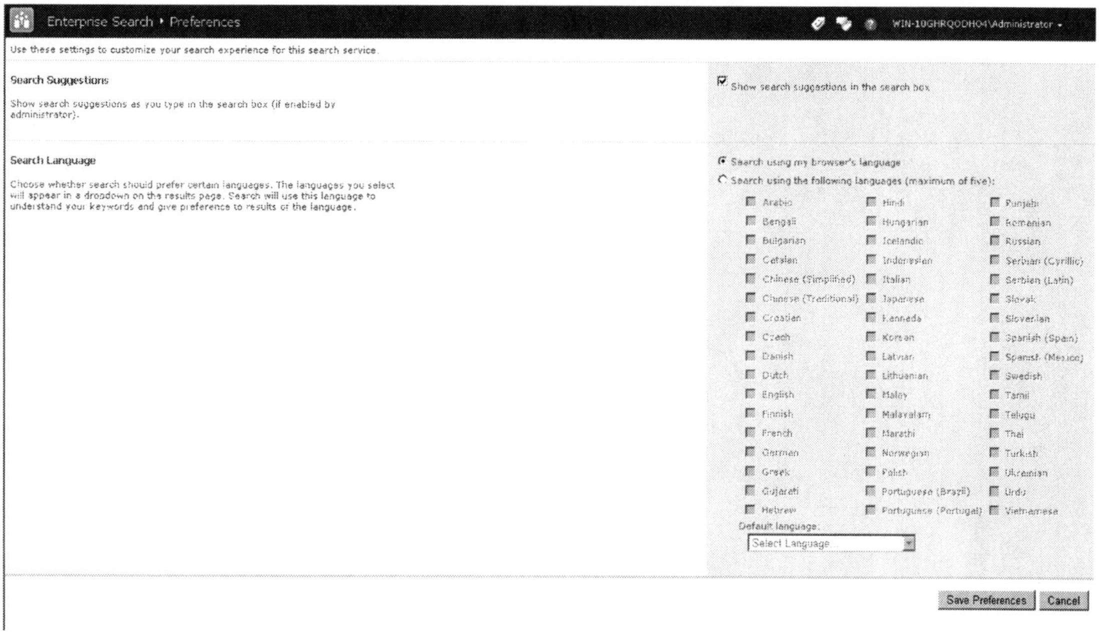

**Figure 5-54.** *Preferences page*

The user can turn search suggestions on and off for the logged-in user profile by checking and unchecking the check box. This setting is ignored if Search Suggestions are turned off on the Search Box Web Part. To specify specific languages to be applied to the search query, the user can select the radio button next to "Search using the following languages". The user can select up to five languages to use during search for the logged-in user profile by checking and unchecking the corresponding check boxes.

# Summary

For users, the ability to quickly and efficiently connect with information is the metric by which a search interface is measured. This chapter has presented a thorough exploration of the SP2010 Search user interface. The chapter explored the basic ways of executing queries, either through the search query box or the search center. It has explained the features and Web Parts available in the All Sites and People search results pages. The SharePoint 2010 query language has been outlined in detail to explain how users can expand and refine searches from the query box. Finally, the Advanced Search and Preferences pages were explained to guide users on how to further refine searches. At this point in this book, you should understand the basic history and terminology around search in SharePoint, be able to plan the infrastructure of a deployment, set up the crawler for various content sources, deploy a search center, and now use the search user interface. The next chapter will deviate from the front-end user interface and explore how to manipulate the experiences of the user interface.

■ ■ ■

# CHAPTER 6

# Configuring Search Settings and the User Interface

After completing this chapter, you will be able to

- Understand and edit settings on search Web Parts

- Understand administrative aspects of user preferences

- Create and edit federated locations

- Understand the behavior of stemmers, word breakers, phonetics, and nicknames

- Manage keywords and synonyms

- Create and manage search alerts

- Understand and manage search suggestions

- Add and modify search scopes

- Manage search tabs and search pages

Every deployment of SharePoint 2010 brings with it a different set of search requirements. For example, the information that is important to an engineering company is very different than the needs of a financial institution. The needs of various user groups within a company are also quite diverse. Users from human resources, marketing, and manufacturing will all navigate to a search center with a different set of goals and expectations. To cater to this diversity, SharePoint has been designed to create flexible search experiences based on the needs of an organization.

The previous chapter provided a thorough overview of the front-end components of the search user interface. It explained the various Web Parts, query syntax, and user-side functionality of search in SharePoint 2010. However, the chapter did not discuss manipulation of the search user interface from an administrative point of view. It did not discuss how to configure a search user interface; it detailed only how to use one that had already been set up. In fact, as noted throughout Chapter 5, many of the features that were discussed are not enabled on the search center by default and must be set up by the administrator. This chapter picks up where Chapter 5 left off by discussing configuration settings for the search user interface. After completing this chapter, you will be able to configure the search experience of your SharePoint 2010 search center and sites.

---

■ **Note** The explanation Web Part features are provided in this chapter only as a review. For full details, please refer to the previous chapter.

---

Throughout this chapter, the focus is on understanding search-related settings within the search user experience in SharePoint 2010. Because of the large number of settings that can be made, we do not discuss every setting for every component, but instead discuss the most important settings of each. The first part of this chapter discusses topics involving the search box, such as setting scopes, redirecting queries, configuring suggestions, and creating fixed query terms. This is followed by a focus on the presentation of search results, the location they are pulled from, the properties that are displayed in the result set, and how to show results from existing federated locations.

The chapter continues to discuss the various settings of the refinement panel. Since this is a significant new feature in SPS2010, we discuss topics such as general settings and how to add new refinement categories in detail. We proceed to discuss the administrative considerations regarding the Preferences page and phonetics. We then look into how to establish keywords and best bets in order to push content to users. An explanation of alert settings is provided before a deep dive into scopes. The chapter concludes by explaining how to create new search tabs on a search center.

Many times search-related settings can be hard to find, and tweaks can cause unforeseen complexities. When describing search settings, we give special attention to implications requiring possible pitfalls and provide recommendations for diagnosing and avoiding common problems. In addition, whenever settings depend on configurations done at the Search service application (SSA) or site collection level, a reference to the appropriate sections will be noted.

# Web Parts

SharePoint 2010 contains new Web Parts as well as significant improvements to existing Web Parts in SharePoint 2007. What is immediately clear from looking at the Web Part settings is how XSL template management and included properties configuration (called columns in the Web Part settings) have been changed to be centrally managed by default from Central Administration. This is covered in Chapter 7. This supports both central management of the look and feel as well as the new federated structure. Another noticeable thing about search Web Parts is the new Locations selector. In SharePoint 2007, the architecture was based on Shared Services Providers. Now it is based on Search service applications (SSA), which are constructed around a federated model. Even searching locations in SharePoint (the SharePoint search index and property store) is a federated search. This is reflected in the new Web Part settings. Federated search is covered in more detail later in this chapter.

## Web Part Settings

Web Part settings are stored individually for each instance of a Web Part. They are also configured directly from the Web Part itself. To start editing Web Parts, click the Page tab on the ribbon and click Edit (Figure 6-1). This will change the page to Edit mode. If the ribbon is not showing, it can be enabled from the Site Actions menu.

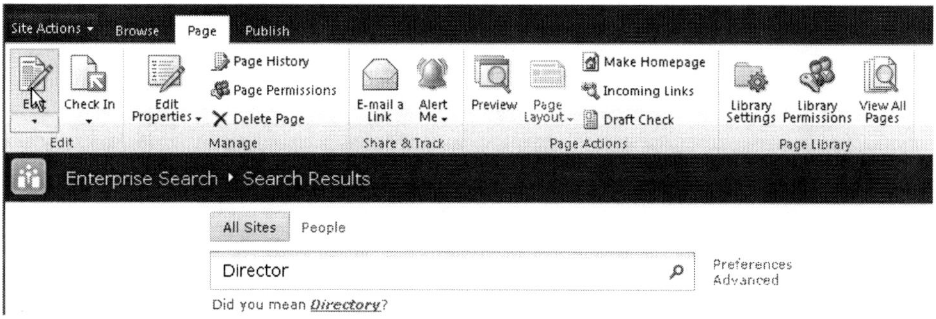

**Figure 6-1.** *Ribbon with Page tab active*

Open the appropriate Web Part context menu, and choose Edit Web Part (Figure 6-2). This will open the Web Part settings menu. Note that the Web Part settings menu is located in the upper right corner of the Web Part page and that the page does not automatically scroll to that location, so it might be required to manually scroll to the top of the page to find the settings menu.

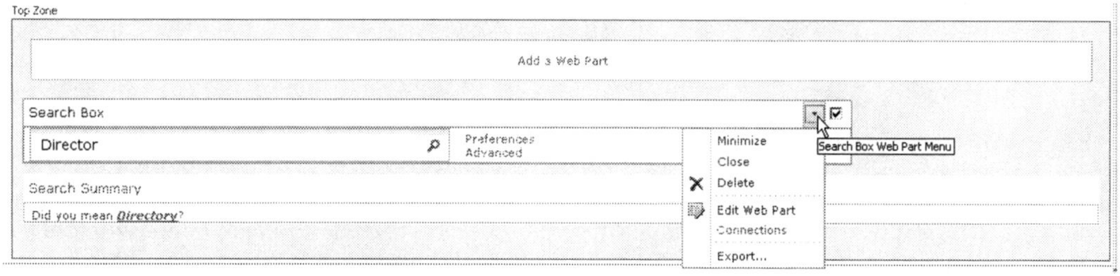

**Figure 6-2.** *Accessing Web Part settings*

The Web Part context menu also contains options for deleting the Web Part or exporting it. Web Parts that are exported preserve their configuration. This means that a configured Web Part can be exported and later imported again either in the same place or on a different Web Part page with the same configuration. The following sections will cover the settings most administrators should know or consider changing when planning to utilize search in SharePoint.

# Search Box

The Search Box Web Part is used to receive the user query input and forward the input to a search results page. In this section, we will look at the following search-related settings (Figure 6-3) of the search box: Scopes, Query Redirection, Query Suggestions, and Additional Query Terms.

*Figure 6-3. Search Box settings*

As with all Web Parts in search centers, both the search pages and the search result pages contain a Search Box Web Part. Those are configured independently. This is especially useful, as the search dialog Web Part on multiple search pages can redirect to the same search result page. This allows a customized look, feel, and behavior of the search dialogs located on different search and search result pages, without the hassle of creating multiple result pages.

## Scopes

The search box can be configured to use scopes in a number of different ways (Figure 6-4). Either a scope can be used implicitly or a scope drop-down can be configured to be displayed. This allows the user to select which scope to search. It is preferable to provide a description for the drop-down label to help users identify the purpose of the scopes. Real-life experience shows that users are often reluctant to use advanced search features, such as scopes, if it is not very clear to them why they can benefit from them.

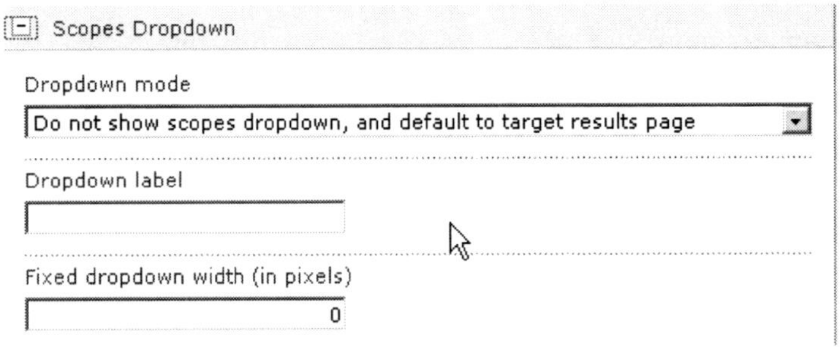

*Figure 6-4. Choosing a scope visibility mode*

From the Scopes drop-down (Figure 6-5), you can configure which scopes should be displayed. This way the search box can be configured to either use hard-coded scope settings or to receive its scope setting from the URL parameter.

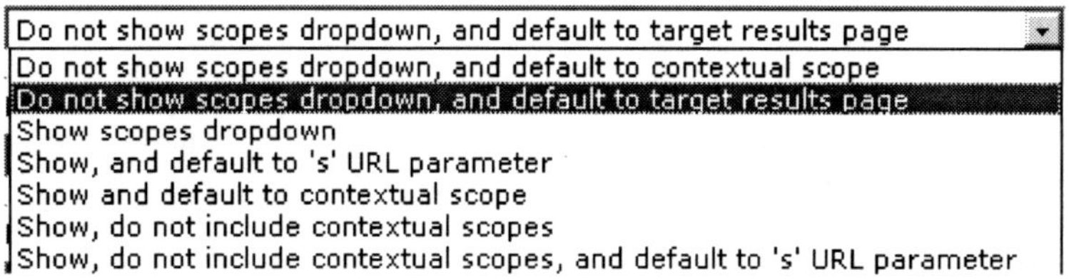

**Figure 6-5.** *Possible scope visibility modes*

"Contextual scope" means the displayed scope selector will show scopes defined for the current site context. The default setting is to use the default scope of the target results page. Other options are to use the URL parameter, which could be relevant if the query is redirected from another search center, or another external link from where a specific scope should be set as default.

## Query Redirection

Query redirection (Figure 6-6) enables the performed query to be redirected to a search results page on another search center. Redirection is especially useful for when putting search dialogs on custom pages outside the search centers. This way the creator can choose which search center should handle the query while still allowing the search to be performed using a specific scope (given that the results page is configured to use the scope from the URL parameter). Query redirections are configured by specifying the "Target search result page URL". The URL should be entered as a relative path.

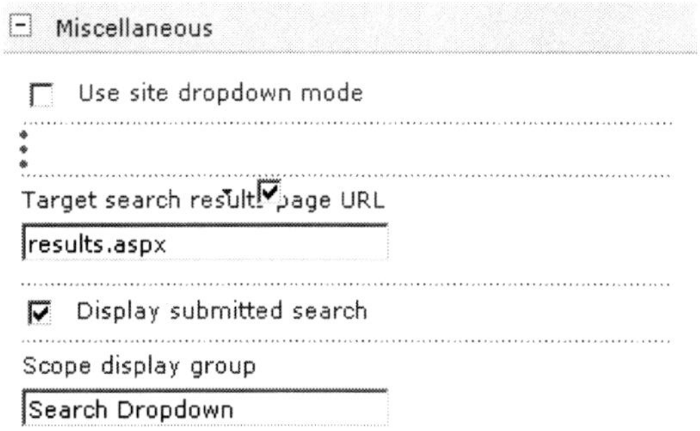

**Figure 6-6.** *Setting query redirection to a specific results page*

The scope display group defines the group of scopes that should be displayed to the user. Managing scopes is described in detail later in this chapter. This way the creator of the search center or the page containing the search dialog can choose which subset of the available scopes to enable for the given search box.

## Query Suggestions

Query suggestions, or search suggestions as they are commonly called, are shown as a drop-down on the search box as the user types in search terms. Search suggestions are shown as "search-as-you-type," if any suggestions exist that match the text in the search box. However, turning on this feature (Figure 6-7) but selecting the Shoq query suggestions check box does have some significant drawbacks that need to be considered. First, the scope from which suggestions are generated is farm-wide, which means that certain search terms might have a different meaning for different departments in an organization. Also it is not always desired that a specific term should yield a search suggestion in all search centers. An example could be that searching for the word "tax" should yield search suggestions on current tax-related issues in a finance department, whereas in the sales department it should yield suggestions on tax related to different product groups and markets instead. Another aspect is secrecy. It might not be desired that everybody have access to suggestions of searches performed by management. These searches might have a private nature. For these reasons, it should be considered whether suggestions are feasible for a given organization or corporation.

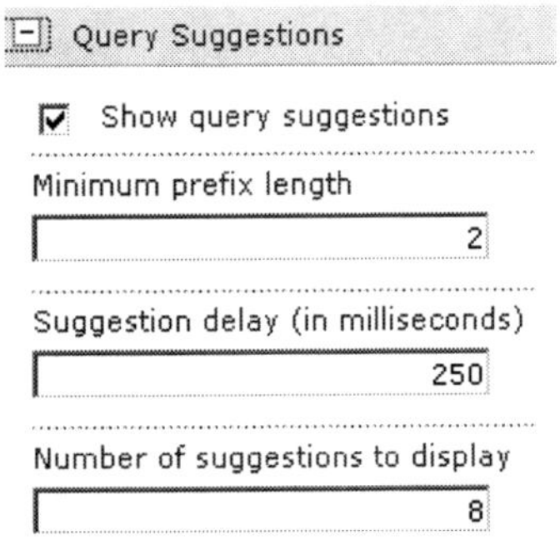

*Figure 6-7. Enabling query suggestions*

Turning on query suggestions introduces some overhead, as new requests to the web application and in turn to the search database are made each time the user enters new text. This can be mitigated to some degree by introducing a suggestion delay and by restricting the number of suggestions to display. If a search box has heavy traffic, it can be a good idea to turn off query suggestions to improve performance.

---

■ **Note** Users can disable query suggestions on the User Preferences page on the search box. Users cannot enable query suggestions on the User Preferences page if they have been disabled on the Search Box Web Part.

---

## Additional Query Terms

In the Query Text Box settings panel (Figure 6-8) it is possible to specify additional query terms. Additional query terms allow the site administrator to define additional terms to be applied to the search. This way the search box can be targeted to specific queries that are feasible in the given context of the search box. In organizations this could be used to further scope the results of a specific search page. For an organization that has a public-facing web site with a lot of subsites each relating to a specific topic, it might be useful that queries performed in the search box or search center of that site return only items relevant to that particular site, but not limited to specific content by the normal scopes group. An example could be a help organization that has country-specific sites. It could limit the search result set of queries performed on each country-specific site to yield only results that contain that particular country name, disregarding the actual location of the result.

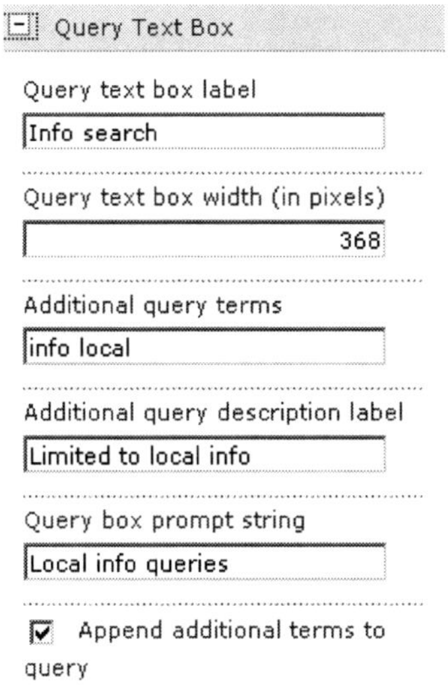

**Figure 6-8.** *Augmenting the query*

If the terms *info* and *local* are specified, as in Figure 6-8, the search result set will now be dependent on these additional terms being present. It is recommended to use the "Additional query description label" and the "Query box prompt string" to give the user hints about the purpose of the given search box, as shown in Figure 6-9.

**Figure 6-9.** *Example of hints when using queries augmented with a fixed keyword*

It is important to understand that adding query terms to limit the search results returned *does not* replace proper security trimming. It should be used only in cases where the context of the search makes it relevant to append query terms to narrow down search results.

# Search Core Results

The Search Core Results Web Part is used to execute and display search results. The query itself is specified as URL parameters. The query can be augmented and/or modified by settings on the Web Part. In this section, we will look at configuring the following search-related settings (Figure 6-10) of the Search Core Results: Location Properties, Fixed/Appended Query Terms and Language, and Metadata and Sorting. Also, on this Web Part the layout of the search results can be customized using XSLT, which is a template that in SharePoint is used to transform the XML output of the Web Part (settings and search results) into HTML, which is then displayed to the user in the browser. Some examples of how to modify the XSLT of the Search Core Results Web Part are given in Chapter 7.

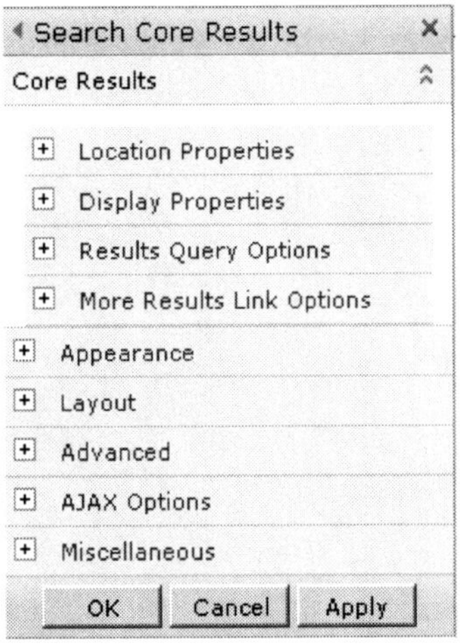

*Figure 6-10. Search Core Results settings*

## Location Properties

Per default the Search Core Results Web Part is unscoped, as shown in Figure 6-11, but it uses the scope defined by the URL parameter "s" if defined. You can configure a default scope to use if no "s" parameter is given. The "s" parameter is especially useful in cases where a direct link to the search results page is given. Such scenarios could be a link on a content page where the link then includes search terms and scopes for a specific topic related to that page. For instance, an organization could have a link to a People search results page for people in a specific department instead of having to maintain that information on the page itself. To set a hard-coded scope, enter the scope name in the Scope text box.

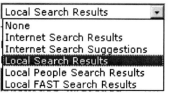

**Figure 6-11.** *Choosing a search location*

The Location property (Figure 6-12) is used to allow selection between local and federated locations. The selected Location property also affects which metadata properties can be included in the search results Web Part.

**Figure 6-12.** *Possible federated search locations*

Local options include the following:

- *Local Search Results*: This is used for normal searching.

- *Local People Search Results*: The only hard-coded scope in SP2010; people searching includes special functionality to support better searching for similar spelled names, etc.

- *Local FAST Search Results*: This is used for normal searching with FAST.

187

Federated options include the following:

- *Internet Search Results*: Federated search returning results from Microsoft's Live Search

- *Internet Search Suggestions*: Federated-related searches (suggestions) from Microsoft Live Search

- *Custom Federated Locations*: Any custom-defined federated locations will also show up as a selectable option.

---

▓ **Note** New locations are added using the Federated Locations page on the SSA, as described later in this chapter.

---

## Fixed/Appended Query Terms and Language

The Results Query Options dialog (Figure 6-13) has options for defining both fixed queries and auto-appending pre-defined query terms to the user's query. It also has a setting for modifying the query behavior by specifying a query language.

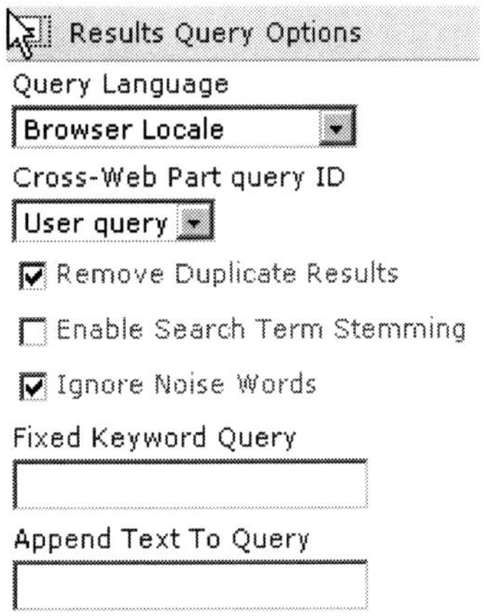

*Figure 6-13. Setting query language and augmenting the query of Search Core Results Web Part*

### Query Language

One of the most important and often ignored options is the query language. All modern browsers allow the user to define a browser language. This is not the language of the browser interface, but the language preference submitted to web sites. The result set returned by SharePoint or most federated locations is affected by the language preference. A common confusion for end users is why certain results are not returned or why they get different results returned when performing the same search on different computers. Setting a default language forces the search to be executed using a specific language, word breaker, noiseword table, and stemming (if enabled).

### Fixed Searches

The Fixed Keyword Query setting is an easy way to define specific searches that do not require user input. The Search Core Results Web Part can be placed on any page. If a fixed keyword query is defined, the results view will automatically be populated with the corresponding results when the user enters that page.

The main reason this is such a powerful option is that it also accepts complex queries. It is possible to set the fixed keyword query to always search and display news from a specific department in a given time frame using a department managed property and one of the date property values.

### Appended Searches

It is also possible to append text to the existing query (similar to the Search Box Web Part). This allows all queries redirected to the given page containing this Search Core Results Web Part to be augmented by this appended text. The relevancy is, for example, if the search center is targeting specific content. Thus the appended text acts as a result set filter.

## Metadata and Sorting

The Custom columns setting, which is configured by editing the Fetched Properties text box (Figure 6-14), is used to specify the metadata to output to the search result XML. This allows custom properties or metadata to be displayed by modifying the XSLT template. In Chapter 7, an example is given of how to add ratings metadata and display it by modifying the XSLT.

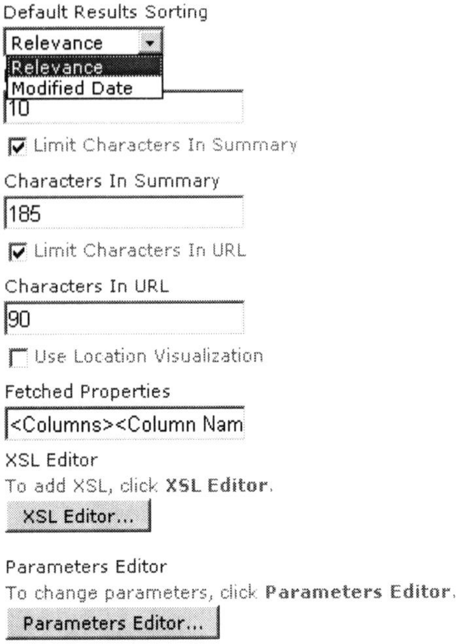

**Figure 6-14.** *Configuring search output*

The Location property, which specifies the location to fetch properties from, affects which metadata properties will be available. For the selected location, only properties relevant to this location are available. The relevant properties are defined at Search service application level if it is a SharePoint location. For other locations outside SharePoint, they are not.

If Use Location Visualization is selected, the fetched properties are automatically populated and the section is grayed out. If it is required to edit which columns to fetch and output, deselect Use Location Visualization. This makes the fetched properties text box editable. If the Fetched Properties are configured to include a property that is not available from the location, that property will not be included in the XML output from the Web Part, which means that it has no effect when used in an XSLT template.

To edit the location visualization, go to the Search service application and open Local Search Results Federated Location. Here a new section for the Core Search Results metadata is added.

The benefit is that it allows a consistent look and feel to be defined for search results on all search centers on the farm. As mentioned this can be overridden locally by unchecking the Use Location Visualization check box and defining which columns to output.

To add a custom column and display it in the Search Core Results Web Part, do the following:

1.  *Check for crawled property.* Make sure the custom property is crawled. This can be done by searching for it in the crawled properties collection on the relevant Search application.

2.  *Create managed property.* Create a new managed property, and map this managed property's custom column crawled property.

3. *Add property to Web Part output*: On the Display Properties group of the Search Core Results Web Part, add the new property to the Columns section by typing the new column name as `<Column Name="custom_property" />`.

4. *Add property to XSL*: Add the column for the custom property to the XSL template such that it gets rendered. This is done by clicking the XSL Editor button, which opens the browser-based XSL text editor. Locate and apply the appropriate rendering logic inside: `<xsl:template match="Result">`.

Another important option is the Default Results Sorting setting. In standard SharePoint 2010 Search, it is not possible to configure sorting for properties other than Ranking and Modified Date. This is possible in FAST search, where sorting can be configured for all metadata properties, including custom properties.

---

▪ **Note** Crawled properties are prefixed by an acronym for its typename. If the custom property is of type string and the name is "`custom_property`", the crawled property will be "`ows_custom_property`".

---

## Top Federated Results

The Top Federated Results Web Part settings (Figure 6-15) are used to execute and display search results from federated locations. They contain the same search settings as the Search Core Results Web Part with the exception of the Location properties. A notable advantage of this Web Part is the option to aggregate results from several locations. In this section, we will look at the following search-related settings of the Top Federated Results: choosing a federated location and using the asynchronous Ajax options. How to create and edit locations is covered later in this chapter.

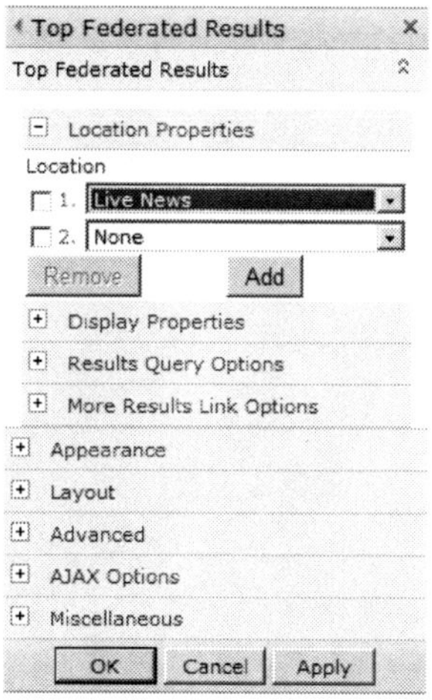

*Figure 6-15. Top Federated Results settings*

## Choosing a Federated Location

To use any new federated location, choose it from the Location drop-down. Alternatively the pre-defined Internet Search Results location can be selected. This searches **http://bing.com** using the OpenSearch 1.1 standard and RSS. To complete the configuration, follow these steps. The results are shown in Figure 6-16.

1. After selecting a location, click Apply, and then OK.

2. Click Stop Editing on the ribbon, and test the new settings with a query.

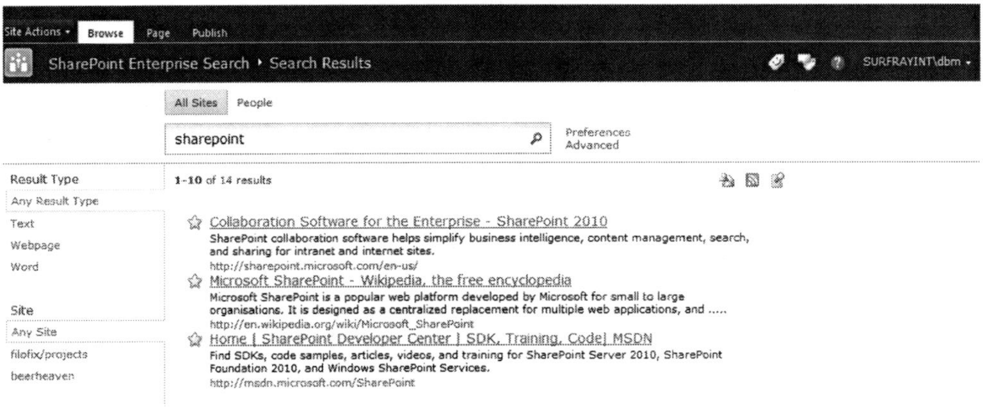

**Figure 6-16.** *Example of top federated results*

## Using the Asynchronous Ajax Options

One of the important but often overlooked features is the option to use asynchronous loading of federated search results (Figure 6-17). Some federated sources may respond slowly, causing the user interface in SP2010 to seem unresponsive.

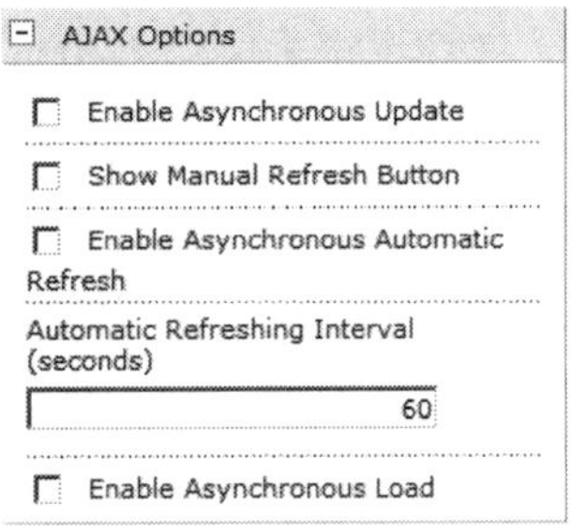

**Figure 6-17.** *Asynchronous loading of external content*

Per default, the user interface will not render until the entire page is ready, which includes fetching all federated search results. To avoid this, it is recommended to use the Enable Asynchronous Load option for federated locations outside your company's control.

# Refinement Panel

A new Web Part in SP2010 is the Refinement Panel Web Part, also known as the refinement panel. The Web Part allows users to drill down through the set of search results based upon managed properties, metadata, and other criteria. One thing to pay attention to is that refiners in SharePoint 2010 are *not* deep refiners. They are based on analysis of a subset of the full result set. Only FAST offers deep refiners. In this section, we will look at the following search-related settings (Figure 6-18) of the refinement panel: "General refiner settings," "Adding custom refinements from managed metadata columns," and "Adding custom refinements from managed properties."

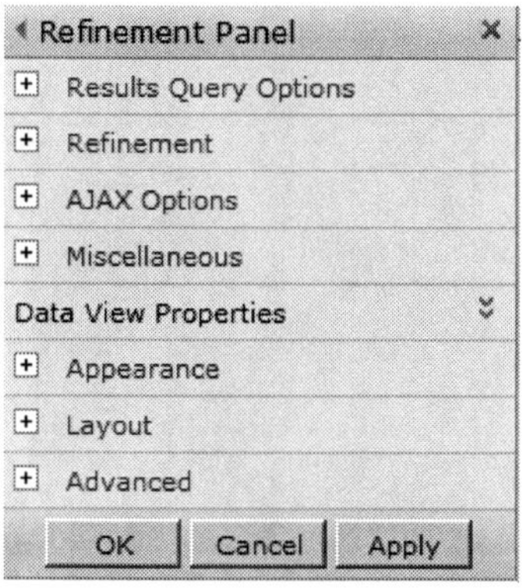

*Figure 6-18. Refinement Panel settings*

To the left of Figure 6-19, the set of refinements that is available out of the box is shown. These are all preconfigured in SharePoint 2010. There are a number of refinements built in, including file type, site, author, modified date, and taxonomy keywords (if any are available).

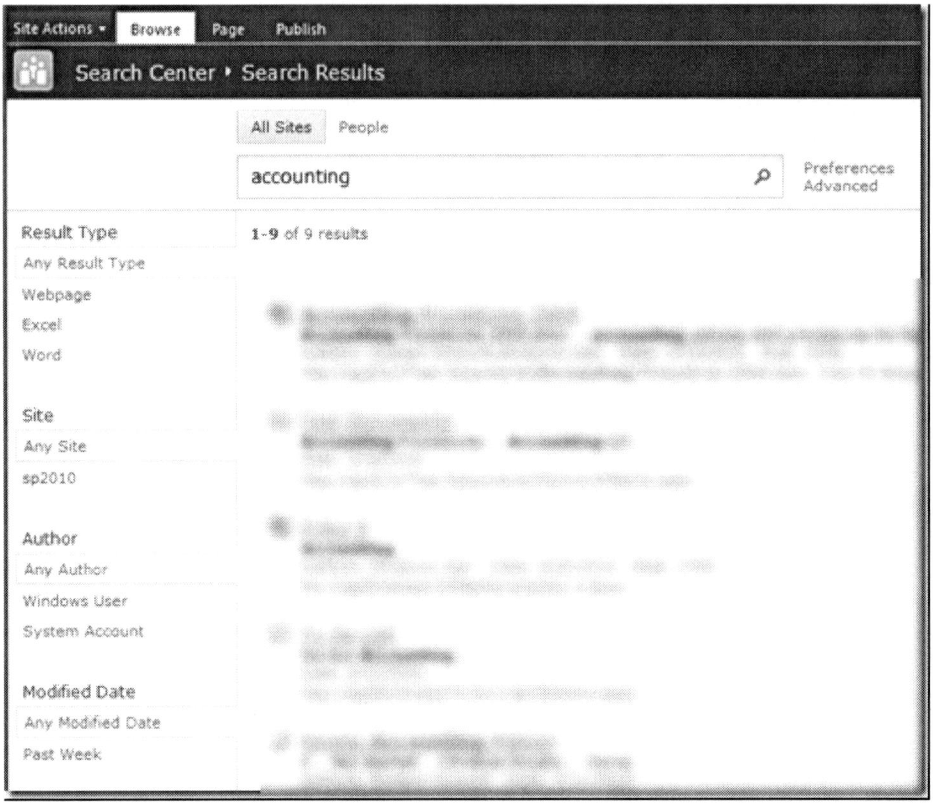

*Figure 6-19. Example of default refiners in SP2010*

## General Refiner Settings

The refiner Web Part has some powerful settings (Figure 6-20) allowing easy implementation of custom refinement categories based on managed metadata columns and managed properties.

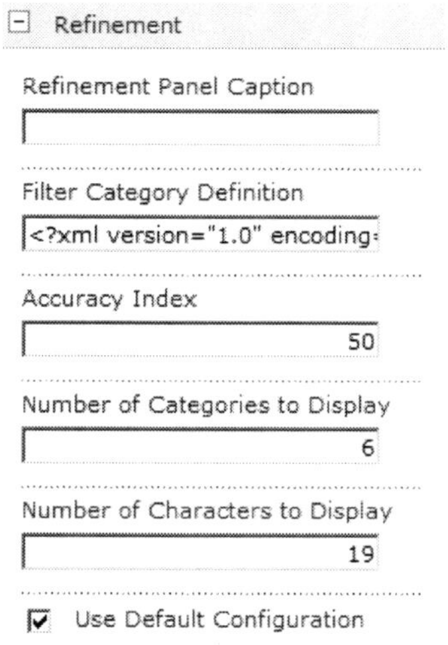

*Figure 6-20. Refinement configuration*

The Filter Category Definition property is a XML field where each category is specified. We'll also look at that later in the chapter.

The accuracy index is the number of results it looks at to determine things to refine. What this does mean is that if there is something unique to refine on but it doesn't occur until result number 51, then it will not be included. The accuracy index has a hard-coded upper limit of 500 to avoid excessive resource usage.

The maximum number of categories to display can be specified. This is set to six by default. Exclusion will be performed by the ordering of the categories in the Filter Category Definition.

The Use Default Configuration check box controls if default or custom values will be used.

---

■ **Note** The Use Default Configuration check box must be unchecked when modifying the filter category definition and other settings. Otherwise any edited settings will not take effect.

---

## Adding a Refiner Category from Managed Metadata Columns

It is very easy to add a new refiner category if the column type is managed metadata. In this case, the SharePoint search engine will automatically create managed properties out of the crawled properties. The only manual step included is to add the appropriate XML to the Refinement Panel Filter Category Definition XML file. It is possible to set many more options than the ones shown in Listing 6-1.

*Listing 6-1. XML for Managed Metadata Column*

```
<Category Title="Field Name"↵
Type="Microsoft.Office.Server.Search.WebControls.TaxonomyFilterGenerator"↵
MappedProperty="ows_MetadataFacetInfo" MoreLinkText="Show More" MetadataThreshold="1"↵
NumberOfFiltersToDisplay="5"/>
```

These are the minimum required options in the XML.

- *Title* is the name of the column or field that the managed metadata is mapped to. *Type* has to be set to TaxonomyFilterGenerator for Managed Metadata fields. The *mapped property* for Managed Metadata fields has to be set to `ows_MetadataFacetInfo`.

Uncheck the Use Default Configuration option, and execute a search that yields multiple values for the added managed metadata column. In the default Filter Definition Configuration file, two categories are per default defined in this fashion. These are Managed Metadata Columns and Tags. The difference between the two is that the Tags category is used for the enterprise keywords, while the Managed Metadata Columns category is used for managed metadata columns. This means that the refinement panel presents two different sources of data. The managed metadata columns are for filtering based on the data coming from the result set, whereas the tags are used for narrowing the search based on keywords.

## Adding a Refiner Category from Managed Properties

If a metadata column is not managed, the crawler needs to be configured to index this column in order to make it available for searching. To accomplish this, a new managed property must be created as follows:

1. Go to Central Administration ➤ Manage Service Applications ➤ Search Service Application ➤ Metadata Properties.

2. Create a new managed property. Add a mapping to the crawled property for your column (e.g., `ows_custom_0x0020_property`), and perform a full crawl on the appropriate content sources.

---

■ **Note** See `http://technet.microsoft.com/en-us/library/ee424403.aspx` for details on managed metadata.

---

3. The crawled property is now mapped to a managed property and can be used in the refinement panel by modifying the Filter Category Definition on the Refiner Web Part.

4.  Add the XML in Listing 6-2 to the Refinement Panel Filter Category Definition XML file. Uncheck the Use Default Configuration option, and execute a search that yields multiple values for the added managed property.

*Listing 6-2. XML for Managed Property*

```
<Category Title="Process Step"
        Description="Process Step of the document"
        Type="Microsoft.Office.Server.Search.WebControls.ManagedPropertyFilterGenerator"
        MetadataThreshold="5"
        NumberOfFiltersToDisplay="4"
        MaxNumberOfFilters="20"
        ShowMoreLink="True"
        MappedProperty="ProcessStep" />
```

The following is a brief description of each line in Listing 6-2.

- *Title:* This is the name of the category to display.

- *Description:* This is the text to be shown as a hint for the filters.

- *Type:* This has to be set to **ManagedPropertyFilterGenerator** for managed properties.

- *MetadataThreshold:* This is the minimum required possible options returned for this filter before the category will be displayed.

- *NumberOfFiltersToDisplay:* This is the maximum number of possible options to show for this category in default view.

- *MaxNumberOfFilters:* This is the maximum number of possible options to collect for this category.

- *ShowMoreLink:* Whether a link should be displayed if more than **NumberOfFiltersToDisplay** is returned

- *MappedProperty:* For managed properties, this is the name of the column or field that the managed property is mapped to.

---

▓ **Note** If Use Default Configuration is checked, the changes will not be reflected in the refinement panel. This is a typical source of frustration. Also, checking it again will override whatever changes have been made, so always back up any configuration made to XML files.

---

## Why Are the Refiners Not Showing?

When the refiners are not showing as expected, this is often caused by one of the following:

- A full crawl has not been executed after the managed property has been created.

- The result set is not big enough to contain data for the relevant column to make the refiner meaningful.

- The refiners are shown in the order they are defined in the XML. For example, if the new refiner category is placed as category number 7, but the refinement panel is configured to show only the first six categories, it will not be displayed in the panel (if the first six categories are shown).

■ **Note** The concept of refiners or faceted search is not part of SharePoint 2007, although a significant number of search centers actually have refiners based on either the faceted search Web Part from CodePlex or the more complex search center offered by the Ontolica product from SurfRay. The latter actually includes numbered refiners for both SP2007 and SP2010.

# Federated Search

Previously in this chapter, it was shown how to select a location to search on the Search Core Results Web Part. Locations are central to the new way search works in SharePoint 2010. Now, the search framework is centered around federation and federated locations.

This section focuses on understanding what federated locations are as well as best practices on how to use them. It also gives a detailed description of typical management tasks related to federated locations.

## Federated Locations

SharePoint 2010 comes with a preconfigured set of locations (Figure 6-21), which includes local locations that are indexed and searched by the SharePoint 2010 search engine. It is, however, sometimes required that content is indexed outside SharePoint. The list of locations can be expanded to include other federated locations as long as they support the OpenSearch 1.0 or OpenSearch 1.1 standards.

Examples of when federation is feasible include the following:

- Large external content sources that are already indexed elsewhere; Wikipedia is an example of this.

- When the scheduled crawler in SharePoint is not optimal—for instance, when content changes rapidly and needs to be immediately available. For these cases a custom crawler and index are better.

- Security setup requires a context not available in SharePoint. This could, for example, be when content is stored on a different isolated domain and the search needs to be performed using a different security context.

- The content is indexed externally and only searched for rarely, which makes it overkill to index it in SharePoint.

- The limitation of 500 content sources in SharePoint forces the use of federated locations.

In some cases, however, it is not feasible to use federation. Examples of this include the following:

- Bandwith between the SharePoint farm and the federated location is too small such that crawling and indexing are not possible with a reasonable performance.

- The content to be indexed is changing rapidly but does not need to be immediately available.

- It is not possible or feasible to index the content externally.

- It is not possible to make the content searchable through the supported OpenSearch specifications.

Federation is configured from the Search service application. To open the federation page, go to Central Administration ➤ Search Service Application ➤ Federated Locations.

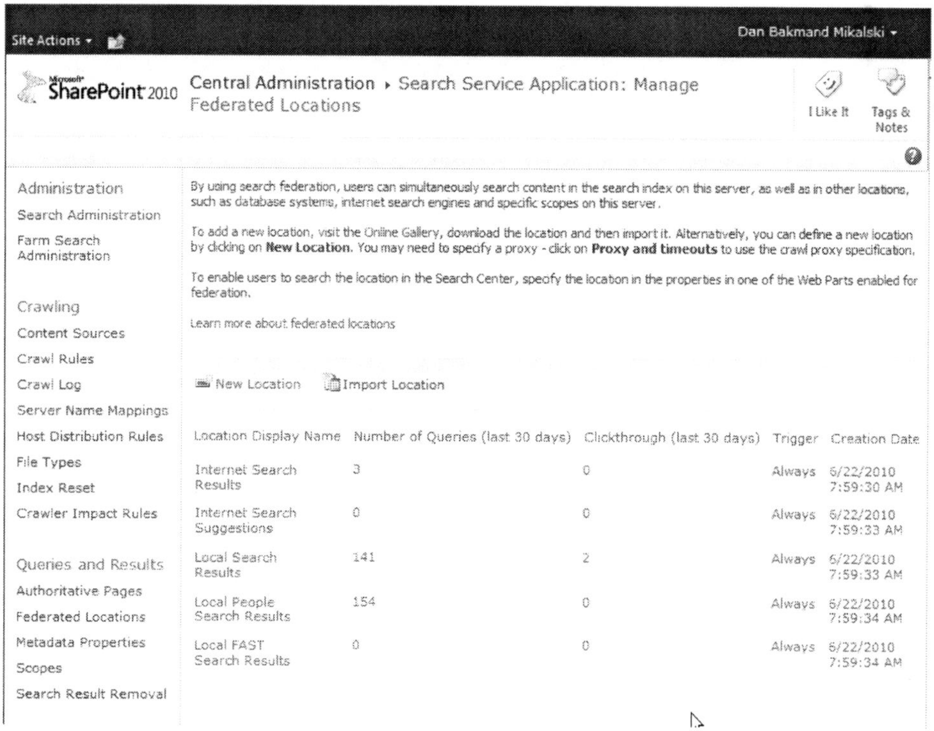

**Figure 6-21.** *Federated Locations page*

A new federated location can be created in three ways:

- *Import Location*: It will prompt for an FLD (Federated Location Definition) file. This file contains all information required to automatically configure the location.

- *New Location*: All settings must be specified from scratch.

- *Copy Location*: Option available on the drop-down of existing locations; this will duplicate that location and its settings.

Which method should be chosen depends on the scenario. For cases where an FLD file already exists, this option is best. Even if the FLD file does not contain the exact configuration needed, it is much easier to modify an existing definition than to create one from scratch. The same thing applies if a definition that is similar to the new one exists. Then it is almost always a better choice to use the Copy option to duplicate an existing location and then modify it as needed. This is generally the best practice with SharePoint. Start with something that works, and then modify it. A lot of developers and IT professionals have spent countless hours trying to solve problems that are hard to identify because they attempted to configure from scratch instead of modifying something that works. SharePoint is not always generous with its error messages.

■ **Note** Federated locations must support the OpenSearch 1.0/1.1 standards.

## Import Location

The easiest way to add a new federated location is to use the location's FLD file for SharePoint 2010 (if one exists). FLD files are typically 15–50 kilobytes. The FLD file contains all the rules and markup required to make it show in the SharePoint federated search Web Part.

■ **Note** Microsoft has published a set of federated search connectors on `http://technet.microsoft.com/en-us/enterprisesearch/ff727944.aspx`.

To add a connector to SP2010 (Figure 6-22), follow these steps:

1. Open the federation page: Central Administration ➤ Search Service Application ➤ Federated Locations.

2. Click Import Location to open the file dialog.

3. Browse to the FLD file, and click the OK button.

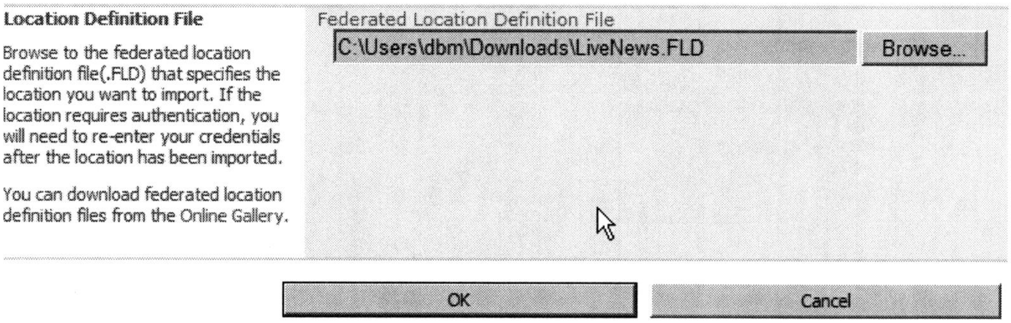

**Location Definition File**

Browse to the federated location definition file(.FLD) that specifies the location you want to import. If the location requires authentication, you will need to re-enter your credentials after the location has been imported.

You can download federated location definition files from the Online Gallery.

Federated Location Definition File

C:\Users\dbm\Downloads\LiveNews.FLD

Browse...

OK                    Cancel

*Figure 6-22. Loading FLD file*

After importing an FLD file, a prompt will be shown with the import result (Figure 6-23). It is not possible to import malformed FLD documents. The important part of this message is the note that the location must be added to a property on the relevant Web Part in the search center.

The location "Live News" was successfully imported.

Click **Edit Location** to modify settings such as the display name, triggers and authentication credentials.
To use the location, it must be added to the properties of a federation-enabled Web Part in the Search Center site.

**Note:** If the location requires authentication, you will need to re-enter your credentials.

Edit Location                    Done

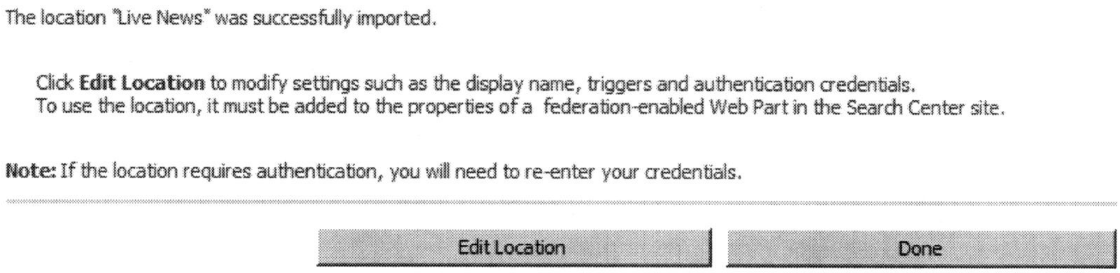

*Figure 6-23. FLD file loaded result*

After successfully importing the FLD file, it now shows as an item in the Federated Locations list (Figure 6-24).

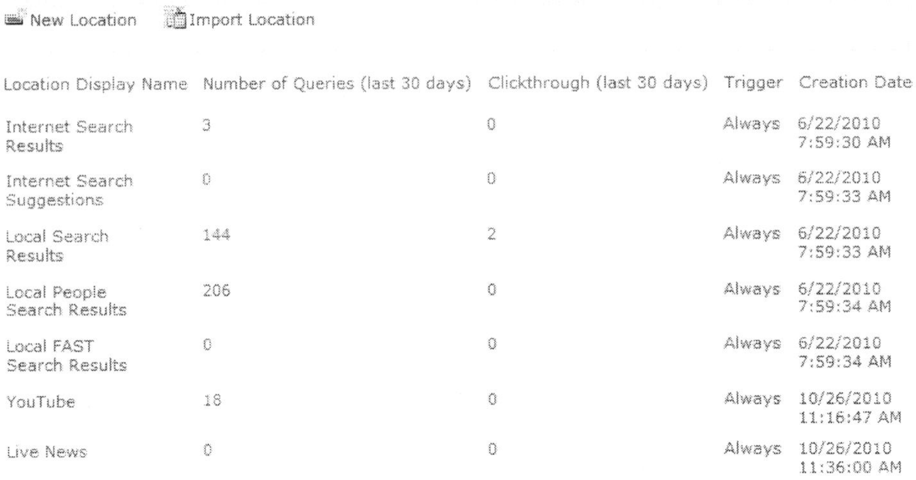

📰 New Location    📑 Import Location

| Location Display Name | Number of Queries (last 30 days) | Clickthrough (last 30 days) | Trigger | Creation Date |
|---|---|---|---|---|
| Internet Search Results | 3 | 0 | Always | 6/22/2010 7:59:30 AM |
| Internet Search Suggestions | 0 | 0 | Always | 6/22/2010 7:59:33 AM |
| Local Search Results | 144 | 2 | Always | 6/22/2010 7:59:33 AM |
| Local People Search Results | 206 | 0 | Always | 6/22/2010 7:59:34 AM |
| Local FAST Search Results | 0 | 0 | Always | 6/22/2010 7:59:34 AM |
| YouTube | 18 | 0 | Always | 10/26/2010 11:16:47 AM |
| Live News | 0 | 0 | Always | 10/26/2010 11:36:00 AM |

*Figure 6-24. Federated Locations page with new locations*

## New Location

New federated locations (Figure 6-25) can be created for both the existing SP2010 index or for external search indexes. SP2010 offers great functionality for easing the configuration of adding external federated sources and displaying results from them.

To add a new federated location to SP2010, do the following:

1.  Open the federation page: Central Administration ➤ Search Service Application ➤ Federated Locations.

2.  Click New Location to open the Create Location page.

3.  Enter the appropriate information, and continue to the next section.

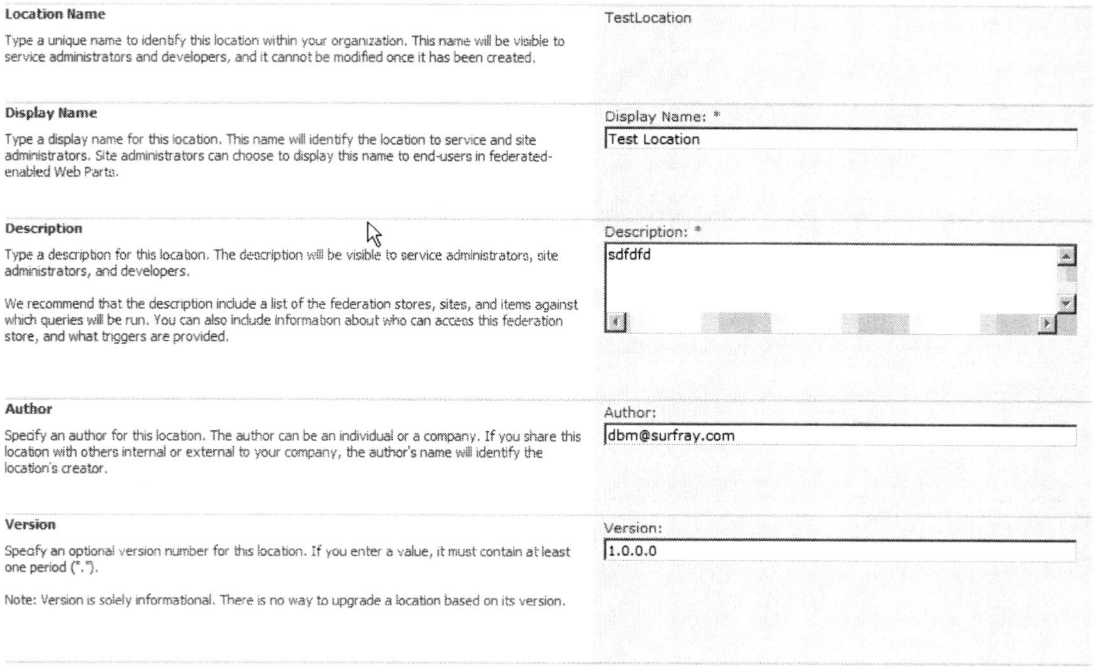

**Location Name**

Type a unique name to identify this location within your organization. This name will be visible to service administrators and developers, and it cannot be modified once it has been created.

TestLocation

**Display Name**

Type a display name for this location. This name will identify the location to service and site administrators. Site administrators can choose to display this name to end-users in federated-enabled Web Parts.

Display Name: *

Test Location

**Description**

Type a description for this location. The description will be visible to service administrators, site administrators, and developers.

We recommend that the description include a list of the federation stores, sites, and items against which queries will be run. You can also include information about who can access this federation store, and what triggers are provided.

Description: *

sdfdfd

**Author**

Specify an author for this location. The author can be an individual or a company. If you share this location with others internal or external to your company, the author's name will identify the location's creator.

Author:

dbm@surfray.com

**Version**

Specify an optional version number for this location. If you enter a value, it must contain at least one period (".").

Note: Version is solely informational. There is no way to upgrade a location based on its version.

Version:

1.0.0.0

***Figure 6-25.*** *Location creation—general settings*

Choose a trigger for the federated search (Figure 6-26). In most cases, this will be set to Always. Filters can, however, be applied to provide logic for when the federated location should be queried.

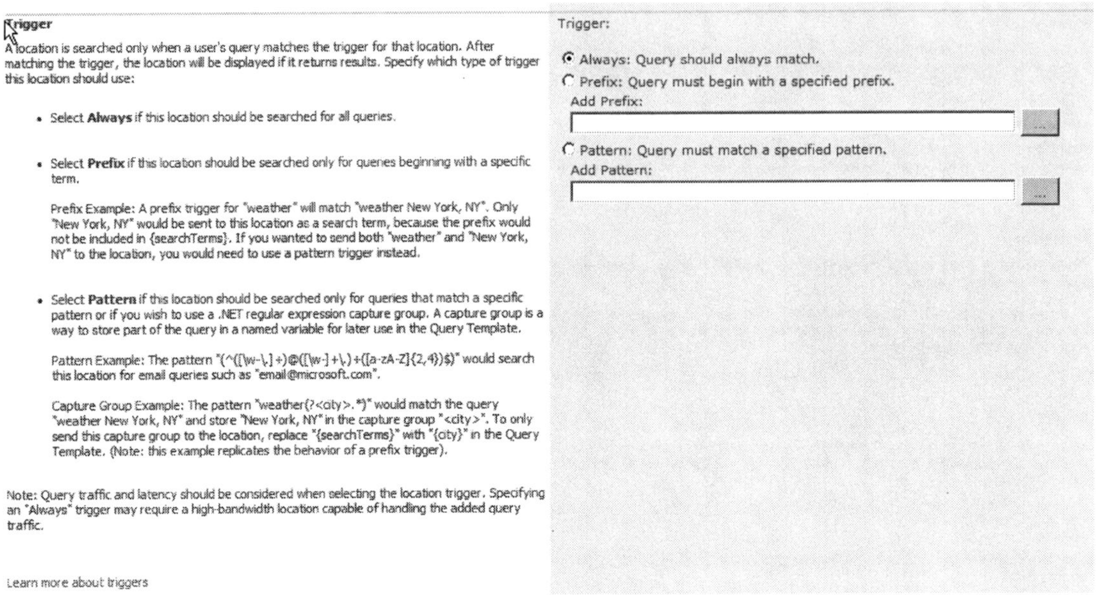

**Trigger**

A location is searched only when a user's query matches the trigger for that location. After matching the trigger, the location will be displayed if it returns results. Specify which type of trigger this location should use:

- Select **Always** if this location should be searched for all queries.

- Select **Prefix** if this location should be searched only for queries beginning with a specific term.

  Prefix Example: A prefix trigger for "weather" will match "weather New York, NY". Only "New York, NY" would be sent to this location as a search term, because the prefix would not be included in {searchTerms}. If you wanted to send both "weather" and "New York, NY" to the location, you would need to use a pattern trigger instead.

- Select **Pattern** if this location should be searched only for queries that match a specific pattern or if you wish to use a .NET regular expression capture group. A capture group is a way to store part of the query in a named variable for later use in the Query Template.

  Pattern Example: The pattern "(^([\w-\.]+)@([\w-]+\.)+([a-zA-Z]{2,4})$)" would search this location for email queries such as "email@microsoft.com".

  Capture Group Example: The pattern "weather(?<city>.*)" would match the query "weather New York, NY" and store "New York, NY" in the capture group "<city>". To only send this capture group to the location, replace "{searchTerms}" with "{city}" in the Query Template. (Note: this example replicates the behavior of a prefix trigger).

Note: Query traffic and latency should be considered when selecting the location trigger. Specifying an "Always" trigger may require a high-bandwidth location capable of handling the added query traffic.

Learn more about triggers

Trigger:

- ⦿ Always: Query should always match.
- ○ Prefix: Query must begin with a specified prefix.
  Add Prefix:
- ○ Pattern: Query must match a specified pattern.
  Add Pattern:

*Figure 6-26. Location creation—trigger settings*

Select the appropriate Location information (Figure 6-27). To query external search indexes, they must support OpenSearch version 1.0 or 1.1. This is not required for the internal search index.

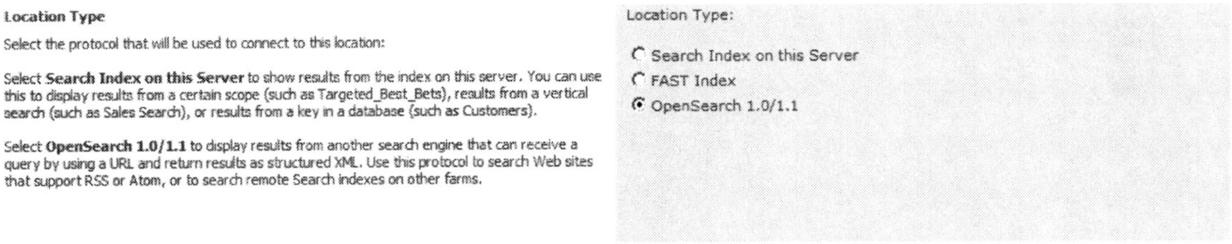

**Location Type**

Select the protocol that will be used to connect to this location:

Select **Search Index on this Server** to show results from the index on this server. You can use this to display results from a certain scope (such as Targeted_Best_Bets), results from a vertical search (such as Sales Search), or results from a key in a database (such as Customers).

Select **OpenSearch 1.0/1.1** to display results from another search engine that can receive a query by using a URL and return results as structured XML. Use this protocol to search Web sites that support RSS or Atom, or to search remote Search indexes on other farms.

Location Type:

- ○ Search Index on this Server
- ○ FAST Index
- ⦿ OpenSearch 1.0/1.1

*Figure 6-27. Location creation—location type*

The query template defines the URL to query and the filters to be applied to the query. For live search, this could be **http://search.live.com/news/results.aspx?q={searchTerms}&format=rss**, as shown in Figure 6-28.

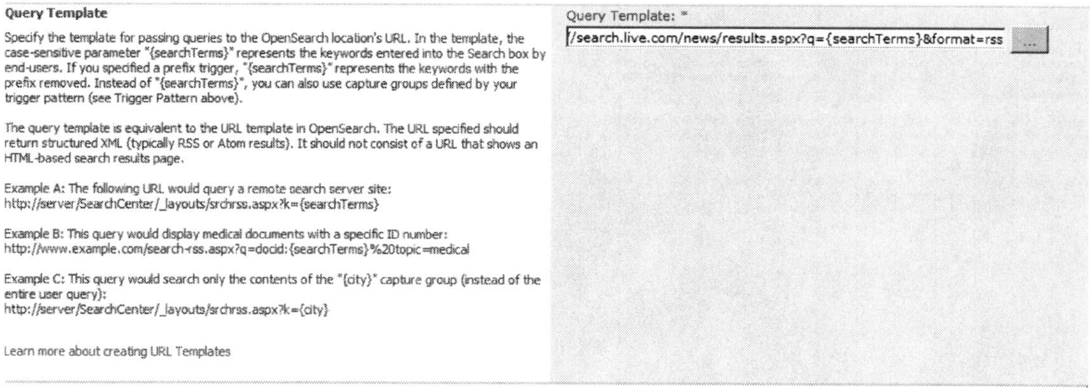

**Query Template**

Specify the template for passing queries to the OpenSearch location's URL. In the template, the case-sensitive parameter "{searchTerms}" represents the keywords entered into the Search box by end-users. If you specified a prefix trigger, "{searchTerms}" represents the keywords with the prefix removed. Instead of "{searchTerms}", you can also use capture groups defined by your trigger pattern (see Trigger Pattern above).

The query template is equivalent to the URL template in OpenSearch. The URL specified should return structured XML (typically RSS or Atom results). It should not consist of a URL that shows an HTML-based search results page.

Example A: The following URL would query a remote search server site:
http://server/SearchCenter/_layouts/srchrss.aspx?k={searchTerms}

Example B: This query would display medical documents with a specific ID number:
http://www.example.com/search-rss.aspx?q=docid:{searchTerms}%20topic=medical

Example C: This query would search only the contents of the "{city}" capture group (instead of the entire user query):
http://server/SearchCenter/_layouts/srchrss.aspx?k={city}

Learn more about creating URL Templates

Query Template: *

/search.live.com/news/results.aspx?q={searchTerms}&format=rss

*Figure 6-28. Location creation—query template*

The "More Results" Link Template box (Figure 6-29) defines the navigation URL that allows the end user to request more results. This is per default disabled on the Top Federated Results Web Part. For live search, this could be **http://search.live.com/news/results.aspx?q={searchTerms}&mkt=en-us&scope=&FORM=LIVSOP**.

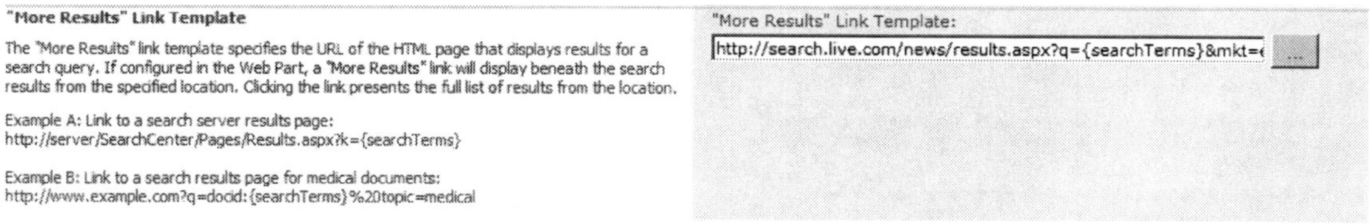

**"More Results" Link Template**

The "More Results" link template specifies the URL of the HTML page that displays results for a search query. If configured in the Web Part, a "More Results" link will display beneath the search results from the specified location. Clicking the link presents the full list of results from the location.

Example A: Link to a search server results page:
http://server/SearchCenter/Pages/Results.aspx?k={searchTerms}

Example B: Link to a search results page for medical documents:
http://www.example.com?q=docid:{searchTerms}%20topic=medical

"More Results" Link Template:

http://search.live.com/news/results.aspx?q={searchTerms}&mkt=

*Figure 6-29. Location creation—"More Results" Link Template box*

The Display setting defines how search results will be presented in the user interface (Figure 6-30). SharePoint 2010 can show results from almost all sources in a nicely formatted manner. Some federated locations, however, might benefit from customized formatting. An example could be YouTube videos if YouTube is selected as a federated location.

**Top Federated Results Display Metadata**

XSL transforms structured XML results returned by the location into HTML, which is shown in the Top Federated Results Web Part. The included default XSL is adequate for most scenarios. To customize how results, text, and images are displayed in the Top Federated Results Web Part, you can edit the default XSL.

Properties determine which metadata is returned with each search result. The default list of metadata is adequate for most scenarios. To customize the metadata displayed on a result, edit the list of returned properties and update the XSL to display the new properties.

Sample data is used to provide a visual preview of the Top Federated Results Web Part when it is edited in a SharePoint Foundation-compatible editor.

☑ Use Default Formatting

XSL:
```
<xsl:stylesheet xmlns:x="http://www.w3.org/2001/XMLSchema"
        version="1.0" exclude-result-prefixes="xsl ddwrt msxs
        xmlns:ddwrt="http://schemas.microsoft.com/WebPart
        xmlns:scwrt="http://schemas.microsoft.com/WebParts
```

Properties:
```
<Columns>
    <Column Name="title"/>
    <Column Name="link"/>
    <Column Name="description"/>
```

Sample Data:
```
<rss version="2.0">
    <channel>
        <title></title>
        <link> http://www.samole.com/</link>
```

*Figure 6-30. Location creation—Top Federated Results Display Metadata options*

It is possible to restrict usage of locations (Figure 6-31). Some search indexes require authentication. SP2010 offers options to use either anonymous access, common authentication, or user authentication. Common authentication is relevant for searching secured internal repositories available to all employees. User authentication is relevant when not all users of the search center with the federated search results are permitted to view the entire source data of the search index.

**Restrict Usage**

Specify whether you want to restrict the sites that can use this location.

Select **No restriction** if site administrators from any site can use this location.

Select **Use restriction** if only site administrators from specific URL domains can use this location. By using this option, you can restrict access to confidential data or limit the number of people who can access the location.

In the **Allowed Sites** list, use a semicolon to separate the start addresses of URL domains. For example, the list "http://site1;http://site2" would ensure that the location can only be used in sites starting with http://site1 or http://site2.

Restrict Usage:

⦿ No restriction: All sites can use this location.
○ Use restriction: Only allowed sites can use this location.
Allowed Sites:

**Specify Credentials**

Specify the access credentials for this location.

Select **Anonymous** when the location does not require authentication.

Select an authentication protocol under **Common** when the location requires authentication, and your company uses a single account that all end-users use to authenticate against the location.

Select an authentication protocol under **User** when the location requires authentication and each user has a unique account to authenticate against the location.

⦿ Anonymous: This location does not require authentication

Common:

○ Basic Authentication - Specify a user name and password
○ Digest Authentication - Specify a user name and password
○ NTLM - Use Application Pool Identity
○ NTLM - Specify a username and password
○ Form Authentication - Specify form credentials
○ Cookie Authentication - Use cookie for authentication

User:

○ Kerberos - User credentials passed automatically
○ Basic Authentication - User provides user name and password
○ Digest Authentication - User provides user name and password
○ NTLM - User provides user name and password
○ Form Authentication - User provides form credentials
○ Cookie Authentication - User provides cookie for authentication

*Figure 6-31. Location creation—Restrict Usage and Specify Credentials options*

■ **Note** When searching federated locations, special attention must be paid to the security implications of allowing queries to be sent to external sources. Most search engines store queries for months or years. If the queries themselves contain confidential information, this will be stored at remote sites. As information is sent on unsecured channels, queries can also possibly be intercepted. It is always recommended to do a security review before using external federated locations.

## Copy Location

New locations can also be created by copying an existing location (Figure 6-32). This is useful if the new location should be similar to an already existing location. Copying federated locations is an easy way to get started with creating a new federated location. SP2010 offers great functionality for easing the configuration of adding external federated sources and displaying results from them.

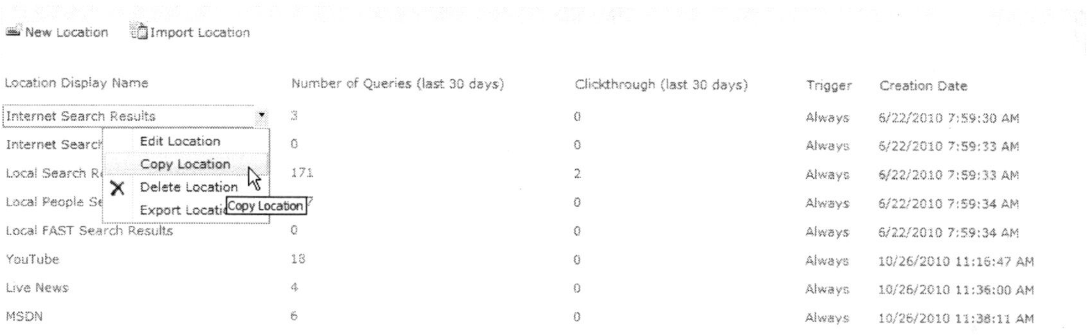

| Location Display Name | Number of Queries (last 30 days) | Clickthrough (last 30 days) | Trigger | Creation Date |
| --- | --- | --- | --- | --- |
| Internet Search Results | 3 | 0 | Always | 6/22/2010 7:59:30 AM |
| Internet Search | 0 | 0 | Always | 6/22/2010 7:59:33 AM |
| Local Search Re | 171 | 2 | Always | 6/22/2010 7:59:33 AM |
| Local People Se | | 0 | Always | 6/22/2010 7:59:34 AM |
| Local FAST Search Results | 0 | 0 | Always | 6/22/2010 7:59:34 AM |
| YouTube | 18 | 0 | Always | 10/26/2010 11:16:47 AM |
| Live News | 4 | 0 | Always | 10/26/2010 11:36:00 AM |
| MSDN | 6 | 0 | Always | 10/26/2010 11:38:11 AM |

*Figure 6-32. Duplicating locations with the Copy Location option*

To copy an existing federated location, do the following:

1.  Click the drop-down for the location to duplicate, and choose Copy Location. After clicking Copy Location, the Create Location page of the new location will open.

2.  On the Create Location page, all fields will be filled out with the same values as the location that is being duplicated, except the Location Name field (Figure 6-33). This field must be unique and is therefore required to be filled before the copy is completed.

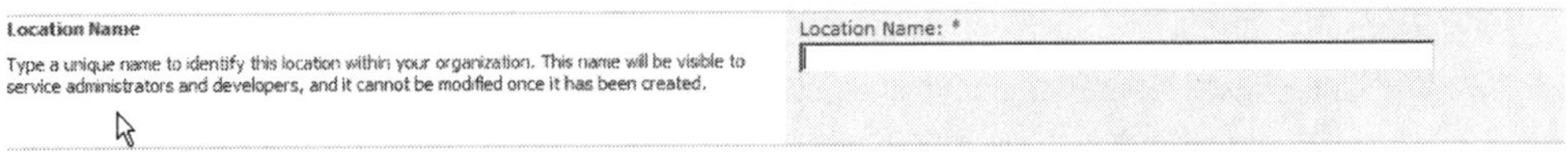

**Figure 6-33.** *Duplicating locations—specify a new unique Location Name*

# The Preferences Page: An Administrator's View

Chapter 5 shows how the Preferences page allows users to set user profile–specific settings for searching. Although this is a very useful feature for users, it is not perfect and does have some drawbacks. This section discusses some of the implications administrators should be aware of.

As mentioned in Chapter 5, the Preferences page is accessed by clicking the Preferences link (Figure 6-34) to the right of the search box.

**Figure 6-34.** *SharePoint 2010 Enterprise Search Center dialog*

## Understanding Why the Preferences Page Improves Search

Letting the user specify settings regarding the search experience directly from the search centers is generally a great idea, as users often have little knowledge about what options exist for tuning their SharePoint experience. This is partly due to the extensive set of possible settings found in the Site settings page (if the user has permission to access this) and partly due to the settings in SharePoint generally being hard to find if not often used. Having this Preferences page will reduce the time required by the administrator or support staff to teach users how to modify the language setting in their browsers and what effect it has. Now this is more intuitive, and most users are expected to grasp the general concept of what this does with less training.

Adding the Preferences link next to the search dialog text box in search centers makes users intuitively aware that they can modify search-related settings and encourages the use of them. The concept is also known from the Google search page, which most users are assumed to be reasonably familiar with.

The Preferences page allows the user to enable/disable search suggestions and to specify the search context language(s) to be used.

## Preferences Scope

The Preferences page is available both in Basic and Enterprise Search Centers. This is obvious as the settings on the Preferences page influence search results from both types of search centers. Preferences are personalized by being bound to a user profile. This way the user will use the same settings regardless of which computer is used to access the search center. In SharePoint 2007, the search context language was based on the browser's language. Preferences are applied globally throughout the SharePoint farm such that they will be the same for all search centers on all web applications.

# Overriding the User's Language Settings

SharePoint 2010 introduces phonetic search and nicknames for People search. As both of these are language-dependent, the Language setting influences the search results returned. The search is performed against all selected languages using stemmers, word breakers, phonetics, and nicknames in all selected languages.

In SharePoint 2007, the administrator has the option of specifying the search context language in the search center to override the browser's Language setting. Even though it is now possible in SharePoint 2010 for users to directly set the language on the Preferences page, this can still be overridden by the administrator. But given that more emphasis has been put on this setting, the administrator needs to be aware of the impact it has on search results. By either overriding the language for search or using the fixed query setting and the Language property to augment the query with a fixed language, this will effectively override whatever setting the user has made. Doing so may cause confusion for users who expect their own Language settings to apply. It is suggested that this gets communicated to users if the Language setting is fixed by the administrator.

On the other hand, giving users access to settings such as the Language setting that directly influences the returned search results can also cause problems from an administrative point of view. Allowing users to define which languages are used for searching reduces the administrator's options for controlling the search behavior and results. This is something that an administrator needs to be aware of when users complain that they cannot find a specific search result.

# Issues to Be Aware Of

Although the Preferences page adds these preferences directly where needed to make the user aware of their existence, it does introduce some problems. The number of settings exposed through the Preferences link is very limited. It allows the user only to turn search suggestions on and off and select the language context of the search.

One important thing that is missed is an easy way for users to learn what a specific setting actually does. In this case, this is actually a significant issue, as both the search suggestions and the Language setting can be difficult for users to grasp if no training or information is provided to them. Still, it is easier than changing the browser's Language setting, as this is something that tends to be forgotten or ignored.

As mentioned earlier, the Search Suggestions feature works only if search suggestions are turned on in the search center. This leads to confusion when the user enables this feature and nothing happens. Although this feature is global for all search centers, it would have been useful to show a warning message to the user on the Preferences page, saying that this feature is not activated on this particular search center as the setting is accessed from the search center where a change is wanted. It might have been a good idea to not include the Search Suggestions feature, as this works only if a site administrator has enabled search suggestions in the search center.

The most important setting from a search perspective is the Language setting. It would have been really useful to create a page only containing this setting. This way the Preferences page would include only the Language option, and the Preferences page could be named accordingly. The argument for why this would be a good idea is that the Language setting influences the returned search result set. Especially for searches that could potentially return search results containing multiple languages, this becomes an issue. An often-heard user complaint in SharePoint 2007 is: "Why are the search results different on my other computer?" The answer in many cases is due to a difference in search context language settings, which in SP2007 were set in the browser's own Language setting. As the Language setting does solve this issue, it would be preferable to expose it more directly.

# Stemmers and Word Breakers

In SharePoint, stemming is used in combination with the word breaker component, which determines where word boundaries are. The word breaker is used at both index and query time, while the stemmer is used only at query time for most languages (exceptions are Arabic and Hebrew). A stemmer links word forms to their base form. For example, "running," "ran," and "runs" are all variants of the verb "to run." Stemming is currently turned off by default for some languages, including English. Stemmers are available only for languages that have significant morphological variation among their word forms. This means that for languages where stemmers are not available (such as Vietnamese), turning on this feature in the search results page (Search Core Results Web Part) will not have any effect, since in such languages an exact match is all that is needed.

Word stemming is not the same thing as wildcard searching, which has to do with doing searches with * in the query. This means you are asking the search engine to find all words that start with the text string and end with anything, since * means match any continuous text string to the end of the word, which in most languages (excluding most East Asian languages) is indicated by a white space. So a search query using * such as "Share*" will return results including "SharePoint," while a search query using the word breaker and stemmer would bring back "sharing," which is an inflectional variant of "share." Wildcard searching and word stemming are often used to refer to the same thing, but they are, in fact, separate and different mechanisms that can return different results—for example:

- Searching for "run" would also return results containing "runs," "ran," and "running."

- Searching for "page" would also return results containing "pages," "paged," and "paging."

Although it would seem obvious to just turn on this feature per default, it does impact how search behaves in ways that might not be desired. Word stemming can affect the relevance of your search query. If some terms have lots of stemming and others have none, one word may now dominate results even if it isn't the priority in the context of what was looked for. Stemming can also negatively affect performance—there will be a delay while expanding the search query to include stemming, and a larger set of results will be returned.

# Phonetics and Nicknames

Phonetics and nicknames are new additions to the search facility in SharePoint 2010. They are targeted at People search and offer significant improvements to the user's ability to find other people inside or outside the organization. This is especially compelling for multinational companies, where incorrectly spelling names or knowing colleagues by nicknames only is common.

## Phonetic Search

Phonetic searching considers alternative spellings and misspellings of a name in the People search results. More specifically, phonetic searching takes into account that many times users know how to say a name but do not know the correct spelling for it. Although this feature is currently isolated to People search, it is the search center that generally presents the largest roadblocks to spelling.

Assume that a user needs to find contact information for a colleague named Geoff Petersen. The user does not know how his name is spelled and instead types Jeff Peterson in the search dialog. Although neither Geoff nor Petersen is an exact match for Jeff Peterson (not even a wildcard match), Speech Server in SharePoint 2010 will return Geoff Petersen as a search result, thus allowing the user to find him based on the combination of first name and surname.

---

■ **Note** Phonetic searching considers only alternative terms based on SharePoint 2010's thesaurus. Cutting a query short and searching for the term Mayn will not necessarily return results for the person with the last name Maynard. For this query to function properly, the wildcard character should be entered at the end—Mayn*.

---

The behavior of phonetic search is influenced by the Language setting. Although the phonetic alphabet is language-independent, as it is based on the International Phonetics Alphabet (IPA), the pronunciation of names can differ between languages.

# Nickname Search

Nicknames add another new facet to People search. As with phonetic search, it is language-specific, but instead of phonetic matching, it works by lookup. Assume a user is searching for a colleague named Michael, with the search context language set to English, but the user knows him only by the nickname Mike. Performing a People search for Mike would then return results for Mike and Michael because of the new Nicknames feature.

As mentioned, the Nicknames feature is language-specific, which means that not all nicknames are valid for all languages. The foregoing example with Mike works for the "en-US" LCID (locale/language ID), which is 1033, but not for the Danish "da-DK" LCID, which is 1030.

The nickname mappings can be found in the table called **MSSLanguageResources**, which is located in the **Search_Service_Application_DB** database (if the default name is used for the Search service application).

To see all nicknames for Michael, the following query can be executed in Microsoft SQL Server Management Studio (database name might differ):

```
SELECT [Phrase],[Mapping],[Locale]
FROM [Search_Service_Application_DB_<GUID>].[dbo].[MSSLanguageResources]
WHERE Mapping ='Michael'
GO
```

Table 6-1 shows the query results. The first column is the nickname. The second column is the name it maps to (Michael in this example). The third column is the Locale ID (LCID) or language variant for which the nickname applies.

*Table 6-1.* *Query Results*

| Nickname | Mapping Name | LCID |
| --- | --- | --- |
| micha | michael | 1031 |
| michi | michael | 1031 |
| mischa | michael | 1031 |
| michal | michael | 1033 |
| michale | michael | 1033 |
| micheal | michael | 1033 |
| michel | michael | 1033 |
| mick | michael | 1033 |
| mickey | michael | 1033 |
| micky | michael | 1033 |
| migi | michael | 1033 |
| miguel | michael | 1033 |
| mike | michael | 1033 |
| mikel | michael | 1033 |
| mikey | michael | 1033 |
| miki | michael | 1033 |
| miquel | michael | 1033 |
| mitch | michael | 1033 |
| chiel | michael | 1043 |
| giel | michael | 1043 |
| machiel | michael | 1043 |

| Nickname | Mapping Name | LCID |
|----------|--------------|------|
| maikel | michael | 1043 |
| michai | michael | 1043 |
| michal | michael | 1043 |
| michel | michael | 1043 |
| michiel | michael | 1043 |
| mitchell | michael | 1043 |

One thing to be aware of is that nicknames might apply both ways, such that Michael is also a nickname for Mike. The same query just mentioned can be changed to view these by changing the mapping in the SQL query:

```
SELECT [Phrase],[Mapping],[Locale]
FROM [Search_Service_Application_DB_<GUID>].[dbo].[MSSLanguageResources]
WHERE Mapping ='Mike'
GO
```

It is possible to add and remove nicknames using the new SharePoint 2010 PowerShell cmdlet. To add the nickname Mike for Michael and vice versa to the Danish LCID, the following can be run:

```
New-spenterprisesearchlanguageresourcephrase –Name Michael -Language "da-DK"↵
 –Type "Nickname" –Mapping Mike -SearchApplication 988218e4-b4f5-4042-b545-c5a6230aab24

New-spenterprisesearchlanguageresourcephrase –Name Mike -Language "da-DK"↵
 –Type "Nickname" –Mapping Michael -SearchApplication 988218e4-b4f5-4042-b545-c5a6230aab24
```

It might take a while for the new nicknames to take effect, as the required job named "Prepare query suggestions" must run before they get applied. The job runs every 24 hours.

Like word breaking, which was outlined in Chapter 1, nicknames and phonetic searches work differently for each language. As long as the corresponding language pack is installed, the language used for a query can be supported by these features. If a user is attempting to search on a language other than his or her current browser language, the user will need to specify the language on the Preferences page. Up to five languages can be queried by the search engine at one time. More details on the Preferences page are provided later in this chapter and in Chapter 5.

# Search Keywords

Keywords are used to configure a relationship between a keyword, synonyms, and a manually defined result set called best bets. Many companies have content where some terms are especially important or have a special meaning. This then leads to a particular query not returning a particular search result or the wanted search result is too far down in the search result set.

Search keywords are a very useful feature in these types of scenarios. They can either be used to define synonyms for particular keywords or to add/emphasize specific search results on the search results page using best bets and the Best Bets Web Part.

Even though this feature is also available in SharePoint 2010, it is especially useful in SharePoint 2010 due to the search statistics available. Now an administrator can find often-searched-for query terms and augment the search results of these with specially selected best bets.

## Managing Search Keywords

The search keywords page is used to create the mapping between keywords and synonyms. Additionally best bets can be configured for each keyword, as shown here. The search keywords page is accessed from Site Actions ➤ Site Settings ➤ Site Collection Administration ➤ Search Keywords.

The first page that is presented is the keywords overview page (Figure 6-35). This page displays a searchable and sortable list of all defined keywords. The list has columns showing the keyword, best bets, synonyms, expiry date, and contact. As it displays almost all relevant information of the keywords, it is easy to get an overview over the keyword corpus.

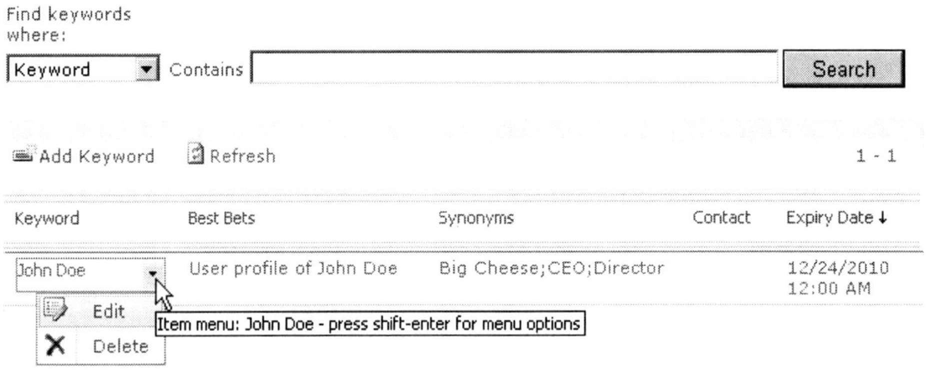

**Figure 6-35.** *SharePoint 2010 Search Keywords list*

New keywords are created by clicking the Add Keyword button. Existing keywords can be edited or deleted by clicking the keyword itself and choosing the appropriate option from its context menu. Choosing Add Keyword or the Edit option opens the keywords editor page (Figure 6-36). This page allows administrators to set the following:

- Keyword phrase

- Synonyms

- Best bets

- Description

- Contact

- Publishing and review dates

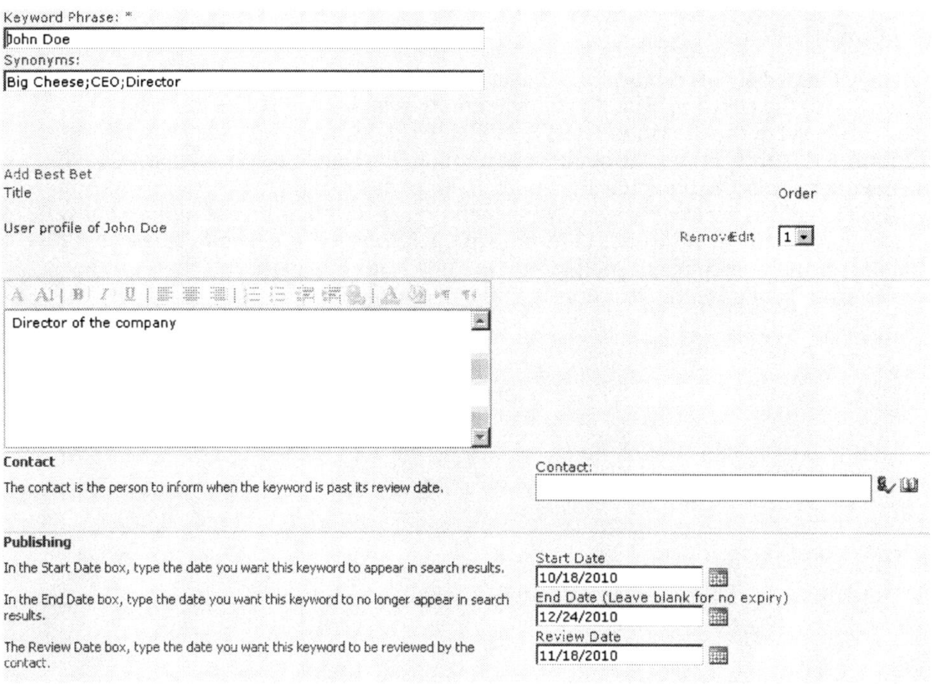

Keyword Phrase: *

John Doe

Synonyms:

Big Cheese;CEO;Director

Add Best Bet

Title                                                                                         Order

User profile of John Doe                                              Remove Edit    1 ▾

Director of the company

**Contact**                                                          Contact:

The contact is the person to inform when the keyword is past its review date.

**Publishing**                                                       Start Date

In the Start Date box, type the date you want this keyword to appear in search results.    10/18/2010

In the End Date box, type the date you want this keyword to no longer appear in search    End Date (Leave blank for no expiry)
results.                                                             12/24/2010

The Review Date box, type the date you want this keyword to be reviewed by the    Review Date
contact.                                                            11/18/2010

**Figure 6-36.** *Search Keywords creation page*

Once a keyword has been created or edited, it is available for search. No crawling is required for keywords to take effect. This enables the creator to immediately test the keyword and synonyms to confirm the behavior is as expected.

## Keywords and Synonyms

The keyword phrase defines the associated search term. No other keyword or synonym can use this phrase. For this reason, it is very important to plan which keywords to use. In the case where a keyword candidate is also a synonym for other keyword candidates, another keyword should be used instead to avoid ambiguous keywords and synonyms. The synonyms define terms that users might search for when looking for the keyword. SharePoint knows if a term has already been used as a keyword or synonym and prevents it from accidentally being used multiple times.

---

▓ **Note** Searching for a synonym to a keyword is *not* equivalent to searching for that keyword. The synonym will return only the best bets for the keywords that the synonym is associated with, not results that the keyword would otherwise return. A search for a synonym is therefore equivalent to a normal search but with added best bets for the keywords that have this synonym defined.

---

## Best Bets and Description

Best bets are a manually defined set of results that will be returned when searching for either the keyword or any synonym for the keyword. The default presentation is shown in Figure 6-37.

Best bets can be displayed to the user in the Best Bets Web Part, disregarding what search results normally would be returned. This way specific results not found in the search can be displayed to the user depending on the query. Another benefit is the ability to emphasize these to the user using either the default presentation as shown here or custom styling techniques. Best bets do not replace any other search results that would normally be returned. Trimming of the normal search results, however, does take place such that the normal search result set does not include results from the best bets set. For more information on how to configure the Best Bets Web Part, see Chapter 5.

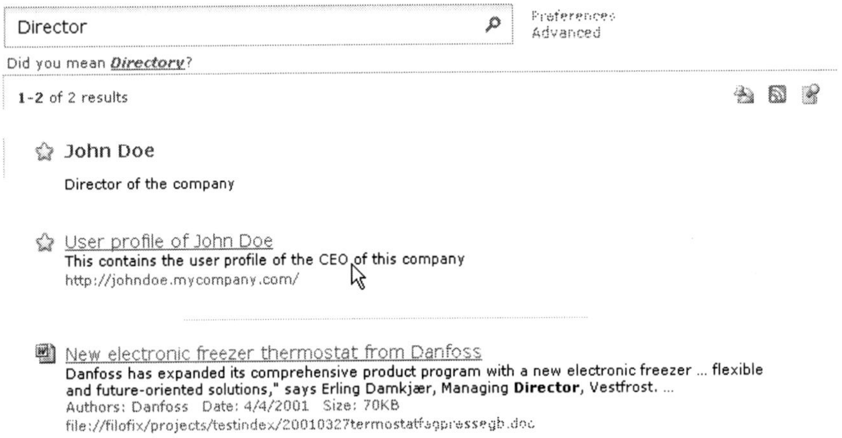

| Director |  🔍 | Preferences<br>Advanced |
|---|---|---|

Did you mean **_Directory_**?

1–2 of 2 results      📤 📰 📋

☆ **John Doe**

    Director of the company

☆ User profile of John Doe
    This contains the user profile of the CEO of this company
    http://johndoe.mycompany.com/

📄 New electronic freezer thermostat from Danfoss
    Danfoss has expanded its comprehensive product program with a new electronic freezer ... flexible
    and future-oriented solutions," says Erling Damkjær, Managing **Director**, Vestfrost. ...
    Authors: Danfoss   Date: 4/4/2001   Size: 70KB
    file://filofix/projects/testindex/20010327termostatfagpressegb.doc

**Figure 6-37.** *Example of search keywords*

A description of the keyword can be added. This description will be shown on the search results page. The description is used to display additional information about a specific keyword and its synonyms. For the keyword just shown, the description is used to provide information about a particular person's job title. This could also be used to show additional information about a specific product name or guidance if searching for keywords known to produce poor results.

## Contact and Publishing

In the Contact field, the user profile of the user to contact with events for the keyword is specified. This way a user can be set as owner or administrator of the keyword. Given the required permissions to edit search keywords, it is suggested that this be the creator of the keyword, or that the Contact be granted permissions to manage keywords. It will complicate maintenance if a third party with no permissions to edit the keyword gets the notifications.

Keywords allow for a start date and end date to be specified. The start and end dates enable keywords to be created before they take effect and to automatically expire at a given date. Searches for this keyword or any of the synonyms will not return best bets outside of the start and end date interval.

This is useful if, for instance, the keyword is relevant only for a time-limited campaign or for other reasons is time-dependent. It also facilitates management if the keyword does not have to be created at the exact time it will take effect. Another use for the end date is to avoid having to delete keywords if, for some reason, they are not wanted for a particular period but might be useful in a future scenario. Then the keyword does not have to be recreated when it becomes relevant again. Simply change the start and end dates to reactivate it.

Keywords also have a review date setting. When the set review date expires, the user defined in the Contact field will get a notification to review the keyword. This mechanism is especially useful in cases where a keyword is relevant for a limited time only, but the exact end date is not known. This way the Contact can be reminded to reconsider the end date or set a new review date.

# Maintenance

One of the biggest challenges with search keywords is the amount of manual maintenance required. Administrators tend to put a low priority on maintaining a meaningful and useful corpus of search keywords after some time. It is therefore important that this task receives focus during normal SharePoint maintenance planning.

Keywords are generally best maintained by non-technical staff. Keyword management, however, does require site collection administrator privileges, and normal non-technical staff is almost never granted this role. Deciding who should be the Contact and generally manage keywords must take this into account.

End dates are often left blank, which means that the search keyword will never expire. There are many situations where this is useful (e.g., for company name aliases, etc.). Often, however, keywords might be relevant only for time-limited products, campaigns, etc., which causes them to exist years after their actual relevancy. Even company names and aliases sometimes change after a longer period. Creating a policy for using the review date setting can counter issues with outdated keywords.

One reason the review functionality of keywords often is not utilized is that it is not clear who should receive notifications and when it requires review. Especially if the Contact leaves the company, this becomes an issue, as the review notifications then might not be caught.

Another challenge with search keywords is their dependency on fixed URLs for associated best bets. When a document or site that is referenced by a best bet is moved or deleted, the corresponding keyword should also be updated such that it doesn't reflect this broken URL in its best bets anymore.

For the reasons just mentioned, periodic manual inspection of keywords should be included in the maintenance policy.

# Suggested Uses for Keywords

Planning how and when to best use keywords can be a challenge. A keyword is not very useful by itself. The obvious use of keywords is to emphasize specific files or sites, but they can also be useful in a number of other scenarios.

Announcements can be created using keywords. For instance, a user who searches for a specific person or product name can be notified that the person has left the company or that the product name has changed to something else.

Ambiguity, where words mean several things, can be explained to the user, using the description to explain the different meanings and possibly give links to a page with more details on the definitions.

Topic policies can be communicated to users. A search for "expenses" could inform the user to contact the finance department for all expense-related information. The same could be the case with profanity, where searches for pre-defined obscene words could give a warning and link to a page containing a profanity policy.

Links to external pages using best bets that make sense for a keyword but are not indexed by SharePoint are useful for associating keywords to sister companies' web sites or other relevant external resources outside direct control of the company. Another use of links to external pages is to associate a keyword such as a customer name with links to all relevant subpages on that customer's web site.

For companies that charge for references, sponsored links can be created to allow customers of that company to get their references emphasized in the search results list at an additional cost. This is not unlike what most larger search engines like Google do.

# Search Alerts Administration

Search alerts in SharePoint are a mechanism to enable users to be notified or alerted by e-mail or SMS text message whenever a specific query would return new results or when the content of existing results has changed. Alerts are personal and can be configured and viewed only by the user who created them.

Search alerts have two requirements for the SharePoint farm configuration:

- Search alerts must be enabled on the Search service application.

- Outgoing e-mail must be configured.

By default, search alerts are deactivated for the Search service applications (Figure 6-38). To enable search alerts, you must use an account that has administrative rights to the Search service application.

**Figure 6-38.** *Toggling search alerts*

To activate search alerts for a Search service application, do the following:

1. Go to Application Management ➤ Manage service applications.

2. Click the Search service application.

3. Locate "Search alerts status", and click the Enable button.

When performing the Reset Index operation for the Search service application, SharePoint will ask if search alerts should be disabled for this operation. This is recommended, as doing this operation otherwise would fire all configured search alerts where the "alert on changes" option is set, which it almost always is.

---

■ **Note** Changes that trigger search alerts are based on the crawled content. An alert can therefore never fire more often than the crawl intervals of the content sources that yield the search results for the specific search alert.

---

# Search Suggestions

Search suggestions (called query suggestions on the Search Box Web Part) work similarly to the Bing search dialog, by providing a list of suggested search terms below the search box while a query is typed, as shown in Figure 6-39.

*Figure 6-39. SharePoint 2010 Enterprise Search Box with search suggestions*

Search suggestions are one of the topics that often cause confusion and are difficult to try out in test environments. This is partially because of the way search suggestions are activated, and partially because they cannot be managed through the SharePoint user interface.

The most important thing to understand about search suggestions is when they are added. Only search terms that yield results that actually get clicked will go into the search suggestion pool. A minimum of six clicks per year is required for the term to show up as a search suggestion.

It is possible to add and remove search suggestions manually. This can be done by using PowerShell commands through the SharePoint 2010 Management Shell.

## Viewing Search Suggestions

To list existing search suggestions, you can run the commands in Listing 6-3 from the SharePoint 2010 Management Shell.

*Listing 6-3. Listing Search Suggestions*

```
$app=Get-SPEnterpriseSearchServiceApplication
Get-SPEnterpriseSearchQuerySuggestionCandidates -SearchApp $app
```

# Adding Search Suggestions

To add new search suggestions, you can run the commands in Listing 6-4 from the SharePoint 2010 Management Shell.

*Listing 6-4. Adding Search Suggestions*

```
$app=Get-SPEnterpriseSearchServiceApplication
New-SPEnterpriseSearchLanguageResourcePhrase -SearchApplication $app -Language en-US↵
 -Type QuerySuggestionAlwaysSuggest -Name "SharePoint Search"
```

This will add the query "SharePoint Search" to the search suggestions list.

The search suggestion will show up in the search dialog only after the Prepare Query Suggestions timer job has executed. Per default it is scheduled to run daily between 1 a.m. and 11 p.m.

To get the search suggestions to show up immediately, run the commands in Listing 6-5 from the SharePoint 2010 Management Shell.

*Listing 6-5. Running the Prepare Query Suggestions Timer Job*

```
$timer=Get-SPTimerJob|? {$_.Name -eq "Prepare Query Suggestions"}
$timer.RunNow()
```

# Removing Search Suggestions

To remove search suggestions, run the commands in Listing 6-6 from the SharePoint 2010 Management Shell.

*Listing 6-6. Removing Search Suggestions*

```
$app=Get-SPEnterpriseSearchServiceApplication
Remove-SPEnterpriseSearchLanguageResourcePhrase -SearchApplication $app -Language en-US↵
 -Type QuerySuggestionAlwaysSuggest -Identity "SharePoint Search"
```

This will remove the query "SharePoint Search" from the search suggestions list. The search suggestion will be removed from the search dialog only after the Prepare Query Suggestions timer job has executed. Per default it is scheduled to run between 1 a.m. and 11 p.m. To get the search suggestions removed immediately, run the following commands in Listing 6-7 from the SharePoint 2010 Management Shell.

*Listing 6-7. Running the Prepare Query Suggestions Timer Job*

```
$timer=Get-SPTimerJob|? {$_.Name -eq "Prepare Query Suggestions"}
$timer.RunNow()
```

# Search Scopes

Search scopes are used to limit the result set by applying rule-based restrictions to the search. Scopes do not require being a subset of a larger result set. They can define individual possible result sets.

The benefit of using scopes is the ability they provide to create a definition for a subset of searchable content or content in the search index. Scopes can then be used by users as an easy way of trimming the possible search results. Scopes can be made easily accessible for users by either creating a search tab with a specially scoped search and results page or by adding the scope selector on a search page and results page itself. Examples of typical scopes could be department-specific content, pre-defined topics, specific content sources, or groups of people in an organization. It is also possible to create aggregate scopes that encompass a number of other scopes.

You can set search scopes at both the Search service application level and at the site administration level. Search scopes set at the Search service application level are available to all sites and site collections within the service application. These scopes cannot be modified or deleted at the site administration level.

SharePoint 2010 now includes the new refiner Web Part, which is described earlier in this chapter and in Chapter 5. The refiner Web Part does offer the user similar functionality to the scopes. For instance, the refiner can allow the user to refine the search results by sources such as sites or by properties such as authors. When planning which scopes to create, this should be taken into consideration, as opposed to planning scopes for SharePoint 2007.

---

■ **Note** To avoid having to wait for SharePoint to update its scopes, go to the Search Administration page, and start an update for the scopes manually by clicking "Start update now".

---

## Managing Scopes

Scopes can be defined at either the Search service application level or site collection level. The only difference here is the availability and grouping of scopes. Availability means that scopes created at the SSA level are available to all sites and site collections throughout the farm. Scopes created at the site collection level are available only to all sites within that site collection. Grouping is possible only on the site collection level. It allows the site collection administrator to define groups of scopes that make sense as a whole. These groups can then be applied to search Web Parts where feasible. Scopes created at the SSA level cannot be changed at the site collection level.

## Scopes at SSA Level

To modify scopes on the SSA level, go to Central Administration ➤ Search Service Application ➤ Scopes. This opens the Scopes list, as shown in Figure 6-40.

Scopes defined at the SSA level are added to a scope pool called Shared. These scopes are always available at the site collection level. At the SSA level, it is also possible to view all scopes defined at the site collection level.

Use this page to view and manage search scopes. The order in which the search scopes appear in this list is the order in which they will appear in the search scope list next to the Search box.

■ New Scope   ■ Refresh

| Title | Update Status | Items |
| --- | --- | --- |
| **Shared (5)** | | |
| People | Ready | 0 |
| All Sites | Ready | 190 |
| testscope | Ready | 5 |
| Documents | Ready | 0 |
| test2scope | Empty - Add rules | empty |
| **http://dev-dbm2010/ (1)** | | |
| sitetestscope | Ready | 92 |

***Figure 6-40.*** *Scopes list page at the SSA level*

## Scopes at the Site Collection Level

To modify scopes on the site collection level, go to Site Actions ➤ Site Settings ➤ Site Collection Administration ➤ Search scopes.

Scopes inherited from SSA are marked as Shared, as shown in Figure 6-41. With the exception of the preconfigured scopes, these scopes are not added to a display group (described later in this section), but placed in a separate group called Unused Scopes. Also new scopes created at the site collection level are placed in the Unused Scopes group unless otherwise specified during creation.

New Scope    Display Groups    Refresh

| Title | Update Status | Shared | Items |
|-------|---------------|--------|-------|
| **Search Dropdown (3)** | | | |
| All Sites | Ready | ☑ | 190 |
| People | Ready | ☑ | 0 |
| sitetestscope | Ready | | 92 |
| **Advanced Search (3)** | | | |
| All Sites | Ready | ☑ | 190 |
| People | Ready | ☑ | 0 |
| testscope | Ready | ☑ | 5 |
| **Unused Scopes (2)** | | | |
| Documents | Ready | ☑ | 0 |
| test2scope | Empty - Add rules | ☑ | empty |

*Figure 6-41. Scopes list page at the site collection level*

## Creating New Scopes

Scope creation (Figure 6-42) is almost the same on both the SSA and site collection levels. Click the New Scope link to go to the Create Scope page. On this page, the scope settings are defined. A scope requires a unique title, which is used to identify the scope. It can also have an optional description.

On the site collection level, it can be selected which display groups the scope should be part of. This Display Groups section is not available when creating scopes from an SSA. The list of display groups reflects the display groups created by the site collection administrator. A scope does not have to be mapped to a display group to be available for search, as it can be specified on the query string, but it must be mapped to a display group to be available for selection by users.

The Target Results page can be set to use the default search results page, or a specific page can be assigned (in case of cross-site collection searches). For some scopes, it would make sense to create a special search results page carefully designed to show search results of a special type. An example of this is the People search page.

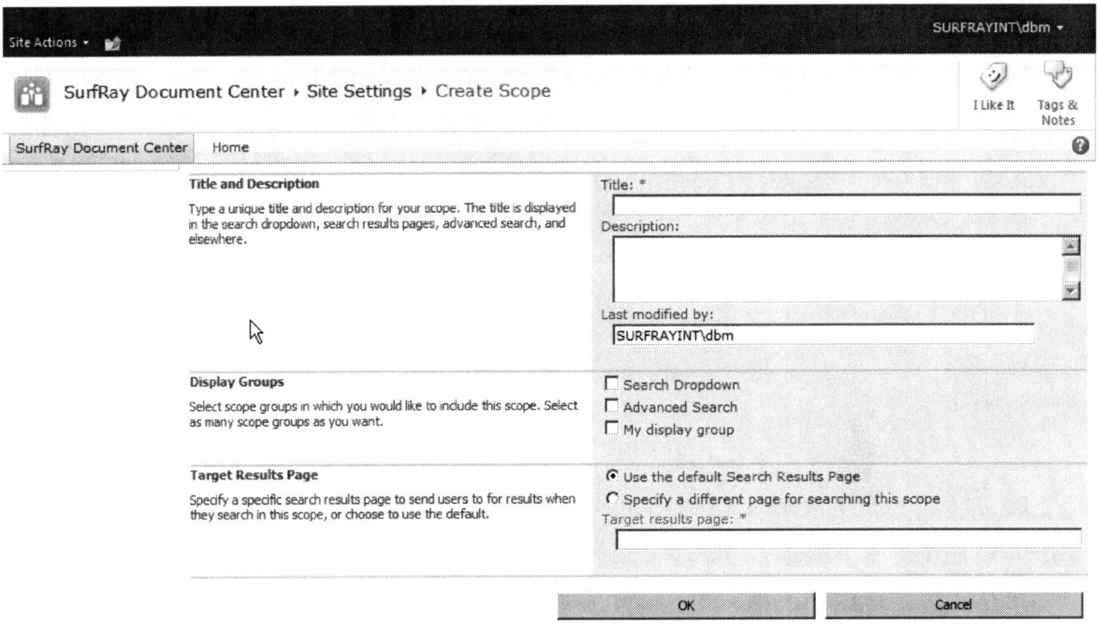

**Figure 6-42.** *Creating a scope*

# Scope Rules

Scope rules can be created by applying AND, OR, NOT rules for a selection of properties. The rule set allows the administrator to specify the trimming of the search index that this scope represents. As mentioned earlier, this can be either content source restrictions or topic filtering. The following types of rules can be created:

- Web address
- Properties
- Content source (not available on the site collection level)
- All content

## Web Address

Rules for web addresses are specified by folder name, hostname, or domain name (Figure 6-43). The effect of specifying an address is that the results will be limited or excluded, based on the address.

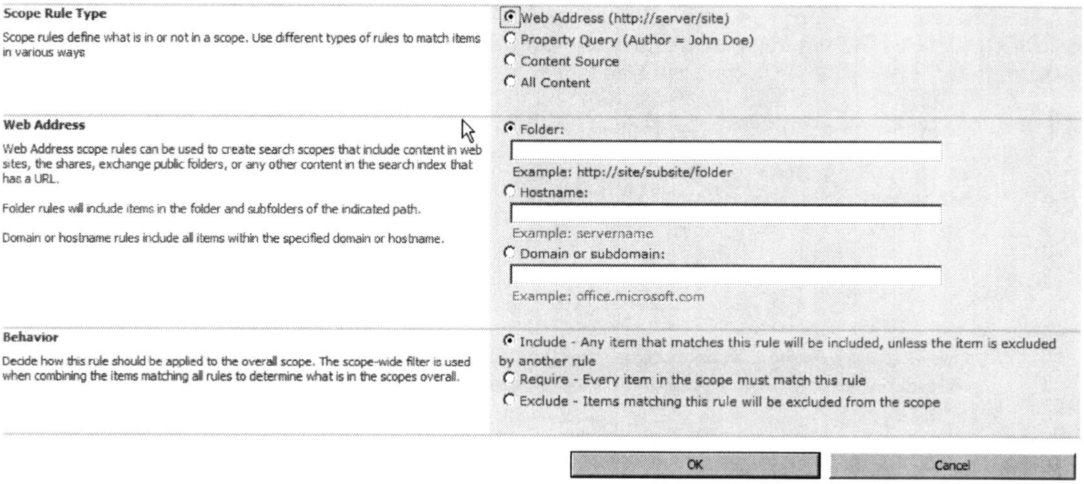

*Figure 6-43. Scope rules—web addresses*

## Property Query

The most often used scope rule is the property query (Figure 6-44). This potentially allows an administrator to create scope rules for all managed properties as long as they are allowed to be used in scopes.

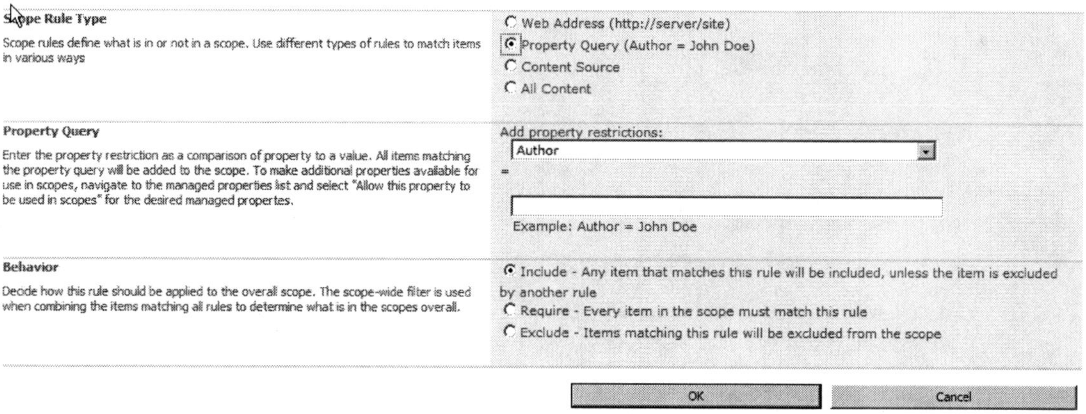

*Figure 6-44. Scope rules—property query*

An often required scope to create is a document scope. Unfortunately this is not possible without performing some additional steps, as the **IsDocument** property cannot be used in scopes per default. The **IsDocument** property defines whether a content type is a document.

The first thing to do is to allow the **IsDocument** property to be used in scopes. This is done on the Search service application. Follow these steps to enable the **IsDocument** property for scopes:

1.  Go to the Metadata Properties list in the SSA, and open the **IsDocument** property (Figure 6-45). Check the "Allow this property to be used in scopes" check box.

2.  Then save the changes.

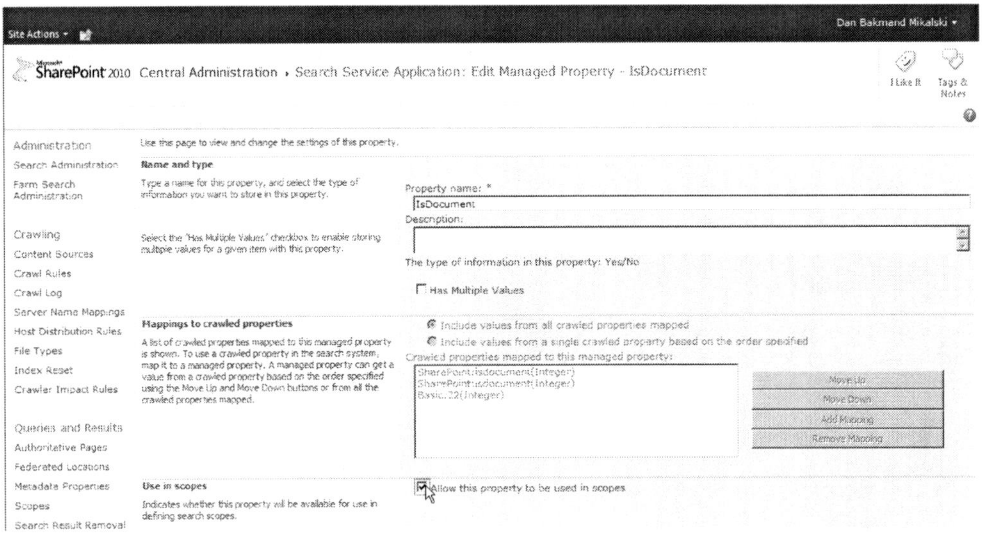

**Figure 6-45.** *Edit Managed Property page for IsDocument property*

Now the **IsDocument** property can be used in scopes. The next steps are to create a document scope and configure it to use the **IsDocument** property.

1.  Go to the Scopes list in the SSA, and click the New Scope button.

2.  Create a new scope with the name Documents (Figure 6-46). Optionally give it a suitable description. Then click OK.

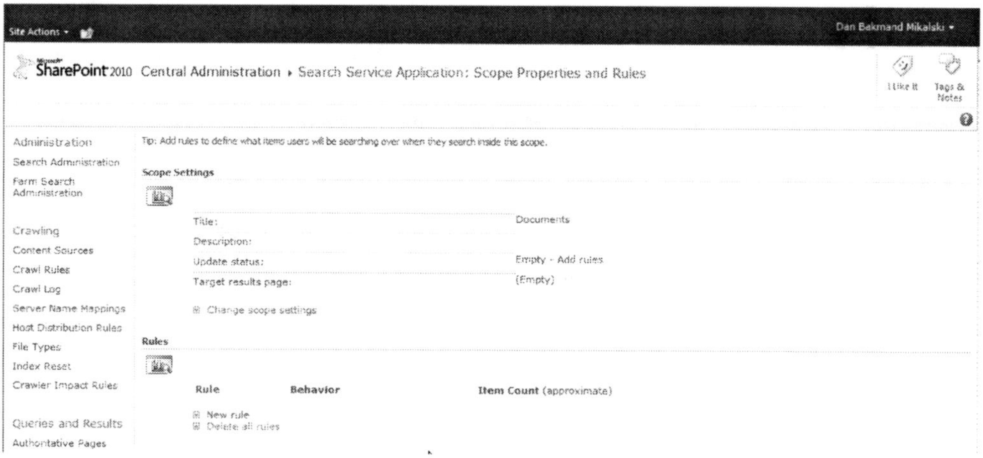

**Figure 6-46.** *Scope overview page for document scope*

With the **IsDocument** property configured and the document scope created, a rule must be created on the scope (Figure 6-47) to make it use the **IsDocument** property.

1. Click the New Rule button.

2. Select the Property Query option for the Scope Rule Type.

3. Enter the **IsDocument** property, and give it a value of 1 in the Property Query setting.

4. Leave the behavior setting as Include, and click OK.

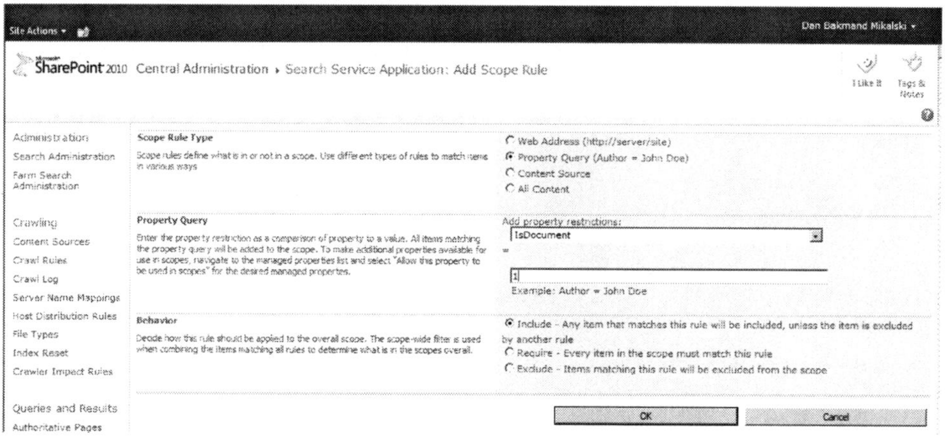

**Figure 6-47.** *Scope rule page with IsDocument rule applied*

Now the document scope is created and can be used on search and result Web Parts to give the user an option to quickly filter content based on whether it is a document.

## Content Source

This rule limits or excludes content from the specified content source. Content sources are the ones defined on the Search service application, including the default content source named Local SharePoint Sites (Figure 6-48). If content sources are to be used in scope rules, care must be taken to make them fine-grained enough to fulfill the requirements of the desired rules. This would typically mean that a content source will be created per file share or groups in a file share, web site, or similar entity.

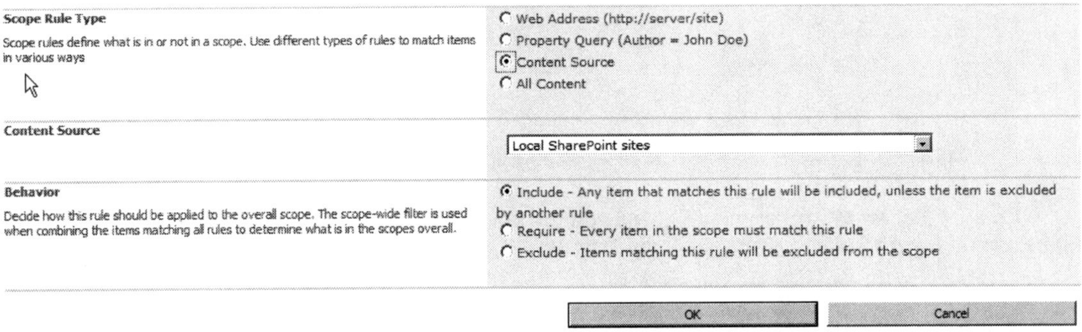

***Figure 6-48.*** *Scope rules—content source*

## All Content

This is the scope rule used by default in search centers (Figure 6-49).

For example, if the goal is to search all content sources except a single one, for the given scope, use this rule to include all content and then use a second rule for the given scope to exclude the appropriate content source.

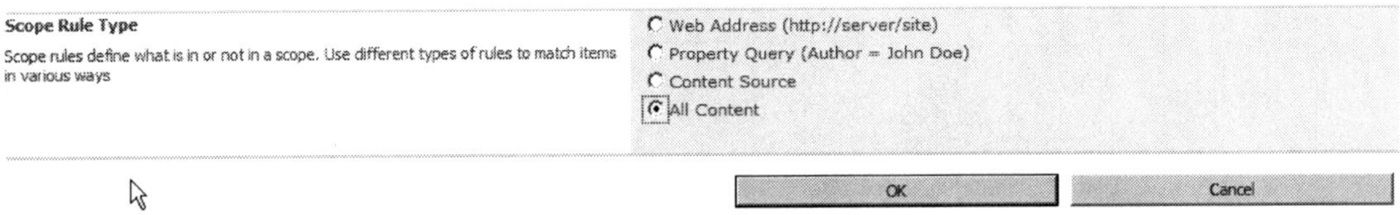

***Figure 6-49.*** *Scope rules—All Content selection*

# Display Groups

For scopes to be usable in search centers, they must be added to a display group in the site collection.

1. Click the Display Groups link to open the Display Group settings page (Figure 6-50).

2. To create a new display group, click New Display Group. This will open the Create Display Group page.

3. To edit existing display groups, simply click the appropriate group name.

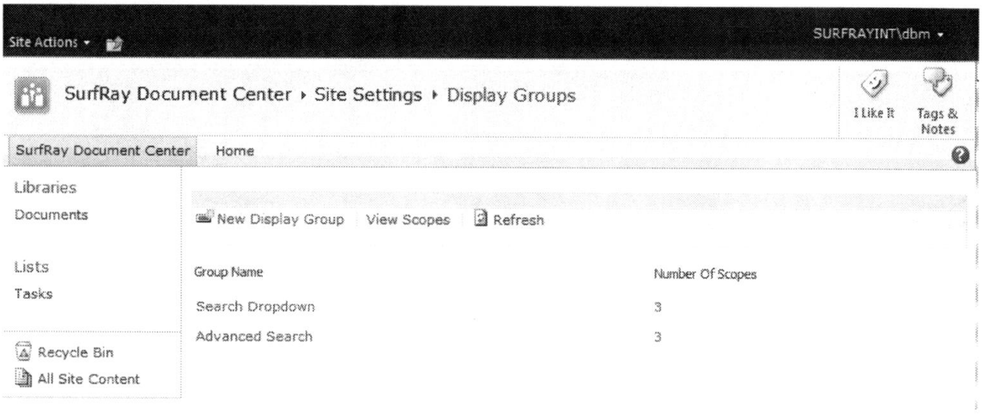

***Figure 6-50.*** *Scope display groups*

On the Scope Display Group page (Figure 6-51), it is possible to define one or more scopes to show in a specific display group. It is also possible to set the default scope and give the group a meaningful title and description.

4. Select which scopes to include in the group and default scope. Then click OK. This will create the new display group.

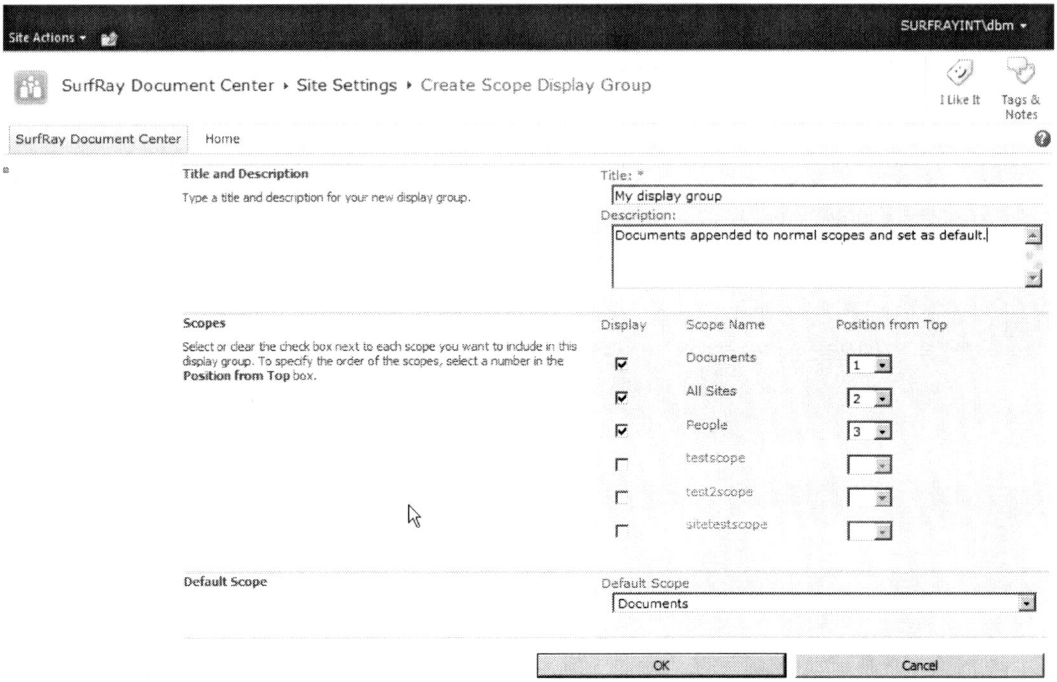

**Figure 6-51.** *Editing scope display groups*

The newly created display group will now be shown on the Display Groups page, as shown in Figure 6-52. It also shows how many scopes are included in the display group.

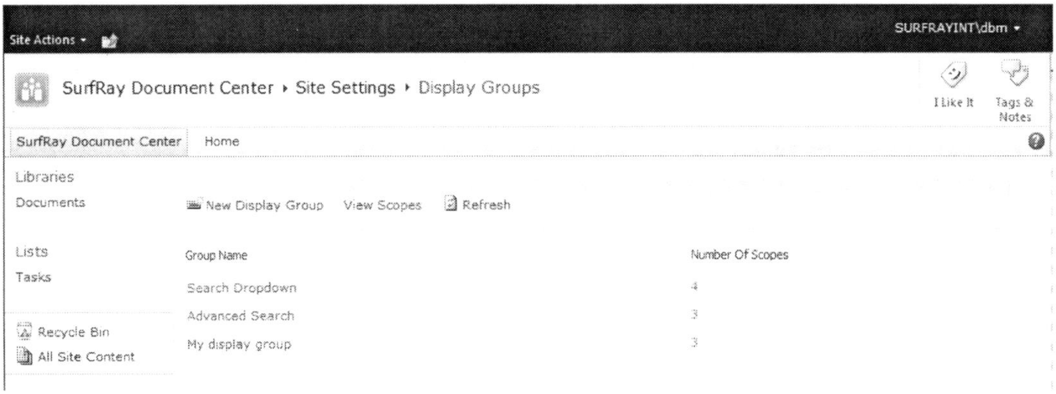

**Figure 6-52.** *Scope display groups with custom group*

5. To use the new display group in a search center (as described in the "Search Core Results" section), set the display group option of any relevant Web Part to the appropriate group name. The Web Part will now use the selected display group, as shown in Figure 6-53.

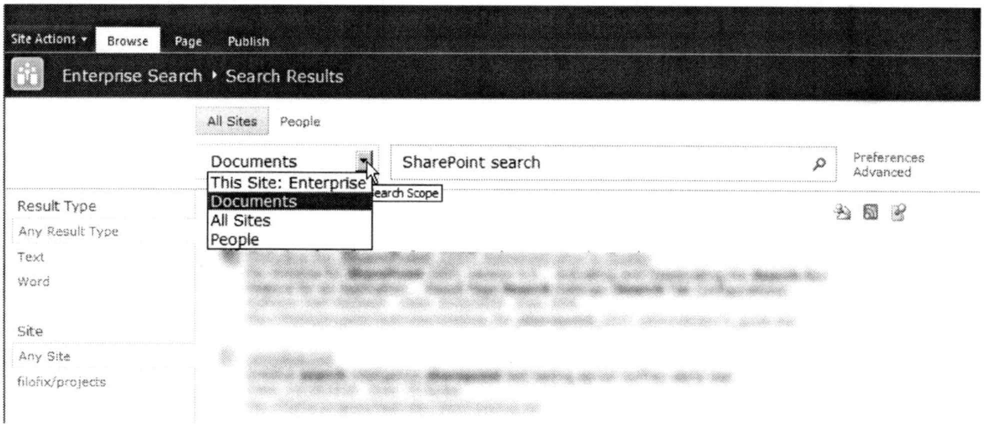

**Figure 6-53.** *Example of search box with custom scope and scope group enabled*

## Adding Search Scope Selector to the Search Box

Most sites contain a search box. Unlike in SharePoint 2007, the search box does not include a scope drop-down. It contains only the "Search this site" search box, as shown in Figure 6-54.

**Figure 6-54.** *The default site search box*

To enable scope selection directly from the search box, do the following:

1. Go to Site Actions ➤ Site Settings ➤ Site Collection Administration ➤ Search Settings. This will open the page for managing the search boxes on this site collection, as shown in Figure 6-55.

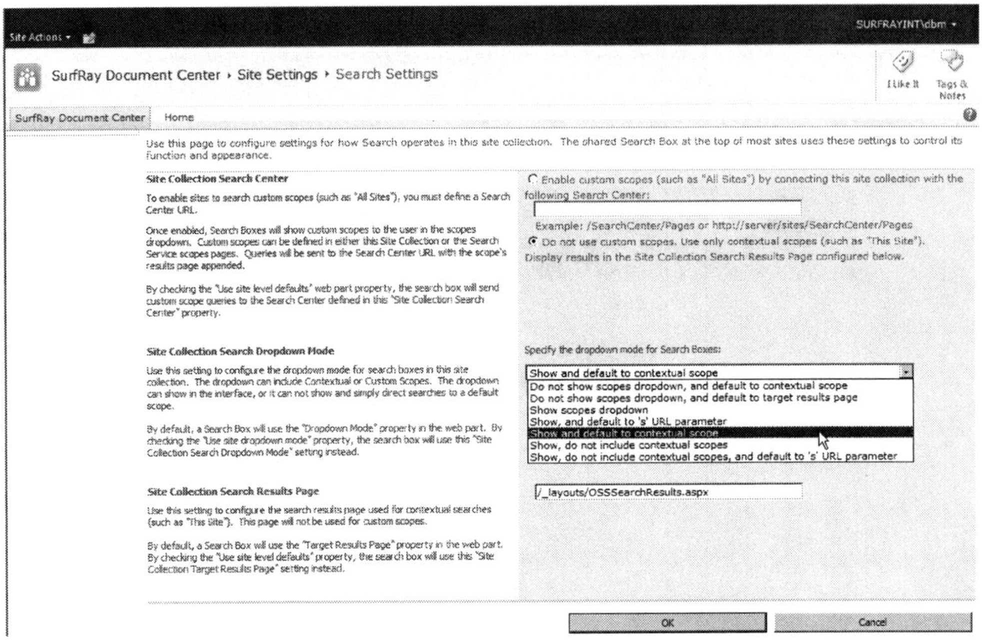

*Figure 6-55. Search settings on the site collection level*

2.  From the Site Collection Search Dropdown Mode section, select the "Show and default to contextual scope" option.

3.  Click OK on the Search Settings page, and validate that the search box now has a scope selector, as shown in Figure 6-56.

*Figure 6-56. The site search box with scope selector drop-down*

# Search Tabs and Pages

Search tabs are a web control displayed on the Enterprise Search Center. The purpose of search tabs is to allow easy navigation between different search pages, each with their own search Web Parts, layout, configuration, and scope. Per default SharePoint creates the All Sites and the People tabs in Enterprise Search Centers, as shown in Figure 6-57.

*Figure 6-57. Search tabs*

The tabs themselves are list items. Separate lists exist for the following:

- Tabs shown on the search pages
- Tabs shown on the results pages

The benefit of search tabs being list items is that it makes all search pages share the same tabs, without affecting the tabs defined for the results pages and vice versa. This way the search pages for All Sites, People, and any other search page share tabs. Similarly the results pages for All Sites, People, and any other results page share tabs.

To add or edit existing tabs, select the Page tab from the ribbon and click Edit to put the page in Edit mode (Figure 6-58). As mentioned before, the tabs editor is not a Web Part but a web control. On the search dialog pages (and also on the results pages), this control is displayed at the top of the page. The location can be changed by editing the page's markup.

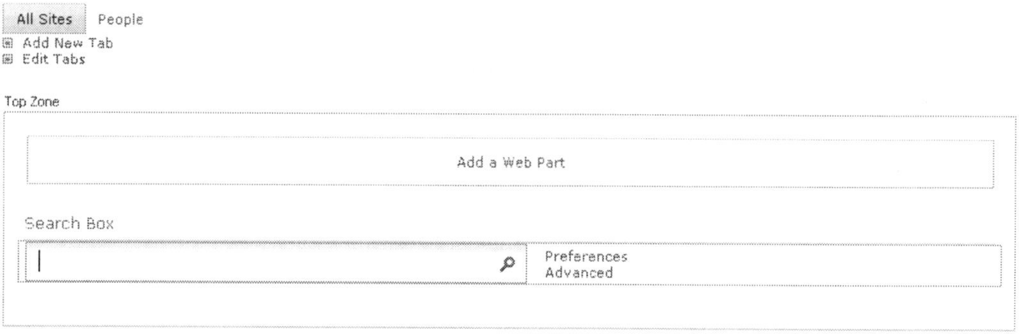

*Figure 6-58. Search tabs edit control on page in Edit mode*

To view, add, or edit existing tabs, click the Edit Tabs link, which opens the list of existing tabs. The list shows the default tabs for an Enterprise Search Center. Adding, editing, and removing tabs is just like managing items in any other list.

On the search pages, three tabs are created per default, but only two tabs are visible on the Search dialog page (Figure 6-59). The two tabs with the tab name All Sites are actually pointing to different pages. The first one is pointing to **default.aspx**, which is the search page normally viewed. The second one points to **advanced.aspx**, which is the page for advanced search. The final tab points to people. On results pages, only two tabs are created per default.

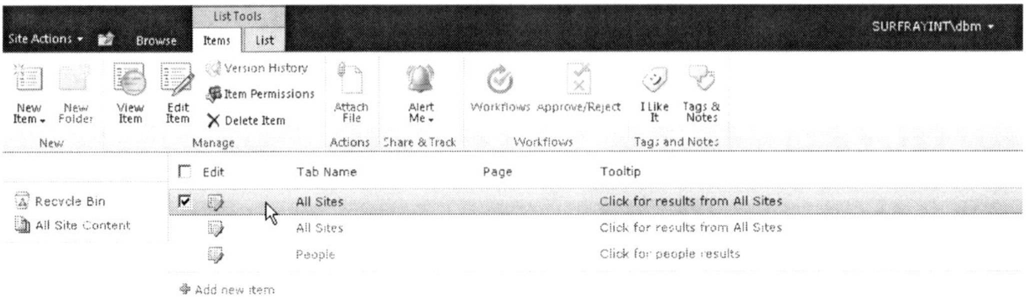

**Figure 6-59.** *Search tabs list*

For new tabs to be meaningful, a new search page or results page should be created. To create a new search page, do the following:

1.  Go to an existing search page.

2.  Click Site Actions ➤ More Options to open the list of page types. The filters in the left menu are useful for quickly finding or trimming down the options to choose from.

3.  Using the page filter (Figure 6-60), three options are displayed, as shown here. Depending on whether publishing is desired, choose the correct page type and click the Create button.

**Figure 6-60.** *Creating a publishing page*

After choosing a page type and clicking the Create button, the Create Page dialog opens (Figure 6-61). Here it is possible to apply some standard information to the new page. The title will be displayed at the top of the page as well as in the title bar of most browsers. The description is displayed just below the title in smaller letters and gives users more detailed information on the intent and usage of the page.

The URL Name specifies the file name of the page. The page is created in a location relative to the site on which it exists. The pages will always be of type **\*.aspx**. It is not possible to create other formats of web pages using this dialog.

The Page Layout section displays the available pre-defined layouts for the given site. If the new page to be created is a search page, choose "Search box" or "Advanced search" from the Page Layout section. If the new page to be created is a results page, choose "Search results" or "People search results" from the Page Layout section.

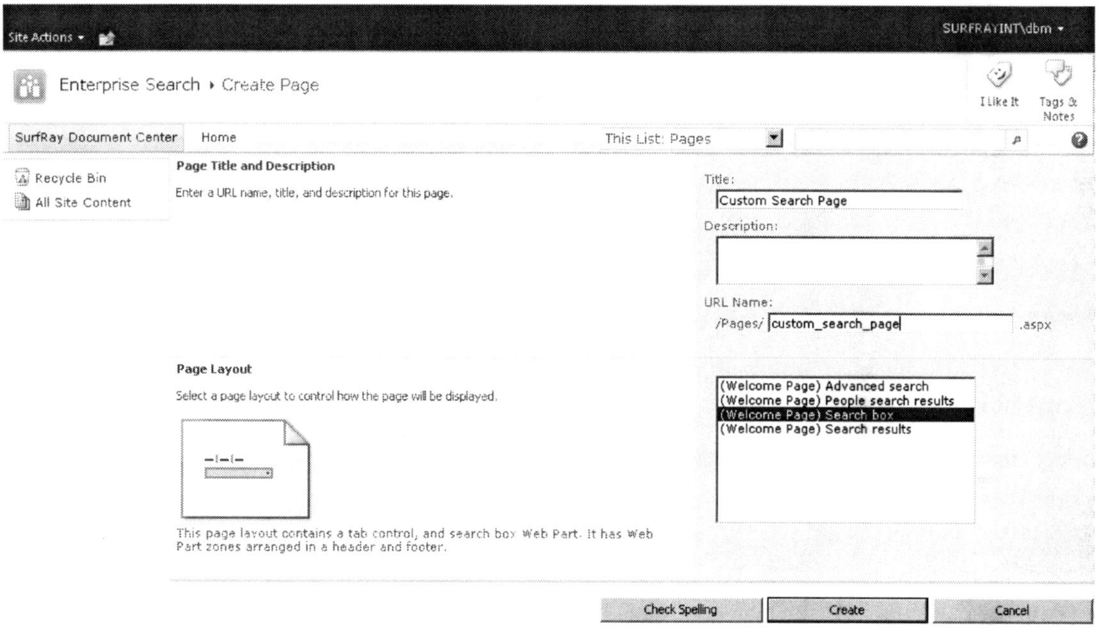

***Figure 6-61.*** *Choosing a page layout of new page*

---

■ **Note** The selection of page layout dictates if "Tabs in search pages" or "Tabs in result pages" will be used.

---

Choose the desired page layout, and click the Create button. The new page will open in Edit mode, as shown in Figure 6-62. For Enterprise Search Centers, this page also include the Tabs web control. Notice that the newly created page is not mapped to a specific tab. This can be done from any of the search pages or search results pages in Edit mode, depending on the target tab group for the new page.

**Figure 6-62.** *New search page in Edit mode*

To add the new search page to the search tabs list, click Add New Tab. This is equal to going to the search tabs list and adding a new item. On the new tab item (Figure 6-63), give the tab a meaningful name and tooltip. The next step is to map the page itself to the new tab. To do this, copy the URL of the newly created page into the Page section.

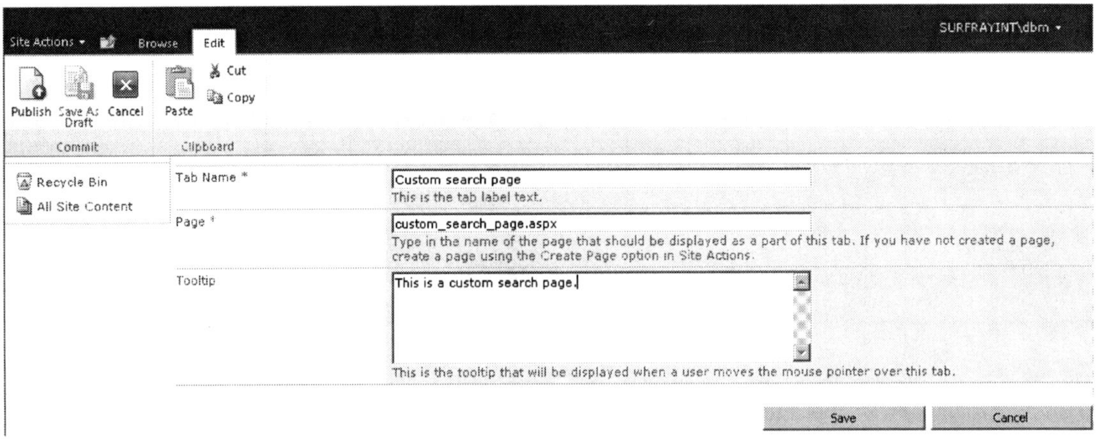

**Figure 6-63.** *Linking new tab to a page*

When the tab name, tooltip, and URL of the target page are entered, click the Save button. A new search tab is now available for the new custom search page and all other pages sharing the same tabs list, as shown in Figure 6-64.

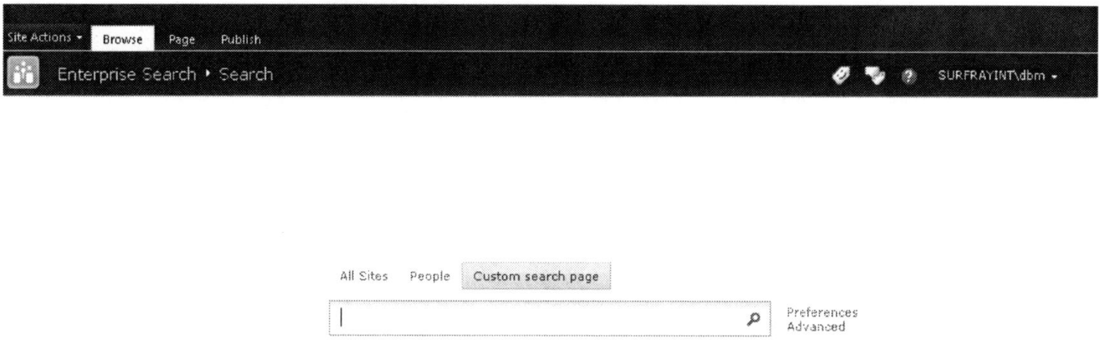

**Figure 6-64.** *Search dialog with custom tab*

Results pages and tabs in results pages are created the same way. Creating new tabs is an option to do more complex search configurations and make them easily accessible to users. In some scenarios, it might be that two tabs differ on the scope they use only when searching. Some of the search settings, such as scopes, are also possible to do on just one page by including a scope selector control, but enabling this as a tab instead of a scope selector is sometimes preferred. It does introduce some maintenance overhead when adding new search pages and search results pages, but it also provides the benefit of being able to fine-tune each page to meet specific demands.

# Summary

In this chapter, we looked at configuring the search-related Web Part settings on the search Web Parts. The focus was on enabling the advanced functionality that is typically utilized in corporations and organizations using SharePoint 2010. This chapter also discussed implications related to different configurations, such as performance issues using search suggestions, etc.

The administrative interface of SharePoint 2010 is vast. This is also true for the search-related settings. Users often experience that it is difficult to accomplish tasks, such as scope or locations management. This chapter assisted the reader in finding his or her way around the multitude of search settings available in SharePoint 2010. We also looked at how to mitigate some common problems the user might experience when configuring certain settings.

There is no possible way to describe every possible configuration of the SharePoint 2010 Search experience, but after finishing this chapter you should be equipped to understand key concepts, predict possible issues, do custom configuration, and leverage the many configuration options offered in SharePoint 2010.

# CHAPTER 7

■ ■ ■

# Working with Search Page Layouts

After completing this chapter, you will be able to:

- Understand master pages in SharePoint 2010
- Apply best practices for modifying layouts of search
- Add and improve navigation in search centers
- Apply custom branded layouts to search
- Use Document Rating in Search and change 'click behavior' of document results
- Understand and configure refiners and the Refinement Panel
- Adding numbered refiners.
- Understand limitations of refiners.

SharePoint search offers endless opportunities for extensions and modifications, but not all are equally easy to perform. This is true for even the most frequently required modifications or extensions.

SharePoint 2010 layout is based on master pages and XSLT. Although it might be trivial to change layout it does introduce some challenges when it comes to the Search interface. A typical extension to the default that corporations require is improved navigation from search centers. Out of the box, SharePoint offers little in terms of navigating from search centers to other sites. This chapter takes a look at different ways to solve this shortcoming including modifying the master page, aspx pages or using a custom navigation Web Part. The techniques described can also be applied to achieve other goals.

Equally important to navigation is the branding and presentation of not only the content sites but also the search experience. Adding branded master pages to search centers is straightforward in SharePoint 2010, but it does introduce some quirks that will be addressed in this chapter. One of the great things about SharePoint is how flexible it is. This is demonstrated through examples on how to utilize the new Ratings property and applying custom 'click behavior' for search results. These examples are designed to introduce the reader to two fundamentally different approaches when improving the search experience and should prove helpful when planning for other similar improvements.

The refinement panel is a novel thing added to SharePoint 2010. It is preconfigured out of the box, but its full functionality is not exposed. This chapter looks at some of the advanced topics on enabling functionality on the refinement panel, with a focus on numbered refiners.

Overall, this chapter introduces best practices on several ways to solve common tasks faced by SharePoint professionals in easy-to-maintain ways. The methods proposed should enable the reader to apply the methodologies to other key requirements as well and understand possible consequences of different configurations of the refinement panel.

# Understanding Master Pages in SharePoint 2010

Master pages provide the ability to separate the layout of the rendered page from the page containing the actual content. Master pages were also a major component in SharePoint 2007, and while backward compatibility has been preserved with a number of new SharePoint 2010 master pages, those new master pages with the version 4 label attached to them are not backward-compatible. However, all version 3 master pages are compatible with SharePoint 2010, although some functionality will be missing.

---

■ **Note** This chapter does not go into the details of how to create master pages. That topic is covered by a number of other books and blogs. Instead, this chapter touches on many of the new master pages provided with SharePoint 2010 and a few general pointers and design hints that are often overlooked concerning solving typical requirements.

---

## v4.master

This is the default team site master page and the one that is suggested as a template when creating a new or custom branded master page. This master page provides the new ribbon bar as well as other UI changes. Also the Site Actions button is moved in SP 2010. It now appears in the upper left corner.

## default.master

If a site is upgraded from SP 2007, it uses this master page per default. The Site Actions button is located on the upper right side, and the UI mainly is the same as in SP 2007. This master page does not include the ribbon bar. The sites using this master page can be changed to use the new version 4 master page, named `v4.master`, or any custom branded master page based on this.

## minimal.master

This master page is close to being the simplest possible. It is used only by the search centers and Office Web Applications. One of the things most people quickly notice when using sites based on this master page is the lack of navigation. It is arguably a significant lack of functionality, and although the purpose is to provide more screen real estate for search results as well as making the search center appear cleaner, it is something that should be changed in most corporate sites. It does make more sense for the Office Web Applications, as they have their own UI. In any case, this is how the `minimal.master` is in SP 2010 out of the box.

# simple.master

This master page is used by the generic SharePoint 2010 pages such as login and error pages. It is not possible to use another master page for these pages. The only option to customize these pages is to create a replacement page and override the existing ones by saving it in the `_layouts` directory on the server.

The following pages use `simple.master`:

- `Login.aspx`

- `SignOut.aspx`

- `Error.aspx`

- `ReqAcc.aspx`

- `Confirmation.aspx`

- `WebDeleted.aspx`

- `AccessDenied.aspx`

# Other Master Pages

SharePoint 2010 includes a lot of other master pages that are typically not required to be manipulated when creating a custom branded layout. It is suggested to leave them unchanged unless a special reason exists for not doing so. These master pages are

- `application.master`

- `applicationv4.master`

- `dialog.master`

- `layouts.master`

- `layoutsv3.master`

- `pickerdialog.master`

- `rtedialog.master`

- `simple.master`

- `simplev4.master`

- `mwsdefault.master`

- `mwsdefaultv4.master`

- `admin.master`

- `popup.master`

# Considerations When Creating a Custom Master Page

The first prerequisite best practice approach before creating any custom branded master page is to create a SharePoint web site. The suggested standard site template to use when creating a site collection is the Team Site template. Using a well-known fully featured site makes it easier to evaluate if the pages show as expected. Once you have a web site created, you are ready to start modifying it.

In any case, when it comes to SharePoint, it is *always* best practice to start creating your custom branded master page based on one that already works. Experience shows that this reduces headaches and avoids spending hours on solving issues related to hard-to-find errors. Using the `v4.master` that comes with SharePoint as a base and trimming it down a bit is usually a good approach. Then initially apply the custom branded template to only one site, and ignore any quirks that you might experience if applying it to your other sites. Only when the master page is behaving as expected on your initial baseline site should it be deployed to the rest of your sites.

Once the base master page for the custom branded master page has been extracted or created, it is best practice to give it a meaningful name. Remember to include v4 in the beginning of the master page name if it is based on a v4 master page for consistency purposes. Then copy it to the `all files/_catalogs/masterpage` folder of the SharePoint farm using SharePoint Designer 2010.

If custom CSS files are required, use SharePoint Designer 2010 to create new CSS files rather than changing the existing ones. They should be saved in the `Style Library` folder. New CSS files will instruct the web browser to overwrite the default SharePoint theme with the new theme that you specified in your CSS file, with the !important syntax. Best practice is to create four separate individual CSS files for header, footer, navigation, and content page.

To make sure the new CSS files work as expected, they should be registered in the custom branded master page with this syntax.

```
<SharePoint:CssRegistration name="/Style Library/APMcss/custom_footer.css"
After="corev4.css" runat="server"/>
```

Begin editing the master page and using the element class and ID name that were declared in your CSS file, until the master page looks like what you wanted.

It is best practice to keep layout consistent throughout our sites. Items that should stay consistent on the sites are

- Header, footer, and other layout segments

- Navigation panes and main navigation controls on pages

- General layout and look of the page; this includes images, border styles, table layouts, etc.

In SharePoint the default layout (as is also a generally accepted layout principle) contains the content in the middle between the header, footer, and navigation panes (Figure 7-1). This way it is the center part of the page that will be updated when navigating and new contents will be displayed in the middle. In the master pages, this is also where the main content placeholder is located.

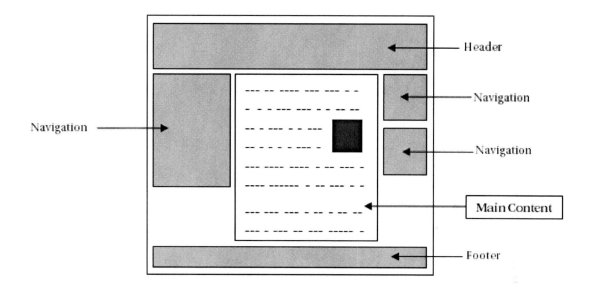

***Figure 7-1.*** *Page organization*

The main content tag is formatted like this.

```
<asp:ContentPlaceHolder id="ConentPlaceHolderID" runat="server" />
```

When any page is created using a custom master page, Web Part zones or content areas should be added only within this custom place holder unless a specific reason exists for doing otherwise.

Once you have finished customizing your master page, it is good practice to create a SharePoint 2010 solution package, so that you can deploy your customized master page to a SharePoint server farm and re-use it for other site collections. Solution packages can be created using Visual Studio 2010. More details on this topic are available on `http://technet.microsoft.com/en-us/library/cc262995.aspx`.

# Adding Navigation to the Search Center

As mentioned, the search pages use the `minimal.master` master page per default. This is a very simple master page with next to nothing on it, not even navigation. This is also one of the most frequently recurring issues people are experiencing, as navigation almost always is an essential part of a corporate web site. The Office Web Applications also use this master page, but for those applications, it makes sense not to include navigation, because it provides more screen real estate, which is a bigger issue for the applications.

Here we will look at different methods for manipulating the search center's layout, exemplified by showing a number of ways of adding navigation to search centers. We also look at how to apply an already existing master page to the search center and some issues related to that. The different techniques applied to solve the navigation issue can also be applied to solve other layout and interaction-related problems.

Which method to choose for solving a particular problem is dependent on a number of decisions, especially the following:

- Is the change required throughout the farm or only on a single page or site?

- How often is the change expected to require updating or other maintenance?

- Should the change automatically apply to newly created pages or be added manually by the site owners and administrators?

It should always be a carefully considered decision which method to use, as redoing it using one of the other suggested methods can require significant work. Firstly, the techniques are so different that almost nothing is re-usable. Secondly, undoing already applied changes based one method before applying a solution based on another method can be tedious and time-consuming. It should also be considered that site owners and administrators might require training depending on the change.

The following are suggestions on when to apply the proposed methods for modifying the layout, in this case adding navigation:

> *Adding a custom navigation Web Part to pages:* Using this method, it is commonly the responsibility of the site owner or administrator to manually add the Web Part. This makes it a very administrative-heavy solution. This can be negated by creating custom site templates that include this Web Part. It does not, however, solve the issue with maintenance if the Web Part is to be removed at a later time, as only future sites would reflect the change. This is, however, also true for all standard SharePoint sites, so it is a well-known issue. In any case, this solution is most suitable for situations where the change should be applied to only certain types of sites or specific sites.

> *Modifying the* `minimal.master` *master page to include navigation:* Making changes at the master page level makes the change both easy to manage centrally and easy to alter and maintain. It does, however, remove the option to control it at site level, unless specific master pages are created for the relevant sites. In a corporation where site content and layout often need some degree of central administration, this is the suggested method.

> *Editing the* `SearchMain.aspx` *pages to include navigation:* Editing the `.aspx` pages themselves can generally accomplish the same things as changing the master pages. It actually offers more flexibility and control over the layout. The benefit of this method is that it allows a change to be applied to all pages on a specific site, without affecting other sites. It is also easy to maintain and update, as any changes will affect both existing and future pages on that site. It does, however, remove the ability to centrally administrate the change, and it makes farm-wide deployment more time-consuming.

## Adding Home and Back Buttons to the Search Result Page

When you create a SharePoint 2010 Search Center, one of the first things you'll notice is that there is no navigation to allow the user to go back to where the user came from or to go to the parent site or top site as seen in Figure 7-2. Obviously the Back button in the browser could be used, but the user should be able to do this from the SharePoint UI itself.

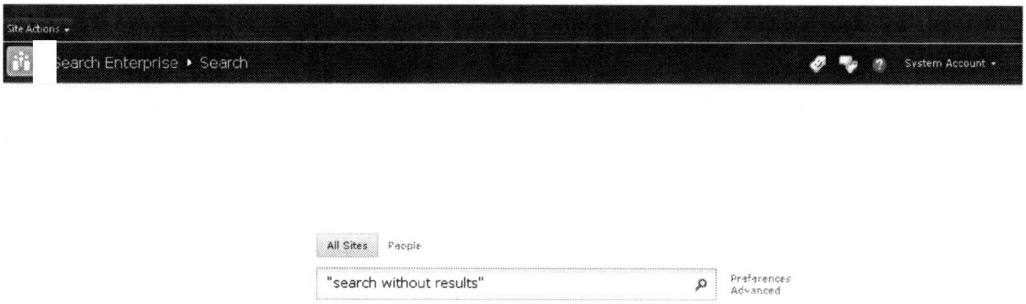

**Figure 7-2.** *Searching for something*

Many use cases can be thought of when determining if this is a real issue. The most common case is when the user searches for something and does not find any desired results (Figure 7-3). This could be done from either a search page or using the search box located on many sites, such as Team Sites, etc.

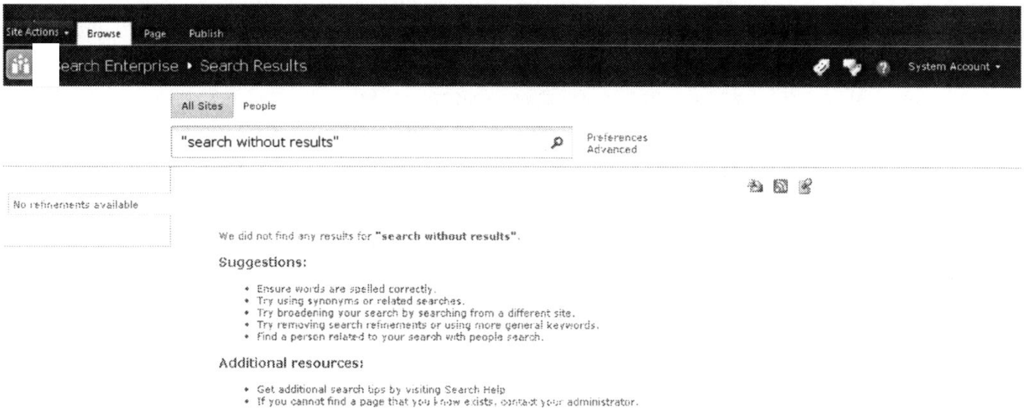

**Figure 7-3.** *Navigation is hidden.*

One way of solving this is to use a Content Editor Web Part that includes Home and Back buttons that are added to the **results.aspx** and **people.aspx** pages. This technique can also be used for a number of other purposes, such as providing quick links or helpful info, but here the focus is on adding dynamic navigation to go back or home.

On the **Results.aspx** page, edit the page and add a Content Editor Web Part. The suggested location is to add it to the left Web Part zone. Give it a meaningful title (e.g., Navigation buttons), and set the Chrome Type to None. Add the necessary icons and text to make it look as required. For the text, that could be Go Home for the home button and Go Back for the back button. For easier deployment, use the existing images from the SharePoint **layouts** folder. That could be **/_layouts/images/hhome.png** for the Home icon, and **/_layouts/images/back.gif** for the Back icon.

Setting the URL for the Home navigation is easy. Just set it to "/" to set it to the site home. However, for the Back button, a little trick is required. Link it to `href="#"`, and set the click behavior as `onClick="history.go(-1)"`.

Now the navigation on the `Results.aspx` page is finished. To avoid repeating this on the `People.aspx` page and other pages where the Home and Back navigation Web Part is useful, it can be stored as a re-usable Web Part.

1. Export the new Content Editor Web Part to your desktop.

2. Upload the saved Web Part to your Web Part gallery. (In the Site Collection Root, click Site Actions, click Site Settings, and then click Web Parts).

3. Give the Web Part a useful name and description, and categorize it.

4. Edit the `People.aspx` page, and add a Web Part, but this time choose the Web Part that is now in your gallery.

An alternative way to deploy this Web part is to copy the following Web Part markup in Listing 7-1 into a text file, change the file extension to `.dwp`, and then upload it to the Web Part gallery so you can re-use it.

**Listing 7-1.** *Navigation Buttons Web Part Markup*

```xml
<?xml version="1.0" encoding="utf-8"?>
<WebPart xmlns:xsi="http://www.w3.org/2001/XMLSchema-instance"
 xmlns:xsd="http://www.w3.org/2001/XMLSchema"
xmlns="http://schemas.microsoft.com/WebPart/v2">
  <Title>Site Navigation Buttons</Title>
  <FrameType>None</FrameType>
  <Description></Description>
  <IsIncluded>true</IsIncluded>
  <ZoneID>LeftZone</ZoneID>
  <PartOrder>0</PartOrder>
  <FrameState>Normal</FrameState>
  <Height />
  <Width />
  <AllowRemove>true</AllowRemove>
  <AllowZoneChange>true</AllowZoneChange>
  <AllowMinimize>true</AllowMinimize>
  <AllowConnect>true</AllowConnect>
  <AllowEdit>true</AllowEdit>
  <AllowHide>true</AllowHide>
  <IsVisible>true</IsVisible>
  <DetailLink />
  <HelpLink />
  <HelpMode>Modeless</HelpMode>
  <Dir>Default</Dir>
  <PartImageSmall />
  <MissingAssembly>Cannot import this Web Part.</MissingAssembly>
  <PartImageLarge>/_layouts/images/mscontl.gif</PartImageLarge>
  <IsIncludedFilter />
```

```
<Assembly>Microsoft.SharePoint, Version=14.0.0.0, Culture=neutral,↵
PublicKeyToken=71e9bce111e9429c</Assembly>
 <TypeName>Microsoft.SharePoint.WebPartPages.ContentEditorWebPart</TypeName>
 <ContentLink xmlns="http://schemas.microsoft.com/WebPart/v2/ContentEditor" />
 <Content xmlns="http://schemas.microsoft.com/WebPart/v2/ContentEditor"><![CDATA[<br/>↵
<a href="/"><img src="/_layouts/images/hhome.png" border="0"/></a> ↵
<a href="/">Home</a>  <a onclick="history.go(-1)" href="#">↵
<img src="/_layouts/images/back.gif" border="0"/></a> <a onclick=↵
"history.go(-1)" href="#">Back</a><br/><br/>]]></Content>
 <PartStorage xmlns="http://schemas.microsoft.com/WebPart/v2/ContentEditor" />
</WebPart>
```

To add the Web Part to a search result page, simply click the Web Part zone where the Web Part should be added and pick the newly created Site Navigation Buttons Web Part as seen in Figure 7-4.

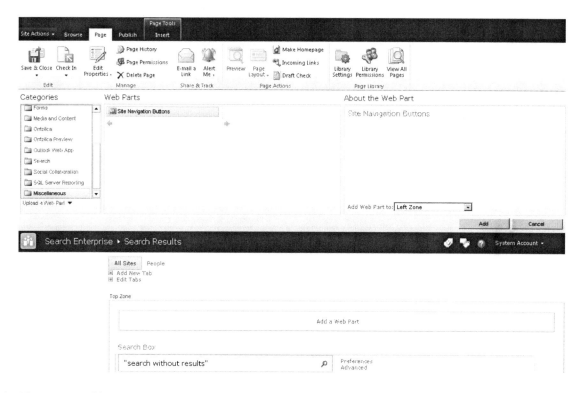

**Figure 7-4.** *Adding navigation Web Part to search result page*

The result should look similar to the one shown in Figure 7-5. Remember that this Web Part can also be used on other pages to keep a uniform look and feel.

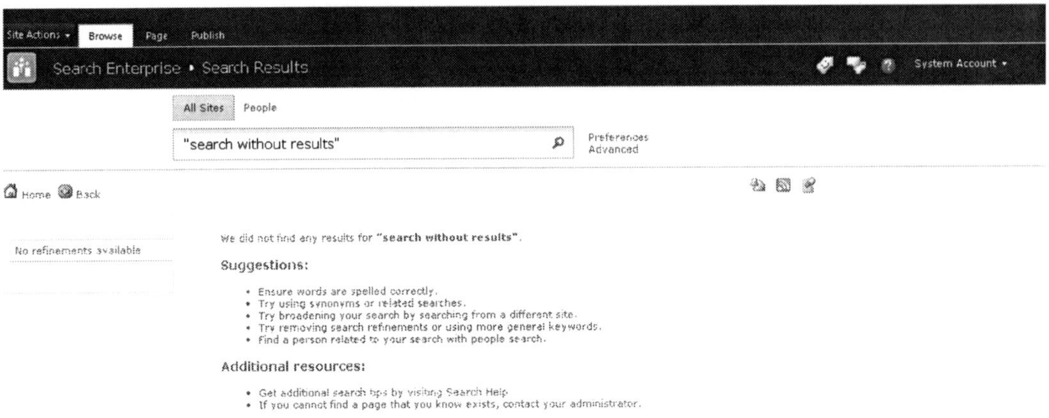

**Figure 7-5.** *Results.aspx page with proper displayed result*

## Adding Navigation to Search Center Master Page

Although the master page `minimal.master` has no navigation, it is possible to add it. This is recommended for most corporations. Assume a user executes a search, gets some search results, and then wants to jump back to the root site. The only way is for the user to modify the URL manually, which is not really a feasible option.

To add navigation to the `minimal.master`, first locate this section in the master page.

```
<div>
<asp:ContentPlaceHolder id="PlaceHolderTitleBreadcrumb" runat="server" />
</div>
```

Add the following markup from Listing 7-2[1] just before the foregoing markup. This places the navigation in the correct location for it to show properly.

---

[1] Microsoft, Kolby H., "change the masterpage of the search center", http://social.technet.microsoft.com/Forums/en/sharepoint2010customization/thread/cd568f4b-6372-480a-b393-ad3d9ab1db84, January 13th 2010.

*Listing 7-2.* *Navigation in* minimal.master *Master Page Markup*

```
<div id="s4-topheader2" class="s4-pr s4-notdlg">
<div class="s4-lp s4-toplinks">
<asp:ContentPlaceHolder id="PlaceHolderTopNavBar" runat="server">
<asp:ContentPlaceHolder id="PlaceHolderHorizontalNav" runat="server">
<SharePoint:AspMenu
    ID="TopNavigationMenuV4"
    Runat="server"
    EnableViewState="false"
    DataSourceID="topSiteMap"
    AccessKey="<%$Resources:wss,navigation_accesskey%>"
    UseSimpleRendering="true"
    UseSeparateCss="false"
    Orientation="Horizontal"
    StaticDisplayLevels="2"
    MaximumDynamicDisplayLevels="1"
    SkipLinkText=""
    CssClass="s4-tn"/>
<SharePoint:DelegateControl runat="server"
    ControlId="TopNavigationDataSource" Id="topNavigationDelegate">
<Template_Controls>
<asp:SiteMapDataSource
    ShowStartingNode="False"
    SiteMapProvider="SPNavigationProvider"
    id="topSiteMap"
    runat="server"
    StartingNodeUrl="sid:1002"/>
</Template_Controls>
</SharePoint:DelegateControl>
</asp:ContentPlaceHolder>
</asp:ContentPlaceHolder>
</div>
</div>
```

Then locate this section in the minimal.master.

```
<SharePoint:CssRegistration Name="layouts.css" runat="server"/>
```

Add this just before the foregoing.

```
<SharePoint:CssRegistration Name="corev4.css" runat="server"/>
```

After these changes, the minimal.master now includes navigation as seen in Figure 7-6. As it is only the search center that uses the minimal.master, it is suggested that this master page is deployed throughout the farm to solve the missing navigation issue for all search centers, both current and the ones created later.

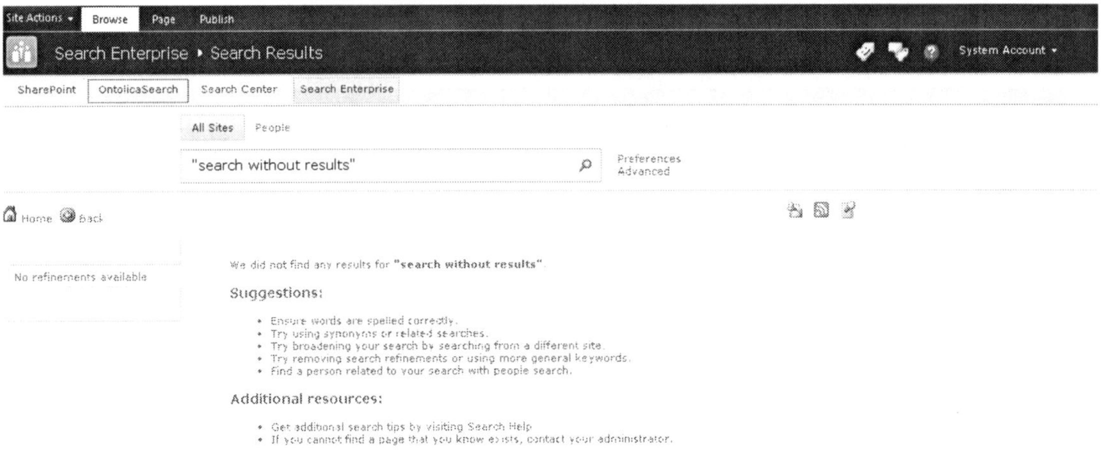

**Figure 7-6.** *Navigation added to* `minimal.master` *screen dump*

## Adding Navigation to the SearchMain.aspx Page

Instead of changing the master page named `minimal.master`, it is also possible to add the top navigation bar directly to the layout of the page. This can be done by adding the following code to the `SearchMain.aspx` page layout.

Begin to edit the page by selecting Edit in Advanced Mode (using SPD 2010). Then locate this section in the `SearchMain.aspx` page. Also do the same for `SearchResults.aspx`.

```
</ContentTemplate>
</SharePoint:UIVersionedContent>
<SharePoint:UIVersionedContent UIVersion="4" runat="server">
<ContentTemplate>
```

Add the markup shown in Listing 7-3 just after the markup shown previously. This way the navigation is added in the right place to make it show exactly as if it were added to the master page using the previously described method.

**Listing 7-3.** *Navigation Markup Added to* `SearchMain.aspx` *Page*

```
<div class="s4-lp s4-toplinks" style="background-image:url(/_layouts/images/selbg.png);
background-repeat:no-repeat;
 repeat-x:left top; background-color:#f6f6f6; vertical-align:middle; min-height:25px;
border-top:1px solid #e0e0e0;
 border-bottom:1px solid #b8babd">
        <SharePoint:AspMenu
           ID="TopNavigationMenuV4"
           Runat="server"
           EnableViewState="false"
           DataSourceID="topSiteMap"
```

```
        AccessKey="<%$Resources:wss,navigation_accesskey%>"
        UseSimpleRendering="true"
        UseSeparateCss="false"
        Orientation="Horizontal"
        StaticDisplayLevels="2"
        MaximumDynamicDisplayLevels="1"
        SkipLinkText=""
        CssClass="s4-tn"/>
    <SharePoint:DelegateControl runat="server" ControlId="TopNavigationDataSource"↵
Id="topNavigationDelegate">
      <Template_Controls>
      <asp:SiteMapDataSource
        ShowStartingNode="False"
        SiteMapProvider="SPNavigationProvider"
        id="topSiteMap"
        runat="server"
        StartingNodeUrl="sid:1002"/>
      </Template_Controls>
      </SharePoint:DelegateControl>
    </div>
```

In the foregoing sample, all the CSS styles come from the SharePoint CSS file named `corev4.css`. These can be changed to fit other requirements for the look of the page. After these changes, the `SearchMain.aspx` and `SearchResults.aspx` pages now include navigation as seen in Figure 7-7. As it is only the search center that uses `SearchMain.aspx` and `SearchResults.aspx`, it is suggested that this page is deployed throughout the farm to solve the missing navigation issue once and for all.

Also notice that the end result from a user's perspective is exactly the same as when adding navigation directly to the master page.

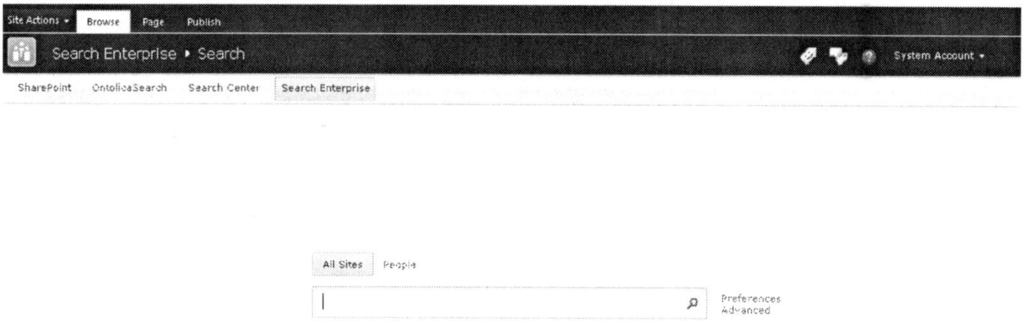

**Figure 7-7.** *Navigation added to SearchMain.aspx screen dump*

# Applying a Branded Master Page to a Search Center

Many corporations prefer to add branding to the front-end layout of their SharePoint farm. Usually this is done on the master pages. Specifically the **v4.master** is often the one that corporations change. This is all fine for normal sites, but in many cases special attention needs to be paid to the search center, as the v4-based master pages break the search center.

## Search Box Is Hiding When Branding a Search Center

Figure 7-8 shows the standard search page in a search center. Pay attention to the search box, as this is the root of the problem.

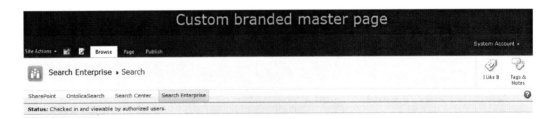

***Figure 7-8.*** *Standard search center search page*

Normally a site collection is created with a search center underneath. Alternatively this is done by creating a publishing portal that already has a search center created. The next step is usually to apply the corporate custom branded master page to all subsites. For a fictive corporation, it could look something like Figure 7-9.

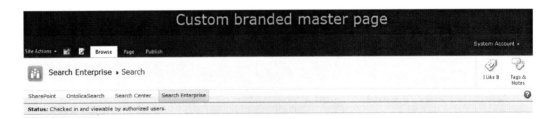

***Figure 7-9.*** *Corporate custom branded master page screen dump from search center search page*

Now the search page has the custom branded layout, but the search box has disappeared. This is because the search center doesn't support the v4 master pages. The search box is not gone; it is actually hidden in the breadcrumb placeholder.

This works just fine when `minimal.master` is applied, but as mentioned, the layout problem, shown in Figure 7-10, happens when trying to apply any of the other out-of-the-box v4 master pages or a custom branded master page simply by clicking the "apply to all subsites" box.

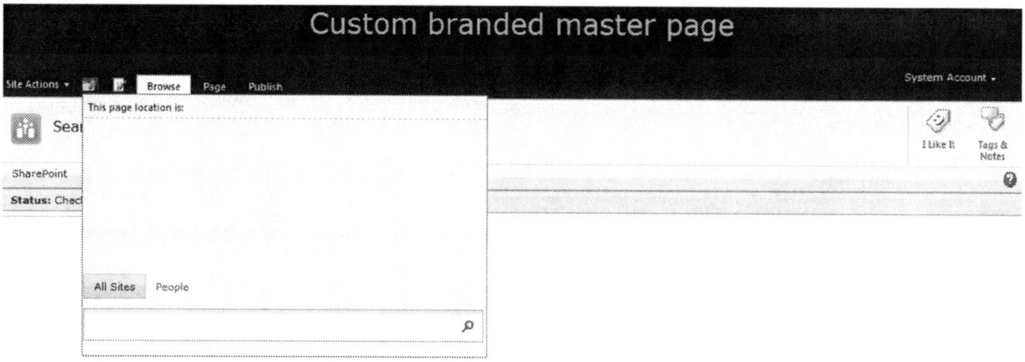

*Figure 7-10. Browse button clicked to show the search box located in the breadcrumb placeholder*

## Making Navigation Visible and Showing the Search Box Correctly

This can obviously be fixed by creating a new custom branded master page based on the `minimal.master` or by adjusting the page layouts in the search center to use the standard content placeholders. In this case, it is recommended, however, to create a new custom branded master page based on the current custom branded master page. With minor adjustments, it can be modified to work with search centers. This approach makes it easier to maintain the master pages in the future.

In Listing 7-4, a copy of the `v4.master` is modified to work with search centers. This is also useful if the purpose is just to add normal navigation to the default SharePoint 2010 Search Center. Basic knowledge about master pages and SharePoint Designer 2010 is assumed.

Make a copy of `v4.master`, and give it a new name like `v4_searchcenter.master`. Then edit the new master page. Then find and remove the tag named `PlaceHolderTitleBreadcrumb`. Now the breadcrumb will work as expected without it being located in the drop-down placeholder.

*Listing 7-4. Removing ContentPlaceHolder Wrapping of the Breadcrumb*

```
<asp:ContentPlaceHolder id="PlaceHolderTitleBreadcrumb" runat="server">
<SharePoint:ListSiteMapPath
runat="server"
SiteMapProviders="SPSiteMapProvider,SPContentMapProvider"
RenderCurrentNodeAsLink="false"
PathSeparator=""
CssClass="s4-breadcrumb"
NodeStyle-CssClass="s4-breadcrumbNode"
```

```
CurrentNodeStyle-CssClass="s4-breadcrumbCurrentNode"
RootNodeStyle-CssClass="s4-breadcrumbRootNode"
NodeImageOffsetX=0
NodeImageOffsetY=353
NodeImageWidth=16
NodeImageHeight=16
NodeImageUrl="/_layouts/images/fgimg.png"
RTLNodeImageOffsetX=0
RTLNodeImageOffsetY=376
RTLNodeImageWidth=16
RTLNodeImageHeight=16
RTLNodeImageUrl="/_layouts/images/fgimg.png"
HideInteriorRootNodes="true"
SkipLinkText="" />
</asp:ContentPlaceHolder>
```

Next, add the PlaceHolderTitleBreadcrumb before the PlaceHolderMain. This will allow the search center to inject the search box in a good location:

```
<asp:ContentPlaceHolder id="PlaceHolderTitleBreadcrumb"↲
 runat="server"></asp:ContentPlaceHolder>
<asp:ContentPlaceHolder id="PlaceHolderMain" runat="server"/>
```

Move PlaceHolderPageTitleInTitleArea (and any supporting HTML) to a hidden panel because this placeholder isn't used the same way in the search center:

```
<asp:ContentPlaceHolder id="PlaceHolderPageTitleInTitleArea" runat="server" />
<asp:Panel visible="false" runat="server">
<asp:ContentPlaceHolder id="PlaceHolderPageTitleInTitleArea" runat="server" />
</asp:Panel>
```

Remove ClusteredDirectionalSeparatorArrow and <h2></h2>. It won't make sense to show these at the top now:

```
<SharePoint:ClusteredDirectionalSeparatorArrow runat="server"/>
<h2></h2>
```

## Adding CSS Styling

To make the master page look correct for search centers, some CSS needs to be added. The CSS styles in Listing 7-5 are added to the <head> section of the master page.

*Listing 7-5. CSS styling of navigation*

```
<style type="text/css">
.s4-ca {
margin-left: 0px;
}
```

```
.srch-sb-results {
background:transparent none repeat scroll 0 0;
}
.srch-sb-main {
padding-top: 20px;
}
.srch-sb-results4 {
margin: inherit;
padding-left: 20px;
}
.ms-bodyareaframe {
background-color: transparent;
}
td.ms-titleareaframe, div.ms-titleareaframe, .ms-pagetitleareaframe {
height: auto !important;
}
.ms-main .ms-ptabrx, .ms-main .ms-sctabrx, .ms-main .ms-ptabcn, .ms-main .ms-sctabcn {
border-color: #eeeeee;
}
.srch-sb-results {
height: auto;
}
.ms-sblink {
display:block;
}
.ms-sblink a:link, .ms-sblink a:visited, .ms-sblink a:hover {
color:#0072BC;
}
</style>
```

Finally, save and publish the new master page. It should be set only for search centers. The result will be that the search dialog now shows correctly as seen in Figure 7-11.

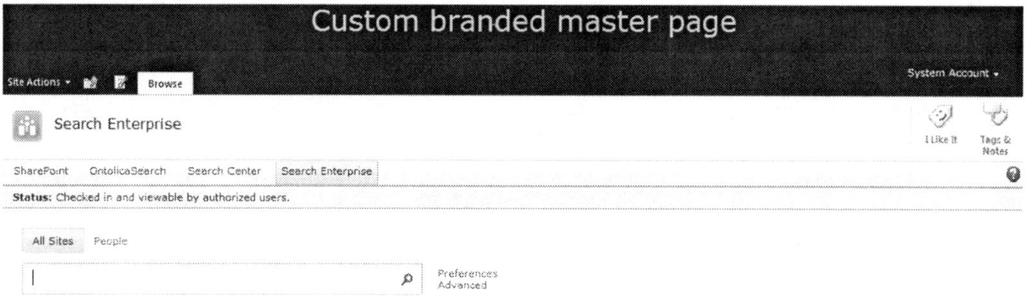

*Figure 7-11. Branded master page*

After these changes, the search center now reflects the custom branded master page in a still easy-to-maintain version. This techniques can also be used to create master pages with search center–specific branding.

# Modify the Search Results Presentation

Search results in SharePoint 2010 offer great opportunities for modification. Many can be done through the UI, but some changes require a little more modification. This section offers some insight into the possibilities through examples of how to add and remove search result information and how to modify the behavior of search results.

## Adding Additional Info to Search Results with XSLT

When searching in SharePoint using default search centers, only a small portion of the available data is actually presented to the user. Often adding new information is as easy as just modifying the XSLT template to display another property value. Sometimes, however, some form of interactivity with the search results is desired. This section focuses on how to enrich the search result UI through an example with ratings.

## Enabling Ratings

To get started, obviously ratings needs to be turned on in at least one list or library. For this example, a document library containing a number of PowerPoint presentations and a few documents is used. To enable ratings, navigate to the document library and choose "List settings" from the ribbon. From the Document Library settings page, choose "Rating settings", which opens a page where it is possible to enable or disable ratings as seen in Figure 7-12.

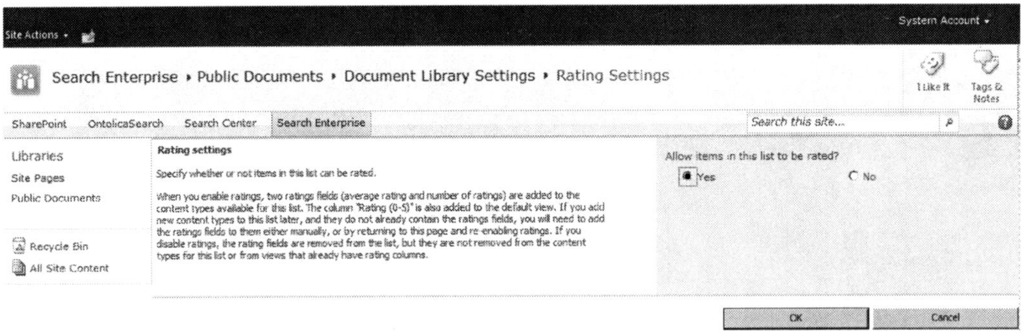

*Figure 7-12. Enabling ratings*

Once this setting is made, a new column is added to the list and to the default view as seen next in Figure 7-13. At this point users can start rating content.

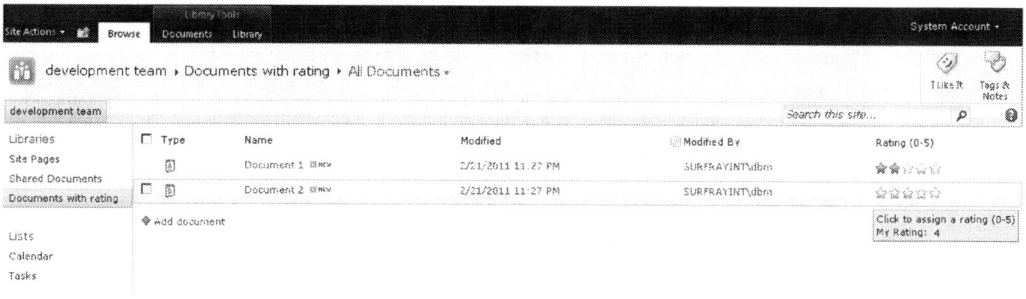

**Figure 7-13.** *Rating controls displayed in document library*

---

■ **Note** When selecting a rating and then doing a page reload, it can happen that the page is not updated with the latest rating due to a delay in processing ratings in SharePoint.

---

As you click the stars and add a rating, this is logged by SharePoint through an asynchronous AJAX call. An automated timer job in SharePoint named Social Data Maintenance Job is responsible for calculating the average ratings. The ratings are stored in the `SocialRatings_Averages` table. The rating information is computed from data in that table.

## Making Ratings Searchable

To allow data (in this case, ratings) to be searchable, it must be exposed as a searchable property. More precisely, this is done by creating a managed property in search to be included in the search results. To create the managed property, a crawled property is required. When the properties are fully configured, perform a full crawl for the properties to become available for searching.

If you are uncertain if these properties already exist, go to the Search Administration page in Central Administration. There open the Metadata Properties link located on the navigation bar to the left, and click the Crawled Properties link. Search for the term "rating." as seen in Figure 7-14.

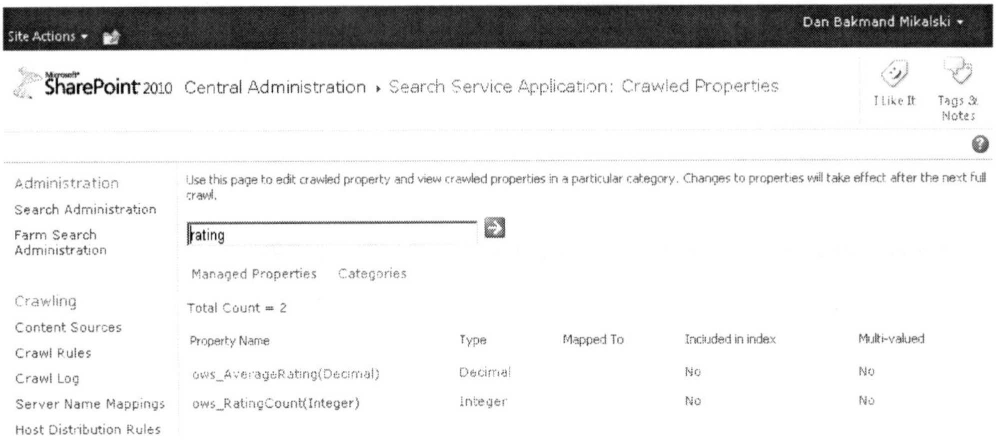

**Figure 7-14.** *Checking properties for rating*

If it already exists, the result should show two hits, one for `ows_AverageRating` and another for `ows_RatingCount`. If no hits are returned, make sure that rating is enabled on a document library, start a full crawl in search, and wait for it to complete.

When the crawled properties exist, then add a managed property for each of the two crawled properties. Begin with the `ows_AverageRating` and create a managed property named "Rating." as seen in Figure 7-15. This value is of a decimal type, and choose the `ows_AverageRating` crawled property for the mapping.

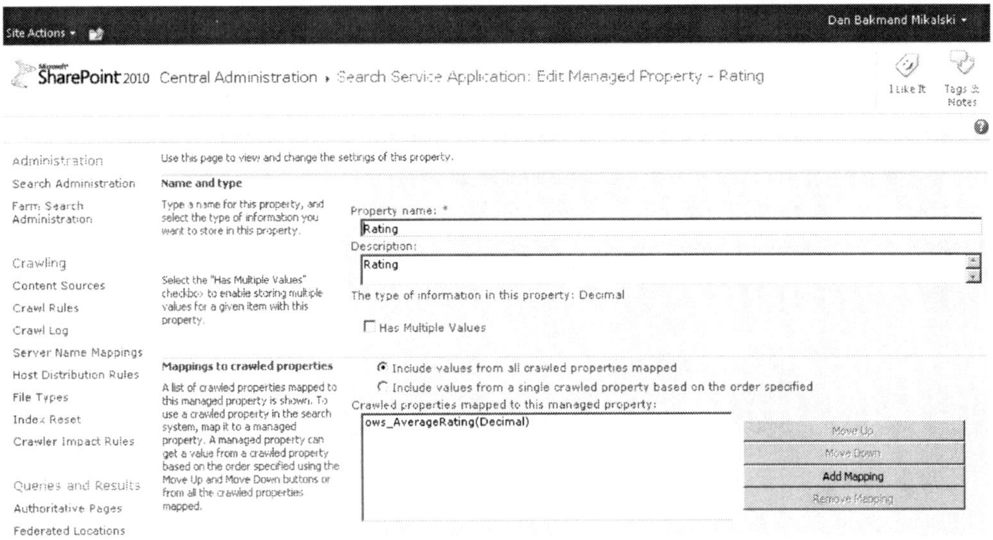

**Figure 7-15.** *Added managed properties for rating*

Next, add a managed property named `RatingCount` the same way as with the `Rating` property. It should be mapped to the crawled property named `ows_RatingCount` and have the type set to Integer. Ensure both of the crawled properties are included in the index. This is done by selecting the "Include values for this property in the search index" check box on each crawled property. After all of these changes have been made, again do a full crawl of search.

---

▪ **Note** An incremental crawl does not update the index when changing managed and crawled properties. When doing structural changes, a full crawl is required. Chapter 3 provides additional details on managing properties.

---

## Adding Ratings to Search Results

When the managed properties are added and a full crawl is completed, the XSL template must be modified to show the rating in the search results Web Part. Open the search results page that needs ratings added to it, and go to edit mode. Now change the following three settings of the Display Properties on the core search result Web Part.

Find the Use Location Visualization setting, and make sure it is unchecked.

Find the fetched properties. Here two new managed properties must be added. It should be expanded to contain these:

```
<Column Name="Rating"/>
<Column Name="RatingCount"/>
```

Find the XSL button and click it. Update the XSL to include the ratings. An example of how it could look is covered next. It is good practice to make a backup of the existing XSL before editing it. This way it is easier to go back to scratch in case the XSL gets wrongly edited.

For ease of use, it is suggested to insert a call template block in the XSL template. For those not too familiar with XSL, this is just a placeholder that displays the XSL formatting template block to apply and which variables to use in the template block. It can conceptually be understood as a method that gets called.

Two variables are required: Rating and Rating Count. These properties are exposed to the formatting template block with the same names for easier reading. The formatting template block is named `DisplayRating`.

```
<xsl:template name="DisplayRating">
  <xsl:param name="rating" />
  <xsl:param name="ratingcount" />
    Rating: <xsl:value-of select="format-number($rating, '#.#')" />
  (rated <xsl:value-of select="$ratingcount" /> times)
</xsl:template>
```

The next step is to include the required markup in the XSL template where the `DisplayRating` template is to be rendered, and the conditions under which it should be rendered. A suitable location in the layout for the rating to be displayed is just before the hit highlighted summary.

Notice that a test is performed to verify that the rating is higher than 0. This is only the case if the item—in this case, documents—has a rating. If the document has a rating, the `DisplayRating` template just shown is called and the rating text is rendered into the layout.

```
<div class="srch-Description2">

<xsl:if test="rating &gt; 0">
  <b>
    <xsl:call-template name="DisplayRating">
      <xsl:with-param name="rating" select="rating" />
      <xsl:with-param name="ratingcount" select="ratingcount" />
    </xsl:call-template>
  </b><br />
</xsl:if>

<xsl:choose>
<xsl:when test="hithighlightedsummary[. != '']">
    <xsl:call-template name="HitHighlighting">
      <xsl:with-param name="hh" select="hithighlightedsummary" />
```

## Viewing and Searching for Ratings

Having performed all the changes required for ratings to show up should yield a result page looking similar to Figure 7-16. It gives the user the possibility to select or ignore a specific search result based on recommendations from other people in your organization directly from the search results list.

This example of showing ratings is very basic. More advanced graphical templates can be applied to further enhance the user experience.

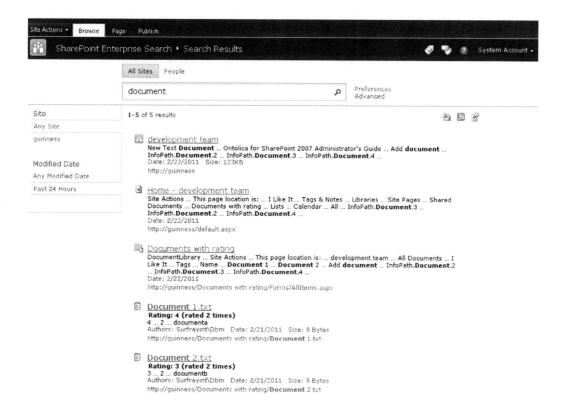

**Figure 7-16.** *Ratings showing in search results*

It is also possible to search for results with a rating higher, lower, or equal to a specific value. This can be done by simply searching for the property.

Rating>3

Rating<4

Rating=3,5

This is very useful for administrators to find documents with poor content that requires updating or deletion. It is equally useful for users to be able to refine or filter by documents that have a certain minimum ranking to avoid getting irrelevant results as seen in Figure 7-17.

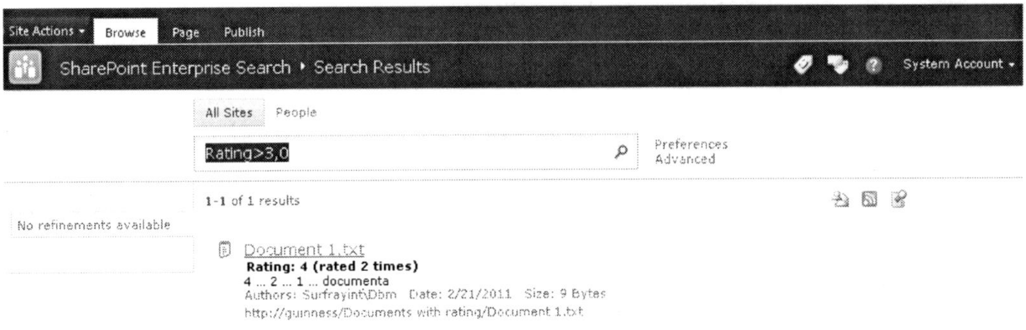

**Figure 7-17.** *Search result based on Rating property and displaying result rating.*

# Removing Metadata from Search Results

Removing metadata is usually a trivial task to perform. All that is needed is to remove the property from the XSL template. For example, there might be a requirement for the `CreatedBy` property to be removed.

To do this, open up the Search Core Results XSL template. Then find and remove or comment out the relevant call template section (shown here in its default form).

```
&lt;xsl:call-template name=&#8221;DisplayAuthors&#8221;&gt;

&lt;xsl:with-param name=&#8221;author&#8221; select=&#8221; author&#8221; &#47;&gt;

&lt;&#47;xsl:call-template&gt;
```

After the XSL is saved, the author or `CreatedBy` property no longer shows in search results.

# Changing Click Action of Search Results

Normal SharePoint behavior when clicking a search result item is to open the source directly. For web sites, this makes good sense but not so much for a lot of document types.

A typical scenario of what the user expects when clicking a document search result is to open a page that displays additional information about that particular search result and possibly a list of available actions and versions. This is available as an option on the search result item drop-down but not the default one when clicking.

The problem is the context switch from SharePoint to the native application of the search result document. The user can either see the loading screen of the document's native application (Figure 7-18) or the document details page in SharePoint, which allows the user to do check-outs, go through version history, and obviously open the document.

**Figure 7-18.** *Standard click action for document results*

The default SharePoint behavior to open the document without warning is a design choice aimed at the user knowing that the document is the right one and wanting to edit or read it. In a search context, this often is not the case.

In those cases, a different action is desired for the search results when clicked. The goal here is to allow the user to make a conscious choice about what to do with the search result.

Other side benefits are that the user doesn't lock the document if it is located on a file share without intent and also to reduce the network load of opening many documents without reason.

To accommodate such a behavior for documents, the default click action can be changed to redirect to the View Properties page rather than opening the document. This requires some rewiring of the search results Web Part.

## Creating a Managed ID Property

Create a managed property and give it a suitable name, for instance `SearchResultID`. Then map it to the crawled property called `ows_ID` with the type Integer. Make sure to include the crawled property in the index. See Chapter 3 for more details on managing properties.

In the Search service application, go to Federated Locations and open the location named Local Search Results. Here the new managed property can be added to the properties of the Core Search Results Display Metadata field like this:

```
<Column Name="SearchResultID"/>
```

When done, do a full crawl to make the property data available in search results.

In the Core Search Results Display Metadata, now click the XSL editor and modify the XSL to include the newly added managed property `SearchResultID` in the Result template match.

```
<xsl:variable name="id" select="id"/>
<xsl:variable name="currentId" select="concat($IdPrefix,$id)"/>
<xsl:variable name="url" select="url"/>
<xsl:variable name="searchresultid" select="searchresultid"/>
```

Now the click action for documents is to be changed. It will be configured to redirect to the View Properties page with the value of the `SearchResultID` property transferred to the View Properties page as a URL parameter.

Fortunately there exists an `IsDocument` property that can be used to check if the click action should be rewired. To accomplish this, find the following XSL from the template.

```
<xsl:attribute name="href">
  <xsl:value-of select="$url"/>
</xsl:attribute>
```

Insert this XSL just after the foregoing. This XSL uses a conditional statement to check if the result is a document. If it is a document, then the `href` attribute is set to the View Properties page with the `SearchResultID` added as a URL argument. Otherwise the `href` value is left unchanged.

```
    <xsl:attribute name="href">
      <xsl:value-of select="$url"/>
    </xsl:attribute>
<xsl:choose>
  <xsl:when test="isdocument='True'">
    <xsl:attribute name="href">
      <xsl:value-of select="concat(sitename,'/Forms/DispForm.aspx?id=',$searchresultid)"/>
    </xsl:attribute>
  </xsl:when>
</xsl:choose>
```

Now the result redirects to the View Properties page for document results (Figure 7-19) and to the URL destination for other types of results. It should be noted that this works for document libraries.

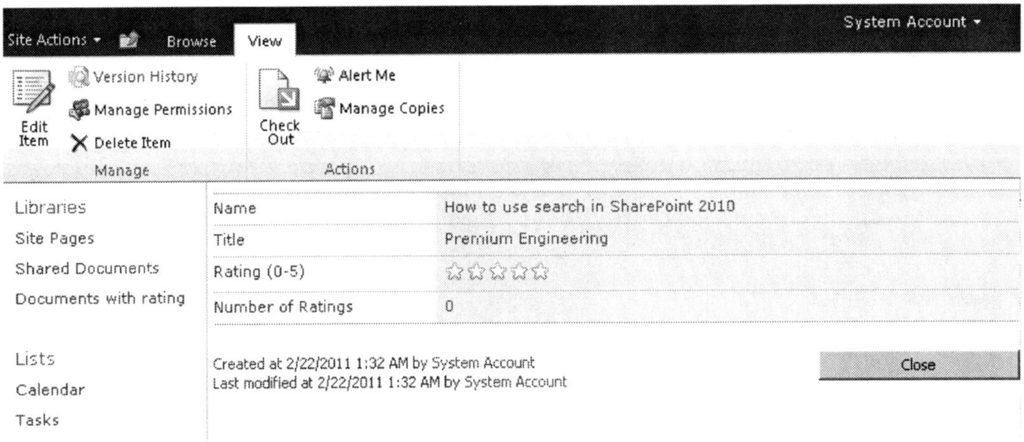

***Figure 7-19.*** *Custom click action for document results*

▓ **Note** The View Properties page also supports a URL argument named source. If set, this defines which page to go to when the Close button is clicked on the View Properties page. This is useful if expanding this example to a live working environment where the user might want to return to the search results after clicking a document result.

# Advanced Topics on Refinement Panel

The refinement panel in SharePoint 2010 is one of the more complex Web Parts to fully utilize. Its behavior is complex and can impose significant performance overhead when searching if configured wrongly. On the other hand, it does also provide a lot of options to leverage, which are not enabled in the default out-of-the-box configuration.

This section will focus on how to easily access and enable some of the most commonly requested features of the refinement panel. It will also discuss possible implications and side effects when enabling these features.

## Adding Refiner Counts

One of the most hyped features of FAST for SharePoint 2010 is deep refinement and numbered refiners that show accurate counts, as seen in Figure 7.20. In FAST this is enabled in the default out-of-the-box refinement panel. SharePoint 2010 does not support deep refinement, but it does support numbered refiners. The functionality is just not enabled per default as seen in Figure 7.21.

Numbered refiners, also known as refiner counts, show the user how many search results refining by each metadata property value will return. This allows the user to quickly determine which rementents are most suitable to apply to get the desired search results. For applications where data set analysis is relevant, SharePoint 2010 is not suitable, as it does not produce accurate numbers and does not even necessarily show all refinement options due to limited precision.

Third-party solutions and free solutions with numbered refiners have existed since MOSS 2007. Examples are Ontolica from SurfRay A/S and the CodePlex refiners. Both offer similar functionality to that of SharePoint 2010, but are more scalable and easily maintained. Especially the Ontolica solution excels in refiner management.

An obvious question, then, is why numbered refiners are not enabled per default in SharePoint 2010. The likely reasons include their limited precision, which disturbs the immediate customer experience, and a desire to lower the default load on the index server. Marketing considerations likely also play a role with hiding this feature to make FAST more attractive compared to SharePoint 2010 Search.

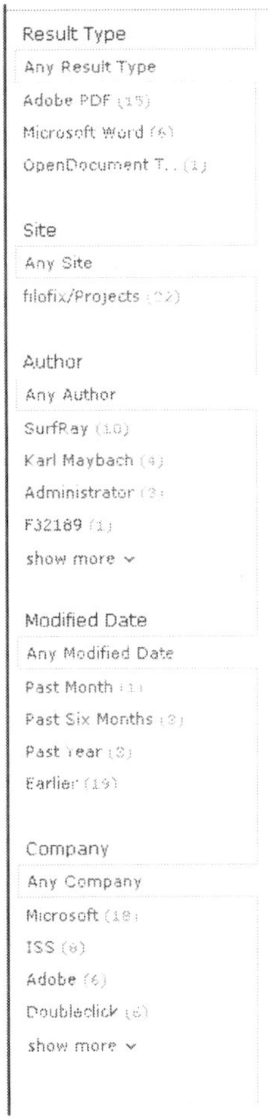

Result Type
Any Result Type
Adobe PDF (15)
Microsoft Word (6)
OpenDocument T... (1)

Site
Any Site
filofix/Projects (22)

Author
Any Author
SurfRay (10)
Karl Maybach (4)
Administrator (3)
F32189 (1)
show more ⌄

Modified Date
Any Modified Date
Past Month (1)
Past Six Months (3)
Past Year (3)
Earlier (19)

Company
Any Company
Microsoft (18)
ISS (8)
Adobe (6)
Doubleclick (6)
show more ⌄

Result Type
Any Result Type
Word
Webpage
PowerPoint
Text

Site
Any Site
filofix/projects
guinness

Author
Any Author
Sbi
Surfray
Lars Thejl
Teater & Dans I N...
show more ⌄

Modified Date
Any Modified Date
Past 24 Hours
Past Month
Past Six Months
Earlier

*Figure 7-20. FAST refiners* 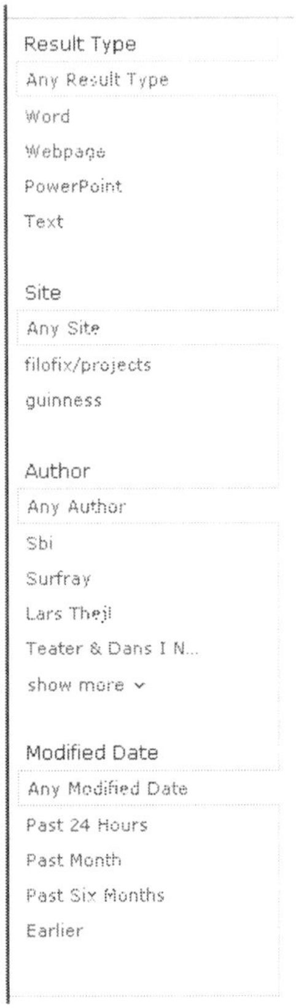          *Figure 7-21. SharePoint 2010 refiners*

To add the counts on the refiners for SharePoint 2010, the Filter Definition category must be edited as mentioned earlier. Details on accessing the refinement panel settings are available in Chapter 6. Open the Filter Definition category XML file.

Refiner counts can be added to individual properties. This allows site administrators to tweak performance, resource requirements, and usability. Refiner counts make more sense for some properties than others. Result Type, Site, and Author are obvious candidates that can benefit from refiner counts, whereas Modified Date is less obvious.

To add a refiner count for a property, the ShowCounts attribute should be added as displayed here. Remember to uncheck the Use Default Configuration check box for the changes to take effect as seen in Figure 7-22.

```
<Category Title="Result Type"
    Type="Microsoft.Office.Server.Search.WebControls.ManagedPropertyFilterGenerator"
    ShowCounts="Count">
```

**Figure 7-22.** *SharePoint 2010 refinement panel with count on selected properties*

## Changing the Accuracy Index

Unlike FAST, which has deep refiners and accurate refiner counts, SharePoint 2010 analyzes a subset of the total result set when determining refinements to show. This also applies to the refiner counts. The value that controls the size of the analyzed subset is called the accuracy index. This value is set on the refinement panel Web Part.

Having imprecise refiners is not per definition an issue as long as it is clearly understood by the users how they work. Often it is very valuable just to know if there are many or few results contained within a particular refinement. In situations like that, it does not matter if the refinement yields 300 or 30,000 results. The target is already achieved by the user being able to evaluate that this refinement does not trim the result set significantly.

Per default, however, the accuracy index that controls how many results are analyzed for the SharePoint 2010 search refinement panel is set to 50, which is too low for most corporations, as global searches must be expected to yield many more results than that. It can and should in most instances be increased to the maximum of 500. This is shown in Figures 7-23 and 7-24. Setting any larger number will automatically change that number to 500. This is hard-coded on the Web Part.

Site

Any Site

filofix/groups (36)

filofix/projects (11)

guinness (3)

Site

Any Site

filofix/groups (489)

filofix/projects (10)

guinness (1)

***Figure 7-23.*** *Accuracy index set to 50*             ***Figure 7-24.*** *Accuracy index set to 500*

Increasing the accuracy index benefits the users, but it is also a costly operation to calculate refinements and counts. It is impossible to give rock-solid measurements on how performance is affected when increasing the accuracy index as it depends on the query and the composition and size of the total result set. It is noticeable when searching when the accuracy index is increased from 50 to 500 for a query that yields a total result set that exceeds 500. A good rule of thumb is to expect the query to take two to five times longer, which means the query can take two times as long to perform when increasing the accuracy index four times. For many smaller queries, the difference is close to non-existent.

---

▨ **Note** A good way of increasing the usability of refiner counts is to increase the accuracy index to 500 and at the same time promote smaller result sets by introducing limited scopes. This generally makes the result sets smaller, thus rendering the refiner counts more accurate. It also increases the query performance.

---

If a higher accuracy is required on SharePoint 2010, a custom programmed solution or third-party solution such as Ontolica from SurfRay A/S is required. Ontolica allows for higher accuracy than the 500 limit. It is also able to estimate the total refinement counts based on the size of the total result set, thus producing much more reliable counts than SharePoint 2010 and with higher performance too. This is amongst others achieved by quantifying on the approximate total result count. To counter the performance hit a user could experience when computing the counts, Ontolica can load the refiner counts asynchroniosly. It should be noted however that although custom and 3rd party solutions in theory can analyze the entire result set and give deep refiners and counts, this is not practical in most cases as it would severely impact performance on large result sets.

# Number of Categories to Display

Refiners are defined in the Filter Definition category XML file. They appear in the order that they are defined. A common issue is that added refiners do not show up or some existing refiner suddenly stops showing, depending on the order in which they are specified in the XML file. This can happen if the number of defined refiners exceeds the number of categories to display. Per default, six categories are displayed at most.

Another reason refiners are not showing can be the metadata threshold (which is discussed next). Well, it won't, if there already more refiners visible that are greater than the number of categories to display. From what I can gather, the refiners are basically rendered in the order they are in the XML, so if you put your refiner at the end and already the refinement panel has rendered the maximum amount, it won't be seen by users.

In the default Filter Definition category XML file, six refiners are defined per default. These are Result Type, Site, Author, Modified Date, Product Category, and Company Size.

If the number of six refiners does not fit in the custom branded page layout, it can be expanded or reduced by changing the number of categories to display. No limit on how many refiners can be added has been found so far. Changing the number to two now displays only the first two feasible refiners as seen in Figure 7-25.

Result Type

Any Result Type

Word (394)

Webpage (62)

Email (2)

PowerPoint (1)

Site

Any Site

filofix/groups (494)

filofix/projects (5)

guinness (1)

***Figure 7-25.*** *Number of categories to display set to two*

Although it should be fairly self-explanatory how to add new refiners, one issue has been raised a number of times: what if the order of the refiners in the XML file should differ from their priority to show? Currently this is not supported in SharePoint 2010. To achieve this, a third-party solution such as Ontolica from SurfRay A/S can be used. This supports such advanced behavior. Alternatively the CodePlex refiners can be modified to also achieve this, but that requires a significant portion of re-programming.

## Metadata Threshold

One of the more difficult settings to work with is the metadata threshold. A common misunderstanding is that this value defines how many different values must be available for a given property. This is not correct. It actually defines how many times the property is found in any of the analyzed search results for the refiner to display.

Assume that the metadata threshold is set to 5 for the Result Type refiner. This refiner operates on the `FileExtension` property. If the analyzed search result set contains only two Word documents and two PDF files, then this refiner will not show. This then also affects how the "Number of categories to display" acts. If a total of ten refiners are defined and the first four do not show, then refiners five through nine will show. If search results often cause most refiners not to be shown due to the metadata threshold, it should be considered to create new refiners targeted at those situations to allow users to always do meaningful refinements. For this reason, it is not advisable to set the metadata threshold too low. Instead new refiners should be introduced.

The metadata threshold value is a byte, which means that the range is [0:255]. In the following example shown in Figures 7-26 and 7-27, the number of categories to display is set to 2 and the threshold is changed from 5 to 250 on the Result Type refiner to illustrate how it works.

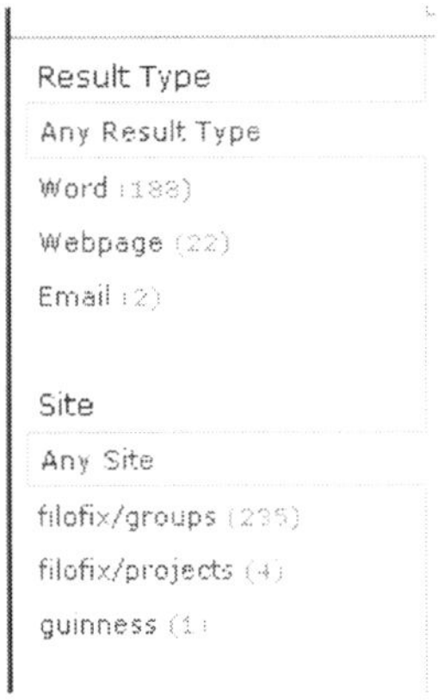

**Figure 7-26.** *Result Type threshold = 5*

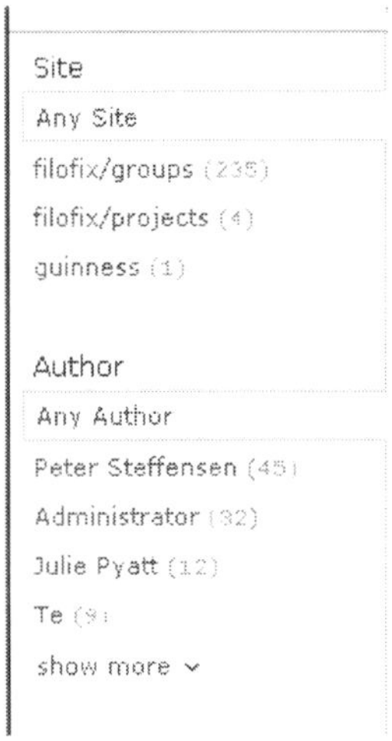

**Figure 7-27.** *Result Type threshold = 250*

## Number of Characters to Display

This is not really an advanced topic but rather a hint of why to use a generally not-used setting on the refinement panel.

The "Number of characters to display" sets how many characters of each refinement option are displayed. The default value is 16, which is often too short to show meaningful information, especially for paths.

It is not uncommon to have names that are longer than 16 characters (Figure 7-28) or paths such as `http://subdomain.domain.org/something/something/something/`. In this case, the limit of 16 is actually not enough to display the actual file and site names on the path. Instead it will be displayed with "`http://subdomain…`" as SharePoint refiners automatically apply the "…" to indicate a partial text. Setting this value too large is not a good idea either, as it wastes screen space. But in general it should be set to some value in the area of 25 to 30, which fits nicely with the standard search layout.

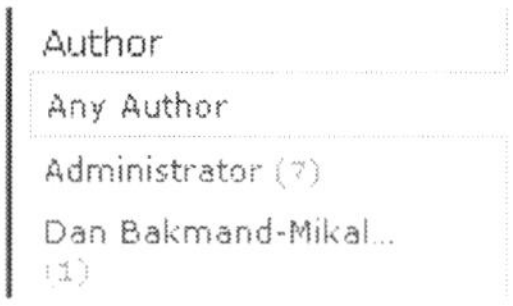

*Figure 7-28. Ending of name trimmed and replaced with "…"*

# Summary

In this chapter on customizing search, the focus was on master pages and some of the quirks involved when working with those in the search context. One issue especially important to notice is how the master pages differ between normal SharePoint pages and the search center pages. This is often a challenge to maintain in custom branded layouts. This chapter offered advice on how to overcome some of the most frequently occurring issues with custom branding search centers.

Another important topic covered is navigation and how this can be improved for search centers. Standard search is somewhat limited with respect to this, but fortunately ways exist for how to improve this. Also the interaction with search results themselves is covered. Arguably the default click action for document search results is unsuitable for the purpose, by defaulting to opening the document rather than letting the user inspect the properties before deciding what to do next. A suggestion for how to change this is proposed.

Adding and removing properties of the search results are described in order to offer insight into some of the extensive possibilities that SharePoint has to offer in terms of customization.

The refinement panel can be customized to achieve improved refinements. With focus on numbered refiners, different options for extending the refinement experience are described and discussed.

# CHAPTER 8

■ ■ ■

# Searching Through the API

After completing this chapter, you will be able to

- Understand the query expression as SharePoint sees it

- Understand the fundamentals of how the search APIs work

- Construct and work with SQL for querying SharePoint

- Create and deploy a custom search-enabled application page

The SharePoint search engine itself can be leveraged for custom development. This chapter focuses on showing the advanced administrator or novice SharePoint developer how the search APIs work in SharePoint 2010. A thorough re-introduction to the query expression is presented, which expands on the already provided description of operators from Chapter 5 and how to organize the query expression to get the desired results.

An example is provided of how to create a custom search-enabled application page using Visual Studio 2010. This search application page provides a base for further exploration and experimentation of the search API in SharePoint 2010.

The purpose of this chapter is to enable the reader to understand and work with the search API. The API itself will not be covered in detail in this book. Instead, the basics of how to invoke it will be covered. Our intent is to provide a solid platform for the reader to expand upon.

## Understanding the Query Expression Parsing Order

Before tackling the API, it's important to review the parsing order of the query expression. Parsing of the query is dependent on the ranking of logical operators. This means defining which operators take precedence over others. The concept is also known from traditional math, where, for example, multiplications take precedence over additions. It can also be said that multiplications have a higher order than additions. An example of this is the following:

```
a=3 +4*5 = 23
```

The result of a is calculated by adding 3 to the sum of 4 times 5. The result in this case is 23 because the multiplication gets executed first.

A normal way of representing the order of computation is to use parentheses. In the math example, the formula would then be written as follows:

```
a=3+(4*5) = 23
```

Using this form of representation makes it easier to understand how a query is executed in the search engine.

## Operator Order

Table 8-1 shows the order of the query operators in SP 2010. This is relevant when constructing queries that contain multiple terms or property restrictions. As always it is possible to overrule this priority using parentheses to group certain sub-expressions.

***Table 8-1.*** *Logical operators in SharePoint 2010 search*

| Order | Operator | Description |
|-------|----------|-------------|
| 1 | AND | The logical AND statement dictates that terms on both sides of this operator have to match the result for it to be returned. It can also be used to group two separate blocks of conditions using the (condition set 1) AND (condition set 2). |
| | + | This is the default operator if no other is specified. A term preceded by this operator must match a result for it to be returned. |
| 2 | NOT | This operator must succeed another term or condition group. The term or condition group following this operator must not be matched in the result if it is to be returned. This operator is similar to using the "-" operator. |
| | - | A term preceded by this operator must not match a result for the result to be returned. |
| 3 | OR | The logical OR statement works similarly to the AND operator, except only one of the terms before or after the OR has to match the result for it to be returned. It can also be used to group two separate blocks of conditions using the (condition set 1) OR (condition set 2). |
| 3 | WORDS | This is not a logical operator but rather a function operator. It should be followed by a comma-separated list of terms surrounded by parentheses. The WORDS operator acts as if there were an implicit OR statement between each item in the list, with the exception of how they rank.

When using the WORDS operator, the terms are treated as synonyms, not individual terms. Ranking of the terms is therefore equal to the total amount of occurrences of any term in the list. If the list contains two terms, and the first is found two times and the second is found three times, the synonym group would be ranked as if five occurrences of the same term were found. |

| Order | Operator | Description |
|-------|----------|-------------|
| 4 | NEAR | Sometimes the relevancy of a search is dependent on not only the terms but also how they appear in the text relative to one another. The NEAR operator allows for queries where the terms have to be close to each other. For logical reasons, this works with free text expressions only. Therefore it cannot be used in a keyword query.<br><br>NEAR can be considered a more restrictive version of the AND operator. |
| 5 | * | The wildcard operator or asterisk character ("*") is used to enable prefix matching. It can process any part of the beginning of a word. Even only one letter followed by the wildcard operator works. It acts as [0...n] random characters, which means it can also be put after the entire term and still match that term. |

For example, take the following user-submitted query:

```
sharepo* search or search near office
```

This would be evaluated as follows:

```
('sharepo*' AND 'search') OR '(search' near 'office)
```

In this example, it is assumed that keyword inclusion is set to All Keywords, which means that there is an implicit AND between keywords.

## Using a Tree Structure to Understand the Query

A good way of understanding how a query behaves is to create a query tree, as shown in Figure 8-1. This way, it is easier to physically view the individual components of the query and evaluate the impact of the operator order. Especially if parentheses are added to the query to manipulate the ordering, this is a helpful way of analyzing the query. The following is an example of a query and the corresponding query tree.

```
sharepo* search or search near office
```

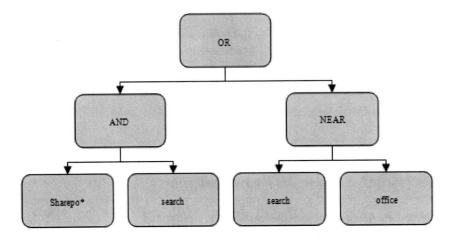

***Figure 8-1.*** *Creating a query tree structure for understanding the search*

If this is to be submitted as a `FullTextSqlQuery`, the SQL would be as follows:

```
SELECT WorkId,Rank,Title,Author,ModifiedBy,Size,Path,Description,Created,Write,Filename,↵
SiteName,SiteTitle,CollapsingStatus,HitHighlightedSummary,HitHighlightedProperties,↵
ContentClass,IsDocument,ContentType,objectid,PictureURL,WorkEmail,CreatedBy,ContentSource,↵
FileExtension FROM SCOPE() WHERE (FREETEXT(defaultproperties,'software') AND CONTAINS↵
(' "sharepo*" AND search ') ) OR CONTAINS('search NEAR office') ORDER BY Rank DESC
```

## Manipulate the Query with Parentheses

You can force a specific ranking of operators in the parsing of the query by combining different parts of a keyword query using parentheses. It is important that the parentheses are closed correctly in such a way that every single left side "(" has an equivalent right side ")". Empty spaces next to the parenthesis do not influence the search result, as they are stripped out by the search expression parser.

Understanding how query parsing takes place and how the order can be modified is important when working with the search API. In the following sections, various ways of using the search API are presented. When creating full text queries or querying through the search web service, the query is passed as clear text. When creating SQL queries, the query is created from a number of aggregated statements. Although this is different from providing one complete query string, the same principle applies.

## The Search API

The SharePoint 2010 Enterprise Search API has changed from using the Shared Services Provider architecture in SharePoint 2007 to using Search service applications in SharePoint 2010. A lot of the engine under the hood is still the same, however. This section focuses on how to do basic search programming in SharePoint 2010. If the purpose is to migrate search code from 2007 to 2010, this should be easy, as search has been abstracted to support code for SP 2007.

Three ways of doing search programming are covered:

- Using the KeywordQuery
- Using the FullTextSqlQuery
- Using the search web service

# Creating a KeywordQuery-Based Search

SharePoint 2010 now has a new way to get the object of the KeywordQuery by using the SearchServiceApplicationProxy. The name of the SearchServiceApplicationProxy is required for creating the KeywordQuery object. The name can be found by navigating to the SSA list. The proxy name is normally the same as the SSA name. Per default this is simply "Search Service Application". If not, then go to Central Administration and open Service Applications to find it.

Having the name of the SearchServiceApplicationProxy, it is now possible to get the proper references required for creating the KeywordQuery object. This is done as follows:

```
SearchQueryAndSiteSettingsServiceProxy settingsProxy =↩
 SPFarm.Local.ServiceProxies.GetValue<SearchQueryAndSiteSettingsServiceProxy>();

SearchServiceApplicationProxy searchProxy =↩
 settingsProxy.ApplicationProxies.GetValue<SearchServiceApplicationProxy>↩
("Search Service Application");

Using(KeywordQuery keywordQuery = new KeywordQuery(searchProxy))
{---}
```

Having the reference to the KeywordQuery object, the search properties can now be configured. SharePoint 2010 introduces a significant number of new properties to configure. In the example below, only the basic properties, that are needed to perform a search, are configured.

```
keywordQuery.QueryText = "Your query text";
keywordQuery.ResultTypes = ResultType.RelevantResults;
keywordQuery.ResultsProvider = SearchProvider.Default;
ResultTableCollection keywordQueryResultsCollection = keywordQuery.Execute();

ResultTable keywordQueryResults = keywordQueryResultsCollection[ResultType.RelevantResults];
DataTable keywordQueryResultsTable = new DataTable();
keywordQueryResultsTable.TableName = "Results";
keywordQueryResultsTable.Load(keywordQueryResults, LoadOption.OverwriteChanges);
```

There are two properties that should receive special attention due to the new, enhanced people-finding abilities in SP 2010: EnableNicknames and EnablePhonetic.

The EnableNicknames property allows for people to be found by their, well, nicknames. This way is it possible to find Andrew by his nickname, "Andy." This is immensely helpful if building custom people finder Web Parts.

EnablePhonetic allows users to find persons even if they do not know the exact spelling of a name. A search for Kristian will return results for "Christian" as well.

One important point of these properties is that they depend on the browser language setting. For instance, the nickname Mike for Michael applies if browser language is set to US or UK, but not if it is set to German.

## Creating a FullTextSqlQuery-Based Search

Sometimes the programmer wants more control over the query. This can be achieved using the `FullTextSqlQuery` class. This class allows the programmer to control the query using SQL syntax, which is often a more familiar language and makes it easier to understand why a query behaves a particular way.

The FROM target object in the SQL has to be set to the `SCOPE()` function, as shown here. If further refinement is required, the scope can be set in a WHERE clause. If the scope is not set, no scope is applied. In the following query, the first name of all persons in the People scope are returned.

```
SELECT FirstName FROM SCOPE() WHERE "scope" = 'People'
```

The SQL select statement can be expanded to return more properties or have more property restrictions. For instance, if the query should be limited to return the author for all documents with a file type of `.pdf`, the following code SQL can be used to perform that search. This assumes the code is executed with the SharePoint context.

The namespace where the SharePoint search types are defined is as follows:

```
using Microsoft.Office.Server.Search.Query;

using(FullTextSqlQuery fullTextSqlQuery = new FullTextSqlQuery(SPContext.Current.Site))
{
fullTextSqlQuery.QueryText = "SELECT Author FROM SCOPE() WHERE \"scope\" = 'All Sites'
        AND CONTAINS(FileType, 'pdf')";

fullTextSqlQuery.ResultTypes = ResultType.RelevantResults;

ResultTable fullTextSqlQueryResults =
        keywordQueryResultsCollection[ResultType.RelevantResults];

DataTable fullTextSqlQueryResultsTable = new DataTable();
fullTextSqlQueryQueryResultsTable.TableName = "Results";
fullTextSqlQueryQueryResultsTable.Load(fullTextSqlQueryQueryResults,
        LoadOption.OverwriteChanges);
}
```

This is a very basic example of how to perform a property search in SharePoint using the CONTAINS predicate. Creating more elaborate SQL queries is covered later in this chapter.

If debugging in Visual Studio 2010, you can then use the data visualizer to see the results. This can be a helpful way of evaluating search results.

## Searching Through the Search Web Service

In SharePoint it is possible to search the SharePoint index not only using the API on a SharePoint server, but also from external locations outside SharePoint, using the search web service. Examples could be custom integrations of search into locally deployed client applications or from other non-SharePoint web sites hosted on other servers.

As opposed to using the API, which, as shown in the previous examples, is straightforward, using the search web service does introduce some new challenges, namely the binding context. Next, it is described how to contact the web service through a console application with the binding context setup from App.Config. The search web service can be called from any code, however, and the binding can be specified directly from code too, where feasible.

## Consuming the Search Web Service from a Console Application

First a reference to the search service soap client is needed. The constructor can either be empty or receive a string with the name of the service binding context to use.

```
SearchServices.WSSearch.QueryServiceSoapClient searchService =
new SearchServices.WSSearch.QueryServiceSoapClient("SearchServiceBinding");
```

It is good practice to verify that the service is actually online before invoking it. This can be done by checking the status message of the soap client.

```
if (searchService.Status().ToLower() != "ONLINE")
        throw new Exception("The search service is not online.");
```

The App.Config file in this example also includes credentials to use when querying the search web service. These credentials are passed on to the search service.

Although it is possible to use anonymous access when searching, it is often a requirement in any corporation that some level of access permissions is set.

```
searchService.ClientCredentials.Windows.AllowNtlm = true;
```

```
searchService.ClientCredentials.Windows.AllowedImpersonationLevel =
        System.Security.Principal.TokenImpersonationLevel.Impersonation;
```

The service is configured to use NT LAN Manager (NTLM) credentials, and the allowed impersonation level is set.

```
String username = ConfigurationManager.AppSettings.Get("SearchUserName").ToString();
String password = ConfigurationManager.AppSettings.Get("SearchPassword").ToString();
String domainname = ConfigurationManager.AppSettings.Get("SearchDomainName").ToString();
```

```
searchService.ClientCredentials.Windows.ClientCredential =
        new System.Net.NetworkCredential(username, password, domainname);
```

At this point, the search service soap client is fully configured and ready to be queried. The web service exposes a method called QueryEx, which receives a XML-formatted query request containing the textual expression to query for. Here the query text is simply "SharePoint AND Search".

```
String queryText = "SharePoint AND Search";
String queryRequestString = "<QueryPacket xmlns='urn:Microsoft.Search.Query'>" +
        "<Query>" +
                "<SupportedFormats>" +
                        "<Format revision='1'>" +
                                "urn:Microsoft.Search.Response.Document:Document" +
                        "</Format>" +
                "</SupportedFormats>" +
                "<Context>" +
                        "<QueryText language='en-US' type='STRING'>" +
                                queryText +
                        "</QueryText>" +
                "</Context>" +
        "</Query>" +
"</QueryPacket>";
```

The request package just shown is the simplest possible request. With the search service soap client configured and the query request ready, the actual query can be executed in order to get a results data set back from the search web service. In real-life applications, there should always be an error handling code and a check on success when contacting the search web service as when calling any other web service. This is left out here for clarity.

```
System.Data.DataSet searchServiceQueryResults = new System.Data.DataSet();
searchServiceQueryResults = searchService.QueryEx(queryRequestString);
```

Finally the results can be retrieved from the search result data set by simply iterating the rows in the returned data set. Each row contains the default properties returned by the search result. Typical properties that are useful are Title, Path, Author, and a Summary of the result.

```
String title, author, path, summary;
foreach (DataRow row in searchServiceQueryResults.Tables[0].Rows)
{
title = row["Title"];
author = row["Author"];
path = row["Path"];
summary = row["HitHighlightedSummary"];
}
```

## App.Config Settings

The App.Config for the application is used to define the default binding. As mentioned, this can also be defined directly in code on the search service soap client object using the API, but it is suggested to use an App.Config whenever possible. This makes it easier to maintain and reconfigure if so needed. As such, this example of the binding is sufficient for most practical uses (Listing 8-1).

***Listing 8-1.*** *Application Configuration file for console application using search web service*

```xml
<?xml version="1.0"?>
<configuration>
<appSettings>
<add key="SearchUserName" value="YourUserName"/>
<add key="SearchPassword" value="YourPassword"/>
<add key="SearchDomainName" value="YourDomainName"/>
</appSettings>
<system.serviceModel> <bindings> <basicHttpBinding>
<binding name="SearchServiceBinding"
                  closeTimeout="00:01:00"
                  openTimeout="00:01:00"
                  receiveTimeout="00:10:00"
                  sendTimeout="00:01:00"
                  allowCookies="false"
                  bypassProxyOnLocal="false"
                  hostNameComparisonMode="StrongWildcard"
                  maxBufferSize="500000000"
                  maxBufferPoolSize="500000000"
                  maxReceivedMessageSize="500000000"
                  messageEncoding="Text"
                  textEncoding="utf-8"
                  transferMode="Buffered"
                  useDefaultWebProxy="true">
              <readerQuotas maxDepth="32"
                  maxStringContentLength="8192"
                  maxArrayLength="16384"
                  maxBytesPerRead="4096"
                  maxNameTableCharCount="16384"/>
              <security mode="TransportCredentialOnly">
                  <transport clientCredentialType="Ntlm" />
              </security>
          </binding>
       </basicHttpBinding> </bindings>
    <client>
       <endpoint address=http://[servername]:[portnumber]/_vti_bin/search.asmx
           binding="basicHttpBinding"
           bindingConfiguration="QueryServiceSoap"
           contract="WSSearch.QueryServiceSoap"
           name="QueryServiceSoap"/>
    </client>
</system.serviceModel>
</configuration>
```

As shown in this section, it is fairly easy to use the search web service for performing searches against the SharePoint index, from outside the SharePoint farm. The drawback here is maintaining the correct binding context if the name or location of the search web service were to change. One way of handling this could be to create a proxy on the organization's primary domain that internally refers to the search web service.

# Creating SQL for the FullTextSqlQuery

SQL query syntax for SharePoint 2010 is similar to that of SharePoint 2007. The most important thing to understand when constructing SQL query syntax is how to parse the input to get a representation that reflects what the user expects and is easily analyzed. This section looks at the different components of the SQL query syntax, what they do, and how to combine them to achieve a specific behavior.

## Creating the Query

Calling and getting results from search engine can be summarized as follows:

1. An instance of the SP query object is created.

2. The query object settings get configured.

3. The SQL is added to the query object.

4. An **execute()** method on the SP query object is called.

5. The return value of the **execute()** method is an SP object of type **ResultTableCollection**.

## Important Configuration Options of the Query Object

The SP query object can be configured with a number of properties. The "must know" properties are as follows:

- Enable stemming

- Trim duplicates

- Ignore all noise query

- Highlighted sentence count (default = 3, range =[0,10] or an exception gets thrown)

- Result types

- SQL query string

- Site context (URL)

- Keyword inclusion

## SQL Query Predicates

The query string supplied to the search engine is constructed from the following predicates. These look like normal T-SQL and should be easily understandable, perhaps with the exception of the SCOPE statement.

- *SELECT*: This states which information you want to get returned from the search engine. These values might be null if they are not available properties for a particular result type.

- *FROM SCOPE*: This is responsible for limiting which areas are searched. The functionality of setting this is currently unclear as it is not easily examined in our test setup.

- *WHERE*: This contains the predicates that are to be searched. These predicates can be FREETEXT or CONTAINS. Predicates can be concatenated with the logical operators AND and OR. The property does not need to be one of the returned properties of the SELECT statement.

- *FREETEXT*: This is in the SP documentation, described as being the best option for finding documents containing combinations of the search words scattered across columns. It is used this way:

  ```
  WHERE FREETEXT(defaultproperties,'SharePoint search')
  ```

- *CONTAINS*: This is best for finding exact matches. It is also used for performing wildcard searches, which is actually also an exact match from a logical point of view but a partial match from a user's point of view. It is used this way:

  ```
  WHERE CONTAINS(' "sear*" ')
  ```

- *ORDER BY*: This instructs the search engine to do a reordering of the returned results by some property.

## Details on Keyword Inclusion

The `KeywordInclusion` property is related to the FREETEXT and CONTAINS predicates. It can be set to one of two enumerations:

- `AllKeywords` (acts as an AND between all keywords in the FULLTEXT predicate)

- `AnyKeyword` (acts as an OR between all keywords in the FULLTEXT predicate)

The value of the `KeywordInclusion` property is set based on how the query tree should look per default. The value `AnyKeyword` typically relates to whether an OR node is implicit when constructing the query tree, and `AllKeywords` relates to implicit AND searches.

It is not be feasible for the user to be limited to use either of the two enumerations. It is therefore possible to override the `AnyKeyword` option by adding a + symbol to the keywords, which basically states that it *must* be contained in the results.

An example could be a query for the following:

```
SharePoint search or engine
```

This would then be evaluated as follows:

```
('SharePoinit' AND ' search') OR 'engine'
With KeywordInclusion = AnyKeyword
```

The SQL would be as follows:

```
SELECT WorkId,Rank,Title,Author,ModifiedBy,Size,Path,Description,Created,Write,Filename,↵
SiteName,SiteTitle,CollapsingStatus,HitHighlightedSummary,HitHighlightedProperties,↵
ContentClass,IsDocument,ContentType,objectid,PictureURL,WorkEmail,CreatedBy,ContentSource,↵
FileExtension FROM SCOPE() WHERE FREETEXT(defaultproperties,'+engine') OR↵
 FREETEXT(defaultproperties,'+SharePoint +search') ORDER BY Rank DESC
```

## FREETEXT and CONTAINS Predicates Format

The format of the predicates is as follows:

```
([<column_identifier>,]'<content_search_condition>' [,LCID])
```

The column identifier can be either a column or a column group. In Ontolica the latter is used by setting it to "defaultproperties", which is also the default value of the search engine if none is set.

The content search condition is different from FREETEXT and CONTAINS and is described individually next.

Localization can be achieved by setting the LCID argument on the predicates, thus allowing for locale-specific searches (language-specific searches). This is relevant not only for words, but also for dates and numeric values, currency format, and more. If no LCID is set, then the systems locale is used.

### FREETEXT

Generally as few FREETEXT statements should be used as possible to improve ranking. If the query can be wrapped into a single FREETEXT statement, that would be the best solution.

The SP search engine removes noise words during indexing and also from the search itself. A search for a noise word will always yield zero results.

A FREETEXT predicate can contain phrases. They must be surrounded by quotation marks.

If more keywords or phrases are present in a FREETEXT predicate, they are implicitly separated by either AND or OR, depending on the KeywordInclusion setting (as described earlier).

### CONTAINS

As opposed to the FREETEXT predicate, the CONTAINS predicate should be used for exact matches.

It has a range of options not available in the FREETEXT predicate. Table 8-2 describes the predicates and arguments available for the CONTAINS predicate. These are then used to create the individual CONTAINS predicates to apply to the query. Multiple CONTAINS predicates can be applied to achieve the behavior desired, if it is not feasible to create one CONTAINS predicate that achieves it. In the case of multiple CONTAINS predicates, they are also separated by Boolean operators, which are required in this case.

**Table 8-2.** *Different uses of the CONTAINS Predicate*

| | | |
|---|---|---|
| Word | A single word without spaces or other punctuation | `...WHERE CONTAINS ('sharepoint')` |
| Phrase | Multiple words or included spaces | `...WHERE CONTAINS('sharepoint search')`<br>Or, to include double quotation marks:<br>`... WHERE CONTAINS('sharepoint ""search""')` |
| Wildcard | Words or phrases with the asterisk (*) added to the end. This is for performing wildcard searching. | `...WHERE CONTAINS ('"sea*"')`<br>Matches "search", "searches", "searching", and "searchable". |
| Boolean | Words, phrases, and wildcard strings combined by using the Boolean operators AND, OR, or NOT; enclose the Boolean terms in double quotation marks. | `...WHERE CONTAINS ('sharepoint' AND '2010' AND 'search')` |
| Near | Words, phrases, or wildcards separated by the function NEAR | `...WHERE CONTAINS ('sharepoint' NEAR 'search')` |
| FormsOf | Matches a word and the inflectional versions of that word | `...WHERE CONTAINS ('FORMSOF (INFLECTIONAL, "search"))`<br>Matches "search", "searches", "searching" etc. |
| IsAbout | Combines matching results over multiple words, phrases, or wildcard search terms | `...WHERE CONTAINS ('ISABOUT ( "sharepoint", "search") ')` |

Words and phrases are similar to those of FREETEXT.

Wildcards are similar to a single word phrase (created by code, not the user).

Booleans can be used either inside a single CONTAINS predicate or to separate a number of CONTAINS and FREETEXT predicates.

As mentioned earlier, it is possible to use either a single CONTAINS predicate with multiple keywords separated by Booleans or multiple CONTAINS predicates that each have only one keyword and separate the predicates by Booleans.

The impact on the query results when using either method or a combination is not known or documented.

FormsOf and IsAbout are not used, and the documentation is not specific enough to make any real estimates on their performance and effect.

An example of a SQL query using wildcards might look like this:

```
SELECT WorkId,Rank,Title,Author,ModifiedBy,Size,Path,Description,Created,Write,Filename,↵
SiteName,SiteTitle,CollapsingStatus,HitHighlightedSummary,HitHighlightedProperties,↵
ContentClass,IsDocument,ContentType,objectid,PictureURL,WorkEmail,CreatedBy,ContentSource,↵
FileExtension FROM SCOPE() WHERE FREETEXT(defaultproperties,'+engine') OR (CONTAINS↵
(' "SharePo*" ') AND CONTAINS(' "sear*" ') ) ORDER BY Rank DESC
```

In the foregoing SQL, there has been a search for the following:

```
SharePo * sear* or engine
```

This is evaluated as follows:

```
('SharePo *' AND 'sear*') or 'engine'
```

Notice how the wildcard keywords are wrapped inside two CONTAINS predicates. According to the documentation, they might as well have been wrapped inside a single one, but in real life, that yields an exception if two wildcards are used within the same CONTAINS predicate. Also notice that there is a '+' operator before the keyword *engine* in the FREETEXT predicate. This way it is specified that the keyword has to exist because an OR-based search always has the following property set:

```
KeywordInclusion = AnyKeyword
```

Otherwise the query would return results that might contain the keyword *engine* but not necessarily. (This appears to be prevented by the search engine, though, as full or empty set queries are not accepted. It seems that at least one word of a predicate has to be matched if the predicate should be evaluated.) If the OR was changed to AND, then KeywordInclusion would be set to AllKeywords and the + would not be set.

# Creating a Custom Search Application Page

In this section, we describe how to create a new application page in SharePoint with search functionality. The example provided is designed to be easy to implement and deploy. Using an application page, which is stored as a physical file on the front-end server, makes it easy to extend and experiment with the query API. The example uses data binding to display the query result data in order to reduce the amount of non-search-related changes required when working with the search API. This example is intended to be easy to understand and extend with more complex functionality. Basic knowledge of Visual Studio 2010 and entry-level knowledge of programming in C#.NET are recommended but not required.

# Setting Up the Solution

Start by creating a new project in Visual Studio 2010 on a front-end server on the farm where the project is to be deployed (Figure 8-2). If this is not possible, the Create Package functionality can be used. Choose the Empty SharePoint Project template, and give the project a proper name. In this example, the project is named SearchApplicationPage.

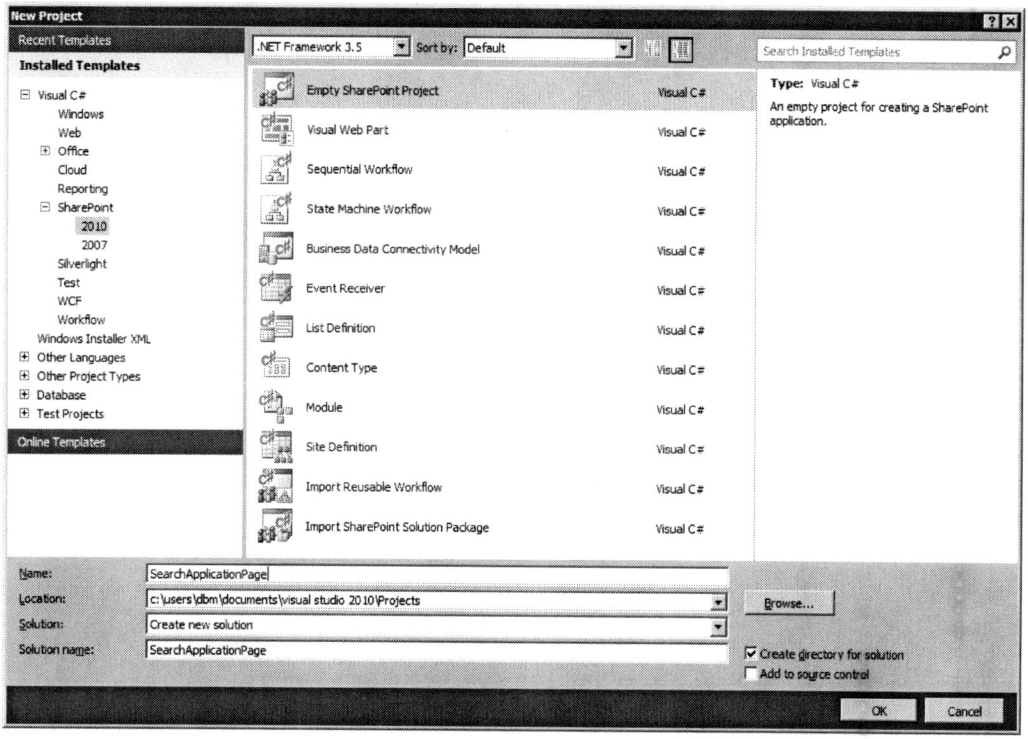

**Figure 8-2.** *Creating a new SharePoint 2010 project*

After creating the project, a prompt appears, asking for the SharePoint server farm URL. Enter the site URL where the solution is to be deployed. The prompt also asks if the solution should be sandboxed or deployed as a farm solution. Choose the option "Deploy as a farm solution" (Figure 8-3). It is always a good idea to validate the site that the solution is deployed to.

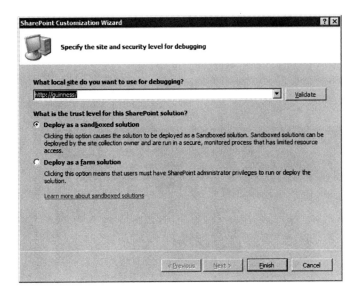

**Figure 8-3.** *Deployment settings*

The next step is to add an application page to the project. In SharePoint 2010, it is best practice to make application pages inherit from the LayoutsPageBase class, which is found in the namespace Microsoft.SharePoint.WebControls. This class is fairly simple but contains common functionality that makes development of application pages easier. When adding the application page, as shown in Figure 8-4, it automatically inherits from the LayoutsPageBase class.

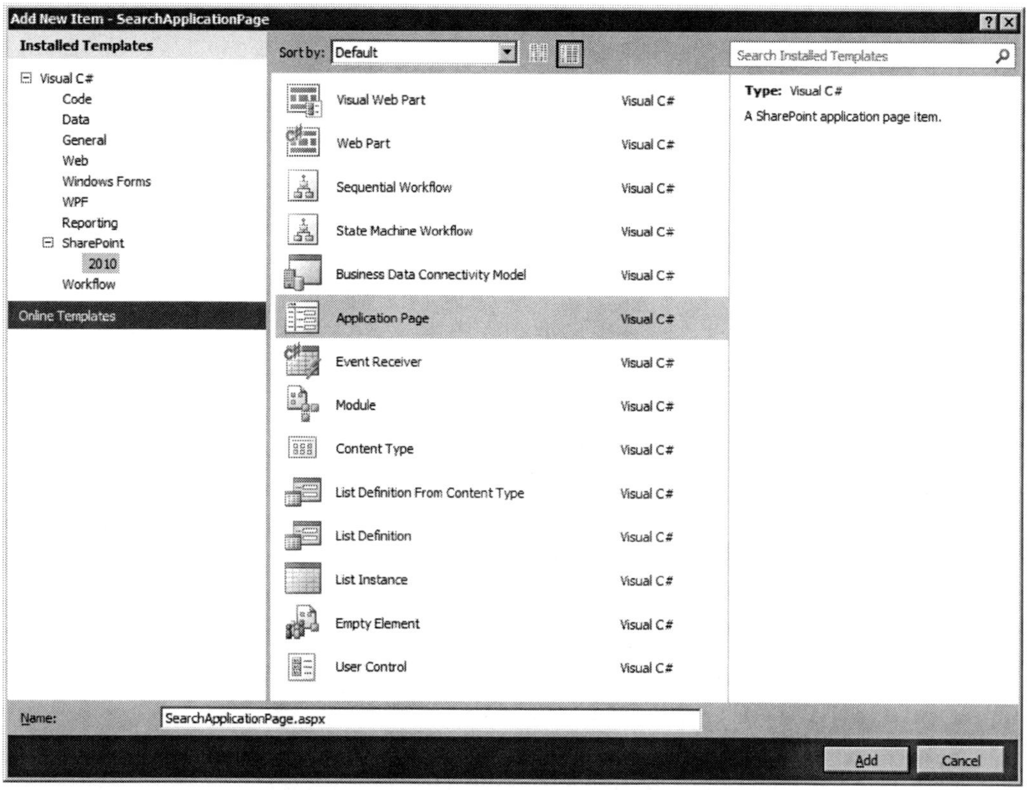

***Figure 8-4.*** *Creating an application page*

Application pages are not available in sandboxed solutions, as they are located in the `Layouts` folder in the SharePoint root folder structure (Figure 8-5). When adding a new application page to the project, as just shown, Visual Studio automatically creates the `Layouts` folder in the project and adds the `.aspx` and code-behind files to it. When the solution is deployed later on, the application page will automatically be added to the `Layouts` folder in the SharePoint root folder structure.

*Figure 8-5. Layouts folder added to project containing application page files*

## Modifying the Application Page Markup

To make the application page useful, some edits to the .aspx page are required. To edit the layout of the application page and to add controls to it, open the **SearchApplicationPage.axpx** file.

First of all, the titles should be changed to something meaningful. Here the PlaceHolderPageTitle is changed to Search Application Page and the PlaceHolderPageTitleInTitleArea is changed to My Search Application Page.

```
<asp:Content ID="PageTitle" ContentPlaceHolderID="PlaceHolderPageTitle" runat="server">
Search Application Page
</asp:Content>

<asp:Content ID="PageTitleInTitleArea" ContentPlaceHolderID=↵
"PlaceHolderPageTitleInTitleArea" runat="server" >
My Search Application Page
</asp:Content>
```

For the application page to have any meaningful functionality, some web controls need to be added. In this example, the application page is used for searching and showing simple search results. For this to work, the following five web controls are added in the content placeholder with the ID "PlaceHolderMain":

- Text box for entering search terms into

- Button for executing the query

- Label instructing user that the text box is for entering search terms

290

- Gridview for showing search results (limited to ten results)

- Label instructing user that the gridview shows search results

When done, the main content placeholder should look like Listing 8-2.

*Listing 8-2. Rendering simple search results using the SPGridView control.*

```
<asp:Content ID="Main" ContentPlaceHolderID="PlaceHolderMain" runat="server">
<asp:Label>Enter search terms</asp:Label>
<asp:TextBox ID="searchText" runat="server" />
<asp:Button ID="searchButton" Text="Search" runat="server" />
<br /><br />
<asp:Label>Search results:</asp:Label>
<br />
<SharePoint:SPGridView ID="searchGridView" AllowPaging="true" PageSize="10"
AutoGenerateColumns="false" runat="server">
<Columns>
<asp:TemplateField HeaderText="Path">
<HeaderStyle Font-Bold="true"></HeaderStyle>
<ItemStyle Width="100" />
<ItemTemplate>
<asp:HyperLink Text='<%# Eval("Title") %>' NavigateUrl='<%# Eval("Path") %>'
runat="server">
</asp:HyperLink>
</ItemTemplate>
</asp:TemplateField>
<asp:BoundField DataField="Write" HeaderText="Edited" ItemStyle-Width="100px">
<HeaderStyle Font-Bold="true"></HeaderStyle>
</asp:BoundField>
</Columns>
</SharePoint:SPGridView>
</asp:Content>
```

Build and deploy the solution to SharePoint by right-clicking the project and choosing Deploy. After it is successfully deployed, the solution can be accessed by entering the following URL into the browser:

```
http://<site url>/_layouts/ SearchApplicationPage/SearchApplicationPage.aspx.
```

At this time, clicking the Search buttons does not perform any action. However, you will see a layout containing a text field for entering search terms, a button for executing the search, and a data gridview Web Part for displaying search results (Figure 8-6).

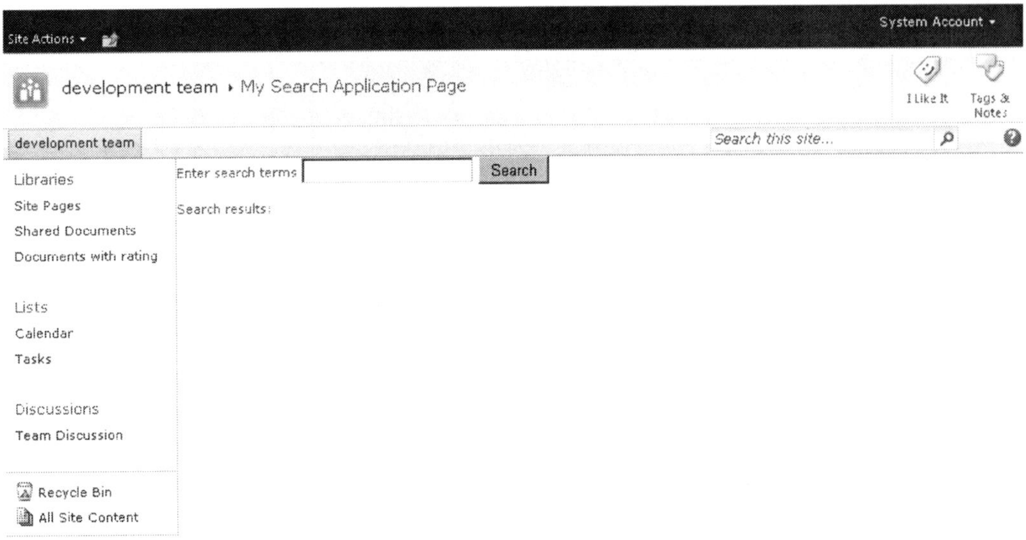

**Figure 8-6.** *Simple search application page layout*

## Adding Code-Behind

Code-behind is the .NET code (C# is used in this book) that implements the logic for the markup. It is executed on the server and can alter the properties of the layout prior to rendering. Adding search capabilities to this application page is very easy. First, the assemblies required for the search API must be added as references to the SearchApplicationPage project (Figure 8-7). This is done by right-clicking the project and then adding references to the following assemblies:

- `Microsoft.Office.Server`
- `Microsoft.Office.Server.Search`

Both assemblies are usually located in the `ISAPI` folder in the SharePoint root folder.

***Figure 8-7.*** *Adding references to the search API*

With the required references in place, only three changes are required in the code-behind file of the application page:

- Adding "using" statements for the namespaces

- An event handler for the button

- A method to invoke from the event handler that executes the search

Open the file named `SearchApplicationPage.axpx.cs`, and add the following namespaces to the top of the file:

```
using System;
using Microsoft.SharePoint;
using Microsoft.SharePoint.WebControls;
using Microsoft.Office.Server.Search.Query;
using System.Data;
```

The file contains the `SearchApplicationPage` class, which has only one default method. This is the `Page_Load` method. Inside the `Page_Load` method, add an event handler for the Search button. Each time the Search button gets clicked, the method called `searchButton_Click` will be invoked.

```
protected void Page_Load(object sender, EventArgs e)
{
    this.searchButton.Click += new EventHandler(searchButton_Click);
}
```

Last, but not least, the code for performing the search is added. This is encapsulated inside the `searchButton_Click` method.

A `KeywordQuery` object is initialized for the current site. Then the result provider is configured as default, which means that it uses SharePoint 2010 Search. The other alternative is to use FAST.

As this solution shows data in only one data gridview, only results of type `RelevantResults` are returned. The implicit operator for multiple keywords or search terms is set to `AllKeywords`. This means that there is an implicit AND between keywords if nothing else is specified. Finally the query text is added—the search terms that the user enters into the text field on the search application page. Now the `KeywordQuery` object is configured, and a search can be executed.

```
protected void searchButton_Click(object sender, EventArgs e)
{

    using (SPSite site = new SPSite(SPContext.Current.Web.Site.Url))
    {
        KeywordQuery query = new KeywordQuery(site);
        query.ResultsProvider = Microsoft.Office.Server.Search.Query.SearchProvider.Default;
        query.ResultTypes = ResultType.RelevantResults;
        query.KeywordInclusion = KeywordInclusion.AllKeywords;
        query.QueryText = searchText.Text;

        ResultTableCollection results = query.Execute();

        if (results.Count > 0)
        {
            ResultTable relevant = results[ResultType.RelevantResults];
            DataTable search = new DataTable();
            search.Load(relevant);
            DataView view = new DataView(search);
            searchGridView.DataSource = search;
            searchGridView.DataBind();
        }
    }
}
```

If executing the search yields any results, the `RelevantResults` are extracted from the search and loaded into a data table. This data table is then used as the data source in a data view. Finally a data binding is applied between the data gridview web control and the data view. Since it has already been determined that some results exist, the data gridview web control will now show these results. Keep in mind that the data gridview is configured to show only the first ten results.

Now deploy the solution again. Click the Search button to perform a search for the search terms and display any results in the data gridview web control (Figure 8-8).

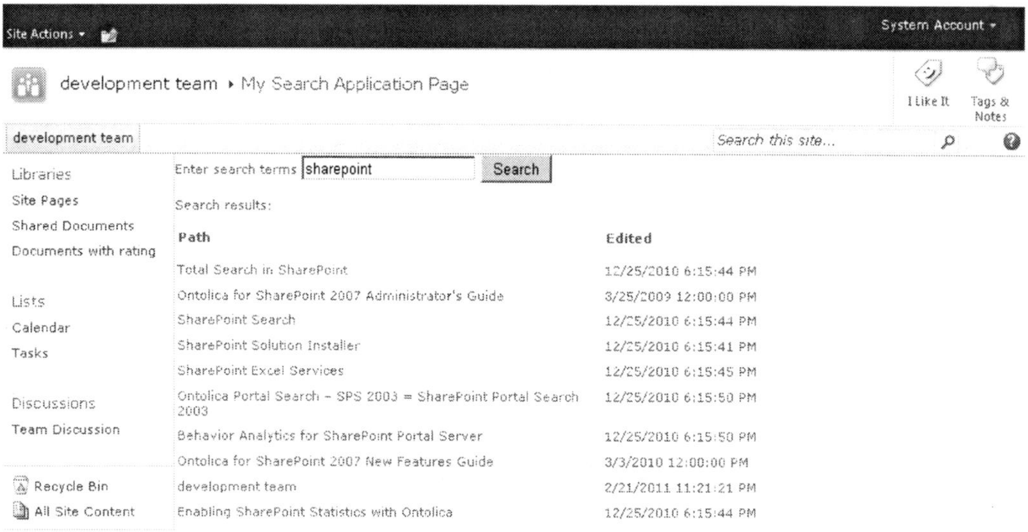

**Figure 8-8.** *Search application page with search results*

# Summary

One challenge when working with search that is often overlooked is how to create proper queries. When dealing with simple one- or two-word queries, this is fairly straightforward, but when more specific or complex queries are required, it can easily become complicated to do correctly. This chapter offered some methods for handling such queries and validating their correctness.

For true coded extensions of the search capabilities in SharePoint, the search API and the search web service are introduced with working code examples of how to use them. The APIs available (keyword- and SQL-based queries) differ in the level of control over the query and how it is constructed. As both require the SharePoint dynamic-link libraries (DLLs) to be present on the machine, this is not always feasible when doing applications intended for execution on client machines. For this, an example is given of how to use the search web service to perform client-based searches and how to create a search-enabled application page.

It is neither possible nor intended that this topic is covered in depth in this book. Rather the intent is to offer the means for the reader to get sufficient knowledge to do further exploration.

# CHAPTER 9

■■■

# Business Connectivity Services

After completing this chapter, you will be able to

- Understand the Business Connectivity Services architecture

- Understand how BCS integrates both inside and outside SharePoint 2010

- Create BCS solutions of simple and medium complexities

- Create custom .NET connectors using Visual Studio 2010

- Configure the Secure Store Service for use by Business Connectivity Services

- Add basic security trimming using Visual Studio 2010

- Understand the potential that BCS exposes for your organization

Business Connectivity Services (BCS) makes it possible to integrate external data sources—typically line-of-business data—with SharePoint 2010. The most exciting features in BCS for SharePoint 2010 are the SharePoint Designer 2010 (SPD 2010) integration, its search capabilities, and Microsoft Office 2010 integration (which is outside the scope of this book).

The new BCS offers similar functionality to the Business Data Catalog (BDC) in SharePoint 2007. In contrast to the BDC, the BCS is accessible to a much wider audience due to its integration with SharePoint Designer 2010. This was not the case with the BDC in SPD 2007. Also, accessing and manipulating LOB data is now easy. With BDC it was relatively easy to read external data, but manipulating external data presented a number of complexities. The new BCS interface in SPD 2010 makes it easy to both define CRUD operations and even aggregate data between different content types across multiple data sources.

Now BCS is available in SharePoint Foundation 2010, which means it is free. This allows for creating complex business-driven solutions at a low cost.

This chapter describes the high-level architecture, capabilities, and components of BCS, with a special focus on search-related topics. Examples will be given of how to use SPD 2010 to create declarative solutions and Visual Studio 2010 to create custom content types using C# and enable searching of these content types.

# BCS Architecture

The architecture of BCS is comprehensive but still makes it easy to use. Considering that BCS can be used for both SharePoint and the MS Office clients, it offers an excellent framework that enables administrators to easily understand and set up BCS solutions that integrate content types from most typical content sources all the way through the pipeline of BCS, finally presenting a data interface in an intuitive way to the end user. Furthermore it allows developers to create new, reusable components as either .NET connectors or custom connectors. BCS can be divided into three layers: presentation, core components, and content sources, as shown in Figure 9-1.

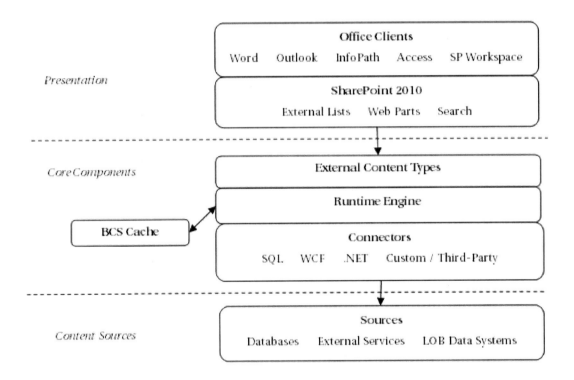

**Figure 9-1.** BCS architecture

## Presentation

BCS presents data that can be consumed or manipulated by SharePoint 2010 and MS Office clients. SharePoint 2010 contains three primary consumers of data exposed through BCS.

- External lists
- Out-of-the-box Web Parts
- Search

# External Lists

SharePoint contains a new list type named external lists. This list acts as any other list, with the exception that an external content type must be defined for the list. It does not support version info and alerts, however, as its data is stored externally.

# Web Parts

BCS Web Parts are similar to those found in BDC for SharePoint 2007. Although BCS is included for free in SharePoint Foundation 2010, BCS Web Parts are included only in the SharePoint 2010 Enterprise edition. Included Web Parts are

- Business Data Actions

- Business Data Connectivity Filter

- Business Data Item

- Business Data Item Builder

- Business Data List

- Business Data Related List

## Business Data Actions

Actions are executed on single results from BCS. The concept is also known from search centers with result actions, which are context-specific actions, such as opening documents in their native application or opening a web page in a new window—in short, actions that differ based on the specific result. Actions are configured by specifying a target URL of an HTTP handler, `.aspx` page, or similar. By adding parameters to the URL, an action can be constructed such that the URL can invoke a translation using the Bing translation service, looking up addresses on Bing Maps, or even invoke special purpose functionality if a custom HTTP handler or `.aspx` page is implemented and deployed. The configured actions for a BCS result are displayed in the Business Data Actions Web Part.

## Business Data Connectivity Filter

The Business Data Connectivity Filter Web Part is used to perform data filtering of SharePoint Web Parts based on values passed from the Business Data Connectivity (BDC) Filter Web Part. A number of filters are included, allowing manual input such as text or date and time, values picked from a list of choices, or fixed values either defined for the site or passed by URL. If a filter exists on a page, the Connections option becomes available on the Edit page. This allows for creating an association or connection between a filter and, for instance, a list view or data view Web Part. This way selected data columns will be filtered based on the defined filter values to show a custom view for a department, user, KPI event, etc.

## Business Data Item

The Business Data Item Web Part shows a single result in a vertical view. A typical use is to show detailed or expanded data of a particular result row from a summarized Business Data List Web Part. The Business Data Item Web Part can be connected to the Business Data List Web Part and respond to selected rows.

## Business Data Item Builder

This Web Part is used to pass a unique identifier from the URL parameter to the Web Parts on the page. Using this Web Part, it is possible to pass the unique identifier across pages containing Business Data Item Web Parts.

## Business Data List

This is a grid view Web Part and the core display method for BCS data, allowing an overview of the LOB data obtained from a BCS source. The key feature is the connection option that allows this Web Part to be connected to detailed view Web Parts and otherwise used for filtering and/or custom actions by clicking a result row.

## Business Data Related List

Sometimes a particular result from one external content type has associations to data in another external content type. The Business Data Related List Web Part is used to show the "many" part of the relationship by using values from other BCS Web Parts or URL-based identifiers to look up associated data for the external content type defined for the Business Data Related List Web Part.

# Search

Search results originating from BCS are displayed in a page called the profile page, when the BCS result item gets clicked or opened. The profile page is an `.aspx` page built with BCS Web Parts. The Web Parts display the relevant BCS entity based on the entity's ID, which is passed to the profile page as URL parameters. Multiple profile pages can be created to accommodate different external content types.

Profile pages are not created automatically for an external content type. Per default, clicking a search result from a BCS source yields the well-known 404 error (page not found). The profile page must be created and configured from the Search service application.

---

▪ **Note** Searching for external content using BCS is available only in SharePoint 2010 Standard and Enterprise versions.

---

# Core Components

The core of BCS is the ability to connect to a large set of data sources using its connector framework. By defining content types from the data sources, the runtime engine is able to execute CRUD operations on these content types. The core components are

- Runtime engine
- BCS Rich Client Cache
- Connectors
- External content types

The runtime engine is responsible for executing BCS operations on the content sources. The runtime engine is integrated into the supported office applications, SharePoint workspace, InfoPath, and, of course, SharePoint 2010. The integration into these applications makes them independent of SharePoint 2010 as a middle layer for using BCS to connect to content sources.

## BCS Rich Client Cache

Business Connectivity Services offers cache and offline features that also support cache-based operations. For users that work with solutions deployed to supported Office 2010 applications (Word, Outlook, SharePoint 2010 Workspace, etc.), they can manipulate external data, even when they are working offline or if the server connectivity is slow or unavailable. The operations performed against cached external entities are synchronized when connection to the server becomes available. It also provides a flexible external data caching mechanism that is as transparent as possible while still enabling the user or application to have explicit control over the content of the cache when required via automatic and manual cleanup.

## Connectors

The BCS connector framework in SharePoint 2010 comes with built-in support for creating external connections to SQL, WCF, and .NET assemblies. In general this covers the majority of connection requirements. It would have been nice, however, if a flat file or `.xml` connector was built in as well. Fortunately the BCS connector framework is designed to be extendable with either custom connectors or custom-made .NET connectors. Later in this chapter, an example will be presented of how to create a .NET flat file connector using Visual Studio 2010.

## External Content Types

External content types are the glue of BCS. They describe the metadata definitions of the external content data, connectivity information, and data access capabilities. This way an ECT provides a reusable schema to be used in SharePoint lists and Web Parts.

The external content type is what the IT professional creates in SharePoint Designer 2010. A typical business requirement for an IT professional is to create an ECT for a customer database. This database might contain names, addresses, payment info, and a unique customer ID. When the IT professional creates an ECT for this data source, the ECT will contain both the column definitions for the required fields as well as names and optionally credentials for the customer database. It will also contain information on which CRUD operations can be executed on the customer database. From the IT professional's point of view, an ECT is a mapping between the external data source and SharePoint 2010. The key difference from BDC in SharePoint 2007 is that the ECT now also contains the full CRUD behavior, whereas in BDC it had to be programmed.

Behind the scenes, an ECT is an `.xml` grammar file containing metadata that describes the ECT. For the ECT to be available, it has to be deployed to the metadata store in SharePoint (or through a click-once package, e.g., Outlook 2010).

Depending on the capabilities of the data sources and connectors, it is possible to create an ECT that provides easy data access with complex logic, such as aggregating data across multiple sources, providing complex transformations, evaluating complex business logic or custom security requirements, or calling systems multiple times in order to provide a single view of data.

---

■ **Note** This book uses the term external content type. Sometimes it is also referred to as an entity. This generally is the term used by developers, as it is the name given to the ECT in Visual Studio 2010. They do, however, mean the same thing.

---

## Content Sources

Content sources are the external part of BCS. They are used by the search engine to index external data. As mentioned, BCS comes with built-in support for connecting to content sources of the types SQL, WCF, and .NET assemblies. Often the content source is made available through installation of Microsoft SQL Server or a data server program that can be accessed and controlled through WCF. In more advanced cases, the content source might provide a .NET API for performing these operations.

On some occasions, the content source does not provide any of the foregoing options for interfacing with the data. In these cases, a developer has to develop either a .NET Assembly Connector or create a custom connector for BCS. Both options have their own benefits and weak points that the developer should be aware of, but it is outside the scope of this book to discuss them.

# Business Connectivity Services Deployment Types

Understanding how and where a BCS solution can be deployed is fundamental when planning how to leverage this new functionality in SP 2010. With the new tool support and wide range of client program support, BCS is a strong candidate to consider when analyzing opportunities to meet business requirements. This section gives an overview of where BCS can be deployed and the general complex levels of deployment.

## Functionality for Normal Users "Out-of-the-Box"

SharePoint 2010 now has out-of-the-box support for users to display external data using BCS in a seamless way. Similarly BCS integrates MS Word 2010, MS Outlook 2010, and SharePoint Workspace with SharePoint 2010 to allow users to use it in a well-known manner. Especially the support for Outlook 2010 was a much sought-after functionality in SharePoint 2007. Little or no administrator intervention is required for users to leverage list data in these applications. In most cases, the permissions setup is the most important step to be conscious about when preparing the SharePoint lists, etc. for use by these applications.

Using the external list, Business Data Web Parts, or the new Chart Web Part in SP 2010, it is easy for users to display external data. It is also possible to extend existing standard lists or document libraries by adding an external data column.

External columns can also be used in MS Word 2010 by creating a Quick Part for content control. This is useful, for instance, when a document template is to reflect the latest available data from the SharePoint-based intranet.

MS Outlook 2010 and SharePoint Workspace provide special integration with SharePoint. External lists can be taken offline from the SharePoint server. This way, users can interact with the data in the external list without leaving the client program. The major benefit is that the integration becomes transparent to the user, since the look and behavior are the same as in Outlook and Workspace. The required add-in for Outlook is installed as part of Microsoft Office 2010.

One thing to be aware of is that offline lists in MS Outlook 2010 and SharePoint Workspace require synchronization. This can be done either automatically or on user request. If automatic synchronization is activated, the default interval is three hours. As the structure of the offline list can change or new views can be added or modified, it is even possible to update the structure or view automatically without any user intervention.

The external content types and external lists/columns for these types of solutions are usually created by an administrator using SPD 2010. The SharePoint ribbon has buttons to make a connection between Outlook 2010 or SP Workspace 2010 and the external list/column.

## Functionality for Advanced Users and Administrators

Some uses of BCS require the administrator or IT professional to perform certain tasks, such as publishing, to make it available to users. It also allows the IT professional to use custom code-based solutions as reusable components. This is particularly beneficial for the way many companies operate, as a consultant company can make components that the internal IT professionals can use and configure to meet changing demands, without having to go back to the vendor or consultant that provided the custom code-based solution for every tiny change to how the component is used. It makes the BCS installation easier, faster, and cheaper to maintain.

InfoPath forms presenting external data can be customized in terms of look and feel. This can be done by adding declarative rules and business logic. It is also possible to add code-behind to the forms. The form is published to the server by the administrator.

SharePoint workflows can be extended with new capabilities through SPD 2010 by adding read and write capabilities to external lists or using custom workflow activities from VS 2010. These must be published in SharePoint.

Site administrators can create Web Part pages based on multiple Business Data Web Parts and Chart Web Parts. By creating connections between the Web Parts, it is possible to create highly customized and information-rich pages with data from most common data sources.

When working with external lists in Outlook 2010, it is possible for users of the Outlook client to create new customized views to show this external data. The custom view can then be saved back to SharePoint. This makes it available as a public view for other Outlook users who use the same external list in Outlook.

Microsoft has a number of applications for creating these solutions. The most common tools are the InfoPath Designer, which is used to create forms, and the SharePoint Designer, which is used to create Web Part pages and workflows. Web Part pages can also be created through the browser. Finally MS Outlook 2010 can be used for creating customized views specifically for Outlook.

# Code-Based Solutions

Code-based solutions are solutions created in Visual Studio 2010 by a developer. These solutions enable the creation of reusable components as either a .NET Assembly Connector to aggregate or transform data from external systems, custom Web Parts, custom workflow activities, code-behind for InfoPath forms, and code-based actions or external data parts for use in Outlook declarative solutions. Code-based solutions are now made easy for developers with built-in support in Visual Studio 2010. In SharePoint 2007, it required advanced coding skills to do anything more complex than data reading. Now the developer can focus on issues such as reusability instead.

A code-based Microsoft .NET Framework solution created in a tool such as Visual Studio can use any element of the public Business Connectivity Services object model and can enable users to interact with external data. It can register with the Business Data Connectivity service by using the BDC object model to present data in SharePoint, an Office 2010 application such as Microsoft Excel, or a custom application. This object model and BCS runtime is installed with SharePoint 2010 and Office 2010. External data can be retrieved directly from the external system while connected, or it can be retrieved locally from the BCS Rich Client Cache, provided it is already available, for instance, from an offline external list in SharePoint Workspace or Outlook. This type of solution can also be used to extend BCS to MS Office applications that are not integrated with BCS. Typically this will be Excel but also PowerPoint.

Alternatively an entire end-to-end solution that leverages the public Business Connectivity Services object model can be created. The deployment process is, however, more difficult, and there is no tool support for this custom connector solution.

In a code-based end-to-end solution, commonly referred to as a custom connector, the developer controls all of the user interface, packaging, and deployment. This type of solution cannot make use of the Business Connectivity Services rich client runtime, which is used by integrated and declarative solutions to integrate data.

---

■ **Note** For most purposes, a .NET Assembly Connector is sufficient to meet business needs, and it is by far the easiest way to go.

---

By using "click once" packages, it is possible to create and deploy new task panes or present external data in external data parts in MS Outlook 2010. This requires a number of XML files to be created and use of the BCS Software Developer Kit to create the package. This book will not go into more details with this, as it is a huge topic on its own, but will just mention the possibility of doing so.

A BCS project type is available to facilitate the creation of .NET Assembly Connectors. An example of a flat file .NET connector is described later in this chapter.

When working with BCS, creating the external content types is the key task to perform by IT professionals. With the new support for creating ECTs in SPD 2010, it is surprisingly easy to do. This is definitely one of the most powerful new additions to SharePoint 2010. It is also possible to create an ECT from the SharePoint site, but SPD 2010 is the better choice when available.

To give an example of creating an ECT, assume a database with customer information (Figure 9-2) that is to be made accessible through an external SharePoint list. The Contact office type is chosen to make it integrate nicely into Outlook as an offline external list.

| | CustomerKey | CompanyName | PhoneNumber | EmailAddress | ContactPerson |
|---|---|---|---|---|---|
| 1 | 1 | Microsoft | 555-xxxxxx1 | mail@microsoft.com | John Doe |
| 2 | 2 | SurfRay | 555-xxxxxx2 | mail@surfray.com | John Doe |
| 3 | 3 | Apple | 555-xxxxxx3 | mail@apple.com | John Doe |
| 4 | 4 | IBM | 555-xxxxxx4 | mail@ibm.com | John Doe |

*Figure 9-2. Sample customer data*

In SPD 2010, connect to a site and open External Content Types from the Navigation menu, as in Figure 9-3. On this page, all current ECTs for the site are displayed. The ribbon has quick access buttons for the typical tasks to be performed.

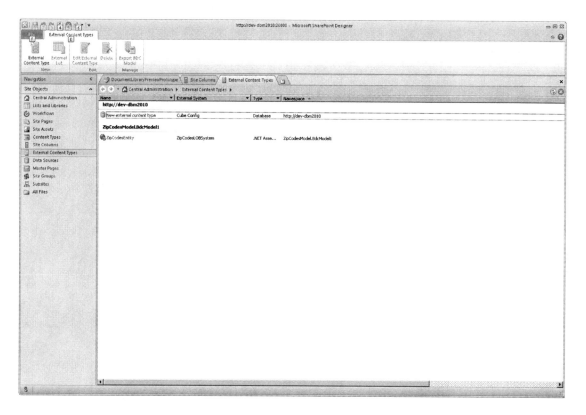

*Figure 9-3. External Content Types window*

The first step is to create a new external content type:

1. Click the New External Content Type button. The External Content Type dialog (Figure 9-4) will be displayed.

2. Enter a Name and Display Name for the external content type. As this example contains contact info, select Contact as Office Item Type in the External Content Type Information section.

3. Click the link named "Click here to discover external data sources and define operations." This opens the Operation Designer dialog.

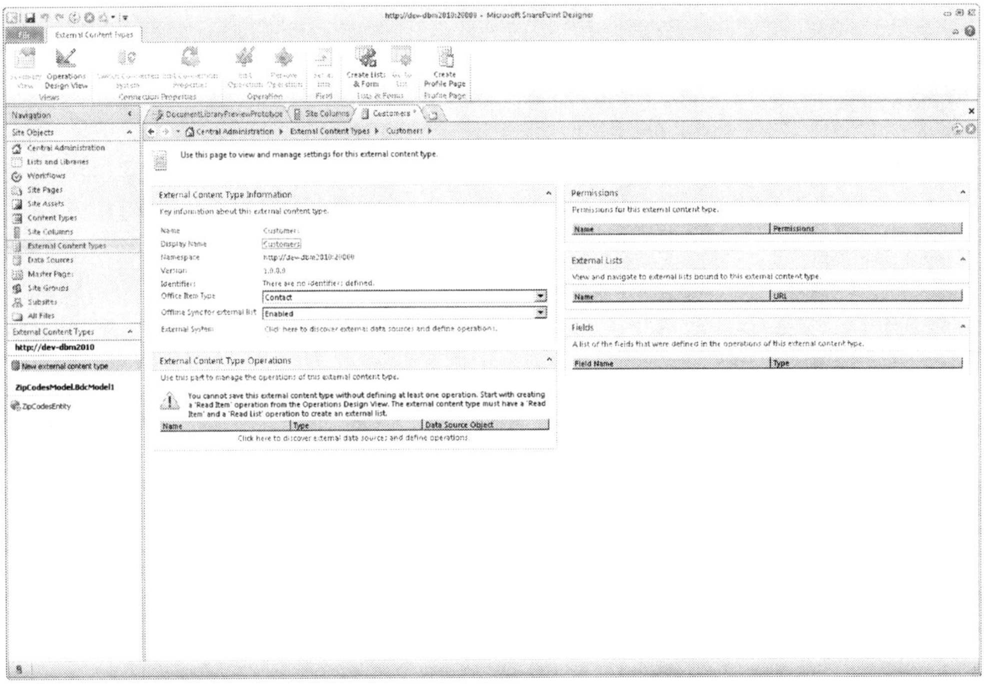

**Figure 9-4.** *Create External Content Type window*

On the Operation Designer dialog, click Add a Connection to connect to the database. In this example, it is called `CustomersDatabase`. This will establish a connection, and the database tables will be displayed. In this example, it has only one table, named `CustomersTable`.

To specify the types of operations that can be performed, right-click `CustomersTable` and select the option Create All Operations, as in Figure 9-5. This will enable all CRUD operations on the database table and open the operations wizard.

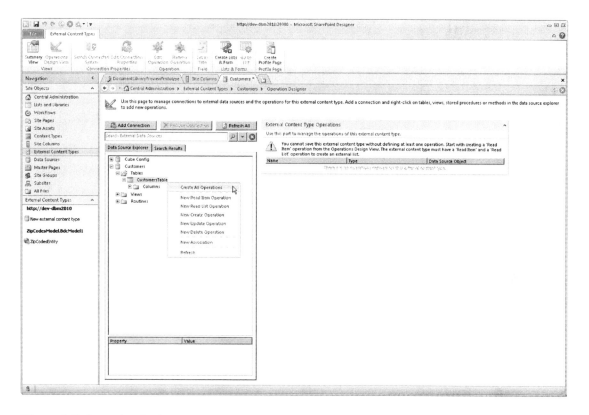

**Figure 9-5.** *Operation Designer*

Use the operations wizard (Figure 9-6) to map columns to the respective office properties. To do this, select the appropriate data source elements such as company name, phone number, etc. in the Properties window and specify the corresponding office property. Optionally a display friendly name can be specified. This name is what is showed later on the profile page for the ECT. Finally choose the column containing the values to be used as unique identifiers.

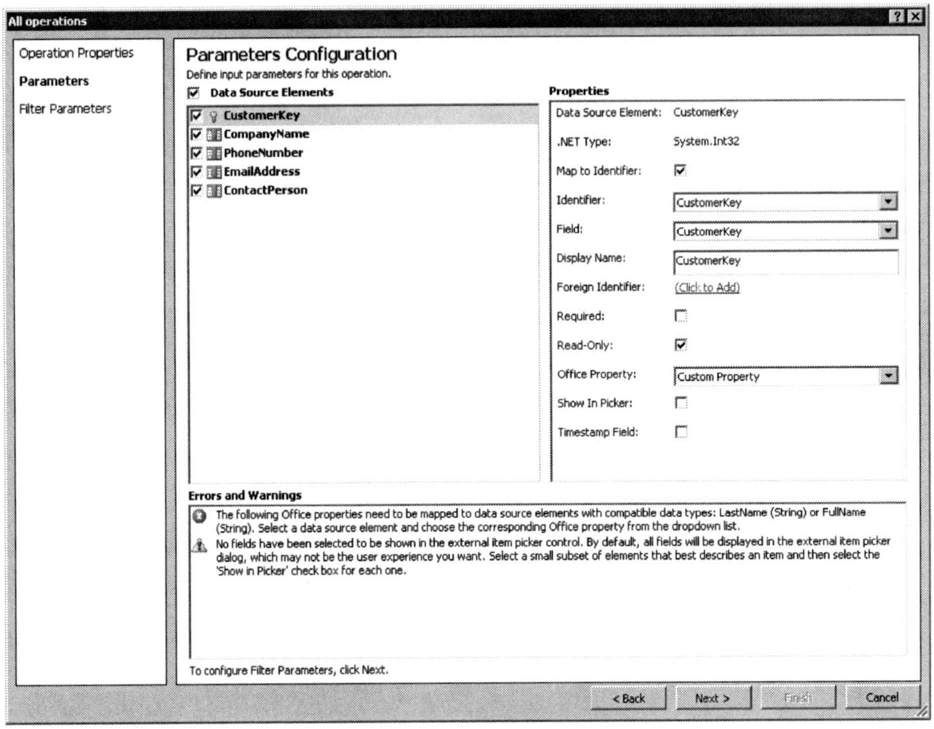

**Figure 9-6.** *Operations wizard*

Close the wizard when done, which returns to the Operation Designer window, shown in Figure 9-7.

---

■ **Note** The wizard gives real-time information on suggested and missing tasks in the Errors and Warnings window. The errors must be resolved before the wizard is completed.

---

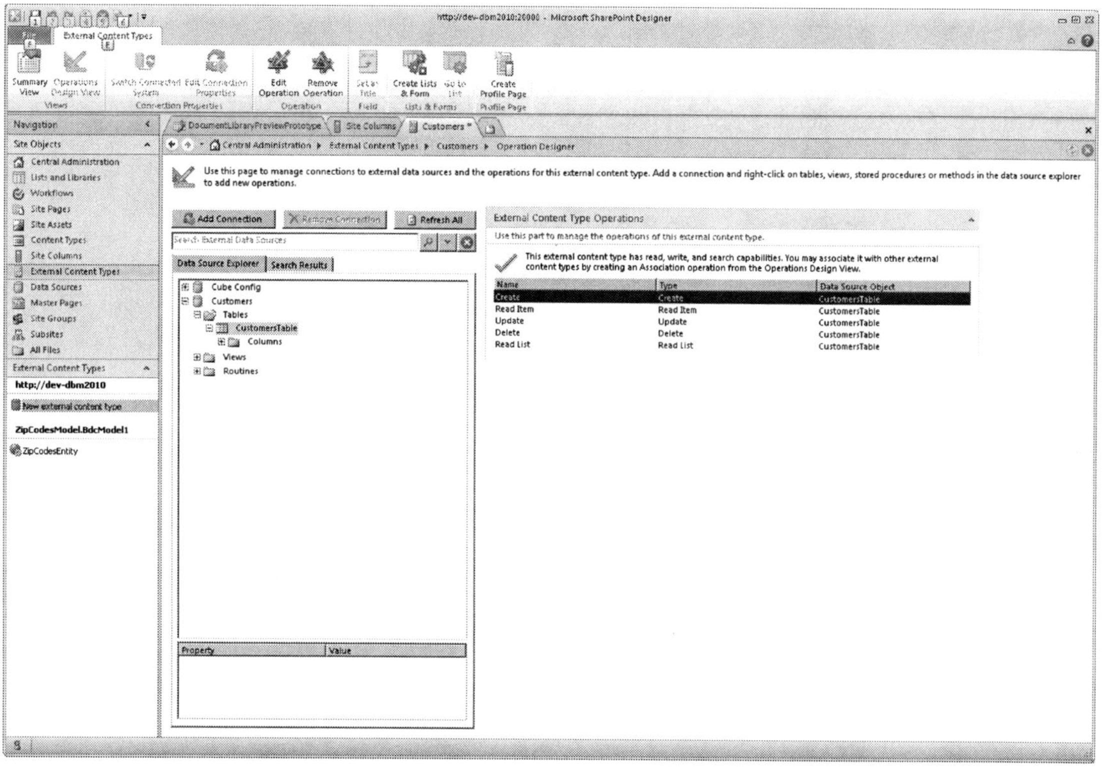

**Figure 9-7.** *Operation Designer*

After completing the wizard, save the ECT by clicking File and Save on the ribbon. The new external data type is saved to the metadata store and can be used for creating new external lists in SharePoint 2010.

Navigate to Site Actions, and view all site content. Select External List, and then click Create. This opens the New External List page, shown in Figure 9-8. Enter the name of the new list, select the External Content Type, and finally click Create.

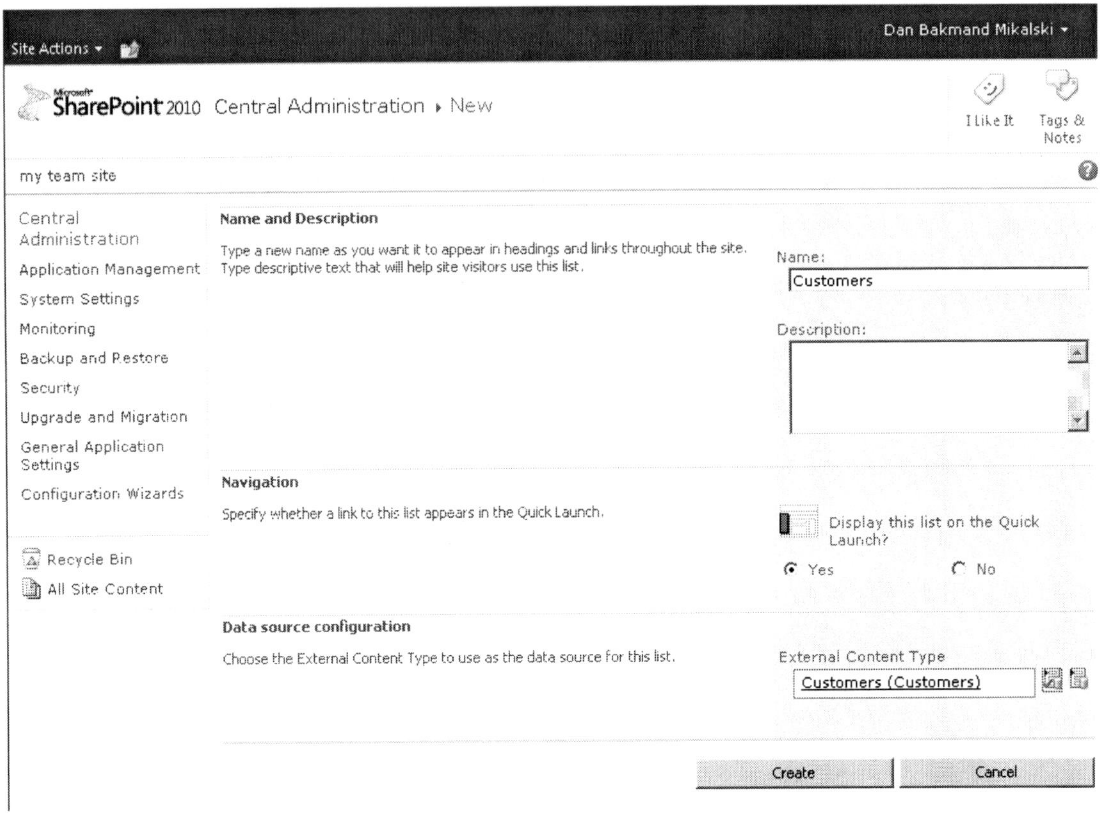

**Figure 9-8.** *Creating an external list*

Before users can access the list, the proper permissions must be configured. Go to the service application for the Business Data Connectivity service. Select the newly created external content type and click Set Metadata Store Permissions, as shown in Figure 9-9.

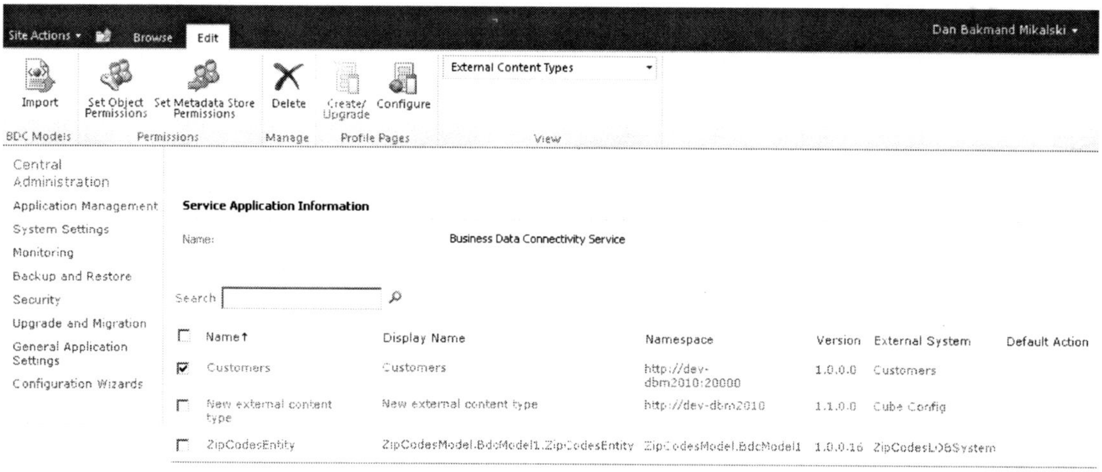

**Figure 9-9.** *Business Data Connectivity service main page*

On the Set Metadata Store Permissions page (Figure 9-10), enter the appropriate user permissions, and click OK. Typically at least one administrative user should have all permissions. As administration here is time-consuming in the case of many users, consider using groups instead for easier maintenance.

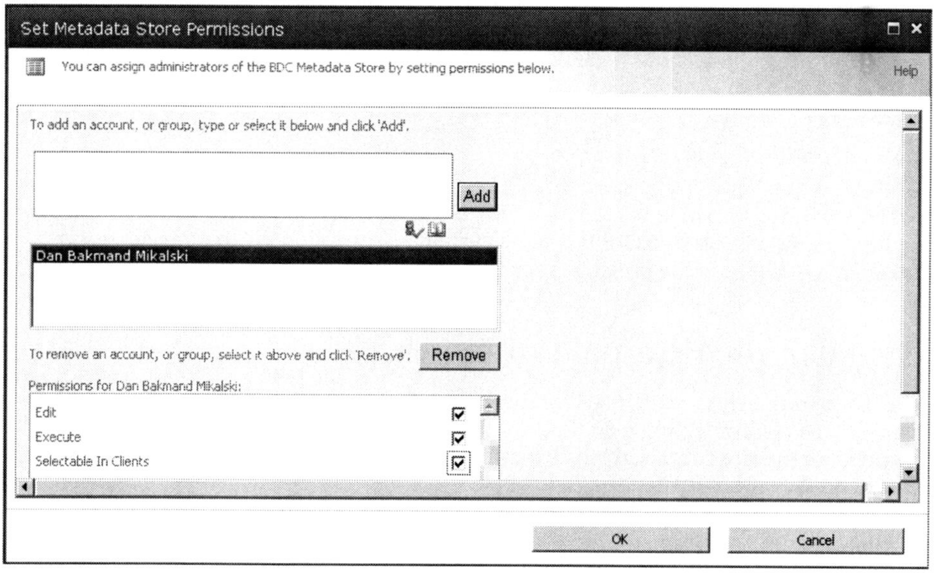

**Figure 9-10.** *Setting metadata store permissions*

■ **Note** If the ECT is to be used in search, make sure to grant the content access account appropriate permissions. In this example, the content access account is set as the author's account.

The new external list looks and behaves as any other ordinary list (Figure 9-11), with the exception of not supporting version history or setting up alerts. Items can be displayed, added, changed, and deleted—for example, changing the `PhoneNumber` in the list updates the value in the `CustomersDatabase` database.

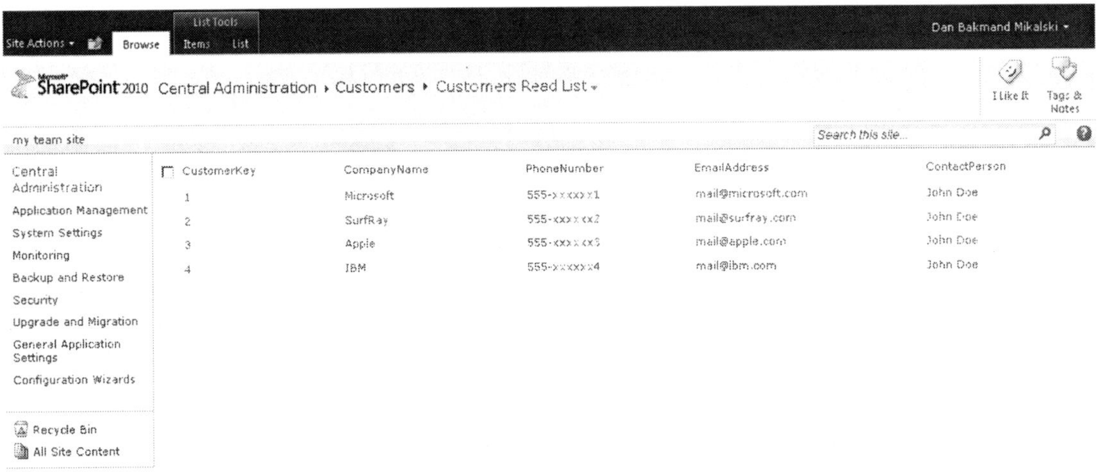

***Figure 9-11.*** *The external list displaying external data*

A key feature of BCS is the option to index the external data and present it nicely as search results. There are some required configuration steps for this to be available. The following sections focus on making the Customers ECT, created in the previous section, searchable.

## Set the Title Field in the External Content Type

It is not required that a title property is configured for the external content types, but this is essential for achieving meaningful search results. It can be configured in SPD 2010.

In SPD 2010, connect to the site containing the external content type. In the Fields section (shown in the bottom right corner on the summary page in Figure 9-12), highlight the Name field of the most meaningful field to use as the title. Click the Set as Title button on the ribbon, and save the external content type by clicking File and then Save on the ribbon.

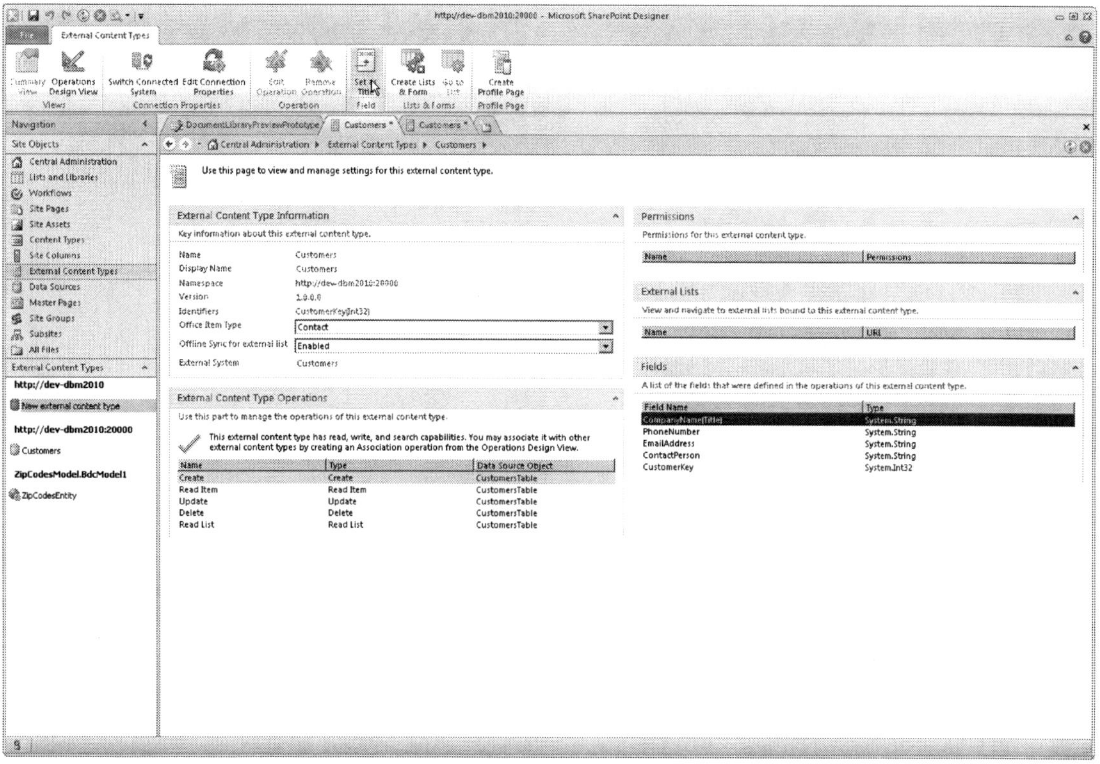

**Figure 9-12.** *Setting the external content type title*

## Creating a Profile Page to Display BCS Results

The profile page is used to display search result items from external content types. Open Central Administration and navigate to Create Site Collections. Create a new blank site to host the profile page, as shown in Figure 9-13. Give it a meaningful name according to the external source it gets paired with. It is important to write down the URL, as it has to be entered manually later.

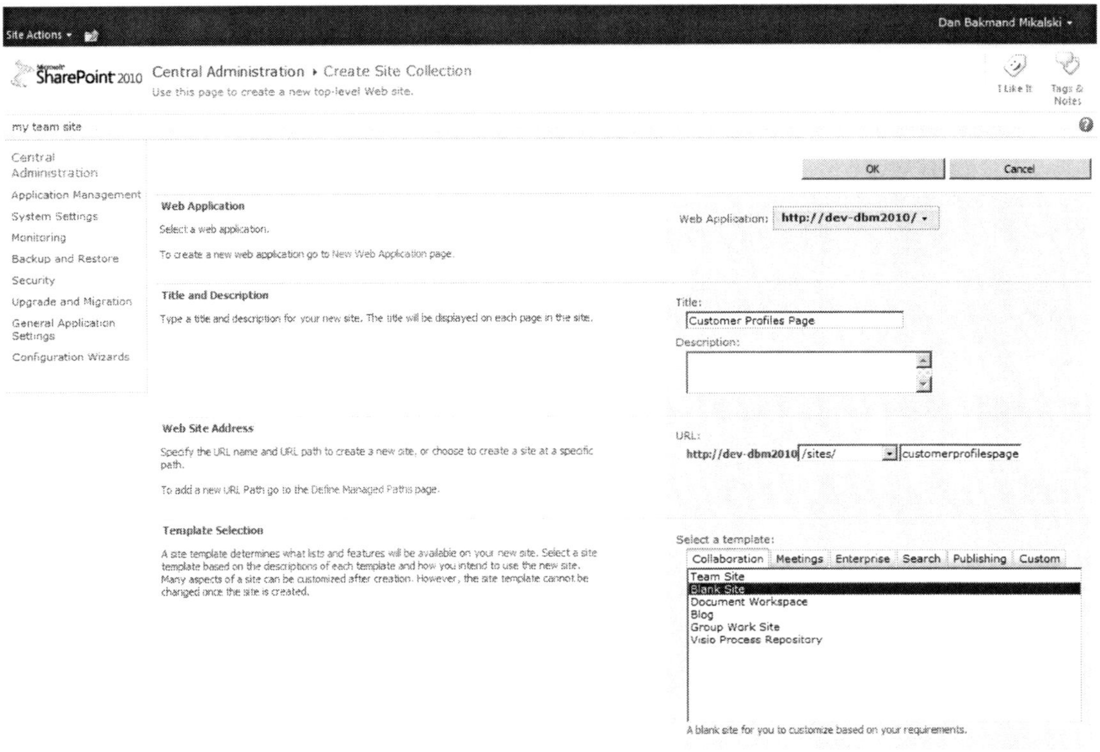

**Figure 9-13.** *Creating a profile page*

Navigate to the Manage Service Applications page in Central Administration, and click the Business Data Connectivity service application. On the Edit tab of the ribbon at the top of the page, click Configure. This opens the dialog shown in Figure 9-14.

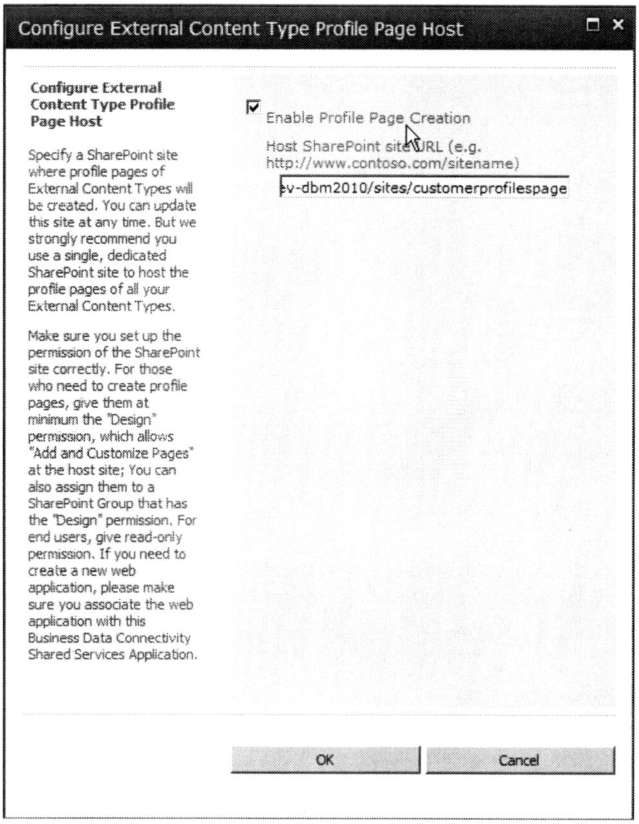

**Figure 9-14.** *Associating the external content type with a profile page*

Enter the URL of the profile page into the Host SharePoint site URL field, and click OK. Select the Customers external content type (or your own ECT) using the check box, and click Create/Upgrade. This will create a new profile page and View action for the external content type. Click OK for the warning in Figure 9-15.

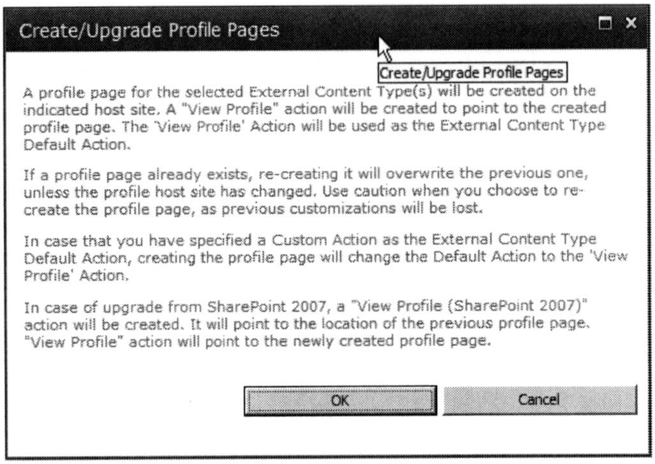

Figure 9-15. *Warning page when creating a profile page*

Clicking OK to the warning will create a new default action pointing to the profile page, with the ID passed as a URL parameter on the query string. A notification that the operation has succeeded (Figure 9-16) will be displayed.

**Create/Upgrade Profile Pages** □ ×

**Profile page creation succeeded.**

1. Customers: Profile page has been successfully created at http://dev-dbm2010/sites/customerprofilespage/_bdc/http___dev-dbm2010_20000/Customers_1.aspx

OK

Figure 9-16. *Confirming the profile page has been created*

# Configure Indexing

Now the external content type is fully configured and ready to get indexed. BCS indexing is easy in SharePoint 2010 compared to BDC in SharePoint 2007. Just add the BCS data source as a new search content source in the Search service application by navigating to the Manage Service Applications page in Central Administration. Click the Content Sources link in the navigation pane, which opens the Manage Content Sources page, shown in Figure 9-17. This page shows a list of all content sources.

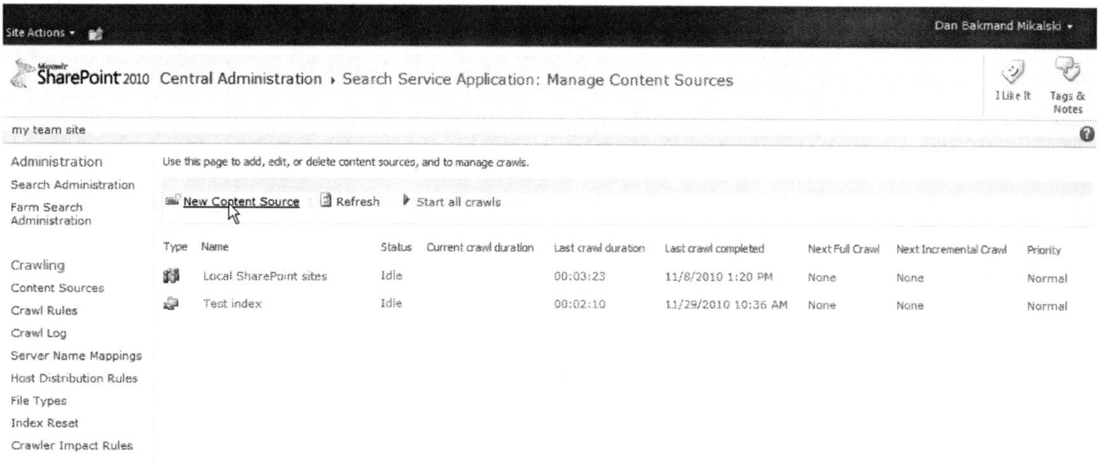

***Figure 9-17.*** *Content sources page*

Click New Content Source, and enter an appropriate name for the content source. Choose Line of Business Data as the content source type, and choose the relevant BCS application and external data source, as in Figure 9-18.

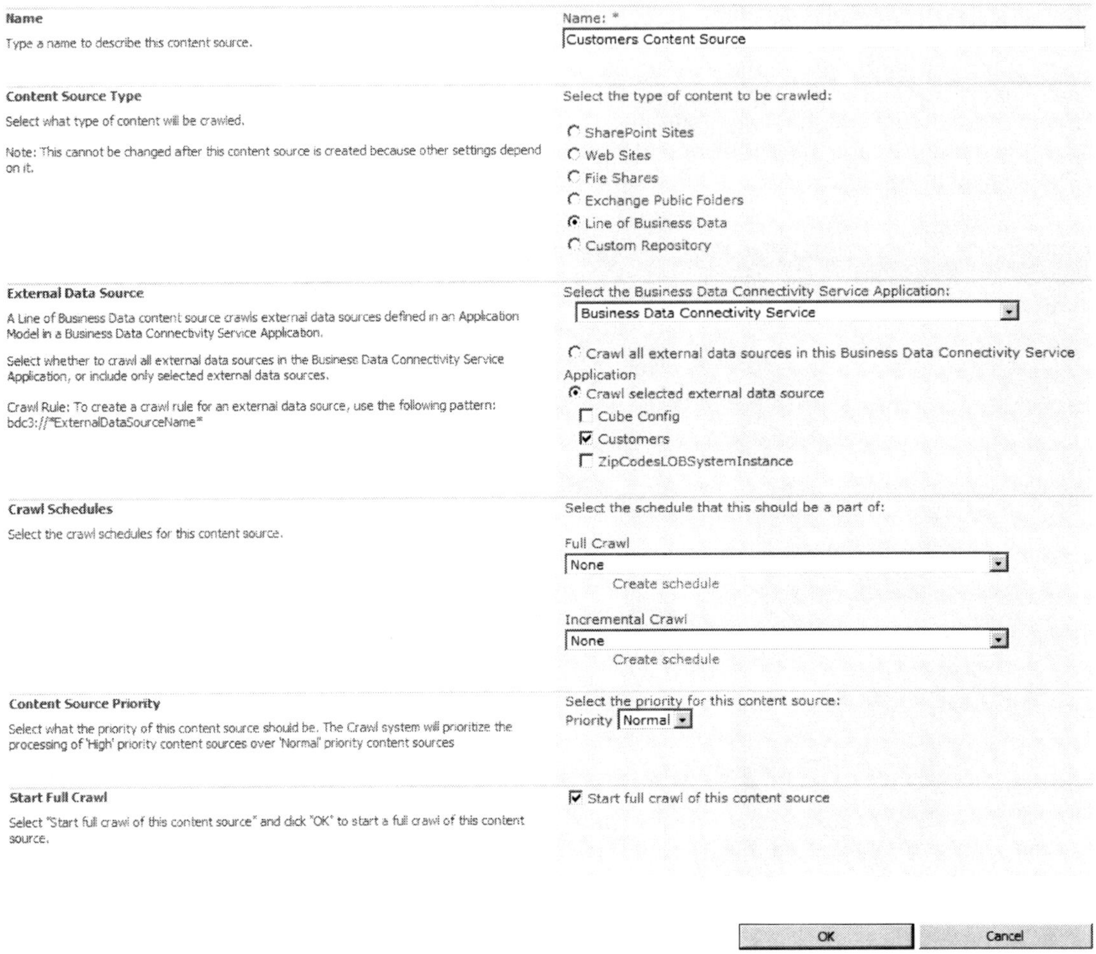

| Name | Name: * |
|---|---|
| Type a name to describe this content source. | Customers Content Source |

| Content Source Type | Select the type of content to be crawled: |
|---|---|
| Select what type of content will be crawled.<br><br>Note: This cannot be changed after this content source is created because other settings depend on it. | ○ SharePoint Sites<br>○ Web Sites<br>○ File Shares<br>○ Exchange Public Folders<br>◉ Line of Business Data<br>○ Custom Repository |

| External Data Source | Select the Business Data Connectivity Service Application: |
|---|---|
| A Line of Business Data content source crawls external data sources defined in an Application Model in a Business Data Connectivity Service Application.<br><br>Select whether to crawl all external data sources in the Business Data Connectivity Service Application, or include only selected external data sources.<br><br>Crawl Rule: To create a crawl rule for an external data source, use the following pattern:<br>bdc3://"ExternalDataSourceName" | Business Data Connectivity Service ▼<br><br>○ Crawl all external data sources in this Business Data Connectivity Service Application<br>◉ Crawl selected external data source<br>  ☐ Cube Config<br>  ☑ Customers<br>  ☐ ZipCodesLOBSystemInstance |

| Crawl Schedules | Select the schedule that this should be a part of: |
|---|---|
| Select the crawl schedules for this content source. | Full Crawl<br>None ▼<br>  Create schedule<br><br>Incremental Crawl<br>None ▼<br>  Create schedule |

| Content Source Priority | Select the priority for this content source: |
|---|---|
| Select what the priority of this content source should be. The Crawl system will prioritize the processing of 'High' priority content sources over 'Normal' priority content sources | Priority Normal ▼ |

| Start Full Crawl | ☑ Start full crawl of this content source |
|---|---|
| Select "Start full crawl of this content source" and click "OK" to start a full crawl of this content source. | |

[ OK ]    [ Cancel ]

*Figure 9-18. Creating a new content source for the LOB data ECT*

Now select "Start full crawl", and click OK. It usually takes a few minutes for the indexer to update and start. When it goes back to idle, the external content source has been crawled.

## Performing a Search

In order to test the search, a site that is configured to perform enterprise searches is required (see Chapter 4). Go to the Enterprise Search Center site, and search for a customer name or other contact detail (if you followed the Customers example). The search should now return results from the BCS, as shown in Figure 9-19.

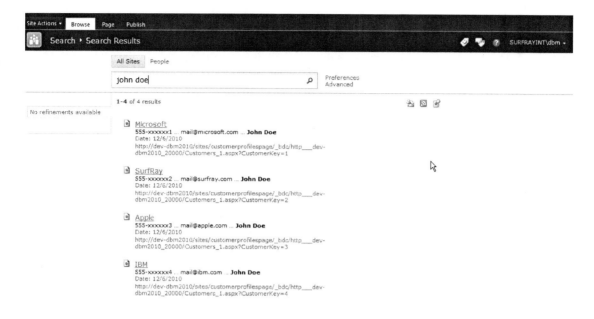

***Figure 9-19.*** *Search results displaying external data*

Clicking a search result from the BCS source opens it in the newly created profile page, as shown in Figure 9-20. The profile page automatically shows the metadata properties from the external content type.

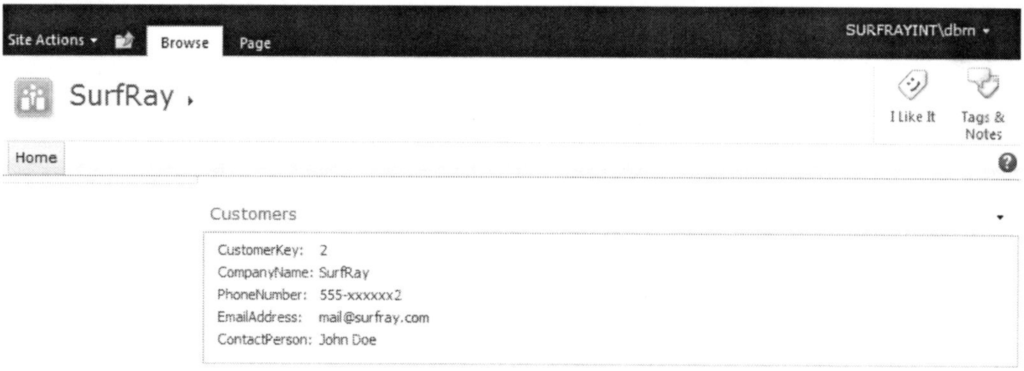

***Figure 9-20.*** *Search results item displayed on the profile page for the ECT*

After following this walkthrough, it should be easy to create and configure searching for other external content types as well.

# Creating a .NET Connector in Visual Studio 2010

One of the major strengths of BCS is how easy it is to integrate with almost any external data source. This section introduces the API and how to use Visual Studio 2010 to create a simple .NET connector. This connector example connects just to a data file but can be extended to connect to more complex data sources. .NET connectors can be discovered through the Discover function in SPD 2010.

## Creating a Sample Flat File Data Source

First of all, we need a flat file with some data in it. Start by adding a `.txt` file on this path on the SharePoint server:

`C:\Shared\zipcodes.txt`

In real-life scenarios, it is likely to be on a file share, but for this example we keep it simple. In this example, the file contains city names and zip codes, separated with a comma and each name/zip pair on a new line. For this example, Danish zip codes are used. The file should look like this:

```
2750,Ballerup
1810,Frederiksberg
1720,Copenhagen West
...
```

## Creating a .NET Assembly Connector Project in Visual Studio 2010

A .NET Assembly Connector is created as the project type Business Data Connectivity Model (BDC Model) in Visual Studio 2010. Open Visual Studio 2010, click File, select New, and then select Project. Choose the Business Data Connectivity Model project type, and name the project ZipCodesModel, as shown in Figure 9-21. Then click OK.

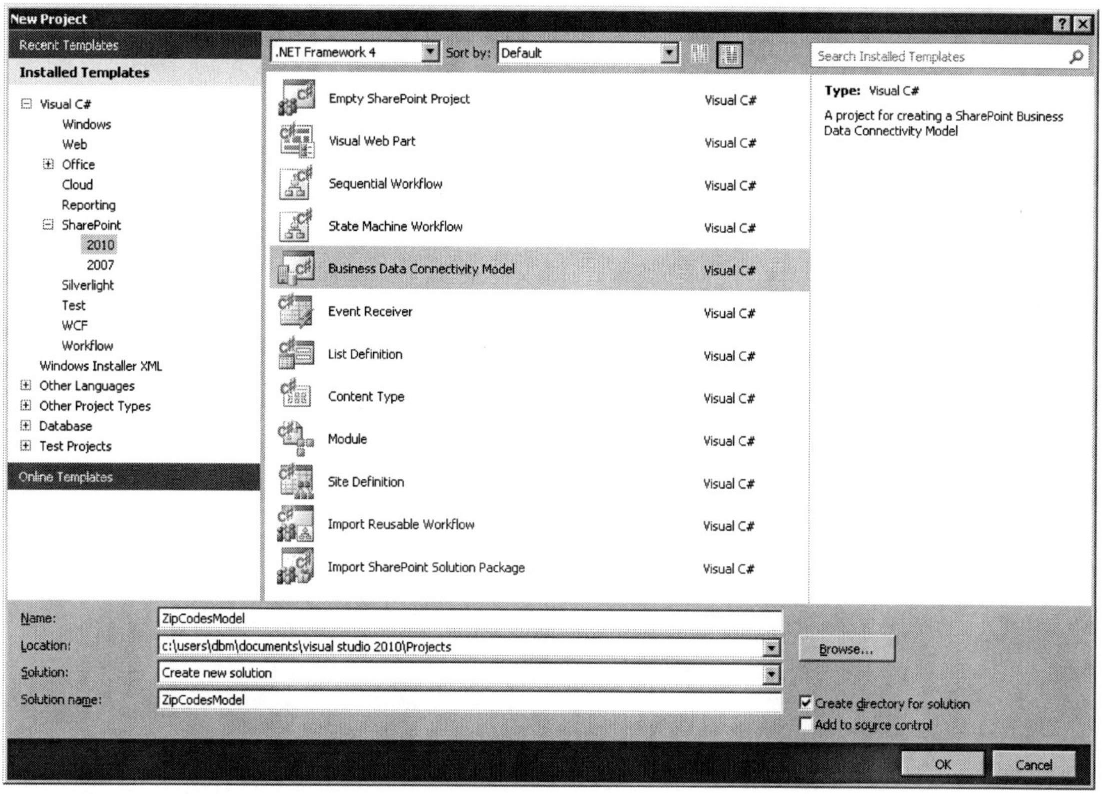

**Figure 9-21.** *Selecting the Business Data Connectivity Model from the Projects window*

Specify the SharePoint site where the model should be deployed (Figure 9-22), and click Finish.

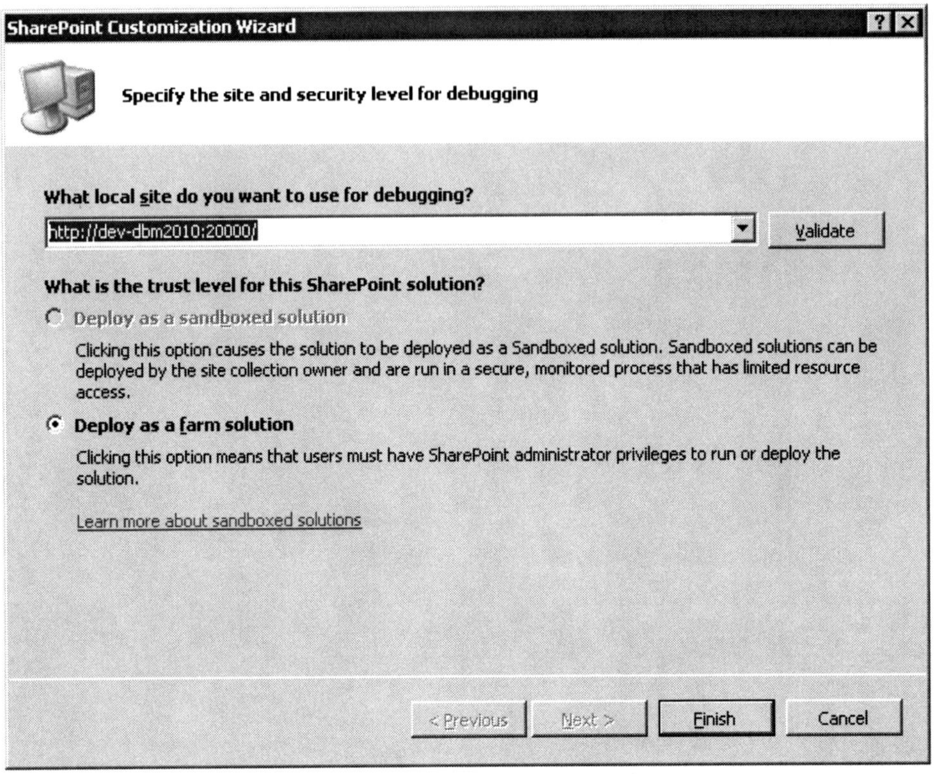

**Figure 9-22.** *Setting deployment site*

Note that BDCM projects can be deployed only as a farm solution. This is because the model has to be deployed to the metadata store.

The BDCM project type creates a number of files automatically. These files shown in Solution Explorer (Figure 9-23) are the minimum required to make a new model and deploy it. If the BDCM is part of a third-party solution, it is likely that an alternative deployment method is used and the feature files and WSP package files can be removed.

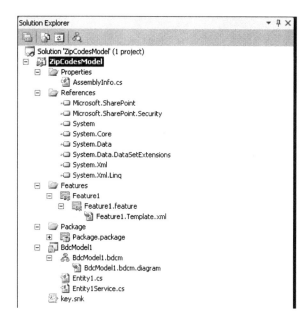

**Figure 9-23.** *Solution Explorer showing the BDC model*

The required references to the SharePoint assemblies are automatically added. A feature for enabling and disabling the BDCM is included, and a WSP package containing the feature and model is added.

The BDC model itself contains a definition of the data source, connection information, and access layer information (query and return type information). The BDC model contains two classes: a class that defines the entity or external content type that this BDC model returns, and a class containing the code used to connect to the data source, query it, and return the entities it contains.

## Creating an Entity (External Content Type)

The first real development task is to create the entity to be returned. It is very important to make sure that the entity contains the appropriate data to fulfill the business requirement for this .NET connector. To do this, the `Entity1.cs` file will be renamed `ZipCodesEntity.cs` and modified to map to the zip codes file.

To rename the file called `Entity1.cs`, right-click it in Solution Explorer and select Rename from the context menu. Type in `ZipCodesEntity.cs`, and click Yes when asked if all references should be renamed.

To modify the mapping, open the entity file by double-clicking `ZipCodesEntity.cs`. Delete the existing properties, and add two new properties called `ZipCode` and `City`. The class should now look as follows:

```
using System;
using System.Collections.Generic;
using System.Linq;
using System.Text;

namespace ZipCodesModel.BdcModel1
{
    public partial class ZipCodesEntity
    {
        public string ZipCode { get; set; }
        public string City { get; set; }
    }
}
```

# Creating an Entity Service Class

The entity service class is this example is used to query the data source—in this example, the zipcodes text file. The output of the entity service class will be one or all objects of the `ZipCodesEntity` class, depending on the operation performed.

Rename the `Entity1Service.cs` file to `ZipCodesEntityService.cs` as with the entity file, and click Yes when asked to update all references.

In Solution Explorer, double-click `ZipCodesEntityService.cs` to open it in code view.

As the data source is a text file, add the `System.IO` namespace, which contains the required classes for reading from the zipcodes text file.

```
using System.IO;
```

Some methods are required for the entity service class to function. The entity service class defines the Finder and Specific Finder methods used to return entities from the data source (zipcodes text file).

`ReadList()` is the Finder method of the BDC model. In this example, it should return all zipcode/city pairs from the data source. The method returns an IEnumerable generic collection of entities, which, in this case, is a collection of `ZipCodesEntity` objects. In this example, the objects are just created in memory, but advanced streaming schemes might be applied if the data source contains larger data sets. The `ReadList()` method can be implemented as shown in Listing 9-1.

***Listing 9-1.*** *Implementation of the* ReadList *Method*

```
public static IEnumerable<ZipCodesEntity> ReadList()
{
    List<ZipCodesEntity> zipCodesEntityList = new List<ZipCodesEntity>();
    TextReader textReader = new StreamReader(@"C:\Shared\ZipCodes.txt");
    string zipCodeEntry;

    while ((zipCodeEntry = textReader.ReadLine()) != null)
    {
        ZipCodesEntity zipCodesEntity = new ZipCodesEntity();

        string[] entityData = zipCodeEntry.Split(',');
```

```
        zipCodesEntity.ZipCode = entityData[0];
        zipCodesEntity.City = entityData[1];
        zipCodesEntityList.Add(zipCodesEntity);
    }

    textReader.Close();

    return zipCodesEntityList;
}
```

The ReadItem(string zipCode) method defines the Specific Finder method for the BDC model. In this example, it returns a ZipCodesEntity object with the zipcode/city pair matching the zipcode argument. The ReadItem() method can be implemented as shown in Listing 9-2.

*Listing 9-2. Implementation of the ReadItem Method*

```
public static ZipCodesEntity ReadItem(string zipCode)
{
    foreach (ZipCodesEntity zipCodesEntity in ReadList())
    {
        if (zipCodesEntity.ZipCode == zipCode)
            return zipCodesEntity;
    }
    return null;

}
```

It should now be possible to compile the assembly, which can be considered a .NET Assembly Connector at this point. Now the BDC model will be created, and the connection to the relevant data source, query capabilities, and return value type are defined.

# BDC Modeling Tools

After defining the entity and service, the BDC model can be created. The BDC model defines how to connect to the data source and how it can be queried. It also defines the type of information it returns. The BDC Explorer and the BDC Designer are used to define the BDC model. Both of these new VS 2010 components are described ahead.

## BDC Explorer

VS 2010 extends the windows list with the BDC Explorer, shown in Figure 9-24. This window is used to create or edit the BDC model.

**Figure 9-24.** *BDC Explorer showing the BDC model*

Just like with Solution Explorer and class view windows, the BDC Explorer is linked to the Properties window. It shows the relevant properties allowing the developer to view and edit the BDC model. Figure 9-25 demonstrates this. When Identifier 1 is selected in the BDC Explorer, the corresponding properties are displayed in the Properties window.

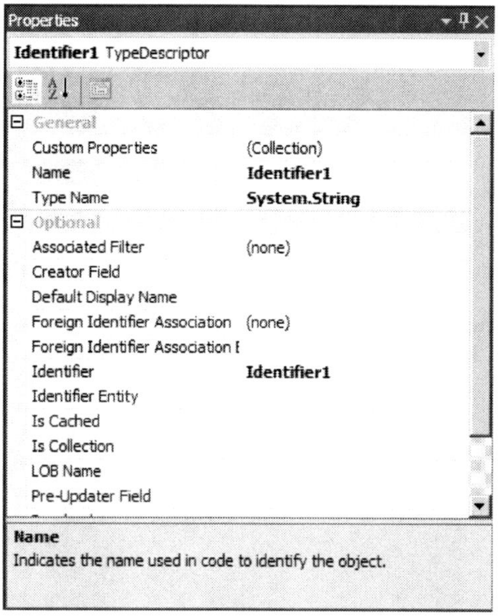

*Figure 9-25. Entity properties displayed beneath the BDC Explorer*

## BDC Designer

VS 2010 includes the BDC Designer (Figure 9-26). This designer window allows the developer to create and edit a BDC model. The BDC Designer works the same way as the BDC Explorer regarding the Properties window.

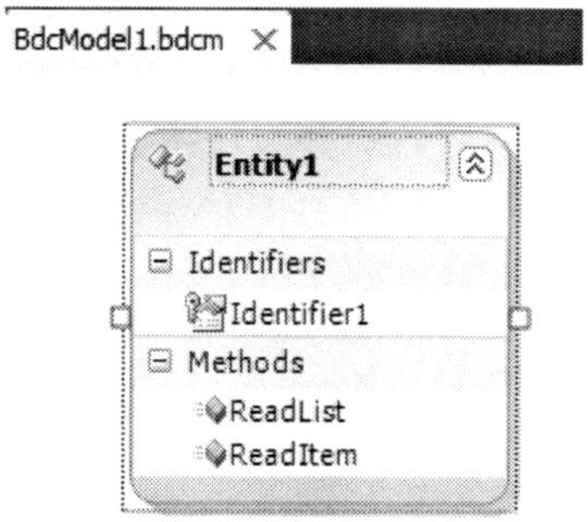

*Figure 9-26. A BDC entity displayed in the BDC Designer*

# Defining the BDC Model

Defining a BDC model is essentially to define the mapping between your .NET Assembly Connector and the BDC. In this series of steps, the mappings between the .NET Assembly Connector and the BDC are defined. To create the mapping, double-click the BDC Explorer to open the BDCModel1.bdcm file in Solution Explorer. The BDC Designer will then open and be visible. From the View menu, select Other Windows. Then click BDC Explorer to open the window.

## Configuring the BDC Model and LOB System

Rename the BDC model to ZipCodesModel, as shown in Figure 9-27. Right-click the second node from the top, named BdcModel1, and click Properties. Change the Name property to ZipCodesModel in the Properties window.

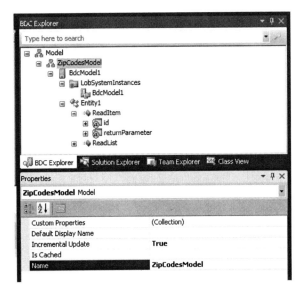

***Figure 9-27.*** *Renaming the BDC model*

The third node from the top (the LOB system) should also be renamed. Change the Name property to ZipCodesLOBSystem using the Properties window, as shown in Figure 9-28.

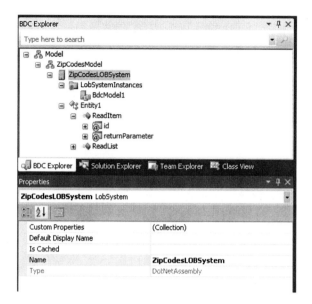

**Figure 9-28.** *Renaming the LOB system*

The fifth node from the top (the LOB system instance) should be renamed to ZipCodesLOBSystemInstance by using the Properties window to change its Name property, as shown in Figure 9-29.

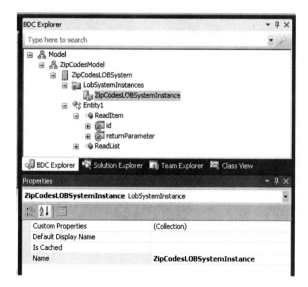

**Figure 9-29.** *Renaming the LOB system instance*

The ShowInSearchUI property on the ZipCodesLOBSystemInstance must be set to allow the ZipCodesLOBSystemInstance to be crawled and searched by the SharePoint search service. If the LOBSystemInstance should not be crawled or searched, this property does not need to be changed. To set the ShowInSearchUI property on the ZipCodesLOBSystemInstance, click the ZipCodesLOBSystemInstance node in the BDC Explorer. Then click the button in the Custom Properties row in the Properties window. Use the Properties Editor to set the ShowInSearchUI property. Give it the data type System.String and set the value to x, as shown in Figure 9-30. Click OK.

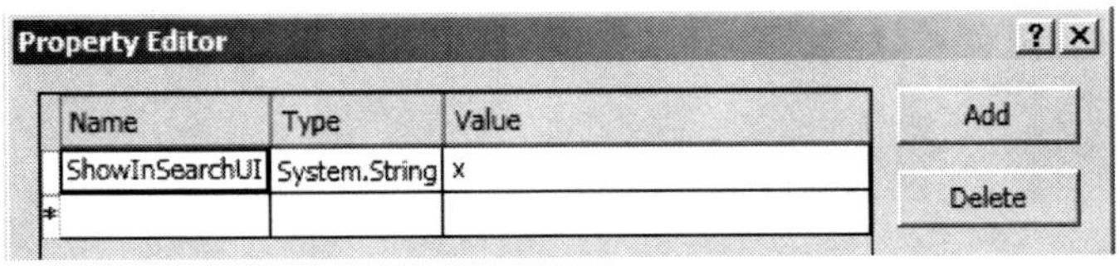

*Figure 9-30. Adding the ShowInSearchUI property to the LOB system instance*

## Configuring the Entity and Entity Methods

The BDC model entity should be renamed to match the entity defined in the .NET Assembly Connector. This is done by selecting Entity1 from the BDC Explorer. Then change the Name property to ZipCodesEntity in the Properties window, as shown in Figure 9-31.

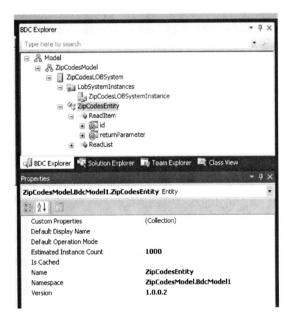

*Figure 9-31. Renaming the BDC model entity*

The RootFinder property on the Finder method must be set to specify the Finder method used to enumerate the items to crawl. If the Finder method shouldn't be used for crawling, this property can be ignored and left unset. The RootFinder property on the Finder method is set in the BDC Explorer by clicking the ReadList node. After that, click the button in the Custom Properties row in the Properties window. Add the RootFinder property, with a data type of System.String and a value of x in the Properties Editor, as shown in Figure 9-32.

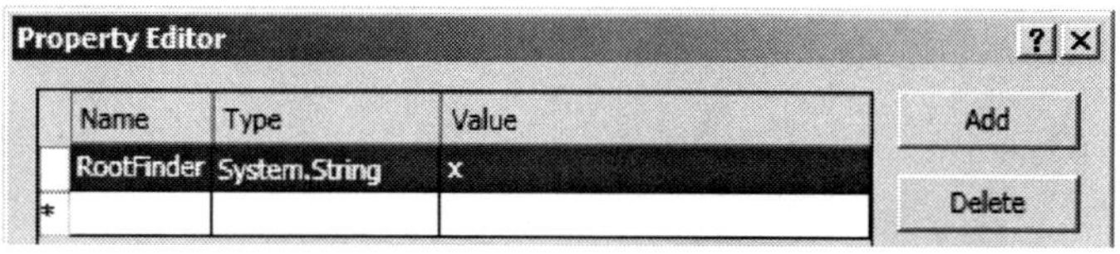

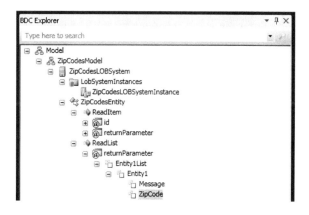

*Figure 9-32. Adding the RootFinder property to the Finder method*

Next, the identifier for the Finder method return parameter is set for the entity. This is done by selecting the Identifier1 node under the Finder method return parameter for the ZipCodesEntity. Then, in the Properties window, change the Name property to ZipCode, as shown in Figure 9-33.

*Figure 9-33. Renaming the Finder method*

Next, set the identifier for the specific Finder method return parameter and the input parameter in the entity. To do so, first select the Identifier1 nodes under the specific Finder method return parameter for the ZipCodesEntity. Then, in the Properties window, change the Name property to ZipCode, as shown in Figure 9-34.

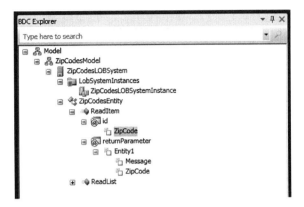

**Figure 9-34.** *Renaming the Finder method return parameter*

Right-click `Identifier1`, and select Rename in the BDC Designer (Figure 9-35). Change the identifier to ZipCode.

**Figure 9-35.** *Renaming the BDC model in Designer view*

The message parameters are not needed, so they should be removed. Right-click the message parameter on the Finder method, and select Delete. This removes the Message node from the BDC Explorer. Repeat this on the specific Finder method. Alternatively delete the entity, and recreate a new "empty" entity.

## Adding Parameters to Map the Data Source

Parameters must be added that map to the data in the zipcodes text file data source. In this example, the only parameter to map is the city name.

In the BDC Explorer, right-click Entity1 and select Add Type Descriptor. In the Properties window, change the **Name** property to `City` and the **Type Name** property to `System.String`, as shown in Figure 9-36. Repeat this for the Finder and the Specific Finder methods.

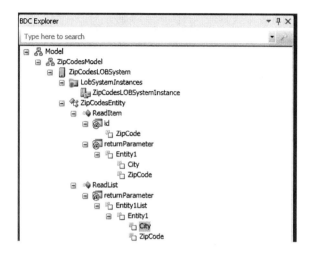

**Figure 9-36.** *Adding parameters to the Finder and Specific Finder methods*

## Configuring the Finder Method Instance

The method instance properties are configured from the BDC Method Details window. This window is also new in VS 2010. Selecting a method in the BDC Designer will display the corresponding method instances in the BDC Method Details window, as shown in Figure 9-37.

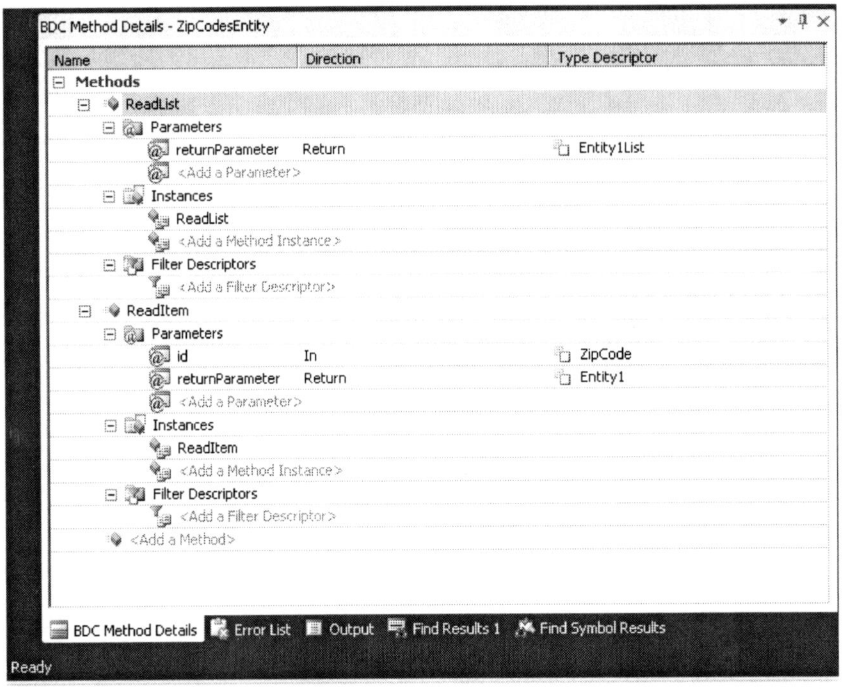

***Figure 9-37.*** *Configuring the Finder method instance*

The Finder method is specified by setting the `RootFinder` property on the Finder method instance. It specifies that this instance is used to enumerate the items to crawl. If the Finder method instance is not to be used for crawling, this property can be ignored and left unset. Click the `ReadList` node in the BDC Method Details window. To set the `RootFinder` property on the Finder method instance, click the button in the Custom Properties row in the Properties window. Add the `RootFinder` property. Set the data type as `System.String`, and set the value to `x`, as shown in Figure 9-38.

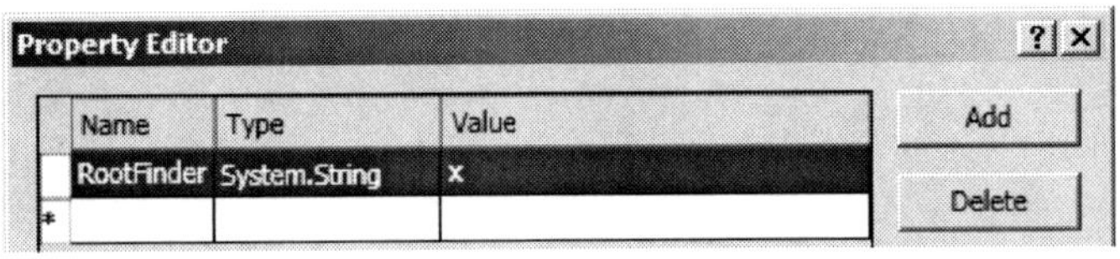

***Figure 9-38.*** *Adding the `RootFinder` property to the Finder method instance*

If the data source contained data suitable for incremental crawls, the `LastModifiedTimeStampField` property on the Finder method instance could also be set. This is not feasible in this example.

## Deployment

Deploying the .NET Assembly Connector is made easy in Visual Studio 2010. Open the Build menu on the top bar, and click Deploy Solution. Now VS 2010 begins to compile and packages the .NET Assembly Connector code, BDC model, and the feature. Finally it creates a WSP, which is the package type used for deploying solutions to SharePoint.

The WSP package is then deployed to the specified SharePoint site. The feature is activated, which registers the external content type associated with this .NET Assembly Connector.

# The Secure Store Service

The Secure Store Service is used to store accounts inside SharePoint to use when authorizing against databases that require authorization, etc. It typically stores credentials in the form of username and password, but it can also store tokens, pin numbers, etc.

The Secure Store Service application works by a scheme being defined providing authentication information. Then the user- or group-level permissions to pass to the database are mapped in the Secure Store application. The Secure Store Service allows connections using the federation, delegation, or impersonation level. In cases of Business Connectivity Services, the mapped credentials are passed from the Secure Store to the data source.[1]

## Configuring the Secure Store Service

In this section and the ones that follow, we will go through the procedure of configuring the Secure Store Service, while explaining the individual steps and configuration options. The first step is to ensure that the Secure Store Service is started:

1. Navigate to Central Administration ➤ Manage Service on Server (Figure 9-39).

2. Locate the service called Secure Store Service.

3. If the Secure Store Service is not started, then start it.

---

[1] Loosely based on `http://lightningtools.com/blog/archive/2010/01/20/bcs-secure-store-services.aspx`.

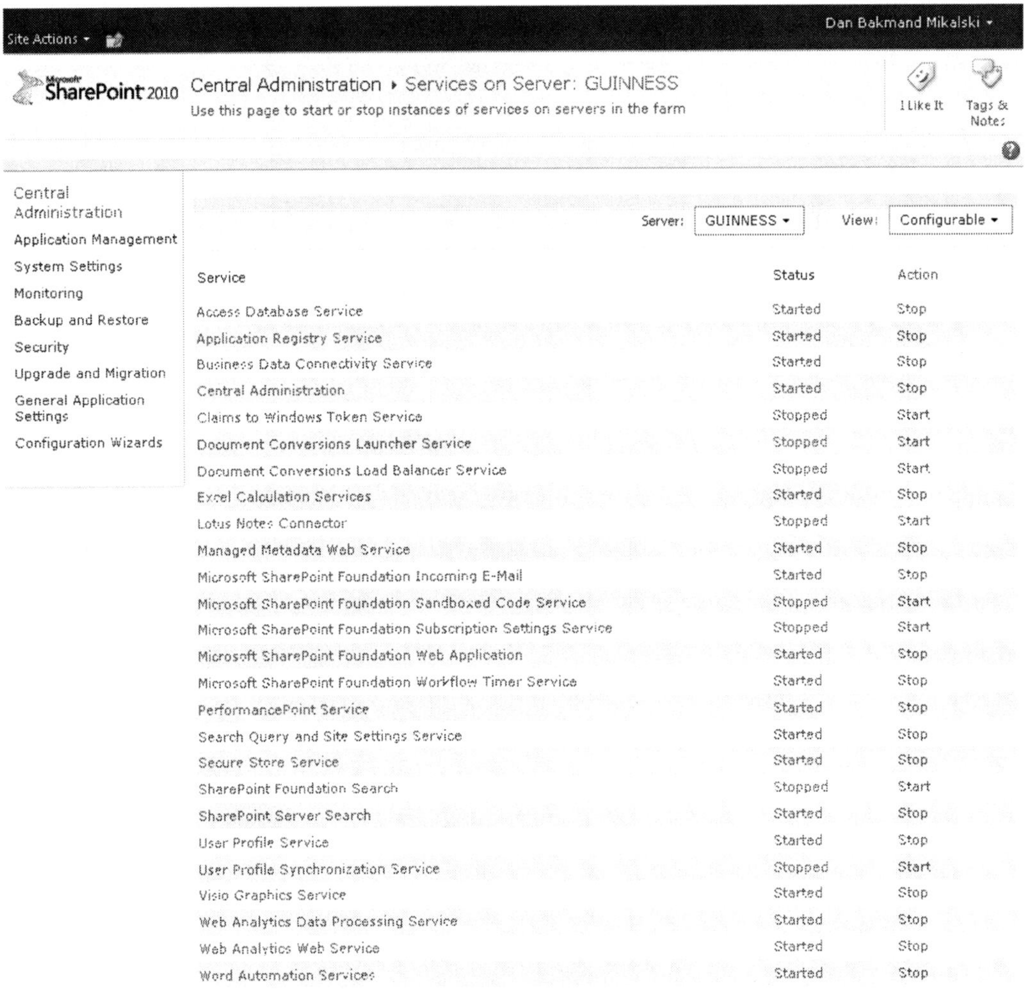

| Service | Status | Action |
| --- | --- | --- |
| Access Database Service | Started | Stop |
| Application Registry Service | Started | Stop |
| Business Data Connectivity Service | Started | Stop |
| Central Administration | Started | Stop |
| Claims to Windows Token Service | Stopped | Start |
| Document Conversions Launcher Service | Stopped | Start |
| Document Conversions Load Balancer Service | Stopped | Start |
| Excel Calculation Services | Started | Stop |
| Lotus Notes Connector | Stopped | Start |
| Managed Metadata Web Service | Started | Stop |
| Microsoft SharePoint Foundation Incoming E-Mail | Started | Stop |
| Microsoft SharePoint Foundation Sandboxed Code Service | Stopped | Start |
| Microsoft SharePoint Foundation Subscription Settings Service | Stopped | Start |
| Microsoft SharePoint Foundation Web Application | Started | Stop |
| Microsoft SharePoint Foundation Workflow Timer Service | Started | Stop |
| PerformancePoint Service | Started | Stop |
| Search Query and Site Settings Service | Started | Stop |
| Secure Store Service | Started | Stop |
| SharePoint Foundation Search | Stopped | Start |
| SharePoint Server Search | Started | Stop |
| User Profile Service | Started | Stop |
| User Profile Synchronization Service | Stopped | Start |
| Visio Graphics Service | Started | Stop |
| Web Analytics Data Processing Service | Started | Stop |
| Web Analytics Web Service | Started | Stop |
| Word Automation Services | Started | Stop |

***Figure 9-39.*** *Services overview*

With the Secure Store Service started, it is now possible to provision a Secure Store Service application as follows:

1. Navigate to Central Administration ➤ Manage Service Application (Figure 9-40).

2. Click the New button on the ribbon.

3. Click Secure Store Service to open the dialog for creating the new service application.

**Figure 9-40.** *Provisioning the Secure Store Service application*

The Create New Secure Store Service Application dialog (Figure 9-41) allows administrators to specify a database where the credentials are stored. The credentials are encrypted and accessible by the Secure Store Service application. To create the Secure Store Service, do the following:

1. Enter a unique service name.

2. Specify the database instance name where the Secure Store database will be created. Also specify a name for the Secure Store database.

3. Choose or create an application pool identity, which the Secure Store Service application will run under. It is suggested to use a unique account for this particular service application for security reasons.

4. Click OK. The Secure Store Service application and proxy should now be created.

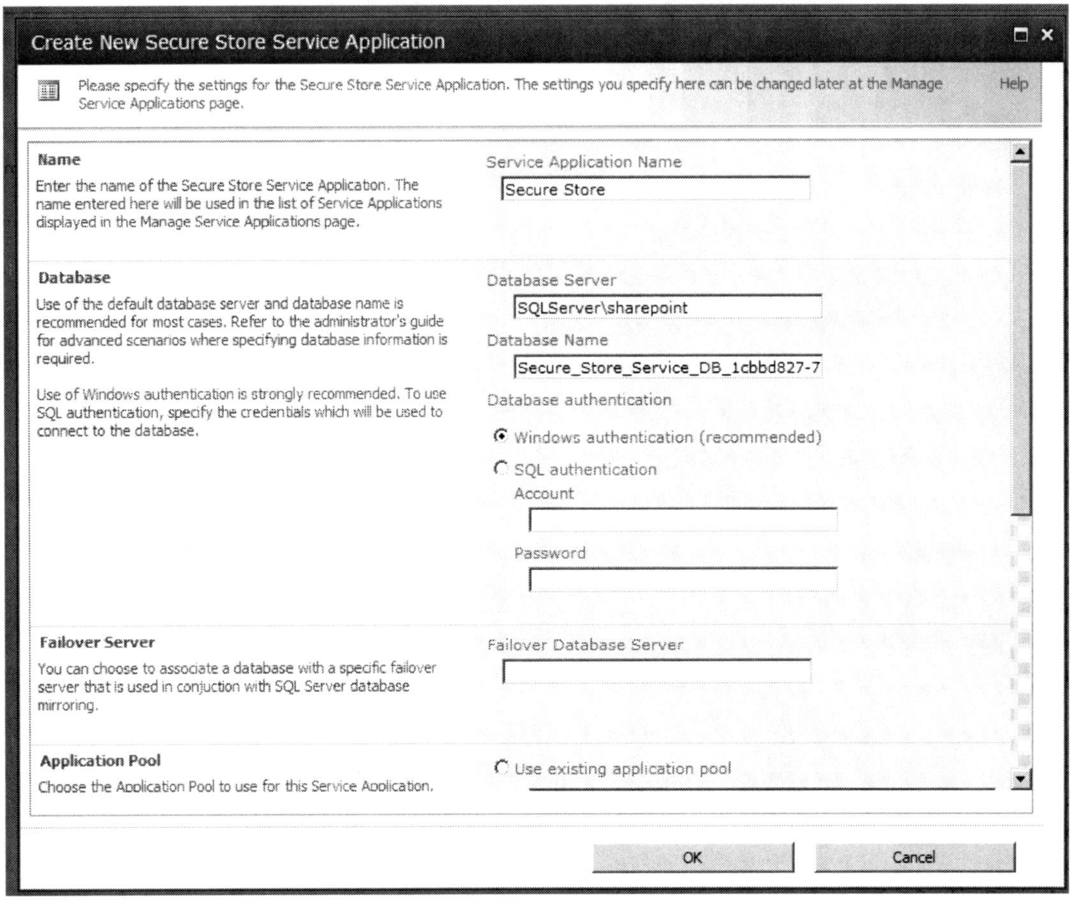

*Figure 9-41. Provisioning the Secure Store Service application*

With the new Secure Store Service application created, it must be configured with a pass phrase (Figure 9-42) that allows it to securely encrypt and decrypt the stored credentials from the database.

1.  Click the Secure Store Service application to begin configuring it.

2.  If it is the first time the Secure Store Service application is being configured, a prompt will appear, asking for a new key to be generated. Click Generate New Key on the ribbon.

3.  Enter a pass phrase, and click OK.

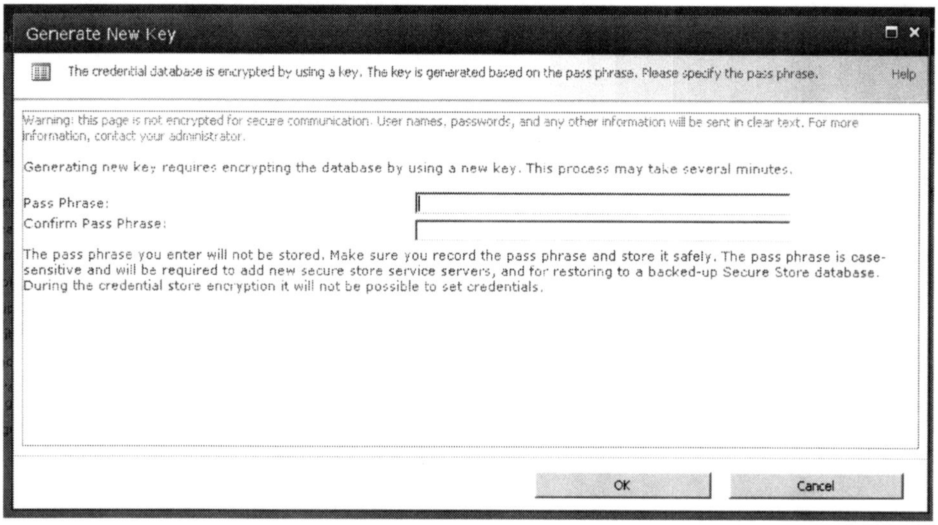

**Figure 9-42.** *Secure Store Service key generation*

## Creating a Secure Store Service Application for Impersonating

For the Secure Store Service to be able to apply the stored credentials, an application must be created that uses these credentials. In SharePoint, this is called a Secure Store Target Application. In essence the impersonation of the securely stored credentials is done through this application.

1. Go to the Secure Store Service application.

2. Click New on the ribbon, as shown in Figure 9-43. This opens the Create New Secure Store Target Application page.

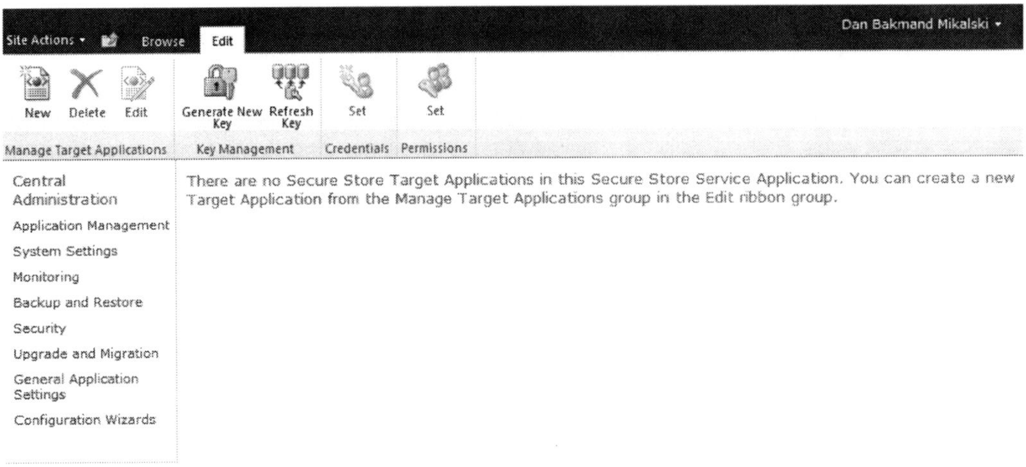

**Figure 9-43.** *Secure Store Service application overview*

On the Create New Secure Store Target Application page, the target application settings are specified. In the example in Figure 9-44, Group is chosen as the target application type. This allows members to be defined whose accounts can be impersonated by another account. This is the most often used scenario. Other options include tickets with a limited valid lifetime. On the target application page, do the following:

1. Enter a unique name for the application. This is not changeable after the application is created.

2. Enter a screen-friendly name and the e-mail address of the administrator, which typically is the creator.

3. Choose the Target Application Type, as described before.

4. Select a Target Application Page URL. A custom URL can be specified to allow mapping this application to a custom page for users to assign accounts, if there is an organizational need for doing so.

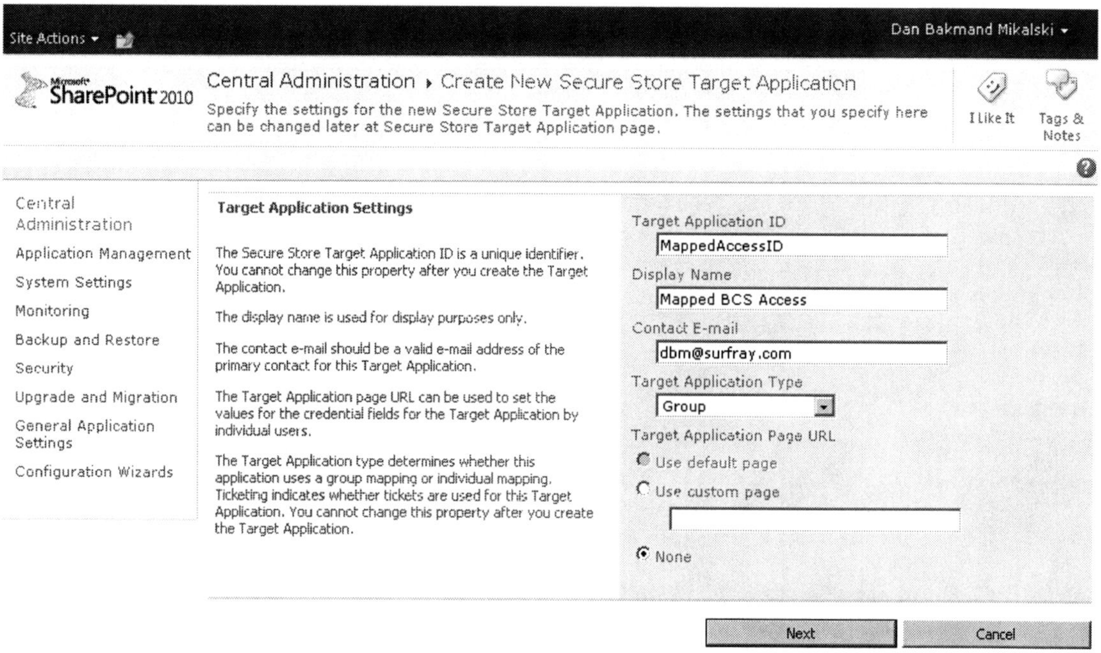

**Figure 9-44.** *Secure Store Service application creation*

To alter the fields and thereby information used by this application, add additional fields that the user will have to fill out to authenticate. The default fields are Windows username and password, as shown in Figure 9-45.

5.  Change fields as required.

6.  Click Next to go to the credentials mapping page.

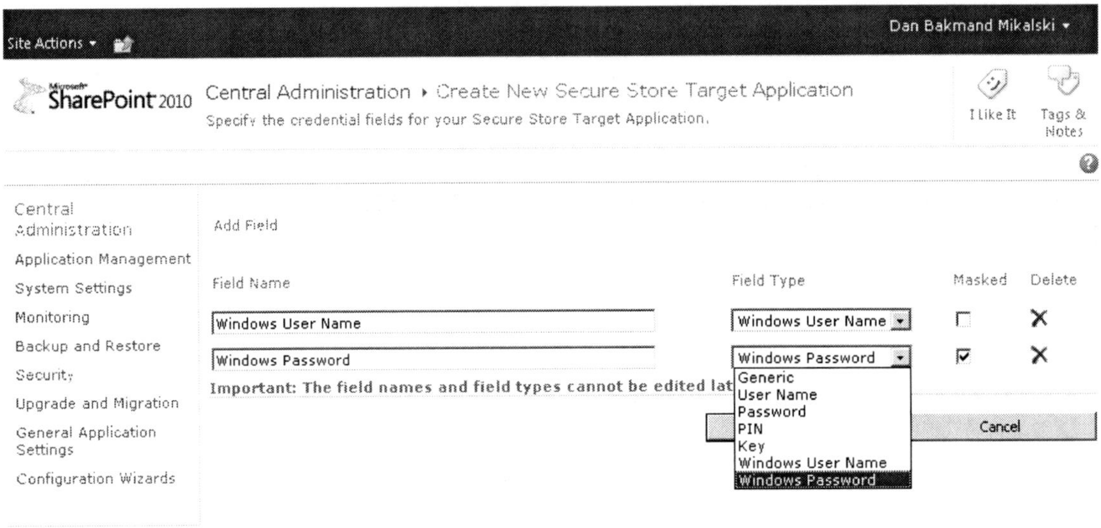

**Figure 9-45.** *Secure Store Service application field mapping*

On the user mappings page, the administrators and members are configured. These are then the members and administrators of the target application. In Figure 9-46, one administrator and two users are added: SP_TestUser1 and SP_TestUser2. It will be explained how to add specific permissions to individual users in the "Setting Permissions" section.

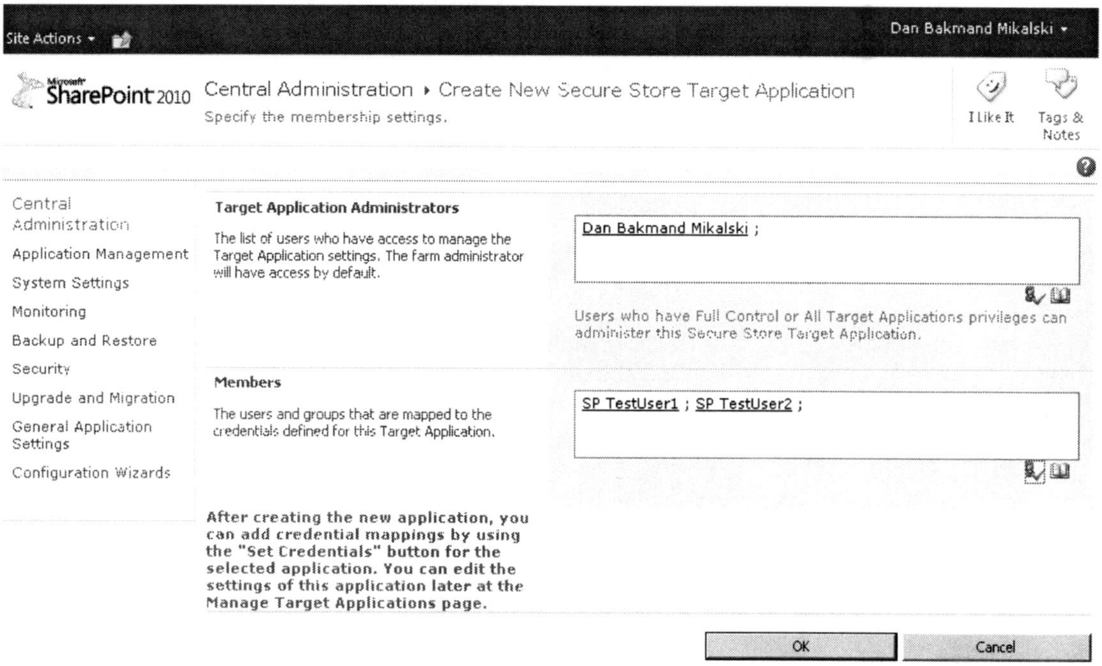

**Figure 9-46.** *Secure Store Service credentials mapping*

Finally click the OK button, and the target application will be created. SharePoint now automatically navigates to the Secure Store Service Application page where the target applications are shown, as in Figure 9-47. It lists the target applications by ID, their types, and display name.

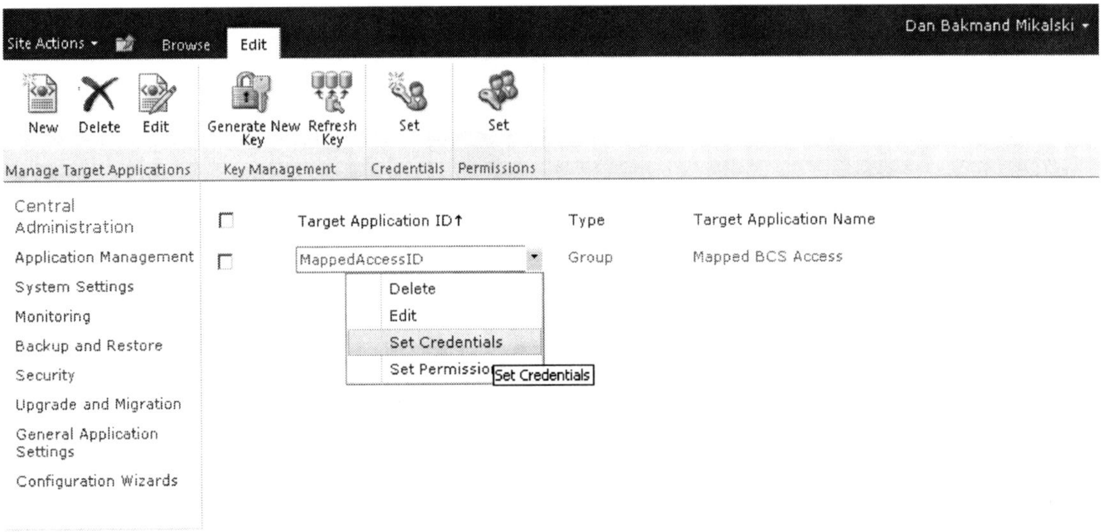

*Figure 9-47. Secure Store Service application overview*

## Setting the Application Impersonation Credentials

Now, the Secure Store Target Application is configured and administrators, members, and credentials type have been defined. At this point, the application impersonation credentials are configured for the members of the target application, as shown in Figure 9-48.

1. Provide one or more credential owners, which are the credentials that map to the custom defined credentials.

2. Enter the Windows username and password(s) to be used when impersonating in the Secure Store Target Application.

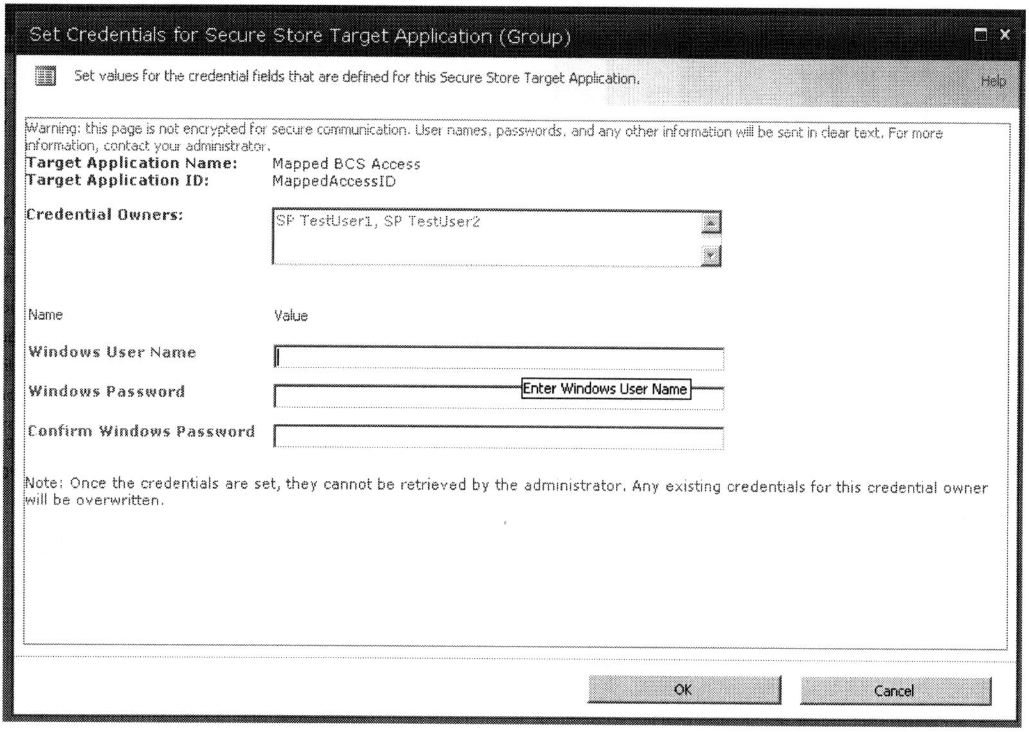

**Figure 9-48.** *Setting the Secure Store Target Application credentials*

With everything configured relating to credentials, the Secure Store Target Application can be used by BCS when creating connections to its data sources, as shown in Figure 9-49.

1. Select a connection type.

2. Enter proper connection details (here it is a SQL Server connection, as shown in Figure 9-49).

3. Enter the target application name at the time of creating a connection to the back end. Given the example data used in the section "Creating an External Content Type," now select the Secure Store Application ID option and enter the application name.

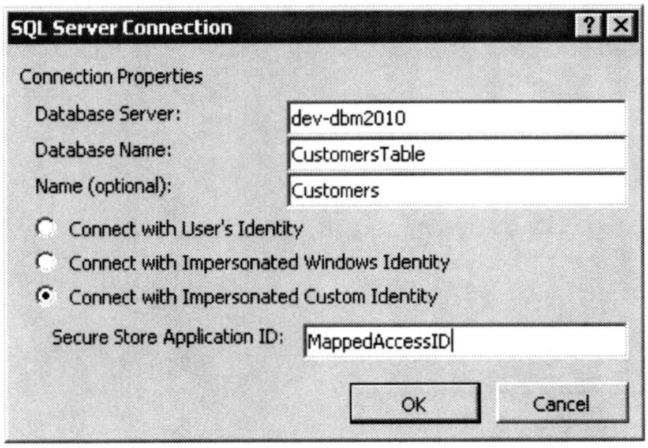

*Figure 9-49.* *Map BCS connection to Secure Store Application ID*

As mentioned earlier in this example, two users were added as members. These users can be delegated individual rights. When these users open an external list based on this external content type, they should be able to see the data pulled from the BDC using the impersonation. For this to work, the users must be members of the BCS application, as the BCS checks permissions using the incoming user account before doing the impersonation and getting the data from the back end. This means that the impersonation is not for communicating with the BCS application itself, but for allowing BCS to get data from its data source. Users still need permissions to access the external content type objects.

## Setting Permissions

Based on the data source created in the previous section, setting permissions on external content type objects is done by doing the following:

1.  Going to Central Administration site ➤ Manage service applications

2.  Selecting the BCS service application just created

3.  Setting permissions on the external content type, as shown in Figure 9-50

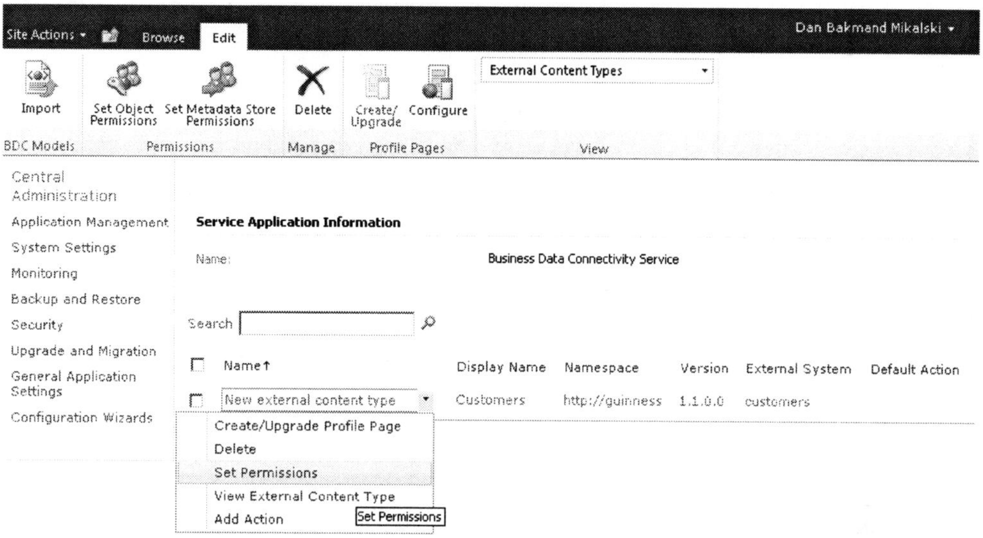

**Figure 9-50.** *Accessing external content type permissions settings*

In this case, the users are granted Edit and Execute permissions on the `customers` external content type object, as shown in Figure 9-51.

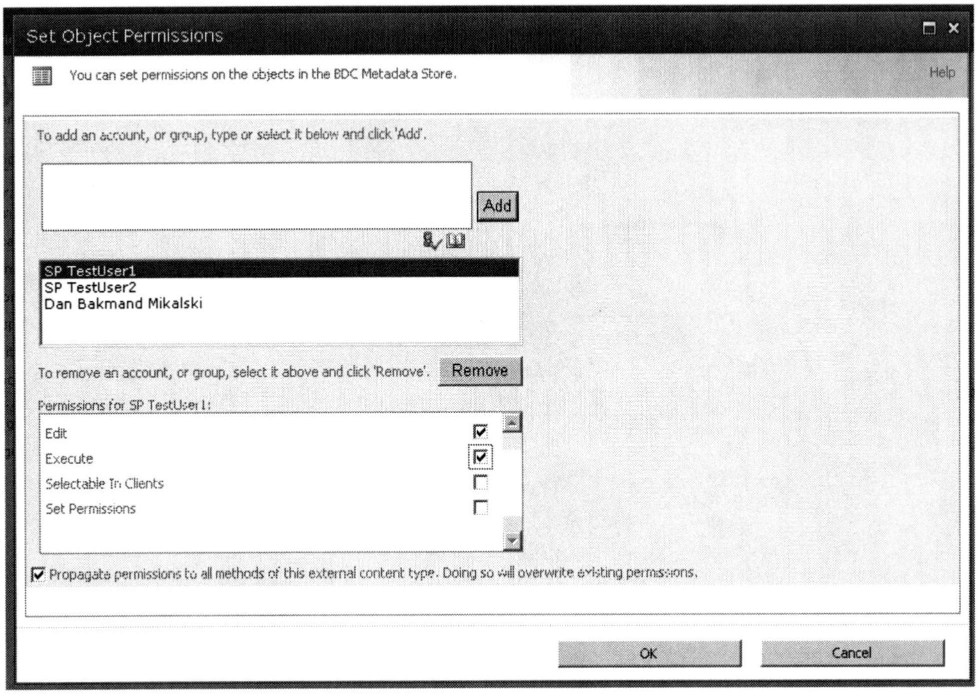

**Figure 9-51.** *Setting external content type permissions*

At this point, the external content type permissions are fully configured and can now be used in BCS Web Parts, external lists, etc. by persons with the appropriate credentials.

# Creating Security Trimmed CRUD Operations on a SQL Database Using Visual Studio 2010

Earlier it was shown how to create a flat file .NET connector using Business Data Connectivity Designer in Visual Studio 2010. Here we will show you how to pull data from an external database into an external list and enable Create, Read, Update, and Delete (CRUD) functions to the external list.[2] The example is based on the same customer data used earlier.

---

[2] Loosely based on http://www.facebook.com/note.php?note_id=338666619441.

This list will implement security trimming by using a rights table that holds security identifiers for each row.

## Connecting Model to Data Source

To begin with, create a new BDC Model project and give it a proper name. Here it is named BdcCustomersModel. To make it easy to use the data obtained from the Customers database, the best way is to add a LINQ to SQL model. LINQ is not the fastest implementation method performance-wise, so if performance is critical, you might prefer to implement a dedicated data adaptor instead.

1. Select the project by left-clicking it.

2. Click Add New Item on the projects menu to open the Add New Item dialog.

3. Select Data templates from the Installed Templates panel.

4. Choose the LINQ to SQL Classes project type from the Templates panel.

5. Give the project a proper name—here it is called "Customer"—and then click Add.

6. Open the Server Explorer, and add a connection to the Customers database.

7. Drag Customers tableand drop it on the Customer.dbml design surface.

At this point, a designer class named CustomerDataContext is automatically added. To allow a connection to be created using a custom connection string, a new class should be added. Name the class CustomerDataContext.cs. Make this class a partial class. Then pass the connection string to the base class through the constructor, as in Listing 9-3.

***Listing 9-3.*** *Data Context for Connecting to a Database with a Custom Connection String*

```
public partial class CustomerDataContext
{
    private const string ConnectionString = @"Data Source=localhost\SQLEXPRESS;Initial⏎
        Catalog=CustomersDatabase;Integrated Security=True;Pooling=False";
```

```
    public CustomerDataContext() :
        base(ConnectionString, mappingSource)
    {
        OnCreated();
    }
}
```

■ **Note** We made the connection string a constant in the code for exemplifying it. In a production environment, it should be added to the Web.Config file in encrypted format. When using your own database, the connection string should be modified to match your database and credential requirements.

## Mapping BDC Model to Data Source

At this point, the BDC model should be mapped to the data source. This involves making a number of entities and specifying appropriate methods. The purpose is to create the interpretation layer between the database and the BDC model. First an entity with an identifier key needs to be created:

1.  An entity named "Entity1" is automatically created. Delete it.

2.  Create a new entity. This can be done using "Drag and Drop" on the Entity from Toolbox and dropping it on the design surface.

3.  Change the default name of the entity to "Customer."

4.  Create a new identifier named, CustomerKey, on the entity "Customer." This is most easily done by right-clicking the entity and selecting the Add Identifier option. This adds a new identifier to the entity.

5.  Give the identifier the name "CustomerKey".

To add functionality, a number of method instances must be added to the entity. This is most easily done by selecting the entity and clicking the <Add a Method> button that appears in the Method Details panel. Create a Specific Finder method on the entity. This will add the ReadItem, as shown in Figure 9-52.

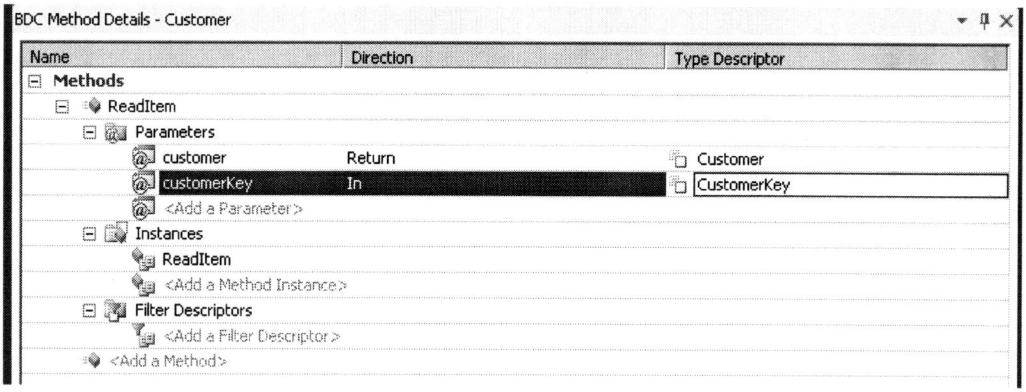

**Figure 9-52.** *Specific Finder method*

As shown in the Method Details panel, the `ReadItem` method has two parameters, namely an `In` parameter, which takes the identifier key, and a `Return` parameter, which is an object instance of the identity type. VS2010 offers some functionality for making it easy to create new methods by copying type descriptors automatically when possible. Therefore it is a good idea to configure those for the Specific Finder method before adding the other methods.

To complete the identifier key configuration, the type descriptor for the return parameter named `CustomerKey` should be added.

1. Open the Method Details panel.

2. Choose the <Edit> command from the type descriptor menu named CustomerKey.

3. In the BDC Explorer, add a type descriptor by right-clicking the CustomerKey, as shown in Figure 9-53, and choose the Add Type Descriptor option. This will create a new type descriptor.

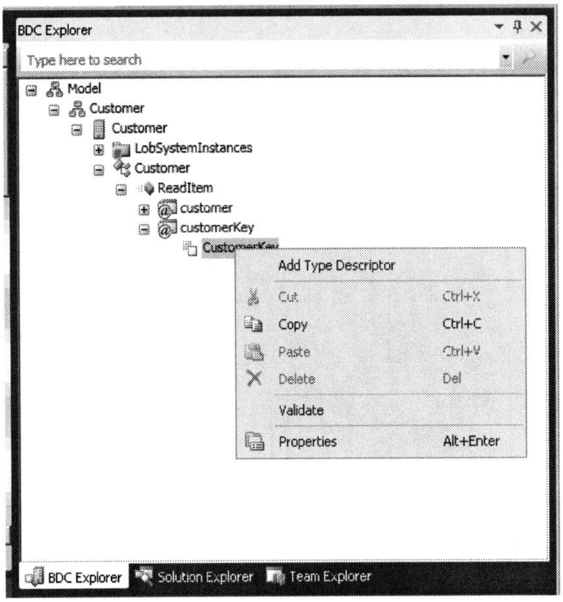

*Figure 9-53. Adding type descriptors*

4. Rename the just-created type descriptor to "CustomerKey", using the Properties panel.

5. Change the `Identifier` property to `CustomerKey`, as in Figure 9-54. This is how the BCS runtime knows that this type descriptor maps to the `CustomerKey` identifier.

6. Change the `Type Name` property to match the type from the LINQ model. In this example, it is not required to change it.

7. Repeat steps 1–6 for all required type descriptors.

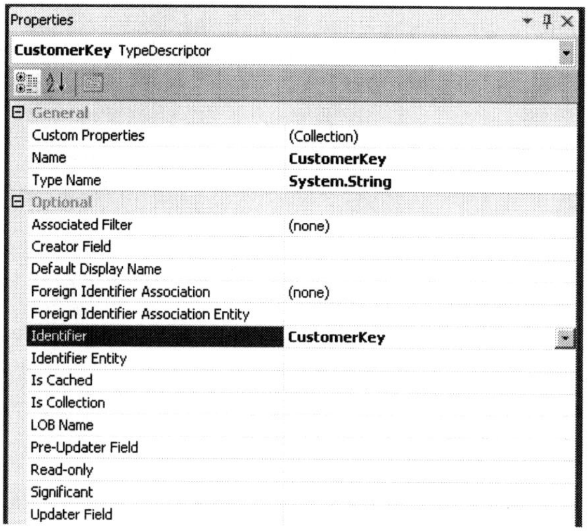

*Figure 9-54. Configuring type descriptors*

When all type descriptors are added as in steps 1 through 7, the type descriptors shown in Figure 9-55 should be visible. It is always a good idea to check the spelling and Type Name properties at this point, as updating them later on can be a pain. Refactoring does not currently support this.

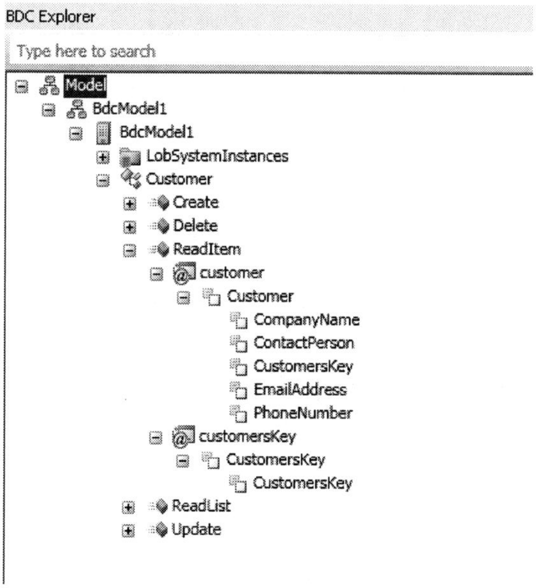

*Figure 9-55. All type descriptors configured*

At this point, the other methods available need to be created the same as the ReadItem (Specific Finder) method. These are the methods that support the BDC operations that are the CRUD operations. To do this, repeat the steps in this section for each of the following methods: ReadList, Create, Update, and Delete. Also counting the ReadItem method, a total of five methods should be defined for the entity named Customer. It is, however, much easier to create the last four methods, as the type descriptors of the return parameters are automatically defined the same way as with the ReadItem method. The BDC Designer automatically applies type descriptors defined in the other methods of an entity and copies them to the newly created methods.

With the required type descriptors in place for the methods, the LOB system–qualified type name of the type descriptor Customer should be defined. This is done by selecting the Customer type descriptor in the BDC Explorer panel. In the Properties panel, its value should be changed from System.String to BdcCustomer.Customer, BdcModel1. This is now the underlying data type of the data structure that the Customer type descriptor returns.

# Adding Code-Behind to Access External Data Source

To implement the logic required for performing the actual CRUD operations, the method body of the methods in the CustomerService.cs code file should be changed to match the code in Listing 9-4.

*Listing 9-4. Implementation of CRUD Operations in the BDC Method Instances*

```
public static Customer ReadItem(string customersKey)
{
    CustomerDataContext context = new CustomerDataContext();
    Customer cust = context.Customers.Single(c => c.CustomerKey == customersKey);
    return cust;
}

public static Customer Create(Customer newCustomer)
{
    CustomerDataContext context = new CustomerDataContext();
    context.Customers.InsertOnSubmit(newCustomer); context.SubmitChanges();
    Customer cust= context.Customers.Single(c => c.CustomerKey ==newCustomer.CustomerKey);
    return cust;
}

public static void Delete(string customersKey)
{
    CustomerDataContext context = new CustomerDataContext();
    Customer cust = context.Customers.Single(c => c.CustomerKey == customersKey);
    context.Customers.DeleteOnSubmit(cust);
    context.SubmitChanges();
}
```

```
public static IEnumerable<Customer> ReadList()
{
    CustomerDataContext context = new CustomerDataContext();
    IEnumerable<Customer> custList = context.Customers;
    return custList;
}

public static void Update(Customer customer)
{
    CustomerDataContext context = new CustomerDataContext();
    Customer cust = context.Customers.Single(c => c.CustomerKey == customer.CustomerKey);
    cust.CustomerKey = customer.CustomerKey;
    cust.CompanyName = customer.CompanyName;
    cust.ContactPerson = customer.ContactPerson;
    cust.EmailAddress = customer.EmailAddress;
    cust.PhoneNumber = customer.PhoneNumber;
    context.SubmitChanges();
}
```

# Adding Security Trimming to .NET Connectors

Being able to do security trimming is important in many corporations. This can be a challenge, especially if the LOB data system uses custom security descriptors. Extending the database .NET connector described in the previous section will show how this can be accomplished. Here we will assume one particular form of security descriptor, but in reality it could be in any format that supports mapping between the user context and the descriptor.

First a rights table must be added to the model to support security trimming. Here we have created a CustomerAccessRights table containing the SecurityDescriptor, Rights, and CustomerKey. The SecurityDescriptor is a binary unique value for a particular user. Rights will contain a simple numeric schema representing user rights to a particular row. It also contains creation rights.

- Read Allowed

- Read / Write / Update / Delete Allowed

No Entry means the user has no rights to this data row represented by the CustomerKey. In a production environment, a different and more fine-grained access rights mapping might be desired, but this should give a good idea about how to implement security trimming that allows multiple users with different access to the same data rows. Given the customer table contains this information, we can create a CustomerAccessRights table containing the security mappings. The SecurityDescriptor should be based on the same method used by the model to trim security. In this example, it is the GetSecurityDescriptor() method displayed in Tables 9-1 and 9-2.

*Table 9-1. Customers Table*

| CustomerKey | CompanyName | PhoneNumber | EmailAddress | ContactPerson |
|---|---|---|---|---|
| 2 | Microsoft | 555-xxxxxx1 | mail@microsoft.com | John Doe |
| 5 | SurfRay | 555-xxxxxx2 | mail@surfray.com | John Doe |
| 6 | Apple | 555-xxxxxx3 | mail@apple.com | John Doe |
| 7 | IBM | 555-xxxxxx4 | mail@ibm.com | John Doe |

*Table 9-2. Customer Access Rights Table*

| Rights | CustomerKey | SecurityDescriptor |
|---|---|---|
| 1 | 2 | <binary data> |
| 2 | 2 | <binary data> |
| 2 | 5 | <binary data> |
| 2 | 6 | <binary data> |
| 2 | 7 | <binary data> |

To add the `CustomerAccessRights` table to the model, add a new LINQ to SQL Classes item to the project and name it `CustomerAccessRights`. In the Server Explorer, add a connection to the `Customers` database if it does not already exist. Then drag the `CustomerAccessRights` table, and drop it on the `CustomerAccessRights.dbml` design surface.

Next the required method for computing the `SecurityDescriptor` is added as in Listing 9-5. This method can be added to the `CustomerService.cs` class that also contains the `Customer` methods. This method computes a security descriptor in the form of a byte array.

*Listing 9-5. Implementation of Method for Getting a Security Descriptor*

```
static Byte[] GetSecurityDescriptor(string domain, string username)
{
    NTAccount acc = new NTAccount(domain, username);
    SecurityIdentifier sid = (SecurityIdentifier)acc.Translate(typeof(SecurityIdentifier));
    CommonSecurityDescriptor sd = new CommonSecurityDescriptor(false, false,
        ControlFlags.None, sid, null, null, null);

    sd.SetDiscretionaryAclProtection(true, false);
```

```
//Deny access to everyone
SecurityIdentifier everyone = new SecurityIdentifier(WellKnownSidType.WorldSid, null);
sd.DiscretionaryAcl.RemoveAccess( AccessControlType.Allow, everyone,
        unchecked((int)0xffffffffL), InheritanceFlags.None, PropagationFlags.None);

//Grant full access to specified user
sd.DiscretionaryAcl.AddAccess( AccessControlType.Allow, sid,
        unchecked((int)0xffffffffL), InheritanceFlags.None, PropagationFlags.None);

byte[] secDes = new Byte[sd.BinaryLength];
sd.GetBinaryForm(secDes, 0);

return secDes;

}
```

Having the Rights table and the security descriptor method in place, the next step is to modify the Customers methods for updating, reading, etc., such that they are trimmed based on the security descriptor. Here (Listing 9-6) the Reader methods are updated to apply security trimming during search.

***Listing 9-6.*** *Adding Security Trimming to the BDC Method Instances*

```
public static IEnumerable<Customer> ReadList()
{
    CustomerDataContext context = new CustomerDataContext();
    CustomerAccessRightsDataContext accessContext = new CustomerAccessRightsDataContext();

    List<Customer> tempCustList = new List<Customer>();
    foreach(Customer customer in context.Customers)
    {
        CustomerAccessRight custAccess = accessContext.CustomerAccessRights.SingleOrDefault(
            c => c.CustomerKey == customer.CustomerKey  && c.SecurityDescriptor.ToArray()
            == GetSecurityDescriptor(Environment.UserDomainName,Environment.UserName));

        if(custAccess.Rights > 0)
            tempCustList.Add(customer);
    }

    IEnumerable<Customer> custList = tempCustList;
    return custList;
}

public static Customer ReadItem(string customersKey)
{
    CustomerDataContext context = new CustomerDataContext();
    Customer cust = context.Customers.Single(c => c.CustomerKey == customersKey);

    CustomerAccessRightsDataContext accessContext = new CustomerAccessRightsDataContext();
```

```
CustomerAccessRight custAccess = accessContext.CustomerAccessRights.SingleOrDefault(
    c => c.CustomerKey == cust.CustomerKey && c.SecurityDescriptor.ToArray()
    == GetSecurityDescriptor(Environment.UserDomainName, Environment.UserName));

if (custAccess.Rights > 0)
    return cust;
else
    return null;
}
```

Using this methodology as a baseline, it is possible to create simple security trimming. When doing security trimming, performance of the trimming mechanism is relevant. Different caching mechanics can be applied with success to increase performance. Also other security descriptor implementations that better fit specific requirements can be implemented using this example as a template for how to approach the topic. Microsoft does provide some resources on this topic.[3]

# Summary

The goal of this chapter was to provide insight into the new Business Connectivity Services framework offered in SharePoint 2010. BCS is in itself an extensive framework out of the box, spanning not only SharePoint but also Outlook, InfoPath, and other Office applications.

One of the powerful capabilities of BCS is its relative ease in creating complex security configurations using the Secure Store Service or programming in Visual Studio 2010. This was much more difficult to accomplish with the Business Data Catalog in SharePoint 2007.

Hands-on examples of how to create and integrate BCS in the organization should encourage the reader to do further exploration of the capabilities. Finally an example of how easy it can be to code a .NET Assembly Connector for exposing an external content type from a data source not supported out of the box should also encourage IT professionals in the organization to view BCS as an opportunity as opposed to the much more difficult and expensive solutions of yesteryear's SharePoint 2007 BDC.

---

[3] http://msdn.microsoft.com/en-us/library/aa374815%28v=vs.85%29.aspx

# CHAPTER 10

■ ■ ■

# Relevancy and Reporting

After completing this chapter, you will be able to

- Understand the basics of search ranking and relevancy

- Be able to make adjustments to affect relevancy

- View and understand SharePoint search reporting

- Use basic best practices to utilize SharePoint Search reports to improve relevancy

- Utilize the thesaurus in SharePoint to add synonyms to search terms

- Tune search with a variety of techniques available in SharePoint 2010

- Create custom ranking models and deploy them with PowerShell

Relevancy and reporting are essential concepts to ensure the success of enterprise search. Understanding how to affect relevancy and react on reporting can help an administrator make search improvements that may have serious impact on the adoption of SharePoint. For all the bells and whistles on an enterprise search engine, the true test of search quality is that for any given query, the desired document or information is returned at the top of the results page. This is easier said than done, and many search users are frustrated by not finding what they are looking for. This gives rise to the demand for more and more search expansion or filtering functionality. If a relevancy model could truly return what users are looking for at each and every search, things like refiners and expanded query syntax would be unnecessary.

Unfortunately, no relevancy algorithm can achieve the goal of always returning the exact document. To compound this, there are a variety of ways that terms can be used to find the same or different information depending on the subjective position of the searcher. Therefore, understanding and being able to modify the search results are key tools for reacting to user demands and improving search.

Another important factor that influences search engine success is the quality of the actual content that is being indexed. Administrators can make great improvements in the quality of search by simply trimming and optimizing the content that is being indexed and searched.

A keen SharePoint administrator should have a clear understanding of how well search is functioning and be able to improve it based on an interactive approach by analyzing and modifying the content to get the best experience possible. To do this, Microsoft has introduced some key features in SharePoint 2010. Those features include the ability to affect the search by adding properties to documents, managing those properties with the Managed Metadata service, adding synonyms to match like concepts and expand queries, and analyzing the successes and failures of the search engine with search reporting.

Relevancy algorithms in search engines are akin to the secret formula in soft drinks. Most search vendors will not reveal their ranking rules, but most are based on basic concepts or on a publicly available and well-known formula such as Term Frequency–Inverse Document Frequency (TF–IDF) or the more advanced BM25.

In aid of the quest for great results, Microsoft has revealed much about its search ranking methods. Not only have they acknowledged that they use a variation of Stephen Robertson's BM25 as the base of SharePoint's ranking algorithm, but they have also exposed a method of modifying or changing that ranking algorithm to match the particular needs of an organization.

First, however, understanding the general mechanism of search ranking in order to affect the quality of results is certainly useful. Therefore, this chapter will discuss the basic concepts that will make a document rise to the top in a SharePoint result set or fall to the bottom. It avoids the mathematics behind the algorithms, as that is a subject for a different book. It will discuss reporting, how to see the successes and failures of the search engine, and techniques that can be applied to modify the way the search engine behaves and eventually improve the search experience. Additionally, it will show how to create your own ranking scheme or modify the existing one and apply it for use in different cases in SharePoint.

# Relevancy Algorithms

Relevancy algorithms can be complicated as there are many elements and considerations to make when attempting to determine exactly which document is best matched to a given term.

Most algorithms, including Google's famous PageRank, are available free to download and inspect from the Internet. However, developers, when creating a ranking algorithm, will almost always add their own modifications to whatever base they are using to create a unique and functional ranking algorithm. Google's present ranking mechanism is certainly exponentially more complex now than it was when its founders first invented it and published it while at Stanford. Whatever the math behind the ranking algorithm, experience and testing can confirm that the ranking in SharePoint 2010 is highly effective for enterprise content and brings relevant documents to the top of the search results page.

As mentioned, SharePoint's default algorithm is purportedly based on an algorithm called BM25. There is some reference to neural networks in literature on the Internet about SharePoint's ranking model. This is supported by a patent created by Microsoft's engineering team, which received US Patent No. 7,840,569 B2 in November 2010. See a link to this patent in the "Further Reading" section. The term neural network means the algorithm is designed to learn from user behavior, something that SharePoint's algorithm certainly does. However, there is no way to actually know that this ranking algorithm is the core of SharePoint's.

To simplify things, however, we can think of an enterprise search ranking algorithm as basically a formula that ranks documents based on the frequency of query terms appearing in the matching documents as well as considering overall comparative document value. SharePoint applies various ranking considerations based on different fields of which a document may be comprised. For SharePoint specifically, these fields are extended to properties and other data associated with the documents. So a single document becomes a collection of differently weighted ranking considerations. These ranking considerations include, but may not be limited to, the following areas:

- Keyword matches
  - Body
  - Title
  - Author properties

- Other property tags
- Intersite anchor
- URL
- Proximity
  - Query segmentation
  - Query term association
- Static document relationships
  - Click distance
  - URL depth
  - File type
  - Length
  - Language
- User-driven weighting
  - Click popularity
  - Skips

The first step SharePoint search takes when receiving a query is to pass the query through a word breaker to ensure the query terms match terms that may be stored in the index. SharePoint has a specific word breaker for each language that can tell where to break compound terms and tokenize them. This word breaking or tokenization happens during both the crawling of terms and the querying of terms to ensure that streams of indexed text are broken into simple items. The neutral or default word breaker in SharePoint breaks terms only for white space or filler characters like hyphens and slashes. Other language word breakers do a more complex analysis based on the grammar of the given language. Some languages have no white space between terms, so they require a special understanding of the characters. Next, the broken or tokenized terms are sent to a stemmer to reduce them to their root form. These terms are finally checked against terms in the index, and a result set is assembled based on all the documents that contain matching terms from the entire corpus. The result set is then prioritized with the item with the highest ranking value at the top of the first page and subsequent matches listed in descending order.

SharePoint search applies what it calls static and dynamic ranking. Static ranking is applied to documents at crawl time and relates to the static elements of the documents, such as distance from authoritative pages, language, file type length, etc. Dynamic ranking is applied at query time and applies value for the specific terms queried, specifically keyword matches, and proximity weighting.

In addition to or in support of these conditions, the factors discussed in the following sections are considered in ranking, but not necessarily in the order they are presented here.

# Keyword Matches

The total number of times the terms appear on the document is, of course, important for ranking. The most obvious element to rank a document as being a match for a given term is the raw number of times that word is mentioned in the document. Documents that mention a specific topic numerous times are likely more relevant for the given topic. Similarly keywords that appear frequently in a corpus will likely have a lower overall relevancy value than those that appear relatively few times in the corpus. For example, a word like the name of the company will likely appear on almost every document. The term frequency–inverse document frequency ranking algorithm that the SharePoint search ranking rules are based upon will lower the overall value of that term and boost terms that appear only in few documents, like product codes or project numbers.

## Terms in the Body Text

Probably the most obvious place to match the terms is in the body of the documents. This is where the bulk of the text will be found and the kind of ranking that most people understand due to the way that global search engines treat web pages. Also, the use of metadata to identify documents is relatively limited o much of documents' thematic value lies in the body text. This is also, unfortunately, the place where it is most difficult to improve content to affect ranking. Having good headings and using accepted terminology are two ways to influence ranking in body text.

## Terms in Titles

Titles are important indicators of a document's purpose. Although there are many poorly titled documents, if a term or phrase appears in the document's title, there is a good chance that the document is about that title. The chance is so good, in fact, that titles are usually given the highest ranking values. Good titling is getting more and more attention in the enterprise, so this ranking value is increasingly effective. Most things in life are given titles by people, including people themselves. And these titles, although sometimes misleading, tell us something essential about the thing that is titled. Therefore, improving titles on documents in an information handling system such as SharePoint is one of the easiest and most useful ways to influence enterprise search ranking.

## Terms in Author Properties and Other Property Tags

Metadata in SharePoint 2010, often referred to as properties, is also important for ranking. Properly applied metadata gives documents purposeful associations to terms and themes that may not be prevalent in the document. One of the most common property tags and most essential to collaboration in SharePoint is the author property. This property is often applied on a number of different document types as well as lists, libraries, and web content. It is also associated with documents that are added to SharePoint, so there is a high probability that a document will have some sort of author associated with it.

SharePoint 2010 has the new ability to include associated metadata with document data in the index, improving search performance for metadata lookup and improving the ranking of documents based on that metadata. It also has the capability of adding inferred metadata based on terms or fields from within the body of the document.

## Terms in Anchor Text

SharePoint 2010 adds ranking value to the documents based on the text in referring links. For sites where users are publishing blogs, wikis, or text content on content managed pages, this referring text consideration can be very useful. When people are placing a link to another document, it is natural to describe what that document is about on the link, and usually a short and descriptive text is used. Considering this in the ranking can have a positive influence but only when it is reasonable to have a descriptive link.

# Proximity

Proximity refers to the relative closeness of the query terms found in a document. However, there is no indication that closeness of query terms that are not in a phrase has any influence in SharePoint search. Tests indicate that a document with two terms that are simply near each other would rank evenly with one that has the two terms at either end of the document. For SharePoint, proximity is based on how terms are grouped into segments or if they are found in phrases.

## Query Segmentation

In multi-term queries and document matches, there are often numerous sets of terms that may match the terms. Some of those sets may match the queries better, based on how the terms relate. For example, the query terms "great search engine" may return a document with the phrase "great enterprise search engine" and "great search for a used engine". Both of these documents have matches for all the terms. However, how these terms are broken into groups can dictate if the document about search engines is ranked above the document about great search. SharePoint takes segmentation rules into consideration when ranking, but such considerations generally offer little influence, and other values like frequency will often override such nuances.

## Query Term Association

When multiple terms are queried in a phrase, terms that appear together in the phrase are naturally ranked highest, and those that are close together are given higher ranking than terms that appear farther apart in a document. If one searches for "Microsoft Exchange", one would expect a document with the phrase in it to appear above a document with the sentence "Microsoft's filings to the US Securities and Exchange Commission." However, there is no evidence that SharePoint discriminates based on word location or closeness outside of phrase matches.

# Static Document Relationships

Static document relationship ranking considerations are those made at crawl time. The crawler breaks the text it streams into the database into what it finds as unique terms and then applies values for the documents in which those terms were found, based on a few factors such as placement in the site, language, file type, and distance from authoritative pages.

## Click Distance and URL Depth

The click distance is the measure of the number of clicks it takes to get from one document to another. There are two elements to consider for click distance: click distance from what is set as or considered an authoritative page, and depth of the document in the site or URL depth. SharePoint site collections have a pyramid structure with one main entry page that leads off to sites, subsites, lists, libraries, pages, and documents. The distance between these is taken into consideration when applying ranking values. Top-level content will get higher ranking, and lower-level content with a deeper click depth will get a lower ranking, because the top-level sites are naturally considered more important and easier to access by users. The distance a document is from an authoritative page also counts. So the ranking can be influenced by setting authoritative pages close to important content. See the section on tuning search.

## File Type

Certain file types are given higher static ranking on SharePoint than others. According to the latest available information, the document ranking order is web pages, PowerPoint presentations, Word documents, XML files, Excel spreadsheets, plain text files, and finally list items.

## Length

Long documents have more terms and would generally be ranked higher than short documents if length were not taken into consideration. Therefore, the ranking is adjusted to consider the density and relative value of the query term to the entire document.

## Language

For sites with documents in many languages, documents in the language of the search user's interface should be given ranking priority over other languages. In some cases, documents contain terms in more than one language or are mostly in one language but have a matching term from another language. In this case, documents are given a static rank at crawl time for the language SharePoint thinks is most likely the main language of the document. Additional ranking value is given at query time once the user's interface language is determined.

## User-Driven Weighting

New to SharePoint 2010's ranking is the inclusion of social elements. This includes the adjustment of static rank values based on whether a document was selected frequently from the search result list.

## Click Popularity

An additional relevancy mechanism in SharePoint 2010 is the weighting of results based on their click popularity in the result set. The links that are chosen for a specific query in a search result list add value to that specific document for that specific search term. Click-through relevancy weighting can help the organization to leverage the expertise of users by allowing them to choose specific documents from a result list and promote them. This is done without any added interaction or specific interaction by the end users. Their well-meaning information discovery helps the entire organization.

■ **Note** The mathematics behind the BM25F relevancy algorithm, which is the base of SharePoint's default ranking algorithm, is explained at `http://en.wikipedia.org/wiki/Okapi_BM25`. Thanks to Mark Stone, technical product manager at Microsoft, for his help with SharePoint's ranking algorithm.

# The Corpus

Understanding the corpus can be a key element to understanding how to monitor and improve search. The term corpus is Latin for body and is often used to refer to the entire set of documents that an organization has. The nature of every organization's corpus is unique. No two organizations will have exactly the same content or even structure of that content. Every organization will also have its own set of accepted terminology and private corporate language. This makes it very difficult to find a search engine, which is basically a text analysis tool that follows a prescribed set of rules, to make sense of and return the best documents for any given query. With that in mind, the quality of SharePoint search in most cases is quite impressive.

When we look at a very large document set, we see a set of terms. This set may be in one or more languages, be comprised of millions or hundreds of millions of documents, and represent thousands of concepts. The value and frequency of these concepts will naturally vary from organization to organization. For example, a religious organization will have a drastically different set of terms and key concepts than an energy company, and a government body will have different terms than a private company.

As with any large body of words, every organization's corpus will have many common terms. There will be a large set of terms that are extremely common to the language they are written in. Then there will be a certain group of terms that are not individually unique to that organization but together represent the key themes that are important to that organization. On the far end of the term set, there are rare terms that appear only very incidentally in the corpus and may not represent any concept core to the important themes of the organization. As we begin to analyze a large corpus, we immediately find many common terms such as (in English) "and", "or", "this", "that", etc. When we have a single document, many of the terms in it are new to the collection of terms the search engine finds. But as the number of documents increases, the chance of a new term appearing diminishes. This experience is explained by Heaps' law (`http://en.wikipedia.org/wiki/Heaps'_law`). See Figure 10-1.

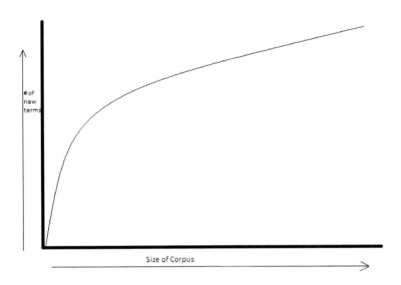

**Figure 10-1.** *Heaps' law shows the diminishing discovery of new terms as document # increases.*

What it tells us as search administrators is that the most common terms are not that interesting to search. These are grammatical or extremely common terms. Probably 80% of the terms used in this book do not directly relate to the key topics covered in the book, but rather are helpers used to explain potentially complicated concepts. On the other side of the graph are terms that occur only very rarely and perhaps randomly. These can often be technical terms, names, and spelling mistakes. For the most common terms, we need a mechanism to ignore these terms. In the case that they are searched for, we do not want to have a ranking war based on the term "the". On the "rare" side, we can either forget about these odd terms or use tools such as synonyms to bring these terms into the core set of theme descriptive terms.

The real goal is to increase the occurrence of terms that have meaning in an organization and apply them to appropriate content—that is, by tagging and the addition of properties. Identifying these terms and the themes they express and then making sure they are associated with the best information about them will help search much more than the most complicated features of a search engine.

## Search Reporting

When it comes to improving usability in SharePoint 2010, reporting is certainly an essential tool. This is especially true for search in SharePoint. Many administrators consider search a "black box" that, when functional, will operate on its own and produce results in some mysterious and wonderful manner. The truth is that search engines are just computer programs that follow a set of rules. Many of these rules we have already seen in the previous section and found to be insufficient at returning the best content for each and every query.

Therefore SharePoint 2010 has some great built-in reporting technology to allow search and farm administrators to monitor overall performance as well as allowing site collection administrators to monitor individual site search success and make modifications to the search behavior as well as the content based on those reports.

Reporting is a key feature in SharePoint 2010 that allows administrators to see statistical information on the behavior of the users and their interaction with the search engine. The reporting mechanism can identify key query terms that are causing frustration for users as well as areas of search that are not working optimally. There are two levels of reporting to administrators in SharePoint, the farm level and the site collection level. These levels are set to allow administrators with different levels of focus in the organization to get the reports that are useful for their particular job function. Farm administrators, who are responsible for the management of the SharePoint farm and its core functionality, can see reports that will help them maintain a working search engine and improve crawling and index quality. The site collection administrator can see reports for his or her site collection and all its sites and subsites. These reports help the site collection administrator optimize the search experience for his or her end users on their own level.

# Farm Level Reports

General search reporting can be found in the Search service application in Central Administration and includes Top Queries and No Result queries. The point of this reporting is to help search or farm administrators learn about the general success and performance of the search engine. Content can be targeted for crawling, crawling errors can be addressed, authoritative pages set, and unwanted results removed based on information from these reports.

This farm-level reporting can help us identify these overall search performance issues and potentially make adjustments to the search engine at the search service to compensate for problems. To access the farm-level search reporting in SharePoint 2010, follow these steps:

1. Open Central Administration on your SharePoint farm.

2. Click Manage Service Applications.

3. Navigate to the Search service application.

4. On the left menu under Reports, there are two types of reports, Administrative Reports and Web Analytics Reports. Choose Web Analytics Reports.

In the base report, we can see the total number of search queries and the average number of search queries per day. This can help the administrator manage load and monitor search for performance. If this number is very high, the administrator should consider adding a query server after investigating the administrative reports (see Chapter 2). If this number is unusually low, the administrator should investigate why users are not searching and confirm that the search mechanism is working for all users. Sometimes poor site setting can restrict access to search or cause other problems that make search non-functional for end users, and they won't even complain.

On the top of the left-hand navigation, we can navigate to the Number of Queries report (Figure 10-2). This will give a more detailed view of the number of queries over time in a graph (Figure 10-3) and the exact numbers for each date (Figure 10-4).

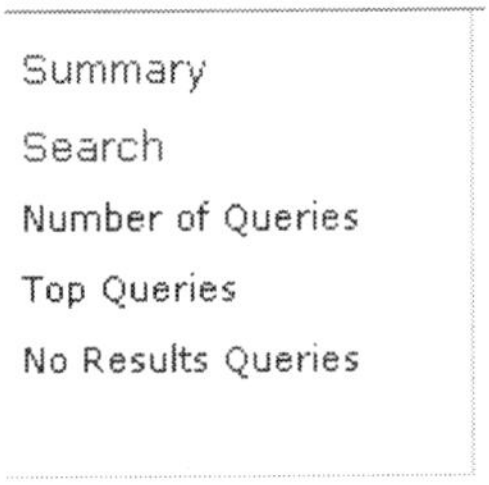

Summary

Search

Number of Queries

Top Queries

No Results Queries

**Figure 10-2.** *The search reports page menu in the Search service application*

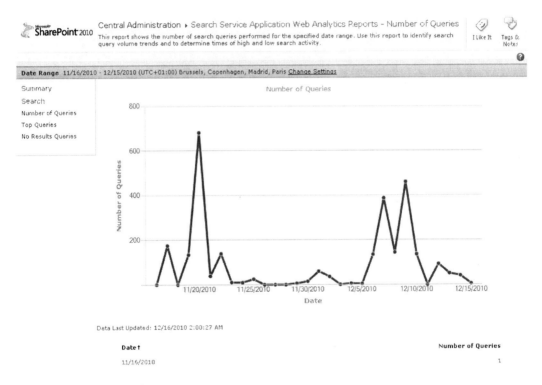

**Figure 10-3.** *Number of Queries page*

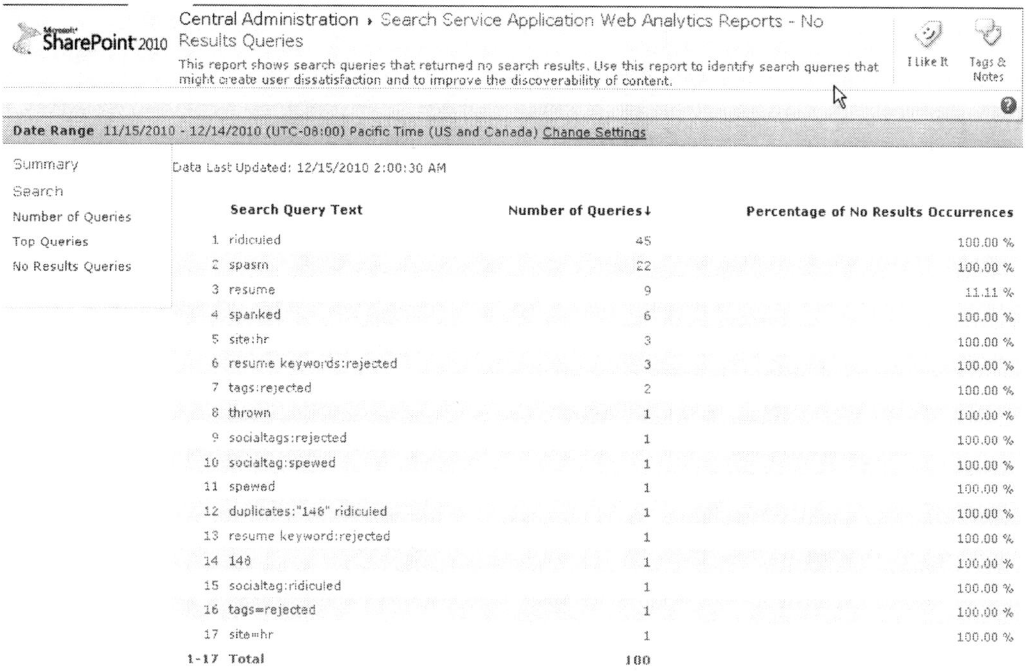


| | Search Query Text | Number of Queries↓ | Percentage of No Results Occurrences |
|---|---|---|---|
| 1 | ridiculed | 45 | 100.00 % |
| 2 | spasm | 22 | 100.00 % |
| 3 | resume | 9 | 11.11 % |
| 4 | spanked | 6 | 100.00 % |
| 5 | site:hr | 3 | 100.00 % |
| 6 | resume keywords:rejected | 3 | 100.00 % |
| 7 | tags:rejected | 2 | 100.00 % |
| 8 | thrown | 1 | 100.00 % |
| 9 | socialtags:rejected | 1 | 100.00 % |
| 10 | socialtag:spewed | 1 | 100.00 % |
| 11 | spewed | 1 | 100.00 % |
| 12 | duplicates:"148" ridiculed | 1 | 100.00 % |
| 13 | resume keyword:rejected | 1 | 100.00 % |
| 14 | 148 | 1 | 100.00 % |
| 15 | socialtag:ridiculed | 1 | 100.00 % |
| 16 | tags=rejected | 1 | 100.00 % |
| 17 | site=hr | 1 | 100.00 % |
| 1-17 | Total | 100 | |

***Figure 10-4.*** *No Results Queries report*

---

■ **Note** The farm-level search reporting shows the search usage statistics for the entire farm. This is important for farm administrators to get an overall view of the search trends and performance of the farm. For more detailed results, site collection reports can be seen at each site collection. However, these reports will cover data only for the individual site collection.

---

# Site Collection Reports

At the site collection level, there is more detailed reporting that will help the site collection administrators to identify areas where content and metadata can be improved to help search as well as add or improve best bets. Site collection reports show the data only for the individual site collection. An organization with many site collections will need to analyze the reports at different collections.

To understand the value of the reports, it is useful to understand the behaviors of search users. The basic mechanism of searching in SharePoint is similar to all search engines. A user enters a query into a search box, either on a search page or on a search field on any page in a SharePoint site. This query of one or many terms is passed to the search engine, and a list of matching hits is displayed in an order the search engine determines best for the given query. At this point, a user looks through the list and does one of a few things. The user can click a document to open it and move on, add terms to the query and search again, refine the result set with refiners, or just leave the search experience and navigate away.

From the search engine's perspective, this creates four basic search behaviors:

1. *Success*: A *successful* search is a search where the user enters a query, gets a result set, looks through the results, clicks a result link, and gets the document that he or she is looking for.

2. *Partial success*: A partial success is where a user enters a query, gets a result set, looks through the results, and clicks a link but gets the wrong document. He or she then goes back and clicks another or searches again.

3. *Unsuccessful with results*: This behavior sees a query entered, and a result set displayed, but no action taken on the results. The user clicks nothing and either searches again or leaves the search experience.

4. *No results*: The user searches but gets a blank search page and a message suggesting search hints.

Although it seems strange, the "no results" behavior is extremely common for enterprise search engines. This is largely due to misspellings, synonym usage, or misconceptions by the end users. When a user searches for something he or she is certain exists or should exist in the organization—a key piece to achieving the information task at hand—and gets nothing, he or she can become extremely frustrated. This makes the "no results" search experience the most acute problem and the one of utmost urgency when optimizing the search engine.

The following reports are available under the Search section in the Site Collection Web Analytics Reports pages:

- Number of Queries
- Top Queries
- Failed Queries
- Best Bet Usage
- Best Bet Suggestions
- Best Bet Suggestions Action History
- Search Keywords

Each one of these report pages displays a different view of the search behaviour of the end users. These reports can help the administrator identify and correct for the failed search behaviour as well as give guidance on how to improve search with built in suggestions. The following sections will cover the important reports and how to best utilize them but first will outline the basic features of all report pages. In the Analyze tab of the ribbon on the report pages, the reports can be adjusted for timespan, filters can be applied, and the reports customized or exported for sharing or further analysis (Figure 10-5). Furthermore, alerts and reports can be scheduled for those that are too busy to remember to look at the reports regularly.

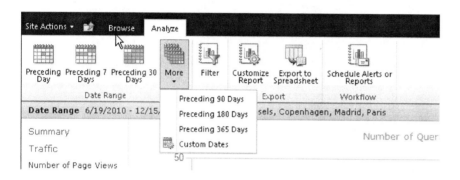

**Figure 10-5.** *Analysis options for reports*

There are some preset timespans available like week, month, or year. In addition, a custom timespan can be set. This data can be exported, and one timespan can be compared to another to perform benchmarking against changes or improvements made to search. The filtering mechanism for search reports allows for filtering based on pre-defined search scopes—that is, any scopes that are already created and used in the search interface. And Customize Reports allows for downloading the report to an Excel sheet to manipulate the reporting parameters. The Excel sheet maintains a data connection to the SharePoint site and will update the data as it changes. Excel makes it easy for administrators to generate custom graphs and work with the report data (Figure 10-6).

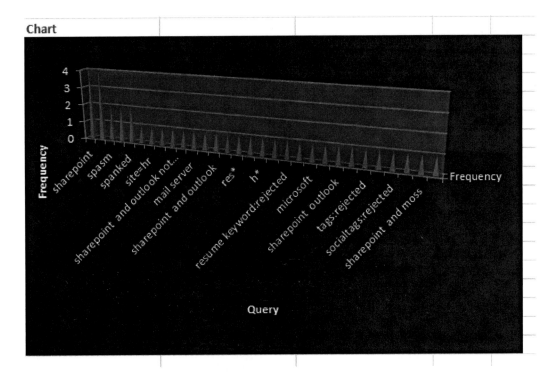

**Figure 10-6.** *A (minimally) customized report in Excel*

## Number of Queries

The Number of Queries report shows the aggregate amount of queries at that site collection and the number of queries per day. It shows trends in search activity from end users. Normally, search should peak mid-week and taper off toward the weekend, depending on what kind of organization is using SharePoint and what the key motivators for information discovery are. This data can help predict load for the site, identify problems with the search engine, or the level of user adoption. If many users are proving frustrated by SharePoint or not fulfilling their information management tasks, a low number of queries could identify a need for training or adoption programs.

## Top Queries

The Top Queries report will show up to the top 50 search queries (Figure 10-7). This will represent the terms that are of the largest interest in the organization. You can see the terms for each query, the number of times each query was searched for, and the percentage in relation to all search queries.

This report gives a good idea of the most common interests in an organization. There are always some surprises in this report for administrators. What users expect to find and what is actually in a site can often be different. Administrators, working with department heads, can help users to align their interests and knowledge information needs with publishing and documentation practices. Sometimes investigating this information can also open up areas of business or collaboration for companies. For example, if all the engineers are looking for policy documents that HR is responsible for but are not included in the Engineering department's site collection, users can be directed to the correct site or search can be expanded to include broader scopes.

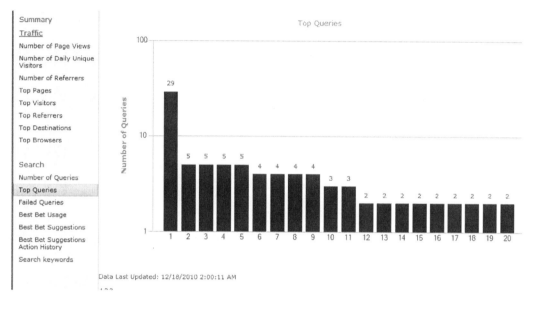

*Figure 10-7. The Top Queries report*

# Failed Queries

Perhaps the most important of the reports is the Failed Queries report (Figure 10-8). If we look at the four basic search experiences outlined in the beginning of this chapter, we will realize that failed queries account for half of the potential experiences. Microsoft groups both no-result queries and no-click queries into the same Failed Queries report. The queries are ranked based on the number of queries and itemized by the percentage of abandonment—that is, those queries where no search result link was clicked. This is important to identify because if people are searching and not actioning the results, they have not technically had a successful search. There are some instances where there is an exception to this, and users may find the information they want within the result set. Search-based applications and search centers with added functionality can make the search results page a valuable information delivery tool in itself. However, for standard SharePoint search, no click can almost always be equated with no success. Therefore, terms with a high rate of abandonment should be taken seriously.

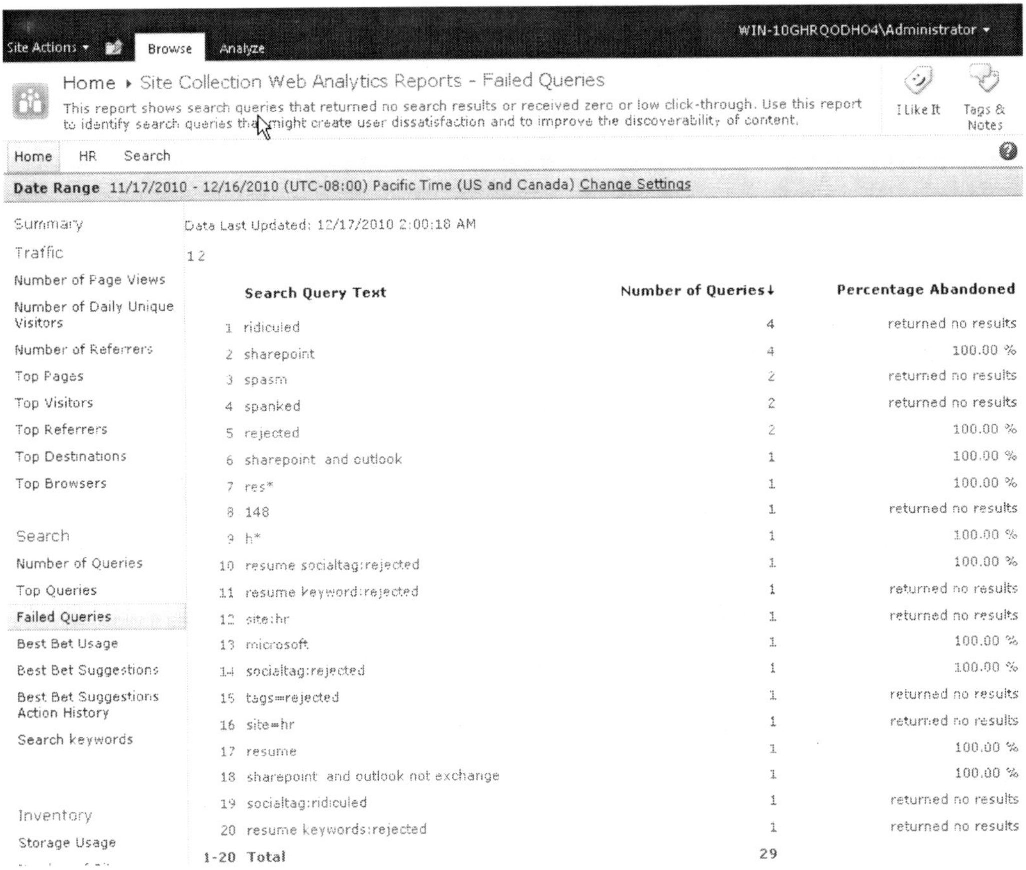

**Figure 10-8.** *The Failed Queries report*

The action points for this report are clear but not always straightforward. The administrator should identify why these terms were search for and why they did not either return a result or receive a click. The case of no result should be followed with an inquiry into what the users are expecting and then providing it. This could mean adding content, adding synonyms in the thesaurus file, or adding tags to existing documents. In the case of low click-through, the searches should be performed and the result list investigated to see why the results were not attractive enough. This could be a matter of poor titles or descriptions, insufficient metadata displayed in the results, or poor ranking. Improving document quality and adding metadata (properties) is a good way forward. Best bets can also be added to give the specific user the best document for the search term at the top of the results page, regardless of the organic result list.

## Best Bet Usage

The Best Bet Usage report will independently report the number of click-throughs that each best bet that is defined gets. This will show if best bets are being utilized over organic search results. If the terms are added to best bets in reaction to data in the Top Queries or Failed Queries reports, benchmarking for the success of modifications using best bets can be tracked. If best bets are not being used, try to change the wording to entice the users to click the best bets as opposed to the organic results or re-evaluate the goal of the searches.

## Best Bet Suggestions

The Best Bet Suggestions report offers suggested best bets based on the data in the other reports. The suggested best bets can be added as easily as clicking Accept or Reject in the report. This is an easy modification for site collection administrators that can improve search with very little effort. However, it requires that the administrator is aware of the reports and visits them regularly.

## Best Bet Suggestions Action History

The Best Bet Suggestions Action History is simply a log of previous best bets suggestions that have been accepted or rejected.

## Enabling Reporting

In SharePoint 2010, the Usage and Health Data Collection service applicationand the Web Analytics service, are installed by default. The Usage and Health Data Collection Service Application is the service that collects the search usage data. The Web Analytics service is the service that then analyzes and makes that data available. Both are necessary to get search reporting.

If the search reports do not contain any data, it is possible data collection has been disabled at the Usage and Health Data Collection service application. This is often done for storage and performance issues. This service application can be found in Central Administration under Manage Service Applications, Usage and Health Data Collection. Make sure Search Query Usage is checked. See Figure 10-9.

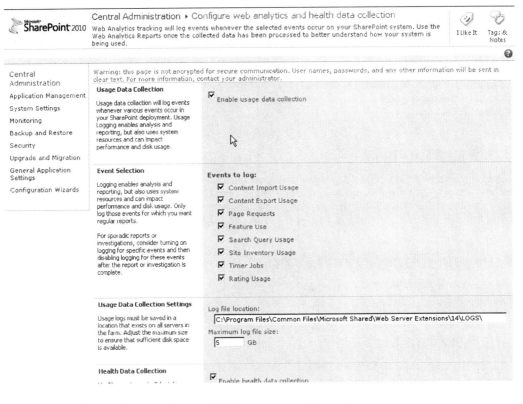

***Figure 10-9.*** *Usage and Health Data Collection service application*

## Displaying Report Data in Site

Another useful way to utilize search results to affect search behavior is to post a list of the most frequently queried search terms. There are advantages and disadvantages to this technique. The advantages are that other users can learn from the previous search queries and find information in a way they didn't think of themselves. However, by allowing them to click the top search terms and fire a search off, they force those search terms to remain in the top search terms as they will remain the most popular simply because they are there to click. Regardless, it can be an informative and interesting piece of information to display and a useful alternative means to access search. To enable display of the top search term on a site or page, edit the page and add the Web Analytics Web Part by clicking the Insert tab on the ribbon and choosing Insert Web Part. When the Web Part dialog appears, choose Content Rollup Web Parts and the Web Analytics Web Part. Add it to the page where you want the top search queries displayed. After the Web Part is on the page, you should choose edit Web Part from the drop-down on the top of the Web Part. Then under Information to Display, choose Most Frequent Site Search Queries. See Figure 10-10.

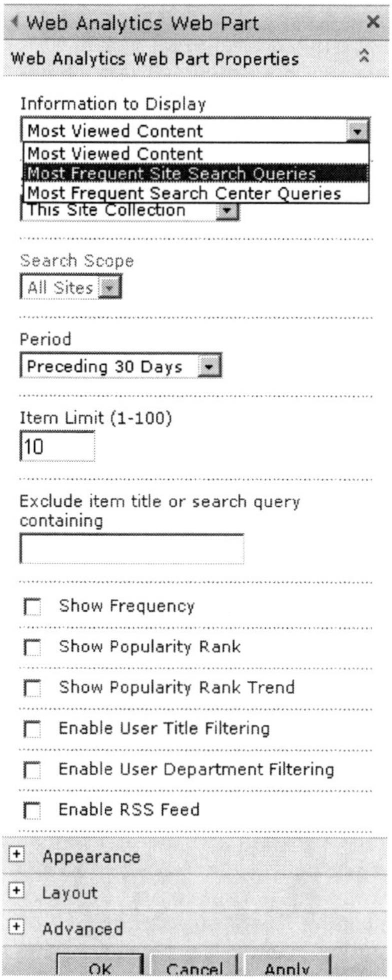

**Figure 10-10.** *Setting the Web Analytics Web Part to display top search queries*

# Tuning Search

Really, the best way to improve the quality of search is to improve the quality of the content being indexed. The computer adage "Garbage In, Garbage Out" applies profoundly to search engines. Poor-quality content will, without exception, result in poor-quality search results. However, improving huge sets of legacy documents imported from a file share or other document storage can be daunting if not impossible. In these cases, it is wise to be critical of the need for such documents and brutal when it comes to trimming old and questionably valuable content from import to SharePoint or crawling by the SharePoint crawler.

The best way to manage document quality moving forward is to have an active training program for SharePoint end users and a coherent tagging and document generation strategy. Word and PDF documents, among others, are often if not usually mistitled, have poor or no metadata, and are not well formatted for search. Having a policy for document authoring and metadata use can lead to a much better search experience and better long-term knowledge management.

Here are some hints on how to improve the quality of content in SharePoint.

1. Make good titles—encourage document authors to title their documents and fill in any metadata on the documents.

2. Convert to `.pdf` wisely. Almost everyone has seen the `.pdf` document titled `Word document.pdf`, or some equally useless `.pdf` title like `untitled.pdf`. This is because no title was given to the document when it was converted from its original format to `.pdf`. By requiring authors to add meaningful titles, administrators and managers can help the findability of information in an organization.

3. Add properties. Use the Managed Metadata ervice to devise taxonomy and teach authors how to use it.

4. Remove old or unnecessary content.

5. Ask users to identify and flag noise documents and click, rate, and share useful ones.

## Authoritative Pages

Probably the easiest administrative way to modify the ranking of the search results in SharePoint 2010 is by the use of authoritative pages. Pages can have additional ranking boost applied to them based on their click distance from an authoritative page. Sites are usually built in a pyramid structure, with an entry page at the site collection level and then a list of navigation links that link sites and subsites. Those sites link to lists and libraries that link to documents. Sometimes links can be provided across sites. SharePoint analyzes this structure and the number of clicks that exist between two documents. Then it applies added value to a page or document's ranking value based on that document's relative location to an authoritative page.

The default authoritative page is the "home page" to your site collection. Therefore, ranking is boosted based on the click depth of the sites, lists, libraries, pages, and documents. As expected, a deep page can have its ranking boosted by linking to it from the main page. The authoritative page setting includes lists and library pages, but individual documents cannot be added.

The Authoritative Pages page can be accessed from the Search service application in Central Administration. The top link under Queries and Results is to the Authoritative Pages page. See Figure 10-11.

Queries and Results

Authoritative Pages

Federated Locations

Metadata Properties

Scopes

Search Result Removal

***Figure 10-11.*** *Link to Authoritative Pages page*

There are three separate levels of authoritative pages (Figure 10-12) that can be set:

- *Most authoritative pages*: Pages close to this page will increase in ranking dependent on the number of clicks from the set page to the page returned in the result set.

- *Second-level authoritative pages*: This performs the same way as authoritative pages but ranks lower than authoritative pages.

- *Third-level authoritative pages*: This performs the same way as authoritative pages and second-level authoritative pages but boosts ranking the least of the three.

And there is one non-authoritative level, which will reduce ranking of entire sites:

- *Sites to demote*: Adding sites to this section will demote all content on that site in the search results.

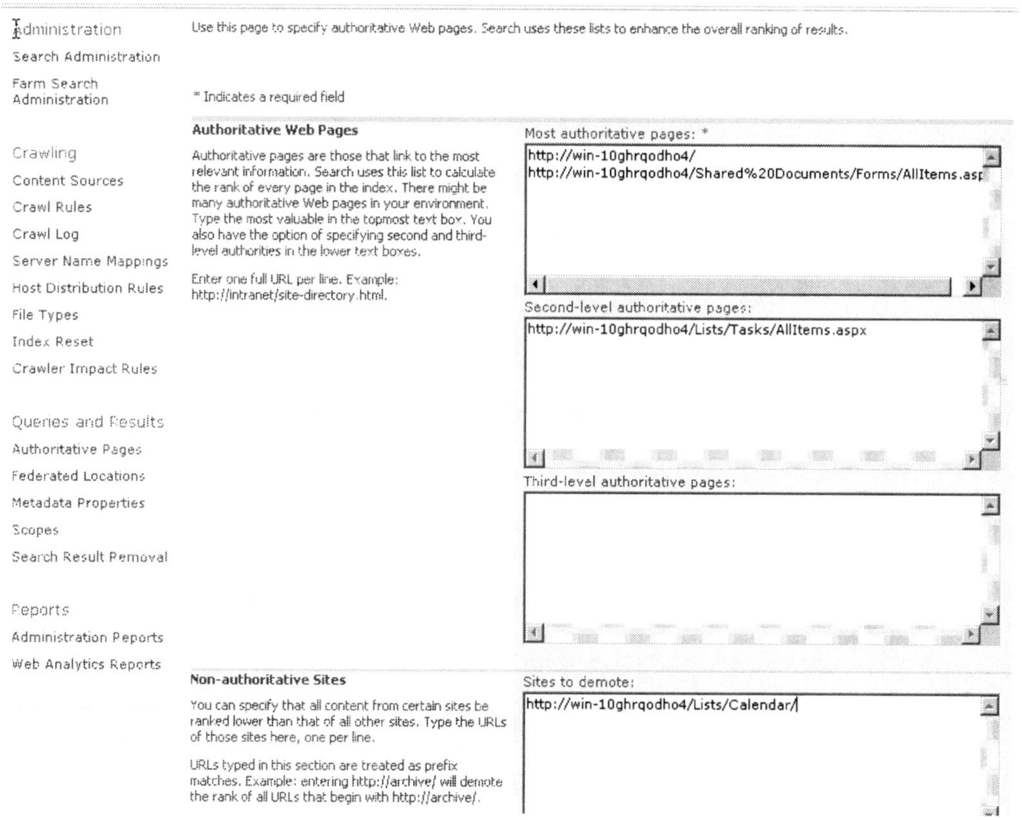

**Figure 10-12.** *Authoritative Pages page*

# Result Removal

In some cases, especially those where very large document repositories are indexed, undesirable results may appear in the result list. In some cases, a document or documents that are buried on a file share may have sensitive information that can be returned in the search results. Searches for "password" or "salary" can often surface these documents. The best way to deal with these documents is, of course, to remove them from the location they are being indexed or restrict them with permissions. However, SharePoint offers a simple mechanism for removing results that are deemed undesirable in the search results. The Search Result Removal feature in the Search service application has a simple field where the administrator can add the URLs of undesired documents.

To add documents to the result removal, do the following:

1. Navigate to the Search service application.

2. On the left-hand menu under Queries and Results, choose Search Result Removal (Figure 10-13).

Queries and Results

Authoritative Pages

Federated Locations

Metadata Properties

Scopes

Search Result Removal

***Figure 10-13.*** *Search Result Removal menu item*

3. Add the URLs of the documents you want removed from search (Figure 10-14).

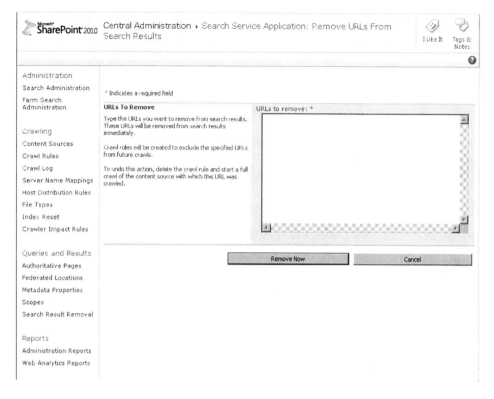

**Figure 10-14.** *Search result removal*

Documents will automatically be removed, and crawl rules will be applied to avoid crawling the documents in future crawls.

# Stop Words

As we saw with Heaps' Law, the most common terms in any corpus do not carry any value for searching. Grammatical terms and helper language that when used in context can convey meaning do not themselves help us to find the information we want. In order to help the search engine avoid ranking documents high that merely have a high density of terms such as "the", these most common terms are set as stop words or noise words in SharePoint's search engine. SharePoint 2010 has one stop word file for each language it supports as well as a neutral file. However, the neutral file is empty by default. All other files have a few of the most common terms for that language in them. More can be added easily by the administrator.

The files are located in `C:\Program Files\Microsoft Office Servers\14.0\Data\Office Server\Config`, where there is a virgin set of files that are copied to the Search service application's specific `config` file when a new Search service application is created. This path is `C:\Program Files\Microsoft Office Servers\14.0\Data\Applications\GUID\Config`. It is best to edit the files in this path at each query server.

The default stop word file for English is called `noiseeng.txt` and contains the following terms.

a
and
is
in
it
of
the
to

These terms can be added to by placing an additional term on each line of the file. Common words in the language may be freely added as long as searching for them would not provide useful results. Some useful additions might be "this", "that", "these", "those", "they", etc.

## The Thesaurus

SharePoint has the capability to match terms with potential synonyms and return documents based on those synonyms. For example, a user may be looking for the project plan for the windmill his or her company is consulting on without realizing that it is actually a wind turbine he or she is searching for (windmills mill grain, wind turbines produce electricity). Searching for "windmill" will not return any hits for his or her query and ultimately cause frustration, and probably a call to the engineers and some laughter and deriding (engineers can be callous). To avoid this, a potential synonym match between windmill and wind turbine could be entered in the thesaurus if it proves to be a common enough mistake to warrant it.

The thesaurus in SharePoint is installed into the same folder as the stop word files, and similarly there is one file for each supported language as well as a language-neutral file, `C:\Program Files\Microsoft Office Servers\14.0\Data\Office Server\Config`. These are a virgin set of the thesaurus and stop word files. When the Search service application is created in the SharePoint farm, SharePoint copies out a set to all query servers in the location `C:\Program Files\Microsoft Office Servers\14.0\Data\Applications\GUID\Config`. If the virgin files are edited, when a new Search service application is created, the edited files will be staged out. But any existing Search service applications and thesaurus files will not be copied over and must be individually edited.

By default, the thesaurus files are lacking any active entries, and the examples within are in comments. So the administrator must edit the files for them to function and copy them out to each query server. The files will be called only if the search is initiated in the specific language context for that file. The different language files are shown in Table 10-1.

**Table 10-1.** *The Thesaurus Files in SharePoint\**

| Language | File name | Language | File name | Language | File name | Language | File name |
|---|---|---|---|---|---|---|---|
| Language-neutral | tsneu.xml | English (United States) | tsenu.xml | Lithuanian | tslit.xml | Serbian (Latin) | tssbl.xml |
| Arabic | tsara.xml | Finnish | tsfin.xml | Malay (Malaysian) | tsmal.xml | Slovak | tssvk.xml |
| Bengali | tsben.xml | French (Standard) | tsfra.xml | Malayalam | tsmly.xml | Slovenian | tsslo.xml |
| Bulgarian | tsbul.xml | German (Standard) | tsdeu.xml | Marathi | tsmar.xml | Spanish | tsesn.xml |
| Catalan | tscat.xml | Gujarati | tsguj.xml | Norwegian (Bokmal) | tsnor.xml | Swedish | tssve.xml |
| Chinese (Simplified) | tschs.xml | Hungarian | tshun.xml | Polish | tsplk.xml | Tamil | tstam.xml |
| Chinese (Traditional) | tscht.xml | Icelandic | tsice.xml | Portuguese (Brazil) | tsptb.xml | Telugu | tstel.xml |
| Croatian | tscro.xml | Indonesian | tsind.xml | Portuguese (Portugal) | tspor.xml | Thai | tstha.xml |
| Czech | tsces.xml | Italian | tsita.xml | Punjabi | tspun.xml | Turkish | tstur.xml |
| Danish | tsdan | Japanese | tsjpn.xml | Romanian | tsrom.xml | Ukrainian | tsukr.xml |
| Dutch (Netherlands) | tsnld.xml | Kannada | tskan.xml | Russian | tsrus.xml | Urdu (Pakistan) | tsurd.xml |
| English (United Kingdom) | tseng.xml | Korean | tskor.xml | Serbian (Cyrillic) | tssbc.xml | Vietnamese | tsvie.xml |

*\*Source: http://technet.microsoft.com/en-us/library/dd361734.aspx*

The file `tsneu.xml` is the language-neutral file that is the default file utilized if no specific language value is passed. On installation it has the following structure and values:

```
<XML ID="Microsoft Search Thesaurus">
<!--
  Commented out

    <thesaurus xmlns="x-schema:tsSchema.xml">
        <diacritics_sensitive>0</diacritics_sensitive>
        <expansion>
            <sub>Internet Explorer</sub>
            <sub>IE</sub>
            <sub>IE5</sub>
        </expansion>
        <replacement>
            <pat>NT5</pat>
            <pat>W2K</pat>
            <sub>Windows 2000</sub>
        </replacement>
        <expansion>
            <sub>run</sub>
            <sub>jog</sub>
        </expansion>
    </thesaurus>
  -->
  </XML>
```

The first thing to do when utilizing it is to remove the comment tags <!-- and -->. This will make the entries active. The first tag to consider is the diacritics sensitivity tag. By default it has a value of zero, which is the setting for off. To enable it, set it to 1. Diacritical marks are marks that some languages utilize to modify the sounds of certain letters, such as accents or umlauts. Many European languages will benefit from diacritical sensitivity. English is not one of them.

The remaining sections are either expansion or replacement. Expansion is used to add synonyms to a given term. If the term in a <sub></sub> tag pair is searched for, the remaining terms in sub tag pairs will also be searched for. Any term in an expansion set will trigger the other terms in the set. Each set of synonyms must be encapsulated in their own expansion tag pair and sub tags.

```
<expansion>
<sub>windmill</sub>
<sub>wind turbine</sub>
<sub>generator</sub>
</expansion>
```

The replacement section is used to substitute a term for another term. This is useful when dealing with spelling mistakes or unused synonyms terms. The query term is not actually searched for, but the replacement terms are.

```
<replacement>
<pat>scarepoint</pat>
<sub>sharepoint</sub>
<sub>SP2010</sub>
</replacement>
```

As is shown in these examples, there can be a one-to-many relationship with both expansion and replacement sections. Microsoft does not recommend more than 10,000 entries in a single thesaurus file. Each entry where a term is defined (<sub> or <pat>) is considered one entry.

Save the thesaurus files as Unicode. If you are editing them in Notepad, this is the default encoding. Other text editors may require special care. After updating a thesaurus file, the Search service application needs to be restarted before changes will take effect. This can be accomplished by opening the services snap-in and restarting SharePoint Server Search 14.

# Custom Dictionaries

Custom dictionaries are lists of words that the search engine may match exactly and pass as a query. These dictionaries supersede the built-in word breakers in SharePoint.

Word breakers are a hidden part of the index and query processes of SharePoint search that manage how terms are handled by the query process. They are small programs or routines that break complex terms into shorter, more understandable terms. As we have seen in the "Stop Words" section, not all words are interesting to search, and the most common ones can be disregarded safely. Similarly, there are many characters that do not conform to the standard conception of what makes up a word. Special characters, such as ampersands (&), dollar signs ($), stars (*), the "at" character (@), and hyphens (-), among many others, are very common in digital information. Many organizations rely on combinations of these characters with letters and numbers to identify documents or products. The "at" character is seen in every e-mail address.

Usually, when put in context, many of these characters can be seen as word separators and hold little contextual value. For this reason, word breakers are employed to break these terms into smaller terms that are more likely to be searched for and make sense. For example, the phrase search-driven application contains a hyphen, linking "search" and "driven". It's common to combine words like this, but I might search for "search driven application" and expect to get results. If the search engine keeps "search-driven" as a single term, I won't find the document with the hyphenated version. Therefore, a word breaker is employed to break apart the term and allow for both variations to be searched.

This doesn't always make sense. Say, for example, an oil drilling company has a pipeline with many valves, and each valve has a unique ID with letters, numbers, and hyphens (e.g., VLV-123-456). If the valve is turned off without checking a document to see what the consequences will be, the whole pipeline could be shut down, or worse, a catastrophic failure could be caused. So, if the word breaker is allowed to break apart the term, all documents with vlv, 123, and 456 on them would be returned. This may be many possible documents and cause a lot of searching (mind you, "vlv 123 456" as a phrase should be returned first—this becomes more problematic when partial terms are searched and wildcards are used). So having the search terms seen as a single term and not broken into its parts can be valuable. This is where custom dictionaries come into play.

Here are the rules that must be observed when creating custom dictionaries:

- Each supported language has its own custom dictionary.

- Custom dictionaries (like stop word files and thesaurus files) should be saved in Unicode.

- Custom dictionaries have the file type `.lex` and are named CustomXXXX, where XXXX is the four-digit hexadecimal language code.

- Entries in the custom dictionaries are not case-sensitive.

- The pipe character (|) is not accepted.

- No blank spaces (white space)

- The pound character or number sign (#) cannot be used at the beginning of an entry, but it can be used within it or at the end, e.g., #Test is not acceptable but T#st and Test# are OK.

- Aside from the foregoing exceptions, any other character is acceptable.

- The maximum length of a single entry is 128 (Unicode) characters.

- There must be a copy of the custom dictionary files on each query server.

Here are the steps for creating a custom dictionary:

1. Create a new text file in a text editor (like Notepad).

2. Add your terms, taking into consideration the foregoing limitations and rules.

3. Save the file with the appropriate file name (e.g., `Custom0009.lex`) in the `%ProgramFiles%\Microsoft Office Servers\14.0\Bin` folder.

4. Restart the Search service application by running `services.msc` from the start menu and restarting the SharePoint Server Search 14 service.

***Table 10-2.*** *Support Languages for Custom Dictionaries and Their Language Codes**

| Language / dialect | LCID | Language hexadecimal code | Language / dialect | LCID | Language hexadecimal code |
|---|---|---|---|---|---|
| Arabic | 1025 | 0001 | Malay | 1086 | 003e |
| Bengali | 1093 | 0045 | Malayalam | 1100 | 004c |
| Bulgarian | 1026 | 0002 | Marathi | 1102 | 004e |
| Catalan | 1027 | 0003 | Norwegian_Bokmaal | 1044 | 0414 |
| Croatian | 1050 | 001a | Portuguese | 2070 | 0816 |
| Danish | 1030 | 0006 | Portuguese_Braz | 1046 | 0416 |
| Dutch | 1043 | 0013 | Punjabi | 1094 | 0046 |
| English | 1033 | 0009 | Romanian | 1048 | 0018 |
| French | 1036 | 000c | Russian | 1049 | 0019 |
| German | 1031 | 0007 | Serbian_Cyrillic | 3098 | 0c1a |
| Gujarati | 1095 | 0047 | Serbian_Latin | 2074 | 081a |

| Language / dialect | LCID | Language hexadecimal code | Language / dialect | LCID | Language hexadecimal code |
|---|---|---|---|---|---|
| Hebrew | 1037 | 000d | Slovak | 1051 | 001b |
| Hindi | 1081 | 0039 | Slovenian | 1060 | 0024 |
| Icelandic | 1039 | 000f | Spanish | 3082 | 000a |
| Indonesian | 1057 | 0021 | Swedish | 1053 | 001d |
| Italian | 1040 | 0010 | Tamil | 1097 | 0049 |
| Japanese | 1041 | 0011 | Telugu | 1098 | 004a |
| Kannada | 1099 | 004b | Ukrainian | 1058 | 0022 |
| Latvian | 1062 | 0026 | Urdu | 1056 | 0020 |
| Lithuanian | 1063 | 0027 | Vietnamese | 1066 | 002a |

*Source: http://technet.microsoft.com/en-us/library/cc263242.aspx

## The noindex Class

One way SharePoint 2010 allows administrators and developers to manage noise in the search engine is by implementing the noindex class value in the HTML of the page. Of course, this works only for web pages or other content written with HTML. Many web pages are largely based on the same templates. These templates include branding and navigation so every web page looks the same or similar and has a similar navigational structure. This is friendly and familiar to web-browsing end users. However, a large number of the important terms for the organization appear on every document. That generates noise in the search engine. Adding this class value to tags in the HTML will tell the crawler not to index the content of those tags and focus only on the terms that appear in the "content" section of the web page.

To include the noindex class, simply find the tag that holds the content that should not be indexed. This is usually a header, footer, news Web Part, or navigation. Add the following values to that tag:

```
class="noindex"
```

It should be noted that some nested tags will require their own noindex class to respect the rule. Here is a typical example:

```
...
<div class="noindex">
<table>
<tr>
<td style="text-align:right;line-height:70%;">
<a href=http://www.prosharepointsearch.com/about.html">About Us</a>
</td>
</tr>
...
```

# Popularity (Click-Through)

Although not something that an administrator can actively modify to improve search, click-through relevancy adjustments can improve search without any administrative influence. This "social search" capability records a number of all the clicks for a given query with the document of choice. This document's ranking value is then, over time, increased to improve its ranking. This is an advantage insofar as the search engine learns based on the experience and knowledge of the end users. It relies on the fact that the end users know what they are looking for in respect to the query they made to find it. And they would naturally click the only document that is the correct one for their query. In actual practicality, this is probably not totally true. Users will click in and out of different documents, looking for the right one. This may or may not adversely affect ranking. However, over thousands, if not hundreds of thousands of queries, a useful pattern should emerge that will help ranking, not hinder it.

Should ranking appear to degrade over time, the Search service application can be removed and a new index, database, and ranking values applied to start again. At this point, there is no other way to manually affect this mechanism.

# Social Tagging

Social tagging is a mechanism in SharePoint to allow users to personalize the content by adding tags to it. The tags can be anything the user wants and are unique to him or her. The tags can affect relevancy as well, helping content be handled by search. The term folksonomy is often applied to this type of user-generated tagging, and it is becoming more and more prevalent on web sites on the Internet. The concept is of a user-generated taxonomy that grows with user experience. Folksonomies can be a useful way to share interests and identify socially interesting concepts but should not be left as the core method for tagging and managing documents' taxonomies. A more managed structure should always be available for end users.

# The Ratings Column

Although not technically part of adjusting relevancy, the ratings column can allow users to filter on results, along with the other search refinement mechanisms to find documents that are considered valuable by other users. The ratings column is a feature in SharePoint that will allow users to give documents in a given library or items in a list a rating by clicking from one to five stars in a column beside the document. Although this may seem trivial in an organization where all documents have value and purpose, if a given list or library is a collection of information on a given topic, the ratings column can allow users to rate and filter based on that what best represents that topic. The rating values can also be displayed on the results page to allow users to quickly identify which documents were ranked useful by their colleagues.

## Adding a Ratings Column

To add a ratings column to a list or library follow these steps:

1. Activate the feature at the farm using PowerShell if it isn't already active. Open the SharePoint 2010 Management Shell and call the following (Figure 10-15):

```
Enable-SPFeature Ratings -Url http://server/site/subsite
```

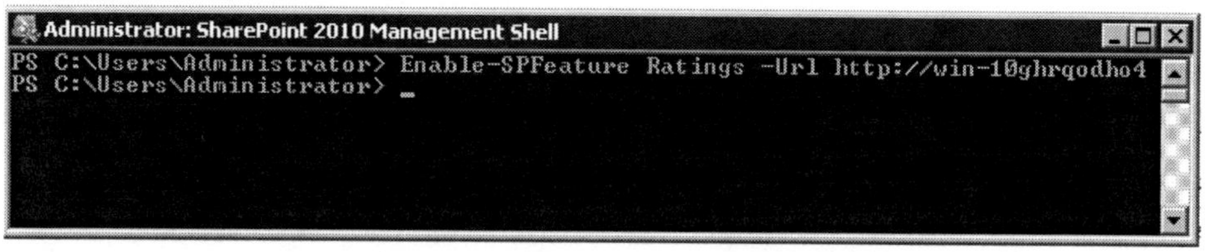

***Figure 10-15.*** *Activating the Ratings feature with Windows PowerShell*

---

■ **Note** SharePoint Team Server Administration (STSADM) is still supported for those more comfortable with it. To enable the feature, run STSADM, which is found in `c:\Program Files\Common Files\Microsoft Shared\Web Server Extensions\14\BIN`. Find `STSADM.exe`, and drag it into a command prompt window with the following parameters: `STSADM.exe -o activatefeature -name ratings -url http://server/site`.

---

2. Navigate to the library or list in question, and click the Library tab in the ribbon.

3. Choose Library Settings in the ribbon, and click "Rating settings" under General Settings (Figure 10-16).

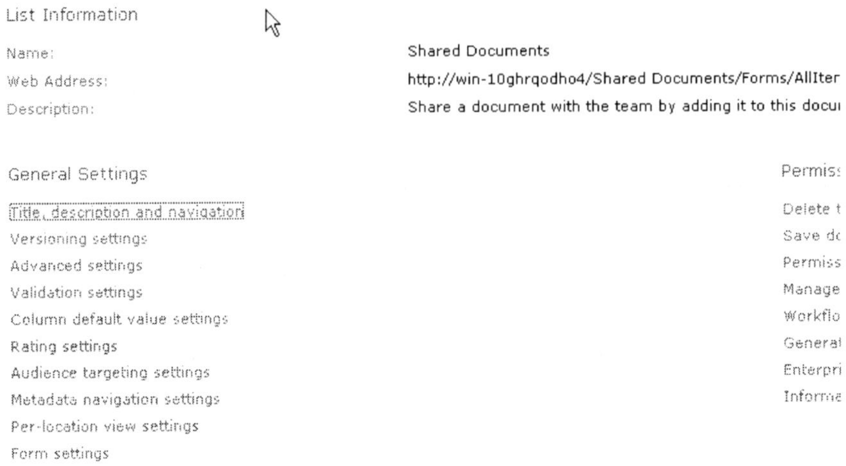
List Information
Name:
Shared Documents
Web Address:
http://win-10ghrqodho4/Shared Documents/Forms/AllIter
Description:
Share a document with the team by adding it to this docu
General Settings
Title, description and navigation
Versioning settings
Advanced settings
Validation settings
Column default value settings
Rating settings
Audience targeting settings
Metadata navigation settings
Per-location view settings
Form settings
Permiss
Delete t
Save dc
Permiss
Manage
Workflo
General
Enterpri
Informa

***Figure 10-16.** Rating settings*

4. Select Yes under "Allow items in this list to be rated?" (Figure 10-17). SharePoint will automatically apply the ratings column to the library or list.

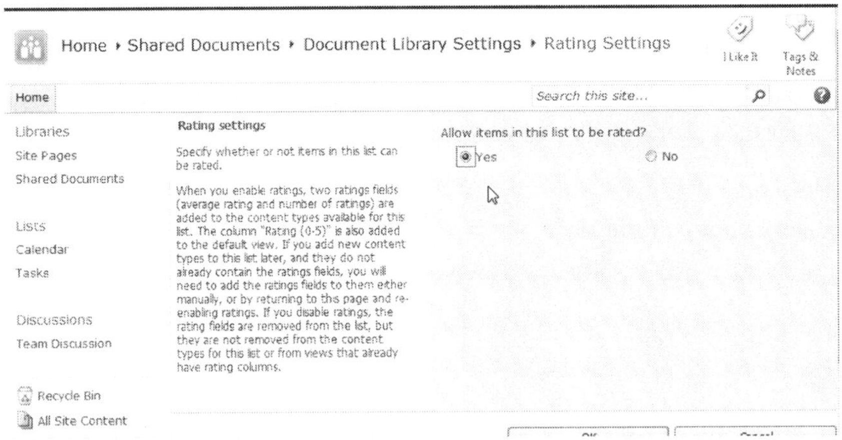
Home ▸ Shared Documents ▸ Document Library Settings ▸ Rating Settings
I Like It
Tags & Notes
Home
Search this site...
Libraries
Site Pages
Shared Documents
Lists
Calendar
Tasks
Discussions
Team Discussion
Recycle Bin
All Site Content
Rating settings
Specify whether or not items in this list can be rated.
When you enable ratings, two ratings fields (average rating and number of ratings) are added to the content types available for this list. The column "Rating (0-5)" is also added to the default view. If you add new content types to this list later, and they do not already contain the ratings fields, you will need to add the ratings fields to them either manually, or by returning to this page and re-enabling ratings. If you disable ratings, the rating fields are removed from the list, but they are not removed from the content types for this list or from views that already have rating columns.
Allow items in this list to be rated?
Yes
No

***Figure 10-17.** Enabling document rating*

5. Run a crawl.
6. Find the `AverageRating` crawled property (`ows_AverageRating`) as shown in Figure 10-18.

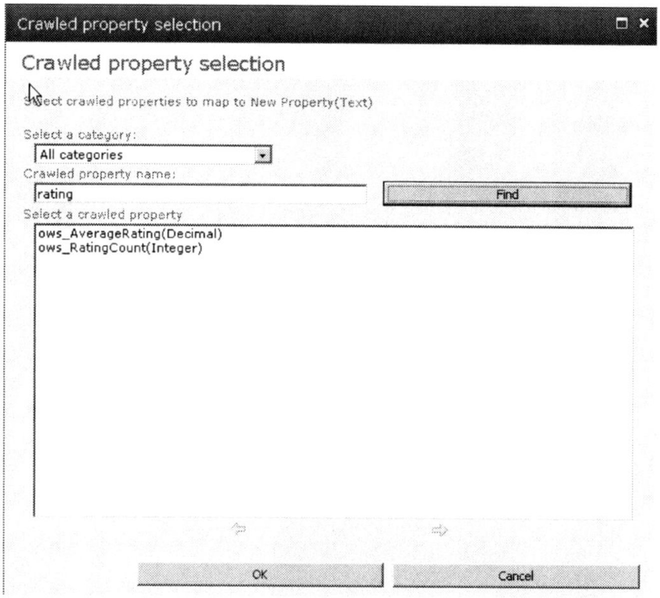

*Figure 10-18. Crawled ratings properties*

7. Create a property called AvgRating, and map ows_AverageRating to it. It should be a decimal property.

8. On the crawled property pages that can be accessed by clicking the crawled property in the Metadata Property Mappings page, check "Include values for this property in the search index".

9. Run a full crawl.

---

■ **Note** Make sure that the property has its values included in the search index. This flag can be set on the crawled property's page. See Figure 10-19.

---

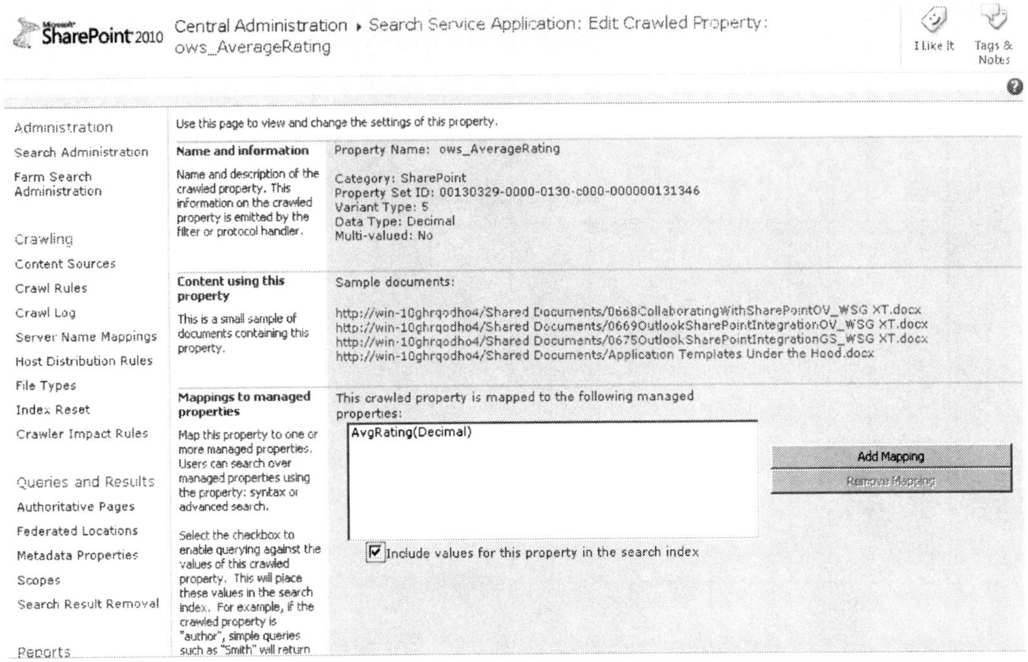

*Figure 10-19. Including values in the search index*

Figures 10-19 and 10-20 are two views of the same mapping, one from the crawled property and one (Figure 10-20) from the mapped property, which is the one we will eventually call from the user interface. One must be set for mapping the crawled property and the other to include its values in the search index.

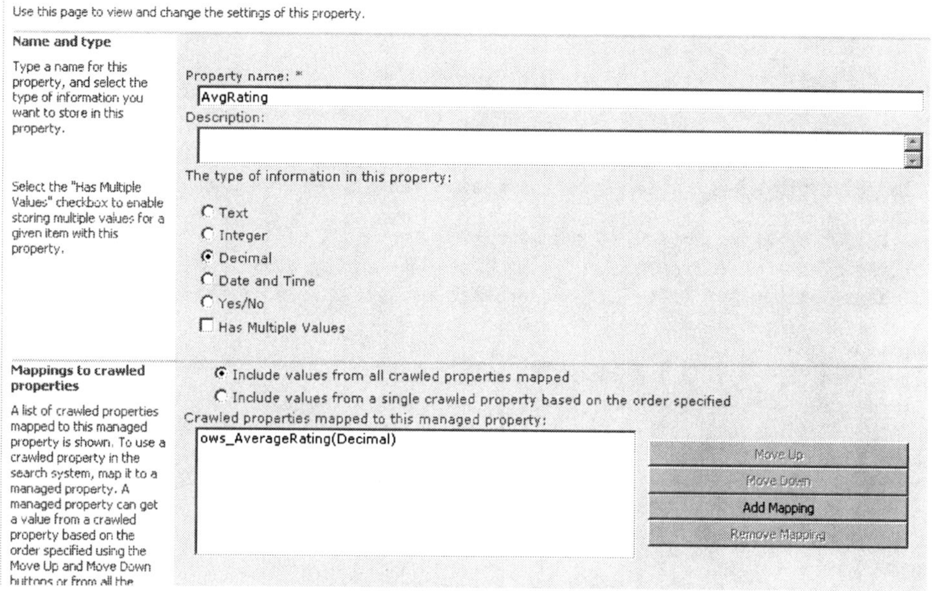

Use this page to view and change the settings of this property.

**Name and type**

Type a name for this property, and select the type of information you want to store in this property.

Property name: *

AvgRating

Description:

The type of information in this property:

Select the "Has Multiple Values" checkbox to enable storing multiple values for a given item with this property.

- ○ Text
- ○ Integer
- ● Decimal
- ○ Date and Time
- ○ Yes/No
- ☐ Has Multiple Values

**Mappings to crawled properties**

A list of crawled properties mapped to this managed property is shown. To use a crawled property in the search system, map it to a managed property. A managed property can get a value from a crawled property based on the order specified using the Move Up and Move Down buttons or from all the

- ● Include values from all crawled properties mapped
- ○ Include values from a single crawled property based on the order specified

Crawled properties mapped to this managed property:

ows_AverageRating(Decimal)

Move Up

Move Down

Add Mapping

Remove Mapping

*Figure 10-20. Adding the* AvgRating *metadata mapping*

## Displaying Ratings in the Results

The next thing to do is to make this rating value visible in the result list. This will help users identify which documents are rated higher by their peers.

To add the ratings values to display on the results page, do the following:

1. Navigate to the search results page, and edit the page.

2. Edit the core search results Web Part.

3. On the right, expand the Display Properties section, and uncheck Use Location Visualization.

4. Add the new column to be fetched from the index. Call it <Column Name="AvgRating"/> and place it anywhere in the list as long as it is after the first <Columns> tag and after the closing columns tag and doesn't interfere with the existing entries.

5. Click XSL Editor. You can now add the XSLT template to control how the stars will be displayed. You should place this in the search results where you want the ratings displayed. A natural place to put it is beside the title. To do this, find the srch-Title3 div tag. Just before this div section closes is the end of the title. It is in the middle of the XSLT and has two closing div tags. Place a call to the template before these closing div tags, as shown in Listing 10-1.

6. Save, click OK on the Web Part editing pane, and stop editing the page.

*Listing 10-1.* *XSLT to display the rating stars<!-- Ratings -->*

```
<xsl:text>&#x20;</xsl:text>
<xsl:choose>
<xsl:when test="avgrating &gt; 0 and avgrating &lt; .75">
                <span class="ms-currentRating"><img class="ms-rating_0_5"↵
 src="/_layouts/Images/Ratings.png" alt="Current average rating is half a star."/></span>
        </xsl:when>
            <xsl:when test="avgrating &gt;= .75 and avgrating &lt; 1.25">
                    <span class="ms-currentRating"><img class="ms-rating_1"↵
 src="/_layouts/Images/Ratings.png" alt="Current average rating is 1 stars."/></span>

        </xsl:when>
<xsl:when test="avgrating &gt;= 1.25 and avgrating &lt; 1.75">
                <span class="ms-currentRating"><img class="ms-rating_1_5"↵
 src="/_layouts/Images/Ratings.png" alt="Current average rating is 1.5 stars."/></span>
        </xsl:when>
            <xsl:when test="avgrating &gt;= 1.75 and avgrating &lt; 2.25">
                    <span class="ms-currentRating"><img class="ms-rating_2"↵
 src="/_layouts/Images/Ratings.png" alt="Current average rating is 2 stars."/></span>
        </xsl:when>
<xsl:when test="avgrating &gt;= 2.25 and avgrating &lt; 2.75">
                <span class="ms-currentRating"><img class="ms-rating_2_5"↵
 src="/_layouts/Images/Ratings.png" alt="Current average rating is 2.5 stars."/></span>
        </xsl:when>
            <xsl:when test="avgrating &gt;= 2.75 and avgrating &lt; 3.25">
                    <span class="ms-currentRating"><img class="ms-rating_3"↵
 src="/_layouts/Images/Ratings.png" alt="Current average rating is 3 stars."/></span>
        </xsl:when>
<xsl:when test="avgrating &gt;= 3.25 and avgrating &lt; 3.75">
                <span class="ms-currentRating"><img class="ms-rating_3_5"↵
 src="/_layouts/Images/Ratings.png" alt="Current average rating is 3.5 stars."/></span>
        </xsl:when>
            <xsl:when test="avgrating &gt;= 3.75 and avgrating &lt; 4.25">
                    <span class="ms-currentRating"><img class="ms-rating_4"↵
 src="/_layouts/Images/Ratings.png" alt="Current average rating is 4 stars."/></span>
        </xsl:when>
<xsl:when test="avgrating &gt;= 4.25 and avgrating &lt; 4.75">
                <span class="ms-currentRating"><img class="ms-rating_4_5"↵
 src="/_layouts/Images/Ratings.png" alt="Current average rating is 4.5 stars."/></span>
        </xsl:when>
            <xsl:when test="avgrating &gt;= 4.75">
                    <span class="ms-currentRating"><img class="ms-rating_5"v
 src="/_layouts/Images/Ratings.png" alt="Current average rating is 5 stars."/></span>
        </xsl:when>
```

```
<xsl:otherwise>
            <b>Not yet rated</b>
            <br/>
        </xsl:otherwise>
</xsl:choose>
<!-- Ratings End -->
```

The ratings should now appear on the result list. See Figure 10-21. This XSLT will check the value of the AvgRating property you have mapped and compare it with ranges between every half unit, starting at three-fourths. This will allow for half ratings based on the decimal values of the ows_AverageRating property, which is an average of all accumulated ratings.

The XSLT uses the built-in image Ratings.png, which is actually a larger image of all ratings stars, and sets them to be displayed using the built-in cascading style sheet (CSS). If the default CSS is changed, the ratings images will not display correctly. There are certainly more clever ways to create this XSLT, but this is a simple start to set the ratings value on the result template.

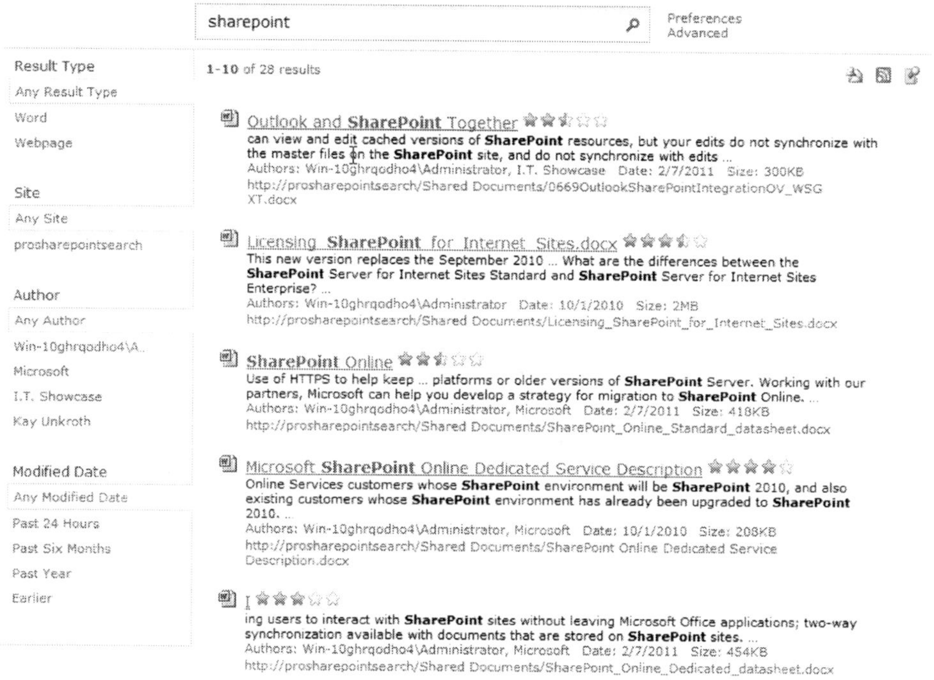

*Figure 10-21. Ratings shown in the search results*

▓ **Note** See Chapter 6 for more information on customizing the default Web Parts.

# Search Keywords and Best Bets

The Search Keywords page in the Site Collection Administration provides a user interface for creating and managing best bets in SharePoint 2010. Keywords that will trigger a best bet or definition can be entered in the Search Keywords section. Additionally, synonyms and responsible contacts can be added. There is a further publishing date mechanism to activate and deactivate time-sensitive keyword campaigns. Best bets and keyword information are added to the top of the search results page for the given keyword search.

To add keywords and best bests, do the following:

1. Go to the Site Settings of the site collection where the best bets and keywords should appear.

2. Select Search Keywords under Site Collection Administration to open the Manage Keywords page, as shown in Figure 10-22.

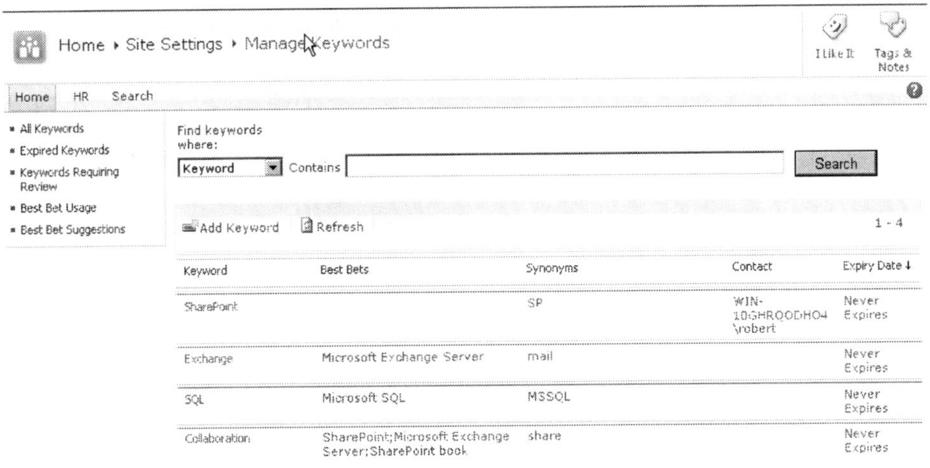

*Figure 10-22. The Manage Keywords page*

The Manage Keywords page lists all active keywords, their best bets, synonyms, contacts, and expiry date. There is also a menu on the left that links to the web analytics reports for the site collection that relate to keyword and best bet activity, and likewise the Web Analytics page has a link to the Manage Keywords page for easy navigation back and forth. This is extremely useful when actioning data in the reports.

To add a new keyword, click Add Keyword and fill out the appropriate fields (Figure 10-23). Synonyms can be defined here to action the best bet for the given keyword as well as any definition or contact required. A contact for that keyword and activation and expiration dates can also be defined.

Synonyms for specific terms will action the best bet but not affect the content of the organic search results.

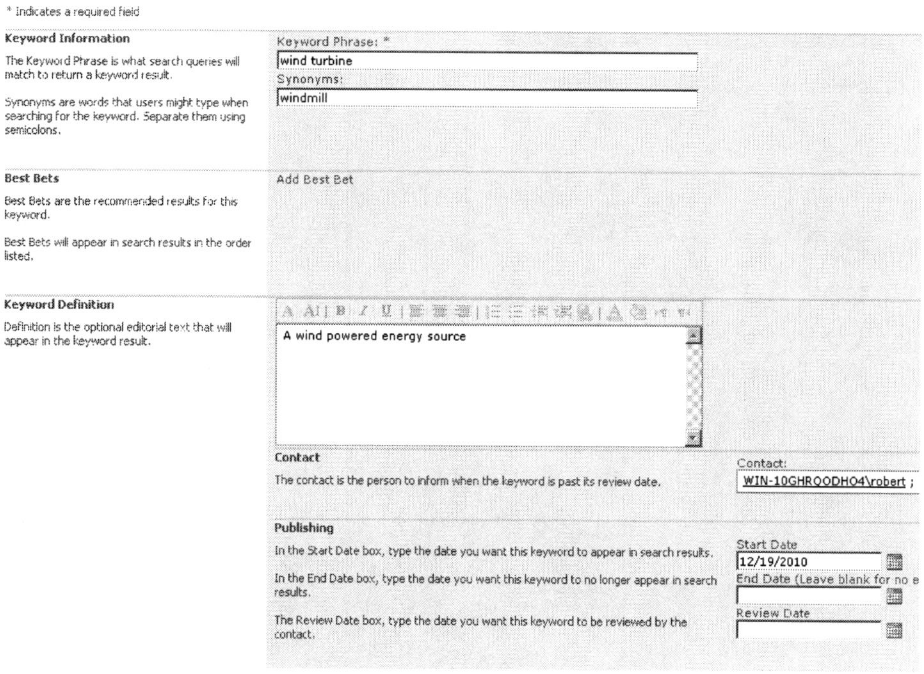

* indicates a required field

**Keyword Information**

The Keyword Phrase is what search queries will match to return a keyword result.

Synonyms are words that users might type when searching for the keyword. Separate them using semicolons.

Keyword Phrase: *

    wind turbine

Synonyms:

    windmill

**Best Bets**

Best Bets are the recommended results for this keyword.

Best Bets will appear in search results in the order listed.

Add Best Bet

**Keyword Definition**

Definition is the optional editorial text that will appear in the keyword result.

    A wind powered energy source

**Contact**

The contact is the person to inform when the keyword is past its review date.

Contact:

    WIN-10GHRQODHO4\robert ;

**Publishing**

In the Start Date box, type the date you want this keyword to appear in search results.

In the End Date box, type the date you want this keyword to no longer appear in search results.

The Review Date box, type the date you want this keyword to be reviewed by the contact.

Start Date

    12/19/2010

End Date (Leave blank for no e

Review Date

***Figure 10-23.*** *The Add Keywords page*

Best bets can be added to each keyword, and several can be added in any desired order (Figure 10-24). However, only one unique URL can be associated with one best bet. Therefore, best bets should be considered as unique links to a specific site. The information in the best bet about that link should be explanatory about the target link and not the keyword. A keyword may have many best bets, but each best bet links to a unique URL. URLs can be as complicated as necessary or as deep in a site as required.

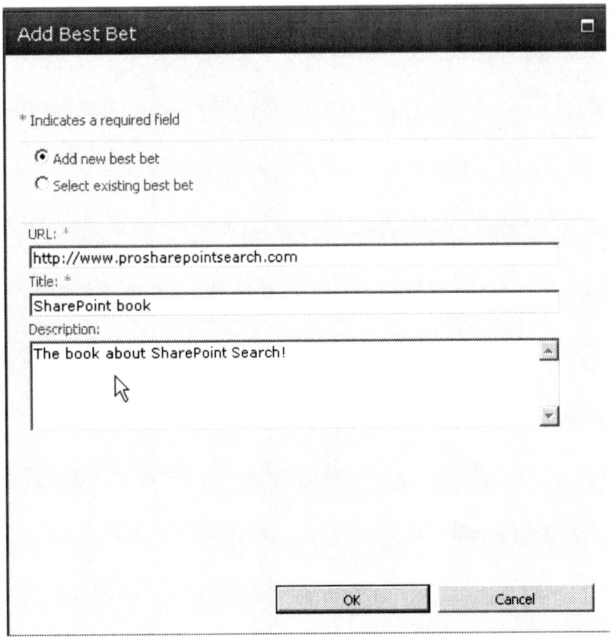

**Figure 10-24.** *Adding a best bet*

If an existing best bet is chosen, SharePoint will list all available best bets. If there are many, administrators can search for the desired best bet. Care should be taken in titling the best bets, as this will be the most likely way of finding the correct one. As each best bet is added to a particular keyword, it is removed from the list of possible best bets. In this way, the same best bet cannot be added to the same keyword twice. After the best bets are added, they can be ordered by importance on the keywords page (Figure 10-25).

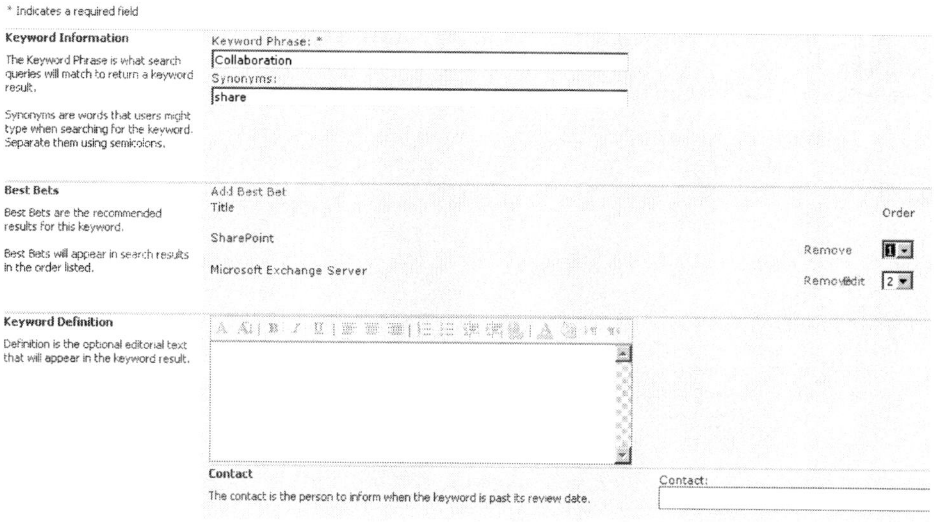

* Indicates a required field

**Keyword Information**

The Keyword Phrase is what search queries will match to return a keyword result.

Synonyms are words that users might type when searching for the keyword. Separate them using semicolons.

Keyword Phrase: *

```
Collaboration
```

Synonyms:

```
share
```

**Best Bets**

Best Bets are the recommended results for this keyword.

Best Bets will appear in search results in the order listed.

Add Best Bet

Title

SharePoint

Microsoft Exchange Server

Order

Remove    1 ▼

Remove Edit    2 ▼

**Keyword Definition**

Definition is the optional editorial text that will appear in the keyword result.

A A | B I U | ≡ ≡ ≡ | ≡ ≡ ≡ ≡ | A A 🌐 🔗

**Contact**

The contact is the person to inform when the keyword is past its review date.

Contact:

*Figure 10-25. Ordering best bets*

# Managed Metadata Service

The Managed Metadata service is a service in SharePoint 2010 that allows administrators to manage terms in an organized manner for use in the columns of lists and libraries. These terms can then be purposefully applied to list items and documents, and the types of values that users can associate with items and documents can be easily managed from a central location.

The Managed Metadata service is especially useful for search because it allows administrators to manage terms that represent concepts and themes that are essential to an organization. This makes it possible to expose important concepts and direct users to use better terms to describe documents and content inside the organization. As mentioned in the section of this chapter entitled "The Corpus," a key goal of the administrator is to reduce the "Garbage In, Garbage Out" trait of search engines. Applying appropriate terms across that corpus can help out a great deal in making garbage into gold.

The Managed Metadata service creates a Term Store, which is basically a database of associated terms called term sets. It can also manage content types. Content types are collections of properties or settings that can act as a container for categorizing documents. Content types can hold metadata, policies, templates, document conversion settings, or even custom features. The documents or list items applied to these content types will then conform to the attributes of their associated content type. Managing these content types in a centralized manner becomes important when dealing with large numbers of lists and libraries in SharePoint. The content type can be defined, used, and re-used across the SharePoint deployment.

Aligning and controlling content types and metadata in SharePoint help search by applying structure to information and extending associated terms applied to that information. Misalignments between existing terms and the terms users expect or use can be remedied by making sure terms and their synonyms are applied to the documents. Administering this in a controlled and structured way with the Managed Metadata service gives the administrator power over such terms.

The Managed Metadata service can produce term sets at a global or local level. Users at a local level can utilize global term sets and their own local term sets but may not use Term Stores local to another site collection or site level.

Follow these steps to accessand set up the Managed Metadata service:

1. Choose the "Manage service applications" menu item on the Central Administrations main page in the Application Management menu. See Figure 10-26.

Application
Management
Manage web applications
Create site collections
Manage service applications
Manage content databases

***Figure 10-26.*** *The Application Management menu in SharePoint Central Administration*

2. Navigate to the Managed Metadata service application. See Figure 10-27.

| | |
|---|---|
| Managed Metadata Service | Managed Metadata Service                Started |
| Managed Metadata Service | Managed Metadata Service Connection    Started |

***Figure 10-27.*** *The Managed Metadata service application*

3. Assign administrators for the service, and save the page. These users will be able to create new term set groups and assign group managers to those term sets. See Figure 10-28.

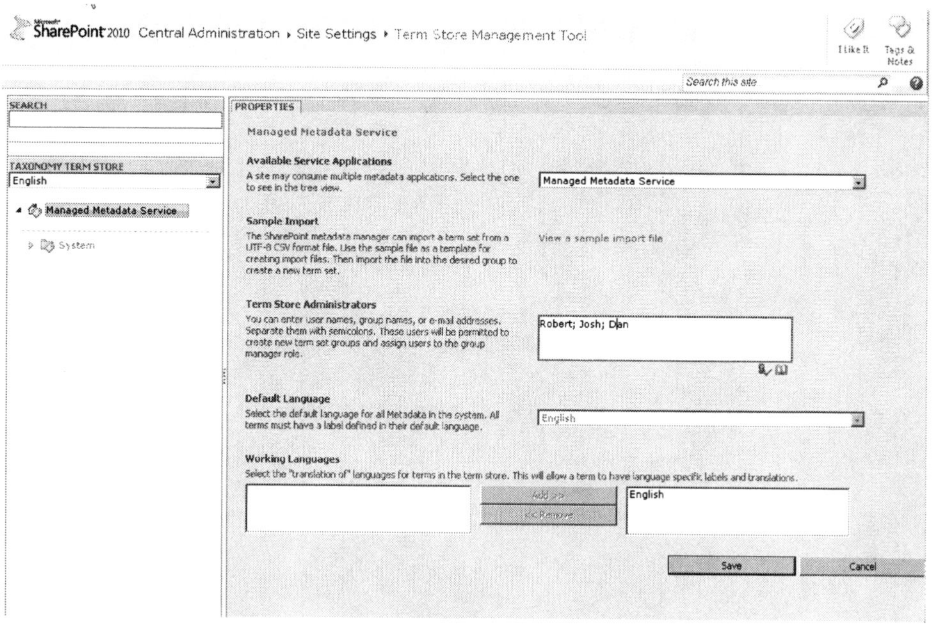

**Figure 10-28.** *Assigning Term Store administrators*

4. Create new groups for term sets, and assign group administrators by choosing the drop-down menu on the Managed Metadata service menu item. See Figure 10-29.

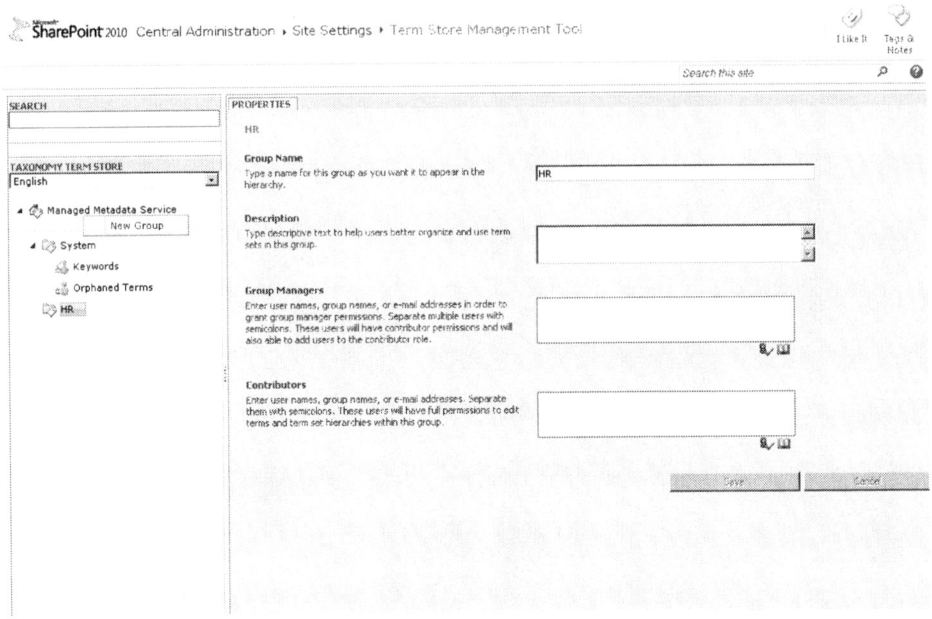

**Figure 10-29.** *A new term set group for the HR department*

5. Create term sets for that group by using the drop-down menu on the new group that was just created. See Figure 10-30.

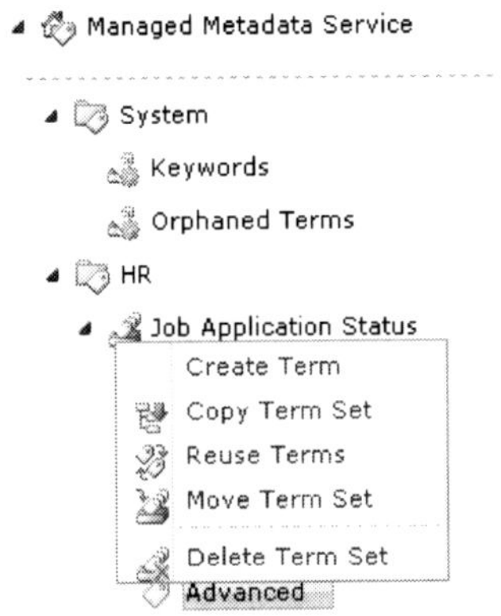

**Figure 10-30.** *Creating terms in the term set*

6. Add additional tiers of terms and sub-terms to that term set.

---

▓ **Note** Term sets can be deleted, but they must be empty of terms to be deleted. Try to plan out term sets well in advance.

---

# Tagging

Now that the term sets have been defined and terms applied, users can have an autosuggest-like functionality when applying social tags and notes to documents. Users should be made aware of the possibility of applying tags to documents. If social tags are applied to documents, a query can be used to find documents of a matching social tag by using the `socialtag:` search parameter in the query box (e.g., resume `socialtag:rejected`). All other property fields can now also be matched with managed metadata.

There is also an easy way to enable Enterprise Keywords features in lists and libraries that, when enabled, can allow a managed metadata field to automatically appear on the Properties page of documents and list items. When enterprise keywords are enabled on the Enterprise Data and Keywords Settings page under the library or list settings page, users will be able to add metadata from Enterprise Keywords fields (Figure 10-31). Additionally, and perhaps more importantly, new columns can be created as a managed metadata type and restricted to the values from a chosen term set in the Managed Metadata service.

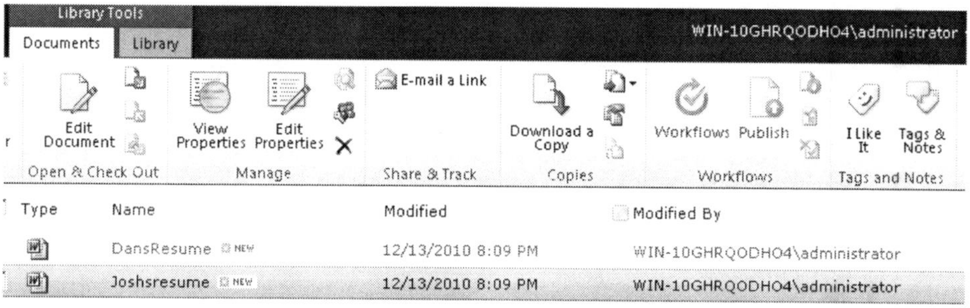

**Figure 10-31.** *A list where tags and notes can be applied to add managed metadata*

As users add their own keywords to document properties in the Enterprise Keywords field, the values are added to the Term Store under the System term set (Figure 10-32). These can then be moved into the appropriate section in the Managed Metadata service. See Figure 10-33. Terms can also be copied, re-used, merged, deprecated, or deleted.

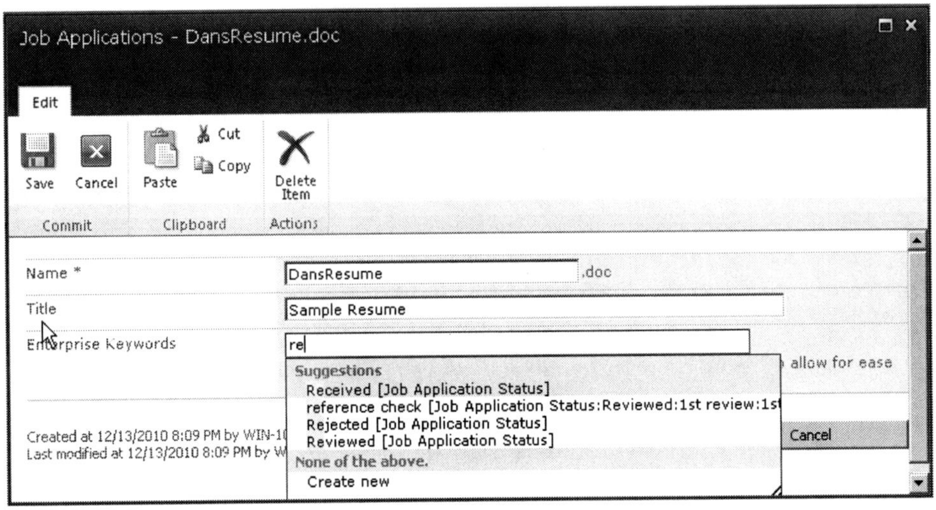

**Figure 10-32.** *Populating the Enterprise Keywords field from the document properties page in a document library*

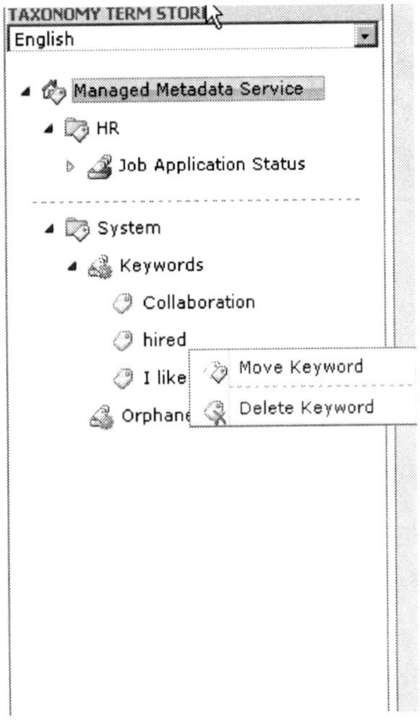

**Figure 10-33.** *Moving a user-defined keyword*

On the Properties page of each term, the term can be given a description and a default label as well as other labels. The other labels act as synonyms for this term, allowing terms with like meaning to be managed together. A single term or a phrase can be a synonym, but each term or phrase must be entered on its own line. See Figure 10-34.

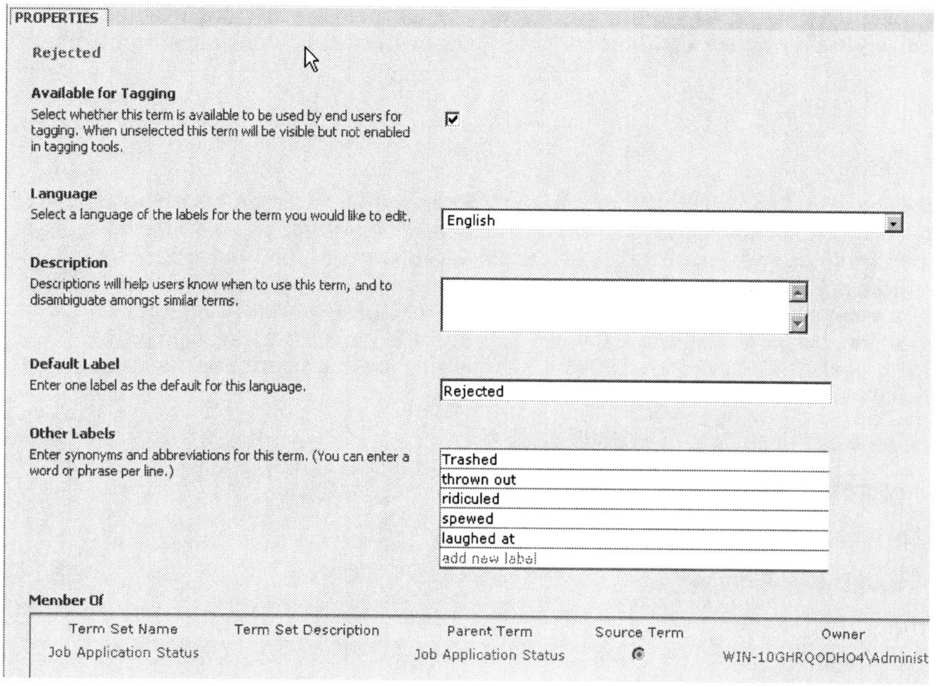

**Figure 10-34.** *Adding synonyms to the term*

Do not expect synonyms mapped to a specific term in a term set to change the results in the search results page. These synonyms are simply a helping hand for users and term managers to find the accepted terms even if they do not know what those terms are. In Figure 10-34, entering "trashed" in the keywords field will give the suggestion for the term "rejected". To implement a synonym for a term that will bring back hits in the search result, use the thesaurus previously described in this chapter.

▓ **Note** Term sets can get very large, so SharePoint has a search function built in for querying them to find an exact node in the hierarchy. This can be useful when additional terms need to be added.

# Custom Ranking

As previously mentioned, every organization has a different set of terms used to describe the themes and concepts that makes the organization unique and successful. This term, uniqueness, combined with a number of other factors, including business process, user bias, language, and purpose, means that even the most clever and complex ranking algorithm will not work for all queries in all cases. In some cases, it may be desirable to adjust the ranking algorithm to slightly change the way that documents are arranged in a result set.

## Built-In Models

Generally speaking, the default search algorithm is the best compromise. Microsoft has invested heavily in improving and testing the default ranking algorithm. The default algorithms also have the advantage that distance, minimum span, and document length considerations are included and cannot be modified in the custom models. But should a clear need for a different ranking model be identified, it is possible to change the ranking algorithm. It is most likely that a metadata-rich environment with extraordinary importance for particular properties will drive the use of a custom ranking model.

Out-of-the-box SharePoint 2010 Search contains the following ranking algorithms that can be used without any adjustment:

- Default ranking model (Main Results Default)

- Expertise Social Distance ranking model

- High Proximity ranking

- Main People Social Distance

- Expertise model

- Name Social Distance

- Name model

- Main People model

- No Proximity ranking

To get a list of these default models and their GUIDs, open the SharePoint 2010 Management Shell and call the following PowerShell cmdlet (Figure 10-35):

```
Get-SPEnterpriseSearchServiceApplication | Get-SPEnterpriseSearchRankingModel
```

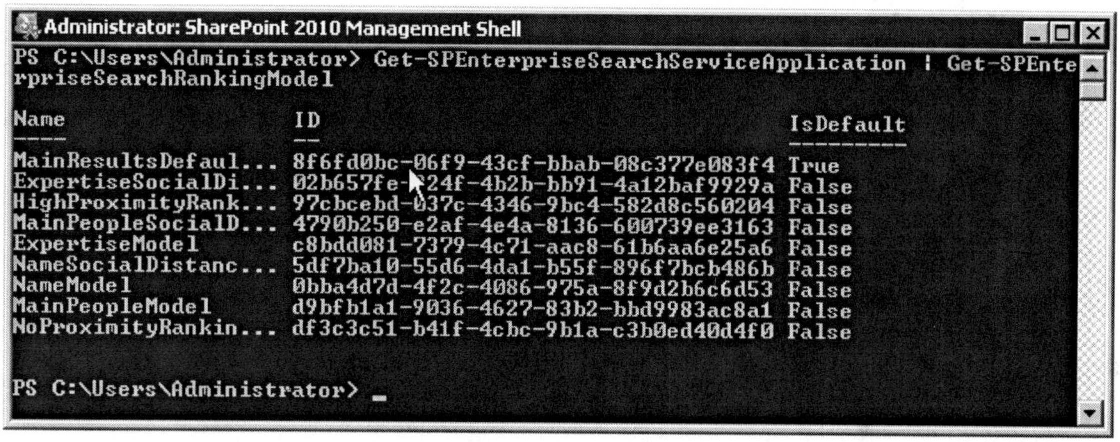

**Figure 10-35.** *Calling the built-in ranking models and their GUIDs*

These built-in alternative ranking models cannot be modified. However, we can see their effect on the search results by simply adding the `rm` parameter and the GUID of the ranking model to the URL of the search results page. For example, the query for SharePoint on our demo site with the No Proximity ranking model would have the URL `http://demo.prosharepointsearch.com/Search/results.aspx?k=sharepoint&rm=df3c3c51-b41f-4cbc-9b1a-c3b0ed40d4f0`, where `k` is the query term and `rm` is the ID of the ranking model. This technique is useful for testing changes to the ranking model but not practical for production implementations. In such cases, the Web Part should be set to use that custom model. See Figure 10-36.

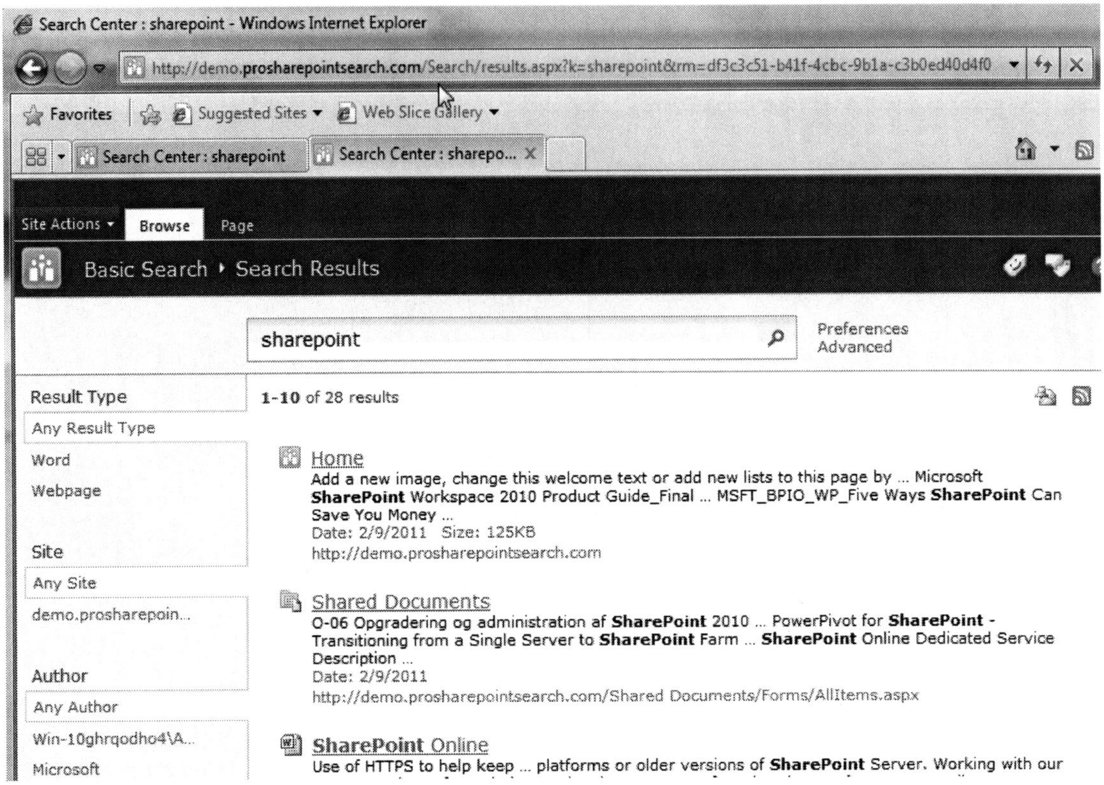

***Figure 10-36.*** *The No Proximity ranking model applied using the* rm *parameter in the URL*

## Custom Models

SharePoint administrators can also create their own ranking models. These ranking models are defined in an XML file that can be added to a new ranking model created in SharePoint by a PowerShell command. The XML descriptor will apply a weighted average of the values that are set in it to the ranking scheme.

Listing 10-2 shows the sample XML descriptor.

***Listing 10-2.*** *The sample XML descriptor.*

```
<rankingModel name="string" id="GUID" description="string"↵
 xmlns="http://schemas.microsoft.com/office/2009/rankingModel">
    <queryDependentFeatures>
        <queryDependentFeature pid="PID" name="string" weight="weightValue"↵
```

```
lengthNormalization="lengthNormalizationSetting" />
    </queryDependentFeatures>
    <queryIndependentFeatures>
        <categoryFeature pid="PID" default="defaultValue" name="string">
            <category value="categoryValue" name="string" weight="weightValue" />
        </categoryFeature>
        <languageFeature pid="PID" name="string" default="defaultValue"
weight="weightValue"↵
  />
        <queryIndependentFeature pid="PID" name="string" default="defaultValue"↵
  weight="weightValue">
            <transformRational k="value" />
            <transformInvRational k="value" />
            <transformLinear max="maxValue" />
        </queryIndependentFeature>
    </queryIndependentFeatures>
</rankingModel>
```

This code is broken into the following:

- *Query-dependent features*: This element contains managed properties that affect dynamic ranking. This element contains a Property ID (PID) that can be extracted from the managed property list using PowerShell, the name of the property (optional), a weight value to apply to the ranking calculation, and an optional length normalization setting.

- *Query-independent features*: This element contains adjustment to static ranking values.

    - *Category features*: This element contains the Property ID, property name (optional), and default value. This adjustment is for properties that have static values (associated with the document) and are small enumerable integers.

    - *Language features*: This element contains the Property ID, name (optional), default value, and weight value. The default value is either 1 or 0, where 1 is the same as the user's locale ID (regional setting) and 0 is not the same.

    - *Query-independent feature* This element requires at least one of the following:

    - transformRational

    - transformInvRational

    - transformLinear

    - transformLogarithmic

---

▒ **Note** See http://msdn.microsoft.com/en-us/library/ee558793.aspx for more information.

---

To set the ranking model on the search center, the core results Web Part needs to be changed or a custom Web Part created that calls the GUID of the desired ranking model.

Use the following PowerShell cmdlet to get the IDs of managed metadata properties. See Figure 10-37.

```
Get-SPEnterpriseSearchServiceApplication | Get-SPEnterpriseSearchMetadataManagedProperty
```

| Name | PID | ManagedType | EnabledForScoping | EqualityMatchOnly |
|------|-----|-------------|-------------------|-------------------|
| AboutMe | 26 | Text | False | False |
| Account | 358 | Text | False | True |
| AccountName | 15 | Text | False | False |
| AssignedTo | 350 | Text | False | False |
| Author | 3 | Text | True | True |
| AvgRating | 400 | Decimal | False | True |
| BaseOfficeLocation | 269 | Text | False | False |
| BestBetKeywords | 12 | Text | False | False |
| CategoryNavigatio... | 314 | Text | False | False |
| CollapsingStatus | 300 | Integer | False | False |
| Colleagues | 394 | Text | False | False |
| contentclass | 261 | Text | True | True |
| ContentsHidden | 175 | Text | False | False |
| ContentSource | 315 | Text | True | False |
| ContentType | 60 | Text | False | False |
| CreatedBy | 340 | Text | False | False |
| Department | 25 | Text | False | False |
| Description | 6 | Text | False | False |
| DisplayDate | 181 | DateTime | False | False |
| DocComments | 130 | Text | False | False |
| DocId | 171 | Text | True | True |
| DocKeywords | 129 | Text | False | False |
| DocSignature | 84 | Text | False | False |
| DocSubject | 128 | Text | False | False |
| DuplicateHash | 299 | Integer | True | True |
| EMail | 351 | Text | False | False |
| EndDate | 346 | DateTime | True | False |
| ExcludeFromSummary | 21474... | Text | False | False |
| ExpirationTime | 182 | DateTime | False | False |
| FileExtension | 319 | Text | True | True |
| Filename | 56 | Text | True | True |
| FirstName | 16 | Text | False | False |
| FollowAllAnchor | 317 | Text | False | False |
| HierarchyUrl | 392 | Text | False | False |
| HighConfidenceDis... | 331 | Text | False | False |
| HighConfidenceDis... | 383 | Text | False | False |
| HighConfidenceDis... | 384 | Text | False | False |
| HighConfidenceDis... | 385 | Text | False | False |

*Figure 10-37. The list of managed metadata properties and their PIDs*

Add the PIDs and the ranking adjustments to the QueryDependentFeature element of the XML, as in the following example:

```
<queryDependentFeature pid="56" name="Filename" weight="50" lengthNormalization="" />
```

The lengthNormalization parameter allows for consideration of document length when considering a particular text value. In the case of managed metadata values, the need for length normalization is probably low because multiple occurrences of the terms are less likely in long or short documents. LengthNormalization should take a value between 0 and 1, where 0 is no length normalization and 1 is maximum consideration.

The `weight` parameter takes a value. There is no clear indication as to what value it should take to increase or decrease relative ranking, as the other ranking weights are not available to compare. A guideline for weighting will be somewhere between a weight value of 1, which is what occurrences in the body text are given by default, and 70, which is what occurrences in a title property are given. It is recommended that several rounds of testing be taken before deciding on the best value.

After the proper ranking values have been applied, a new ranking model needs to be created based on the XML. The XML must be applied as a string when creating or setting the new ranking model. To create a new ranking model, open the SharePoint 2010 Management Shell and call the following PowerShell cmdlet:

```
Get-SPEnterpriseSearchServiceApplication | New-SPEnterpriseSearchRankingModel↵
 -rankingmodelxml '{the entire xml string with spaces removed}'
```

However, it is better to create a a `ps1` file with the command and then run it from the command prompt so that it can be more easily edited and re-used. Create a text file, and add the foregoing into the text file. Then save it as `CustomRanking.ps1`. Drag that file into the PowerShell console.

Listing 10-3 is an example ranking model. It is only an example and has no useful ranking affect. A GUID is needed. There are several ways to generate a GUID—there are even web sites available to generate one if necessary. When creating a custom ranking, make sure the PIDs match the actual property values.

*Listing 10-3. An example ranking model*

```
<?xml version='1.0' encoding='utf-8'?>
<rankingModel name='Pro SharePoint Ranking'
              id='D51BD02D-2FE4-4712-9DF1-30AD432AC2A1'
              description = 'Pro SharePoint Ranking Model'
              xmlns='http://schemas.microsoft.com/office/2009/rankingModel'>


        <queryDependentFeatures>
                <queryDependentFeature name='Title' pid='2' weight='0'
lengthNormalization='10.0000000000'/>
                <queryDependentFeature name='Keywords' pid='356' weight='0'
lengthNormalization='5.0000000000'/>
                <queryDependentFeature name='Description' pid='6' weight='0'
lengthNormalization='50.0000000000' />
                <queryDependentFeature name='Status' pid='359' weight='0'
lengthNormalization='20.0000000000'/>
        </queryDependentFeatures>

        <queryIndependentFeatures>
                <queryIndependentFeature name='DistanceFromAuthority' pid='96'
default='5'            weight='0.0000000000'>
                        <transformInvRational  k='0.1359244473'/>
                </queryIndependentFeature>

                <queryIndependentFeature name='URLdepth' pid='303' default='3'
weight='0.0000000000'>
                <transformRational k='1.2170868558'/>
            </queryIndependentFeature>
```

```
            <queryIndependentFeature name='DocumentPopularity' pid='306' default='0'
weight='0.0000000000'>
                    <transformRational k='1.2170868558'/>
            </queryIndependentFeature>

            <queryIndependentFeature name='DocumentUnpopularity'pid='307' default='0'
weight='0.0000000000'>
                    <transformRational k='1.2170868558'/>
            </queryIndependentFeature>

            <categoryFeature name='Priority' pid='347' default='0'>
                    <category name='Low' value='3' weight='25.0000000000'/>
                    <category name='Medium' value='2' weight='50.0000000000'/>
                    <category name='High' value='1' weight='100.0000000000'/>
            </categoryFeature>

            <languageFeature name='Language' pid='5' default='1' weight='1.0000000000'/>
        </queryIndependentFeatures>

</rankingModel>
```

## Setting the Results Webpart to Use Custom Ranking Models

Now that there is a custom ranking model and it has been tested using the rm parameter and appears to be ranking as desired, the core result Web Part or a custom results Web Part needs to be set to always obey that ranking model. To do this, the Web Part needs to be exported, modified, and imported back into the site. The DefaultRankingModelID property must be applied to the Web Part with the GUID of the custom ranking model, because there is no exposed setting in the Edit Web Part pane.

To add this property to the .webpart file, follow these steps:

1.  Find the results page where the Web Part that will be modified resides. Click Site Actions, Edit Page.

2.  On the results Web Part, choose the Web Part edit menu and choose Export. See Figure 10-38.

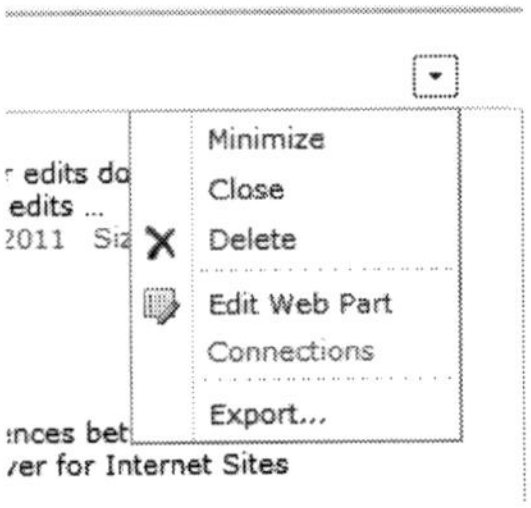

*Figure 10-38. Export Web Part*

3.   Save the Web Part to your drive, and open it in a text editor.

4.   Find the `DefaultRankingModelID` property.

5.   Open the SharePoint 2010 Management Shell, and call the following PowerShell cmdlet to find the GUID of your custom ranking model:

`Get-SPEnterpriseSearchServiceApplication | Get-SPEnterpriseSearchRankingModel`

6.   Copy the GUID into the `DefaultRankingModelID` property on the Web Part. Make sure the property tag is properly closed.

```
<property name="DefaultRankingModelID" type="string">8f6fd0bc-06f10-43cf-bbab↵
-08c377e083f4</property>
```

7.   Go back to the results page, and delete the existing Web Part.

8.   Choose Add Web Part on the Web Part in the Web Part zone where the previous Web Part was.

9.   Under the categories section, there should be an Upload Web Part button. Click it, and upload your modified Web Part. See Figure 10-39.

**Figure 10-39.** *Upload the modified Web Part*

10.   Choose Add Web Part again, and add the new Web Part.

11.   Publish the page.

Now the results should reflect the new custom ranking. If there is more than one result Web Part on the page, all results Web Parts will display ranking based on the model found in the first results Web Part on the page.

# Summary

In this chapter, we looked at generic concepts of search engine relevancy and how they can help us to understand and eventually improve SharePoint 2010 Search. We also went over some concepts about how terms are matched with documents in a collaboration portal. The reporting features of SharePoint 2010 were outlined and some suggestions on how administrators can use these features were given. In addition, a number of built-in search enhancement features such as setting authoritative pages, removing unwanted results, adding stop words and synonyms, creating custom dictionaries, utilizing the `noindex` class, and tagging documents were covered.

Also, the Managed Metadata service was outlined. Although this service is not only search-focused, its proper use can improve content and make search function much better. Additionally, a small UI tweak to add the ratings column to search was given as an example of how search can be further integrated into SharePoint's extended features. Finally, custom ranking models were described and instructions given on how to create and apply a custom model.

# Further Reading

Here are some suggestions for further reading or more details on the topics covered in this chapter.

## Relevancy

For information on the math behind base search ranking algorithms, see `http://en.wikipedia.org/wiki/Okapi_BM25`.

For Microsoft's neural network ranking algorithm patent, see `www.freepatentsonline.com/7840569.html`.

For further reading on Heaps' Law, see `http://en.wikipedia.org/wiki/Heaps'_law`.

## Reporting

For information on reporting and health monitoring in SharePoint, see `http://technet.microsoft.com/en-us/library/ee681489.aspx`.

## Tuning Search

For how to configure authoritative pages, stop word files, the thesaurus, and custom dictionaries, see `http://technet.microsoft.com/en-us/library/cc262796.aspx`.

## Custom Ranking

For MSDN guidance on custom ranking models and the example schema, see `http://msdn.microsoft.com/en-us/library/ee558793.aspx`.

Although this MSDN blog post by "Kundu" is somewhat dated, the principles still apply to SharePoint 2010 and can give some insight into adjusting custom ranking: `http://blogs.msdn.com/b/kundut/archive/2009/10/15/relevance-in-sharepoint-search.aspx`.

# CHAPTER 11

■ ■ ■

# Search Extensions

After completing this chapter, you will be able to

- Plan for extending SPS2010 Search through free and purchasable third-party additions

- Recognize limitations of SPS2010 resolved by third-party additions

- Navigate the marketplace of SharePoint solution vendors

- Asses the need for additional search web parts, document visualization, and automatic classification

- Determine if a replacement for the SharePoint 2010 search engine is necessary

- Budget for the relative cost of third-party additions

Thus far, this book has focused on how to get the most out of search in SharePoint 2010 with in-house resources. It has focused on setup, use, configuration, customization, and basic custom development. While these are the vital components of working with search in SharePoint, it should be recognized that like all software, the platform is not without its limitations. Many SharePoint 2010 deployments will require functionality beyond that supported by the basic platform. In some cases, it may be prudent to begin development of custom solutions to meet business needs. Depending on the needs, however, custom development may be found to be too expensive, time-consuming, risky, or even impossible. In these situations, it may be necessary to turn to external resources.

This chapter explores the limitations of SharePoint 2010, and the most popular functions that are added to the platform to offset those limitations. It explores the business needs that may require add-on solutions, and reviews vendors with commercial software solutions. It takes a look into free add-on solutions through open source project communities, and provides general outlines of when replacements to the SharePoint 2010 search engine, such as FAST Search Server for SharePoint 2010 SharePoint (FAST) or the Google Search Appliance, should be considered. The concepts in this chapter are designed to be surface-level overviews of the available options, but do not go into deep-level detail. There are many resources available that are dedicated to each solution mentioned, and this chapter should be treated as a guide for when to seek out those resources.

# Extending Search Beyond In-House Development

Microsoft has an extensive network of partners, consultants, developers, and software vendors that support SharePoint 2010. In the summer of 2010, just after the release of SharePoint 2010, Microsoft released that it had 390,000 partners worldwide supporting its vast array of software. Furthermore, 95% of Microsoft revenue at that time stemmed from partners. It is safe to assume that no matter the feature needs of a company, there is probably a Microsoft partner available that can assist to custom develop or sell a pre-developed solution to meet the requirements.

Most third-party enhancements are either solutions that meet back-end needs beyond the user interface, or user-side features such as Web Parts. To review, Web Parts are ASP.NET server controls, and act as the building blocks of SharePoint. They allow users to modify the appearance, content, and behavior of SharePoint directly from the browser. Web Parts allow for interaction with pages and control the design of a page. These building blocks provide all the individual bits of functionality users may experience within a SharePoint environment. SharePoint 2010 comes with over 75 Web Parts to meet the dynamic needs of organizations, but it would be impossible for Microsoft to include Web Parts in SharePoint 2010 that meet every feature need for every organization using the platform. When search user features beyond those included with the platform are required, "custom search" Web Parts are needed.

Custom Web Parts can range from adaptations of existing Web Parts to meet new business requirements, to completely original Web Parts that are built from scratch. Since the user experience in SharePoint flows through Web Parts, application pages, and ASP.NET controls, all add-on solutions will contain some combination of custom Web Parts. There are, however, specific point solutions built to add one or more Web Parts to meet specific feature needs. These range from free open source projects from sites, such as CodePlex, individual purchasable Web Parts, such as those offered by Bamboo Solutions, to broader packages of Web Parts, such as those offered by SurfRay's Ontolica Search product.

In addition to custom Web Parts that cater directly to user functionality, there are many other solutions available that cater to back-end needs. These needs may range from better metadata tagging and improved taxonomy, to more index- and crawler-focused solutions such as iFilters and connectors. Although portions of these solutions are composed of Web Parts, they also tie into the underlying architecture and layers of SharePoint that the user does not interface with directly. They nonetheless greatly affect how users interact with content and navigate SharePoint.

# CodePlex and Open Source

When faced with a need beyond the out-of-the-box capabilities of a platform, it is common to look to open source solutions. Open source software is that which provides the end product's source materials. Generally, open source software is provided at no cost in the public domain, leading to its attractiveness as a first step for enhancements.

CodePlex is Microsoft's open source project hosting web site. The site provides a medium for people to request projects to be made by independent developers, share their own developments with the public, find solutions already in the works, and download solutions made by other people. The best part about CodePlex is that all of the solutions and downloads are free. CodePlex brings together programming hobbyists, professional developers who want to share their skills, and those new to Microsoft technologies with a problem to solve. The site provides a medium for these people to collaborate on projects and distribute their work at no cost.

There is a vast range of projects hosted through CodePlex, and the number is constantly growing. At the end of 2010, CodePlex was hosting nearly 20,000 open source projects for the Microsoft community. Projects are usually driven by a need to add point solutions to Microsoft technologies prior to the need being addressed by Microsoft. For example, MOSS 2007 did not include a search refinement

Web Part. Since the ability to refine search results by managed properties was common to many other search technologies, and widely popular on web sites, users began requesting the feature more and more. Either by request, or on their own, someone began working on a search refinement solution for MOSS 2007 to meet this need. The first release (version 1.0) of this MOSS Faceted Search Web Part was in September 2007, and it was downloaded several hundred times.

Over the course of the next several months, the solution received several updates fixing bugs such as security policy issues and XML formatting. In early 2008, the programmer-released version 2.0 of the MOSS Faceted Search Web Part brought many major fixes to the Web Part and extended its features. Bugs such as malformed queries, security enhancements, and disappearing functions were addressed. New features such as multi-thread processing, facet icons, and the ability to exclude certain facets were added. In addition to the Web Part, version 2.0 included guides to configuration and styling. The solution became increasingly popular, with over 15,000 downloads. Version 2.5 was released in July 2008, about six months after version 2.0. It was titled to be the first Enterprise release with continued bug fixes and the new ability to be integrated with the Enterprise Library, support for advanced search, support for language refinements, enhanced error visualization, and support for "OR" queries. In January 2009, the Web Part author uploaded version 3.0 of the solution, but unfortunately the solution was not complete. A year later, version 3.0 of the solution had still not been fixed, and the download was eventually rolled back to version 2.5.

The development history provides a perfect example of a project life cycle for a CodePlex project. It brings to light the benefits and concerns for using open source solutions. The solution was and still is free to anyone who would like to use it. Organizations that experienced successful, bug-free deployments of the Web Part had a chance to benefit from a search navigation feature that was not included with SharePoint until the release of SharePoint 2010. Development of the software was taken care of for them at no cost, and they only needed to allocate resources for its installation and configuration.

Organizations that implemented one of the earlier releases of the MOSS Faceted Search Web Part needed to be mindful of several bugs in the software. Since the solutions available on CodePlex are open source, organizations that experienced problems with the Web Part could not hold the developer accountable for resolving issues. They could report bugs in the review section, or message the author through the web site's messaging system, but did not have a guarantee for action. As was seen with the 3.0 release, continued development of CodePlex projects is not guaranteed, and organizations need to be cautious of the software and version downloaded.

For some organizations, using open source software available through CodePlex is the best solution to custom development needs. Generally, organizations that meet this profile have development resources in-house, and use open source solutions as a jumpstart to in-house development. When properly leveraged, some developers can build on open source software, and use it to jump straight into the more advanced stages of development. This is a common practice for consultants and system integrators with limited solution development time lines. Companies may also not have budgets allocated to software purchases beyond the base SharePoint 2010 platform. These companies can leverage CodePlex projects to enhance their environment without additional software costs.

## Getting the Most Out of Your Open Source Products

It is important to follow a few best practices when using any open source solution, including those available on CodePlex. Most importantly, never install open source solutions directly into a live production environment. While it is never recommended to test software in production without first deploying to a development environment, the rule must be drastically stressed for open source software. These solutions are not tested by Microsoft, and as a result should not be blindly trusted to work without bugs. A proper QA test cycle should always be done on open source solutions prior to adding them into a production environment. Although they may be time-consuming to resolve, problems resulting from software testing in development do not necessarily stand as a detriment to an organization as a whole. By contrast, if a major problem is first experienced in a production environment, the consequences are significantly more severe.

Before installing a download from CodePlex, read the reviews and discussions for the release. These are comments added by others who have downloaded the software. Reviews are generally comments about whether a user had a good or bad experience with the solution and why. Discussions provide insight into problems that may be experienced with the download so that they can be avoided. Problems may be minor or avoidable, but these discussions are generally the best knowledge base for getting ahead of potential issues when testing. They may also provide insight into how to make certain configurations.

At the end of 2010, there were about 300 active CodePlex projects addressing needs in SharePoint 2010. The most popular download is the SharePoint 2010 Manager, which adds a SharePoint object model explorer. It gives administrators the ability to browse every site on a local SharePoint 2010 farm and view every managed property within the farm. It also allows administrators to update properties and data in the SharePoint object model directly from one consolidated explorer view through the tool.

---

■ **Note** The SharePoint 2010 Manager project can be found at `http://spm.codeplex.com/`.

---

## Additional Search Related Projects

Some additional search-related projects include a Wildcard Search Web Part, which allows for the wildcard syntax to be added implicitly to every query. The SharePoint Google Directions Web Part (Figure 11-1) allows for federated queries to Google Maps instead of the default Google Web Search. This Web Part provides a query field in SharePoint 2010 for starting and ending directions, and when executed, the query is executed through Google Maps and returns the results in a second browser window.

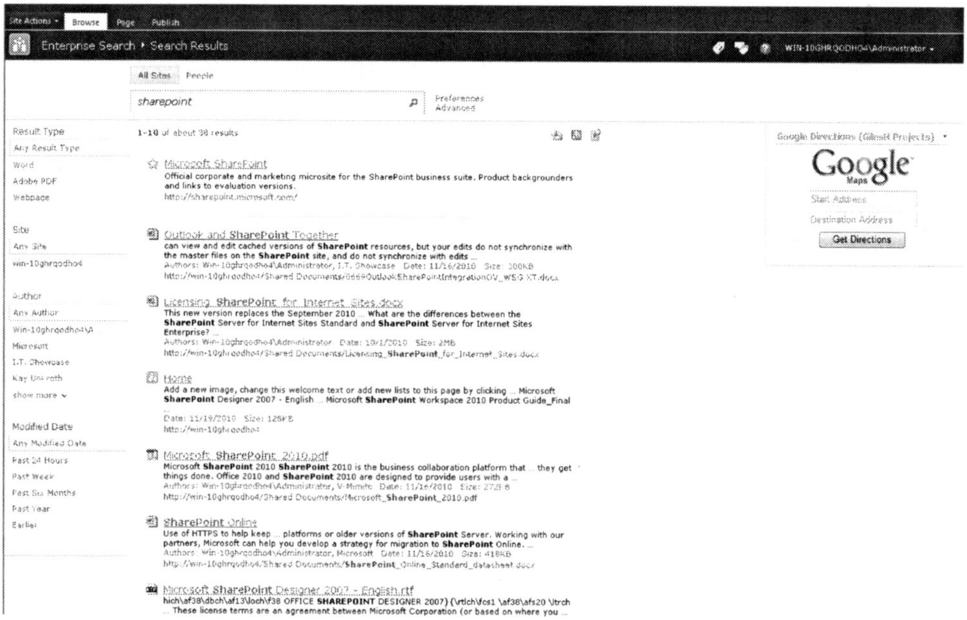

**Figure 11-1.** *CodePlex Google Directions Web Part*

The SharePoint 2010 Managed Metadata Web Part creates a user navigation control from a Managed Metadata column assigned to a list or library (Figure 11-2). This allows for user navigation of a term set related to a column in a list or library.

**Figure 11-2.** *CodePlex SharePoint 2010 Managed Metadata Web Part*

The SharePoint Outlook Connector makes it easier to upload e-mails from Microsoft Outlook to SharePoint, and attach SharePoint documents to an e-mail message (Figure 11-3). This improves on the standard process, which requires users to save e-mails to their desktops before uploading through the SharePoint user interface. It also allows users to bypass the need to download SharePoint documents to a local drive before attaching them to an e-mail.

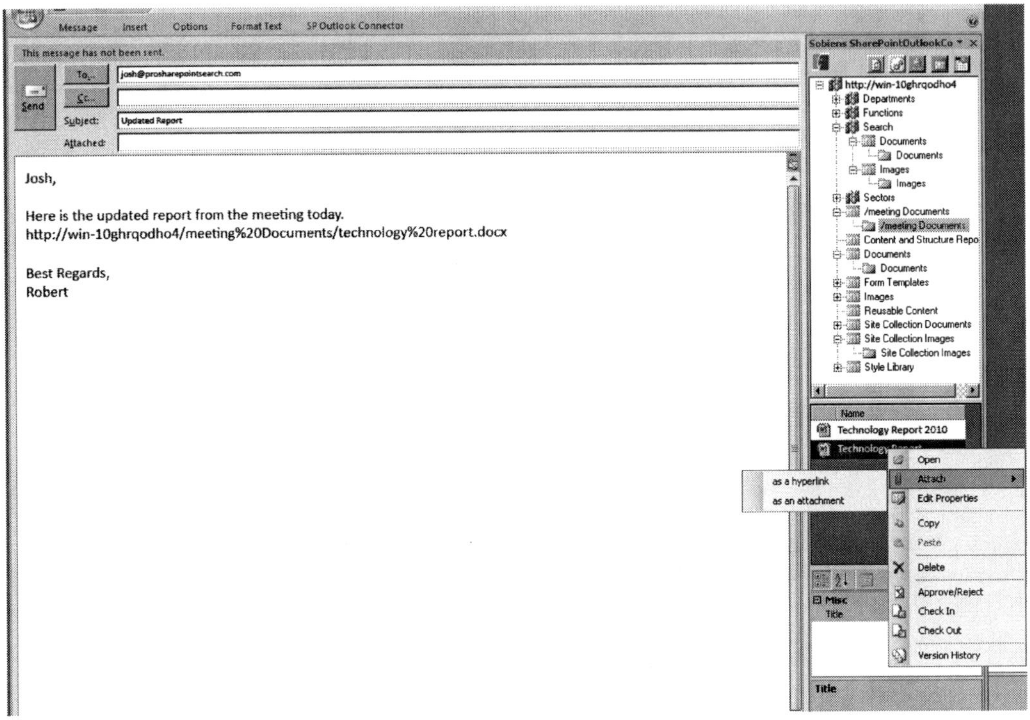

*Figure 11-3. CodePlex SharePoint Outlook Connector*

■ **Note** The Web Parts mentioned in this section can be found at the following links.

http://wildcardsearch2010.codeplex.com/

http://gileshgoogdirections.codeplex.com/

http://metadatawebpart.codeplex.com/

http://spoutlookconnector.codeplex.com/

These projects provide a general idea of the broad range of solutions that can be found on CodePlex. As needs evolve, and SharePoint 2010 matures, many more solutions and projects will appear on the site over time. While CodePlex is not the only place to find open source solutions for SharePoint 2010, it does house the most abundant collection and is a good place to start looking for solutions.

# Commercial Solutions

The rest of this chapter focuses on commercially available solutions. Unlike open source projects such as those found on CodePlex, solutions made available through Microsoft partners are generally well tested and supported by the developing vendor. Popular commercial solutions bring the benefit of stability and support, which is vital to organizations that rely on their SharePoint deployments. Reliable vendors can be expected to resolve problems when they arise and assist with successful implantations, unlike open source projects, which run the risk of any number of failures or consequences to an environment.

## User Interface Enhancements

Chapter 5 provided a thorough look into the SharePoint 2010 Search user interface. It outlined the major features and Web Parts that are included with the platform. Chapter 8 provided details on how to build custom Web Parts in the event those included with SP2010 do not meet all of an organization's needs. It may, however, be a better option to search for commercially obtainable solutions to enhance the search user interface. While this book could not cover the entire scope of every potential addition to the search user interface that an organization may want to utilize, this section attempts to point out some of the most frequently deployed features.

Search user interface enhancements may range from simple formatting and branding with custom XSLT, to completely new navigational functionality that provides for more fluid navigation. Users may complain that they are returning too many results in a search result set, and that the SharePoint 2010 search refiner Web Part is not allowing them to refine on their necessary properties. This may be the result of poor metadata since the search refiner Web Part is simply allowing for pre-defined property restrictions to be executed on the search result set. Users may recognize that although they know a particular suggestion should be appearing in a refinement category, it isn't. This may be because the items with the property they want to use do not appear until late in the result set, and SharePoint 2010's search refiner Web Part considers only the first 50 items. They may want to see how many results are included in each refinement option. Users may notice that while they can navigate into the site refinement category, they cannot backtrack without starting over. The list of requests for improvement could continue, and, depending on the user's needs, they are valid considering the limitations of just the search refinement Web Part included with the platform. This does not even consider the additional features users may request that are not even within the scope of the Web Parts included with SharePoint.

Since the way users work with SharePoint is many times quite different than how site designers originally expected, anyone planning a SharePoint deployment should expect demands for improvements. The user interface is generally the first point of complaint to be brought to the design team's attention because it is the only layer users directly touch. Unlike the components that drive the user interface, when users notice something wrong or a feature they would like to have, this is the only layer where they may be able to easily express their needs. If metadata or taxonomy is poor, users unfamiliar with the technology know there is an issue, but can rarely express the exact problem. By contrast, if a user knows he or she needs the site to include a tag cloud like the blog he or she regularly visits, that need is more easily verbalized. SharePoint designers and administrators should be prepared to handle these user interface needs during initial testing and well after a rollout.

# Individual Commercial Web Parts

To meet the broad and evolving range of search user interface needs, many vendors have brought purchasable solutions to market. The individual Web Parts available from companies such as Bamboo Solutions and SharePoint Boost provide a starting point for meeting specific user enhancement needs. Bamboo Solutions, for example, offers a List Search Web Part. The Web Part allows users to search multiple lists at once, and return the results back into a single consolidated list. In SharePoint 2010, prior to this customization, searches can be directed at either all lists, or one list at a time, but cannot combine results from several specific lists. The Web Part can accept the standard SharePoint 2010 BOOLEAN operators in a query and then return results with customized columns and sorts. After search results are returned from the lists, the user can rearrange column orders and print the search results. This feature has a number of real-world applications such as searching for client information scattered among several lists or searching for a product across several catalog lists. The List Search Web Part is available in simple and advanced versions that cater to different customization needs. The features of each option can be found in Table 11-1.

*Table 11-1.* *Bamboo Solutions List Search Web Part Features*

| Feature | Simple | Advanced |
|---|---|---|
| Specify the list to be searched, view to use to display the search results, and the fields within the list to make available for use as search criteria | X | X |
| Specify a set of lists to be available for the user to select from for searching | | X |
| Constrain a search to a single list without having to create an index and search scope | X | X |
| Display search result hits by individual list item | X | X |
| Identify a view associated with the list to use to display the search results, allowing the designer to specifically define the look and feel of the search results list, including columns and sorts | X | X |
| AND/OR operators to be included in the search criteria | | X |
| Group search results | | X |
| Allows user to select ALL or ANY words to join search columns | X | X |
| Ability to rearrange search results column order | X | X |
| Ability to print search results | X | X |

| Feature | Simple | Advanced |
|---|:---:|:---:|
| Ability to search keywords in all list columns | X | X |
| Users have the option to select available lists | | X |
| Disable lookup fields to control Web Part performance | | X |
| Translate the Web Part into English, French, German, or Spanish, or customize translation for the language you need | X | X |
| Customize the look and feel of the Web Part by modifying the HTML Source and CSS | X | |

Unlike open source solutions, such as those found on CodePlex, these solutions are tested and supported. While caution should always be used whether testing new features from open source, Microsoft, or other commercial vendors, a significantly greater trust can be put into well-reviewed commercial solutions. Although commercial solutions may require an initial financial investment, when compared with the costs of fixing broken solutions or repairing a crashed SharePoint portal, the investment is easily justified in most cases. For most environments, the cost of lost productivity due to a portal crash dwarfs the cost of software licensing. Individual Web Parts are generally available at a fairly low cost and can be obtained through an online purchase system. Although all vendors in this space have different price structures, straightforward Web Parts can be expected to cost less than US$1,000.

■ **Note** Full details on the List Search Web Part available from Bamboo Solutions can be found at http://store.bamboosolutions.com/pc-35-1-list-search-web-part.aspx.

For environments that require more complex enhancements to the search user interface, there are many other solution packages on the market. These solutions usually include a broad range of search enhancements including various features for refining search results, suggesting alternative queries, taking action on results, entering more advanced queries, or integrating search into other business processes. These solution sets include a package of Web Parts to directly enhance the user experience, but may also add additional functions such as databases for analytics or workflows for search-based processes. They can also be categorized into two distinctly different paradigms: those that extend SharePoint search, and those that replace it. The second of these options is reviewed later in this chapter.

# Comprehensive Commercial Search Extensions

Extensions that directly expand the search functionality of SharePoint 2010 are offered in solutions such as SurfRay's Ontolica Search and BA Insight's Longitude. Search extensions of this kind can sit on top of SharePoint 2010 and leverage the search architecture that is already in place. This provides for some benefits and downsides when compared with the more well-known "enterprise" search solutions such as FAST, Google, and Autonomy. By utilizing SharePoint 2010's search pipeline, administrators need to manage only one crawler and index. This keeps management in one consolidated interface, instead of spreading jobs out between several different search solutions. For organizations without extra expendable employee hours each week, the time saved not having to manage two sets of physical and software architecture is invaluable. In addition, by using only enhancements that directly build on top of SharePoint, security and permissions are preserved. For organizations with strict security and privacy concerns, the avoidance of managing additional permission sets is critical to controlling availability of restricted information.

## Ontolica Search

Ontolica Search, the SharePoint search extension offered by Microsoft partner SurfRay, can add a broad range of additional search features to a SharePoint environment. Unlike the individual Web Parts offered by vendors such as Bamboo Solutions, which meet one specific need, Ontolica Search addresses a broader need for search improvements. All of the features in Ontolica rely on the SharePoint search engine. They pass queries to SharePoint, retrieve information, display that information to users, and allow manipulation of the returned data. While there are additional functionalities in the solution, search features can be categorized as focusing on the four main areas.

- Faster access to information

- Refinements to filter results to the most relevant items

- Actionable results to facilitate business processes

- Experience populated suggestions for query adjustments

## Accessing Information Quickly

Ontolica Search connects users with information faster from any page with a query box. While SharePoint 2010 includes the ability to enable query boxes to present thesaurus-generated suggestions, this solution can provide a list of the top search results for the entered query. As a user enters a query, Ontolica Search returns a list of the most relevant results, which can then be actioned (Figure 11-4). This allows users to check out the more relevant items directly from the page they are on without ever navigating to the search center.

**Figure 11-4.** *Ontolica Search As You Type feature*

## Enhanced Refinements

When it comes to the search center, users find a broad range of additional refinement options beyond those available with SharePoint 2010. The search refiner Web Part has been upgraded to present the number of results in each refinement suggestion (Figure 11-5). The site refiner category allows users to drill in and back out of taxonomies using a breadcrumb navigator. Also, possibly most important, the refinements can analyze up to 2,000 items in a result set instead of just the first 500.

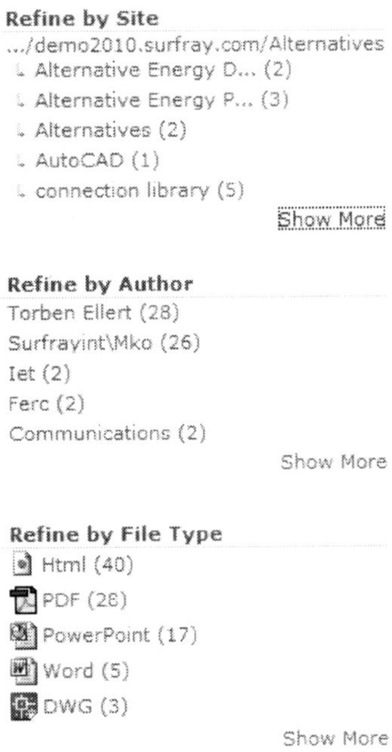

**Refine by Site**

.../demo2010.surfray.com/Alternatives
∟ Alternative Energy D... (2)
∟ Alternative Energy P... (3)
∟ Alternatives (2)
∟ AutoCAD (1)
∟ connection library (5)

Show More

**Refine by Author**

Torben Ellert (28)
Surfrayint\Mko (26)
Iet (2)
Ferc (2)
Communications (2)

Show More

**Refine by File Type**

Html (40)
PDF (28)
PowerPoint (17)
Word (5)
DWG (3)

Show More

*Figure 11-5. Ontolica search refiner Web Part*

In addition to the search refiner Web Part, Ontolica Search also adds the ability to rearrange search results and group them by managed properties. Unlike the search refiner Web Part, which allows users to select one property from a result set, this option allows users to see multiple properties but skip past those that are irrelevant. Finally, the solution provides the ability for administrators to set up quick filters. These are radio buttons or check boxes below the query field that allow users to select pre-defined combinations of property restrictions. SharePoint administrators can customize these to offer users an alternative to building common property restrictions on the advanced search page. These features can be seen in the following figure of an uncustomized Ontolica search center on SharePoint 2010 (Figure 11-6).

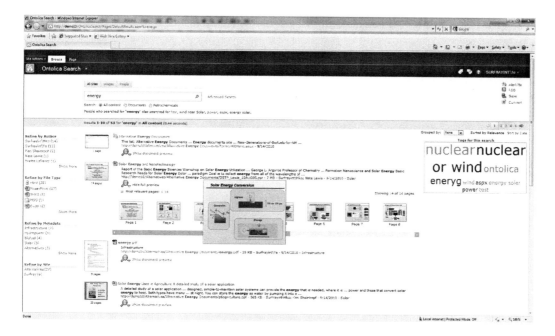

***Figure 11-6.*** *Ontolica search center on SharePoint 2010*

## Actionable Results

Actionable items and documents are a common feature throughout SharePoint, but the ability is lacking in search. Ontolica Search provides a drop-down on search results so that users can execute actions on them (Figure 11-7). The default action taken when clicking different search result types in SharePoint 2010 was discussed in Chapter 5. This drop-down provides a broader range of default actions, such as the ability to check out Microsoft Office documents directly from the search results page, setting alerts on individual results instead of entire result sets, and executing an e-mail containing the item's link through Microsoft Outlook. In addition to these default actions, custom actions, processes, and workflows can be added.

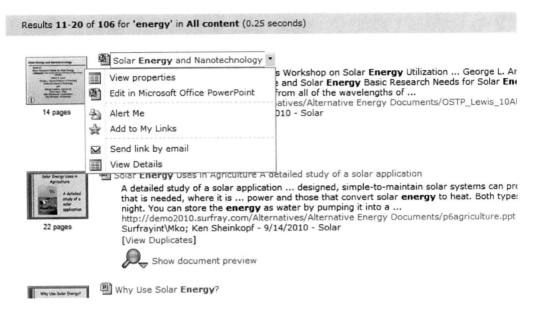

**Figure 11-7.** *Ontolica search result actions*

## Query Suggestions

The final focus of Ontolica Search is to provide experience-driven query suggestions. On the back end, Ontolica Search contains a business intelligence database cube that gathers a wide range of statistical data from the SharePoint farm. This data is gathered from IIS logs, Central Admin logs, and logs from the use of the tool itself. Ontolica then processes this data and makes it available through a wide range of statistic reports, such as the most popular search terms, queries that returned no results or did not result in a user clicking a result, and storage trends. This information can be used for a wide range of business intelligence, marketing, and search engine optimization needs. It is also used to present query suggestions to end users.

Ontolica Search presents suggestions in three formats, which include autosuggestions in the query field, related queries, and a tag cloud Web Part. When a user is executing a search query in the search center, the autosuggest feature provides a drop-down of query suggestions similar to the SharePoint 2010 Search suggestions. The related query Web Part and tag cloud Web Parts guide users to additional queries that may be useful. Just like SharePoint 2010, these suggestions are based on the aggregated experiences of users. Where these suggestion features differ from SharePoint 2010 is in the scope of suggestions. SharePoint 2010 can provide suggestions based only on the experiences of all users within the farm. Ontolica's suggestion features, however, can be isolated to a search center, the user's department, or the entire company. This means that users can receive search suggestions based off of the experiences of users in their own department, and do not have to receive suggestions based off of the entire company. This is quite practical in that the types of queries done by people in the sales department are most likely very different from those executed by the HR department. Suggestions are not cluttered with those helpful only to users in other departments.

# Customize Search without Programming

In addition to adding a broad range of additional refinement, action, and suggestion features to SharePoint 2010, Ontolica helps overcome the complications of customizing the search experience. Ontolica's features are easily customizable and as stated previously, can all be set to cater to specific user groups, even with only one search center. For example, users from the Human Resources, Marketing, and Engineering departments require very different experiences from search. To give each of these departments a different search experience in SharePoint, separate search pages would need to be created and maintained for each department. With Ontolica however, users can all access the same search page but received customized refinements, search suggestions, and relevancy.

Ontolica also provides administrators with simple tools to leverage metadata and expose it in the search UI without any custom development. For example, customizations such as adding new search refiners for custom properties or even a new search field on the advanced search page can be made by non-technical administrators. The following table summarizes the major differences between SharePoint 2010 and Ontolica Search.

*Table 11-2. SharePoint 2010 and Ontolica Search Feature Comparison*

| Feature | SharePoint 2010 | Ontolica Search |
|---|---|---|
| Boolean Search (AND, OR, NOT, NEAR) | X | X |
| Wildcard Search (*) | X | X |
| Numbered refiners with exact counts | | X |
| Accuracy index limit | 500 items | 2,000 items |
| Query Suggestions | X | X |
| Audience Targeted Query Suggestions | | X |
| Related Queries | X | X |
| Audience Targeted Related Queries | | X |
| Tag Cloud Web Part | | X |
| "Did You Mean" Related Content | X | X |
| Search As You Type | | X |
| Advanced People Search | X | X |
| Image Search | | X |
| Visual Best Bets | | X |

*Continued*

| Feature | SharePoint 2010 | Ontolica Search |
|---|---|---|
| User selected result sorting models | Limited | X |
| Search Result Grouping (Clustering) | | X |
| Search Result Action Menus | | X |
| Audience Targeting for all web parts | | X |
| Customization without programming | | X |

# Vendor Notes

Many vendors, including Bamboo Solutions and SurfRay, offer free trials of their solutions. This allows for testing prior to a purchase. Make sure to allocate appropriate time for setup of the solutions during testing. Ask vendors about the installation, setup, and customization time needed so that realistic time resources can be dedicated. It is also recommended to do research on the experiences of others who have tested products as vendor estimates may be for best-case scenarios, and not the norm. While first-hand experiences are the best judge, investigating the experiences of others may uncover problems with solutions that may not be immediately apparent.

Take note of system resource requirements and other secondary costs. Many solutions, especially those reviewed later in this chapter, require large amounts of setup time, regular maintenance, professional services, and additional hardware that can rapidly increase costs and time demands. Asking the right questions and doing sufficient research will help to paint a full picture of the real costs associated with the software and the amount of time needed to maintain it after rollout.

Ask users what they would like to see improved. While this should seem obvious, many times technical teams run off of the assumptions of what needs to be improved without directly asking those affected. While users may not be able to verbalize a solution, they can express their problems. If users complain that they get too many results in their search result set, look into improvements in scopes, filtering capability, and duplicates. If users complain that they can't find items they know exist, look into improvements in tagging, iFilters, permissions, and content sources. Here are a few questions that are essential to determining the improvements that will resolve real findability problems.

- *Are users seeing too many irrelevant results high in their search result set?* If this is the case, consider adding a custom sorting option so that users can shuffle results based on the properties that are important to them. Set up additional managed properties, and make the fields required to complete when users upload new items to SharePoint. Add additional refiners based on the managed properties that are most widely used. Leverage third-party Web Parts that provide results based on user context or add additional refinement capabilities. Create more specific document libraries, and create processes that make users upload their documents into their relevant libraries. Create scopes for users to search against specific content libraries.

- *Are users unable to find items in search that they know exist?* It is first important to check that the location of the content is accessible to SharePoint search. Full details on how to do this are provided in Chapter 3. It is then necessary to make sure the content of the desired item is searchable. The content of certain file types, such as PDFs, is not accessible to SharePoint's index without the appropriate iFilter. Make sure that any necessary iFilters are installed and working. If SharePoint is able to correctly index items and they are still not appearing to users, check the items' managed properties. SharePoint places a large weight on managed properties when determining relevancy. Adding more defined properties and clarifying ambiguity greatly increases SharePoint search relevancy. This can be done manually or with third-party classification solutions. If users are using keywords that are not within the content or properties of a document, create synonyms to tie their query terms to keywords associated with the document. For frequently required items, set up a best bet for query terms that promote the item to appear at the top of a search result set.

- *Are users finding items they shouldn't be able to view?* Check that user permissions have been correctly established. Make sure only those users who should have clearance to certain sites, content types, and content sources are set to access restricted content. This may be a problem with LDAP or Active Directory security. If permissions are set correctly, make sure that sensitive documents are correctly tagged as restricted content types. This can be done manually or with auto-classification tools such as those reviewed later in this chapter.

Finally, it is always important for real users to go hands-on with solutions prior to production rollouts. Improvements are much harder to make once a solution has gone live. Set up a development environment that mirrors production, and have real users work on it for a week. Ask them for feedback on improvements and use the advice. If improvements are requested with a small test group, the complaints can be expected to be compounded on a production rollout.

# Visualization

Visualization of documents has seen a drastic increase in popularity since the release of MOSS 2007. Users demanding faster recognition of documents have fueled the development of solutions that show them their documents before the requirement to take action on them. This set of functionality can now be found on Google's web page preview, Bing's visual search, and even Windows Explorer's preview pane. As users take hold of this concept and use it in their personal lives, it is safe to expect that they will begin to demand it in their business environment.

While search visualization is also a search user interface improvement, the feature is so popular that it requires its own focus. Microsoft has taken note of the need for users to quickly differentiate between documents from whatever program they are using. The Windows Explorer preview pane was first introduced in Windows Vista, and received vast improvements in Windows 7. This feature is extremely useful in that users see the content of a file without the need to open a specialized application. Unfortunately, Microsoft did not decide to include this feature in SharePoint 2010 without the FAST Search Server for SharePoint 2010 add-on. This feature undoubtedly broadens the gap between SharePoint 2010 and the enterprise add-on discussed later in this chapter.

## Scanning Options

The popularity of the visualization feature has not gone unnoticed by Microsoft partners. There are several vendors with solutions built to add document preview functionality into SharePoint 2010. The available visualization solutions greatly range in the needs they address. For example, KnowledgeLake's Imaging for SharePoint product assists with scanning documents into SharePoint, searching scanned-in unstructured content, and viewing scanned documents directly in SharePoint. It adds a Silverlight-based viewer to view common document types such as Office documents, PDFs, and most image files. It focuses on the time it takes for organizations to store and process large amounts of paper data. KnowledgeLake's solutions are designed to address both the input and retrieval of documents in SharePoint. This feature set is extremely useful for organizations with large amounts of paper documents to manage such as those in the legal, healthcare, financial services, utility, and insurance verticals. For these types of companies, the ability to transfer paper documents into digital files that can be more easily stored, organized, and retrieved is a paradigm-shifting solution to old problems.

## Lightweight Document Viewers

Other solutions, such as Atalasoft's Vizit, BA-Insight's Longitude, and SurfRay's Ontolica Preview, take slightly different approaches to SharePoint document viewing and imaging. Like Windows Explorer's preview pane, these products embed a lightweight document viewer to quickly view files in the SharePoint browser (Figure 11-8). They enable users to view full-page documents and compare files directly from lists and search results.

Ontolica Preview is primarily designed to cater to search. Unlike other visualization solutions, Ontolica Preview goes beyond simply displaying files in the browser. It has the ability to understand the unstructured data within documents, and connect this content to search queries. The solution can understand the user's search query, cross-reference it with a target file, and highlight the occurrences of terms from a search query within the document. Ontolica Preview quickly guides users to the information they are looking for within a document by noting the pages where query terms appear most frequently, and displays high-resolution previews of pages with the highlighted keywords.

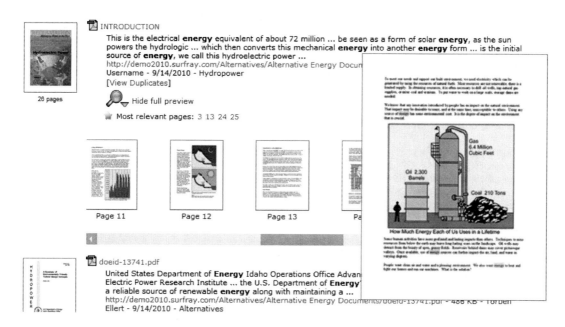

**Figure 11-8.** *Ontolica Preview*

## Other Options

A third option, Vizit, takes some notes from KnowledgeLake Imaging and Ontolica Preview. It provides some scanning ability, but not nearly the extensive scanning features provided by KnowledgeLake. Vizit provides lightweight previews and the ability to compare documents, but does not present previews with hit highlighting and relevant pages. It does, however, provide the ability to annotate documents and clean them like the KnowledgeLake product. Each of these products meets a slightly different range of visualization needs in SharePoint. The best solution for one organization may not be so for another. It is important to analyze the needs of users, and select the enhancement that best fits their needs, budget, and the complexities the organization is prepared to handle.

## Choosing the Best Option

Table 11-3 provides a high-level overview of the viewing features provided by each solution. This does not reference every feature, as all three solutions do offer additional search and scanning. For full details and up-to-date information on product improvements, it is always best to contact each vendor directly.

*Table 11-3. Visualization Product Comparison*

| Product Feature | KnowledgeLake Imaging | Ontolica Preview | Vizit Pro |
|---|:---:|:---:|:---:|
| Support for Office documents, PDF, and raster image formats | X | X | X |
| Support for vector image, archive, and database formats | | X | |
| Full-page document viewing | X | X | X |
| Thumbnail views of documents | | X | X |
| View multiple documents at once | X | X | X |
| View document sets | X | X | X |
| Search query highlighting within previews | | X | |
| Links to relevant page based on search queries | | X | |
| Zoom in and out or fit-to-width viewing | | | X |
| Rotate and flip documents | | | X |
| Ability to "find similar" with embedded searching | X | | |
| View pages of documents immediately without waiting for the entire document to download | X | X | X |
| Annotate documents using text, image stamps, highlights, lines, and sticky notes (TIFF/PDF only) | X | | X |
| Clean up documents with border removal, page de-skew, and hole punch removal | | | X |
| Rearrange pages and remove pages from documents | | | X |
| Split documents or merge different documents together | | | X |
| Encrypt selective pages and portions of PDF and TIFF files | X | | |
| Scan and index documents without ever leaving the SharePoint interface | X | | X |
| View or modify SharePoint column properties with access controlled by SharePoint security | X | | X |
| Automatic population of metadata from scanned documents | X | | |

■ **Note** The products listed in this section can be found at the following locations.

www.knowledgelake.com

http://surfray.com/

www.atalasoft.com/products/vizit

# iFilters

Not all file types can be crawled by SharePoint 2010 out of the box. To expand the supported file types, Microsoft developed iFilters, which act as plug-ins for the Windows operating system. iFilters allow SharePoint to index file formats so that they are understood by the search engine and are searchable. Without an appropriate iFilter, SharePoint cannot understand the content of files and search within them. iFilters allow the index to understand the file's format, filter out embedded formatting, mine text from the file, and return it to the search engine.

The subject of iFilters was first introduced in Chapter 1. Chapter 3 dove into the concept in more detail, and provided a thorough walkthrough detailing the installation of Adobe's PDF iFilter, and the RTF iFilter available from Microsoft. While these walkthroughs in Chapter 3 provided the steps for setting up iFilters, they focused only on these two file formats. There are hundreds of other file formats that organizations may need to index with SharePoint 2010.

iFilters are available for most major file types through a variety of vendors. In addition, there are usually several vendors offering iFilters for the same file type. Not all iFilters work the same, and depending on the amount of content being crawled that includes file types requiring an iFilter, crawl performance may be drastically different depending on the installed iFilter. Slower iFilters result in slower crawl time since SharePoint's index takes longer to understand the content of files. The PDF iFilter, for example, is undoubtedly the most frequently implemented iFilter. The crawl time for the three most popular PDF iFilters can be found in Figure 11-9.

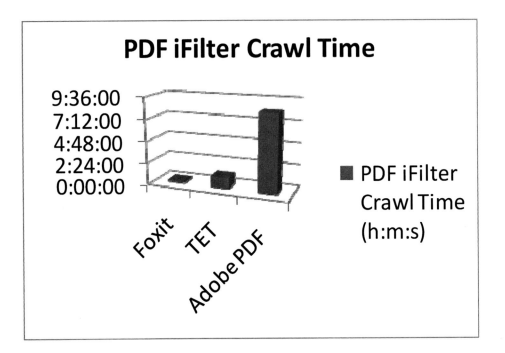

***Figure 11-9.** PDF iFilter crawl times*

---

■ **Note** Crawl time comparison is based on a data set of 22,559 PDF files in 84 folders, 15.7GB of data total. Full details on the testing resulting in this comparison can be found at http://blogs.msdn.com/b/opal/archive/ 2010/02/09/pdf-ifilter-test-with-sharepoint-2010.aspx.

---

While Adobe does offer a PDF iFilter at no cost, it is not the most efficient solution. Several third-party vendors, such as IFilter Shop, Foxit, and PDFlib, offer their own versions of a PDF iFilter. The most popular is most likely the Foxit PDF iFilter 2.0, which, according to Microsoft speed tests, works 39 times faster than the free Adobe offering. The most significant crawl speed differences can be found on machines with multi-core processors, as Foxit's iFilter makes efficient use of multi-threading support. In addition to being the fastest PDF iFilter available, unlike Adobe's iFilter, Foxit provides 24/7 technical support for their product. Also while Adobe's PDF iFilter can index page contents and file attributes, Foxit's PDF iFilter can also index PDF bookmarks and PDF attachments. The license cost for the Foxit PDF iFilter 2.0 is around US$700 and US$100 for annual maintenance per production server. Non-production servers cost US$450 per server. A feature comparison of the PDF iFilters available from Adobe, PDFlib, and Foxit is shown in Table 11-4.

*Table 11-4. PDF iFilter Feature Comparison*

| Product Feature | Foxit PDF iFilter | PDFlib TET PDF iFilter | Adobe iFilter |
|---|---|---|---|
| Extract PDF content | X | X | X |
| Extract PDF attributes | X | X | X |
| Extract PDF bookmark | X | X | |
| Extract PDF attachments | X | X | |
| Add log settings | X | X | |
| Extract PDF metadata | Some | Yes | Some |
| Indexes XMP image metadata | | X | |
| Performance | Fastest | Faster | Slow |

▓ **Note** More information about the PDF iFilters referenced in this section can be found at the following locations.

www.foxitsoftware.com/

www.adobe.com/support/downloads/detail.jsp?ftpID=4025

www.pdflib.com/products/tet-pdf-ifilter/?gclid=CPrc6cbv5aUCFYXD7QodJHeC1A

www.ifiltershop.com/

In addition to indexing PDF file types, organizations may need to work with countless additional document types. Companies that focus on engineering, manufacturing, or design may need to index DWG-format CAD files, for example. Vendors such as IFilter Shop and Ransdell & Brown, Inc. offer iFilters that support this. IFilter Shop also offers a wide range of additional iFilters such as ASPX, MSG, Microsoft Project, PostScript, RAR & ZIP archives, vCard, Windows Media Audio and Video, and Adobe XMP. While these are just a few of the vendors that offer iFilters, there is an entire community of developers and consultants dedicated to enhancing Microsoft technologies. Ask for their advice, consult the forums of the company that produces the content type, and compare solutions. No matter the environment's content needs, there is most likely a solution available.

---

■ **Note** More information about the iFilters referenced in this section can be found at the following locations.

www.dwgindex.com/DWGFilter.html

www.ifiltershop.com/

---

# Taxonomy, Ontology, and Metadata Management

For those new to SharePoint, or even knowledge management systems, the terms taxonomy and ontology are probably tied to experiences in a biology class. Taxonomy is the practice and science of classification. Originally used to classify organisms, the use of taxonomies has spread to classifying things and concepts by underlying principles. Taxonomies can be seen in the organization of companies with an organizational chart. Organizational charts classify people by who they work with, who they work for, and who works for them. Taxonomies can be found in company product catalogs. A company may sell shoes, but it may classify them into groups such as size, gender, season, or color. Each of these properties is considered to be a node, and all of the shoes are cataloged into one or more nodes. A more expanded taxonomy may contain several subsets for each node. For example, to create more accurate groupings, shoes may first be grouped by gender, and then by season. Taxonomies allow for information to be organized into a hierarchical structure so that it is easier to manage and understand.

While similar in concept, ontologies are a bit broader than taxonomies, as they apply a larger and more complex web of relationships between information. Ontology is a formal connection of knowledge and connecting concepts within a domain. Instead of simply grouping information together into silos, ontologies define relationships between individual items. Ontologies are the foundation of enterprise architecture and, as a result, vital to the ability to catalog and understand information within SharePoint.

Although taxonomies and ontologies are not the only key to search, they are a significant building block for effective navigation. Without relationships between documents, teams, people, and sites, SharePoint 2010 would be a vast blob of content without any framework. Searching for managed properties would work, but SharePoint wouldn't be able to understand the difference between the property that defines a file as a PDF and the one that defines its author. Users could not scope searches to specific sites because sites are taxonomic silos of information. Searches could be executed for people, but users could not see organization charts or the documents they created.

SharePoint 2010 makes significant improvements over its predecessor in taxonomy management. MOSS 2007 did not provide taxonomy management tools, and, as a result, managing schemas and classifying content against them was difficult to impossible. Taxonomies could be designed only with very limited nodes and subsets. These setbacks resulted in potentially oversimplified taxonomic structure. SharePoint 2010, by contrast, provides a powerful toolset for creating and managing taxonomic structures. This helps organizations leverage SharePoint for the backbone of their cataloging and knowledge management needs.

# Automated Classification

Building taxonomies is only half of the solution. While SharePoint 2010 allows for the taxonomic structure to be designed, it falls short of automatic mechanisms for classifying items into the taxonomy. Farm structures can be built, but items cannot easily be organized into the structure. Features are in place for users and administrators to manually assign documents into taxonomic structures and tag them with metadata, but this process can be cumbersome and inaccurate. Unfortunately, people are inefficient and inaccurate at tagging items. Too often, general terms such as *meeting notes, sales report, policies*, and *manual* are tagged to large amounts of unrelated documents by users, which dilutes the specifics of the item. It is extremely common to find the name of the company that owns the portal on documents. If an employee of the company American Ninjas Associated searches for the term *Ninja*, they are probably going to return a massive amount of irrelevant results because the company name was tagged as metadata. In fact, the most relevant metadata in most environments is the properties SharePoint automatically creates such as author, file type, and upload date.

Because the search engine heavily relies on metadata for refinements and relevancy, the efficiency of search is directly affected by the quality of metadata. If items are incorrectly tagged or stored in the wrong location, they cannot be found in search. Organizations may seek to improve search relevancy by creating more thorough document upload processes that request more specific information and providing better training on what to include in document tags. These options still rely on the inaccuracy of people and their opinions instead of strictly designed rules and ontology. Although SharePoint 2010 cannot automatically add most metadata to items, there are several Microsoft partners with commercially available solutions to assist. There are several well-established solutions to help auto-classify SharePoint data, such as Smartlogic's Semaphore, MetaVis's CLASSIFIER, and Concept Searching's conceptClassifier.

# conceptClassifier

Concept Searching's conceptClassifier can automatically classify content in SharePoint 2010 against any available taxonomy. It integrates with the SharePoint 2010 Term Store and can process any content that is indexed by SharePoint. It then applies conceptual metadata to content and auto-classifies it to the Term Store metadata model. The metadata it produces is then stored as SharePoint properties. Authorized users can view, manipulate, and add additional tags as necessary using a form that integrates with the standard SharePoint 2010 Web Parts. This greatly reduces the time resources and inaccuracies that come with manual tagging.

The Taxonomy Manager component provides the ability to get instant feedback and automatic suggestions for terms from the client's own content to automate the term creation and building the hierarchical model. Management, testing, and validation are done in conceptClassifier, and terms are written back into the Term Store in real time.

Figure 11-10 shows the conceptClassifier Taxonomy Manager component interface. In this image, the Avionics and Sensors node is highlighted on the left panel. This shows the taxonomy hierarchy where nodes can be added, moved, or deleted. On the right panel are the clues (terms) that have been automatically or manually generated from the organizational content.

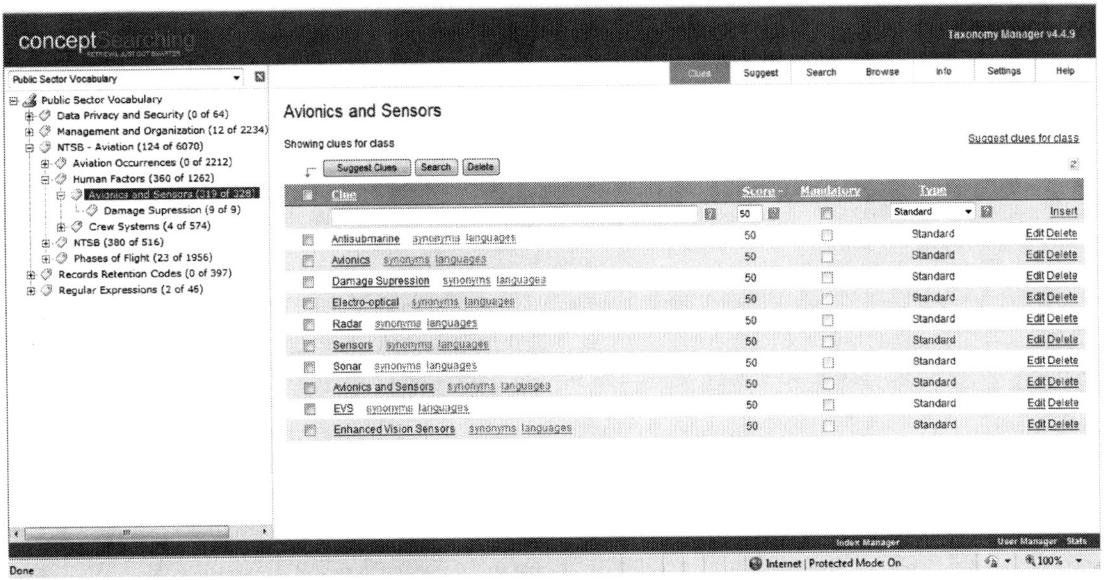

*Figure 11-10. conceptClassifier Taxonomy Manager component interface*

The user can add terms manually, provide a score, make the clue mandatory, and select the type. Clue types supported include the following:

- *STANDARD*: Single words and phrases

- *CASE-SENSITIVE*

- *DOCUMENT METADATA*: Partial matching on metadata values

- *PHONETIC MATCHING*: Ability to locate topics regardless of spelling variations

- *REGULAR EXPRESSION*: Any regular expression can be used, such as part number, credit card numbers.

- *CLASS ID*: Can be classified only if parent or grandparent is classified

- *LANGUAGE FILTERS*: Individual topics limit individual clues to specific languages.

Document movement feedback is also available to tune the taxonomy. This provides the mechanism to evaluate the changes on the taxonomy in real time without the need to reclassify the content. The feature will display the new classifications based on changes made to the scores. Indicators show how the score changes will impact the classification.

Indicators include the following:

- Document remains classified with a higher score

- Document remains classified but with a lower score

- Document remains unclassified and the score does not change

- Document will now become classified

- Document either stays or becomes unclassified

conceptClassifier can greatly increase document classification accuracy by leveraging multi-word concepts in its matching algorithms. Unlike SharePoint 2010's native tagging mechanism, which forces users to enter one potentially ambiguous word to define a concept, Concept Searching's tool can apply compound term processing to classify unstructured documents against taxonomies.

Figure 11-11 shows conceptClassifier's Term Store integration. All changes made in conceptClassifier or in the Term Store are immediately available, without the need to import or export. Classification rules for Avionics and Sensors are illustrated, showing the same node as the previous screenshot but from within the Term Store. The conceptClassifier taxonomy component provides the ability to manage, validate, and test the taxonomy(s). It also ensures that content will be correctly classified to improve findability in search, records management, and compliance.

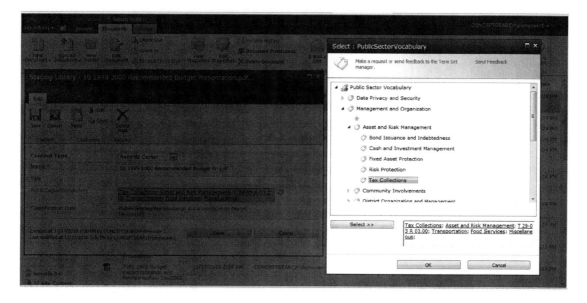

*Figure 11-11. conceptClassifier Term Store integration*

In addition to automatic concept extraction and classification, conceptClassifier also provides more advanced classification rules. These allow the tool to recognize the difference between single word and multi-word concept or phrases. It can understand existing metadata such as file type and storage location. The tool understands spelling variations based on phonetics much like the phonetic search in people on SharePoint 2010. It can also understand patterns such as part number and addresses. Finally it can recognize hierarchical relationships between topics and automatically detects the dominant language in a document.

Beyond the need for well-designed taxonomy and metadata to drive the ability to find information, it is also necessary to control sensitive information. For SharePoint deployments with organizationally defined sensitive information such as *For Official Use Only* (FOUO), *Personally Identifiable Information* (PII), and *Personal Healthcare Information* (PHI), accurate document classification means more than efficiency. For organizations with this type of information, poor classification leaves portals open to security breaches. Concept Searching's conceptClassifier can be used to automatically detect sensitive information or potential security breaches. It can do this by detecting patterns and cross-referencing them to associated vocabulary. Documents that the tool finds to meet certain suspect parameters can be tagged appropriately and locked down if necessary. This feature can also automatically change the file's content type so that workflows and permissions management can be automatically initiated to protect potentially sensitive documents.

In Figure 11-12, content has been automatically classified using one or more defined taxonomies. Based on the conceptual metadata and organizationally defined descriptors, documents are classified and, where appropriate, the content type has been automatically changed. The second and third document contained social security numbers and Personally Identifiable Information (PII); therefore the content type was changed to PII Document and the two highlighted documents will be routed to a secure repository where Windows Rights Management can be applied.

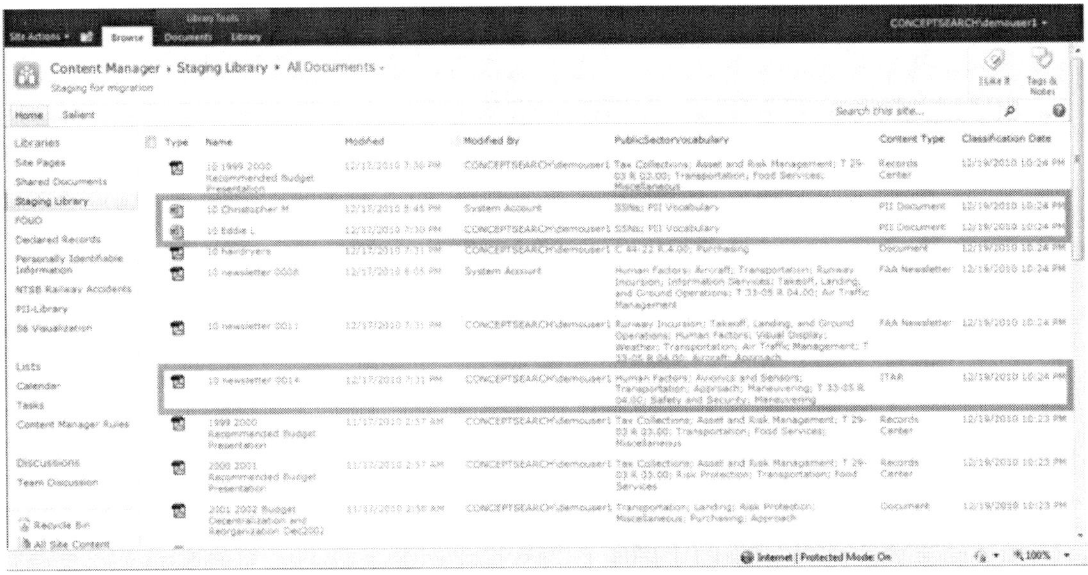

***Figure 11-12.*** *conceptClassifier automatically tagging sesitive documents*

The time it takes to install and set up contentClassifier is relatively limited considering the massive effect it can have on an environment. The product is downloadable in 30 minutes, contains a menu-driven setup, and from an administration perspective is easy to use. The taxonomy capabilities are also very easy to use, especially considering the amount of time it takes to create them in out-of-the-box SharePoint 2010. There are, however, no solutions that can completely operate autonomously without some administrative attention. Taxonomies do need to be managed and maintained. The tool was designed to provide this capability through the interactive features designed for subject matter experts (business users) as opposed to highly technical taxonomy specialists. SharePoint environments never remain static, so time is required for ongoing management of the taxonomy.

While these are not all of the features of Concept Searching's conceptClassifier, this does provide an initial idea of the available functionality in this and other classification solutions. While auto-classification is not the only way to improve information within taxonomies and ontologies, it is most certainly a great place to start.

## Choosing the Best Option

The previous chapter reviewed a few other approaches to improving relevancy using the features included in SharePoint 2010. In addition to their auto-classification solutions, both Smartlogic and Concept Searching vendors offer additional tools for managing taxonomies and ontologies. A comparison of the auto-classification solution features for these two vendors is shown in Table 11-5.

***Table 11-5.*** *Auto-Classification Products*

| Feature | SharePoint 2010 | Smartlogic Semaphore | Concept Searching |
|---|:---:|:---:|:---:|
| **Vocabulary support** | | | |
| Hierarchical Term Store (taxonomy) | X | X | X |
| Native read/write integration without the need to import/export terms | | X | X |
| Synonyms | X | X | X |
| Multi-language | X | X | X |
| List management (folksonomy and authority) | X | X | X |
| Relationship definition (ontology) | | X | X |
| **Model support** | | | |
| Poly-hierarchical taxonomy structure | Partial | X | X |
| User-definable model structure | | X | X |
| Expandable term information | | X | X |
| Text mining to identify candidate terms | | X | X |
| Ontology collaboration and review tools | | X | X |
| Extensive reporting management and control | | X | |

*Continued*

| Feature | SharePoint 2010 | Smartlogic Semaphore | Concept Searching |
|---|---|---|---|
| Open, ability to layer standard Microsoft and other reporting tools | | X | X |
| Term approval workflow and audit log | | X | X |
| Term Store management with instant feedback and term suggestions | | X | X |
| Easy rollback | | | X |
| Import, combine, organize, and harmonize models | | X | X |
| Enterprise model management | | X | X |
| Distributed taxonomy management | | X | X |
| Controlled vocabularies from organization's own content | | X | X |
| Automatic content type updating based on organizationally defined vocabulary and descriptions | | X | X |
| Automatic declaration of documents of record and routing to records center | | X | X |
| Automatic identification and lockdown of data privacy assets | | | X |
| **Navigation support** | | | |
| Configurable and multiple best bets | One only | X | X |
| Concept mapping | | X | X |
| Taxonomy browse-as-you-type | | X | |
| Ontology and knowledge map browsing | | X | X |
| Dynamic classification summarization | | X | |
| Taxonomy navigation | | X | X |
| A–Z listing | | X | |

| Feature | SharePoint 2010 | Smartlogic Semaphore | Concept Searching |
|---|---|---|---|
| Classification & text mining support | | | |
| Manual tagging | X | X | X |
| Assisted classification | | X | X |
| Automatic rules-based classification | | X | X |
| Incremental library classification | | X | X |
| Classification hierarchy support | | X | X |
| Classification strategy support | | X | |
| Compound term processing | | | X |
| Classification from SharePoint to other repositories | | | X |
| Classification of non-SharePoint content | | X | X |
| Content migration | | X | X |
| Semantic processing for driving SharePoint workflow | | X | X |
| Classifies all SharePoint content (libraries, blogs, wikis, pages, discussion threads) | | X | X |
| Entity extraction | | X | X |

# Replacing the SharePoint Search Engine

As this book has extensively shown, SharePoint 2010's native search capabilities are capable of handling the broad needs of most organizations. The index architecture can be scaled out to handle around 100 million items, custom connectors can be built through the BCS so the index can access custom content sources, and the user interface can be customized as needed to help users connect with content. While the capabilities of SharePoint 2010 Search are extensive, some organizations may need functionality beyond that which is supported by the native platform. Depending on the needs, custom development may be the most appropriate option. If custom development does not match an organization's time requirements, budget, or available skillset, third-party tools can be added to build out SharePoint 2010's functionality. There are, however, certain cases where these options still do not address the needs of an organization. In these cases, it may be necessary to replace SharePoint 2010's search architecture.

Readers that have followed this book in its entirety to this closing section have certainly found SharePoint 2010's search capabilities or available add-ons to meet the majority of their needs. As pointed out throughout this book, search in SharePoint 2010 does have its limitations, some of which can be overcome only by completely replacing the search architecture. For those readers who have hit a wall with SharePoint 2010's limitations, it is necessary to review some of the most popular solutions to replacing SharePoint search.

Before looking into solutions to handling the limitations of SharePoint 2010 Search, it is first important to review the limitations pointed out throughout this book. Many of the front-end user interface limitations have been reviewed in Chapter 5 and throughout this chapter. These include limitations such as the number of suggestions that can be presented for each refiner category, a lack of document previews, and the limited ability to customize search interfaces to user context. These limitations can be overcome through commercially available SharePoint extensions. Back-end limitations, by contrast, are directly tied to the core architecture of the search solution. Back-end limitations include those such as the number of items that can be indexed, the ease of access into content sources, and manipulation of relevancy. A summary of the major back-end limitations can be found at the end of this section in Table 11-6. Unlike the front-end user-side features, which can be enhanced through simple customization or commercial extensions, back-end limitations require complete replacement of the search architecture and index pipeline.

## Replacement Considerations

The decision to replace the search components in SharePoint 2010 is not one that should be taken lightly. While there are many search engines available that can integrate into SharePoint 2010, none does so without consequence. All search engine replacements will require additional time to set up, configure, and manage. They can bring advantages; but for many organizations the disadvantages brought by the complexities of mixing technologies in one farm do not justify the change. When analyzing potential replacements for SharePoint 2010 Search, it is important to fully understand the answers to these questions.

- *Do I need to index more than 100 million items?* SharePoint 2010 is capable of handling up to 100 million items if properly scaled. There are few organizations in the world that break this limit. For organizations that need to index more content than SharePoint 2010 is capable of supporting, replacing SharePoint 2010's native search pipeline is necessary. This is the single most compelling reason to replace SharePoint 2010 Search.

- *Do I have an enterprise agreement for SharePoint?* Currently, Microsoft's replacement of the native SharePoint 2010 search engine, FAST Search Server for SharePoint 2010, is available only to deployments of the enterprise version of SharePoint. Organizations that purchase the extension must be at the ECAL level.

- *Do I have the time to manage a more complex enterprise search engine?* While some enterprise search engine replacements are marketed to be easier to manage, all bring the inherent complexity of another major solution to manage. Unlike a search extension, which adds onto SharePoint, replacing the search engine requires management of a second set of search index architecture and software. The time it will take to rebuild sites, manage metadata, secure permissions, and maintain additional physical servers should be taken into account.

- *Can the additional user interface features I need be achieved through an extension of SharePoint or do I need to replace the core search engine?* It makes no sense to replace the entire search engine just to achieve deep numbered refiners. Comparatively inexpensive commercial solutions are available to meet these more basic needs. Unfortunately, countless enterprise search engine replacement projects are started on this illogical premise. Well-managed organizations don't pay hundreds of thousands of dollars for the complexity of a search engine replacement when a simple Web Part will fix the need. Before determining that SharePoint search needs to be replaced, first look at how it can be enhanced. Enhancements are generally much less expensive, time-consuming, and disruptive to users.

- *Do I have the budget?* Enterprise search engines are expensive. Be prepared to allocate a budget starting at US$30,000 for a minimal search engine replacement such as a single-server Google Search Appliance. For enterprise-level search engines such as Autonomy, Endeca, or FAST Search Server for SharePoint 2010, be prepared to expect software costs that start at US$100,000. Then be sure to appropriately budget for additional hardware, professional services, maintenance, and training.

If, after analyzing answers to these questions, the organization still needs to replace SharePoint 2010 Search, there are many solutions to consider. Enterprise search providers such as Endeca, Autonomy, Coveo, Google, and FAST all offer solutions that can replace SharePoint 2010's search architecture. The enterprise search engines offered by these companies are designed to be extremely scalable and crawl a broad range of content sources. In addition, they allow administrators significantly more influence over the index pipeline and relevancy. Each enterprise search provider caters to a slightly different set of needs. Considering the significant investment and impact, if an organization needs to replace SharePoint 2010 Search, it is best to contact each vendor and conduct a thorough analysis of the available options.

The most widely popular replacements for SharePoint 2010's native search are the solutions offered by Google and Microsoft.

# Google Search Appliance

Google's offering, the Google Search Appliance (GSA), is designed to be a straightforward plug-and-play solution to enterprise search. It is a packaged combination of a standard rack-mounted server and administrative software that can be plugged into a server rack to provide an instantly scalable on-premise search solution for web sites and intranets.

The GSA found a rise in popularity in MOSS 2007 for several reasons. Sadly, the most noteworthy reason for the popularity of the GSA is its brand presence, since it is offered by the world's leading global search provider. Implementations on SharePoint also increased on SharePoint due to new migrations from file shares to MOSS 2007, which saw a drastic jump in popularity over its predecessors. Many organizations owned Google Search Appliances for their web sites or file shares, and found a way to justify them in MOSS 2007. Its uptake also greatly benefited from the limited search architecture scaling available in MOSS 2007. The GSA was able to take advantage of a brute-force approach to searching massive amounts of documents spread across many content sources. Simply adding another GSA decreased crawl times and increased the maximum index size as well as search speed. It provided benefits over MOSS's search user interface, which included dynamic navigation, advanced query syntax, query suggestions, automatic spellcheck, and result groupings based on topic. It also opened up a broad range of reporting and analysis features through Google Analytics not available in MOSS 2007. Some of these analytics can be seen in Figure 11-13.

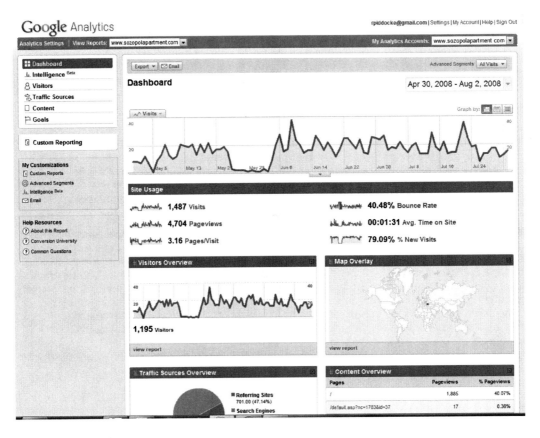

***Figure 11-13.*** *Google Search Appliance Analytics*

With SharePoint 2010, it is apparent that Microsoft took note of the loss of market share around search. The majority of the features that made the Google Search Appliance stand out in the MOSS 2007 era were integrated into native SharePoint 2010. The search user interface features such as related queries, query syntax, and refiners have all been integrated into SP2010. Figure 11-14 shows the GSA search experience on the platform, and it is helpful for understanding the basic user interface differences. In addition to the decreased gap in the user interface, with the capabilities of the BCS, developers can more easily connect SharePoint to a wide range of content sources. SharePoint 2010's native search architecture is also significantly more scalable than MOSS 2007. SharePoint 2010 also provides a much broader suite of search analytics through the newly introduced Web Analytics reports discussed in the previous chapter.

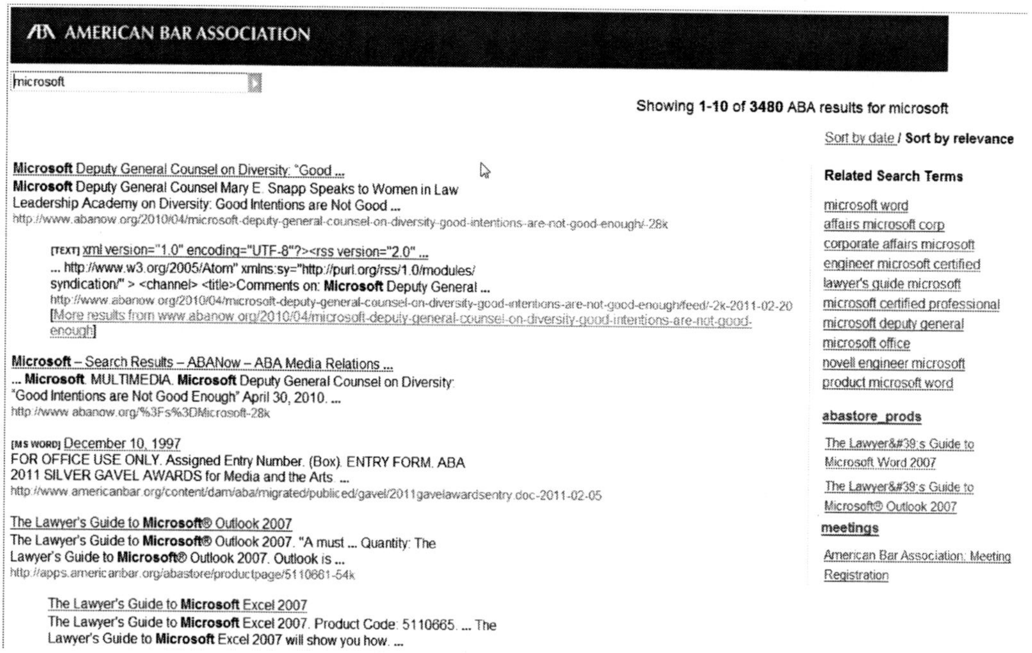

**Figure 11-14.** *Google Search Appliance results in SharePoint*

While the improvements in SharePoint 2010 Search greatly reduce the feature gap between the Google Search Appliance and SharePoint, there are some remaining benefits to Google. Depending on the GSA model an organization chooses to implement, the index is marketed to be infinitely scalable to billions of items. By contrast, SharePoint 2010's index is capped around 100 million items. The GSA does support more content sources out of the box without knowledge of the connector framework. This is important for organizations that want to easily connect to content located in EMC Documentum, IBM FileNet, Hummingbird, Lotus Notes, Oracle Content Server, and SAP KM.

It is also noteworthy to mention that Google's relevancy is primarily beneficial in the public domain. The factor of relevancy combined with a questionable history of security is partly the reason most GSA deployments can be found on public sites and not intranets. The technique of crawling global web sites is quite different than the techniques used to provide relevant search results on an intranet. Global search engines are used to connect people with general information scattered around the Web. They function similarly to the yellow pages, in that people are frequently searching for general concepts and not specific items. For example, like the yellow pages, on a global search engine, users may search for general concepts, such as shoe stores in their city. They are not frequently searching for a specific pair of shoes located at a specific branch of a store. If users want to find a specific pair of shoes at a specific store, they do a global search to find the store's web site, and then call or search again within the web site using the site's search engine. The user experience when searching within intranets is quite the opposite. They are generally looking for a specific item, authored by a specific person, within a specific site. The ability to present relevant results based on this specificity is what makes SharePoint's relevancy shine on intranets.

Although the Google Search Appliance is one of the least expensive options for replacing SharePoint 2010 Search, it is still not cheap. Management of search still requires time and attention. Setup time is slightly less than the amount of time necessary to set up search in SharePoint 2010, but not drastically reduced. Pricing for the appliance, which includes both hardware and software, is based on the number of indexed documents. At the end of 2010, pricing for the basic appliance model started around US$30,000 for a two-year contract and the ability to index 500,000 items. The basic model can be scaled to support up to 10 million items, and the more powerful model can support up to 30 million items per appliance. Unlike most enterprise search platforms, which charge a one-time license fee and annual support, Google licenses the GSA in two- or three-year leases. When the contract period expires, the unit stops serving data. It can then be returned or replaced with initiation of a new contract.

■ **Note** Google's search appliance is not the same as Google Mini. Google Mini is a simple search engine for use with less than 100,000 items, and is primarily designed for web sites. SharePoint 2010's search capabilities are significantly more advanced than Google Mini, and as a result it would not be a viable replacement for SharePoint search.

## FAST Search Server 2010 for SharePoint

In Wave 14, Microsoft has decided to attack alternative enterprise search engines head-on. In early 2008, Microsoft acquired the Norwegian enterprise search vendor FAST Search and Transfer (FAST). Established nearly a decade earlier, FAST was one of the world's leading providers of high-end search and business intelligence solutions. Its platform, FAST ESP, is a highly customizable and scalable search engine capable of meeting a seemingly endless array of search- and intelligence-based business needs. By acquiring FAST, Microsoft took a significant step toward alleviating its deficiencies in the search marketplace.

Since the acquisition, Microsoft and the FAST Group have been hard at work to integrate FAST's search technologies into Microsoft's more mainstream infrastructure solutions. While some of these technologies are available in native SharePoint 2010 Search, the release of FAST Search Server for SharePoint 2010 established Microsoft as a real player in the enterprise search space. FAST Search Server for SharePoint 2010 is a replacement for the SharePoint search architecture. It integrates seamlessly into SharePoint 2010 with a familiar interface and by picking up settings, permissions, and metadata. FAST Search Server for SharePoint 2010 is not an extension to SharePoint 2010 Search, however; it is a replacement, since it does require dedicated servers and adds a completely different index pipeline.

■ **Note** FAST Search Server for SharePoint 2010 should not be confused with its stand-alone enterprise search platform, FAST ESP. FAST ESP is a service-oriented architecture used to build search-derived applications.

FAST Search Server for SharePoint 2010 can greatly expand the user interface and the search back end for enterprise SharePoint deployments. The platform includes all of the features of standard SharePoint 2010 Search and adds additional user interface features such as advanced sorting, document previews, deep numbered refiners, and visual best bets. Advanced sorting allows for a broad range of additional search sorting options beyond SharePoint 2010's standard relevancy. This feature is similar to the "display relevance view option" and "display modified date view option" in standard SharePoint 2010, but provides more extensive sorting such as size, document rank, created date, and modified date. These sorting options can also be customized to meet the specific needs of a deployment. Figure 11-15 shows the default options made available with this feature.

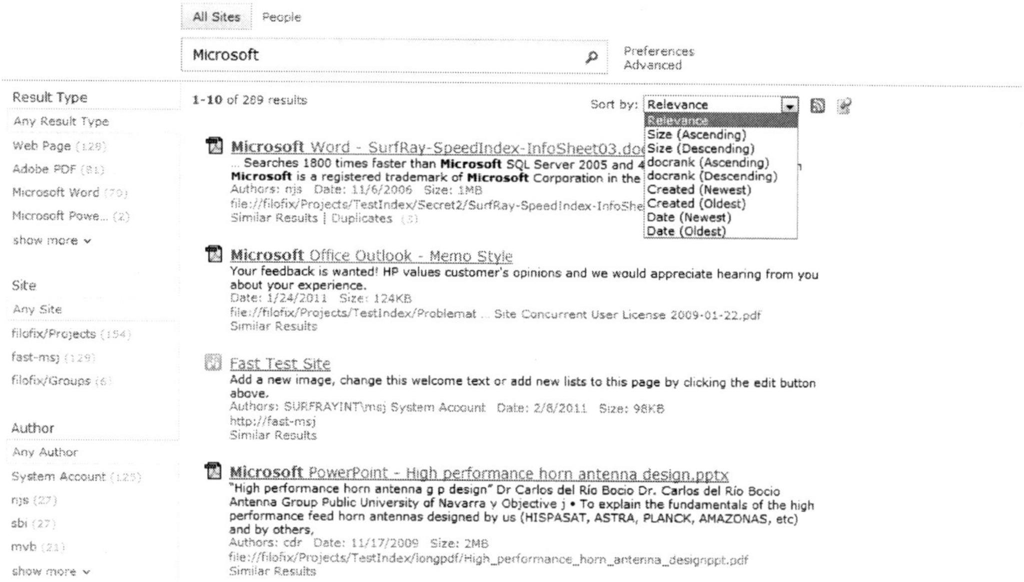

**Figure 11-15.** *FAST Search Server for SharePoint 2010 advanced sorting*

One of the most popular features of FAST Search Server for SharePoint 2010 is the document thumbnail and preview feature. This is a very limited version of the visualization functionality reviewed earlier in this chapter. FAST Search Server for SharePoint 2010's document preview is made available through the use of SharePoint Office Web Applications (OWA), so previews are available only for Office documents. More specifically, first-page thumbnails are available on the search results page for Microsoft Word and PowerPoint files. Full document previews are currently available only for PowerPoint files (Figure 11-16). For FAST's thumbnail and document preview to function, the document must be stored on a SharePoint 2010 site that has OWA enabled. While this does provide a nice visualization enhancement for SharePoint, clients using the search replacement should be aware that previews for Office files other than Word and PowerPoint are not supported and users must have OWA enabled on their browsers. This does lead to the restriction that users cannot preview PDF, Autodesk, or other Microsoft Office file formats. Caution should also be used when deploying this feature to public sites or those that are expected to be accessed via mobile devices, where the installation of OWA cannot be reasonably assured.

*Figure 11-16. FAST Search Server for SharePoint 2010 PowerPoint preview*

---

■ **Note** Visualization solutions, such as SurfRay's Ontolica Preview and BA Insight's Longitude Preview, can be added to FAST to support broader content types.

---

FAST Search Server for SharePoint 2010 greatly enhances the Best Bets feature to allow for multiple visual best bets. Unlike SharePoint 2010 Search, which allowed for only one best bet per keyword, multiple suggestions can be tied to a single keyword using FAST. In addition, with FAST, Best Bets can use HTML for graphical best bets similar to those found on web sites instead of the simple text suggestions provided with SharePoint. This is especially beneficial to organizations that wish to use SharePoint 2010 on public-facing deployments. Figure 11-17 shows the difference between best bets in SharePoint 2010 and those available in FAST for SharePoint. The visual banner is a FAST best bet, whereas the second item titled *sharepoint* with a star is a standard SPS2010 best bet.

***Figure 11-17.*** *FAST Search Server 2010 for SharePoint best bets*

The popular search refinement Web Part is also greatly enhanced in FAST for SharePoint. Instead of providing plain, shallow refinements that can analyze only the first 50 items in a result set by default, FAST's refinements are deep and numbered (Figure 11-18). This allows for refiners based on the aggregation of managed properties for the entire result set. This has the significant benefit of refinement options reflecting all items matching a query. It does, however, take a significant amount of memory from the query server for large result sets, so enabling this feature should be done with caution. For deployments of FAST for SharePoint with more limited hardware or a high query frequency, the option remains available to display refinements based only on the aggregation of properties for the top 100 search results.

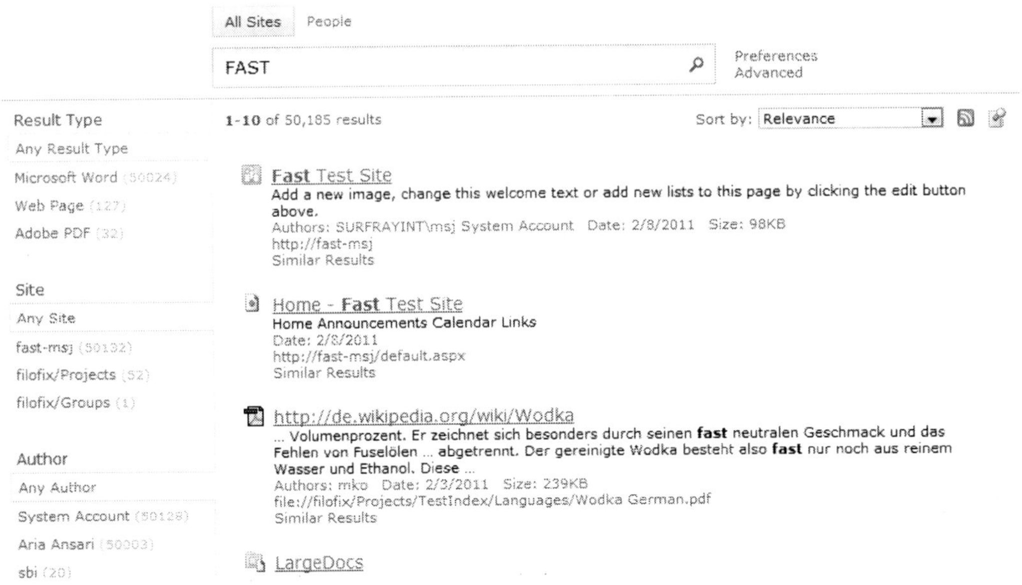

**Figure 11-18.** *FAST Search Server for SharePoint 2010 deep refiners*

FAST Search Server for SharePoint 2010 can also enhance the user interface by providing different result relevancy, best bets, and refinement options based on user context. This allows the search interface to be catered toward user groups. For example, when searching for the keyword "expansion," people logged in from the sales group may get a best bet for documents outlining the strategy to increase sales figures in a new geography. People in this department may also get search refinements based on product groups or sales territories. If a user from the human resources department executes the same query, FAST Search Server for SharePoint 2010 can be configured to provide a different experience for that user based on his or her department. The user in the human resources department that searches for the keyword "expansion" could get a visual best bet for hiring policies in a newly established department. The search refinements may include fields such as department, clearance level, or policy type.

All of these user-side features can be added through significantly less expensive search extensions, such as those reviewed earlier in this chapter. The features that make FAST Search Server for SharePoint 2010 stand out are those on the back end. FAST Search Server for SharePoint 2010 replaces SharePoint 2010's search architecture with an extremely scalable search engine. While SharePoint 2010's native search index can handle up to 100 million items, FAST Search Server for SharePoint 2010 can be scaled to index billions of items while retaining sub-second query times. Like the Google Search Appliance, scalability is dependent on licensing and hardware. FAST Search Server 2010 for SharePoint requires its own dedicated hardware. It cannot be installed on the same server as SharePoint Server 2010. The minimum hardware requirements include a dedicated server with 4GB RAM, 4 CPU cores, and 50GB of disk space, but 16GB RAM, 8 CPU cores, and 1TB of disk space on RAID are highly recommended to achieve the intended performance. Due to the enterprise nature of the search engine, however, most deployments contain about four servers dedicated to FAST Search Server 2010 for SharePoint.

In addition to an extremely scalable index, FAST provides much greater control over the index pipeline. SharePoint 2010 Search was designed to make access to powerful search relatively simple. As a result, some limitations were implemented in what can be manipulated in regards to relevancy during indexing. SharePoint 2010's index pipeline can be considered a black box, with very little ability for manipulation. SharePoint 2010 and FAST's default relevancy is designed to provide accurate results on intranets against large sets of different data. Each organization's needs are different, and because relevancy is perceived differently among different users and organizations, it may be helpful to tune relevancy according to specific needs. Organizations that wish to directly influence relevancy algorithms can do so using FAST Search Server for SharePoint 2010. Administrators with programming and Windows PowerShell experience can blend multiple rank components such as content context, authority, term proximity, and quality. Keyword-driven, statistic, dynamic, and linguistic relevance can all be manipulated to affect the order of items in a result set.

FAST allows administrators to extract metadata at index time, execute business intelligence activities on the fly, and build custom queries using FAST's proprietary FQL query language. FAST's metadata extraction is similar to the auto-classification solutions reviewed earlier in this chapter, although it does require a bit more manual attention. Metadata can be extracted from the plain text within items as they are indexed, even if no formal structure exists within the file. This allows for significantly improved connection of structured concepts and properties to documents. This metadata can then be used to enhance search relevancy and provide more accurate refinement options to users.

Finally, much of the real potential for large enterprises that choose to implement FAST Search Server for SharePoint 2010 is tied to the ability to use it for a core to custom search-based application (SBA) development. Microsoft has taken the first step to pulling search technologies out of the search center and into other applications. For example, FAST can be connected to business intelligence solutions such as Excel workbooks and Reporting Services reports. This allows for advanced discovery of statistical information that may be useful for management teams to understand how employees are working and utilizing data. It also provides the ability for marketing teams to use search to understand how clients may be navigating a public SharePoint site or what best bets are most effective in converting site browsers to clients. Developers and consultants can utilize the FAST Search Server for SharePoint 2010 as the core infrastructure for advanced systems or portals that rely on information access and reporting. Examples include search-based applications such as research and development portals, product support dashboards, supply chain management trackers, and compliance tools.

As mentioned earlier, FAST Search Server for SharePoint 2010 is licensed separately from SharePoint 2010. Unlike the Google Search Appliance, which includes everything needed in one package, organizations that wish to implement FAST must purchase hardware, Windows Server, SQL, and FAST Search Server licensing. Users must have the enterprise client access license (ECAL) to access the FAST features. At the end of 2010, pricing per server for FAST Search Server 2010 for SharePoint started at about US$22,000.

## Choosing the Best Option

This section was meant to provide only a high-level overview of the most popular options for replacing SharePoint 2010's native search engine. There are entire books dedicated to this subject, and any organization that finds that its needs reach beyond the capabilities of SharePoint 2010 should seek the guidance of an experienced consultant. Considering the financial and time investments required to implement enterprise search engines, even those that are marketed to be simple, a thorough analysis of the best solution to meet an organization's particular needs should be conducted. A hasty jump into a mixed platform may prove to be a costly waste of resources if better hardware or user interface extensions would meet needs with greater efficiency. Table 11-6 will assist with an initial analysis of options.

*Table 11-6. SharePoint 2010, GSA, and FAST Comparison*

| Feature | SharePoint 2010 | Google Search Appliance | FAST Search Server 2010 for SharePoint |
|---|:---:|:---:|:---:|
| Front end | | | |
| Basic search | X | X | X |
| Scopes | X | | X |
| Search enhancements based on user context | | X | X |
| Custom properties | X | | X |
| Property extraction | Limited | | X |
| Query suggestions | X | X | X |
| Search as you type | | X | |
| Similar results | | | X |
| Visual Best Bets | | X | X |
| Sort results on managed properties or rank profiles | | | X |
| Shallow results refinement | X | X | X |
| Deep results refinement | | | X |
| Result clustering | | X | X |
| Document Previewers | | | X |
| Alerts | X | x | X |
| Query federation | X | X | X |
| Windows 7 federation | X | X | X |
| People search | X | X | X |
| Social search | X | X | X |

| Feature | SharePoint 2010 | Google Search Appliance | FAST Search Server 2010 for SharePoint |
|---|---|---|---|
| **Back end** | | | |
| Taxonomy integration | X | | X |
| *Multi-tenant hosting | X | X | |
| Rich web indexing support | | X | X |
| Support for MySites, profiles pages, social tagging, and other social computing features | X | X | X |
| Automatic relevancy tuning by document or site promotions | Limited | X | X |
| Manually tunable relevance with multiple rank profiles | | X | X |
| Language support for most Latin-based languages | X | X | X |
| Language support for Asian characters | | X | |
| Real-time language translation for queries and results | | X | |
| Metadata extraction during indexing | | | X |
| Integration of advanced BI tasks | | X | X |
| Access to line-of-business (LOB) data systems | X | X | X |
| Site map auto-generation for global search engines | | X | |
| Topology scalability | Multiple servers | Multiple servers | Multiple servers |
| Maximum index capacity | Approx. 100 million items | Billions | Billions |

■ **Note** One especially important item to note from the previous table is that unlike standard SharePoint 2010 and GSA, FAST Search Server for SharePoint is not capable multi-tenant hosting. FAST Search Server must be deployed on a farm dedicated to a single SharePoint customer and cannot be offered through hosting providers as a shared service.

# Summary

This chapter has described the basic ways SharePoint 2010 can be enhanced using third-party solutions. Both open source and commercial solutions are available to expand SharePoint's search features and meet needs beyond what is capable with the native platform. Enhancements range from simple Web Parts, to document preview panes, to auto-classification tools. In extreme cases, where SharePoint 2010 cannot be enhanced through configuration, custom development, or commercial enhancements, the search capabilities can be replaced with alternative enterprise search engines. This final chapter provided the footing for investigation of solutions to search needs beyond this book. There are extensive libraries of knowledge catering to possibilities that are opened up through SharePoint 2010 Search. Leverage those resources to explore the endless possibilities for enhancement.

# Index

CPSIA information can be obtained at www.ICGtesting.com

228012LV00007B/1/P